MODERNISM

Savage Reprisals (2002)
Schnitzler's Century (2001)
My German Question (1999)
Mozart (1999)

THE BOURGEOIS EXPERIENCE: VICTORIA TO FREUD
Pleasure Wars (1998)
The Naked Heart (1995)
The Cultivation of Hatred (1993)
The Tender Passion (1986)
Education of the Senses (1984)

Reading Freud: Explorations and Entertainments (1990)
Freud: A Life for Our Time (1988)
A Godless Jew: Freud, Atheism, and the Making of Psychoanalysis
    (1987)
Freud for Historians (1985)
Freud, Jews and Other Germans: Masters and Victims in Modernist
    Culture (1978)
Art and Act: On Causes in History—Manet, Gropius, Mondrian (1976)
Style in History (1974)
Modern Europe (1973), with R. K. Webb
The Bridge of Criticism: Dialogues on the Enlightenment (1970)

THE ENLIGHTENMENT: AN INTERPRETATION
Vol. I, The Rise of Modern Paganism (1966)
Vol. II, The Science of Freedom (1969)

Weimar Culture: The Outsider as Insider (1968)
A Loss of Mastery: Puritan Historians in Colonial America (1966)
The Party of Humanity: Essays in the French Enlightenment (1964)
Voltaire's Politics: The Poet as Realist (1959)
The Dilemma of Democratic Socialism: Eduard Bernstein's Challenge
    to Marx (1952)

MODERNISM

THE LURE OF HERESY

From Baudelaire
to Beckett and
Beyond

PETER GAY

W. W. NORTON & COMPANY

New York London

FRONTISPIECE: Marcel Duchamp (1887–1968), *Nude Descending a Staircase, No. 2* (1912). Exhibited at the Armory Show of 1913 in New York, it was cruelly nicknamed "explosion in a shingle factory" but became a key exemplar of modernism in action.

For information about permission to reproduce
selections from this book, write to Permissions,
W. W. Norton & Company, Inc.,
500 Fifth Avenue, New York, NY 10110

For information about special discounts for bulk purchases,
please contact W. W. Norton Special Sales at
specialsales@wwnorton.com or 800-233-4830

Manufacturing by R.R. Donnelley, Harrisonburg
Book design by Barbara M. Bachman
Production manager: Anna Oler

LIBRARY OF CONGRESS
CATALOGING-IN-PUBLICATION DATA

Gay, Peter, 1923–
Modernism : the lure of heresy from Baudelaaire to Beckett and
beyond / Peter Gay.—1st ed.
p. cm.
Includes bibliographical references and index.
ISBN 978-0-393-05205-3 (hardcover : alk. paper) 1. Modernism (Art) 2. Arts,
Modern—19th century. 3. Arts, Modern—20th century. I. Title.
NX454.5.M63G39 2007
700.9'034—dc22   2007025903

W. W. Norton & Company, Inc.
500 Fifth Avenue, New York, N.Y. 10110
www.wwnorton.com

W. W. Norton & Company Ltd.
Castle House, 75/76 Wells Street, London W1T 3QT

1 2 3 4 5 6 7 8 9 0

TO MIMI AND DORON

CONTENTS

Part Three: ENDINGS

..

LIST OF
ILLUSTRATIONS

Color illustrations of August Renoir, *The Swing*; Andy Warhol, *Brillo Box*; Andy Warhol, *Marilyn*; and Guggenheim Museum, Bilbao, that do not appear in the text are included in the color inserts.

The man of letters is the enemy of the world.

—*Charles Baudelaire*

To describe the fatal character of contemporary things
the painter uses that most modern recourse—surprise.

—*Guillaume Apollinaire*

PREFACE

THIS BOOK IS A STUDY OF MODERNISM, ITS RISE, TRIUMPHS, AND decline. As the reader will quickly discover, it is the work of a historian; I shall disregard chronology when I find that useful or necessary, but my dominant direction will be to move forward from past to present, from chapter to chapter, and within each chapter. It is a historian's book, too, in that I have not stayed within the confines of formal analysis of novels and sculptures and buildings, but will, if briefly, place the works of modernists into the world in which they lived.

Yet the book is not a history of modernism, which, given the mass of available materials, would be almost unthinkable in a single volume, or else reduced to nothing better than a pile of thumbnail sketches. Where are William Faulkner and Saul Bellow among the novelists? William Butler Yeats and Wallace Stevens among the poets? Where are Francis Bacon and Willem de Kooning among the painters, and why have I said so little about Matisse, and then only as a sculptor? Was it reasonable to skip composers like Aaron Copland and Francis Poulenc, or Richard Neutra and Eliel Saarinen among the architects? Can I justly hope to cover path-breaking movie directors by confining myself to four of them? Where are topics like opera and photography? In a history, I would have had to find room for them all. But, as the introductory section, "A Climate for Modernism," should make clear, I have looked for what modernists had in common, and the social conditions that would foster or dishearten them.

I have, then, treated painters and playwrights, architects and novelists, composers and sculptors as exemplars of indispensable elements in the modernist period. But I have aimed to make my choices, selective as they are, to add up to a usable definition of modernism, its scope, its limits, and its most characteristic expressions. I should emphasize at the outset that in making my selections I have not been guided by my political views, at least not consciously. I have after all provided detailed observations for such key modernists as the Fascist Knut Hamsun, the bigoted High Anglican T. S. Eliot, and the hysterical anti-feminist August Strindberg. I deplore their ideologies, but I found them vital witnesses. Yet, as I have said, the point of this study is not to compile an expansive catalog of all the strands and leading figures in modernism, but to examine their presence in culture and to discover, if possible, whether they coalesce to define a single cultural entity. My slogan has been that of the Founding Fathers: *E pluribus unum*.

BUT WHERE IS FREUD? Does he not belong, after all, among the most dramatic of modernists? Certainly, when we assess Freud's taste, we must deny him that title. In art, music, and literature, he was a perfectly conservative bourgeois. He admired Ibsen but was silent about Strindberg; he liked among living novelists the skillful craftsman and socially sensitive but scarcely avant-garde John Galsworthy, and seems not to have known the novels of Virginia Woolf, even though she and her husband Leonard were his English publishers; the pictures on his walls reveal no sign of response to Austrian moderns like Klimt or Schiele, and his furniture shows that the experimental designs of Viennese modernists had made no inroads on him. His principled opposition to the received social and cultural attitudes of his class lay elsewhere.

Indeed, when we note the reluctant, usually bitterly antagonistic reception of Freud's ideas across the twentieth century, especially on sexuality, his uncompromising role as a dissenter quickly becomes apparent. If much of the Freudian view of the human animal present and past appears to be fairly commonplace today, that is so because for a century much of the respectable world has made its progress toward him. It has adopted phrases from the psychoanalytic dictionary—sibling rivalry, defensive maneuver, passive-aggressive—without acknowledgment. Hence it is not far-fetched to describe the first set of sympathetic colleagues who began weekly meetings in Freud's Viennese apartment from 1902 on as an avant-garde in the healing professions, especially after that Wednesday group graduated to become the Vienna Psychoanalytic Association. It was, and remained, at war with conventional medicine and psychiatry, and was firmly led by a single, confident innovator. As we shall see, F. T. Marinetti, the dominant figure among the Futurists around the time of the First World War, and André Breton, among the Surrealists in the 1920s, occupied rather similar positions. They were the Freuds of their clans.

THE IMPACT OF FREUD'S psychoanalytic theories on modern Western culture has not yet been fully mapped. Indirect as much of it was, it was certainly enormous, especially among educated bourgeois, whose tastes were also inextricably implicated in the origins and progress of modernism. Whether it is the matter of parents speaking to their children frankly about such delicate topics as where babies come from; a loosening of the meaning of family, so that unmarried couples living together are no longer shocking as they once were; a markedly growing acceptance by society for what used to be called perversions like homosexuality and lesbianism; a sharply increased awareness of the ravages that human aggressiveness can cause—sharply increased but, as recent history teaches only too painfully, not enough to influence policy; and other, similar cultural habits. This is not to deny that in some circles, the Freudian way of thinking remains as indigestible as it was a century ago.

But not, I must emphasize, for me. I am aware that there are still debatable, and still debated, clinical and theoretical issues in psychoanalytic thinking like the causes of dreams, the maturation of female sexuality, and the healing properties of the talking cure as against the ministrations of medication. But these are matters that, however they are eventually resolved, will not make Freud's (and his followers') ways of thinking about the mind, its functioning and malfunctioning, irrelevant. His view of human nature, to summarize it tersely, features placing mind into its natural world, which means that it is susceptible to causal laws, whether physiological or psychological; the devious, inadequately recognized activity of the dynamic unconscious; and the inescapable lasting discord between libido and aggression. The psychoanalytic technique of fostering free association in his patients was the equivalent of the Impressionist painter taking his easel out of doors or the modernist composer abandoning traditional key signatures. Freud, the self-declared scientist of the mind, was in sizable company in making contradictory feelings—ambivalence—central to his picture of the world. This tragic vision renders a life of conflict an essential element in history—including that of modernism.

This, very briefly, is my way of seeing human existence in the pages that follow. I have utilized this Freudian perspective most directly whenever I thought it helpful. But even when it makes no explicit appearance, it lies at the heart of my historian's reading of the decades when modernism helped to define the realities of social and cultural life in the nineteenth and twentieth centuries.

I have not ventured to offer a psychoanalysis of modernism. On this crucial point, I have been Freud's loyal follower. When it came to the roots of artistic genius, he accepted the inconvenient assertion that psychoanalysis really has no comprehensive explanation to offer. In 1928, in an essay on Dostoevsky, he made a well known concession that has rarely been taken as seriously as it deserves to be when he laid it down that "before the problem of the *Dichter*," the novelist and the poet, "psychoanalysis must lay down its arms." In these pages I have not tried to go Freud one better. But readers, no matter how they feel about Freud's contribution to their understanding, should be alert to my conviction that, however brilliant, however determined in their enmity to the aesthetic establishment of their time, modernists were human beings, with all the accomplishments and all the conflicts that psychoanalytic thinking would attribute to them.

—Peter Gay
Hamden, Connecticut, and New York City, January 2007

MODERNISM

A CLIMATE
FOR MODERNISM

ODERNISM IS FAR EASIER TO EXEMPLIFY THAN TO DEFINE.
This intriguing situation is in itself a tribute to its diverse riches. Its exemplars cover so vast and varied a terrain—painting and sculpture, prose and poetry, music and dance, architecture and design, theatre and movies—that shared ancestry or common ground must seem implausible. Some years ago, Justice Potter Stewart of the U.S. Supreme Court declared that while he could not define pornography, he knew it when he saw it. Noteworthy modernist works, whatever their genre or their claim on the world's attention, leave precisely that impression.

No wonder that attempts at a comprehensive assessment of modernism are likely to be befogged by commentators, enthusiasts, and avid merchants of the culture industry. The same uncertainty attaches to the quick label stuck on individual works of art and literature: in truth, from mid-nineteenth century through the twentieth, "modernism" has been applied to innovations in every domain, to any object that can boast a modicum of originality. Not surprisingly, then, cultural historians intimidated by the chaotic, steadily evolving panorama they are trying in retrospect to reduce to order have sought refuge in a prudential plural: "modernisms."

This compliment to the turbulence that pervades the modern marketplace for art, literature, and the rest shows due respect for an imaginative individuality that has for almost two centuries ignited spirited debates over taste, its expressiveness, morality, economics, and politics, and over their psychological or social origins and implications. But to renounce the admittedly imprecise, all-embracing singular "modernism" is ultimately an unsatisfactory strategy. For there is something about certain prints, compositions, buildings, or dramas that we classify as "modernist" without hesitation or fear of contradiction. A poem by Arthur Rimbaud, a novel by Franz Kafka, a piano piece by Eric Satie, a play by Samuel Beckett, a painting—*any* painting—by Pablo Picasso, all offer trustworthy testimony to what we are attempting to identify. And over all these classics there broods the saturnine, trimly bearded face of Sigmund Freud. Each carries its own credentials. *That*, we say, *is modernism.*

Yet for historians of culture, the mere shock of recognition is not enough, and I have written this text as an attempt to be at once more wide-ranging and more concrete. To the best of my knowledge, no scholar has ever tried to map all the manifestations of modernism as making up a single historical epoch. I have already hinted at the reasons for this failure of nerve: to paraphrase what G. K. Chesterton once said about Christianity, it is not that defining modernism has been tried and found wanting, but that it has been found difficult and not tried. Whatever cultural symptoms of modernism we explore, the particular threatens to overpower the general.

True, modernists were on the whole less enthusiastic about the political or doctrinal middle of the road than the extremes. For all the liberalism of key figures like James Joyce or Henri Matisse, moderation struck many a modernist as bourgeois and boring—two epithets they were disposed to treat as synonyms. But this should astonish no one: almost by definition they felt, as inveterate risk takers, most at home at the frontiers of the aesthetically safe, or beyond them. The one thing that all modernists had indisputably in common was the conviction that the untried is markedly superior to the familiar, the rare to the ordinary, the experimental to the routine. Hence, perhaps the most illuminating metaphor we can employ in our search for larger commonalities is that of a large, interesting, far-flung family, distinct in its individual expressions but joined by fundamental links as families are bound to be.

My purpose in these pages, then, is to show that a substantial amount of credible evidence gathered across all the fields of high culture provides unity amidst variety, a single aesthetic mind-set, a recognizable style—the modernist style. Like a chord, modernism was more than a casual cluster of avant-garde protests; it added up to more than the sum of its parts. It produced a fresh way of seeing society and the artist's role in it, a fresh way of valuing works of culture and their makers. In short, what I am calling the modernist style was a climate of thought, feeling, and opinion.

CLIMATES, EVEN EMOTIONAL CLIMATES, change, which is to say that modernism had its distinct history—like all histories both internal and external. I shall spell out the most telling details of its internal history— the traffic of artists with other artists, or themselves, and with the institutions that directly impinged on their fortunes—in the chapters that follow. For its part, the external history of modernism, which fits it into its environments, is quite as relevant to my enterprise, since the movement at once expressed its culture and changed it. Hence later in this introduction I provide a quick survey of the economic, social, and intellectual (not excluding the religious) backgrounds that fostered or obstructed avant-garde enterprises. The achievements and the failures of modernism are incomprehensible without its stage settings and costumes, which were more than mere receptive, passive decor. Their outer worlds were both the agents and the targets of urgent modernist agendas. The unmatched Russian impresario of modern ballet, Sergei Diaghilev, is supposed to have told his choreographers, "Astonish me!" It was a good modernist slogan.

"MAKE IT NEW!"

1.

FOR ALL THEIR PALPABLE DIFFERENCES, modernists of all stripes shared two defining attributes, and I shall investigate both in the chapters that follow: first, the lure of heresy that impelled their actions as they confronted conventional sensibilities; and, second, a commitment to a principled self-scrutiny. Other possible criteria of classification, no matter how promising, all failed: political ideologies, though inviting, cannot serve to define modernism, since it is compatible with virtually every creed, including conservatism, indeed fascism, and with virtually every dogma from atheism to Catholicism. History shows that modernists have bitterly fought one another over basics of belief, or unbelief.

What I am calling the first of these defining qualities, the lure of heresy, is no mystery. The modernist poet who pours obscene content into traditional meters; the modernist architect who eliminates all decoration from his designs; the modernist composer who deliberately violates the traditional rules of harmony and counterpoint; the modernist painter who exhibits a rapid sketch as a finished picture—they and their allies drew satisfaction not only in having taken a new, an untried, a revolutionary path—their own—but also in the sheer act of successful insubordination against ruling authority. Such emotions are impossible to quantify, but it appears likely that perhaps half the joy of making a radical picture or house or symphony must have derived from the creator's satisfaction to have bested the opposition. The jaunty slogan that Ezra Pound introduced for his fellow rebels before the First World War, "Make it New!," tersely summed up the aspirations of more than one generation of modernists.

Proof texts abound. When Frank Lloyd Wright was designing the Guggenheim Museum in New York in the 1950s, he advertised its coming glories as the first decent art museum in the history of the world. More modest—to give but one more example—in 1940, Matisse was overcome by crippling doubts about his creativity. "I am paralyzed by some element of conventionality," he wrote to his friend and fellow painter Pierre Bonnard, "that keeps me from expressing myself as I would like to do in paint." He soon conquered his anxiety, but what matters here is his devotion to, and yearning for, absolute artistic autonomy, all guidance emerging solely from within. And with the passage of the decades and the spread of modernist art, this assertion of personal sovereignty came to govern the consumers of culture quite as much as its makers. The artists' willingness to speak, paint, sing freely, audaciously, "from the heart," would be matched by their publics' willingness to appreciate—and to acquire—their self-revelations.

The central significance of the second criterion for modernism, the commitment to a principled self-scrutiny, which entails an exploration of the self, had far deeper roots than unconventionality. The hunt for the secrets of human nature has been conducted through the centuries by introspective thinkers from Plato to St. Augustine, Montaigne to Shakespeare, Pascal to Rousseau. In their animated advocacy of human autonomy, Denis Diderot and Immanuel Kant, writing during the mature Enlightenment, might qualify as protomodernists.

The modernists, then, had worthy ancestors. For them, self-scrutiny or scrutiny of their subjects became essential to their unorthodox enterprises. Beginning around the 1840s and more daringly as the decades went on—I am casting Charles Baudelaire, in preference to all other heretics, as modernism's first hero—poets made esoteric departures in their disdain for traditional verse or decent subject matter as they rehearsed the expressive possibilities of language. Novelists began to investigate their characters' thoughts and feelings as never before. Playwrights came to put the subtlest psychological conflicts on the stage. Painters started to turn their backs on art's age-old privileged vehicle, nature, to seek nature in themselves. Music in its modernist guise grew for ordinary listeners more inward, less immediately rewarding, than ever.

Once launched, these self-directed tendencies assembled most of the essential ingredients of modernist practice during the Romantic decades in the age of the French Revolution and its aftermath. Celebrated—or notorious—Romantics set a tone for rebellious nonconformity. Byron and Shelley, Chateaubriand and Stendhal exhibited a defiant libertinism in their private lives; Friedrich Schlegel derided bourgeois marriage as a sham, while several decades after him, Marx and Engels charged that it was just a sordid business deal, a higher form of prostitution.

This uninhibited Marxist critique of middle-class self-censuring society was part of the revolutionary atmosphere across the Continent in 1848—I have borrowed it from the *Communist Manifesto* published that year—and enjoyed only limited attention at the time. Modernists, certainly, at least in these early years, dealt in somewhat less inflammatory slanders, although at his most enraged Gustave Flaubert, the great modernist in fiction, with his first novel, *Madame Bovary*, came close.

Flaubert's malicious caricature of the bourgeois deserves a moment of particular attention, for it became a model in modernist circles. Anti-bourgeois fury runs through his extensive, brilliant correspondence and his published writings like a recurrent nightmare. His bourgeois is stupid, greedy, complacent, philistine, but also all-powerful. In a famous letter, he called himself "bourgeoisophobus," a description all the more instructive in its introduction, no doubt casual, of a psychiatric term. His hatred of the middle classes took the form of a phobia amounting to an irrational inability to see his society as it really was.

In short, his portrayal of the hated bourgeois is an indiscriminate libel that lacks all sociological specificity and, with that, all reliable substance. Flaubert lumped together into his caricature workingmen, peasants, bankers, tradesmen, politicians, the inescapable and proverbial grocer, all but a select coterie of writers and artists—his friends. Uncritical reliance on such testimony has distorted the social history of modernism almost beyond rescue.

This fatal flaw did not prevent admiring readers, through generations, from following his lead. Only a few anti-bourgeois, like Emile Zola, equaled him in his sectarian malice, but Flaubert's tone became common coin among nineteenth-century modernists all too prepared to condemn a whole social class for the failures of their own inventions. Nor could twentieth-century modernists improve on this nineteenth-century name-calling. In 1920, the Italian modernist painter Mario Sironi, soon to make himself the Fascists' reliable artistic spokesman, drew an illustration of a desolate cityscape in which three sinister figures lurk in a corner, one armed with a pistol, another with a knife, apparently waiting to assault a respectable-looking—that is to say, bourgeois—man walking toward them wholly unaware of what awaits him. The laconic caption for this class-linked drama: "Antiborghese." There is no evidence that Sironi disapproves in the slightest of the thugs prepared for their victim.

Mario Sironi,
Antiborghese (1920).
A curious sample of the
avant-garde's
detestation of the
bourgeoisie, here
coarsely in Italian.

This hostility survived. It is striking how little changed across the decades in the modernists' sheer hatred of the commonplace bourgeoisie. One instance must suffice: the inventive Pop sculptor Claes Oldenburg, famous among other delightful outrages for the gigantic red-tipped lipstick erected on top of caterpillar tracks—now housed in the courtyard of a residential college at Yale—declared in 1960 that bourgeois toyed, and only toyed, with imaginative innovations. "The bourgeois scheme is that they wish to be disturbed from time to time, they like that, but then they envelop you, and that little bit was over, and they are ready for the next." What was needed, Oldenburg thought, was an "elevation of sensibility above bourgeois values," one that would "restore the magic inherent in the universe." This is an instructive accusation: Oldenburg held with the Romantics, whether secular or devout, more than a century and a half before him that the middling orders had robbed the world of enchantment, which it was the supreme duty of creative spirits to restore. Yes, the self-appointed spokesmen for their modernist tribe insisted: bourgeois did want to make things new, but not too new.

The verbal aggressiveness that modernists lavished on their opponents from the beginning was not quickly matched in unconventional masterpieces. But cultural heretics presided over a few scandals that kept middle-class anxiety at a high level: Manet's famous nude, *Olympia* (painted in 1863 but exhibited in the Salon only two years later); Algernon Charles Swinburne's *Poems and Ballads* (1866), with its steamy allusions to masochism and other sexual specialties favored by superannuated English schoolboys; a widely circulated, pitiless assault by French men of letters—Baudelaire, Flaubert, the Goncourt brothers, and, a little later, Zola—on the hopelessly uncivilized bourgeoisie, the tone-setting element, as they saw it, in the land of philistine grocers. It was not until the 1880s that modernists began to produce crops of historic works with impressive energy for some four decades and more. Then, in the late 1920s and early 1930s, as we shall see, this astonishing energy waned (though not permanently) in the face of triumphant totalitarianism and a worldwide depression.

2.

THE DECADES CLUSTERING AROUND the turn of the twentieth century, then, were pivotal for the career of modernism; they deserve, and will receive, the bulk of space in this study. It was a far from tranquil time in the arts: sensational, deeply unsettling stylistic experiments were disrupted by the First World War, the shaping catastrophe of our modern age. Its outbreak, its savagery, and its length—it dragged on from August 1914 to November 1918, with long, murderous stalemates particularly on the western front—astonished even those powers, principally the Austrians and the Germans, mainly responsible for the bloodletting. The culture wars that had agitated all the arts were, of course, as nothing compared to the casualties exacted by the military conflict. But they were startling enough: Expressionist poems, abstract paintings, incomprehensible compositions, plotless novels were together making a revolution in taste. And after the war was over, modernists went on with their work.

Not as though nothing had happened. Many modernists served in the army, some of them suffered breakdowns, others were killed at the front. But by and large, once peace had broken out, they took up largely where they had left off. Marcel Proust did not change his style during the war, but introduced it in the last volume of *A la recherche du temps perdu*. Max Beckmann's canvases showed a new awareness of horror and death. Walter Gropius was brought to political consciousness by the war. And postwar artists used the war almost as much as it used them.

The historian notes the curiously uneven impact of this world conflict, this appalling breakdown in the concert of nations. It proved irreparable in politics, in economic relations, in cultural attitudes, in the death of empires. But viewed against the emergence of modern barbarism, the war showed itself comparatively inconsequential on canvas or in print. The avant-gardes of the 1920s, innovative as they seemed, mainly harvested what the prewar years had sown, when aesthetic innovations had crowded one upon another. Each modernist instance, whether from 1880 or 1920, confronted, fascinated, or repelled contemporaries—whether experienced as urbane or primitive, authentic or fraudulent, magnificent or quite simply incomprehensible. A modernist short story or string quartet was an opportunity seized, an act of aggression, a slap at what Henrik Ibsen disdainfully called the "compact majority."

THE COMMOTION THAT THE WAR YEARS generated in high cultures, and that did not grow any clearer in retrospect, has not been the only source of confusion for historians studying modernism. The stature of avant-garde masterworks changed across generations; some were even absorbed into the very canon their authors professed to despise and had worked to discredit. With time, offensive (or at least startling) innovations in the theatre, the museum, or the concert hall lost their power to outrage. The infuriated balletgoers who in 1911 noisily disrupted the premiere of Nijinsky and Stravinsky's *Rite of Spring* were followed by audiences that found this potent amalgam of radical score and radical choreography far from indigestible and really quite enjoyable. It is an apparent self-contradiction but a historical fact that modernist works, produced to provide an aura of heresy, should end up being called classics.

It is telling, after all, that the experiences of seeing or reading or hearing certain distinctive modernist works—Adolf Loos's Steiner House in Vienna, August Strindberg's *Dream Play*, Igor Stravinsky's *Firebird*, Pablo Picasso's *Demoiselles d'Avignon*—speak with undiminished vitality to consumers of high culture today, though they all predate the First World War. Yet they are as stunning, as *modern*, as Frank Gehry's Guggenheim Museum at Bilbao, completed only a few years ago. If chronologically ancient, these older works remain pieces of the living history of culture and give that history much of its life—and its perplexities.

MISREADING MODERNISM

1.

AMONG THE GROUNDS FOR MISREADING MODERNISM, one, particularly prominent, was that the ground of battle was sabotaged from the start by aggressive combatants' willful misunderstandings of their opponents. The legends that formed around the lives of modernists further obscured the social realities: insouciant, romantic bohemian squalor, as portrayed at mid-nineteenth century in Henri Murger's fiction (given wide circulation and unearned authority half a century later in Giacomo Puccini's opera about the joys and pains of starving for art), was more fable than fact. By midcentury, few painters or composers were still eking out a picturesque, penniless existence in fifth-floor walk-up garrets, living in unmarried bliss. In reality, there never had been very many of them, and most avant-garde artists grew comfortable, some of them even prosperous. Radicals became rentiers; by and large, nineteenth-century avant-garde writers or composers, however they started out, eventually grew into solid citizens. The absorptive capacity of a cultural establishment that modernists had worked so hard to subvert was nothing less than impressive.

Hence, with a few agreeable exceptions, the debates among rivals for public favor in the arts were dialogues of the deaf. All reached for what combatants in such disputes commonly turn to: gross oversimplifications and, with that, equally gross exaggerations of their distance from the "enemy." Fanatics at both ends of the spectrum enjoyed exposing the wickedness of the other and acted on the aggressiveness that their own mythmaking permitted them to release and rationalize. The most vehement spokesmen for the modernists presented themselves as professional outsiders, and the establishment treated them as noisy, willful amateurs whose plays did not deserve to be performed, paintings did not deserve to be exhibited, novels did not deserve to be published. And modernists gladly confirmed their status as pariahs by cultivating the painful pleasures of victimhood.

The historian who takes these agitated battle cries at face value is bound to perpetuate rather than expose cherished fairy tales. It seemed all so straightforward to traditional artists, critics, and audiences: modernists appeared like a coherent front of scofflaws or mavericks massed against the solid verities of time-honored high culture and, usually, Christian faith. Authorized spokesmen for that culture from monarchs to influential aristocrats denounced these dissidents as immature or worse, immoral, as madmen and bomb throwers.

In this inflamed atmosphere, anti-modernists produced judgments notable for their vehemence, for their obstinate refusal to appreciate whatever case the rebels were able to muster. But few among the innovators alarmed their culture from the simple need to be alarming. Surely some among them worked at being offensive, and the general public obliged them by being offended. Yet all too often the responses of the establishment were plainly out of all proportion to the shocks that aroused them. When Ibsen's *Ghosts* was first performed in London in 1891, reviewers threw around incendiary epithets, evidently enjoying themselves as they mouthed their inflamed denunciations. Granted, the play dares to mention sexual irregularities and has a principal character collapse in an attack of syphilitic insanity. But it hardly deserved to be called a "disgusting representation," an "open drain, a loathsome sore unbandaged, a dirty act done publicly." Nor was it an instance of "gross, almost putrid indecorum," or its author "a crazy, cranky being" who was "not only consistently dirty, but deplorably dull." What most strikes a later reader in these effusions is their uncontrolled hysteria, the helpless hyperbole of good citizens under assault, being made to face hitherto repressed truths about their lives.

In short, the modernists were justified in believing that they had something important to say that "decent" artists would not, actually could not, say. Knut Hamsun wrote *Hunger* (1890) and succeeding fictions to remonstrate against what he condemned as the psychological superficiality of other novelists. Vasili Kandinsky gradually eliminated all allusions to nature in his canvases until by 1910–11 there were none left because he believed that all other painters had failed to capture the mystical nature of existence. Strindberg staged his early naturalistic dramas, *The Father* (1887) and, a year later, *Miss Julie*, as critical responses to the well-made, sexually discreet plays then ruling the stage, and a decade later reversed the direction of his modernist protest with Expressionist closet dramas like *A Dream Play*. T. S. Eliot launched his provocative verse—*Prufrock and Other Observations* came out in 1917 and *The Waste Land*, that undisputed modernist classic, in 1922—at a time when, as he put it, "the situation of poetry in 1909 and 1910 was stagnant to a degree difficult for any young poet to imagine." These modernists had well-defended bastions of culture to assail and drastic departures to offer. For all their frivolous appearance, they knew what they were attacking. For all their overstatements, they were serious.

Candor about sexuality, always a sensitive topic and in the modernist age still hedged about with tenacious taboos, was not the only subject susceptible to censure. When in 1905, at the Salon d'Automne in Paris, Henri Matisse, André Derain, Maurice de Vlaminck, and like-minded artists exhibited their latest paintings, reviewers denounced their glowing, exuberant canvases as "pictorial aberrations" due to "color madness"; they reminded one reviewer of the "naïve sport of a child who plays with the box of colors he just got as a Christmas present." The automatic dismissal of these artists, quickly but not affectionately nicknamed *Les Fauves*, "the Wild Beasts," became a trope in debates over high culture. Speaking of childhood: like other modernists exploring their inner lives, Paul Klee saw his playful creations set aside with the condescending observation that a seven-year-old could have produced such smears. To the most determined antagonists of those trying to make it new, modernists of all persuasions were an undifferentiated mass of vandals, incompetent in technique and untalented to boot.

2.

THE MOST STRIDENT AVANT-GARDE ORATORY lent a certain color to these charges. Looking back at the rhetoric many modernists allowed themselves to deploy early and late, one finds statements that rivaled the conservatives' language in their extremism. One favorite modernist topos was the urgent necessity to destroy those havens of reaction, the museums. As early as the 1850s, the French Realist critic and novelist Edmond Duranty had suggested that the Louvre, that "catacomb," be burned to the ground, an idea that the Impressionist painter Camille Pissarro happily endorsed some two decades later. The demolition of these "necropolises of art," he thought, would greatly advance the progress of painting. Indeed, at their most bellicose, modernists refused to entertain any traffic with what Gauguin snidely called "the putrid kiss of the Ecole des Beaux-Arts."

The urgent desire to erase the canon achieved widespread and lasting popularity among advanced circles. Before the First World War, bellicose Italian Futurists, not unexpectedly, made it an ingredient in their immoderate program of aggression against contemporary culture. "We want to demolish the museums, the libraries," exclaimed Filippo Tommaso Marinetti, the group's founder, in his *Initial Manifesto of Futurism* of 1909, "combat moralism, feminism, and all opportunistic and utilitarian acts of cowardice." Hostility could hardly go further short of direct action.

This ferocity had enough staying power to survive the First World

J. Lemot
(1847–1909),
*Gustave Flaubert
Dissecting
Madame Bovary*,
in *Parodie* (1869).
The great
analytical novelist
caricatured as his
destructive self.

War. When the experimental American photographer Man Ray landed
in Paris in 1921, he was taken aback to hear the inflammatory talk in the
artists' cafés he frequented: "Unfortunately when I got over here I got
tied up with the avant-garde movement, which despised museums,
which wanted to destroy them." Yet, in spite of all this provocative
posturing, strange as it seemed, modernist artists could fantasize about
finding wall space in the very museums they wanted to set on fire.

Modernists, then, were no less impassioned than their adversaries,
no less unjust. Their principal villain was, of course, the bourgeoisie,
and the most prestigious aggressor remained Flaubert. The "perspiring

philistine," as Robert Louis Stevenson called the bourgeois, was a figure of fun or of menace, ridiculous or looming; modernists treated him
as being quite incapable of appreciating original creations. Abundant
evidence to the contrary, Victorian and later modernists lampooned the
solid burgher everywhere, in plays, in novels, in poems, in cartoons, in
paintings, and asked their audiences to sneer or laugh at him.

WHAT IN THE HEAT OF COMBAT, then, looked only too clear-cut—the
war of the new against the old, as most history books have it—was
actually an intricate pattern of skirmishes interrupted by truces and
muddled by changes of front. The modernists' favorite battle cry,
"*There* is the enemy!," seems to be more securely grounded than it
really was. Granted, to see modernists and lovers of the conventional
as implacable adversaries has much to commend it. But, like all sweeping statements concerning the history of culture, this one, too, must
make abundant room for exceptions. At the least it requires fine-tuning.
What psychoanalysts call the narcissism of small differences moved
many modernists to slander their allies almost as vehemently as they
did the most benighted philistine.

With some unexpected consequences: the abuse that modernists liked
to bestow on their adversaries served to divert attention from the fact that
their own camp was little more unified than that of the establishment they
were fighting. Yet there is ample evidence that this perceived unanimity—
the self-presentation of willing allies—was never absolute. Gauguin criticized the Impressionists for being the slaves of visual probability;
Strindberg detested Ibsen's problem dramas; Piet Mondrian was disappointed that Picasso should have "failed to advance" from Cubism to
abstraction; Virginia Woolf had strong reservations about Joyce's obscenity; Kurt Weill made scathing comments about the compositions of his fellow modernist Erich Korngold; Josef Albers, the disciplined abstract artist
who became famous for his series *Homage to the Square*, was so deeply
offended by the Pop antics of Robert Rauschenberg, whom he had taught
at North Carolina's Black Mountain College, that he consistently claimed
never to have heard of him.

Probably the most consistent, and most irritating, subverter of avant-garde concord was the Spanish painter Salvador Dali. As eager to astonish the public with his pronouncements as with his bizarre, often distasteful Surrealist canvases, he gave the back of his hand to all his modernist competitors. He was destined, he told the world, "to rescue painting from the void of modern art." If modernists condescended to bourgeois, they could also condescend to fellow modernists, or at least find them wanting in aesthetic courage or discrimination.

Even more startling, from the beginning years, led by none other than Baudelaire, some modernists earnestly tried to make peace with the guardians of taste. These efforts are less well known than sensational confrontations but quite as interesting. Reviewing the Paris Salon of 1846, Baudelaire dedicated his observations to the bourgeoisie. Virtually supreme in French culture, he wrote, it was the most reliable resource for painters, poets, and composers, and as founder of great art collections, museums, and symphony orchestras. Hence, contemporary bourgeois were "the natural friends of the arts." Half a century after Baudelaire, and in his spirit, Guillaume Apollinaire, lyrical poet and friend to all that was avant-garde in his time, pathetically appealed to the generosity and large-mindedness of his middle-class readers. He begged them to recognize that avant-garde authors were filled with goodwill toward their bourgeois audiences, aiming only to lead them to hitherto unfathomable vistas of beauty and profundity: "We are not your enemies. / We want to give you vast and strange domains / Where mystery in flower spreads out for those who would pluck it." And, rather astonishingly, he asked for their pity.

In later years, reflective avant-garde spirits recognized that their vaunted individualism, which presumably freed them from the burden of the past, the vulgarity of their time, and the oppression of the powerful, was often compromised by the desire for companionship and reassurance. In the 1960s, in late retrospect, the brilliant American critic Harold Rosenberg, himself firmly committed to the modernist revolution, savagely derided the current crop of cultural heretics as "the herd of independent minds." A cartoon in *The New Yorker* brought this piece of self-criticism to the educated masses: in a painter's studio

"Why do you have to be a nonconformist like everybody else?"

From *The New Yorker*, June 28, 1958.

swamped with incoherent abstractions a woman is berating an artist who is clearly the author of these unsalable horrors, "Why do you have to be a nonconformist like everybody else?"

AN ARRAY OF PREREQUISITES

1.

IF THE CONFLICTS WITHIN THE MODERNIST FAMILY provided ample problems for avant-garde poets and painters, its struggles with the social forces among which they must live were quite as delicate. Modernism was touched at all points by the society from which it drew its lifeblood. To reiterate: in order to flourish, modernism required the support of social and cultural preconditions. Thus—to take a single instance—it is too obvious to require demonstration that modernists needed a relatively liberal state and society to function at all. Severe and consistent censorship of verbal or pictorial representations regarded as blasphemous, obscene, or subversive created a climate of repression singularly hostile to modernist innovation. Again, their works show that the modernist age could have arisen only at an advanced stage in Western civilization, at a time when certain social habits and attitudes worked in its favor, even when they did so hesitantly, erratically, and unintentionally. True, a fostering climate could not have, by itself, guaranteed the emergence and survival of modernism, and potent obstructions from any of its essential prerequisites would have frustrated its most strenuous efforts. In other words, modernism is unthinkable without a substantial and influential number of patrons and clients affluent enough, free enough, and disposed enough to support it.

Without confessing to economic determinism, I shall begin by sketching in the economic background. The seedbed for modernism was assembled from the widely distributed prosperity in industrializing and urbanizing states. The factory system—emerging first in England in the late eighteenth century, increasingly flourishing there and, after some delays, in Belgium, Germany, France, and the United States through the Victorian decades—was the precondition for the mass production, and, with that, the mass consumption of consumer goods, including the fine arts. The railroad, to its first astonished observers a modern miracle, created a spectacular means of transporting passengers and freight; between the late 1820s and the 1860s, it created a tightly woven network of rail lines across industrializing countries, and changed population patterns and commercial opportunities forever. Newly devised financial instruments and vast banking empires provided the capital supporting an unprecedented market for wealth. And, as we shall see, modernism grew along with this expansion.

Art historians have often observed that modernism was mainly an urban phenomenon. Victorian cities, growing at breakneck speed, built theatres and concert halls and induced consumers to fill them, founded conservatories and orchestras and amassed recruits to perform in them. It was in cities that public-spirited citizens established institutions of high culture throughout the century: the Frankfurt Museum, designed as a haven for all the muses, was founded in 1808; the New York Philharmonic Orchestra in 1842; the Hartford Atheneum in 1844; the Amsterdam Rijksmuseum in 1885. This was the bourgeois elite at its best, a middle class unknown to Marx. In contrast, a mere handful of modernists settled in remote hamlets to escape what depressed them as the nervous-making haste and noise of city life: German poets and painters had Worpswede for a retreat, French painters Brittany. Small towns with solid cultural traditions like Jena became pioneering centers of artistic activity. Still, modernism would have been unthinkable without London and Amsterdam, New York and Chicago, Munich and Berlin. And practically everyone agreed at the time that Paris was the cultural capital of a territory far larger than France. In his autobiography, *Ecce Homo*, Nietzsche, the good European, laid it down: "As an *artist* one has no home in Europe but Paris." It was the drastically modernized city of the 1850s and after that he had in mind.

The modernists' reliance on enlightened middle-class support, far from the simplistic generalizations they offered, underscores the contention that their cultural revolution could only have thrived in recent times. In earlier ages, patronage for the arts had been the monopoly of selected, tone-setting makers of taste: monarchs, aristocrats, princes of the Church, and in a few mercantile hubs like those in the Netherlands, an affluent minority of commercial magnates. The artworks that have survived from medieval and early modern centuries into ours, whether as stately mansions or precious objects in museums, demonstrate that many exalted clients had fulfilled their obligation to beautify sanctuaries and palaces, often munificently and tastefully, either out of piety, the pressure of self-display, the love of beauty, or a compound of them all.

This was to change. By the nineteenth century, modern heirs of Maecenas began to usurp the place of long-established cultural philanthropists, while anonymous publics, nearly all of them bourgeois, provided composers and playwrights with leeway to maneuver among, even to undermine, governing tastes. Perceptive Victorians were not blind to this revolution. In the middle years of Queen Victoria's long reign, Lady Elizabeth Eastlake, who was an experienced observer of the English cultural market and, as the wife of Sir Charles Eastlake, director of the National Gallery in London, particularly well informed, wrote: "The patronage which has been almost exclusively the privilege of the nobility and the higher gentry was now shared (to be subsequently almost engrossed) by a wealthy and intelligent class, chiefly enriched by commerce and trade." And these divisions in modernist aggression were sharpened by the way that avant-garde art, literature, and music spread beyond exclusive coteries of cultural aristocrats to attract sizable audiences. The term "bourgeoisie" grew a little more flexible, especially in its lower ranges.

Public institutions, most of them founded or greatly expanded

Claude Monet (1840–1926), *The Gare Saint-Lazare: Arrival of a Train* (1877). A characteristic text for the urbanism and modernism of the Impressionists.

in the nineteenth century, served as recruiting agents for the tastes of the future. From midcentury on, the Victorian decades became a time of lending libraries, free days at museums, accessible and reasonably priced popular tracts about some astonishing offerings, cheap seats in theatres

and concert halls, an explosion in the commercialization of culture, and the popularization of inexpensive reproductive techniques like lithography and photography. That is obvious enough; the proliferation of modernist tastes is after all a central element in their history. But it is essential to recognize that the new profusion of cultural objects, addressed to ever-expanding audiences, did much to increase their diversity.

Modern wealth derived from many sources and this underwrote the differences in local avant-garde tastes. Maturing capitalism showed extraordinary ingenuity in devising techniques for harnessing resources: employing massive numbers of clerks for escalating bureaucratic tasks in commerce, manufacturing, government, and service industries; devising new legal entities such as the corporation for enlisting supplies of capital; transforming the mass production of goods by intensifying the division of labor, standardizing tasks, and developing more efficient machinery; speeding up transportation and communications with revolutionary improvements in the mails, roads, and canals. And while the age of modernism took wing, mechanization, it has been well said, took command. And so, when contemporaries praised the locomotive as the founder of a new world, they were right.

These decades of dizzying transformation saw the gradual (never quite complete) dismantling of the mercantilist state intervention that had once regulated economies. Although that retreat from paternalism also generated festering, unsanitary slums and the heartless exploitation of labor, the horrors that came to be known, too politely, as "the social question," it released unexampled entrepreneurial energies. Anxious and angry social critics denounced the way capitalists deployed these energies as selfish and unscrupulous, and in large part it was. But inventions like the typewriter, the Atlantic cable, the telephone stood as agents of capitalism in a wealth-creating machine that enormously enlarged the circles of the flourishing middle classes in Europe and the United States alike. Untold numbers of bourgeois earnestly attended art exhibitions with dollars, pounds, and francs loose in their pockets.

To these adult pupils in the aura of high culture, money was time. They were a breed that around midcentury crowded the recitals of virtuosi like Franz Liszt and Jenny Lind, took their honeymoons in Italy to devote themselves, Baedeker in hand, to furthering their education in painting and architecture. This, too, was the age of domestic entertainments that relied on amateur sopranos or pianists as part-time virtuosos, often indifferently gifted but usually heartfelt. The sincere bourgeois love of music has been another casualty of the bias of implacably hostile observers: cynical anecdotes to the contrary, playing music at home for invited guests was, often enough, something better than a trap set by young women in search of suitable mates.

2.

JUST WHAT PLEASURES BOURGEOIS liked to spend their surplus money on obviously depended heavily on time, place, opportunities, their degree of political elbow room, familial habits, and a host of private motives. Liberty was no guarantee of good taste, any more than were spare funds; but—as modern totalitarianism proves, if proof be needed—lack of liberty was the lethal adversary of the inner freedom without which a creative spirit would be nothing more than a cog in a predictable, government-run machine. If the sorry reputation that has been foisted on bourgeois culture had been all one could report about the Victorians and their heirs, there would have been no modernism.

Throughout the modernist age, the agitated question remained whether, and just how much, one could expect the middle classes, or the growing number of the highly educated, to rise above the crude appetite for mere diversion that cultural Cassandras diagnosed them as craving above all else. Cultural pessimists, usually journalists writing for the better monthlies, or publicity-hungry academics with a fluent pen and a superior attitude, had no doubt about the inescapable triumph of the philistine. The coming mass society, they largely agreed, would be catastrophic for the arts. It would enable each ignoramus to tell the world that he knew nothing about art but knew what he liked. Hence, pedagogic campaigns to acclimatize masterworks among the literate would produce not the elevation of vulgar taste but the vulgarization of elevated taste. In a century when larger and larger proportions of the male population were being admitted to the active political public, when the push for universal literacy was producing large numbers of what their self-described "superiors" called the half-educated, and when trade unions were giving a voice to the hitherto mute, this collective worry was perhaps natural. But it was also self-satisfied, unjust, and arrogant. We cannot escape the fact that snobbery was a powerful side effect in the modernists' appraisal of publics that so plainly failed to understand them. This much is certain: a number of modernists were democrats, but modernism was not a democratic movement.

3.

THE PROSPECTS OF A DEMOCRATIC CULTURE were of particular concern to modernists, and cultural critics from de Tocqueville to Max Weber undertook to analyze social realities with the classic tools of sociology. The archetypal item in this informal social science literature is a little known article by an equally little known German cultural bureaucrat, Alfred Lichtwark. His short article titled "Publikum" was published in 1881, five years before he was appointed director of the Hamburg Kunsthalle, the city's leading museum. In that essay, Lichtwark divided the publics for art into three categories: the masses, the educated, and the chosen few. The first, he asserted, the largest segment in Germany and any other country, is almost wholly ignorant about past art and at best aware of a few etchings after two or three Raphael *Madonnas*. The second consists of cultured individuals with minimal art historical information; they tend to idealize some single period and, no better than the unteachable mob, lack all interest in modern art. The third is a "highly select" minority. "These are the rarest and the most reliable ones. To be in touch with them is like a revelation, for what they possess as a gift of nature—good taste and their own good judgment—can never be quite attained by means of education." Unfortunately, Lichtwark added gloomily, they play only a negligible role in Germany's artistic life.

This extraordinary statement is worth pausing over. Its cultural pessimism was in tune with the preponderant view that only a chosen

Leopold von Kalckreuth (1855–1928), *Portrait of Alfred Lichtwark* (1912), director of the Kunsthalle, Hamburg, who became controversial for slyly and slowly buying not-yet-popular French Impressionists.

minority can ever mobilize the erudition and the psychological flexibility needed to seek out and appreciate whatever goes beyond the commonplace and the trifling. Most people will never give up treating paintings, dramas, and novels as sheer distractions or moralizing lessons. Lichtwark partially subverted this view by pointing out that his favored few might be recruited "from the most varied of social strata," from men "who have taken the most diverse educational paths." But like most of his fellow cultural critics, Lichtwark considered the bulk of the educated bourgeoisie incapable of setting aside its material interests. And in this conviction, he forged a loose partnership with the anti-bourgeois ideologists in the avant-garde. Yet—and it was an important qualification—the true lover of art, he thought, with his almost mystical faith in exceptional individuals including no doubt himself, was not predestined to class or wealth. For some of them, education was not enough; for others, it was not necessary. He was committed to the interesting idea that there is more to taste than money.

BEHIND THESE ANTI-PHILISTINE declarations was the artist, rising in social acceptability. Modernism could never have got off the ground without the impassioned leadership of self-confident craftsmen feeling in no way collectively inferior to their clients. Humility was not a desirable trait in a cultural rebel. Not all the artists' pride in their calling, which became common enough in the nineteenth century, was wholly realistic, certainly not at the beginning. Shelley's much-quoted declaration about poets being the unacknowledged legislators of the world was the elaboration of a fanciful wish rather than the analysis of a social reality. The limiting "unacknowledged" did give the boast a tinge of reasonableness. And unacknowledged the artists remained; but respectability was within their grasp.

Celebrated, almost legendary masters from earlier times had shown the way. Michelangelo, the "divine" genius who could afford to defy a pontiff; Alexander Pope, who, selling his translations of Homer by subscription, escaped the customary subservience of courting noble applause and financial patronage by prefacing works with servile dedications; Samuel Johnson, whose immortal letter of 1755, rejecting the unwanted patronage of Lord Chesterfield, could, if the bourgeoisie ever had a coat of arms, serve as its device; Mozart, who in 1781 broke his servile position at the court of the archbishop of Salzburg to live in Vienna as a freelance composer and soloist the last ten years of his life.

By the Victorian decades, some, many, early patrons made imaginative novelists, architects, sculptors socially acceptable in the houses of the rich who supported their work and welcomed their friendship. In an age when writers could regard themselves as lords of the imagination, they could—and often did—look down with contempt on the bourgeois whose grandfathers had in turn looked down with contempt on theirs. It was their improving social status that allowed so many modernists to indulge their narcissistic disposition. Modernism was as much a matter of morale as of money and liberty.

THIS RICH AND COMPLEX environment greatly eased the advent of modernism, but it also drew on another epochal development that permitted it to mature into a movement more substantial than a mere distraction for bored aesthetes. Well before 1900, Western civilization seemed to be entering a post-Christian era, and modernists were deeply involved in these developments. Cultural change, as we have seen, was drastic, ubiquitous, and irresistible, and attitudes toward religion were not exempt from it. As Holbrook Jackson noted in 1913 in a well-informed survey, *The Eighteen Nineties*, the term "new" had been proliferating in titles for decades—the New Drama, the New Woman, the New Realism, and the rest—deplored by conservatives as a cover for light-headed adventurism and hailed by more liberal spirits as the signature of, well, a new age.

The historian must move warily here; for on the subject of religion, the laws of uneven development within and among societies defeat virtually every generalization. To begin with, established sectarian beliefs retained masses of loyalists in the middle classes, the very classes from which secularists also drew most of their recruits. Voltaire's call to action, *Ecrasez l'infâme,* a legacy from the eighteenth century, survived as a slogan that anti-clericals and anti-Christians continued to find only too relevant. That infamous thing, conformist belief—at least among churchgoers—buttressed by conformist churches, seemed to be enjoying more lives than a cat.

The guardians of divine truths and magical rituals, Protestant,

Catholic, and Jewish alike, might moan over the escalating secularism of nineteenth-century society, but they could also look with some satisfaction on places of worship still unquestioned, still crowded, still soundly endowed. The grip of religious bodies on education might be slipping, but they were still a cultural and political force to be reckoned with. And most countries still tied a privileged denomination to state power; the United States, which with its late-Enlightenment Constitution outlawed an established Church, was still an exception. France, that hotbed of revolutions and secular ideologists, did not decree the separation of church and state until 1905, after more than a century of wrangling.

Certainly "Post-Christian" was not synonymous with atheism. Quite the contrary, the nineteenth century was a golden age for incubating new dogmas, or for old dogmas brought into modern times as they borrowed prestige from contemporary physics, chemistry, and biology, disciplines that—even skeptics admitted—were clearing up mysteries that had been thought beyond rational explanation. That is why Madame Blavatsky notoriously advertised her version of Theosophy as a synthesis of theology, philosophy, and science. That is why, in calling her creation "Christian Science," Mary Baker Eddy, a persuasive saleswoman for her new sect, encapsulated in two key words the appeals most likely to gain the adherence of Victorian men and women.

Indeed, the very advances of scientific explanations called into being a diverse, at times desperate response; mysticism in many guises flourished as it had not done for centuries. It inundated Western civilization with a sundry menu of spiritualist dogmas all the way from primitive credulity to sophisticated logic chopping, from séances devoted to Tarot cards and table moving to semi-scientific researches into unexplained psychological phenomena. To find a congenial doctrine among the varieties of spiritualism was a welcome move for thousands, educated and uneducated alike, who could no longer accept the Christian legend of a divine Saviour and the tales surrounding his brief appearance among humans—really, when you think about it, a highly improbable story—but found it repugnant to embrace what they thought the chilly, deadening materialism of natural science.

Modernists prominently participated in these fierce debates. In fact, joining the crowded array of contenders for faith, avant-garde artists advanced their own candidate, the religion of art, cultivating what they called "art for art's sake." If, as some modernists reasoned, the age of priests was a thing of the past, perhaps the age of artists was poised to succeed it. But, understandably, the general response to this specialized theology was tepid. It was too abstract, too distant from the common predicaments that most religions address, to find crowds of worshippers. Hence, most modernists were more active in the negative side of these debates, working to destroy religion rather than to create a new one. Arthur Rimbaud, that brilliant, perverse schoolboy who compressed a career of heterodox poetry into five youthful years of feverish productivity, wrote in 1873 in *Une Saison en enfer*, "One must be absolutely modern." Not long before his death in 1903, Gauguin, in a diatribe against the Catholic Church, put succinctly what being absolutely modern meant: "What must be killed so it will never be reborn: God."

Around the turn of the century, this was still a subversive message, but no longer very original. Nietzsche, the most eloquent rhetorician of subversion, had proclaimed the death of God and the bankruptcy of prevalent morality more than a decade earlier. About that time, George Bernard Shaw, a Nietzschean among playwrights, defined his task to be making the comfortable uncomfortable, and that is what Nietzsche set out to do. He fell silent in early 1889 after an irreparable psychotic breakdown. But at the time of his death eleven years later, his stirring message, at once aristocratic and anarchistic, had begun to reach, often to intoxicate, a sizable and enthusiastic public.

To Nietzsche's mind, on the lookout for half-truths and cultural hypocrisy, no deception was more obstinately resistant to correction than self-deception. God might be dead, but only a handful of his contemporaries had accepted this crucial fact of human existence. Most people, he believed, were still being victimized by that old, ingenious Judeo-Christian conspiracy that had induced the masters to yield to the slaves. To make this great swindle plausible, the sly victors had imposed on their betters under the aegis of respectable morality and religious faith. If anyone fitted the description of heretic in chief in a century half ready for the revelation, it was Friedrich Nietzsche. More than anyone else, he provided his world with a climate for modernism.

THIS CLIMATE, THE ESSENTIAL prerequisite for the modernist revolution, was an atmosphere in which society could accept, however reluctantly, drastic departures from settled artistic habits, entertain unfashionable opinions about beauty, and tolerate conflicts among styles. For a century and a half and more, experimental playwrights and poets, architects and painters found themselves at once rejected and celebrated, decisively transforming a culture that was both resistant and excited to witness this insurrection. Slowed down by the First World War and virtually exterminated in the 1920s and 1930s in totalitarian countries, it bounced back into vigorous life in 1945 once again, to make it new. Then, in the 1960s, it died, as historical periods will. Or did it? That is a question I shall raise in its proper place.

Not that every artistic innovation deserved to triumph or even to survive; the productions pouring out from the modernist cornucopia were not automatically admirable. Still, it remains my essential point that modernism amounted to a double psychological liberation, for consumers of high culture as much as for its producers. It provided artists with a license to take their insubordinate fantasies seriously, to look unblinkingly at the canons that had for so many centuries dictated their subject matter and their techniques, to decide whether a modification— or, more radically, an overthrow—of reigning standards was called for, and that *they* would be the ones to carry through the revolution.

The way that artists profited from this climate far outstripped the public's ability to appreciate their exhilarating originality. T. S. Eliot once famously warned that most humans are unable to tolerate very much reality. This may hold true even for modernists. It may be that the greatest illusion they treasured was their conviction that they had overcome all illusions. But, however the future may come to judge them, at their best they left works that survived them and that will survive us.

PART ONE

FOUNDERS

Edouard Manet (1832–1883), *Charles Baudelaire*
(1869). One among several portraits of the
pioneering modernist by an artist the Impressionists
much admired.

1.

PROFESSIONAL OUTSIDERS

THE HEROISM OF MODERN LIFE

1.

NO SINGLE POET, NO SINGLE PAINTER OR COMPOSER can securely claim to have been the "onlie begetter" of modernism. But the most plausible candidate for that role was Charles Baudelaire. For the history of modernism, he is— along with a chosen few like Marcel Duchamp or Virginia Woolf, Igor Stravinsky or Orson Welles—absolutely indispensable. His original, immensely stimulating art criticism, his candid autobiographical ruminations, his influential translations of Edgar Allan Poe's dark tales for a French audience, his defiance of accepted boundaries in his deeply personal poetry—above all, that poetry—bear the stamp of a founder.

Like the modernists who came after him, he was a Realist with a difference: He detested the mind-numbing reproduction of the world in conventional poems or paintings, and at the same time, like the most sophisticated Romantics, had no patience with unchecked subjectivity. "What is pure art according to the modern idea?" he asked, and answered his rhetorical question: "It is to create a suggestive magic, containing at the same time the object and the subject, the world external to the artist and the artist himself." Subjective responses always remained of cardinal significance to him. Reviewing the Paris Salon of 1859, in his straightforward words, he wrote: "If an assemblage of trees, mountains, rivers and houses, that is, what we call a landscape, is beautiful, it is not beautiful by itself but through me, my personal grace, through the idea or the feeling I attach to it." A work of art is complete only when the consumer as it were cooperates with it.

BAUDELAIRE WAS BORN in 1821, to a prosperous and well-connected family. It was a France very different from the nation in which, still a young man, he would achieve notoriety as a dandy, bohemian, and poet of impressive daring. Well before he was thirty he had, with the rest of the country, lived through two royal houses. The Bourbon dynasty, restored after Napoleon's final defeat in 1815, had worked hard to re-create the clerical Old Regime as though the French Revolution had never happened. It signally failed; and in 1830, after discontent had given birth to a new revolution, Louis-Philippe, an Orléanist prince saddled with the misleading nickname of "bourgeois" king—there was in fact very little that was middle-class about his thinking—came to the throne. His platform was ostensible devotion to moderate policies. He styled himself "King of the French" rather than "King of France." He abolished censorship. He guaranteed freedom of the press. But the guarantee lasted less than five years and the dynasty only eighteen. After yet another change in regime, the February revolution of 1848, France briefly tasted the experience of a Second Republic. By December of that year, Louis Bonaparte, the canny and treacherous Nephew of a greater Uncle, was its president. His betrayal of the regime he had sworn to uphold was only a matter of time.

Aside from these stirring events, Baudelaire experienced a revolution at home. Adored by his mother and in virtually sole possession after his elderly father died, he was soon compelled to share her with a dashing rival, Lieutenant Colonel Jacques Aupick, a decent, civilized man who became her second husband when Charles was eight. Though Baudelaire at first got on with his stepfather, he never quite worked through his expulsion from paradise. He cultivated scrapes at school, but fortunately he soon discovered his gift for poetry. For some years, though, his search for the *mot juste* did not keep him out of politics. During the 1848 revolution, he made an appearance on the barricades as a republican. But then, on December 2, 1851, President Louis Napoleon rudely closed the republican interlude with a *coup d'état*. A year later he made himself Emperor Napoleon III, a disheartening sequence of events that permanently soured Baudelaire on political activism.

Yet his presumably unpolitical talents could not save him from public controversy. His career documents, in an extreme form, the interaction of politics and modernism, the difficulty of keeping matters of verse apart from matters of state. In 1857, he was put in the dock for his volume of poems, *Les Fleurs du mal*, the foundation of his enduring fame. With an indignant show of wounded propriety, the imperial government charged him with blasphemy and obscenity. The scandalous corruption in the highest circles of the Second Empire, now six years old, made this prosecution look almost like a preemptive strike anticipating denunciations of libertinism in high places. Neither Baudelaire nor his publisher had intentionally defied the authorities, but in effect his poems were testing the boundaries of the permitted, and naturally it was the state that was drawing the map. The verdict was to suggest that most respectable Frenchmen, and Frenchwomen, wanted to keep intact fences of moral control that *Les Fleurs du mal* proposed to tear down.

The prosecutor entrusted with the case, Ernest Pinard, assiduously reminded the court just how risky it is to censure a work of literature, but insisted that this book contained poems deserving to be banned for their lasciviousness. The dry rot infesting contemporary French civilization must be stopped! The court was swayed by much of Pinard's earnest rhetoric. It rejected the charge of blasphemy, but agreed that six poems were obscene, fined Baudelaire 300 francs, and decreed that the offending verses be deleted from any future edition. This decision, like the trial as a whole, shows an advanced but anxious society on the verge of making room for radical dissent from dominant social ideals. Not only had the prosecutor taken care to express his respect for the vocation of literature, but the court had diligently enumerated the places where Baudelaire had crossed the line. Much of the history of modernism during the decades that followed, in France and elsewhere, would be filled with maneuvers to permit, or refuse, public access to avant-garde literature.

As expected, the six poems that the court had outlawed were among Baudelaire's most erotic. More than one portrays his naked mistress's colorful and seductive body. Nor did he hesitate to enlist explicit sexual fantasies in the service of poetry, as in "A celle qui est trop gaie," perhaps the best known of these outlaws. In this shocking declaration of amorous ambivalence—"I hate you as much as I love you"—the poet captures a reliable way of punishing, in astonishing and appalling images, his lover's "joyous flesh." He will inflict a wound in her side and, giving "vertiginous pain," pour his "venom," that is, his syphilitic blood, into these "new lips." One can see why Baudelaire was, and long remained, an outsider to respectable French society:

> Pour châtier ta chair joyeuse,
> Pour meurtrir ton sein pardonné,
> Et faire à ton flanc étonné
> Une blessure large et creuse,
>
> Et, vertigineuse douceur!
> A travers ces lèvres nouvelles,
> Plus éclatantes et plus belles,
> T'infuser mon venin, ma soeur!

He was fully aware of his extreme audacity, and hoped that he might garner the sympathy of readers—at least of some—who might not dare to acknowledge his poetic genius. In the famous Introduction to the 1861 edition of Les Fleurs du mal, now stripped of the six offenders, Baudelaire apostrophized his "hypocritical reader" as his intimate brother: *hypocrite lecteur—mon semblable—mon frère!* But he had few brothers. He would have many, and illustrious, sons, however. And so, in retrospect, Baudelaire appears as the first in a distinguished line of cultural rebels who would gradually weaken and then partly erase the perception of obscenity and blasphemy as crimes, and do their utmost to destroy the distinction between public and private life.

IN LATE 1863, BAUDELAIRE explicated his telling phrase, "the heroism of *modern life*," in a series of articles devoted to the gifted French illustrator Constantine Guys, whom he praised for his "powerful originality." What distinguished Guys in Baudelaire's eyes was his search for the beauty of his time. Academic artists, he wrote, have dwelled on the distant past, and neglected "particular beauty," the "beauty of circumstances," for love of "general beauty." The beauty Baudelaire championed was to be found not in the glamour of politics and war, but in "the spectacle of fashionable life," of elegant carriages, smart grooms, nimble footmen, lovely women, and beautiful, well-turned-out children. Here was one good reason why, as I indicated earlier, modernism flourished mainly in great cities.

Baudelaire's modernism, then, principally included "the ephemeral, the fugitive, the contingent," and one best discovered it by strolling through the teeming streets of the metropolis. Only the open-eyed habitual *flâneur*, only the "passionate observer" who "sets up house in the heart of the multitude," will do it justice. Since Paris is, like London, an "immense picture gallery," the modern artist—that is to say, the artist of the modern—will properly read "the immense dictionary of modern life" in its ambiance.

With such faultlessly anti-historicist views, Baudelaire was speaking for a still small but growing minority of artists who were turning their back on the classical and Christian past. The incomparable artist Honoré Daumier's ridiculing Homeric heroes, and the no less gifted composer Jacques Offenbach's lampoons of legendary Greek immortals like Helen of Troy or Ulysses were symptomatic of independent minds who were beginning to question, and hoping to subvert, the time-

honored hierarchies of the arts. In company with the aesthetic revolutionary Baudelaire, they staged a humorously aggressive self-liberation
from prescribed ancestor worship. Daumier's brilliant lithographs
made the current French regime, whether the Orléans monarchy, the
Republic, or the Second Empire, the target of his wit and unmatched
draftsmanship; Offenbach's wicked operettas, including *Orphée aux
enfers* and *La Belle Hélène*, humanized grandiose figures, divine and
mortal, from ancient Greek literature, thus contributing their share in
the making of a modernism free of deference.

This shift took time. In the decades after his death in 1867 at forty-
six, the author of *Les Fleurs du mal* gradually came to command an
extraordinary following. Looking back in 1935, that once highly
regarded American poet Edna St. Vincent Millay, who had translated
some of his verses, could call Baudelaire without fear of contradiction
"the most widely read poet in France today." She might have added that
he was not only a highly readable poet but also one highly esteemed by
the cognoscenti. And his public was international.

The elevation of Baudelaire to the literary canon was in short a
strictly posthumous affair. In December 1865, profoundly disheart-
ened by the French public's indifference or implacable hostility to his
work and overwhelmed by debts, he had written from self-imposed
exile in Belgium as an outcast aware of his loneliness: "I like nothing
so much as being alone." He had little choice. True, he enjoyed an
extensive acquaintance among poets, musicians, and painters, talked
literature with seasoned professionals and promising beginners,
attended salons and soirées. Baudelaire was no hermit; as his acquaintances had good reason to know, he was loyal, generous, and open to
the world. But in his lifetime that larger world never quite returned
the compliment.

The qualities that made Baudelaire subversive also isolated him. In
July 1857, Flaubert, just acquitted after his own trial for obscenity and
blasphemy in *Madame Bovary*, thanked him for a copy of *Les Fleurs du
mal* in terms rare for a novelist given far more to disparagement than to
praise: "You have found the way of rejuvenating romanticism. You
resemble no one (which is the first of all qualities)." It was a singular trib-

ute from an authority whom Baudelaire valued as a kindred spirit. "You resemble no one"—nothing could be a more heartfelt accolade for a modernist! Granted, his writings, poetry and prose, had won a certain reputation. But he was generally disreputable as a bohemian who consorted with prostitutes and ladies of the demimonde, and who frequently sought out what he had christened "artificial paradises" and would write about vividly—the blissful and destructive dreamland of hashish and opium. He did not regard himself as a *poète maudit* for nothing.

No wonder, then, that Flaubert's enthusiasm should be as singular as it was extravagant. As early as 1855, Baudelaire had published a group of poems in the respected *Revue des Deux Mondes*—they would reappear in *Les Fleurs du mal*—that garnered some vicious reviews damning the author with immoderate adjectives. Upon publication, Gustave Bourdin reviewed *Les Fleurs du mal* in *Le Figaro*, widening the gulf yawning between the reading public and the avant-garde artist. Bourdin thundered that Baudelaire's verse made him doubt the poet's sanity; they showed the squandering of promising gifts. Their sexual explicitness particularly agitated him. "Never, in the space of so few pages, have I seen so many breasts bitten—no, even chewed!—never have I seen such a procession of devils, fetuses, demons, cats and vermin." These straitlaced denunciations illustrate the endemic conflict between respectability and the avant-garde at its most naked in the early decades of modernism.

WHAT MADE *LES FLEURS DU MAL* a founding document of modernism was, even more than its explicitness, Baudelaire's ability to merge formal clarity and licentious subject matter, the strictest rule-bound sonnets and the grossest metaphors. It is significant that Flaubert should have thought highly of Baudelaire's "asperity, with its niceties of language." In fact, the never-ending debate over whether Baudelaire was at heart a romantic or a classicist is an accolade to his ability to blend literary discipline with the efflorescence of his erotic imagination. A conventional versifier may excel in his control, a libertine in his freedom; it was Baudelaire's gift of joining technical control to emotional scope that made him so extraordinary a model for modernist poets. His assiduous followers took his unreserved praise of the imagination seriously, particularly when he joined it to verbal proficiency, because he demonstrated that he practiced in his verse what he preached in his pronouncements.

Through the decades, Baudelaire's admirers would say over and over that his voice was the voice of poetry pure and simple. It offered no political, ethical, or religious program; it did not try to impress its readers with rhetorical flourishes; it emerged from feelings, not ideas. For Baudelaire, form was a vessel that receives substance to mold into an appropriate shape. He found, to borrow a phrase from one of his most consistent admirers, T. S. Eliot, an "objective correlative" for whatever he wanted—or perhaps better, needed—to express. It followed, and particularly applied to Baudelaire (Eliot made much of this point), that the morality or immorality of a poem depends not on its subject matter but on its treatment.*

Baudelaire made his reader see, then, perhaps in some degree to share, his moods and his experiences. Some of the poetic pictures he drew were unsurprising—the sea as mirror, a ship reaching harbor, angels clad in gold—but he made even these familiar images serve fresh ends, as he gave voice to his existential despair, and grimly celebrated his liaison with Jeanne Duval, his mulatto mistress, whom soon after meeting he set up in an apartment of her own. Duval was an actress with strictly limited acting skills, and their long-term affair, frequently disrupted by quarrels, often appears in his poems, in which he celebrates her beauty, sometimes passionately and sometimes with freezing distance. Whatever suffering she put him through, she was, if ambivalently, the heroine of *Les Fleurs du mal*. She was, to him, mysterious and fascinating:

* Baudelaire commended Flaubert's *Madame Bovary* for showing that "all subjects are equally good or bad according to the manner in which they are treated." As C. K. Stead points out, Eliot's "essay on Baudelaire, or, to take another example, his remarks on Ford's *'Tis Pity She's a Whore*, show that he does not consider a poem is immoral for saying, or describing, 'immoral' things. A poem is 'moral' only in being '*complete*,' in being healthy, a true mimesis of 'things as they are,' a product of the individual sensibility in tune with 'the Nature of Things.' "

> *Tes yeux, où rien ne se révèle*
> *De doux ni d'amer,*
> *Sont deux bijoux froids où se mêle*
> *L'or avec le fer.*

> *Your eyes, where nothing reveals itself*
> *Either sweet or bitter,*
> *Are two cold jewels in which are mixed*
> *Gold with iron.*

These are lines rare in their conventional similes.

Other metaphors were all his own. In "Spleen. Quand le ciel bas et lourd," one of his most quoted poems, he visualizes the defeat of Hope as despotic, atrocious Despair triumphs by picturing a low, heavy sky weighing like a lid on a spirit moaning under long troubles, while Hope like a bat flaps its timid wings against the wall. And in "A celle qui est trop gaie" (already quoted as a witness), he shows, freshly, his frequent anguish. Plainly, Baudelaire did not find even sexual pleasure an unmixed delight. He was persistently preoccupied with human suffering—and not only his own. As the title of his collected poems hints, he chooses to deal with sin and its price, with evil and its flowers. One day, he reports, he had discussed with some acquaintances the greatest pleasure that love can give, and listened to an array of answers—to receive affection, to gratify pride, to produce new citizens for one's country—but had maintained, when his turn came, that the true pleasure of love was "the certainty of doing *evil*," something that "both men and women know, from birth, that nowhere but in evil do they find gratification." Baudelaire the dandy and social outcast was faithful to his mission as a poet, and to honest reports to the world of himself. His mixed emotions, all deeply experienced, belong on the record—he wanted, he said, to undress his heart wholly—*mon coeur mis à nu*. No other confessor, not even Jean-Jacques Rousseau, had ever been able to show himself quite so naked as this revolutionary poet. This is the way modernism begins, not with a whimper but a thrill.

As his stock in the literary marketplace steadily rose in the twentieth century, Baudelaire became a valuable enough property to have ideologists try to enlist him as a secret ally, with T. S. Eliot showing the way. "His comprehensiveness itself," Eliot wrote, "makes difficulty, for it tempts the partisan critic, even now"—as late as 1930—"to adopt Baudelaire as the patron of his own beliefs." Curiously, Eliot himself was not innocent of such appropriations, and thought Baudelaire a believer, if a heterodox one. His business, he wrote, "was not to practice Christianity, but—what was much more important for his time— to assert its *necessity*."

Eliot was not alone in trying to rescue Baudelaire for the party of traditional faith. For decades, French Roman Catholic publicists and historians like Etienne Gilson and François Mauriac took Baudelaire's guilt-ridden broodings on damnation—*his* damnation—as proof that he was trying to be a Christian entering through a back door. But this informal campaign to hijack Baudelaire for the cause of Jesus was doomed from the start, for *Les Fleurs du mal* and his other texts simply do not support such pious readings. Still, repeatedly launched and repeatedly abandoned, this crusade attests indirectly to Baudelaire's singular importance for the modernist canon. He became a writer one wanted if possible on one's side.

2.

BAUDELAIRE, FOR ALL HIS ACTIVE SOCIAL LIFE, was one of the great solitaries of modernism. There is something romantic about the lonely avant-garde artist: the poet communing with the muse on long, unmapped walks, the composer in a rustic retreat opening himself up to melodies and harmonies unheard by lesser makers of music, the novelist correcting proofs in a crowded café taking no notice of the animated clientele filling the place with talk and smoke. The larger and noisier the crowd clamoring around him, the more tightly will the creative loner wrap himself in his productive segregation.

This portrait of the inspired maker of sublime cultural artifacts at work suggests that real originality is never collective—which makes it thoroughly modern, since the creative individual (only partially glimpsed during the Renaissance) was little regarded until the age of the Enlightenment. Before then, virtually everybody knew that the ancients, or the Church, or the Bible, had thought and said it all, leaving room at most for some intelligent elaboration. As recently as the eighteenth century, writers and thinkers praised, with Alexander Pope, what oft was thought but ne'er so well expressed. For philosophes like Voltaire and his clan, Cicero was still the unsurpassed authority on matters of ethics and statecraft. In sharp contrast, the claim of being first and alone in the field became a central feature in the competitive modernist enterprise, which conjured up the figure of the inventive spirit who neither wants nor needs ancestors or company, except, of course, for his muse. In this idealized sketch, the avant-garde artist makes up a club with a membership of one.

To call originality a romantic idea calls up individualists like Stendhal and Benjamin Constant, to say nothing of Byron and Beethoven. But its deepest foundations reach down to the Enlightenment. I recall Montesquieu's boast that his work had no fathers, or the Encyclopédistes' rejection of any authority apart from reason and experience, or Kant's definition of enlightenment as a condition in which the true adult has shaken off all immature dependence. With their ideal of autonomy, these audacious intellects worked to budge mankind's attention from past to future. Their imagination, whether artistic or scientific, suggested the most decisive of oedipal triumphs, making paternal guidance unnecessary or, more drastically, having disposed of the father—creative energy liberated by parricide. Not all modernists were quite so unfilial. We will encounter many among them who treated past achievements with respect, even if they felt certain that they had risen above them.

But—there is always a "but" for the historian of culture—like all generalizations, this stark, quixotic figure, the maker of the new untouched by his past or his world, is often a simplistic idealization. As we shall see, some modernists, like the great anti-artist Marcel Duchamp, disenchanted by the inability of their fellows to adopt their ruthless iconoclasm, had no use for collective action or even a collective ideology. Yet most modernists—the abstract pioneer Vasili

Kandinsky a striking exemplar—joined or founded artistic cliques of like-minded outsiders, rebelling, inventing, suffering together. True, a few mavericks, among them Paul Gauguin, who ended up living among South Seas natives, strangers, and inspirations, or Emil Nolde, bending his ear to his innermost promptings immured in a North German fishing village, pursued their painting in demonstrative separation from respectable, mediocre contemporaries and, for that matter, from innovative fellow artists. But these conspicuous exiles, the most single-minded of professional outsiders, were the exception rather than the rule. The majority of nineteenth- and early twentieth-century artistic rebels sought emotional security in the confederacies we know as avant-gardes.

OUTSIDERS LIKE THE MAKERS of modernism collected psychological dividends from *being* outsiders, but they nearly all paid for their prominence. They could glory in notoriety—that was certainly true of late nineteenth-century bohemian circles in Munich and Paris, of Dadaist protesters against the First World War, or of self-promoting Surrealists like Salvador Dali. They could treasure being called names—immoralists, lovers of the ugly, even madmen—as proof that their work was making a difference: one of them, Oscar Wilde, will appear later in this chapter to testify. But their rejection of an artistic and popular consensus, their very originality, exposed them to the hazard of walking a solitary path. The unsuccessful collaboration that Vincent van Gogh tried to stage with Paul Gauguin at Arles late in 1888 was a symptom of his frantic effort to break through his isolation. He, like other modernists, wanted to be alone in company. The avant-gardes crowding the cultural scene of the nineteenth century were largely founded to make collective individualism possible.

These searches for approving and stimulating company were eased by shared hatreds as much as by mutual affection: few modernist groups were more stable than those formed around a single enemy—the Academy, the censors, the critics, the bourgeoisie. In the history of modernism, such alliances of convenience and fondness were potent agents for advancing the good cause. In the protracted debates that late in the nineteenth century raged in the better periodicals over the merits of tradition-minded artists compared to those of the innovators, avant-gardes were the self-appointed spokesmen for the new.

There is something singularly apt about the name "avant-garde," which troublemakers among artists, writers, and philosophers began to give themselves, or had bestowed on them, well before mid-nineteenth century. In a time of dramatic change, artistic avant-gardes prided themselves in pointing their culture in the right direction. Indeed, this metaphor, evoking brigades of subversive painters or poets in martial action, was so appropriate because it was, of course, borrowed from military usage. It called to mind the spirited vanguard of an army on the way to battle, sounding the trumpet and flourishing the flag. Cultural avant-gardes were nothing if not bellicose, stoutly proclaiming the merits of their cause, the perils of their exposed position, and the fatal shortcomings of the smug establishment that dared to oppose—and vastly outsell—them. In a time of successive enlargement of the prosperous middle classes, when the very nature of patronage significantly became more and more the business of the bourgeoisie, artists could spread their cultural and political wings more widely than ever. This, in a word, was the age in which we must seek the origins of modernism.

It is therefore significant that as early as 1821 Shelley should have been able to imagine poets as the unacknowledged legislators of the world; perhaps even more significant that eighteen years later, it should have been a second-rate author like Edward Bulwer-Lytton, a prolific, once highly appreciated English novelist and playwright, who coined the phrase, now trite from overexposure, "The pen is mightier than the sword." The notion was in the air.

Whatever avant-gardes called themselves, they left no doubt that they were at war with dominant, "official" styles of thought and practice. That is what the remarkably unconventional German playwright and short story writer Heinrich von Kleist meant early in the nineteenth century when he called his high-temperature dramas "extreme theatre." In the same decades, accepted ideas were under similar pressure from impatient and militant minorities that included, as Honoré de Balzac noted in 1846, such dissenting ideologues as "Communists, Humanitarians, philanthropists." Theirs was a stance for activists. In 1890, the French writer Pierre Loti, in a representative passage, extolled his avant-garde faith, "quite remote from the resignation of my ancestors." Subservient acquiescence—passivity, complaisance, deference to authority—was in the avant-garde's vocabulary only to be denounced.

Yet, fitting as "avant-garde" seems in its transferred meaning, in one respect it departed from its original usage. The leaders of an army, feeling the sting of hostile fire, marched toward the enemy ahead of their troops, but experimental painters and the rest turned their guns on their own rear guard. Their enemy was largely within. What William Morris, like other seditious progressives, denounced as "the philistinism of modern society" called for an intense critique of the culture in which the modernists were compelled to live. Around 1900, after decades of increasingly intense preparation, after enlarged voting rights in many countries—if not yet for women—full-fledged modernists would carry on this civil war with even greater determination. Ezra Pound's much-quoted slogan, "Make it New!," was implicit in all the rebels' programs, which, whatever their detailed proposals, stood for liberation from the burdens of the past. There was in the present age much that was regrettable, much (especially in decent taste) that deserved to be eradicated. But the cure, the modernists believed, was at hand—in their revolutionary views.

3.

BAUDELAIRE WAS A PIONEER even in coining the avant-garde principle of necessary contemporaneity. He had already said it early: *il faut être de son temps*. In his writings as in his conduct, he personified the conviction that the creative artist must not remain fixated on classical antiquity, chivalric medievalism, or bucolic idylls. Rather, he must appreciate what he called, a little unexpectedly, the heroism of modern life—the teeming metropolis, fashionable ways of enjoying oneself, even the unpretentious uniform of present-day bourgeois, the black frock coat.

A great French modernist, Edouard Manet, who was on friendly terms with Baudelaire and extravagantly, if justly, admired by progressive painters, said precisely the same thing: "The fact is, our only duty is to extract from our epoch what it has to offer us, without at the same time ceasing to admire what preceding epochs have done." In his work, he captured bourgeois at leisure in the Bois de Boulogne or, dressed up in their finery, at the Opéra. And in his portraits, he painted contemporary novelists and poets sympathetic to, or participants in, modernism like Emile Zola and Stéphane Mallarmé, and thus further underscored his own timeliness. It is not extravagant to read his paintings as Baudelaire's program on canvas.

This holds especially true of Manet's much-praised and much-debated *Olympia*, the nude he painted in 1863 and exhibited at the Salon two years later. Historians who enjoy such bureaucratic precision have called this canvas the first modernist painting, and, unproductive though preoccupations of this sort may be—there are other plausible candidates for the title, including Manet's own *Déjeuner sur l'herbe* (1863)—one can understand why. The painting flouted contemporary aesthetic and ethical standards in the most aggressive way. Manet had not idealized his model or resorted to the accepted respectful distance between the artist and the model—at least while she was posing. He had not given her a name borrowed from Roman history, Greek mythology, or natural phenomena, each of which would have been a fig leaf for her ostentatious nudity. And, to startle viewers even further, he evoked the past and the present at the same time: the seductive young body comfortably stretched out on her snowy pillows for the viewer's delight, self-confident and unashamed, is at once a free interpretation of Titian's *Venus of Urbino* and the portrait of a young Parisienne.

Still, *Olympia* got a mixed reception from reviewers, so steeped in moralizing, so offended by the model's energetic nakedness, that Zola, still a young radical journalist, defended this shameful entry to the Salon with an extreme disclaimer. He gave it a purely formal reading, arguing that the supposed subject matter of *Olympia* was really of no consequence: the painting was a brilliantly composed harmony of colored patches. A truly masterful artist could be in tune with his time without necessarily falling into obscenity or blasphemy. It was not a persuasive argument, but Manet showed his gratitude, and his collegial cordiality, by inserting a small copy of *Olympia* into his portrait of Zola. Here was more proof that advanced artists and writers really believed that *il faut être de son temps*.

4.

IN ITS EARLY DECADES, from midcentury on (to return to Baudelaire's principal occupation), avant-garde poets embodied the principle of this need for modernity with exceptional vigor. Their verses, and their increasing resort to that intermediate genre, the prose poem, stood out for intensity of feeling, audacity in subject matter, and originality of expression, all united by a characteristic effort at psychological penetration. Their commitment to their own time challenged poets to take as close a look inward as outward, perhaps closer, animated by frank, even painful honesty. In May 1871, when he was all of seventeen, Arthur Rimbaud, precocious and dissolute, said it plainly in a famous letter to a friend, Paul Demeny: "The first study of the man who wants to be a poet is the knowledge of himself, complete." A seer is made, not born, and must prepare himself for his vocation "by a long, gigantic, and rational *disorder of all the senses*. All forms of love, suffering, and madness; he searches himself." This is an "unspeakable torture when he needs all his faith, all his superhuman strength where he becomes all men: the great patient, the great criminal, the one accursed—and the supreme Scholar!" To write poetry worthy of survival requires hard, indeed exhausting work. Who but a philistine could disagree?

Uneasy about the flatness or inauthentic heroism of much contemporary verse, poets joined the forces of dissent not in France alone. Almost from the start, modernism was a cosmopolitan phenomenon. It was not a wildfire spreading from a single, identifiable source; much depended on individual artists or cultural prejudices and the strength of censorious government inhibitions. Ibsen was an acceptable playwright in Germany years before he conquered Britain. The young Eliot found French Symbolist poets far more thrilling as models than any versifier writing in English. Stravinsky could be applauded in France for decades before his Russian compatriots heard his splendid ballets. Again and again, Paris was the creative place from which the infection spread; but not as often as Frenchmen, especially Parisians, claimed to believe.

All through the history of modernism, there were important international encounters of modernists, literal meetings that will find their place in these pages. In 1881, during his American lecture tour, Oscar Wilde went to visit Walt Whitman, one outsider interviewing another. They talked about poetry. When his host wondered whether he and his friends would renounce Tennyson and other leading versifiers of the previous generation, Wilde thought that they might. True, he said, Tennyson was "of priceless value." But he acknowledged that, regrettably, this national icon had withdrawn from his age. "He lives in a dream of the unreal. We on the other hand, move in the very heart of today." This was a modernist speaking.

Wilde's host had no reason to disagree with his British guest. The poet, Whitman had written in the preface to *Leaves of Grass*, "is a seer . . . he is individual . . . he is complete in himself." And he is supremely contemporary, flooding himself "with the immediate age as with vast oceanic tides." The result: startling, unparalleled confessions felicitously expressed. In his prudent reticence, Whitman was something of an exception among contemporary modernists, virtually forced into a measure of discretion by law and custom. Hence, unlike Paul Verlaine, who did not banish his sexual tastes from his verse, Whitman virtually defied his audience to read between his lines as he shammed a robust heterosexuality. There is much talk in Whitman's *Leaves of Grass* of manly, comradely love, but there is no "Sonnet of the Asshole," a joint production by Paul Verlaine and Rimbaud, who between 1871 and 1873 did more together than compose joint sonnets. And Algernon Charles Swinburne, the representative of French modernist poetry in Britain, let the world know, even if with some indirection, that the pain he had learned to love in his public school was his greatest pleasure.

One particularly striking element in this subversive literature was that much of the time its authors poured their poetic passion into traditional vessels, heady new wine into musty old bottles. Even Rimbaud, playful and inventive as he was, wrote some fine sonnets. But it was also Rimbaud who championed the cause of formal innovation: "Let us ask the *poet* for the *new*—ideas and forms." These new forms included typographical experiments, obscene images, untried verse meters, complicated metaphors, eccentric and difficult formulations.

No poet among the nineteenth-century modernists was more eccentric and more difficult, intentionally, than Stéphane Mallarmé, aiming, as he put it, to "give a purer sense to the words of the tribe." Characteristically, Wilde, basking in his acquaintance with that master, praised his talent for being incomprehensible, at least in French—though he became comprehensible, Wilde typically added, in English translation. For Mallarmé, the late nineteenth century was a time of crisis for literature but also a time of "a great new freedom." For the first time "in the literary history of our nation, in this endeavour to disengage the ultimate essence, the soul, of whatever exists and can be realized by the consciousness, in this dutiful waiting upon every symbol, by which the soul of things may be made visible; literature, bowed down by so many burdens, may at last attain liberty, and its authentic speech." This Symbolist agenda was, with all its moderation, an expression of great hope. After the conclusion of the Franco-Prussian War in 1871, with the decisive defeat of France, there had been peace in the Western world, and good prospects for that peace to hold. As international trade rose with the decades, more and more influential personages in business, banking, and industry, even among some military men, preferred peace to war not only for economic but also for cultural reasons.

The key modernist words, each an act of aggression against the academic establishment, were all in Mallarmé's text, explicit or implied: "soul," "symbol," above all "consciousness" and "liberty." And they gave all modernists, poets naturally included, their cultural assignment. They must strike through the masks of superficial celebration and mourning to reach the deep essence of life in their own soul, and, as newly liberated artists, do so now.

ART FOR ARTISTS' SAKE

1.

BY 1867, THE YEAR OF BAUDELAIRE'S DEATH—Queen Victoria had been on the throne for thirty years and the name "Victorian" had begun to be a target of some mockery—playwrights, architects, composers, poets, novelists, and other makers of high culture who longed for social respectability had largely acquired what their forebears had long struggled for. There were still patches of ground, especially in Central and Eastern Europe, where artists had not yet wholly cast off the status of servant. But in Western Europe and the United States, they could make friends with, and marry into, the upper middle classes or the gentry, and make grand claims for the autonomy and the dignity of their vocation.

Their cause could only prosper from the spectacle of aristocrats like Lord Byron or the vicomte de Chateaubriand, who did not disdain writing poems or novels, and even getting paid for it. Even a few German states timidly joined this status revolution: Goethe and Schiller were raised to the nobility. That von Goethe was also a hardworking public servant in the duchy of Weimar and von Schiller a professor lecturing on the philosophy of history at the University of Jena did not exactly injure their social transfiguration. But their sober occupations were not the main reason for their elevation, which they largely owed to their literary fame.

The elbow room that aspiring avant-garde artists, like their more conventional colleagues, needed was more than mere celebrity. What they craved was an ideology, a solid validation of their lofty modern status. In 1835, toward the end of the promising early years of the French July Monarchy, Théophile Gautier's naughty *Mademoiselle de Maupin*, this declaration of independence in behalf of literature, proved an impressive statement. Gautier, all of twenty-three, prefaced the novel with a long, racy manifesto, which championed what would come to be called, tersely, "art for art's sake." In view of its historic import and its place in the career of modernism, it should really be called "art

Portrait of Théophile Gautier (1811–1872), poet, novelist, reviewer,
the most quotable advocate of art for art's sake.

for artists' sake," for it was a strong plea for the maker of beautiful objects as much as an appreciation of the objects themselves. It rejected the classic division between the two, which had long separated art (highly admired) from the artist (socially disdained.)

Art, so this modern doctrine goes, serves no one but itself—not mammon, not God, not country, not bourgeois self-glorification, certainly not moral progress. It boasts its own techniques and standards, its own ideals and gratifications. "I don't know who said it, I don't know where," Gautier wrote, "that literature and the arts influence morality. Whoever he was, he was doubtless a great fool." All that the arts produce is beauty, and "nothing that is beautiful is indispensable to life." The good looks of women, the charms of music and painting, are valuable to the extent that they are useless. "Nothing is truly beautiful but what can never be of use to anything. Everything that is useful is ugly, for it is the expression of some need, and human needs are ignoble and disgusting, like men's own poor and feeble nature. The most useful place in a home is the latrine." Nothing could be plainer.

Art for art's sake was in fact too direct a proposition for many advanced writers or painters to support it wholeheartedly. And yet— which is why the doctrine had broader impact than its limited explicit popularity would have indicated—anti-bourgeois, anti-academic artists were only too pleased to exploit its implications without fully subscribing to its principles. Cultural pessimists all the way back to Plato had believed that the wrong kind of poetry or the wrong kind of music have pernicious effects on morals; at the other extreme, believers in the innate goodness of human nature found it hard to abandon the hope that the right kind of poetry or music would purify conduct. Many modernist heretics retained some of the old faith that painting, the drama, the novel have a moral mission, whichever side an artist was on—for every Joyce or Schoenberg, creating for his own sake, there was a Strindberg or an Eliot working under the pressure of powerful social and religious convictions. In effect, art for art's sake was a radical assertion in behalf of nineteenth-century artworks, as well as of their makers' claim to sovereignty: the artist is responsible to no one but himself, and herself, except perhaps to other artists.

Anxious conservatives reviled this lofty self-appraisal as a typical symptom of modern arrogance.* Yet this is what England's most influential aesthete, the late nineteenth-century Oxford don Walter Pater, one of Oscar Wilde's much-quoted forebears, essentially meant with his famous pronouncement, "All art constantly aspires toward the condition of music"; or, more baldly stated, the purpose of art is art. This, too, is what the young Swinburne, still an untamed devotee of dissident French poetry, meant when he defended his first volume of verse, widely disparaged as immoral, by insisting that he had written his *Poems and Ballads* as "adult art," with a purity of its own. "All things are good in its sight." Whether his verses could be "read by her mother to a young girl" or not was perfectly irrelevant. In short, it did not take much for the cult of art to blossom into the cult of the artist. This is the cult—the cult of oneself—that James McNeill Whistler, the most barbed and most gifted spokesman for the aesthetic movement, represented in all its glory.

One can trace this development in modernist manifestos. A most articulate instance were the declarations of self-proclaimed Belgian painters who, in late 1871 after five years of working closely together, published the journal *L'Art Libre*, complete with a "Profession of Faith." It told the world that they were their country's cultural avantgarde, who represented "new art," with its "absolute freedom from directions and tendencies, its character of modernity." With confidence in the relative cultural liberalism of their country, they stood ready to assure the victory of "Modern Art" by battling "reactionary coalitions" that would try to stop them, turn them aside, or slow them down. "We want free Art. That is why we fight to the death those who want it enslaved." In its second number, *L'Art Libre* followed up this jaunty declaration of war with a solemn agenda: "Today, artists are, as they have almost always been, divided into two parties: conservatives at any

* In 1895, in *Die Grenzboten*, an eminently respectable German periodical with strong conservative leanings, an anonymous author deplores "the claims of the modern school," which has "the creative artist simply stand above the domain of theoretical art criticism. The artist marches ahead, creatively, he places the new before us; should the public not understand him, should what he has created fail to fit into the aesthetic clichés of the critics, still he must follow him."

price and those who think that Art can survive only on condition of transforming itself. The first condemns the second in the name of the exclusive cult of tradition." The identification of modern artists with the hallowed cause of Art can hardly be closer than this.

By this time, the pathetic caricature of the artist and his bitter struggles with poverty and neglect, though fading in reality, remained a familiar protagonist in fiction. In the literary imagination at midcentury, he was the destined outsider, the victim of the philistine present and the prophet of a less commerce-ridden future. Balzac's *Le Chef d'oeuvre inconnu*, the model for the genre, with its artist doomed never to finish his masterpiece, dates back to 1831. One of its best known offspring, *Manette Salomon* of 1867, was the Goncourt brothers' contribution to this literature. The two brothers, Edmond and Jules, intimate collaborators until Jules's death in 1870, were assiduous (if one-sided) chroniclers of their high-society Paris, and realistic novelists. *Manette Salomon* follows the fate of artists, two of whom seek only the truth of the modern. But both necessarily fail: society is too strong and too vulgar for them to realize their ideals. One is compromised by his inability to sustain the necessary quasi-religious asceticism—that is, the authentic religion of art; the other is destroyed by his infatuation with an irresistible, man-eating model, more loyal to her greedy and possessive family than to Art, let alone to artists.

By making that model a Jewess, the Goncourts introduced a presumably new peril to authentic modernism, one that nineteenth-century anti-Semites found easy to explore. The role of Jews in the modernist movement deserves more study than it has enjoyed. This much, though, seems obvious enough about the decisive critical decades of modernism: the emergence of Jews to full citizenship, the access to economic affluence, the opening of social opportunities, though often halting, made Jews, much like other bourgeois of their time, important beneficiaries and supporters of modernism. Their particular strength, though even that was far from overwhelming, lay among the middlemen of the arts: art dealers, publishers, critics, journalists, scholars, producers of plays and exhibitions, and other indispensable promoters of avant-garde culture. Yet, for all the widely

credited talk of Jews as exceptionally devoted to the modernist enterprise, there was really no such thing as Jewish modernist taste. Jews
bought Salon pictures as well as Picassos, resisted compositions by
Schoenberg far more often than relishing them, commissioned
tradition-minded architects in strong preference to hiring a loyal pupil
of the Bauhaus.

The Goncourts' generalizations about their principal adversary, the
bourgeoisie, are no more reliable than their slanders of Jews. Everywhere
(we have seen it before) the middle strata of society were finely differentiated and, more often than not, gained both social and legal positions
considered unthinkable a century before. But the Goncourts make cultural history easy for themselves. Bourgeois are all alike. Hence, the true
modern artist finds that "traditions, the ancients, are the stones of the past
lying heavily on our stomach." Aware of this, the modern artist must
shake off these loads by nourishing his hostility to a class that cannot tell
apart a slick production from an authentic work of art. Thus *Manette
Salomon* tries to document that the bourgeois society of its time invariably subverts the authentic by the meretricious. But the work is more a
mediocre and tendentious fiction than a dependable analysis. There were
social critics in those days who deserved criticism themselves.

THE SEEDBED FOR THE principle of art for art's sake had been planted
decades before the emergence of modernism with the idealization of
selected monuments in the world of literature, painting, and music.
While the glorification of artists' lives was anything but new—one
thinks of Vasari's biographies of Renaissance painters, to go back no
further—it received downright worshipful forms during the Romantic
decades, at least for outsized celebrities like Goethe and Beethoven.
These two, in sharp contrast to lesser fellow artists, mere mortals, were
canonized as secular saints whose possessions adorers treated like
relics. This pious vocabulary is worth noting.

Beethoven let posterity take care of his image. Not Goethe: if he
became a legendary figure, he was in large part the maker of his own
myth. He was distinguished and long-lived, dying at the advanced age

of eighty-two in 1832. During his long lifetime, he carried on a large and enlightening correspondence, explained himself in detail in his autobiographical writings, permitted—in fact invited—readers to draw biographical inferences from his voluminous poetry and prose, and gladly received visitors who faithfully recorded his sage pronouncements. The most faithful of these, Karl Eckermann, Goethe's Boswell, published his conversations with the Master in two separate volumes, in 1836 and in 1847, which both, interestingly enough, became and remained best-sellers.

This devout attitude, though it did not remain uncontested, survived through the nineteenth century and beyond, producing its share of clichés. It had its undignified moments, like the adulation of, and intrusive curiosity about, dazzling idols like Niccolò Paganini, adding up to a high form of gossip. But the spiritual tone of voice thought proper for literary and musical geniuses was more serious, and more consequential. So intelligent and professional a musician as Robert Schumann did not hesitate to celebrate Beethoven as a "high priest" officiating "at the high altar of art." Only Richard Wagner went him one better: in his essay "Pilgrimage to Beethoven," he observed that Beethoven's music was a guarantee that "my redeemer liveth," and left no doubt that his living redeemer was indeed Beethoven. In its early stations on the road to the sanctification of artists; in its distorted, almost childish simplicity, it laid the groundwork for the modernist self-confidence that would smoothe the way to success. Only the language of admiration changed, growing subtler but without giving up the religious tone. It was simply irresistible.

In 1855, Eduard Hanslick, on his way to becoming the "czar" of music reviewing in Vienna, a man who prided himself on his independence and his freedom from sentimentality, visited Weimar for a look at the houses of Goethe and Schiller. The latter was "generally accessible" and "thousands had been moved and edified as in a church." In Goethe's mansion, only the rooms housing Goethe's collections, his plaster casts and minerals, were open to the public. Though offended by this "insulting aristocratic contrast," Hanslick approved of the care with which the Master's "precious relics" had been preserved.

2.

THE CULT OF ART so easily turned into the cult of the artist because that spiritual vocabulary—"high priest" and even "redeemer"—became so commonplace among nineteenth-century artists and their admirers. In this increasingly post-Christian age, the sheen of unconditional devotion to higher things had not yet lost its luster. At the end of the eighteenth century, William Blake had pronounced that "Christianity is Art," and set it off against the worship of money. Half a century later, Arthur Schopenhauer gave such talk intellectual respectability, and in the 1890s, the popular German poet and playwright Richard Dehmel, to give but one instance, spoke for a tribe of new believers when he told a friend bluntly, "My Art is my religion." In these years the French critic Camille Mauclair wrote a book titled *The Religion of Music*. And in 1906, Shaw, in *The Doctor's Dilemma*, has the amoral artist Louis Dubedat pronounce his blasphemous creed on his deathbed: "I believe in Michael Angelo, Velasquez, and Rembrandt; in the might of design, the mystery of colour, the redemption of all things by Beauty everlasting, and the message of Art that has made these hands blessed. Amen. Amen." Shaw took care to capitalize "Beauty" and "Art," as Flaubert had done half a century before him. No doubt Art had become, at least for some, a new religion, a substitute for a fading Christian faith.

But the religion of art cannot claim to have been very successful; its rhetoric was too obviously empty and forced. Yet it retained partisans beyond the First World War. In 1920, the well-respected Italian art critic and cultural commentator Margherita Sarfatti, for years Mussolini's mistress, turned back to the old romantic fantasy. "Life imitates art," she wrote in the Fascist newspaper *Il Popolo d'Italia*; "artists are the spiritual guides who determine unawares the future attitudes of the general populace." The fantasy of the artist's omnipotence died hard.

3.

THE ADVANCED CIRCLES that backed art for art's sake were small but enthusiastic and eloquent. By the second half of the nineteenth century, the phrase had become a favorite slogan among aesthetes, often as recognizable by their dress as by their opinions. Among their most conspicuous representatives, some of them, notably Gautier, Swinburne, Huysmans, Whistler—and, once again, Baudelaire and Wilde—often almost literally wore their aestheticism on their sleeve. But to take this fashionable service to self-display as defining Wilde, probably the most extravagant of them, is to trivialize his magnitude as a cultural icon. With all his lightheartedness, as we shall see, he ended up as a martyr to the religion of art, a major figure in modernism as it was reaching toward its height.

Wilde founded no school, nor could he have done so; there could never have been a second Oscar. "The only schools worthy of founding," he once said, "are schools without disciples." His originality faced in two directions: he surpassed his followers no less than his ancestors. When he worked within a tradition, as with his dramas, he emancipated himself at the end to produce a masterpiece, *The Importance of Being Earnest*, that only he could have written. When he proclaimed, and practiced, art for art's sake, he developed a version of the doctrine that the originators would have found extravagant; he placed the critic even higher in his hierarchy of creative spirits than the artist whose work he criticizes. William Butler Yeats, who came to know Wilde in the late 1880s, called him "a man of action, exaggerating, for the sake of immediate effect, every trick learned from his masters." That is a little harsher than it need be, but it is true that for the sake of being up-to-date, Wilde, ever militant, took his avant-garde persuasion beyond the dreams of Gautier or Baudelaire.

OSCAR WILDE WAS BORN in Dublin in 1854 to well-connected Protestant middle-class parents—his father an eminent eye specialist, his mother a voluble poet and quite as fervent an Irish patriot as her husband. He shone at Magdalen College, Oxford, sporting a rare double first, celebrated for his repartee in the common room and the exquisite china in his own rooms. He was already an aesthete, and never changed. Even his political ideology, an idiosyncratic anarchistic socialism, was an outgrowth of his aestheticism: the abolition of private property and the family would create, he argued, a "true, beautiful, healthy individualism." He enchanted (though at times also put off) attentive audiences in Britain and the United States with well-constructed lectures on the decorative arts and practical household hints. His life's mission, he declared, was to make the world love beauty. Modernism had no campaigners more amusing in their propaganda work than Oscar Wilde.

He prospered in private life no less. In 1882, he acquired (all sources agree) a pretty, intelligent, well-read, and devoted wife. He charmed parties with his quick wordplay and quotable pronouncements. In the years that followed, he won his credentials as a controversialist with astute and forceful book reviews and combative essays on literary criticism. Even though some suspicious readers of *The Picture of Dorian Gray* (1891) found disturbing symptoms of perversity, they took this dark, widely discussed tale seriously. And even after his catastrophic appearances in court in 1895 both as accuser and defendant, a rout to which I shall return, even after he ended up in Her Majesty's prisons as number C. 3. 3., he could still count on a few—a very few—sympathetic friends. He died in Paris in 1900, remaining an aesthete to his last curtain call, traces of his mordant humor intact to the end. He told one of his last visitors, "My wallpaper and I are fighting a duel to the death. One or the other has to go." Predictably, this was a bout he must lose, though he was also, poignantly, a victor, transfiguring his cherished aesthetic ideal into life for art's sake.

WILDE'S LIFE WAS A persistent skirmish with the party of conformity. His much-admired wit attests to his utter seditiousness. More than a device for capturing or retaining the attention of his audiences with his "fluent paradoxes," in James Joyce's admiring words, it was his preferred way of demonstrating that what most of his contemporaries thought profound and true was superficial and false. Wilde's wit is hard to imitate but easy to analyze. Again and again he would take an accepted cliché or a commonplace and reverse it. One instance, the most-quoted Wildean epigram of them all, must suffice, this one reported by Ada Leverson, one of his steadfast followers during his months of trials. Speaking of the way that Dickens had handled Little Nell's demise in *The Old Curiosity Shop*, Wilde told her, "One must have a heart of stone to read the death of Little Nell without laughing," at once ridiculing the truism to which virtually every reader of Dickens, all too ready for tears, would have subscribed and offering an aesthetic alternative.*

No doubt, Wilde's epigrams could be too slight or too strenuous to do his critical work effectively. But his quip about the death of Little Nell is not just funny; it raises in a single sentence interesting questions about the sociology and history of taste, and about the relations of a writer to both. No wonder that Shaw should have called Wilde "Nietzschean"—Nietzsche, too, could be dazzling in his sentences, and, like Wilde, skeptical about the permanence of claims to truthfulness. The philosopher and the playwright, each in his way, shared the hazards inherent in the modernist ambiance and thus, as energetic immoralists, dared to live in precarious circumstances.

There were times when, more alert to his antagonistic milieu than most fellow modernists, Wilde showed himself aware of the risks he was taking. In 1886, almost a decade before his days in court, he famously likened the artist's life to a "long and lovely suicide," and professed no regrets that it should be so. One now reads these words, with their tragicomic mixture of casualness and solemnity, as remarkably prescient. Yet on the surface, at least until the spring of 1895, Wilde's life seemed charmed if not exactly placid, a succession of triumphs as a higher journalist and an adventurous playwright scarcely marred by a few setbacks. As early as 1881, in *Patience*, Gilbert and Sullivan had exploited him as a celebrity worth lampooning, having not

---

* In a memorable passage in praise of the imagination, Wilde built his case by a sequence of outrageous paradoxes: "Many a young man starts in life with a natural gift for exaggeration which, if nurtured in congenial and sympathetic surroundings, or by the imitation of the best models, might grow into something really great and wonderful. But, as a rule he comes to nothing." For, Wilde continues, "he either falls into careless habits of accuracy, or takes to frequenting the society of the aged and the well-informed. Both things are equally fatal to his imagination, as indeed they would be fatal to the imagination of anybody, as in a short time he develops a morbid and unhealthy faculty of truth-telling, begins to verify all statements made in his presence, has no hesitation in contradicting people who are much younger than himself, and often ends by writing novels which are so like life that no one can possibly believe in their probability."

just one but both male protagonists impersonate him. Such gentle attention served to protect him, for a while.

By this time, cartoonists were turning Wilde into a distinctive target for thousands of newspaper and periodical readers in the United States almost as much as in Britain, with his eccentric suits, extravagant neckties, and languid pose, clutching a lily or leaning against a sunflower. He spent valuable hours and exquisite care on his appearance, his speech, his instructions to his barber, his presentations of self on private and public occasions. "To become a work of art," he once wrote, "is the object of living," and he certainly believed that he was sincerely pursuing that agenda. One Christmas, when Wilde and his family were living in a small house in Chelsea, they invited Yeats to dinner, and the guest later recorded: "I remember thinking that the perfect harmony of his life there, with his beautiful wife and his two young children, suggested some deliberate artistic composition." No wonder Wilde made excellent copy, more serviceable than more humorless fellow avant-garde writers. And, except for the end, he did not object to the publicity. It kept him in the news, which was where a dandy, a work of art for artists' sake, clearly belonged.

4.

BUT THERE CAME A TIME, during his months on trial, when the public attention he had courted became a plague to him. Wilde's trials have been exhaustively examined, but their place in the career of modernism deserves further exploration. He was—we recall Yeats's impression of perfect domestic harmony—to all appearances a happy family man. But in 1886, he let a student, Robert Ross, seduce him, and from then on homosexual themes pervaded Wilde's social life, his travels, even, though more subtly, his writings. It was as though, after embracing the dangerous dogma of art for art's sake, he took on a second burden: the love that dared not speak its name. In 1891, already firmly committed to what his most right-thinking contemporaries called criminal conduct, he met Lord Alfred Douglas, who was to coin this famous definition of same-sex infatuation a year later.

Oscar Wilde with "Bosie," early 1890s, Wilde's most passionately adored and most viciously self-centered lover.

Wilde's discovery, "Bosie," was sixteen years younger than the writer who became his lover and his victim, blond, pallid, slight, a very minor poet, extremely moody and demanding. He could be charming when he wanted to be. Unfortunately for Wilde, though, he did not want to be charming most of the time but quarrelsome and vicious, utterly self-absorbed, capricious, and unscrupulous about cadging money from his celebrated lover. Wilde, though at times compelled to protest against Bosie's cruel whims, was helplessly in love; he took Douglas on trips and paid and paid, financially and emotionally.

While in those years the love that dared not speak its name was draped in euphemisms like "Greek love"—the technical term, "homosexuality," had been coined as recently as 1869—the century made a large issue of it. Scientific research into its origins and nature, or special pleading masquerading as scientific research, became a common pursuit.

Until a fanatic for truth like André Gide came along, homosexuality was practiced clandestinely, and religious believers exploited it, or rumors about it, as a stick for beating the avant-garde, as though there were something effeminate about the new music, the new poetry, the new theatre. Newly founded empires—Italy in 1870, its German counterpart in 1871—introduced legal codes as other countries revised old ones. Some states decriminalized homosexual congress between consenting adults, while others, like France, which had erased it from the criminal code during the Revolution, had never turned their back on that progressive act. But there was an important exception to this liberalization of the anti-sodomy laws of direct concern to Oscar Wilde: Great Britain. In 1885, the Labouchère Amendment added to the Criminal Law Amendment Act of that year criminalized "acts of gross indecency" between men who, if convicted, could receive sentences of two years of prison with hard labor. Henry Labouchère said later that he had introduced his amendment after reading a horrifying report on male prostitution and noted the irrational variety of ways the authorities were handling these acts throughout the country. Thus, Wilde was to be caught by a legal, perfectly logical, if inhumane, gesture. It would nearly kill him.

DOUGLAS DRAGGED HIS famous lover through ferocious quarrels, but Wilde refused to send his "gold-haired angel" packing. Only too willingly, he let Douglas introduce him to a life of debauchery. Each of them took his pleasure freely with others, increasingly with youngsters who made love for money. With every new partner, the risk of blackmail increased, but Wilde found the ready availability of beautiful boys whether in London or in Algiers irresistible. Then, in February 1895, Douglas's father, the marquess of Queensberry, on bad terms with Bosie and fiercely opposed to his attachment to Wilde, left a scribbled note at Wilde's club: "To Oscar Wilde, posing Somdomite." Wilde, not amused by the misspelling and failing to note the escape hatch that "posing" would give the explosive nobleman, imprudently sued for libel.

Inevitably, he lost his suit; the image of a concerned father eager to shield his son from iniquity, and evidence that Wilde had indulged in unsavory assignations, carried the day for Queensberry. And, since the names of prominent politicians had been introduced in the proceedings, the authorities felt obliged to prosecute Wilde instead. His first

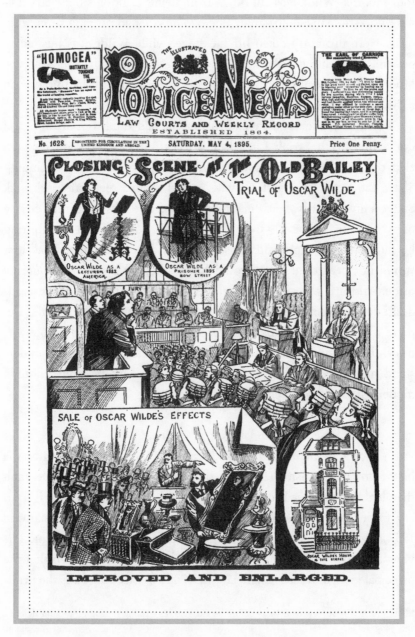

Police News, London (1895). Wilde on trial in the popular press.

trial ended in a hung jury, but in a second trial, in late May, his peers found him guilty as charged, and the judge sentenced him to the maximum, two years of hard labor.* With rude suddenness, in the space of four months, Wilde was cut down from being London's lionized playwright to stigmatized criminal. The two hits he had running simultaneously were promptly taken off the stage, while Wilde was hustled to prison. The religion of art, as I have hinted before, had its martyrs. Modernists contemptuous of hypocritical respectability had no reason to be surprised.

Why did Wilde not escape abroad, as he had ample opportunities of doing after his first trial? Literary historians and biographers have puzzled over the question for a century. Most sympathizers, including Shaw, the Leversons, and his wife, urged him to seek safety abroad. Sadly, a little angrily, he turned them down. The reasons for his course of action—or inaction—were complicated. Bosie, intent on injuring his father publicly and ready to sacrifice Wilde to his own oedipal fury, would not hear of it. Nor would his mother, in misplaced maternal pride. And it is plausible that he was driven by a largely unconscious desire for punishment, seeking a long but far from lovely suicide. But there was another probable motive: Wilde's self-image as a heroic witness for the kind of cultural elite that the vulgar always fail to understand and never fail to persecute. I cannot say it often enough: modernism was not a democratic movement.

THE LARGER MEANING of the Wilde case, then, lies in its bearing on the history of modernism. His trials did more damage to the defendant than had their prosecutions to Flaubert and Baudelaire. And it is a far cry from the Nazis' exhibiting "Degenerate Art" across Germany in 1937 as a matter of state policy. But it remains a traumatic moment. The view among a solid majority of commentators has long been that the principal instigator and beneficiary of Wilde's conviction was the prud-

* The young Ernest Newman, years before he amassed his striking reputation as a music critic and biographer, wrote that Mr. Justice Wells's denunciation of the degenerate defendant amounted to "the bovine rage of the Philistine."

ish, insipid, resentful middle-class public, impatient to disgorge its rage against a self-proclaimed culture hero who had snobbishly sneered at the morals and the tastes of ordinary citizens. In his authoritative biography of Wilde, Richard Ellmann speaks for a consensus as the trials were about to start: "Victorianism was ready to pounce."

Why? No doubt, Wilde had been provocative; he had made enemies, particularly among literary men who had smarted under the lash of his reviews. He had irritated others with his self-confident pronouncements, with his addiction to paradox, his flaunting what others were doing on the sly. There had been deep, unspoken anxiety among many who had watched Wilde in public; the apostle of pleasure had questioned their character; and now, a convicted felon, he had involuntarily vindicated it.

But there was even more to it than this: the sheer offensiveness of his art-as-religion enterprise. The response of the English press is revealing. Most reputable newspapers like the *Manchester Guardian* gave the trial only modest coverage. Other high-quality dailies like the *Pall Mall Gazette* and *The Times* treated the affair as newsworthy and entertaining, quoting from the attorneys' speeches, the defendant's testimony and the judges' comments, but studiously refrained from moralizing, refusing to feed their readers' self-righteousness.

And, significantly, those newspapers that did welcome the chance to sermonize—by no means the majority—placed Wilde's debacle in moral and cultural terms. The *St. James's Gazette*, which approved of the stern sentence meted out to the "perverted criminal," saw it as a necessary reproof to Wilde's ethical relativism, to the "New Tolerance" that had been poisoning "our art, our literature, our society, our view of things." The newspaper saw the proliferation of styles in novels and paintings and the experimental attitude toward subject matter—in a word, modernism—as a direct offspring of Wilde's libertinism. He was dangerous less because of his tainted loves than the intermingling of his erotic tastes with his "religious" advocacy of art for art's sake. Perhaps still more appalling, ran this analysis, the coexisting and collusion of these two "perversions" had served as a foundation for Wilde's haughtiness as an artist, permitting him to feel superior to ordinary mortals.

What mainly brought him down, then, was that for juries, Wilde, even though he disavowed it, appeared to be firmly committed to art for art's sake at its most extravagant. Thus he wrote, shockingly, in the preface to *The Picture of Dorian Gray*: "There is no such thing as a moral or an immoral book. Books are well written or badly written." In his libel suit against Bosie's father, he put this position on the public record. His martyrdom is inseparable from his enthusiasm for what the *Westminster Gazette* called the "unwholesome tendencies" in the art and literature he practiced and praised. Except for their libertarian impulse to commend laissez-faire in private matters, avant-garde artists had no general position on acceptable sexual behavior. Nor did homosexuals or lesbians dominate these circles. It is easy to compile a list of them— Rimbaud, Verlaine, Proust, Gide—but their sexual conduct did not define their cultural epoch. What mattered most in the Wilde case was his insistence that life and literature are two things apart, a point of view that ran directly counter to what creative spirits had believed through the centuries. In holding that trying to reform the morals of the public through novels, plays, and poems is inartistic and a sheer waste of time, Wilde invited an anxious response. And in anxiety, vindictiveness is a natural consequence.

That art for art's sake had originated in France did not make it any more acceptable to those not fortunate enough to be French. But in the end it is significant that Yeats, that powerful modernist poet, wanted Wilde to stay and face his accusers. That self-sacrifice, Yeats believed, did much for Wilde's reputation: "he owes to that decision half of his renown." This is not very convincing. Wilde's lasting fame rests on his writings, far more than on his willingness to accept suffering he could have escaped. But Yeats had a point: the stake of avant-garde thinking in Wilde's history was considerable. Granted, his martyrdom, like many martyrdoms, was largely in vain. Neither the autonomy of art nor the sovereignty of the artist was much advanced by it. But Wilde's consistent aestheticism, his courage to be pilloried as an eccentric, became a wry kind of model for a few choice spirits who would carry their defiant modernist individualism into the twentieth century.

2.

IRRECONCILABLES AND IMPRESARIOS

1900

OSCAR WILDE DIED IN 1900, IN A SHABBY PARISIAN hotel room, in the city that had been the vital center of modernist activity for decades. By the turn of the century, the Impressionists (of whom more soon) had been exhibiting their canvases, each of them a protest against Salon art, for over twenty years and were finding themselves overtaken by painters more subversive even than they. Georges Méliès was showing his experimental films. Auguste Rodin was producing, at a rapid rate, portrait busts and ambitious, controversial statues, and, about this time, was beginning to enjoy the rewards of fame. Shortly before, in 1896, Alfred Jarry had launched the Theatre of the Absurd with his remarkable vulgar play *Ubu roi*. And only eight years earlier, in 1888, Edouard Dujardin had started a new epoch in fiction with *Les Lauriers sont coupés*, introducing unprecedented *monologues intérieures* into the novel. The Eiffel Tower, a marvel of modern engineering erected for the Paris World Exhibition of

1889, painted during its construction by Georges Seurat and shown dancing in Robert Delaunay's playfully distorted canvases, dwarfed the city.

Together, these and other scandalous, or at least discomfiting, cultural events centered on Paris appeared as massive assaults on the bastions of the respectable arts. This seemed the right moment for Claude
Debussy, himself an irreproachable modernist, to repeat by now stale
insults against the philistine bourgeois herd mind, and to assert that
"art is of absolutely no use for the masses." Wilde, then, left the stage
at a time of cultural turmoil, which he had done much to provoke.

France was, at the time, heatedly embroiled in the Dreyfus case, the
trial of Captain Alfred Dreyfus, a distinguished military man of Jewish
origins, convicted in late 1894 of selling sensitive materials to France's
traditional adversary, the Germans. The case grew into an *affaire* that
split the country, as it exploded far beyond a simple case of espionage.
It brought together on one side discontented monarchists still reluctant
to accept the Third Republic that had been France's latest incarnation
since the early 1870s, modern anti-Semites who were making a political
game of hating Jews, and principled believers in the honor of the
French army which had pushed for Dreyfus's conviction.

The pro-Dreyfus party consisted largely of believers in the republic
and won impressive support from artists, writers, and intellectuals.
Emile Zola, chief among the school of French Realist novelists, and the
undisputed champion of the Dreyfusards, launched a celebrated appeal
to reverse the verdict of guilty. His argument—correct, it turned out—
was that Dreyfus had been framed and that the incriminating pieces of
evidence were forgeries. Families divided on the issue, friendships broke
up over it. Modernists who shared a principled detestation of Salon art
found themselves in diametrically opposed camps: Edgar Degas was a
furious anti-Dreyfusard, Claude Monet almost as emotional on the
other side. But the Third Republic, in real danger of collapse, survived.
In 1906, Dreyfus was vindicated, reinstated, and promoted.

NOT ALL WAS CONFLICT, though. Also in 1900, Paris, seasoned in staging world's fairs, hosted an exhibition of the arts and industry more

grandiose than any of its predecessors. A particularly interesting feature of this *Exposition Universelle* was the *Exposition Décennale*, a gathering of paintings and sculptures produced in the 1890s and selected by juries in the participating provinces. It proved a model of tolerant eclecticism. Camille Pissarro, a respected elder among the Impressionists—Cézanne proudly advertised himself as his pupil—indignantly predicted to his son Lucien, himself a painter, that the fair would be odious, "a monstrosity— bazaar, music hall," But, overcrowded as it was and incoherent in its aesthetic message, the comprehensive, downright overwhelming survey of recent work by sculptors and painters gave room to an international array of subversives: Rodin, Matisse, Maillol among the first; Renoir, Degas, Corinth, Munch, Balla, Vlaminck, Ensor, Vuillard, Nolde among the second. The sheer mass of exhibits invited criticism on artistic and political grounds, but at least the artists identified as members of the modernist camp had a chance, however limited, to shine. Even extreme dissident outsiders like Gauguin, Cézanne, and the young Picasso were represented by several canvases.

Yet the *Exposition Décennale* was more a truce, or a fortuitous result of the selectors' tastes, than a solid peace between modernists and the establishment. *L'affaire Caillebotte*, which had erupted in Paris in the mid-1890s, shows subterranean crosscurrents of hostility breaking into public notice. Gustave Caillebotte, heir to a fortune made in textiles and real estate and a notable painter—a Realist with Impressionist touches—died in 1894 and left to the state a splendid collection of paintings he had largely bought from his friends, all of them Impressionists. Plainly aware just what to expect from the enemy, he worded his will carefully and explicitly forbade having his bequest exiled to provincial museums or hidden in some storeroom. They must, he specified, first be shown together in the Luxembourg, a Parisian museum devoted to the work of living artists, and then transferred to the Louvre. Caillebotte's sixty-seven paintings and pastels included five Cézannes, four Manets, eight Renoirs, seven Degas, sixteen Monets, nine Sisleys, and eighteen Pissarros.

The response from leading spirits at the Beaux-Arts was vehement. Within the next two years, as negotiations with the Luxembourg pro-

ceeded, they rose in defense of academic art. The elderly Jean-Léon
Gérôme, in his early seventies, a faultless academician whose paintings
had won top prizes at the Salon and been acquired by connoisseurs,
maintained that the sort of art Caillebotte had gathered meant "the end
of the nation." The makers of such "dung," he said, symptoms of
"great moral depravity," were anarchists and madmen. In 1897, when
the Luxembourg finally showed the selection of forty pictures from
Caillebotte's legacy that it had accepted in a compromise, Senator
Hervé de Saisy took the floor in the Senate to deplore
this resolution. It polluted, he protested, the prized collections of the Luxembourg with unhealthy and decadent art. In retrospect these sound like forlorn voices,
futile reactionaries attempting to derail the irresistible
march of Impressionism. But to rely on them alone is to
write history from the victor's triumphant bulletins. At
the time, the conquest of modernism was still far from
assured, the inner freedom it offered a far from clear
dividend for the art-loving, and art-buying, public.

A NEW WAY OF SEEING

1.

TO GRASP THE GATHERING POWER of Impressionism,
it is best to begin at the beginning. In April 1874,
Claude Monet, not yet a familiar name to collectors,
joined twenty-nine like-minded anti-academic painters
in a crowded group show in Paris. They garnered
mixed reviews, with the unenthusiastic ones more mem-

Gustave Caillebotte (1848–1894),
Paris, a Rainy Day (1877).
This large oil is probably
his most famous canvas.

orable largely because they were to strike posterity as so laughably obtuse. The exhibitors, we read, lack all talent, they violate the elementary rules of painting, they have covered naïve canvases with scribbles that would be charming in a child but are revolting, in fact nauseating, debaucheries in an adult. Yet one of the canvases, Monet's *Impression, Sunrise* (*Impression, soleil levant*), painted two years before, achieved a somewhat factitious immortality. Later art historians and critics have fastened on this painting for supposedly giving its name to what would

prove to be the most momentous gathering of avant-garde artists in the nineteenth century. Impressionist paintings monopolized the entrance chamber, filled with lovely and nowadays hideously expensive pictures, in the palace of modernism.

In truth, the labels "Impressionist" and "Impressionism" stood from the first as a collective designation that included, in addition to the work of Monet, that of his most interesting associates: Pissarro, Sisley, Renoir,

Degas, Berthe Morisot, the young Cézanne, and a slightly older major artist, Manet, who refused to join the exhibition yet whose canvases the participants unanimously admired. This correction, placing credit where it belongs, underscores the ability of contemporary critics to recognize from this opening exhibition onward that they were face to face with a groundbreaking approach to painting. In 1876, Edmond Duranty (the writer, we recall, who wanted to burn down the Louvre) christened it

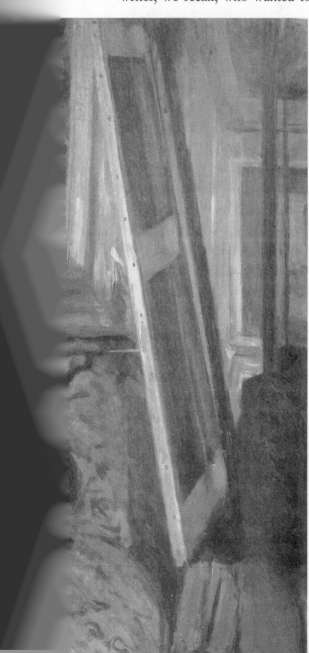

"The New Painting." It was a style and more than a style: it was a new way of seeing.

The new painting was, of course, not wholly new. Two English masters, John Constable and J. M. W. Turner, whose work French artists came to appreciate, had already painted out of doors earlier in the century and brilliantly sought to capture the impact of rain, clouds, and sunlit scenes on their sensibility. Again, the young Monet enthusiastically praised the more recent Barbizon School of landscape artists, notably Constant Troyon, Théodore Rousseau, and Charles-François Daubigny, as true students of nature, a compliment he extended to Jean-Baptiste-Camille Corot.

Other painters had much to teach the Impressionists, such as Gustave

Gustave Caillebotte, *Self-Portrait* (1892). A rare self-portrait by the greatly gifted semi-Impressionist.

Courbet, with his powerful, tough-minded realism, and the Dutch artist Johan Barthold Jongkind, who specialized in luminous harbor scenes, and whose career as an early Impressionist was badly damaged by his drunkenness. The Impressionists never denied this ancestry; but they were aware, too, that they had taken these painters' unconventional experiments to unfamiliar levels and, consolidating themselves as a movement, had indeed made painting new. Over and over we shall see that modernist breakthroughs were less often abrupt, wholly unforeseeable innovations than a gradual, step-by-step conquest of uncharted territory.

The artists who organized this historic 1874 exhibition must have had an inkling of its possible importance. They formally incorporated themselves as a Société Anonyme des Artistes, Peintres, Sculpteurs, Graveurs etc., sharing the expenses and, they hoped, the profits. In the end, after their show closed on May 15, the expenses greatly exceeded the profits and, prudently enough, the society dissolved itself. It was not surprising that Monet, who had put a price tag of 1,000 francs on *Impression, Sunrise*, failed to sell it. The vocabulary of Monet's harbor scene, as that of most among his fellows, was still too unfamiliar, too distant from common aesthetic perceptions, even among sophisticated tastes, to find buyers easily. The first serious collectors of Cézanne, to give but one instance, were eccentrics: an impecunious dealer in art supplies, a country doctor who dabbled in art, a midlevel customs official. The time when the monied would discover these artists was still two or three decades away, and by no means predictable when this exhibition opened its doors.

MONET'S *IMPRESSION, SUNRISE*, depicts the harbor of Le Havre, misty with daybreak. The water is gray, dappled with faint dark gray and black touches; two small boats, jet black, dominate the center; the buildings in the middle distance and looming cranes emerge from a veil of retreating darkness; the sun, still low on the horizon, is an orange-red disk reflected in the water as indistinct squiggles, and the sky is mottled as the morning beats back the night. Altogether truly an impression, a highly accomplished impression, looking far more casual a piece than it really was. A characteristic specimen of the new painting, it tells no stories and offers no lessons; it does not aim at making its viewers more devout, more moral, more patriotic, or for that matter, more sexually aroused. Like other Impressionists, Monet had painted it outdoors, capturing the fleeting moment.

And he was certainly deliberately, fiercely, up-to-date. Almost by definition, Impressionist painters were carrying out Baudelaire's influential agenda to lavish all their attention on the present in which they lived and to which they responded. History painting, a highly honored genre favored to secure medals at the Salon, did not interest these subversives in the least. In 1868, the proto-Impressionist painter Eugène Boudin, who had been Monet's teacher and inspiration, wrote to a friend that the time for artists to be in tune with their moment had come. To paint the people of one's period was "now making its way, and a number of young painters, chief among whom I would put Monet, find that it is a subject that until now has been too much neglected." A self-doubting but persistent chronicler of small, modest beach scenes, Boudin was announcing the program of an avant-garde that could come to prosper beyond the imagination of most modernists.

To be sure, the Impressionists' introspective stance had an objective correlative: their subjects—landscapes, cityscapes, portraits—are plainly recognizable, but not spectacular, not picturesque, and virtually interchangeable. Their paintings are paintings, nothing more, with energetic, striking, visible brushstrokes and high color, calling attention to themselves as paintings. They seem to have been dashed off quickly; a prevalent criticism of Impressionist canvases was that their makers had not taken the trouble to finish them. This was a serious, if understandable, misreading, but that much is true: Impressionist paintings were reports from the interior. Renoir is reputed to have replied to the question whether he painted from his head or his heart, "*Non, mes couilles*—my balls." Had he known of this statement, Freud, for whom the erotic origins of art were obvious, would have been gratified.

In and of itself, the Impressionists' productive self-absorption, which cheerfully violated the canons of academic painting, made many art lovers of their day feel uneasy and cheated. They were used to seeing meticulous finish: every button of an officer's uniform correctly rendered, as in the highly prized, and priced, Gérômes; they expected an erotic charge: every nude in an antique or Oriental scene voluptuous, provoking fantasies, as in the no less expensive Cabanels. They wanted for their walls paintings of sturdy peasants, anecdotes that made them smile, grand battle scenes, respectful portrayals of Jesus or the Virgin Mary that would direct their thoughts to higher things. But the Impressionists offered them humble

fare, nothing more than sketches. There were presumably authoritative gallery visitors who thought them not worth a comment. In 1877, Harper & Brothers published S. G. W. Benjamin's well-illustrated *Contemporary Art in Europe*, which, in a sizable chapter on France, does not waste a single word on Monet and his friends.

This silence is an eloquent, if involuntary, tribute to the revolutionary impact of Impressionist art on its time; an impact that, in view of how familiar, even innocuous that art seems nowadays, requires an exercise of the historical imagination to appreciate.* Significantly, contemporaries gave these artists a political twist to link them to the anxieties haunting the French, just getting used to their Third Republic, far more than any ideological consensus among the Impressionists. We recall that between 1868, when Monet and Renoir had fully developed the Impressionist idiom, and 1874, the year of the first "Independent" exhi-

* In his authoritative study of the avant-garde, Renato Poggioli has justly noted that "impressionism, for all its placidly serene inspiration and the quiet integrity of its work, must be considered a genuinely avant-garde movement, perhaps the first coherent, organic, and consciously avant-garde movement in the history of modern art."

Claude Monet (1840–1926), *Impression, Sunrise* (1872). This famous rendering of the harbor at Le Havre was widely credited with giving Impressionism its name.

bition (until 1886 there were to be seven more), the country suffered a series of humiliating and sanguinary blows: in the fall of 1870, a humiliating war against Prussia; in the spring of 1871, brutal and bloody civil strife, concentrated on Paris, launched by pitiless government troops against the "forces of sedition" who had refused to bow to the peace treaty imposed on France by a gloating victor.

And for a worrisome stretch of time, no stability. In 1874, France was no longer an empire but not yet a secure republic. During those years, nearly everything could be interpreted as political, and the Impressionists, too, were enlisted—by others—in the sanguinary drama that divided France into irreconcilable camps. Some commentators preferred the label "Intransigent" to that of "Impressionist," linking these loosely allied painters to extremists. "The Intransigents in art are holding hands with the Intransigents in politics," an anonymous journalist charged in *Le Moniteur Universel* in 1876; "nothing could be more natural." To this conservative, and to others like him, artistic subversion was the twin, or at least a close relative, of political subversion. To its opponents, modernism was, in a word, dangerous.

Actually, the Impressionists' political convictions ranged from anarchism to liberalism to reactionism. What *was* true was that they were trying to be objective about their subjectivity in their art, which was thus irreconcilable with all time-honored academic ideals where the inner life of the artist played no part. They certainly deserve the name of authentic modernists. In 1878, Théodore Duret, perhaps the most active supporter of the Impressionists among critics, put it perceptively in a pamphlet, *Les Peintres impressionistes*, in which he defined their essence as an assertion of the most profound individualism. Each of their landscapes, still lifes, or genre scenes documented their responses to external stimuli in defiance of the accepted principles of art taught in academies and studios alike.

While the Impressionists were generally not very articulate about their motives and their aims,* a few comments gleaned from their let-

---

* Some of them, it is fair to add, were not even interested. Renoir has been quoted as saying, "Don't ask me whether painting ought to be subjective or objective. I don't give a damn."

ters or interviews amply support this reading of their sense of themselves as individualists, as artists with a new, highly personal ideal. Thus, early in September 1868, Boudin defended his distinctly unfashionable style of painting outdoors after nature, and decided that, however strongly others might object, "I still persist in following my own little road, however untrodden it may be, wishing only to walk with a surer and a firmer step." On virtually the same day, desperately unsuccessful with his paintings and literally near starvation, Boudin's friend Monet expressed the same conviction. Writing to his fellow Impressionist Frédéric Bazille from the provinces that he was glad to be away from the capital with all its distractions, he asked rhetorically: "Don't you think that one is better off alone with nature? One is so completely preoccupied with what one sees and hears in Paris, if one is to remain strong; what I do here will at least have the merit of not resembling anybody, because it is simply the expression of what I've experienced by myself." *What I do here will at least have the merit of not resembling anybody*—a declaration of independence, of artistic autonomy and uniqueness which, we remember, Flaubert had told Baudelaire was the first of all qualities.

2.

THIS "FIRST OF ALL QUALITIES" was not confined to France. Not long before his death in 1896, Sir John Everett Millais, Bart., probably Britain's most famous painter, reflected on this quality most emphatically, drawing on the wisdom gained in half a century of making pictures. In 1848, still plain Mr. Millais, he had joined two close friends, Dante Gabriel Rossetti and William Holman Hunt, and four other youthful artists, also students at the Royal Academy of Art in London, to found the Pre-Raphaelite Brotherhood. The group, first advertising itself a little mysteriously with the abbreviation "P.R.B.," vowed to restore the purity and vitality of English art by rescuing it from the deadening monotony of academic instruction. The sheer hatred of academies of art, whether in London or Vienna or Düsseldorf, runs through the history of modernist painting like a leitmotif. Rebels

Berthe Morisot (1841–1895), *On the Balcony* (1871–72). Though occasionally patronized by her fellow Impressionists, Morisot was a gifted and versatile artist.

denounced them as the nemesis of talent and true feeling. What the Pre-Raphaelites wanted was artistic truthfulness, a recognition of the authentic coloration of nature all across the canvas, and, a little paradoxically, access to the spirit of their time by going far back in the history of art to the honest painting that had been so fatally sidetracked (in

Ruskin's dramatic phrase) by the "vapid fineries," which elsewhere he calls the clear and tasteless poison, of Raphael's work.

Now, Millais joined praise of contemporary English art to a solemn warning: "But while we look around and congratulate ourselves on the number of young men whose brilliant talents hold out such bright promise of worthily upholding the English school, we must not forget that only by insistence upon their *individuality* of conception and expression can they hope to advance to the first rank." The emphasis was Millais's. Like the avant-garde clusters that came after the P.R.B.— much, in fact, like the Impressionists—the Pre-Raphaelites were united more by what they detested than what they valued. Though their paintings exercised considerable collective influence and their prolific output would figure prominently in British museums as so many Pre-Raphaelite masterpieces, the most talented members of the P.R.B. soon drifted apart to pursue their own particular way with the brush. And Millais, that articulate onetime rebel, ended up much as a number of other modernists did, tired of their outsider status: an ornament to society, president of the Royal Academy, and a baronet. It is a demonstration of the absorptive capacity of modern bourgeois society.

FATIGUE WAS NOT the only reason for rebels changing fronts. Growing acceptance of the new by patrons and clients, too, could be a drain on rebellious energies; an embrace could be as stifling to modernists as obstruction or censorship. But that did not happen with the Impressionists who survived into the twentieth century. Monet, the archetypical Impressionist, who died in 1926 at the age of eighty-six, grew if anything bolder in his last years, and it was not his problematic eyesight that drove him to his experiments. His late landscapes, the waterlilies, willow trees, and the Japanese bridge on his Giverny property, seem almost abstract in their emphatic brushwork, their intense identification with the tangled scene before him. The link to nature, though, held secure; these paintings show the outdoors through Manet's schooled and impassioned perceptions.

The passage of time blurred the sharp outlines of Impressionist rad-

icalism for the educated public, and the name grew into a lazy generalization. The divergences and quarrels among the new painters
remained of interest mainly to experts; Manet's consistent refusal to
exhibit with the Independents, Degas's unique classicism, Seurat's scientific study of color theory, Cézanne's almost autistic reinterpretation
of nature, could all be assimilated into a single family, delightful, colorful artists all, whom it was a pleasure to look at and hard work to differentiate. In 1892, the English critic Charles W. Furse alerted his readers
that they were "probably familiar with the use of the term impressionism. It is one of the commonest in the art jargon of the day and bears
with it the peculiar advantage of being, to most people, a mere phrase,
utterly intelligible, and consequently suggestive of high culture." He
was no doubt exaggerating the imprecision of art talk, but not by much.

The accessibility of Impressionist art grew with the inventions of
modern communication. Innumerable and inexpensive reproductions,
more and more in relatively faithful color, made these canvases easily
available to thousands of people looking to decorate their walls; some
of these consumers, usually young, would grow into collectors who
could afford the originals. Worse, an international array of painters,
trendy and influential, known as the *juste milieu*, claimed the prestige of
Impressionism for themselves while smoothing down its more daring
innovations. No wonder that affectionate adjectives like "pretty" or
"charming" abounded, taking the bite out of the Impressionists' individuality and trivializing their tough and honest subjectivism.*

Meanwhile, financial opportunities beckoned for Impressionists.
Not for Sisley, whom his fellow Impressionists thought the equal of
Monet: down to his death in 1899, he was in unremitting financial
straits, often compelled to sell some of his finest landscapes for 1,000
francs or less. Not for Pissarro, who through the years eked out a mod-

---

* Some of the most contemptuous critiques of the Impressionists' supposed insipidity were
offered by rival modernists. Here is Paul Signac, after Seurat the most eminent (and politically
the most radical) among the Neo-Impressionists, commenting on a sale of Sisleys in 1887: "The
public and the buyers are certainly snapping up second- and third-rate artists. What is Sisley? A
middle-class, prettified Monet that people will fight over to decorate the living rooms of apartments rented for 4,800 francs on Boulevard Haussmann. . . ."

Paul Cézanne (1839–1906), *Mont Sainte-Victoire* (1885–87). One of many instances of Cézanne doing his favorite landscape.

est living with his art. It was Monet whose prices rose spectacularly year after year. As a young painter, he had sometimes been, like several of his painter friends, destitute enough to satisfy the requirements of a sentimental writer for a poor but happy *vie bohème*—he even claimed to have made what looks like a halfhearted attempt at suicide in 1868. But that dismal condition did not last. As early as that same year, he sold a painting for 800 francs; and in 1879, he earned over 12,000 francs, a sum that a professional man, a physician, a lawyer, a higher government official would have regarded as a banner year. Yet he tripled that income in the early 1880s, and in 1895, he reached the economic stratosphere by making more than 200,000 francs. The Americans, the barbarians whom so many Europeans liked to denigrate as materialistic and uncultivated, made him a millionaire.

But this rapid-fire outline history of Impressionism in glory does an

Alfred Sisley (1839–1899), *Snow at Louveciennes* (1878). A fine Impressionist representation of what the art critic Robert Hughes has aptly called "the landscape of pleasure."

injustice to the power and persistence of conservative tastes. The market for old masters, or for academic contemporaries, did not fade in view of the Impressionist surge. If Louisine Havemeyer, Mary Cassatt's friend, bought Manets and Monets, her husband, Henry, who had engrossed the American sugar market, bought Rembrandts, some of which were even by Rembrandt. James Simon and Eduard Arnhold, two of imperial Germany's richest men—both known as *Kaiserjuden*, Jews on fairly close terms with Wilhelm II—were important collectors, with Arnhold graduating to Renoirs and Cézannes after casting off safer, more traditional art, and Simon specializing in painters of the Italian Renaissance.

Some of the most assiduous art lovers of the late nineteenth century spent their disposable income on the stars of the Salon. In the approving company of fellow millionaires in Baltimore, William T. Walter put together an impressive collection that included Barbizon canvases but featured Gérômes and similar aesthetically correct masters. The highest price he paid was a fantastic 128,000 francs for Meissonier's *1814*, showing a stern-looking Napoleon astride a white stallion. Some civilized and sensitive lovers of art retained reservations about the Impressionists' appearance of insouciant spontaneity. Henry James, who did think them "decidedly interesting," cautioned against the "latent dangers of the Impressionist practice," and called them, not uncritically, "the Irreconcilables." And for many, Irreconcilables these modernist agitators remained.

MIDDLEMEN AS PEDAGOGUES

1.

THOUGH THEY TOOK PRIDE in their rebelliousness, the most isolated modernists were never alone, whether irreconcilable or not. They had fellow rebels as allies, of course, but, quite as important to them, they were surrounded, especially from the nineteenth century on, by cultural middlemen who advertised, and profited from, their talents. Impresarios shepherded violinists and sopranos from concert hall to concert hall, art dealers tried to persuade their acquisitive customers that their collections would be nothing without this or that gem from their stock, producers of plays and operas tempted audiences with spectacular staging, literary and art critics spoke for, or against, innovators in as authoritative a tone as they could muster. They, and other middlemen of culture, intervened in the making of taste, trying to entice lovers of art, music, and literature, many of them new to the culture market, to rise above easy entertainments and learn to appreciate the sophisticated, the difficult, the unconventional.

To be sure, there had been such intermediaries for centuries: art auctions appear in the sixteenth century, art dealers in the seventeenth, managers arranging concerts for composers and performers in the eighteenth, and so do reviewers of books, recitals, and exhibitions. But in the Victorian decades, with the spectacular new prosperity among the middling orders, all this grew into an industry. The public market in the arts, as distinct from commissions handed down by the aristocratic and the commanding, was transformed almost beyond recognition.

BY MID-NINETEENTH CENTURY, then, the beginning years of modernism, these middlemen were amassing enough influence to channel—and create—demand. Around 1870, there were more than a hundred art dealers in Paris alone. Since collecting presupposed the ready availability of free-floating cash, its history is irrevocably interwoven with maturing capitalism. Once private citizens began to be seriously engaged in the cultural market, works of art became, more than ever, a commodity.* This commercial activity could be, and in the nineteenth century often was, a pedagogic enterprise. If any demonstration is needed of Adam Smith's famous invisible hand of capitalism—the unimpeded (and legal) activities of self-interested merchants producing unintended benefits to society—it is here. Businessmen of culture offered and sold artistic products, whether dramas, drawings, or volumes of poetry, and with the same gesture advanced the aesthetic cultivation of the buying public.

Without these aides, modernism would probably have remained the special province of a few monied and eccentric amateurs rather than swelling into an irresistible avalanche that would enforce fundamental transformations in taste. The great cultural upheaval that was the work

---

* I want to note here that the ugly, now fashionable term "commodification" utterly fails to convey the complexity of the transactions between dealer and buyer. It grossly slights the latter's aesthetic, strictly non-commercial passions. Besides, art had been, at least in part, a commodity for two millennia.

of the modernists was in part a matter of large numbers: though philistine taste continued to command the buying habits of the majority among the prosperous, a pro-modernist minority could revolutionize one cultural domain or another, if it only had enough money to back up its astonishing desires, and it usually did.

Admittedly, much of the time that invisible hand of commerce in culture, far from raising the general taste, only leveled it. Art dealers, booksellers, concert managers were under pressure to give their market what it obviously wanted rather than take the trouble of breeding it up to recognize, and despise, readily digestible gratifications. Salesmen of high culture could not help noticing that diverting stuff was easier to dispose of than complex, profound, in short, demanding work. And so, all too many entrepreneurs showed off sentimentality as emotional depth or flogged kitsch as everyone's natural favorite. They could count on a certain indolence in aesthetics on the part of their prospective customers, perfectly understandable among people not sufficiently versed in the subtleties of musical or literary composition and too tired to give them the attention they needed and deserved.

But the easy choices that concert entrepreneurs, gallery owners, or museum directors made in their efforts to provide pleasure did not always spring from sheer cynicism as they confronted well-heeled parvenus. These middlemen between producers and consumers were not necessarily men of avant-garde tastes themselves. Yet they were only part of the story, since in the society in which modernist protests were beginning to take root, a growing segment of possible audiences looked for progressive tuition in the arts, even—or particularly— when it contradicted the commonplaces they had grown up with. Thus cultural entrepreneurs could serve as public preceptors, at least some of the time for the better. One often forgotten role of capitalist is that of educator.

TWO IMPORTANT DEALERS, Knoedler in New York and Durand-Ruel in Paris, document their convoluted share in the history of modernism. Knoedler, a family firm with unfailingly safe tastes, was founded in 1846

and continued to expand with the years, moving more than once from its downtown Manhattan quarters to other, ever more opulent mansions. By 1895, the firm had opened branches in Paris and London, a way of acknowledging the provenance of most of its stock. The house made little effort to keep up with changing tastes; the American magnates who became its regular clients—John Jacob Astor, Collis P. Huntington, J. P. Morgan, H. O. Havemeyer, a gathering of multimillionaires—consistently supported its conservative bent. For many decades, the real money was in old masters, the Knoedlers' specialty. If, in 1870, the firm managed to extract $16,000 from William H. Vanderbilt for a Meissonier, they charged Andrew Mellon over $1 million

Paul Durand-Ruel (1831–1922). The Impressionists' most daring and most consistent dealer for decades.

for a Raphael *Madonna*. Not that they wholly slighted contemporary schools—they hung the modest, attractive landscapes of the Barbizon School on their walls, and a few living American artists. But for Manets, to say nothing of Cézannes, American collectors had to go elsewhere.

They had to go to Paul Durand-Ruel. From its beginnings in the early 1870s, his art gallery had bought Impressionists at low prices, paying these artists anywhere from 140 to 500 francs a canvas, and selling them at a reasonable markup. This enterprising buccaneer bought up roomfuls of paintings at a time or undertook to purchase a favorite artist's complete production. His raid on Manet's studio in 1873, when he picked up twenty-three paintings for 35,000 francs, proved immensely profitable to him as he disposed of these treasures at from 4,000 to 20,000 francs apiece. And his contract, dating from 1881, to buy anything that Pissarro would paint in the future gave Durand-Ruel a virtual monopoly on that modernist's output, which at the time was selling for a mere 300 francs a canvas, and netted ten times that much and more.

Durand-Ruel, then, was a speculator with a taste for the future. The painters he mainly admired, he said—the Impressionists—"are worthy of being included in the most beautiful collections." In a world in which conformist tastes were under strong pressure but continuing to have their partisans, art dealerships could be found on every side. It is worth noting that in the midst of his aesthetic radicalism, Durand-Ruel was a consistent reactionary in matters of religion and politics, a good Catholic and loyal monarchist—yet another refutation of the legend that modernists are unswervingly on the left.

There were years, especially in the late 1870s, when Durand-Ruel was in financial difficulties, and temporarily dried up as a source of support for French modernists. But he recovered and the Impressionists recovered with him. In 1883, he sent a selection of his rich holdings, including his Impressionists, to Boston. Wealthy Americans had come to Durand-Ruel's gallery in Paris, and now he came to them. By 1886, he had opened a branch in New York. It was a shrewd and profitable move. Although American reviewers continued to express doubts about the new painting with aesthetic objections familiar from Europe, enough Americans became art enthusiasts as converts to Impressionism. The power of dealers was not the least element in helping to accomplish this revolution.

ANOTHER POTENT TEACHING INSTITUTION in the arts, that of critic, aimed at consumers of culture rather than its producers, developed a relationship with the arts more ambiguous than with dealers and impresarios alike. "There is a certain portion of the reading public," the *Musical Times and Singing Class Circular* of London noted in 1889, "whose minds are of so invertebrate an order that they are either unwilling or unable to form an opinion for themselves. To them any statement proceeding from an authoritative source appeals with convincing force." Unfortunately, too many appealing sources deserved less authority than they claimed.

Especially in mid-nineteenth-century France, when that new institution, the large circulation newspaper, acquired ever wider readership, the field of literary journalism was overrun with venal hacks whose opinions were not their own. They wrote what their editor ordered them, or the artists they covered bribed them, to write. Balzac's depiction of them in *Les Illusions perdu* as a morass of unscrupulous scribblers in the Paris of the 1840s is a caricature, but only slightly overdrawn. These professional philistines spoke only to, and made more, philistines. Avant-garde artists had neither the money nor the inclination to win them over.

Corruption, though, was only a relatively minor threat to avant-garde artists compared to the incurable ignorance or inadequate cultivation among critics. In 1891, Henry James lamented the overflow of literary chatter fueled by writers utterly unqualified to pronounce on such sacred subjects as contemporary fiction or poetry, music, or painting. The very multiplication of printed opinion in the Victorian age was, he wrote, summoning up his most resonant organ tones, a "catastrophe," amounting to "the failure of distinction, the failure of style, the failure of knowledge, the failure of thought." This was a little too grimfaced. After all, the century suffered no shortage of perceptive critics, from William Hazlitt to Bernard Shaw, not to mention James himself.

One French art critic, Théophile Thoré, was responsible for nothing less than the discovery of Jan Vermeer, among the greatest of seventeenth-century Dutch painters. And these journalists worked in a brilliant professional company—producers of masterpieces who doubled in well-informed criticism: writers like Theodor Fontane and Oscar Wilde, composers like Hector Berlioz and Robert Schumann, poets like Charles Baudelaire and Théophile Gautier, painters like James McNeill Whistler and Max Liebermann. All of them, far from denying new talent or resisting change, forcefully wrote in behalf of both.

But the critics' erudition and sympathy, no matter how extensive or lively, were no guarantee that they would be receptive to modernist experiments. Being only human, the finest of them could be tone-deaf in one register or another. Perhaps the most respected of literary critics whom virtually all educated French readers took as their guide, Charles-Augustin Sainte-Beuve, failed to appreciate some of the fresh talents that audiences would come to greet as the first of the modernists. His vigorous praise of Flaubert's *Madame Bovary* in 1857 promptly after its publication displays his perceptiveness and generosity toward an original contemporary master. But later critics of this critic, most famously Marcel Proust, found him too much the historical and biographical judge to recognize the revolutionaries in his time. And it is true, Sainte-Beuve spoke highly of Baudelaire, but, it seems, not highly enough, and his record on other outsiders is not radiant. In short, modernists were compelled to fight their way partly against the critics whose goodwill they would have valued and whose verdicts posterity has wondered about.

2.

THE NINETEENTH CENTURY witnessed the rise of other new men of power, museum administrators, a breed whose backing many avant-garde artists (apart from those who wanted to burn museums down) highly appreciated and whose opposition they judged extremely damaging to their cause. The Victorian century was an age for the founding of museums in every civilized country, and the men chosen as directors occupied strategic posts. Strategic and exposed: they had to maneuver between boards of directors or a busybody ruler on one side and the art-loving public on the other. Hence a complex code of conduct, demanding at once flexibility and firmness, was of particular significance for them, more significant even than scholarship. They were cultural diplomats in trying posts, art collectors in the public interest and with the public's money. This meant that they had to nurture being ingratiating without being servile. And of all late nineteenth-century museum directors, the one most strikingly equipped with such weapons was Alfred Lichtwark, who as we know had presided over Hamburg's Kunsthalle since 1886. I have learned from him before; he is worth learning from again.

In 1891, Lichtwark commissioned Max Liebermann to paint a full-length, life-size portrait of Carl Petersen, Hamburg's principal mayor, to inaugurate a new "Collection of Pictures from Hamburg." It was a risky move: Petersen, white-haired, handsome, carrying his advanced age with impressive dignity, belonged to the old local elite and was not known to be a devotee of artistic experimentation. For his part, Liebermann, a native Berliner well known for his wit, by then one of his country's best known painters, bore the stigmata of being an iconoclast: many called him, a little imprecisely, an Impressionist, even though he was a relatively mild sort of modernist. That he was also a Jew did not help him in some quarters. But, more important, his detractors huffed that he was a champion of ugliness in art.

Liebermann's sizable and enthusiastic clientele, which included Lichtwark, did not agree. In his choice of subjects, he was noted for crowded genre scenes—children in an Amsterdam orphanage, without pathos—and for portraits, chiefly of prominent professional men. He had honed his style under the impress of contemporary French and seventeenth-century Dutch artists—Théodore Rousseau for the first, Frans Hals for the second—whose paintings he visited and revisited on annual tours to the Netherlands and France. Then living in Munich, two decades before the Petersen commission Lieberman had secured widespread publicity, twice. He had painted a realistic twelve-year-old Jesus in the Temple with no attempt to idealize the priests or, for that matter, the Saviour—a scandalous canvas that generated an ugly debate, including harsh speeches in the Bavarian legislature. And he had sold a large painting showing peasant women in a barn plucking geese, the *Gänserupferinnen*, for 3,000 Deutschmarks, a substantial sum that amounted to about two years' pay for a skilled craftsman. Since then, his palette lightening, he had come close to seeing the world through modernist French eyes.

Still, Lichtwark thought he could take a chance on Liebermann. He had met the man and liked him, visited and corresponded with him, and two years before had bought one of his paintings for the Kunsthalle. A knowledgeable art historian with firm tastes, Lichtwark was the model of a museum director, a public servant who worked hard and skillfully at satisfying his board and the museumgoing public. As Gustav Pauli, his successor, wrote of him, he "was brilliant company, and won people over by a mixture, as fortunate as it is rare, of forthrightness and discretion." He made his life, Pauli added, as though he were speaking of Oscar Wilde, "into a work of art."

It is an extravagant tribute. But one can justly say that Lichtwark, by making the Kunsthalle into a school for consumers of art, put his gifts to good use in the service of the new. In 1903, lecturing on "Museums as Educational Institutions," he made a point that modernists could only applaud: "As long as museums do not ossify, they will have to transform themselves. Every generation will offer them new tasks and demand new achievements from them." Reading such thoughtful words from a museum director, an artistic revolutionary would have thought it a good thing that he kept his radicalism intact.

THAT LICHTWARK could gather so much power shows that hierarchical though it was, German society, certainly Hamburg's society, was porous enough to grant access to selected outsiders. The son of an impecunious miller, born in 1852 in a rural outpost of Hamburg, he spent most of his childhood in the city conscious of his poverty and fiercely determined to escape it. His intellectual gifts, wedded to a nagging ambition, led to a career as a teacher; and then, in his late twenties, after finally attending a university and serving an apprenticeship in Berlin museums, he made his leap into administration. His appointment to the directorship of the Kunsthalle—he was thirty-four—gratified his highest aspirations: it made him, the social outsider, into an insider. Whatever controversies he faced, he retained his post until his death in 1914.

If anyone could have sold Hamburg's elite on Liebermann, it would have been Lichtwark. But the Petersen commission proved more problematic than he had expected. Petersen detested the portrait and denigrated it as tasteless, too relaxed, a mere caricature. If it was an experiment, it was an experiment gone wrong. The mayor's fellow patricians did not venture to disagree. This response put Lichtwark the diplomat to work. To lower the temperature of the controversy without having to give up the portrait, he kept it from being shown until 1894, and then only behind a curtain. It was not until 1905 that he dared to exhibit the work in full public view. He had saved the Liebermann for the Kunsthalle.

He had also probably saved his job, and that mattered to him, enormously. Once a teacher, now he had a whole city and, with his publications, a whole country as his pupil. He wrote fluently and took every opportunity to put his words into print. Since he was interested in almost everything, he wrote about almost everything—interior decoration, gardens, primitive art, neglected local painters, photography, furniture, art education, even paintings. He was convinced that good taste, far from being confined to poems or paintings, is a pervasive quality expressed in the house one builds, the garden one plans, the table one sets.

These excursions into the byways of taste struck him as an essential part of his pedagogic role. A severe but perceptive judge, he was convinced that contemporary Germany was sadly deficient in the finer aesthetic feelings. Nor did museums alleviate the situation. The art they now exhibited was just that: exhibition art, "an art without a home, without connections, aimed solely at the passing effect." Lichtwark in short was a modernist with a sense of tradition, in some ways the most useful ally an avant-garde could hope for, since he could speak to conservatives without a sense of alienation. The country, he wrote, and not just Hamburg, must learn to build on certain cultural habits in the arts;

but, lacking them, one must create them. "Without that, we will not arrive at culture."

These were stark realities, Lichtwark believed, yet far from being grounds for despair, they should be a call to action. To hanker for a vanished authentic high culture was to squander time and energy; only a level-headed look at who needed to be educated, how urgently, and in what, could ever produce improvement. That is why Lichtwark spent so much valuable time observing, and reflecting about, the art-consuming public and its ways. We have already encountered his classification of that public, showing true lovers of art few in numbers and far from influential. That lament dated from 1898.

With passing time, he grew no more optimistic; if anything, the German *Bürgertum* depressed him even more. "Whoever looks at the bourgeoisie from the standpoint of art and the artist," he had written in 1898, "will not be fond of it. A parvenu with all the disagreeable traits of the type, it is swell-headed with its success, opinionated, arrogant, the born and sworn enemy of all artistic independence, the patron and protector of all those who flatter its vanity and its narrow outlook." Such people had no visceral appetite for art and had, sadly enough, succeeded in reducing architecture, the decorative arts, and painting to their own low level. A tradition-hating modernist face to face with the German buying public around the turn of the century would not have taken exception to this scathing verdict.

As Hamburg's foremost art teacher, Lichtwark used his own Kunsthalle, naturally enough, as his preferred forum. Forced to meet opposition, as he often was, he would move as boldly as he could, as prudently as he must. His tastes, in part cultivated as strategies, were unusually diverse: he was a loyal son of his city, a patriotic German, and a cosmopolitan modernist. This hardworking eclecticism enabled him to sponsor exhibitions of forgotten local painters (his own most sustained scholarly enterprise was a bulky two-volume study of Hamburg portraitists), to rediscover virtually unknown, now highly regarded, German Romantics like Philipp Otto Runge and Caspar David Friedrich, and to introduce recent French painters to German museums that few had encountered before. He was the first director to add Courbet, Manet, Monet, Sisley, and Renoir to the Kunsthalle collection. When we consider the contemporary *affaire Caillebotte*, which demonstrated vehement French resistance to modernist painting, the German situation did not seem very different.

But, wisely, Lichtwark would buy only one, or at most two, of these avant-garde rebels, compared with literally dozens of Liebermanns, who, though derided as an Impressionist, was at least a German Impressionist. He was opening the door to the moderns a crack, smartly refusing to flood his galleries with them, especially since most of his modernist purchases were foreign—worse, French. Yet his heart was with these adventurers who defied the Salon.

In fact, nothing pleased him more on his hunting trips for the Kunsthalle than to look at the Impressionists. In 1899, he visited their favorite dealer, Durand-Ruel, to renew cordial acquaintance with the Sisleys, Renoirs, and Pissarros on show there. This, he reported to the supervisory commission that governed the Kunsthalle, was "one of the most interesting exhibitions one can see." It was free of charge, but even so there were few visitors. If we charged admission, Durand-Ruel told him, no one would come. "The public rebels against everything beautiful." Apparently the French, too, needed to learn how to see. But not Lichtwark. Monet, he exclaimed, was "always the same and always different, though sworn to a formula, always equally excellent and yet progressive." They might sneer at him and his associates, but the Impressionists "will remain the great survivors." He would do his part to make his prediction a reality.

That he had some high-ranking colleagues in his corner could only solidify Lichtwark's taste for the new painting wherever it originated. His counterpart in Berlin, Hugo von Tschudi, director of the National Gallery there, was one supporter whose combat with the old guard he watched with particular relish and some anxiety. "There is a circle in Berlin," Lichtwark wrote in 1897, "whose vital interest it is to regard the famous inscription on the front of the National Gallery, 'To German Art,' as a program for its acquisitions and to allow no foreign things to enter." Tschudi's adversaries, he added, were employing two arguments in their effusions: "Patriotism and hatred of so-called modernism—*das sogenannte Moderne.*" An unholy combination of the two was the heart of their campaign, led by the elderly Carl Schuch, specialist in landscapes and still lifes, several of whose canvases were at Lichtwark's Kunsthalle, and Anton von Werner, a German Gérôme, the leading, certainly the most highly paid, academic painter of crowded patriotic scenes—a victorious battle, the proclamation of the German Reich at Versailles in January 1871, and the like—everyone present painstakingly drawn and instantly recognizable. "For us," Lichtwark told the administrative committee, "this quarrel is of direct interest because Werner and Schuch, using Hamburg's reactionaries, are trying to sow weeds among our wheat. Werner's and Schuch's pamphlets are being distributed in Hamburg by the hundreds." Aggressive avant-garde artists were not alone in those years in taking up arms.

Words were not the only weapon. Money was quite as effective, often more so. In the quarter century that Lichtwark presided over the Kunsthalle, it had become a routine lament among museum administrators that invading tourists from the United States, spendthrift and voracious, were raising prices not just for Rembrandts and other old masters, but for modernist art no less. True, perhaps, but European museum directors were quite as greedy in the competition for first-rate paintings as any American. Granted, they could not arbitrarily exceed their annual budgets to snag a particularly desirable—and expensive—canvas, but they could shift proportions within their subventions, or beg particular financial backing for special acquisitions. Lichtwark's commissioning Liebermann to do the portrait of *Bürgermeister* Petersen could never have been financed without a private subsidy.

And so, when it came to advancing the fame (and elevating the price) of controversial modernists, European museum directors were the Americans' most assiduous rivals. In 1912, Lichtwark was, as so often, in Paris, and bought a splendidly animated Renoir, rare in his oeuvre, an elegant young Parisienne on horseback in fetching riding habit accompanied by a boy on a pony—for just 90,000 Deutschmarks. In retrospect, the 3,000 marks that Liebermann had got for his

Gänserupferinnen forty years earlier—there was relatively little inflation in those times—becomes a real bargain.

This, then, was the scene around 1900, when modernism was maturing and scored, with the Impressionists, its first triumphs. But as we move to its core in the central chapters that follow—chapters devoted to each art separately—we shall find that victory was never guaranteed for modernists, whether poets, painters, playwrights, or architects. Even success could prove a failure.

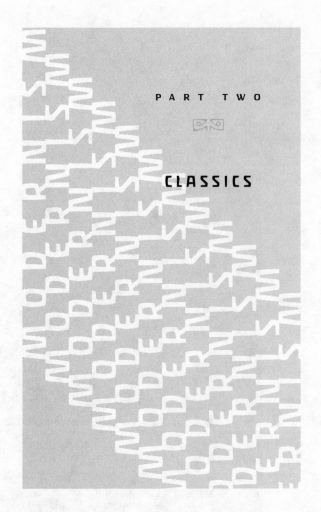

PART TWO

CLASSICS

Edvard Munch (1863–1944), *The Scream* (1893). Munch's most
celebrated rendering of an inner state—*his* inner state.
Modernist art at its most subjective.

PAINTING AND SCULPTURE— THE MADNESS OF THE UNEXPECTED

WELL BEFORE 1890, THE PACE OF ARTISTIC INNOVA-
tion, already lively, measurably accelerated, mainly in Europe.
Nearly every year brought astonishment, at times displeasure,
to audiences attending concerts, readings, or the theatre. Novelists with literary aspirations grew more demanding with
their readers; serious poets asked their audience to be familiar
with esoteric lore; experimental composers showed contempt
for music one could easily listen to; inspired architects, tired of
copying the historical models they had been taught in their
academies, audaciously tried out new materials and untested
spaces. Modernists in all domains of high culture seemed to
be embarked on an express train to the future. But the most
spectacular aesthetic revolutionaries in those years were the
painters.

From that perspective, the Secessionist mini-rebellions
that erupted among German and Austrian painters during
the 1890s were symptomatic of a mounting discontent with
aesthetic conventions, as one school of anti-academic artists
soon succeeded, and often felt itself superior to, its prede-

cessors. The Secessionists, rebels against the regimented and powerful academies of art in Berlin, Düsseldorf, Munich, and Vienna, were, for all the protests of traditionalists, relatively mild subversives. They retained the mimetic ideal, but loosened up their brushstrokes, sometimes heightened their colors, and added ordinary people—working families and peasants—to their chosen subjects. Secessionist canvases sold well, but in the end their straddling between traditionalism and adventurism proved to be not radical enough for the art of the twentieth century.

Alert contemporaries noted that the shifts of generation to generation among painters had never been so rapid and abrupt as during the years before the Great War. Advanced spirits marched under the common flag of modernism, but they finely differentiated themselves by more insignia than there were basic artistic divergences. Impressionism, Post-Impressionism, Neo-Impressionism, Symbolism, Expressionism, Orphism, Cubism, Futurism, Suprematism, Neo-Plasticism, Surrealism, accompanied by the Nabis and the Fauves, crowded progressive exhibitions and began to invade art histories around the turn of the twentieth century and after.

This carnival of names matters to the student of modernism, for the most influential among them, notably the Impressionists and the Expressionists, whether christened by supportive or by dubious viewers, impressively underscored the inward impulses at the core of their art. These painters put history, genre, ancient myth, certainly the assiduous imitation of external reality aside, as they principally listened to their intimate reactions in their search for objective aesthetic correlatives. Indirectly but potently, their canvases were confessions. To be sure, some of this name-giving (or name-calling) was tendentious. *Fauves*, or Wild Beasts, a scarcely flattering label for André Derain, Henri Matisse, and Maurice de Vlaminck, whose high-spirited, aggressively colored canvases first shocked the public in 1905, was excessive: their landscapes were exuberant commentaries on a recognizable world.

The profusion of labels underscores what has been noted before: an unquenchable appetite for an identity by painters cut loose from traditional standards, an often anxious eagerness to form or join a school with a distinct agenda that would recognize their special gifts and give them their share in the great rebellion against the commonplace. They were loners together and apart. And they thought themselves both important and necessary. As Giorgio de Chirico, the undisputed spokesman for the Italian Metaphysical School of painters after the war, put it with his usual grandiosity in 1919: "A European era like ours, which carries with it the enormous weight of infinite civilizations and the maturity of many spiritual and fateful periods, produces an art that in certain aspects resembles that of the restlessness of myth. Such an art arises through the efforts of the few men endowed with particular clearsightedness and sensibility." Although comparable tumults roiled the waters in the other arts, composers or playwrights or choreographers were not so quick as the painters to provide themselves with new identities.

These were times, then, for rudely questioning long-honored rules in all the arts, for mocking highly paid established virtuosos, for sending into retirement well-loved stylistic formulas, outworn religious prescriptions, self-protective pruderies, and anachronistic mannerisms that together had dominated the cultural landscape for so many centuries. But the triumphs of the new were not yet assured. As modernists everywhere complained, consumers who blindly trusted in tradition and complacently preferred easily digestible kitsch to the more arduous labor of providing lasting aesthetic pleasure were influential and tenacious. In Berlin, in December 1901, Germany's Emperor Wilhelm II, who claimed expertise in the arts as much as almost anything else, gave a festive speech that was memorably, if slightly, misquoted for calling the modern painting now spreading across Western culture "gutter art."* He did not literally say so, but by and large he meant it. And there were many educated Germans with no tie to the imperial court, and not just Germans, who agreed with him.

---

* Paraphrase of a speech by Emperor Wilhelm II celebrating the completion of the Siegesallee, a preposterous "Victory Avenue" built on his orders in Berlin, featuring thirty-two statues of his Hohenzollern predecessors. The oration became internationally irritating because it accused the arts of all nations, excepting only the German, to be sure, of degeneracy. He did not literally use the term *Rinnsteinkunst*—"gutter art." What he said was that a nation can cultivate its role as a model for others only if the ideals of art have penetrated into the lowest strata and "when art lends its hand to lift up instead of descending into the gutter." But it was the paraphrase quoted here that became famous, or notorious.

Most modernists exploited this imperial insult as an incentive. They knew—or at least told one another for mutual reassurance—that whatever the Kaiser might say, by following their star they were on the right path to artistic truth. The losses seemingly attached to their bold subjectivity were really hidden gains: the mimetic precision that had for so long served as the touchstone for good taste in painting and sculpture, fiction and drama, was to them inexcusably old-fashioned. In short, modernists considered Ezra Pound's famous injunction, "Make it New!," a professional, almost a sacred obligation. And it was the avant-garde painters who were the first, and the most highly visible, cultural revolutionaries.

IF IN THE COURSE OF TIME, avant-garde artists got on the express train to the future, a smaller but still significant number of them got off at some critical point. Such a farewell could divide close friends. Consider Mary Cassatt, happily settled in Paris since 1874 in voluntary, agreeable exile, financially independent and close to Degas, the only American painter ever to exhibit with the Impressionists. She was the most persuasive educator in the cause of modernism, converting rich visitors from the home country to the new painting, doubtless doing more to domesticate radical innovators like Manet in the United States than the most assiduous art dealer. Yet she found that the latest directions in painting left her cool, even hostile. In 1912, she urged her close friend Louisine Havemeyer, whom she had earlier persuaded to amass an outstanding collection of modern French artists including Courbet and Manet, to sell her Cézannes, whose popularity, she was sure, "*cannot* last." Surely, "the whole boom" for Cézanne "is madness and must fall."

Early in the following year, she worried that her Louisine had grown too fond of Matisse, who was to her mind nothing better than a "*farceur*," a humbug. She had an explanation for Matisse's brilliant colorful experiments on canvas. "If you could see his early work! Such a commonplace vision. Such weak execution, he was intelligent enough to see he could never achieve fame, so he shut himself up for years and evolved this [style] and has achieved notoriety. My dear Louisa," she concluded with a bold generalization, "it is not alone in politics that anarchy reigns." Cassatt chose a convenient way of dismissing an artistic heretic she could not, or would not, comprehend: she called Matisse a fraud and interpreted his freedom as license. Yet there were a few lovers of modernist explorations—evidently Mrs. Havemeyer was one of them, since despite her fondness for Courbet, she had plainly shown an interest in the radical Matisse—who did manage to leap over the shadow of youthful enthusiasms. But that ability required an acrobatic agility that was rare. Modernists, it appeared, tested the aesthetic flexibility not just of cultural conservatives but quite as much of fellow modernists.

Louisine Havemeyer was not the only persistent supporter among pro-modernist lovers of art to encounter resistance among intimates. Some of them, like Arthur Schnitzler, had to battle with themselves. The most resourceful playwright, novelist, and short story writer in the late Austro-Hungarian Empire, more supple and adventurous than his fellow Viennese modernists, he made the supreme topic of sexuality his specialty. It even earned him Freud's admiration for his perceptiveness, which he displayed with a felicitous amalgam of wit, daring, and precision. The appreciation of the new was natural to him, yet even he reached a point where novelty stepped over the boundaries of his ability to react with anything but bewilderment and disapproval. In early 1913, Schnitzler visited an exhibition of Picassos in Munich, and after years of applauding Picasso's far-reaching assaults on academic realism found his latest turn downright unintelligible. "The earlier paintings extraordinary," he recorded in his diary. "Vehement resistance to his current Cubism."* The conflicts of modernists with traditionalists, fellow revolutionaries, and themselves made for disorderly history, but it was always stimulating, never dull.

* Arthur Schnitzler diaries (*Tagebücher*), February 8, 1913. He had, as it were, got off this future express once before: In December 1908, he had heard the Rosé Quartet perform Schoenberg's revolutionary Second Quartet, Opus 10, the first important largely atonal composition, and, with other members of the audience, he balked. "I do not believe in Schoenberg," he confided to his diary. "I immediately understood Bruckner, Mahler—should I fail now?" December 21, 1908. By that time, this flexible listener projected his inability to follow the latest, most dramatic step toward modernist music on the composer and denounced Schoenberg, much as Cassatt had denounced Matisse, as a swindler—see April 4, 1912.

SELF-ABSORPTION: EXPRESSIVE INWARDNESS

1.

OF ALL THE WAYS that modernist painters could exhibit their innermost being, making explicit self-portraits put them into the closest possible touch with their viewers. These looks into the mirror were monuments to subjectivity, normally not pathological enough to qualify as acts of narcissism but assertive enough to serve as documents of self-absorption. They added up to a record of intense preoccupation with the self that procured the artist a tentative immortality and at the same time attested to his respectability. The despised and rejected rarely painted self-portraits. To be sure, the modernists had not invented the genre; as so often, here, too, they lived off their past. Some of the most celebrated, most expressive self-portraits date back at least four centuries, to Albrecht Dürer, who had shown himself in a variety of imaginative poses, including the Man of Sorrows. And Rembrandt's legendary series of self-revelations from apprenticeship to old age—he did at least seventy-five of them—became an object of virtual veneration. The modernists knew, and admired, self-portraitists who had gone before them. But they were not simply fitting into a tradition. Their tributes to stellar precursors were common among them, yet they were also in the grip of their own problematic selves.

The passion for self-portraiture among modernists was not all exuberance. Their painting had a substantial depressive side; it was as deeply engaged in exhibiting misery as sheer satisfaction in professional competence. Not that neurosis was a precondition for artistic gifts; this causal linkage has never been clinically established, though in the decades of modernism the supposed tie between them became a favorite topic for psychologists and a popular cliché among the educated. And life history after life history during the modernists' classic period seemed to lend support to the theory that insanity and brilliant brains actually were near allied.

All too popular late nineteenth-century treatises by the German cultural critic Max Nordau and the Italian criminologist Cesare Lombroso,

both of them doctrinaire, fastened the unprovable—and inaccurate—
link between genius and madness in the general consciousness. Indeed,
Vincent van Gogh and Paul Gauguin, among the greatest, certainly the
most important, of modernist painters, sufficiently exhibited the
expected symptoms: the first shot himself to death after a succession of
terrifying psychotic breakdowns; the second deserted his wife and five
children and his thriving career as a stockbroker to spend the rest of his
days in distant, impoverished exile, painting, painting.

The oeuvres of these two masters of expressive inwardness attest to
the substantial share of self-portraits in the careers of modernist
painters determined to carry further the aesthetic revolution launched
by the classic Impressionists. With their fairly rapid conquest of collectors, Monet and his associates had forced the door to unconventional
art, and the generation that followed them, half grateful, half insistent
on their own originality, poured through. I recall Gauguin's complaint
that the Impressionists were painting "without freedom, always shackled by the need of probability." It was a frontier that he and others in
his party were determined to cross. They would paint horses blue,
Christs yellow, faces green, and devote close attention to such "inartistic" motifs as shoes and chairs. As the greatest among Symbolists (a
comprehensive label borrowed from modernist French poetry associated with the verbal experiments of Mallarmé), they labored to capture
their deepest personal responses to the world rather than rendering that
world as accurately as was in their power.

In short, though both Gauguin and van Gogh thought the Impressionists' subversion of Salon art eminently worthy of respect, their own
paintings offended dominant conformist tastes so decisively that the
exhibitions winning them a larger market would be largely posthumous. Van Gogh had shown a handful of paintings before his suicide in
1890, but was not launched on his rise into universal favor and astronomic prices until 1901, with an exhibition at the Bernheim-Jeune
gallery in Paris. And the Salon d'Automne, also of course in Paris, put
Gauguin on the map in 1906, three years after he had died in the Mar-
quesas virtually unknown outside a tight coterie of admirers. Both
came to painting late, but once they did, they pursued their vocation

with obsessive, religious fervor. When they painted self-portraits, they did so for themselves, and, as we shall soon see, for one another.

VAN GOGH, BORN IN THE NETHERLANDS in 1853, worked for a time as a teacher and lay preacher in England and did not start painting seriously until his late twenties; he did not reach Paris until 1886. The city, bustling with artistic insurgents, gave him a quick liberal education in the latest styles as he absorbed the canvases of the Impressionists and met fellow subversives, including Gauguin. But it was in the feverish last two years of his life, from February 1888 on, that he developed his final, inimitable manner working in and around sun-drenched Arles. And it was there that in the fall of that year he tried to construct an idealistic community of painters, proposing Gauguin, whom he modestly admired more than he did himself, as *chef de l'atelier*. The scheme failed, largely doomed by Gauguin's prickliness and van Gogh's erratic behavior—the notorious episode of van Gogh cutting off part of an ear took place just before Christmas—and both went on to paint their masterpieces alone.

Few modernist artists felt as driven as van Gogh to explain how much of himself, and just what, he was pouring into his art. His frank, notably informative letters to his art dealer brother Theo, who supported him emotionally and financially, or to his sister Wil, read like exhaustive museum labels for his paintings. In fact, his self-portraits and his other canvases—interiors, still lifes, landscapes, urban snapshots, or portraits—form a seamless web of indiscreet self-disclosure. He painted everything else just as he painted himself, with the same sense of barely tamed energy, the same urgency, the same heavy impasto, the same distinct brushstrokes. Whether he painted irises or interiors, wheat fields under a lowering sky or his face swathed in bandages after assaulting his ear, all were in their way auxiliary confessions. Yet his explanatory letters indicate that he did not think his canvases spoke for themselves.*

---

* Perhaps the best known of these comments are the letters about *The Night Café* of 1888, an interior with which van Gogh paid overdue rent to his landlord at Arles. "I have tried to express the terrible passion of humanity by means of red and green," he wrote to his brother Theo in February. "The room is blood red and dark yellow, with a green billiard table in the middle; there are

His explicit self-portraits did say a great deal. Van Gogh painted himself some forty-one times, doing the finest of them toward the end. The first dozen or so, painted in Paris, still have the look of a promising beginner's work, but by early 1888, he could take reasonable pride in his final Parisian efforts. "It isn't an easy job to paint oneself," he wrote from Arles that summer; "at any rate if it is to be *different* from a photograph." He ruefully acknowledged that his almost skeletal head, appearing more foursquare than in earlier versions, his short red beard tightly trimmed, his cheekbones prominent, might remind a viewer of death. Why not? After all, the advantage of his Impressionist technique was to capture inner truths: "It is not banal, and seeks after a deeper resemblance than the photographer's." The democratic lens, an invention that van Gogh despised, was to his mind doomed to register mere surfaces.

After he had found his style, van Gogh could reach for the subtler resemblances he prized. With bruising honesty he refused to prettify his countenance: he shows it ashen, at times greenish, the cheeks sunken, or bearing the marks of his mental breakdowns. And not his face alone. His characteristic brushwork, nervously laid on in staccato parallels or vertiginous swirls, makes his clothes and his chosen background serve self-disclosure no less. One of van Gogh's most eloquent autobiographical statements is not a literal self-portrait but a much-reproduced, deeply disturbed and deeply disturbing painting of Saint-Rémy at night. The town is lit up by stars and an impossibly pointed moon, all circled by agitated haloes that intimate a losing struggle to master mental suffering by translating it into art. And the last paintings read as though repression is failing to keep his anxieties from overwhelming him. Whether labeled self-portraits or not, they serve as images of his mind.

GAUGUIN'S SELF-PORTRAITS are very different from van Gogh's, but no less enlightening. A direct comparison between them is particularly

---

four lemon-yellow lamps with a glow of orange and green. . . . I have tried to express, as it were, the powers of darkness in a low wine-shop, and all this in an atmosphere like a devil's furnace of pale sulphur—all under an appearance of Japanese gaiety and the good nature of Tartarin" (the cowardly "hero" of several novels by Alphonse Daudet).

appropriate because in the early fall of 1888, as van Gogh was trying to persuade Gauguin to join him at Arles, he proposed that they should each paint themselves for the other. Both did so. Van Gogh depicted himself as a Japanese bonze, the member of a priesthood committed to a religion of nature that strongly appealed to him. He is serious, even grave, posing in front of a neutral green background, stressing his gaunt looks and gazing beyond the viewer. In sharp contrast, Gauguin's self-image reads like a protest against respectability, like a message from an eccentric, determined outsider defying a commonplace world. His loyal friend, the artist Charles Morice, rightly commented on Gauguin's "legitimate ferocity of a productive egotism." He painted himself for his friend van Gogh as a free spirit in a prison culture, displaying his character and his conflicts by aggressively distorting the outlines of his head, exaggerating the wicked hook of his nose, and, with his anti-naturalistic color, putting his exceptional self on stage.

Even if we did not know his astonishing life history, this self-portrait would proclaim Gauguin a buccaneer glorying in the role he had created for himself: to paint and seek salvation, as he would in far-flung sea voyages, rural Brittany, and, most remotely, Tahiti. A youthful self-portrait of 1883, showing him at the easel, is still relatively tame. By 1888, in the self-portrait for van Gogh, he sought more magnificent effects. Significantly, he described the painting, in a letter to his painter friend Emile Schuffenecker, as "one of my best efforts, absolutely incomprehensible (upon my word) being complete abstraction." The whole, he added, with its color "remote from nature," amounted to a statement—a statement in good modernist fashion, we may add, about himself. No wonder that he and van Gogh called themselves "symbolists." Their thrilling artistic innovations required a close look beneath surfaces to be understood.

Later Gauguin self-portraits bear out his intense self-dramatization. Just a year after the painting dedicated to van Gogh, he showed himself looking much like a stylish devil, holding a writhing little snake between his fingers as though it were a cigarette, and crowned by a halo—if he is a devil, he seems to be telling the viewer, he is a fallen angel. Others among his self-portraits are if anything still more provocative. He is

Christ in agony in the Garden of Gethsemane or on his way to Golgotha and death; he smuggles distorted fragments of his face into still lifes and statuettes and clay pots. One of the most striking self-portrayals, dating from 1893, has him holding the tools of his trade, and is suffused with what looks like strong artificial light: the dominant brick red background seems to have spilled over to the face, which, with the sidelong glance from half-closed eyes and the odd attire—astrakhan cap and blue cloak over a dark brown jacket—marks him out as the enemy of bourgeois decorum. These instances of artistic candor stand at the outer edges of self-expression this side of a madhouse.

IF VAN GOGH AND GAUGUIN were in their self-portraits determined to declare their innermost selves without bourgeois reticence, another great modernist painter of self-portraits, Paul Cézanne, gave away quite as much, though more subtly, by aiming to give away nothing. Few students of Cézanne have missed the studied impersonality in the scores of paintings and drawings he did of himself. It fits them effortlessly into the highly individual, intensely alive architectural modern classicism that became his mark in his mature work. In the 1860s, a young painter learning his craft—he was born in Provence in 1839—Cézanne specialized in imaginary scenes of melodramatic brutality: rapes, orgies, murders. Nor was his earliest self-portrait, dating from around 1861 and painted after a photograph, much more inhibited in its emotional exhibitionism. He transformed his rather round, commonplace face into a gaunt, threatening presence, pulled together the black eyebrows into a brooding frown absent from the snapshot, and curved the mustache to make himself scowl. More faithful to his state of mind in the painting, it seems, than in the photograph, he has portrayed himself as a troubled, perhaps angry young man.

But with the early 1870s, after he had undergone an informal training with Pissarro—though always resolutely his own man, he shared the Impressionists' palette and exhibited with them more than once—his unconscious grew cannier. The striking transformation of Cézanne's art from expressive self-disclosure to expressive self-control is a vivid instance of sublimation. He gave up inventing episodes of extreme sexual and aggressive violence and mastered his urges with apparently cool, distant, carefully thought-out landscapes, interiors, portraits, and those astonishing late constructions, the commanding canvases of Bathers. As he slowly developed into the sovereign source of twentieth-century art—Picasso and Braque in their Cubist phase were only the most eminent of his many disciples—he would organize arrangements of ripe, round, luscious apples on a disheveled tablecloth, or two card players face-to-face, or return again and again to paint his beloved Mont Sainte-Victoire. Strange, demanding paintings all of them, violating perspective and straining natural shapes, they are mute witnesses to a sensual nature fiercely held in check. It is no wonder that his breakthrough to fame was delayed to 1907, through a sensational retrospective at the Salon d'Automne a year after his death.

Cézanne's most important self-portraits, largely concentrated in two decades from the mid-1870s to the mid-1890s, seem if anything even more consciously, almost desperately, reserved. He subordinated everything—shapes, colors, his bald head and broad shoulders—to his overall design. He contrasted his boldly curved shiny pate with a strong diamond-shaped wallpaper design in the background or held his palette as though it were an extension of his right arm. He looks worried, unkempt, always distant. He laid on the colors with short, visible parallel strokes to proclaim the presence of a painting far more than of a person. And he painted his eyes, which the ancient truism has it are the windows of the soul, as opaque, impenetrable. For all that, the blank stares that Cézanne bestowed on the viewer were accomplices to an irresistible indiscretion. His self-portraits betray the very secret he aimed to keep: he was a man who all his life tried to impose order on an unruly, perhaps chaotic self.

The self-portrait sketches—Cézanne did more than twenty of them—were less thoroughly designed and they document his appearance more spontaneously. In fact, two or three of these quick reflections show a worry line over the bridge of the nose, or lips tightly pressed together, making him look recessive and careworn. All in all, Cézanne's artistic reactions to his inner turmoil shore up Freud's assertion that try as they will, humans cannot keep their secrets. Conflicts will out, defying efforts at concealment; however handled, they leave traces along the way. This must be true particularly for the world of modernism, freed of so many constraints on self-expression. Whatever the reasons, in his last years Cézanne, feeling defeated and solitary, stopped doing self-portraits altogether, only showing that indiscretion can take many forms, including silence.

2.

SO FAR, ALL THESE MODERNIST self-portraits have been unsmiling, even solemn affairs. I cannot repeat often enough that their art emerged as much from distress as from exuberance, perhaps even more. But at least one seditious painter, James Ensor, not much happier it seems than Cézanne, managed to treat his neurotic predicaments with that rarity among modernists: wicked humor. Less celebrated than modernists like Gauguin or Cézanne, he was probably the best known among Belgian modernists and the most garrulous if disturbing of self-portraitists. He was born in 1860 in the bathing resort of Ostend, where his parents kept a souvenir shop, featuring cheap tourist china and, during carnival, cheap masks. It was from shards of such childhood memories and from traumas—quarreling parents, a domineering Flemish mother whose looming power he never shook off, an ineffectual English father who found solace in the bottle—that Ensor built up his artistic universe. Those who knew him recalled that his talk tended to the macabre.

So did his thoroughly anti-academic art; his morbid symbolism is obtrusive to the point of obviousness. He managed to annoy even *Les XX*, the progressive clan of Symbolist Belgian painters, vigorous critics of Salon art, with whom he was associated for years. Significantly, the leading expressive device he featured in his work was a skeleton, sometimes several on the same canvas. They are busy with rather comical, often domestic tasks, making themselves at home in Ensor's rich fantasy life. One skeleton is comfortably ensconced in an upholstered easy chair glancing at Chinese objects; another is sketching; still another is playing a clarinet. He shows oddly dressed skeletons huddling around a stove to get warm; cannibalistic skeletons who battle with brooms and brushes over a hanged man labeled "Stew"; and a fleet of flying skeletons, the largest wielding an enormous scythe, terrorizing a crowd that tries to flee. In Ensor's largest, most renowned painting, *The Entry of Christ into Brussels* of 1888, a throng mills about the Saviour riding a donkey, while a top-hatted skeleton dominates the foreground.

Evidently unwilling to trust his viewers to understand his message, Ensor liked to insert explanations into his pictures. In one gruesome self-portrait, *The Dangerous Cooks*, he has a white-robed waiter ready to serve up his, Ensor's, head on a platter to a party of nauseating banqueters and has painted a large label identifying him stuck into the top of the skull. By 1900, when his impious inventiveness was beginning to desert him, he had painted, etched, and drawn himself more than twenty times, and his blizzard of self-portraits appears in retrospect as so many sphinxes without a mystery. They are droll acts of aggression against the conventional art-loving public he despised. Ensor's aim was to infuriate his viewers, and he succeeded. An etching of 1887, *The Pisser*, is characteristic; it shows a man relieving himself against a wall scribbled over with childish graffiti and bearing the legend: "Ensor is a madman." A Romantic out of his time, a belated E. T. A. Hoffmann, he persistently exhibited his conviction that only the insane, certainly not the bourgeoisie, have the truth.

Ensor's self-portraits are raids not simply on the public but on himself. A tall, handsome man, conscious of his looks, with regular features, turned-up mustache, and well-trimmed beard, he persecuted his appearance with savage wit. In the first of his self-portraits, dating from 1879 when he was not yet twenty, with its smiling assertion of his stature and cheerful flecks of color, he still managed to be decorous. A few drawings and a later self-portrait of 1880 remained within the confines of what a well-educated gallerygoer would have a right to value. But in his self-presentations, such lapses into conventionality were exceptional. His best known and more characteristic self-portrait, dating from 1883, has him glancing askance at the viewer from under a flowered woman's hat, complete with drooping feathers.

For all his lifelong malaise, then, Ensor knew how to extract dividends from his anguish. No doubt, his sufferings were real enough. He did two self-portraits titled *Demons That Torment Me*, beset by vaguely human monsters with twisted limbs, multiple sets of eyes, and jagged wings reaching out to him in menace. The second of these includes a gravestone marked J. ENSOR, 1895. His need to be provocative was a cry for attention and apparently a bid for revenge. The intriguing carnival masks that figure so prominently in his work play a double role. They call up memory fragments of a childhood spent around his family's shop, and they stand as tokens of his mutinous conviction that humans wear disguises—petty bourgeois like his parents more damnably than most—that the artist in pursuit of truth must tear from their faces. He liked those masks, he told a friend, "because they hurt the feelings of the public that has received me so badly." Not all of Ensor's fury and dejection remained unconscious.

To make matters harder for him still, his art suggests that he was ambivalent about the lower-middle-class milieu from which he came. He found it stifling and yet somehow welcoming. Two paintings of 1881, *Afternoon in Ostend* and *The Bourgeois Salon*, are quiet, cheerful, dimly lit interiors that speak not of disdain but of comfort. Naturally, Ensor's efforts to escape the world he hated and needed were at best partly successful: he rebelled in his art but for most of his life remained mired in his family's ambiance. In a chalk drawing of 1886, *Self-Portrait, The Painter Sad and Sumptuous*, he emerges somber-faced from an ornate wardrobe as though, kept caged in by the massive furniture, he is aching to get out.

With this record, Ensor's self-portraits read like brave efforts at coming to terms with an unpalatable self-perception. In one of them, *Strange Insects* (1888), he anticipated Kafka's "Metamorphosis" as he fitted his head to the body of an oversized cockroach. Imprisoned in such a life, death must often have seemed preferable; that is what he seems to be saying in his patented shocking manner with an etching of 1888, *My Skeletonized Portrait*. He shows himself at three-quarter length, buttoned up in a tight-fitting coat, the features of a skeleton superimposed on his face. His imagination nourished by this grim self-image, Ensor did an etching of a recumbent skeleton, its upper body propped up by a pillow, titled *My Portrait in the Year 1960*. And around 1896, he gathered all his spleen to show himself fashionably dressed at the easel with a death's-head for a face: one skull leers down from its perch at the top of an easel while others grin at him from the wall. Ensor's self-portraits are graphically visualized nightmares, and modernist culture gave him permission not only to suffer but also to express them.

In several of his revelations, Ensor's claim to victimhood hardened into an identification with the most famous victim in history: Jesus Christ. Like Gauguin, he claimed the sufferings of the Saviour for his own. Repeatedly, he drew the redeemer tormented by Satan and his legions, and in one explicit drawing, *Ecce Homo, or Christ and the Critics*, Ensor is Christ, with tousled hair and ravaged face, hemmed in between two dour bourgeois accusers. That was a touch of secular, not religious megalomania: Ensor, the atheist, saw Christ as a great man, not a god. In one drawing, *Christ Watched by Angels*, done in deliberately naïve style, he has three angels praying by the side of the dead naked Jesus, who bears Ensor's features.

This blasphemous and pathetic identification reached its climax in a much-reproduced colored drawing of 1886, *Calvary, called Ensor on the Cross*. One is instantly reminded of Gauguin. A crowd, mainly in modern dress, stands and kneels around the three crosses. Ensor hangs in the center, brilliantly lit by haloes and the sun's rays, while a personage decked out in a top hat stabs this mock-Christ with a lance bearing a flag with the name "Fétis," one of Ensor's most energetic critics. In changing the "INRI" above Christ's head to "ENSOR," he makes the explicit even more explicit.

A principled modernist in this as in all else, Ensor reveled in his subjectivity. "My work has been purely personal through and through," he wrote in 1899. "This personal vision has, I think, borne me up into higher regions." In the same document he called himself "an exceptional painter." No doubt he was; yet in his self-observant and self-expressive time, when artists could share their most furtive feelings with the world, he was by no means as isolated as he thought. But he remained an acquired taste for the few. He died in 1949, his talents long dissipated.

To be raised to a barony by the Belgian state in 1929 was a late recognition he largely considered an insult after a lifetime of neglect.

3.

VAN GOGH, GAUGUIN, CEZANNE, ENSOR, were in their self-portraits the painters of present-day alienation. The Norwegian Edvard Munch, among the most brilliant of modernists and Ensor's almost exact contemporary but far more sober—his dates are 1863 to 1944—was the painter of its identical twin, present-day anxiety. He explored what he thought he saw in the world around him and, even more, felt in the world within. In this double task, Munch was, as we know, in good company. Baudelaire and Manet had said decades before that an artist—particularly they meant, of course, what we would call the modernist artist—must engage with his own time, and Munch, like his fellow heretics, did precisely that. He paid the usual price: being misunderstood, neglected, rejected, but enjoying occasional appreciation. Cézanne, too, though rarely very articulate, believed himself yoked to the avant-garde of his time, and said that a good painter expresses what is most advanced in his own day. It necessarily followed, since only a few free spirits were "advanced," that more conventional contemporaries were bound to regard modernist makers of self-portraits as inartistic, unsettling, wedded to ugliness.

Munch's self-portraits were no exception to this fate. He was born on a Norwegian farm and suffered through an appalling childhood. His mother died when he was five, and his father, a physician generous with his assistance to the poor, was a depressive disciplinarian with a volcanic temper who practiced draconic harshness and was subject to episodes of near-psychotic religious dread. "Disease, insanity and death were the angels which attended my cradle," Munch later recalled, not without reason. His lifelong preoccupation with nonconformist authors like Kierkegaard, Dostoevsky, and Nietzsche, still widely treated as outside the cultural mainstream, only strengthened his subversive worldview. As a student, he embraced conventional artistic doctrine; it was not until his early twenties that he found the inner freedom to draw on his early life, a painful but principal source of inspiration he never relinquished. In 1889, he went to Paris, and that stay, with his exposure to Monet, van Gogh, and other professional outsiders, provided the vocabulary he needed to develop his unique amalgam of Symbolism with Expressionism and to investigate—and portray—his inner turmoil to the full.

The very titles of Munch's canvases lend plausibility to this claim: *The Sick Girl* and *Jealousy*; *Death and the Maiden* and *Death in the Sick Chamber*. His motifs ranged more widely than this, and he worked for many years on a vastly ambitious, never completed project, the "Frieze of Life," intended to show "life in all its fullness, its variety, its joys and sufferings." But the sufferings greatly outnumbered the joys—not quite so extreme as van Gogh's perhaps, but close enough to resemble barely concealed breakdowns. No wonder that in Munch, Eros, ever present, appears as more of a menace than a blessing, a source of guilt and shame. If, in *The Kiss* (1895), he shows a fervent pair of nude lovers embracing, melting into one another, in the slightly earlier *The Day After* (1894) he has a young woman, partially unclothed, clearly exhausted, lounging on the bed on which she has evidently spent the night in sexual gratification. And *Ashes*, an oil from the same year, hints at what looks like another, this time calamitous morning after: a distraught-looking young woman, standing, facing the viewer, grasps her tousled hair while a man cowers at the edge of the canvas, his head turned away. One of Munch's paintings, *Vampire*—a subject to which he returned more than once—has a long-haired woman biting the neck of a man who passively submits to the assault, while in a companion piece he shows a man biting a woman's naked breast.

Munch's best known picture, *The Scream*, widely considered the quintessence of modern angst, which he revisited in several versions from 1893 on, shows a scantily articulated figure—whether man or woman is impossible to determine—its hands clasped to its cheeks, its eyes staring, its mouth wide open, standing on a long bridge, with ominous clouds swirling around. We have it from Munch himself that the idea for this portrait of a nervous fit came to him after experiencing an overpowering anxiety attack. But usually its untold thousands of viewers have generalized his nightmarish vision and read *The Scream* as the artistic epitome of the nervous unease that observant contemporaries thought was haunting crowded and bustling urban existence in the 1890s. Munch was neither a prophet nor a sociologist; he meant his disturbing output, laid out with powerful precision, to be essentially a personal confession. In 1932, in a most illuminating self-revelation, he wrote to the German art critic Eberhard Griesebach: "My art is actually a self-manifestation—*Selbstbekundung*—and an attempt to clarify my attitude toward the world. It is in a word a kind of egotism. . . ." But art lovers, awed by Munch's impressive talent, celebrated his paintings as testimony to larger realities. We know how intently modernists desired to be relevant to their time, and one way of being relevant was, as the reception of Munch shows, to function as a symptom of a culture in crisis.

MUNCH MADE IT IMPOSSIBLE to count the number of his self-portraits since he deliberately kept several of his paintings ambiguous as to the gender of the sitter. But they were abundant and agitating; solitude, like death, makes its presence obtrusive. In one, of 1906, the artist sits conspicuously alone at a restaurant table with a bottle of wine, the wineglass and the plate in front of him empty. In another, of 1915, he stands, naked, his hand placed familiarly on a skeleton. Again, he shows himself as a Sphinx, endowed with ample breasts. Later, in 1930, he drew himself as a corpse lying before Dr. K. E. Schreiner, his physician. One of the earliest self-portraits, dating from 1895 when he was thirty-two, probably the one most frequently reproduced, has him staring straight at the viewer—that is, at himself in the mirror—with a skeletal arm lying across the bottom, lest too much cheerfulness break in. Whatever the public's take on his work, what always remained primary for Munch was self-revelation through self-absorption.

SELF-ABSORPTION: THE GERMANS

1.

THEN THERE WERE THE GERMANS, a culture long eminent, or notorious, for its soulfulness. At mid-nineteenth century, when modernism was in its apprentice years, Heinrich Heine sarcastically noted that while the French owned the land and the British the sea, his fellow Germans had control of the sky. It is perhaps no coincidence that Munch's first international exposure should have been in Berlin. In 1892, he exhibited fifty-five paintings for his first large-scale showing. But the presentation, sponsored by the Verein Berliner Künstler, became a scandal: it was closed after a week following a split vote of the association and an infuriated debate in the press. One of Munch's most impassioned supporters, the eccentric Polish novelist Stanislaw Przybyszewski, illuminated the hidden grounds for the resistance to Munch: his art, he wrote, represented the direct expression of the painter's unconscious, his "naked individuality," an assault on bourgeois propriety. The display of the inner self could, it seems, go too far. To put it bluntly, Munch's Symbolism demanded too much from most viewers. For defenders of academic art, Munch's canvases were not art at all.

Germans thinking of self-portraiture took pride in being the compatriots and proud heirs of the sixteenth-century Albrecht Dürer, the first and probably greatest modern self-portraitist. His only rival was Rembrandt, and among German art historians, he too was a good German. Whatever Rembrandt's motives for his self-preoccupation may have been (much like Dürer, he left precious little autobiographical material for the historian), late nineteenth-century cultural and political German nationalists exploited him as a pawn in the campaign to prove their country's superiority to other, lesser cultures in inwardness—*Innerlichkeit*. For political purposes, the Dutchman Rembrandt was conveniently granted German citizenship.

That backward glance—in tune with other modernists, the Germans did not disdain the past for the sake of the present—proved highly useful to patriots, who needed as much support as they could mobilize. That the main impulse of modernism's thrilling dispensations radiated out from Paris only hardened the opposition of the German art establishment. Yet cultivated German taste was by no means solid in its hostility to the new painting.* In Berlin, in Hamburg, even in con-

---

* For the record, I should note briefly that there was nothing unusual in premodernist times about a painter painting himself. Velázquez did so, as did Rubens, Poussin, Reynolds. In mid-eighteenth

servative Munich, partisans of the new engaged in a contest of wills and money against the bearers of tradition, with the outcome uncertain.

Schooled in romanticism and metaphysics, German artists and critics strove for profundity more heartily and more systematically than their counterparts in other countries: far from being embarrassed by Heine's witty critique of German inwardness, they liked to contrast their own spiritual nature with English and French, notably French, superficiality. In full accord with this self-congratulatory stance, nineteenth-century German painters sought to render the depths of human life and death, mainly death, decades before modernist temptations invaded their nation. In 1872, the German-speaking Swiss painter Arnold Böcklin—a hero to German art lovers best known for his self-invented mythology featuring tritons and mermaids—most famously painted among other self-portraits one in which, in the vigor of life, he stands palette and brush in hand listening closely to the phantom violin that a skeleton behind him is playing. Three years later, the highly successful German painter Hans Thoma virtually copied Böcklin's invention by showing himself, too, listening to death. He enjoyed this confrontation enough to repeat it twice more in later self-portraits. These artists in turn had followers eager to use the skeleton as a prop, all of them, as German commentators a little pompously noted, "poets with a paintbrush." In 1896, Lovis Corinth varied this familiar theme with a half-length self-portrait in a sunny studio, robust and shirt-sleeved, a skeleton hanging from an iron hook near him.

CORINTH PROVIDES A BRIDGE to German modernism. He was, with Max Liebermann, Germany's most eminent semi-Impressionist, though unlike the French, he did vigorous canvases on historical themes. His self-portraits, including drawings and etchings, add up to scores: from 1900 on, at the age of forty-two, he painted himself at least

---

century, Anton Raphael Mengs, Germany's most important painter, did at least fifteen self-portraits. And Anton Graff, whose career reaches into the nineteenth century, set some sort of a record, even outdoing Rembrandt, by painting himself eighty times or more.

once a year, on his birthday. But in 1911 he suffered a debilitating stroke and the self-portraits he did after that catastrophe, always candid, show a wounded, haunted face. Famous for his fleshy nudes and virile attitudes, Corinth had represented himself in 1910 in knight's armor holding his smiling, buxom nude wife, Charlotte, in his arms. The title: *The Victor*. A year later, he became and remained a victim. He could still paint, but in a slapdash, somewhat tremulous style, as though his damaged body had imposed an extravagant version of Expressionist touches on him.

Perhaps Corinth's most speaking presentation of his modernist self in oils is dated, precisely, August 3, 1913. On vacation in the Tyrol, he represents himself in jolly local attire complete with a jaunty hunter's hat decorated by a feather. But in striking inconsistency to his costume, he stares at the viewer sad-eyed and frowning. And near the brim of his hat he has written a laconic message: "Ego." Here he is on view, his pathos exhibited as honestly as he could manage.* Later, his widow stoutly confirmed that he meant what he had written on that canvas. Her husband's self-portraits, she wrote, had been "very serious and critical encounters with his own ego." Corinth's never-interrupted exploration of his appearance is just one more proof of the point that Gustave Courbet had made half a century before when he called his self-portraits his autobiography. The Germans' indefatigable display of the ego was a valuable clue to the self.

2.

HOW FAR THIS SELF-DISPLAY reached became evident in the work of Ernst Ludwig Kirchner, with his candor the German Munch. In Kirchner, anxiety was endemic, blatant, and painful. His characteristic attack, a nervous, jagged line and Expressionist color, made his work, after a time of eclectic experimentation, instantly recognizable, though Kirch-

---

* Picasso, who painted a literally uncountable number of self-portraits, anticipated Corinth in this self-reference. In 1900, when he was nineteen and starting to acquire a reputation as an original craftsman in Barcelona, he did an elegant, flattering watercolor sketch of himself and inscribed it "Yo."

ner himself trumpeted his stylistic uniqueness at the expense of the diverse masters—Munch, van Gogh, and Gauguin—who had helped to make him the artist he became. Though a loner among the modernists, in 1905 he helped to found, and soon dominated, a circle of young German Expressionists, *Die Brücke*, in Dresden. We have seen it before: there were times when even an artistic hermit like van Gogh—and Kirchner—craved the support of allies.

His group's name—"The Bridge"—was well chosen only if one read it as a conduit to the future. After all, as principled insurgents the *Brücke* artists were intent on blowing up bridges to the past or to the timorous present. The contrast with the French Fauves, who first exhibited their canvases in the same year, is instructive. For all the unappreciative reviews their intense, brilliant landscapes garnered, the leading Fauves—Matisse, Vlaminck, and Derain—were trying to synthesize new and old; as Elie Faure laid it down in his preface to the catalog of the exhibition, "the revolutionary of today is the classic of tomorrow." Revisiting the almost literally dazzling canvases of their first group show, one finds the Fauves a relatively tame collection of innovators. Only Matisse continued to revolutionize painting and, as a lifelong modernist, to remain ahead of the pack of artists maintaining that they had shaken off the trammels of bourgeois Salon taste.

The shock provided by the Fauves was sharp but short. Matisse went his own way to find new drama in domestic settings; Vlaminck retired to more conventional paintings; only Derain remained faithful to the "savage" pure colors that had made him and his colleagues the talk of Paris. In 1906 and 1907, his dealer, the perspicacious Ambroise Vollard, sent Derain to London to recapitulate Monet's success with his atmospheric scenes of the Thames, and, though he did not repeat what Monet's London had vaguely promised, the sketches and canvases that Derain brought back to Paris were authentic Fauve productions, with London's skies, water, ships, and public buildings powerfully represented in his favorite reds and blues. Appealing as they were—and are—they did not make a school, as avant-garde painters found inspiration elsewhere.

Thus, the *Brücke* painters, the Fauves' contemporaries, looked back with favor on only a handful of outsiders, and had no patience with the idea of sharing in a great tradition. They were bolder than most of their contemporaries; they painted and did woodcuts or lithographs in shared studios, ran cooperative exhibitions, published manifestos, and invited sympathetic art lovers to join them. Their self-proclaimed aim was to modernize painting in Germany. The pictures produced in the various Secessions in Berlin, Munich, and elsewhere, however anti-academic they might proclaim themselves to be, struck them as too timid, too compromising, scarcely adequate to the artistic possibilities offered by the turbulent metropolitan centers of their day.

In contrast, Kirchner was preeminently a painter of the modern city. Dresden and Berlin were his laboratories, though during long stays at Swiss sanatoria he demonstrated that his nervous technique could make landscapes, too, seem electric. Still, urban life was his métier, with unembarrassed nudes, clearly city products, in his studio; provocatively dressed ladies of the night swaggering on street corners; crowds flood-ing the sidewalks of Berlin. But he was not a copyist of externals; he insisted rather that his art was a revelation of inner vibrations. "The modifications in form and proportions are not arbitrary," he wrote about his painting, "but serve to make the spiritual expression large and forceful." That is why—an important disclaimer—"color, too, is not that of nature but one born from the painter's design intentions." This color creates, he added categorically, "in connection with the other col-ors in the picture, a certain resonance which expresses the painter's experience." The artist, he said over and over, forms a world rather than represents it. He was never a humble photographer of mundane reality.

Not even Kirchner's self-portraits could be simply labeled realistic. They were Expressionist notations registering less his momentary appearance than his disorientation in a world at war, his sexual appetites, or his precarious mental condition. Clearly his face and his body fasci-nated him; rivaling Rembrandt, at least in quantity, he painted, drew, and etched himself at least eighty times. Especially just before and dur-ing the war, when he seemed in a prolonged mental crisis, he unbur-dened himself with self-portraits, passionately. There is Kirchner delirious with morphine—all these done between 1914 and 1918—

Kirchner the drunkard, Kirchner in uniform with a nude model standing behind him and his right arm amputated or shot away. The last is a particularly frightening image open to a variety of interpretations, most of them apparently excessive. He was not making an anti-war protest, nor depicting himself castrated.* It was Kirchner the neurotic sufferer.

In 1937, the Nazis added to his malaise by including his paintings in the catalog of proscribed "Degenerate Art"—the most vicious rebuff of modernist painting any twentieth-century regime would ever enact—the final ground for despair in an artist as labile as Kirchner. His suicide the following year at fifty-eight seemed almost predictable. Surely, no German modernist exceeded his devotion to studying and exhibiting his self down to the roots except for one, the masterly Max Beckmann.

3.

IN HIS OWN HIGHLY PERSONAL WAY, Beckmann was a philosopher with a paintbrush. Without committing himself to doctrines like Schopenhauer's or accepting what he called the "nonsense" of Theosophy, he perused both. All his days he fished in deep intellectual waters, agonizing over the meaning of life—and of himself. In this enterprise, unsystematic but heartfelt, Beckmann's self-portraits were an essential element, never a casual interlude to relax from some more strenuous project. They are among his most potent—and most appealing—creations, as they emphasize his squarish head, jutting chin, and balding forehead, all modeled with a sure hand and notable control of color. He punctuated his work with self-portraits from the beginning of the twentieth century to 1950, the year of his death, in drypoints, woodcuts, lithographs, drawings, and paintings. More than once, he smuggled his likeness into the ambitious, large-size triptychs he began to paint after the war.

---

* The search for the real meaning of a wounded Kirchner's self-portrait in uniform may serve as a caution against over-reading. He had no front-line traumas to work through, and his political attitude toward the war was complicated, so that the convenient interpretation of this painting as either a symbolic representation of castration or an anti-war protest is far too simplistic.

One of Beckmann's earliest self-portraits, dating from 1901 when he was seventeen, is a striking exercise in technique, an etching that shows him open-mouthed, screaming, But at the heart of his intentions was the substance of his being rather than the flashy pirouettes he had learned to perform. He paints himself soberly dressed, a cigarette dangling from his right hand, or in a tuxedo, with the cigarette in his left. Again, he shows himself as a painter, improbably wearing a hat, holding a brush and a palette. He is a clown or a pedestrian on a swarming city street, a musician holding an unnaturally bulbous saxophone, a husband with his wife—twice, with his first and his second. He is in Amsterdam in self-imposed wartime exile with three friends, or alone, crowding out all background with his massive head. Again, in a brilliant half-length self-portrait of 1948—it remains one of his most memorable self-displays—he shows himself in a red and black–striped jacket holding a horn, one of his favorite props. His moods are as varied as his attire: truculent, frightened, defiant. He is everywhere in his art.

As Beckmann saw himself changing, he faithfully reproduced what he saw in the mirror as the history of his face. The Great War, which he barely endured as a medical orderly at the cost of a breakdown, left permanent scars on him, as it did on so many modernists. Violence, murder, and grisly death increasingly dominated his choice of subject; to capture and convey his cosmic gloom, Beckmann utilized stark Expressionist distortions in figures and colors. They marked audacious steps beyond the diffident innovations of German Secessionists that he had found so congenial as a young artist. Probably his best known self-portrait, a woodcut of 1920, attests to that postwar Beckmann. He has sharply etched his features: the eyes, almost closed, are inexpressive slashes of black, the corners of the mouth, unsmiling, are drawn down. The picture documents that, if for the most part postwar modernism lived off ideas and techniques developed before 1914, it did so in a novel, more cynical, at times more despairing vein.

Curiously enough, it was in 1938, in London, after the Nazis had included his work in their "exposure" of "Degenerate Art," that Beckmann took a rare opportunity to speak of the intentions underlying his art. They amounted to an acknowledgment of the subjective pressures that oriented so much modernist painting. He prudently stayed away from political comment. All the more reason to speak with some freedom about his motives for taking his face and figure as a subject, as he so often did. "All objective spirits," he said, "press toward self-representation—*Selbstdarstellung*. I search for this self—*Ich*—in my life and in my art." True objectivity implied subjectivity. This hunt was, to Beckmann's mind, every artist's most urgent and most demanding assignment. "Since we still do not know what this self really is, this self to which you and I give expression, each in our own way, we must push toward its discovery more and more deeply. For this self is the great, veiled mystery of existence." He characterized himself as "immersed in the problem of the individual," and tried "to represent it in every way. What are you? What am I?" he asked. "These are the questions that incessantly pursue and torment me and perhaps also play a certain role in my art." His "perhaps" was unnecessarily guarded; these questions were all over his work.

THIS OVERVIEW of modernist painters as specialists in self-portraiture should leave no doubt that as audacious pioneers in the pursuit of their inner life, all of their canvases, whether unambiguously showing the painter's face or not, were at least in some regards self-portraits. They were, if sensitively and attentively read, part of a great confession. This was true even, indeed especially, of major modernists who turned their back on representation altogether.

MYSTICAL MODERNISM

1.

IT HAPPENED ON ONE LATE AFTERNOON in Munich with twilight approaching, probably in 1909 or perhaps 1910—Vasili Kandinsky, who tells this story himself, rarely troubled his memoirs with prosaic and precise indicators like dates. He was returning to his studio after a day's sketching and quite inadvertently was about to invent abstract art. "Suddenly," he recalled, "I saw an indescribably beautiful canvas soaked in an inner glow." He rushed over to the perplexing painting on which he saw only forms and colors. The explanation quickly seized him: "I knew for certain that the object harmed my picture." A faithful rendering of reality somehow now appeared to be the supreme barrier to art. His conclusion was utterly sweeping: "the aims (and thus the means) of nature and art are essentially, organically, and by universal law different from each other." He had made a pictorial statement that owed nothing to the external world.

Whether Kandinsky's reminiscence is a trustworthy report on a dazzling insight or (which is more likely) the dramatized condensation of a more protracted retreat from the ideal of mimesis, thus to pit art against nature was an epochal event in the history of modernism. As we shall see, most artists who in these heady years cut the links to external realities reached that decisive point only after years of working toward the style that was to make them famous. Their pilgrimage—to them it seemed nothing less—was an instructive illustration of, and tribute to, the individualism that lies at the core of modernism, with its passion for the thrilling and the shocking and its sovereign disregard of conventions. Plainly there were more ways than one to encompass artistic self-revelations.

Kandinsky was one of three great modernist painters—Mondrian and Malevich were the others—who accomplished the task of undressing his heart (in Baudelaire's phrase) in obedience to a mystical sense of reality. No doubt, Kandinsky's mysticism was the triumph of personal urges over professional training. Born in Moscow in 1866, he was schooled, and well schooled, in law and economics, but gave up a career in the "real world" and moved to Munich in 1896 to study painting. He made himself into a skilled draftsman and painter of strongly colored, sometimes storytelling landscapes. And he showed himself, for all the isolation he was steering toward, an inveterate founder and joiner of unconventional groups. Yet he found none of his incessant activity to be satisfying in any way. If he looked for an artistic language to express his most private emotions, it was a new, cosmopolitan vocabulary he wanted. And around 1910, about the time he saw his canvas on its side and in dim light, he felt that he had reached his goal. Non-representational art with no reference to subject matter was on its way.

Not long before Kandinsky broke through to abstraction, this individualistic subjectivity found weighty academic support in a powerful confrontational treatise by the German aesthetician Wilhelm Worringer. In his thesis *Abstraction and Empathy* (1908), which he billed, underscoring its emphasis on mind, as a "Contribution to the Psychology of Style," Worringer argued that modern aesthetics had "taken the decisive step from aesthetic objectivism to aesthetic subjectivism." What matters in art—or rather, what should matter—are the emotions it arouses. If a "psychology of the need for art" is ever written, he maintained, it "would be a history of the feeling about the world and, as such, would stand alongside the history of religion as its equal." Modernists could only welcome so emphatic a champion. "The value of the work of art, what we call its beauty," Worringer wrote, "lies, generally speaking, in its power to bestow happiness." It followed that all kinds of artworks, whether primitive or sophisticated, figurative or abstract, derivative or innovative, could assert validity independent of conventional aesthetic hierarchies or moral uplift. Kandinsky, Worringer seemed to be saying, had every reason to feel entitled to produce what and how he pleased.

Kandinsky's radical divorce between art and nature, however inconsistently maintained,* was not a purely aesthetic decision. It was an expression of his homemade, rather ramshackle mystical system, concocted of Russian folk tales, the Theosophical dogmas of Madame Blavatsky, an exceptional susceptibility to musical as much as visual stimuli, and a sense of mission to rescue spirituality from the corrosive effects of contemporary "materialism." The modern world, Kandinsky believed, much as German Romantics had done a century before, had lost its soul and desperately needed to be re-enchanted, and art alone could do that.

---

* It is hardly astonishing that Kandinsky the amateur metaphysician sometimes contradicted himself, even on fundamentals. Thus in 1921 he wrote: "Abstract art does not exclude a connection with nature, but on the contrary, the relationship with nature is growing stronger and more intense than ever."

Vasili Kandinsky (1866–1944), abstract etching (ca. 1925). For the abstract painters of Kandinsky's time, such art might be wholly unrepresentational, but all were tied, in the artists' minds, to spiritual impulses.

Altogether, his "philosophy" added up to a heavy dose of recycled romanticism, that vague catchall term that Kandinsky liked to claim as his own. "If today there should be a new objectivity—*neue Sachlichkeit*—let there also be a new romanticism," he wrote in 1925, and added, "the meaning and content of art is romanticism," which meant to him a creative, highly unorthodox creed that, without rigorously excluding the intellect, placed the artist's and the viewer's feelings at the heart of aesthetic experience. That there were many who disagreed with him, modernists and others, and that he was aware of it, emerges from his wishful, almost wistful, formulation—"let there also be a new romanticism." Its prospects were on the whole dim; but Kandinsky's plea once again illustrates the sheer variety of modernist motivation.

THIS RATHER LAME Romantic revival was gaining some popularity around the time of the First World War, after half a century particularly hospitable to new pieties, or to old pieties tailored to modern tastes. We have noted it before in cults like Theosophy, anthroposophy, Christian Science, and a bewildering menu of beliefs ranging from primitive credulity about messages from the beyond to the civilized and earnest investigations of the English Society for Psychical Research, all of them determined to offer soothing alternative philosophies of life more cheerful than the ideology of science. The hunger for a spiritual message holding out hope that death is not the end seemed impossible to satisfy by the spectre of a frigid, law-governed universe. Hence, one version of spiritualism or another became the superstition of intellectuals and the educated. If all officially recognized denominations had proved bankrupt, if the holy story the Bible tells was incredible, then the authentic kernel of the sacred—these would-be believers convinced themselves—must be preserved and allowed to ripen free from old-fashioned sectarianism. It was in this turbulent atmosphere that a wing of modernists, among whom avant-garde painters were prominent, cast their impatience with conventional styles of thinking like impious positivism into religious form. Kandinsky was prominent among them.

Nor did he hesitate to say so. In his best known, extensively read and widely translated essay, *On the Spiritual in Art* (1912), he noted, rummaging through notions recent and remote, that the "inner-essential" similarity between simpler times and the present would reveal "the seed of the future." This teleology would have sounded distinctly unfashionable to anyone imbued with the scientific mentality, but it was a posture far from peculiar during the heyday of modernism—even among modernists.

ABSTRACT PAINTINGS, soon practiced by a small but persistent cohort of modernists working in Kandinsky's wake, confronted art critics with some unprecedented risks: one proposed reading of these canvases seemed as good as any other. Kandinsky says somewhere that the more interpretations one of his paintings invited, the better. If he seriously believed that—and apparently he did—he must have judged each of them a rousing success. "None of the statements that he made about his own works," one of his most respected analysts, Hans K. Roethel, has written in some dejection, "gives any interpretation of their meaning; his comments add to their mysteries rather than reveal them." Through the years, to his death in Paris in 1944, he continued to play with his forms; once he had discovered abstraction, he never abandoned it.

During his early years as an iconoclast, mainly spent in and near Munich, Kandinsky juxtaposed splashes of vividly contrasting irregular patches of color and spots in other colors invading the larger fields, often adding a dramatic streak of black traveling across the canvas. Some of the shades he chose were suggested by his reading in Theosophy, but all emerged from an inner, unidentifiable pressure. In his years in Moscow from 1916 to 1921—he supported the Russian Revolution and actively engaged in teaching and administration in the new regime until he found that his modernist abstractions were not welcome—he began to organize his figures more rigidly than before. He drew clearer, sharper outlines, relying in part on circles, straight lines, and half moons, but continued to paint mysterious shapes overlapping and brushing up against one another.*

---

* This was not a purely internal development. Kandinsky was responding to the abstract canvases of his fellow Russian modernists, like the Suprematist Kazimir Malevich and the Constructivism developed by, among others, the great designer El Lissitzky.

The small forms Kandinsky used at times made for a humorous symphony, some of them hazily resembling, but never truly imitating, structures appearing in nature. He introduced teasing shapes that could be interpreted as the portals of a cathedral or a horseback rider, but this only made his inventions appear more esoteric. Not even his mood— or the mood he intended to express—ever seemed unambiguous. From the time he adopted abstraction, then, his paintings were almost liter- ally indescribable. He worked vigorously, often in troubling uncer- tainty, on each of his pictures, and all that his audiences could do was to experience them. In short, what I am calling the lure of heresy could be quite as unsettling to the creators of abstract art as to its appreciators. Kandinsky's pictures only resembled one another.

2.

BY THE END OF THE FIRST WORLD WAR, the clan of abstractionists had grown to a small but fervent bevy of aesthetic extremists. Not all of them regarded their output as a form of worship; the witty French artist Robert Delaunay, for one, with his vividly colored swirls worked not to articulate a religious message but to exhibit a color theory. Yet at least one leader in the non-representational camp, the Russian Kazimir Malevich, deserves particular attention because the paintings he did from the late 1910s to the early 1920s in his Suprematist phase—it was a name he had coined—were the most sweeping exemplars of modernist non-objective art. Like Kandinsky imbued with Russian folk religion, and unlike him, occasion- ally identifying the artist—himself—with God, Malevich reduced paint- ing to elements more distant from nature even than Mondrian's. In 1913, he exhibited a black square within a white rectangle, and five years later, topped this seditious canvas with a slanting white square inscribed in a white square of a barely different hue. To appreciate the appearance of *White on White* required not just artistic open-mindedness but keen eye- sight. Beyond this monochrome there was only an empty canvas.

For Malevich, his simple-looking paintings were the incarnation of a spiritual ideology. He wanted to put something in the place of noth- ing, artistic sensibility as a substitute for capitalistic greed. "By Suprematism," he wrote, "I mean the supremacy of pure feeling or sensation in the pictorial arts." As he recalled his awakening, it had been "in the year 1913 in my desperate struggle to free art from the ballast of the objective world" that he had "fled to the form of the Square." That square, he insisted, was not empty, but "rather the experience of object-lessness." Such thinking took art—and of course the artist—very seriously indeed. When Malevich maintained that the time was ripe for a new religion, he meant a new aesthetic.

3.

FOR ALL THE POTENT CONTRIBUTIONS of Russian artists to the modernist revolt, the one among them whom even a large museum-visiting public can instantly identify was a Dutchman, Piet Mondrian. As a young painter, Mondrian had done some striking naturalistic landscapes, but he was to shift away dramatically from such conventional subjects. Like many other modernists, Mondrian was a driven man, obsessed by a gnawing discontent with bourgeois taste and a consuming need to strike out beyond it. Speaking freely to a few friends about his states of mind and the meaning of his painting, he would emphasize the compulsion under which he worked. His gradual move toward the celebrated grids was a partly painful, at least mesmerizing, effort for him. In some deep ways, he never ceased wrestling with his father's rigorous Calvinism, which he at once rejected and incorporated. His studios and apartments—whether in Amsterdam, Paris, or New York—attested to his secular religiosity; to an asceticism never overcome: everything in its place, nothing superfluous by way of ornament.

This internal propulsion meant that once sure of his mission, Mondrian could be receptive to other artists' work only to transcend it. Late in 1911, he moved at the age of thirty-nine to Paris and continued his artistic education. Yet he was determined not to fall into dependency. He found Picasso deeply impressive but, no longer intimidated, remained incredulous about the supposed originality of the great Cubist's talents. True, he confessed, he admired the Impressionists, the Post-Impressionists, and the Fauves, but—it was a large reservation—

"I had to seek the true way alone." The pious formulation—"the true way"—is revealing.

That true way was the path to what Mondrian called "pure reality." The brilliant landscapes of his early years, which alone would have secured his artistic reputation, gradually gave way to highly colored figurations that looked a little like a pointillist on a binge—still recognizably windmills or dunes, but increasingly patterns that existed for their own sake. Then from 1908 on he moved step by small step toward non-representational art. His trees and his dunes still looked like trees and dunes, but less and less so. His famous two still lifes with ginger pot (1911–12) were Cubist in inspiration, and the trees he painted in these years were stripped of all but bare trunks and branches, as though a mighty storm had blown away every trace of foliage. He was beginning to title his paintings "Composition," reducing his commitment to the imitation of nature to a minimum. Later, explaining what "Neo-Plasticism" meant to him, he noted that "denaturalization" is "one of the essential points of human progress; it is of the greatest importance in neo-plastic art." In 1914, in one of his important transitional canvases, Mondrian painted what he called a *Pier and Ocean* that, without its title, would have seemed no more than a fairly crowded jumble of straight lines and elongated crosses. By 1917, he was experimenting with splashing colored rectangles across his canvases; it was only a matter of time before he would bring straight black lines and colored rectangles together. That moment came around 1920; the rectangles once in place became almost sacred to their maker.

It had been a long pilgrimage. As early as 1915, taking a walk with a friend in the Dutch artists' village of Laren, and talking about the effect of moonlight on landscapes, Mondrian abruptly broke out: "Yes, all in all, nature is a damned wretched affair. I can hardly stand it." Like Kandinsky, he was a seeker. Both drew their mystical notions largely from Theosophy, and—this is most important—took their painting to be more than mere painting, a form of prayer. Both found in their art the solution to their religious perplexities, as they resolutely turned their back on nature.

Mondrian did so literally, all through his life. In 1939, he fled Paris for London, and late in 1940, he migrated from Great Britain to the United States, his now-celebrated abstract rectangles known mainly to a select circle of American collectors. Among the artists who befriended him in his last few years—he died in 1944—was the abstract painter Robert Motherwell, who could afford to take, and enjoyed taking, his Dutch fellow artist out to dinner. The two sometimes went to Tavern on the Green, an old New York standby that fronts on Central Park. When the weather was fine, Motherwell reports, the two would take a table outdoors, and Mondrian would insist that he sit with his back to the park's lush greenery.

This was not an abrupt reversal by an old man threatened with senility. Nor was it just a matter of taste; it attests to his conviction that the more the human animal escapes from the authority of nature, the more civilized it becomes. In building great cities, in the triumphs of technology and science, humans had far outstripped nature; it was up to painting now to catch up with the engineers. For the mind—on this point Mondrian never wavered—has a vast creative potential and, as his work increasingly showed, at least for him requires no external source of inspiration. The vision that underlay Kandinsky's abstractions was replaced, in Mondrian, with a stripped-down structure; those who watched him paint could attest that he trusted his intuition alone in his search for a lasting artistic form. As a faithful, in fact, an extreme modernist, for Mondrian subjectivity was all.

THOUGH THEIR ARTISTIC aims and religious inspiration were close cousins, in their external appearance and social presence Mondrian and Kandinsky were as different as two artists can possibly be. Kandinsky was sociable and gregarious, Mondrian austere and, though never without friends, a solitary explorer. Kandinsky could never be without female companionship. Mondrian was, even though there are a few reports (all of uncertain reliability) about some unhappy romantic attachments, very much the professional bachelor. Those who had observed him noted that the one dance he truly liked was the Charleston, in which one does not touch one's partner. Kandinsky was

Piet Mondrian (1872–1944), *Composition with Red, Yellow and Blue* (1937–42).

a born educator, spending eleven years as a professor at the incarnation of German modernism, the Bauhaus, until it closed in 1933, teaching drawing and wall painting with enthusiasm and consistently enjoying gratifying popularity with his students. Mondrian kept publishing the same rhetorical effusions about his private doctrine, "Neo-Plasticism." Kandinsky invented ever new forms for his pious quest. Mondrian, after settling on his celebrated grids, varied them only in accord with a minutely calibrated program.

For all his isolated pioneering, Mondrian pursued his devout modernist agenda with a small band of companions, as obsessive in his public role as he was in his private studio. In 1917, he helped to found an avant-garde journal, *De Stijl*, with such like-minded Dutch colleagues as Theo van Doesburg, to establish a "spiritual community among artists" who together would create "a collective style." In one of its manifestos, Mondrian and his colleagues insisted that "plastic" modern art, the art that reconciles technology and artistry and that ought to inform architecture and painting alike, "must derive not from exterior vision but from interior life, not from imitation but from representation." This aesthetic ideology (with Mondrian's rigidity a new kind of orthodoxy) would among other things confine itself to "the horizontal-vertical order" and thus exclude "the diagonal and the curve." Such doctrine, at once sweeping and detailed, was a most serious matter admitting of no exceptions. When in 1924 the volatile van Doesburg introduced the diagonal into his painting, overtly contradicting *De Stijl* principles, Mondrian took this act to be outright treason and broke with the group and van Doesburg. Neo-Plasticism was not to be trifled with.

Unadulterated Neo-Plasticism came in 1919, when the curveless, unmodulated canvases we associate with Mondrian entered his repertoire. For half a dozen years in Paris, he was compelled to paint flower pictures to eke out a scanty living; it was not until 1926 that American collectors like Katherine S. Dreier discovered him and permitted him to live by his serious—I am tempted to call them religious—paintings alone. But nothing diverted him from his mission, certainly not poverty; nothing moved him to moderate the simple rules governing his painterly procedure: placing perfectly straight horizontal and vertical bands across the canvas and having them frame rectangles confined to red, blue, and yellow as well as three "neutral" tints—black, white, and gray. Ever simplifying, by the late 1920s his paintings consisted of a few (sometimes only two) lines, one strictly horizontal and the other no less strictly vertical, animated by a single patch of color. It was only in the 1930s that he recomplicated his canvases slightly, at times doubling the black bands, at times turning his canvases to make them a lozenge. But the fundamental grid remained inviolate.

In the light of that consistent severity, Mondrian's last canvases, his *New York* and *New York City I*, his *Broadway Boogie Woogie* and *Victory*

Boogie Woogie, come as a surprise, cheerful and animated, the stripes brightly colored instead of black. These exuberant paintings represent, I believe, the emergence—or reemergence—of a certain carnal vitality in Mondrian, an ability to depart from his dearly held dogma of the rectangle as a resistance to sensual pressures, no longer fully expressive of him as he experienced New York, which is to say, Manhattan. New York was, to his mind, a triumph of civilization, with its impressive rectangular piles of steel and glass, its noisy energy a happy counterweight to nature's silences. Had he lived on, and in New York, he might have reclaimed some of the erotic vigor he had so artfully, so anxiously denied with his sober grids, expressing his relentless resistance to the tension of curves and play of colors without which sexual life is largely unthinkable.

As a loyal modernist, Mondrian was modern also in his conviction that a true artist must belong to his age. Looking back in 1941, three years before his death in New York, he expressed his confidence that he was consistently working "in accord with the spirit of modern times." He interpreted that spirit to be a search for freedom—from conformity, from academicism, from commercialism. The modern art he had learned to practice was, he said emphatically, "*a liberation from the oppression of the past.*" It was a principle by which he lived. Since his death, Mondrian's patterns have been assimilated (not surprisingly) into mercantile culture. Reproductions or imitations of his grids have appeared in shop windows, advertisements, book jackets, even women's clothes. The lure of heresy has abated; as the sense of novelty has faded, the desire to own one of his modernist pieces intensified. No wonder that potential buyers can recognize his art instantaneously. But it would be unhistorical to forget how alien his work once seemed.

PICASSO ONCE DEFINED modern art as a sum of destructions. But the motivations of abstract artists show this definition to be incomplete, however felicitous it appears to be. The three abstractionists on whom I have concentrated—Kandinsky, Malevich, and Mondrian—were intent upon constructing, and displaying, a religious worldview that would help to repair the spiritual losses generated by the materialistic culture they were forced to live in. I cannot emphasize enough that the sources of the modernist rebellion in the arts rose from all quarters of the political, intellectual, and emotional world. What they did share was a powerful sense of opposition to that world as it was, and a hunger for spirituality.

ANARCHISTS AND AUTHORITARIANS

1.

AS THE GREAT WAR kept on its murderous march, modernists, fed up to the gills with the military-political complex that dominated their lives and killed their friends, began to characterize the situation with just one word: "insanity." True, some Britons subscribed to the sentiment inscribed on a London statue for the heroic English nurse Edith Cavell, shot by the Germans in 1915 for aiding British soldiers behind the enemy's lines: "Patriotism is not enough. I must have no hatred or bitterness for anyone." True, some Germans despised the popular slogan, "God punish England!" and kept in touch with their old "enemy" friends in messages sent through neutral countries. But these civilized minorities scarcely influenced policy. The official line on both sides was chauvinism, encouraged and even enforced by censors, adorned by pious talk of divine missions and divine support. After the madness was over, Freud would sarcastically note that both the Allies and the Central Powers had enlisted God for their side, a pair of incompatible claims that, he thought, had done little for His reputation.

This was the poisonous atmosphere in which Dada, the singularly disrespectful anti-art lobby, emerged and, for a time, flourished. The very question, Who invented this ludicrous name, Dada? has never been satisfactorily settled, a sign of the free-floating confusion in which this non-movement lived. It was revolutionary, but not without its precursors. The most significant proto-Dadaists included important artists like Giorgio de Chirico and the far more radical Marcel Duchamp, who single-handedly demonstrated the lengths an anti-artist could go to kill art—or at least try—by inventing new examples of it.*

---

* Duchamp deserves, and will get, a section of his own below.

Dada's program, to the extent that it had one, was simple, wholly negative. Tristan Tzara, a Romanian multilingual poet and effervescent organizer, probably the liveliest and most tenacious among Dada's founders, put it tersely: "The beginnings of Dada were not the beginnings of art, but of disgust." Its votaries had grown convinced that all artists, including the most uncompromising anti-establishment schools, had betrayed their true subversive vocation by collaborating with bourgeois exploiters and philistines. "The Dadaist," wrote the Berlin poet Richard Huelsenbeck, another founder, in 1920, recalling the war years, "considers it necessary to come out against art, because he has seen through its fraud as a moral safety valve." Art, was the Dadaists' message, had been so fatally compromised that it could not be a matter of purifying, of improving, of renewing it. The point was to destroy it.

This was, of course, a self-contradictory assignment; the very effort to do away with art inescapably produced art, and some of that made interesting contributions to the modernist rebellion. The often imaginative work of the Dadaists was a tribute to the freedom of their fancy, but they soon divided into irreconcilable parties: the absolutists, like the inventive Spanish painter Francis Picabia, insisted that "every page" for which a Dadaist is responsible "must explode, whether through seriousness, profundity, turbulence, nausea, the new, the eternal, annihilating nonsense, enthusiasm for principles, or the way it is printed. Art must be unaesthetic in the extreme, useless and impossible to justify." In dramatic contrast, political activists like George Grosz, the maker of unforgettable anticapitalist propaganda, insisted on Dada's left-wing agenda. When the issue was revived in the mid-1920s with Surrealism, it was more or less resolved in favor of possible Surrealist art: André Breton, the poet, critic, and maker of manifestos who set the tone for the movement, decided that there was such a thing, provided it sprang from irrational mental roots—from dreams, hypnosis, hallucinations, and free association.

THE BIRTHPLACE OF DADA was Zurich, in neutral Switzerland. Not coincidentally: it was a city relatively free of the compulsive interference with public speech in belligerent countries. On February 2, 1916, the German writer Hugo Ball sent out an invitation to the Zurich public to attend the opening three days later of the newly founded Cabaret Voltaire. Its announced purpose was to "create a center for artistic entertainments." Its chosen name was infelicitous for a place that would specialize in outlandish Dadaist manifestations; as the father figure for the Enlightenment, Voltaire was the proponent of rationality, standing at the opposite extreme from the Dadaists' carefully cultivated absurdities. And the entertainments Ball had promised turned out to be exercises in black humor, each of them designed to show up the pretentiousness, the sordidness, the bathos of any art susceptible to ridicule—as all arts seemed to be. "Dada," proclaimed Tzara, "is using all its strength to establish the idiotic everywhere." No matter how idiotic Dadaist performances would be, they were to their makers' minds the essence of good sense compared to a war that seemed to have no aim except mass slaughter.

Even though Dada did not succeed in establishing idiocy at Cabaret Voltaire or anywhere else, it certainly rehearsed it vigorously, often spontaneously, and sometimes with very funny routines. Before long, it opened branches, mainly in Berlin, Paris, and New York, run by disaffected exhibitionists who tended to follow the lead of the Zurich originators. Dadaists read out nonsense poems or sang strange songs of their composition, performed in preposterous costumes and dressed up in masks in which they took great pride. One particularly dazzling number, always sure to receive a lively response from the audience, was the *poème simultané*, with three "actors" reading three different poems at the same time. This organized chaos was, of course, an infuriated reflection on the larger, more lethal chaos outside the Cabaret Voltaire's walls.

The most spectacular event in Zurich's Dada was also its swan song. It came on April 9, 1919, in a hall crowded with expectant supporters. The usual performers were on stage insulting the audience, reading from yet-to-be-completed manuscripts, reciting preposterous verses, presenting an awkward modernist ballet, and—the hit of the evening—offering a simultaneous poem read by not three but twenty participants. That this choir of declaimers could not always keep its collective rhythm surprised no one. But, in any event, the Dadaists could not surpass this evening, and besides, peace had broken out. Looking back from midcentury, leading modernist art critics like Clement Greenberg and Harold Rosenberg did not take Dada very seriously, except for seeing the Pop artists of the 1960s, in Rosenberg's view, as Dadaists revived. If Pop was the second age of ingenuity, that oddly assorted pair, Dadaism and its successor Surrealism, were the first, exploring the kind of inwardness that made most modernists comfortable. If these fairly self-sufficient centers of unconventionality allowed art any legitimacy at all, they gave artists the widest field imaginable for discoveries.

2.

It was on organizational strategies that the two parted company. Whereas Dada represented organized anarchy, Surrealism was a one-man authoritarianism. Its leading spirit, André Breton, decreed who would be admitted as a member of his group, and prescribed its intellectual orientation. For him, Surrealism was not a doctrine of art but one of unconscious ideas made manifest. In the midst of a paragraph of praise for Picasso in his first *Manifesto of Surrealism*, published in 1924 when he was twenty-eight, Breton spoke contemptuously about "that lamentable expedient which is painting." Freud was more important to him than Picasso. Indeed, in the whole history of modernism, only one avant-garde, Surrealism, frankly acknowledged its vast debt to psychoanalysis. It could have been even larger: Breton's knowledge of Freud's views was superficial more than profound, but that did not keep Freud's name and some of his ideas from Breton's short list of modern authorities.

In Breton's famous *Manifesto*—a statement he had been debating, revising, and experimenting with for five years—he pleaded for the possibilities of a Surrealist art. It was a curious document, far longer, far more personal, than such declarations of purpose usually are. It listed the names of the faithful, commented on the evolution of the author's thinking, and explicated its checkered prehistory that, Breton argued, included Shakespeare, Swift, Sade, Baudelaire, Rimbaud—scarcely a catalog to make good bourgeois happy. But this implicit declaration of hostility—Sade? Rimbaud?—did not trouble Breton and his followers: in their books, as they had been for modernists for almost a century, bourgeois remained the enemy incarnate.

Breton's *Manifesto* also contained his formal definition of Surrealism: "Pure psychic automatism, by which one intends to express verbally, in writing or by any other method, the real functioning of the mind. Dictation by thought, in the absence of any control exercised by reason, and beyond any aesthetic or moral preoccupation." Hence, "the omnipotence of dreams" and "the undirected play of thought" belonged among the central tenets of Surrealism. This definition bluntly affirmed that for Breton, the creative juices of a true painter or poet can never generate action through planning and calculation, and that the overwhelmingly rationalist philosophies of the nineteenth century had badly distorted that fundamental truth. Hence, the only painting acceptable to Surrealism would be the kind arising from the unconscious, and one that candidly advertised its irrational origins. If painters of the Dada persuasion had left any interesting artwork for posterity, it had been mainly their inventive way with the unconventional typography of front pages for one of their ephemeral journals; but several painters in the Surrealist camp, whose primary allegiance was essentially to their own inner urges, made canvases of impressive originality, resembling one another only in using a remnant, even a small one, of the external world for their subject matter.

3.

The most literary among the Surrealist painters was the Belgian artist René Magritte, whose lifetime specialty was the incongruity between a title (or caption) of his painting and the work itself, or between the subject of the work and sober reality. The most famous of these, often reproduced and much discussed, was *La Trahison des images* (1928–29), which shows a clearly delineated pipe accompanied by a handwritten denial: "*Ceci n'est pas une pipe.*" Reflecting, years later, on his turn to painting as a career during the First World War, Magritte was lucid about his confrontational intentions as he gradually became aware of them: "My interest lay entirely in provoking an emotional shock." In an autobiographical account, he singled out a melodramatic moment of

René Magritte's famous *La Trahison des images (Ceci n'est pas une pipe)* (This is not a pipe) (1928–29).

truth: He was being shown a reproduction of de Chirico's daring *Song of Love* (1914), in which a plaster head of Apollo shares top billing with a large rubber glove. Moved to tears by the experience, the future suddenly lay open to Magritte: to force the incongruity of surface realities into shocking harmony.

Perhaps the best explication of the puzzles that Magritte sets the viewer is to regard them as visual puns. They are far more quickly explained than, say, Dali's crowded and peculiar compositions. Magritte's *The Red Model* (1935) has a pair of low boots that end up as naked feet in the region of the toes; *Philosophy in the Boudoir* (1947) depicts a nightgown on a coat hanger with two firm, luscious breasts emerging in their proper place. Among his most admired ideas, tried several times, he shows a landscape painting leaning against a window looking out on precisely that landscape. *The Collective Invention* (1934) has a fish lying on an empty shore with oceanic waves making a strong background, and a woman's long legs of human size attached to the fish's body.

His commentaries on well known paintings are just as ghoulish.

In *Perspective: Madame Récamier by David* (1951), he substitutes a coffin mimicking a sitting figure for David's sensual portrait. Such inventions—and there are many like them—have an unsettling quality that characterized his work for decades. Once having formulated his recipe, Magritte never departed from it, and though this predictability made his paintings less surprising than they might have been, they are for the most part witty enough to make them a pleasing, if not a profound, aesthetic experience.

Breton admired Magritte greatly, and praised his "supreme originality" and the "capital importance of his intervention." Surrealism, he wrote, had been indebted to a sizable list of painters, the first of whom was Max Ernst. Like many other modernists, Ernst was not a native Parisian (he was born in Germany in 1898), but went to Paris to find his niche in the world of art. Given to hallucinatory experiences even as a boy, his imagination found ample room for play in the atmosphere of the world's capital for modernist art. His range as draftsman and maker of graphic series was unsurpassed, and reflects the sheer attractiveness of Surrealist doctrine.

4.

IN HIS LONG LIFE as master of surrealism, Breton found perhaps a dozen artists worthy of being numbered among representatives of its art. Of these, two deserve our special attention: Joan Miró and Salvador Dali. They stand at opposing ends of modernism: Miró as the pure artist, Dali as the incorrigible publicity hound. Few modernists have given art-loving publics so much unadulterated pleasure as Miró. The museum devoted to his work in his hometown, Barcelona (itself an exercise in modernist design by Miró's friend, the great José Luis Sert), provides an agreeable, comprehensive ramble through his persistently evolving styles, a rarely ceasing debate with himself as he poured out paintings, drawings, sculptures, designs for carpets and ballets and tableware. It was not until the mid-1920s—he was born in 1893—that he reached the audaciously colorful version of Surrealist painting that underwrote his international reputation. He had made himself into an artist devoted to insistent color and somewhat mysterious patterns, though never forgetting unmistakable reminiscences of the external world.

Miró's *Person Throwing a Stone at a Bird* (1926) is an early masterful instance: a ruthlessly simplified human figure—the head is a near circle with an eye its only feature; the body is an enlarged curving shape ending up in a huge single foot; the throwing arm is a straight thin line that bisects the figure—stands on a beach, with the sea and the sky providing a tranquil backdrop. He had said in those years that he wished to "assassinate painting," but that was one of those sayings that historians would do well to resist. He was no Dadaist: Miró wanted to transform—or rather, subdue—painting to fit the demands of his imagination. Even his Surrealism was a more individualistic affair than Breton liked. There were occasions when Breton extravagantly lauded Miró as the most Surrealist artist of them all, but when Miró, in his impatience, lent his talents to designing costumes for the Ballets Russes, Breton disapproved: it was not revolutionary enough. This criticism did not divert Miró from pursuing what he deemed his destiny as an artist, to whom his imagination alone issued orders.

DALI'S PLACE AS AN ARTIST is far less secure. George Orwell, in an early appraisal, got it right: "The two qualities that Dali unquestionably possesses, are a gift for drawing and an atrocious egoism." Without the first he would never have been able to gratify the second. He was a spectacularly endowed and thoroughly trained craftsman, and showed his talents and his learning from the beginning. His distaste for modern art, loudly proclaimed, was well known, and his admiration for the immensely successful, soundly academic Meissonier unsurprising. With a bow to widespread interest in psychiatry, Dali defined his artistic procedure as the "paranoiac-critical method," which amounted to the "spontaneous method of irrational knowledge based upon the critical-interpretive association of delirious phenomena."

Breton might have been displeased with the implicit rationalism of a "critical" method no matter how paranoiac, but the amusing social presence of the new recruit—Dali had, inevitably, visited Paris and met the Surrealists in 1928—and his peculiarly "Freudian" paintings, converted him to the young, hyperactive Spaniard. Dali, one of the greatest self-advertisers that the modernist age was to see, had an easy triumph among the art-loving and newspaper-reading public. His staring eyes—Freud, upon meeting him, called them "candid" and "fanatical"—and his striking, turned-up mustache made him a natural target for press photographers.

More, his paintings, if at times only with their titles, hinted at scandalous erotic mysteries exciting to philistines. An important early Surrealist canvas, showing what looks more or less like a man's head beset by vermin and a young woman performing oral sex on a crippled man, bore the title *The Great Masturbator* (1929). But the painting that made him something of a household name was *The Persistence of Memory* (1931), with its melting (but still legible) watches draped over various surfaces in a barren landscape. In short, Dali tried in a roundabout way

Salvador Dali (1904–1989), *The Great Masturbator* (1929). A characteristic painting by this self-advertising Spanish Surrealist.

what the Pop artists would attempt to do directly three decades later: to blend aristocratic and vulgar art into a synthesis. And that synthesis, low as it was, pleased the millions.

PICASSO: THE ONE-MAN BAND

1.

PICASSO COULD DO ANYTHING—brilliantly. He might enjoy taking time out to gossip with adoring visitors, especially fellow Spaniards, attend a bullfight, or hunt women; still, he was enormously productive. He worked steadily, rapidly, and resourcefully. To give but a single example: in that magnificent cycle of a hundred etchings he did between 1930 and 1937 for Ambroise Vollard, one of his most important dealers, he produced forty of them, all variations on an artist in his studio, in a feverish creative rush within two months, between March and early May 1933. And he made most of the breaks from his studio routine serve his art, for his conversations, his entertainments, above all his sexual conquests regularly lived on in his work. In a busy, varied, and very long life—he died in 1973 at the age of ninety-two—he spread his vast oeuvre across an astonishing spectrum, painting, drawing, sculpting, making graphics and ceramics. From virile youth to impotent age, he generated a literally uncountable mass of self-portraits, trying every conceivable medium and inhabiting most conceivable roles: Picasso the dandy, the lover, the artist, the carouser, the clown, the friend, even the monkey, and the diminutive aged voyeur watching younger couples at sex. He launched styles, modified styles, lampooned styles with unquenchable originality until his final years. In short, he was a one-man band among the modernists.

He was born in Malaga in 1881, the son of a third-rate painter who spent his life teaching the subject he had mastered so inadequately. Even as a boy, Picasso, endlessly scribbling, demonstrated that he would succeed in the craft in which his father was so grossly failing. His mother, whose maiden name, significantly enough, Picasso adopted for his artist's signature soon after he went off on his own, was his firm supporter whenever there was a conflict within the family. It is reasonable to suppose that her unconditional love for him stood model for the feelings Picasso thought he had a perfect right to claim from the many women who stirred his passions in adult life. In 1895, the family moved to Barcelona, a city that Picasso would regard as his own. By 1900, he was in Paris for the first time, but it was not until 1903 that he made a permanent move to the capital of art. It was his way of saying farewell to his father, but not to Spain. In years to come, many would come to think of Picasso as a French painter, but he always remained a Spaniard at heart.

He once famously said, in a broad hint to his future biographers, that he wanted to leave to posterity as complete a documentation of his life as he could muster.* Actually he did not date his early pictures, not even those of the Cubist years where such specificity would have been most helpful to students of his work. But it is true that for Picasso, life and art meshed more closely than in most other artists. His works were, in the most elevated possible sense, *oeuvres d'occasion*. A shift in style, then, *might* reveal—it is imperative not to be more definite than this— that a new woman was occupying his bed. But urges other than erotic cravings or gratifications also roused him to action, above all aesthetic conundrums calling for aesthetic solutions. He often made art quite literally for art's sake.

It has long been fashionable, even among psychoanalysts, to discount motives originating in a drive for mastery, a painter's enthusiasm, say (to take one of the favorite games of Picasso's maturity), for depicting a nude body in multiple perspectives literally inconceivable to other painters. But walking around his model was only one of many artists' games Picasso liked to play. He ached to solve technical problems that were not even problems for his fellows. At all events, whatever he etched or painted became a work of art under his hand, an act of free translation of reality, a tribute to his genius.

The uniformly recognized trajectory of his work, that much-discussed succession of Picasso's styles, was in no way predictable. Each innovation emerged from inner monitions, from an imperative

---

* Picasso: "Why do you think I date everything I do? Because it's not sufficient to know an artist's work—it is necessary to know when he did them, why, how, under what circumstances."

need to experiment. He would not be confined to a particular style, not even one he had invented himself. In his life as an artist, Picasso's untrammeled ability to play—the only activity, Friedrich Schiller had said more than a century before him, in which man is truly human— provided his audiences with repeated surprises. And himself no less: "Painting is stronger than I am," he said late in life. "It makes me do what it wants." It was this invaluable passivity before the demands of art, given productive guidance by his craftsman's self-discipline, that made Picasso so protean a modernist.

Protean and unsurpassed: the Blue and Rose periods after 1900; the Cubist years incubating from 1906 to reach their full realization four and more years after; the neoclassical canvases that dominated the early 1920s; the imaginative series of etchings a decade later; the left-wing political phase from the late 1930s; the dazzling parodies of historic masterpieces after the end of World War II, are the principal styles we associate with Picasso. In fact *Les Demoiselles d'Avignon*, probably his most radical painting, first sketched in 1906 and completed the following year, discloses an evolution in his styles on a single canvas. Two of the prostitutes, on the right, painted somewhat later than the other three, have faces reminiscent of ancient Iberian and African masks, attesting to Picasso's newly acquired interest in that kind of art, and sharply distinct from the other three faces. If prompted by some inner urge toward innovation, he could not wait. Painting was indeed stronger than he was.

EACH OF THESE STYLES WOULD have been productive enough to guarantee Picasso prominence in the forefront of modernist art.* But one of them, Cubism, calls for particular attention, for more than all the oth-

* This is not to maintain that Picasso's styles were hermetically sealed against one another. In 1906, when he was already contemplating his epochmaking *Demoiselles d'Avignon* with its unprecedented distortions of the human face and figure, he painted one of his loveliest oils, *La Toilette*, which depicts a stunningly beautiful, realistically rendered nude arranging her hair, as she stands before a mirror held out to her by a fully dressed servant. Again, in the same year, he painted some heavyset nudes who anticipate the vaguely neoclassical figures he would explore after the First World War.

Pablo Picasso (1881–1973), *La Toilette* (1906). Picasso could paint anything, and this lovely canvas shows his realism at its best.

ers, it made a momentous modernist statement about the autonomy of art. Neo-Impressionists had flouted nature with their arbitrary colors. Abstract painters were aiming to make nature irrelevant. Cubists for their part would concentrate on the first, without feeling it necessary to adopt the second, of these choices. They found inspiration in Cézanne's still lifes that conquered amazed artists in that exposition of 1907, paintings in which tables and chairs and bowls of fruit violated the simple rules of linearity and perspective they necessarily obey in nature. Picasso's tributes to Cézanne are many and highly visible—one modernist cheerfully in debt to another.

For centuries, painters had faced the task of providing an illusion of three-dimensionality in a two-dimensional medium. Tricky as it was, painters manipulated shapes and gradations of color. Now the first Cubists and indisputably the greatest, Pablo Picasso and Georges Braque, rejected these time-honored solutions: they were intent on making works of art that would not let the viewer forget their distinct essence as human products. They shattered surfaces that in nature belong together and reassembled fragmented reality by transforming a curved object like a woman's breast or a man's cheek into some strange geometric contour that resembled virtually nothing, certainly not a breast or a cheek. In a word, the Cubists deliberately misrepresented the world of objects, giving the viewer the chore of putting the fragments together into a recognizable semblance of actuality. Curves survived in Cubist art, but they were upstaged by straight lines, by rectangles, and, as contemporaries noted with some amusement, by cubes. Beauty seemed far from the Cubists' intentions, yet some of their canvases, Braque's *Still Life with Violin and Pitcher* and Picasso's portrait of Ambroise Vollard, both of 1909–10, are astonishing in the sheer aesthetic pleasure they give. Modernist painters were not committed to beauty, but there were those among them who made it.

The Cubist style was long-lived enough to go through noticeable phases. After the austerity of the founding years, the time of Analytic Cubism, its successor, Synthetic Cubism, worked with a brighter palette and its canvases intensified their alienation from nature with stenciled inscriptions and arbitrarily added pieces of paper. Soon

Pablo Picasso, *Portrait of Ambroise Vollard* (1909–10).
A brilliant early Cubist canvas of one among Picasso's dealers.

Picasso and Braque were joined by others, until a distinct faction of
Cubists emerged. But the importance of Cubism ranged far beyond the
half dozen members of a newly formed avant-garde. All of modernist
painting drew dividends from the dismemberment that the Cubists
were visiting on their subject matter: it was like a license granted artists
to reassert their high status in a striking variety of ways. And this, too,

was the most significant role that Picasso played in his lifetime. No modernist asserted the artist's sovereignty more forcefully than he did.

2.

THE EXTRAVAGANT DEFORMATIONS to which Picasso could subject the human face and figure, sometimes quite viciously, make it easy to forget that he was one of the most exquisite draftsmen in twentieth-century art. He did a graphite portrait of Vollard in 1911, a pencil drawing of his friend, the poet Guillaume Apollinaire, in 1916, an oil portrait of his son, Paul, in 1923, each breathtaking in its utter loveliness, in the sure touch and expressive energy of his line, each a picture that an academically committed artist would have been proud to claim. They make the delighted viewer think of Rubens, that sublime master of the pen. He did others, equally traditional, equally distinguished. He was aware of his gift: commenting on the training of artists, he insisted that drawing must come first and complained that it was not being sufficiently fostered in his day. His own essays in traditional draftsmanship are persuasive evidence that the most determined iconoclast among modernist painters could score his effects with old-fashioned techniques.

Picasso's technical mastery of his professional instruments was so complete that he could confidently render any attitude, any gesture, any emotion. We can read the dazzling riches he left to the world with his portrayals of men and women, to say nothing of minotaurs, as an impressive if unintended representation of the gamut of human nature, in particular the instinctual drives in moments of extreme excitement. Unintended: there is no evidence that Picasso ever read a line of Freud or for that matter any other psychologist. But he energetically put the drives and their vicissitudes through their paces. Of course, obviously, for any painter major or minor—or any poet or playwright—sexuality and aggression are indispensable raw material. What distinguished Picasso was the animation, at times the brutality, with which he fixed love and hate on canvas and paper, and his uncanny skill in finding aesthetic equivalents for them with an unmatched force of expression and intensity of vision. That is why his triumphant talent as a draftsman was so essential

to Picasso's achievement: he could draw anything, and did. The constraints of good taste, which would have kept academic artists from such
forthrightness, never stopped him—probably never occurred to him.

Thus, in painting and sketching sexuality, he often spurned the
mask of sublimation. Inhibition was not in his vocabulary: lust pulsates
in his work, including his self-portraits. There he is, lying in bed, partly
dressed, being serviced orally by a nude long-haired brunette; there he
is (probably) returning the compliment to a naked young woman who
is obviously relishing it. When he was not a protagonist, he was no less
candid. No wonder conservative critics denounced his art as porno-
graphic. He had a wide repertoire, and several kinds of couplings at his
disposal, some of them physically impossible ones.

Between August 29 and September 9, 1968—Picasso was then
eighty-six—he did a cycle of twenty-five highly explicit etchings of
Raphael and his famous model, La Fornarina, making love. Raphael was

Pablo Picasso, *Raphael and La Fornarina* (1968). One etching in a series of
twenty-five—he was then eighty-six years old—that took the candid depiction
of sexual intercourse (unsentimental, athletic) to its limits.

a perfect foil for Picasso: still the most idealized painter for the nine-teenth century (except perhaps in Germany, where he had to compete with Dürer), an artist, it was widely supposed, killed at thirty-seven by too much sex with La Fornarina. He starts the series with the couple, as it were, warming up; the first and even more the second in the sequence document that Raphael is ready to perform. Picasso always had a special affection for genitalia, particularly the female ones, which he liked to show prominently, even in exaggerated, at times menacing, size. And he makes the couple's amorous activity all the more tantalizing by intro-ducing a voyeur, usually in the guise of the aged Pope Julius II, who watches the couple embrace athletically. Indeed, the portraits of his mis-tresses while a love affair was still flourishing exhibit a sense of unmixed joy and an appreciation of good looks that make these pictures virtual declarations of love. Fernande Olivier, Dora Marr, Françoise Gilot, Jacqueline Roque, all of them exceptional beauties, were highly pleasing subjects, however unrealistically he would picture them. Even some of the late etchings in the Raphael cycle betray a certain tenderness between the lovers. He was too much the old-fashioned Spaniard, too much the self-centered misogynist, to dwell long on the affectionate aspects of love, but they are there, and charming to see.

3.

SOME OF PICASSO'S most powerful depictions of aggression exhibit varied mixtures of cruelty and subtlety. At times, as in *Guernica* (1937), he concentrates on the victims of war; at times, he immortalizes his own hostile impulses. Little aroused his rage more visibly than his grievances against women. He transformed some of his female sitters into voracious harpies or grotesque skeletal ogres with unrecognizable faces dominated by murderous teeth. It would be too mechanical to read these portraits as a direct paraphrase of his troubles with one mis-tress or another; he was too imaginative for that.* At the same time,

---

* Roland Penrose, in my judgment rightly, makes this point perfectly clear: "It would be crude and untrue to suggest that he portrayed his companions as beauties during the first flush of love and as monsters when conflicts begin to arise between them."

though, having so many expressive means available to him, he did not hesitate to record love turned into hate—the strongest of hatreds—with no pity for the object of his rage.

What is more, he invented nasty episodes that illustrate unbridled hostility with no sense of disapproval on his part: we have a telling drawing of a muscular naked man beating a cringing naked woman, another of a woman being strangled. More central to his work, he imagined rapes with fair frequency, it seems with almost sadistic relish. Like love turned to hate, rape is a transformation of emotions, libido turned into aggression. The more harmless among these scenes show centaurs carrying off protesting nudes, but more often, Picasso expends his virtuosity on the act itself. Most revealing among these encounters between power and weakness are his representations of a minotaur raping a woman. The minotaur, which made its most frequent appearance during the 1930s in Picasso's etchings, was for him a fundamentally ambiguous being, and hence all the more intriguing. In Greek legend the son of a queen and a sacrificial bull, equipped with a human body and a bull's head, there is something bestial about him and something divine.

And so, Picasso imagines a genial and sociable minotaur, most famously in an etching of 1933, the minotaur carousing with an artist, both holding their wineglasses, and two models, both of them deliciously naked. But in the same year, he also devised two harsh scenes with the minotaur crudely overpowering a woman incapable of resistance. Yet again in the same year, he has a minotaur leaning over a tranquilly sleeping girl, his right hand affectionately stroking her cheek. The inner world, Picasso seems to be saying, is neither simple nor rational, and whoever experiences it as simple and rational has not really seen it. That, one might say, is more a banal than a profound observation. But original or obvious, Picasso's vision captures it all.

L.H.O.O.Q.

PABLO PICASSO MUST be in the forefront of any responsible account of modernism. But Marcel Duchamp is the truly indispensable icon for its history. Other nonconformists undertook to revise, reshape, reinvigorate the craft they had learned to practice and distrust, but Duchamp's oeuvre invites the suspicion that he actually aimed at abolishing art as such. His motives defy full interpretation, for all his agreeable if selective openness; to make them particularly hard to read, he was, somewhat like Ensor, endowed with a sly sense of humor. His fondness for puns and word games was notorious; his irony pointed, though rarely wounding—a typical French gift, his admirers thought. Hence the historian must take his pronouncements with prudent reserve.

This much is beyond dispute: Duchamp was thoroughly alienated from accepted aesthetic conventions and in love with originality. Asked after the First World War—he was born in Normandy in 1887 to a respectable bourgeois family, with two artist brothers—why he had stopped painting, he replied, it seems quite sincerely, that his reservoir of inspiration had run dry. Certainly, repeating himself was anathema to him. Duchamp was partial, as he put it in his inimitable way, to "the madness of the unexpected."

This, too, is plain: what he derided most heatedly and most consistently was what he damned as "retinal art," painting and sculpture that appeal to the eye alone. He was in his way an intellectual. The only kind of art he cared about was art that was somehow smart and alert; ideas for a work mattered to him more than the finished product. In short, it seems only reasonable to take him as intent not on discovering novel principles for art but on delivering its funeral oration. Art historians who in recent years have announced the death of art usually give Duchamp the credit—or the blame—for killing it. With his "readymades" (to which we shall return), a creation peculiarly his own, he remains the most promising suspect; he was at the scene of the crime, heavily armed, for decades before later suspects, like Andy Warhol, were born.

FOR ALL HIS EMINENCE among modernists, Duchamp, the supreme anti-artist, obviously did not perform on the stage of the new art alone. As we have seen, the atmosphere in the arts after 1900 was heavy with new ways of giving voice to old feelings, and with questioning self-evident principles that had served well for centuries. Old-fashioned Realists prized the hoary anecdote, often retold, about the ancient Greek artist so skillful that real birds pecked at the grapes he had painted. But now unnatural colors and deliberately distended shapes had become occasions not for criticism but for applause; the artist's response to his inner and outer world came to matter more than his fidelity to the model. Attacks on photographic conformity became commonplace among advanced spirits. I have already quoted Picasso as calling modern art "a sum of destructions"—it is a felicitous definition.

Duchamp made his first notable contribution to the demolition of conventional art not in Paris but in New York, a reminder of the growing cosmopolitan reach of modernism. In February 1913, the epochmaking International Exhibition of Modern Art, an ambitious large-scale show of modernist paintings that introduced American art lovers to the latest developments at home and abroad, opened in the armory between Sixty-seventh and Sixty-eighth Streets on Park Avenue. It amused many, outraged not a few, and changed some art lovers' tastes forever. Duchamp submitted four canvases, most famously the *Nude Descending a Staircase, No. 2*. It had not been well received at home: in 1912, the Salon des Indépendants had refused to show it and so, undiscouraged, he tried his luck abroad.

He had been toying with Cubist-like forms for about two years, and this painting epitomized his current preoccupation with rendering motion in a stationary medium. His *Nude* was a humanoid figure of indeterminate gender—probably, though not very distinctly, female—captured as it were at successive moments. The picture proved a sensation among visitors to the Armory Show. They crowded around this odd rectangular cluster of structures, perplexed, irritated, stimulated to pointed jokes. One periodical launched a poetry competition seeking the most apt description and cartoonists tried their hand at caricaturing what struck them as an offense in oils. For some obscure reason, among epithets, of which there were many, "an explosion in a shingle factory" carried the day.

But it was his "readymades" that secured Duchamp a place at the front of the avant-garde of avant-gardes. He launched them in 1913, fittingly as a lark, with no utilitarian, let alone aesthetic intentions, by mounting a bicycle wheel on a white kitchen stool. This gesture stands as a historic moment in the calendar of modernism. *Bicycle Wheel* generated consternation even among urbane, ostensibly liberated artists, gratifying Duchamp's wish to needle them by exceeding anything they

SEEING NEW YORK WITH A CUBIST

The Rude Descending a Staircase
(Rush Hour at the Subway)

J. F. Griswold, "The Rude Descending a Staircase," *The Evening Sun*, New York (March 20, 1913). Lampooning Duchamp's famous painting (see frontispiece).

had ever dared to imagine. Was this wheel a bad joke, a misplaced hobby, a deliberate insult to art?

It took Duchamp some time, three years in fact, to trump the outlandishness of *Bicycle Wheel*. His chosen battlefield would be New York, where Duchamp was among the organizers of another vast show of contemporary art. He bought a full-sized porcelain urinal, turned it bottom up, and painted on it the "signature": R. MUTT (after the plumbing manufacturer, J. L. Mott, who had produced the piece), and the date: 1917. He called it *Fountain*. This readymade shocked some of Duchamp's closest modernist friends as simply obscene and certainly inartistic, and after some furious debate, the board, of which Duchamp was a member, rejected the fixture on the official ground that it was not a work of art, a desperate gesture proclaiming—in the age of Duchamp! —that there was a distinction between art and other objects. Duchamp promptly resigned, and the public would never see *Fountain*, which gave the "sculpture" even more notoriety.

This incident, his second rebuff on the part of artists who were his friends and presumably allies in the modernist venture—the refusal of the Indépendants in 1912 to show his *Nude* was the first—wounded him more deeply than he ever acknowledged. He admitted in a late interview that the action of the Indépendants "gave me a turn." And he argued that it had actually done him a favor: "It helped liberate me completely from the past." But the persona he constructed for himself as a young man and that served him well all his life was one of supreme indifference to the outside world. He retired to privacy and made anti-art.

Whatever the response to his adventures, Duchamp's imagination was far from exhausted. In 1919, he came up with *L.H.O.O.Q.*, a postcard-sized reproduction of Leonardo da Vinci's *Mona Lisa*, "improved" with a thin military mustache and a tiny goatee. The initials he put beneath the picture, read out, in French, "*Elle a chaud au cul**—

* Sensational though Duchamp's slightly doctored *Mona Lisa* seemed, and seems, to be, it is worth noting that he was not the first to toy with celebrated images. Newspaper cartoonists had been doing it for years (see the cartoon of Flaubert as surgeon, p. 14). In 1887, Coquelin Cadet devised a photo-relief illustration for *Le Rire*, titled "Mona Lisa with a Pipe," depicting the mysterious lady smoking a large pipe and blowing smoke rings (see p. 342).

Marcel Duchamp (1887–1968), *L.H.O.O.Q.* (1919).
Mona Lisa "improved"; one of Duchamp's most
notorious readymades. (See also p. 342.)

she has a hot ass." This was a minor joke, but those who saw it or
heard of it made much of the act of vandalism. Duchamp's reputation
as the bad boy of art was established, and each of his gestures only
confirmed it.

THE IMPLICATIONS LURKING in this outrageous combination of wordplay and defaced masterpiece proved devastating: if fiat can make anything art, if calling something art or perhaps signing it is enough to

turn it into art, then nothing can distinctively be art. Subjectivity must run rampant. At the least, all the established criteria (and, for that matter, all modernist criteria) for judging a painting or a piece of sculpture—composition, color, message, craftsmanship, verisimilitude, tactile feel—will have lost their relevance. Nor did Duchamp's work after the First World War show any intention of slackening his search for unfettered individuality; his constructions remained as bizarre and unique as ever. Between them, the famous complicated piece, *The Bride Stripped Bare by Her Bachelors, Even*, known as *The Large Glass*, on which he worked for eight years (1915–23), and which has given interpreters much gratifying work to do, and the late *Etant donnés* (1944–66), a meticulously assembled peephole show of a provocative nude woman first exhibited in 1969, the year after his death, show that he was in no mood to compromise.

But, true to himself, Duchamp subverted even his subversions. He advised patrons like Peggy Guggenheim, who, with limited funds, had

Marcel Duchamp playing chess (his favorite game) at the Pasadena Art Museum (1963); the result of this game is unknown.

Marcel Duchamp, *Nude Descending a Staircase, No. 2* (1912).

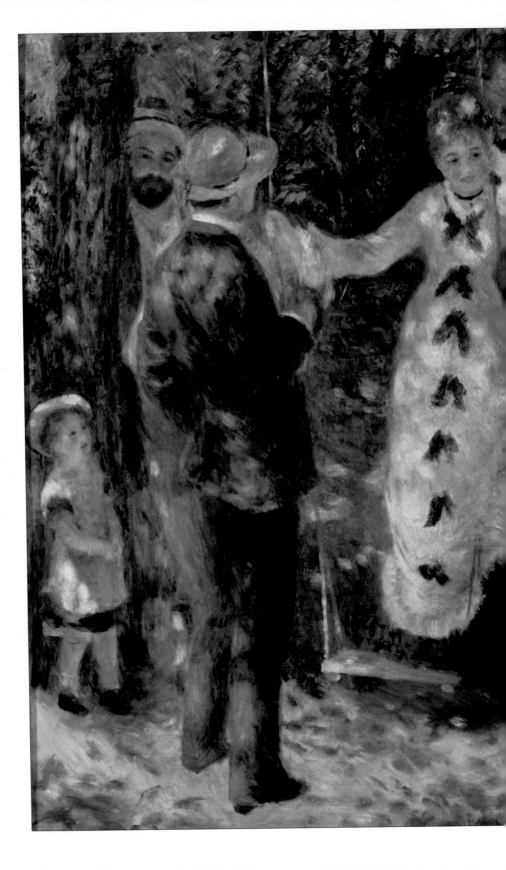

Alfred Sisley,
*Snow at
Louveciennes*
(1878).

Berthe Morisot,
On the Balcony
(1871–72).

Auguste Renoir, *The Swing* (1876).

Paul Cézanne,
Mont Sainte-Victoire
(1885–87).

Umberto Boccioni,
*Development of a
Bottle in Space*
(1912).

Claude Monet, *Impression,
Sunrise* (1872).

Pablo Picasso, *La Toilette* (1906).

Henri Matis
Reclining Nude
(192

Constantin Brancusi,
Bird in Space (1923).
He would return to this purest
of modernist abstractions,
an enormously influential work,
with a variety of materials.

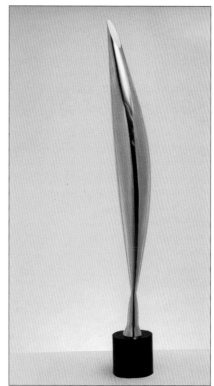

Marcel Duchamp, *L.H.O.O.Q.* (1919).

Edvard Munch, *The Scream* (1893).

to confine her lust for paintings. He taught her, she said gratefully, to understand the differences among the latest schools in modern art. Yet, for all his friendships with outsider collectors and outsider painters, all his sound, disinterested advice, he consistently refused to join even the most unconventional alliances, such as the Dadaists, with whose extremism he had much in common. In 1967, not long before his death in Neuilly, reflecting about the Surrealists whom he knew and appreciated, he said it most plainly: "I myself have never had a part in any such group explorations of unknown lands, due to that something in my character which prohibits me from exchanging the most intimate things of my being with anyone else." He kept alive his deserved reputation as an exception in an age of avant-garde collectives.

Still, Duchamp was no megalomaniac. He was the supreme smasher of icons. Robert Motherwell, in fact, called him "the great 'saboteur.'" But, as his help to keep modern art alive testifies, he cannot really have believed that he could destroy art single-handed, or even with allies. If he ever toyed with such Samson-like notions, he would have needed only to survey his career, especially in the United States, to prove himself a failure in such a foolhardy enterprise: his rich American friends and clients, particularly the principal among them, Walter and Louise Arensberg, would have set him straight.

The Arensbergs may stand as the ideal patrons of modernists, of whom there were many. Well off and well educated (if having graduated from Harvard and undertaking to learn Italian well enough to translate Dante is a dependable sign of a good education), married young to a classmate's sister even better off than he, Walter Arensberg had all the material preconditions for patronage in hand. He had no interest in going into his father's steel business or, it soon turned out, any other, and so all he needed was a spark to inflame that inexhaustible greed for objects known as collecting, whether it strikes a ten-year-old schoolboy or a fifty-year-old lawyer. And that came, with dramatic suddenness, with the Armory Show. Arensberg's appetite for possessing contemporary art awoke and, as such appetites often behave, would not be extinguished in his lifetime.

The Arensbergs—after Louise Arensberg bought into her husband's enthusiasm—in addition to buying other first-rate modernists like Picasso, Braque, Klee, and Brancusi, collected Duchamps avidly. They bought directly from the artist, whose close friends and grateful hosts they soon became and remained, or acquired Duchamps that had somehow fallen into the hands of other less fanatical collectors. They were democratic patrons. And, childless, as they grew older and less robust in health, they were the target—sometimes they thought the victim—of overtures from museum directors across the country. After long, suspenseful, often bitter wrangling, they left their important holdings to the Philadelphia Museum of Art, where they now reside, including Duchamp's puzzling large-scale construction, *The Large Glass*, and *Etant donnés*.

The irony is only too obvious, part of the explanation just how enemies of museums end up in museums. Here, in Philadelphia, are all the Duchamps the Arensbergs could manage to amass. And Duchamp himself, that self-proclaimed nemesis of art, actively participated in installing his work in one of the country's largest "mausoleums," the kind of crypt for dead artists that activists had long wanted to burn down, open for viewing by visiting art lovers as though they were conventional classics. We have noted it before: it is a mistake to underestimate the absorptive gift of the middle class, particularly when it has money to spend and taste to use it well.

ANTI-MIMESIS

1.

MODERNISM WAS AN IDEAL PLAYGROUND for sculptors. Much like avant-garde painters, they developed the most unpredictable agendas once they felt liberated from neoclassical rules. Their resemblance to painters was in fact no mere coincidence; the sculptors' modernism was less a rebellion against their nineteenth-century predecessors than an extended footnote to contemporary avant-garde painting. Auguste Rodin, the indisputable principal sculptor of the age, stood somewhere between the fronts of the rebels against the skillful imitation of nature, particularly the human body, on one side, and the conservative practitioners of the historic task on the other. Born in 1840, he never left the broad naturalistic ground of accurate representation—Matisse recalled him authoritatively issuing the advice, "Copy nature!"—but at the same time he amazed, even outraged, much (though by no means all) of the art-loving public with his experiments. His notorious life-size *Balzac* of 1897, the bulky novelist boldly wrapped in a neutral, covering cloak, roused a storm of protests. In 1906, in an encounter that has engaged the attention of art historians, the young Matisse visited the great man to show him some of his drawings. It led to nothing, except to Matisse's conviction that the master's piecemeal way with carving figures, a separate hand modeled here, a separate leg modeled there, could never appeal to him. "I could only envisage the general architecture of a work of mine," he wrote, "replacing explanatory details by a living and suggestive synthesis." Rodin was an all-purpose irritant to the tradition-minded, but not the ancestor of modernist sculpture.

Rather, it was the radical painters who set that sculpture loose on its twentieth-century adventures. And they were adventures in subjectivity. This collaboration of distinct genres was eased by double talents: the most important modernist sculptors were also painters, often better

Henri Matisse (1869–1954),
Reclining Nude III (1929).
Matisse, though increasingly a
painter, often returned to
certain sculptural subjects, like
the reclining nude.

known as painters than as sculptors. Degas, Matisse, and Picasso were only the most celebrated of them; others also used the needle, the pencil, and the brush as perfectly ordinary instruments in their work. Once established after undermining the ideal of interpreting nature, these progressive painters showed sculptors how to move away from mimesis by example rather than precept.

Their disciples had an inkling of this. "While my technical liberation," wrote David Smith, the most prominent American maker of large metal pieces, in 1952, "came from Picasso's friend and countryman González, my aesthetics were more influenced by Kandinsky, Mondrian, and Cubism." He might have added Picasso himself, a not insignificant if occasional sculptor in his own right. Beyond doubt, Smith commented, "since the turn of the century, painters have led the aesthetic front both in number and in concept." He confirmed his diagnosis three years later in a lecture at the University of Mississippi: "Cubism freed sculpture from monolithic and volumetric form as Impressionism freed painting from chiaroscuro." The Spaniard Julio González who liberated Smith was a sculptor whose welded pieces incited him to try steel and iron as materials. He, too, followed the modernist path: born in 1876, he moved to Paris in 1900, and became a friend of Picasso's. But what mattered most was that painters had subverted the ancient imperative of replicating nature; this emancipation gave sculptors opportunities that were almost literally unlimited. The history of modernist sculpture reveals that they explored almost all of them.

Some well known early modernist sculptures actually leave the impression of being three-dimensional Cubist pieces. Picasso's bronze *Head of a Woman* (1909–10) reimagined facial surfaces as an assemblage of gently pointed rectangles, but still left the sitter's face identifiable as a face. The Futurist Umberto Boccioni's *Development of a Bottle in Space* (1912) exploded the contours of a bottle to have its fragments playfully adding up to a complicated assemblage—but still a bottle. And Jacques Lipchitz's *Guitar Player* (1918) largely retained the natural shapes of a man, including a recognizable hand touching a guitarlike four-sided object, to leave viewers with a strong suggestion of a real musician strumming a real instrument. Not surprisingly, the mod-

Umberto Boccioni, *Development of a Bottle in Space* (1912). Like other Italian
Futurists, Boccioni stressed "dynamism" as the dominant modern reality that
art, including sculpture, must embody.

ernist sculptors who left some semblance to the external world in their
work at least partly overcame public skepticism. It seemed as though
viewers were aching to find a trace they could associate with their
common experience, and responded gratefully when they made out a
familiar form. It required less of an imaginative effort than the purely
abstract pieces.

THE SCULPTOR WHO probably fulfilled the "naturalist" version of the
modernist program most satisfactorily was Henry Moore, born in Castle-
ford, Yorkshire, two years shy of the twentieth century, a rare glory in
English high culture that boasted few memorable artists in his field. In a
long career, the kind of portrayal to which he returned most frequently
was a recumbent figure, whether executed in stone, which Moore largely

used before the war, or bronze, to which he increasingly turned. He made monumental figures, often complicated with a rounded, irregular void created by a strategically placed arm or leg. Nature was never far from his mind: he insisted, instructively, that the best place to view his work was out of doors, in productive symmetry with the scenery.

At times, Moore involved his public in the risky pleasure of absorbing the whole of the carved shape he had made by placing two masses in close juxtaposition; this would force viewers to fill in the intervening emptiness in order to construct a single figure in their minds. Occasionally, he celebrated maternity with a mother and child, but the supreme emotion was stimulated by what he called his "form-experience," his response to shapes that stayed in his mind; they left a feeling of solidity, of a sober, weighty form resting on firm ground. Moore and Barbara Hepworth, a fellow Yorkshire sculptor (who went further toward pure abstraction than he normally did), were both proponents of direct carving, whatever substance they were shaping. This fidelity to their material kept their loyalty to nature alive, at least in the background.

But the autonomy of sculpture remained their ideal. The charm of Moore's smooth surfaces made his pieces an exceptional pleasure, a defiant yet calm rejection of mimesis leaving agreeable, or at least impressive, intimations of the human shape. "More than any other sculptor," the American art historian and museum director William R. Valentiner, a consistent admirer, wrote about Moore, "he expresses our deep longing for a closer connection with the elemental forces of nature as found in primeval deserts, mountains and forests, away from cities, away from the artificial life guided by intellect instead of emotional energies," a not very coherent but profound sentiment that conventional sculptors could never come close to conveying. Moore, who lived until 1986, managed to translate his personal voyage to the interior into deeply expressive images.

2.

MOORE'S AND HEPWORTH'S WORKS document that sculptors who clung to nature, no matter how distantly, were giving themselves wide latitude. But obviously those who discarded any intentional resemblance as an abject surrender to outworn neoclassicism enjoyed even more unconstrained freedom. The range of their imagination was largely private, partly unconscious, but in any event without boundaries. Some of the abstractionists, like Alexander Calder, subjected their constructions to homemade logic: in his much-admired mobiles, which he kept reinventing in engaging variations, Calder subjugated arrays of wire, wood, and gaily colored aluminum ovals or leaflike shapes to a precarious balance in which each element had its place. These inventions moved quietly, without collapsing, with a breath or the touch of a breeze upon them. It is an emblem of the collegiality of modernists that when in 1949 Calder showed Marcel Duchamp these constructions for the first time and asked his advice just what to call them, Duchamp baptized them *"mobiles"* without hesitation.

Calder's mobiles lacked gravitas, but their wit—a quality, we know, in notably short supply among modernists—carried them a long way toward bridging the abyss between avant-garde and middlebrow taste. Another dazzling humorist among modernist sculptors was Picasso, who during the years went through bouts of constructing some severe, but more often amusing sculptures. It was, for Picasso, mainly a matter of *seeing* what others had not seen: to his alert eyes, one could combine a bicycle seat and handlebars into a bull's head; one could use a small model of an automobile for the head of *Monkey with Young*. In forcing objects to serve his purposes—certainly purposes for which they had never been intended—Picasso was once again affirming the artist's untouchable supremacy.

In this atmosphere, then, in which anything was possible, the subjective contribution to the making of art—for modernist sculptors no less than for modernist painters—was triumphant. There was no court of appeal against the artist's choices. He might link his creation to a public source. Russian artists at work in the first, still libertarian, phase of their Revolution saw themselves as giving exuberant expression to the new world they were helping (they thought) to make a reality. They did not all wait for the 1917 Revolution: in 1914, the Russian sculptor Vladimir Tatlin went to Paris to apprentice himself to Picasso. Unfortunately, Picasso was not interested, but Tatlin saw enough of Cubism to start back at home on a series of abstract sculptures; his "counter-reliefs," he called them. They were imaginative structures that had nothing to do with traditional Realism. What made Tatlin famous was a maquette of a celebratory tower, *Monument to the Third International*, on a commission from the Department of Fine Arts in 1919. Soviet agencies were still comfortable with modernist independence in those days. Not for long.

Tatlin's tower was never built. It would have been almost impossible to realize at any time; intended to be substantially taller than the Empire State Building, it consisted of an intricate interweaving of steel spirals and glass rectangles, with one of its three central cores rising aslant above the rest of the internal spaces, these spaces providing ample room for offices and auditoriums. More conspicuous still, Tatlin's design would have been in uninterrupted motion, turning on its axes at three different, carefully regulated speeds. It was a splendid instance of what Russians in a revolutionary spirit came to call Constructivism, a style in which external realities had no share and the question of appropriate materials became central.

This is not to say that abstract sculptors never ventured into the territory of the opposition. Just as Picasso in the 1920s painted savage oils that harshly caricatured his mistresses but recognizably depicted, however distorted, women on canvas, so did Constructivist sculptors sometimes gesture toward reality, even though their renditions, the product of absolute freedom, were likely to be mutilated into unidentifiable shapes. The work of David Smith, for example, veered between gigantic metal pieces unrelated to anything but to his other constructions and table-sized "portraits" that vaguely resembled human figures. And González's wrought-iron sculpture, *Woman Combing Her Hair* of 1936, may stand for dozens of the "representational" experiments of abstract artists. For all its title promising a figurative likeness, *Woman* appears like a far-fetched parody of what it purports to be, using an accumulation of wires and curved metal fragments that depicts a woman's head only because its maker said so.

IN FACT, THE CRAFTSMAN as sole authority on the meaning of a piece of sculpture became the norm, at the very least the starting point, for learned interpretations. One brilliant beneficiary of this preempted authority was the Romanian sculptor Constantin Brancusi. His reputation reached great heights during his lifetime—his dates are 1876–1957—a position he has never lost. To David Smith, he was quite simply "our greatest living sculptor," and other professionals admired and followed him in their own creations. His commitment to simplicity and his fidelity to whatever material he was working with became a generally accepted slogan.*

Brancusi's most notable single piece is *Bird in Space*, first done in highly polished marble in 1923 and the next year in bronze, a most congenial material. It is probably the most famous modernist sculptural piece of them all, a slender, elongated object slightly fattened up in the middle and standing on one end. As with most of Brancusi's oeuvre, this invention stands as an extreme instance of reductionism; some of his best known sculptures are barely inflected egglike compositions "representing" a sleeping child or (we are told) Prometheus. By titling the cool, remote, very handsome *Bird in Space* as he did, he invited the viewer to see it as a bird's wing. Thus, once sculptors had shoved the ideal of imitation aside, the supremacy of the artist, resembling the supremacy of the biblical Adam naming the animals, reached a stratospheric height that most modernists had aspired to, but scarcely imagined for themselves.

3.

AS SOME SCULPTORS ADDED to modernism's store of wit, a few of them enriched its supply of eroticism. The most interesting exemplar is once again from Brancusi; his *Princess X* of 1916 made for a scandal,

---

* It is important to keep in mind that Brancusi's passion for simplicity was far from simple. "Simplicity," Sir Herbert Read has rightly said, "is not a goal, but one arrives at simplicity in spite of oneself, as one approaches the real meaning of things."

Constantin Brancusi, *Bird in Space* (1923). He would return to this purest of modernist abstractions, an enormously influential work, in either bronze or marble.

not excluding the seemingly sated modernist mecca of Paris. One need not be an erotomaniac to see the polished bronze piece as a partly erect penis complemented by testicles, or perhaps the double ball-like shapes at the bottom as breasts. Even avant-garde artists were shocked: when the piece was exhibited at the Salon des Indépendants in 1920, it was promptly withdrawn, simply too suggestive for these progressive spirits. Just as Duchamp's *Fountain* of 1917 had roused the displeasure of his fellow modernists as tasteless and inartistic, so Brancusi's reduction of the body to physical organs—especially these organs—standing for the whole seemed beyond the pale of decency. Avant-gardes were rarely unified ideological parties; one modernist's boldness was another modernist's obscenity.

4.

SOME AMONG THE PIECES I have briefly discussed here—Brancusi's *Princess X* of 1916 and Duchamp's *Fountain* of 1917—go back to the First World War. They show that once sculptors were liberated from mimesis, they did not hesitate to take advantage of their newfound freedom. After 1945, avant-garde sculpture, with its enormous range but with no visible, consistent development, has kept this profusion alive. Sculptors began to use electrical wiring and modern plastics and fiberglass for lit pieces, to make convoluted string constructions internally illuminated by neon tubes, to pile up identical, faithfully painted Brillo boxes, and to construct dead white plaster human beings modeled from real people.

Not all these modernist self-exhibitions have been charming, or meant to be. Some painfully dwelled on the atrocities of the twentieth century, some celebrated the heroism of French Resistance fighters. But a few of them, like several of the welded and painted constructions by the English sculptor Anthony Caro, have had a less strenuous agenda. Perhaps the most admired among Caro's abstract constructions is the *Early One Morning* of 1962: a long, hollow assemblage with a sizable rectangular steel plate at one end reaching out, as it were, to the other end, a tilted cross, with several steel elements between them, the whole painted an attractive red. Its appeal is hard to explain, but it is immediate.

Anthony Caro, *Early One Morning* (1962). Caro, a prominent English sculptor, has influenced other modernists with his intellectually powerful constructions.

A few postwar artists like Caro have been influential, serving as inspiration to lesser colleagues. But most of them have taken pride in their uniqueness. And for sculptors at least in the current chaos of ideas and production, where individuality has become a commonplace, where almost anyone is a modernist, the epithet "modernism" virtually loses all concrete significance—a strange turn of events that marks a rare reversal in our account. Which is another way of saying that the market for neoclassical sculpture has largely collapsed and nothing very orderly has taken its place.

A famous episode involving Brancusi strongly suggests that the future of modernist sculpture is likely to be less stormy than its past. In 1926, he sent one of his most elegant pieces, *Bird in Flight*, on which he had been working for more than three years, to the United States for a one-man exhibition. But the inspector from the Customs Service refused to allow it free entrance as a work of art. Seeing it as "an object of manufacture," he demanded a duty of 40 percent. Brancusi, baffled but not defeated, paid the imposition under protest, and took the agency to court. If the exaction had prevailed, the sales of Brancusis—and other modernist pieces—would have been greatly hampered. But the courts found for Brancusi, a fine instance of "bourgeois" embracing the modernist dispensation. Such pleasing denouements were rare, but not nearly so rare as doctrinaire modernists have maintained. Conventional bourgeois society, too, could embrace the unconventional.

PROSE AND POETRY — INTERMITTENCES OF THE HEART

THE NEW FICTION

IF BUYING AVANT-GARDE ART WAS CONFINED FOR THE most part to prosperous bourgeois who had the resources to acquire it and the space to hang it, judging what to many seemed the escapades of modernist literature lay open to a far larger public. Here the principal criterion to capture attention was sales. But there was one salient feature that modernist painters and modernist novelists had in common: both produced imperishable masterpieces, permanent monuments in the history of high culture.

Yet the acceptance of the new fiction was far from easy. For most readers consuming novels in the second half of Queen Victoria's reign, the games that modernist writers were beginning to play seemed like systematic betrayals of a well-tested, cordial relationship between author and audience. Avant-garde novelists asked the public to commit itself to a concentrated attention that more complaisant writers were sparing it. As commercial publishers were only too well aware, readership for the imaginative prose on the horizon was bound to be restricted; it was almost predictable that the classics among modernist novels should encounter impediments to publication and distribution, and would register far smaller sales than what the avant-garde learned to call middlebrow fiction.

What art critics were saying about the consumption of paintings applied to what literary critics said about the consumption of novels. They saw three reading publics: by far the largest consisted of the "barbarian" masses, with no awareness of demanding fiction and inevitably content with shallow fare; the second, much smaller, though still substantial in numbers and with easy access to high culture, feeling superior to the multitudes but reluctant to spend the time and effort an avant-garde novel would exact; and finally, a small elite, an aristocracy of novel readers open to innovations and experiments. Modernist literary critics dismissed the largest of these reading publics, the philistine majority, as simply unteachable. Occasionally, they broke out with diatribes against the horrors of modern democracy, and found it inconceivable that its denizens would ever read, let alone buy, a modernist novel. They were, if anything, even more disdainful of readers with middlebrow tastes who, after all, enjoyed the advantages of schooling and a degree of leisure. And their denunciations did not abate even after modernist fiction had become more familiar.

THIS ARISTOCRATIC SKEPTICISM about readership was, if not admirable, perfectly understandable. Much like the most inventive modernist painters, writers of modernist fiction generated, apart from sophisticated satisfactions, certain anxieties in their audiences by their sheer unpredictability—uneasiness, even suspicions, about their essential intentions. What would they think of next? In the days of the classic nineteenth-century novel, readers rarely asked such a question. An author's name on the title page aroused fairly precise expectations: Thackeray did not gratify readers quite like Trollope, Turgenev not quite like Tolstoy. But the pleasures each provided were relatively straightforward; the reader could concentrate on the tale rather than its teller.

This was the most conspicuous difference between traditional novelists and their modernist successors. Writers of conventional fiction did not particularly call attention to their techniques. But anti-establishment novelists did. They appeared much like expert magicians whose dazzling pyrotechnics kept reminding their audience of their presence on stage. Not that enthusiasts for a modernist writer like Robert Musil, say, or Italo Svevo, necessarily failed to become engrossed in his fictions. They could and did, but they retained a touch of watchfulness for a manipulative hand at work devising new tricks.

Expectedly, the old-fashioned novel confronted its characters with interesting complications and worked to sustain an atmosphere of suspense, raising prospects of alternate endings. There were surprises in those fictions, turns of fortune that an ingenious author threw in the characters' path like so many sticks. But these tensions had to be resolved at the end. Unequivocal final clarity, with each surviving personage in its proper place, was an indispensable element in the tacit agreement readers made with their authors—they expected nothing less. And, often, nothing more.

Then, late in the nineteenth century, a few venturesome novelists, lured by the promise of modernist subjectivity, declared themselves unsatisfied with the rewards of the Realism then dominant in fiction. The hard-won triumph of Emile Zola, which many regarded as a sign of progress in an age of storytelling stifled by polite evasiveness, was soon under attack, as it were, from the left. In 1891, Thomas Hardy, in a severe critique of the brash, outspoken, fashionable Realists, commended a literary agenda more searching than the scientific exploration of surfaces. "A sight for the finer qualities of existence, an ear for the 'still sad music of humanity,'" he wrote, quoting Wordsworth, "are not to be acquired by the outer senses alone, close as their powers in photography may be. What cannot be discerned by eye and ear, what may be apprehended only by the mental tactility that comes from a sympathetic appreciativeness of life in all its manifestations, this is the gift which renders its possessor a more accurate delineator of human nature than many another with twice his powers and means of external observation, but without that sympathy." There were inner realities, he was certain, that novelists had too assiduously overlooked.

Not long after, in 1899, the English poet and critic Arthur Symons, in his perceptive and prescient polemical essay, *The Symbolist Movement in Literature* (reading it marked an epoch in T. S. Eliot's literary self-education), observed that Hardy's implicit program was in the process of being realized. He noted with pleasure the developing "revolt against exteriority, against rhetoric, against a materialistic tradition" and the "endeavour to disengage the ultimate essence, the soul, of whatever exists and can be realised by the consciousness." It was through symbols, Symons argued, that "the soul of things can be made visible; literature, bowed down by so many burdens, may at last attain liberty, and its authentic speech." Symbols are realities as real as the amount a fictional character earns and the kind of house she lives in, in important ways more real. Exteriority, rhetoric, materialism—those, the early modernists charged, were the regrettable traits that had corrupted the fiction of the time in precisely the way that academic art had corrupted painting. Symons's heady vision of a literally soulful future for the novel raised questions of tone, of tact, of vocabulary, of insight. The modernists' critique of current fiction, searching to find ways of penetrating to the dark heart of their invented characters, made the novel into a maze as mysterious as it was delightful.

For one thing, modernist novelists dramatically reversed the customary allocation of space, devoting extensive passages to a single gesture or disposing of a protagonist in less than a sentence. In the opening volume of *A la recherche du temps perdu*, Marcel Proust takes two full pages to analyze M. Swann's first kiss with Odette, the courtesan he will eventually marry; in Virginia Woolf's *To the Lighthouse* (1927), one of her two supreme works of art—*Mrs. Dalloway* (1924) is the other—we learn of Mrs. Ramsay's death, the true protagonist of the novel, in passing, literally in a parenthesis. These novels are high points of modernism to which I shall return. For another thing, plot, the logical sequence of events so obligatory in Victorian fiction, lost much of its appeal. In Dickens, in Tolstoy, in Fontane, even in Flaubert, there is a great deal of action, all the time. Not so in modernist novels. In 1918, the English novelist May Sinclair, reviewing the first volume of Dorothy Richardson's modernist sequence, *Pilgrimage*, noted in some astonishment: "In this series there is no drama, no situation, no set scene. Nothing happens." It was the passionate voyage to the interior, its celebration of subjectivity coupled with the regular flouting of the rules of novel writing, in a word its inherent difficulty, that made modernist fiction a scandal with the philistine.

Part of this scandal was, of course, the frankness with which modernists—at least some modernists—treated sexual relations. What earlier novelists had only glanced at, with mildly suggestive, equivocal circumlocutions, now lay open. Subtext became text, though for some decades within limits. The historic taboo that had protected the private sphere of the Victorians—not necessarily shamefacedly but certainly stoutly—was beginning to crumble, and modernist writers did more than their part in its demolition. The French led the way, and more repressed cultures did not thank them for it, even though English or German readers avidly consumed piquant imports from Paris and eventually followed them at a safe distance. Flaubert, the Goncourt brothers, Zola and his followers redefined what was called the dignity of literature. Henceforth, at least for liberated spirits, proof of that dignity would lie not in the social position of fictional protagonists or the respectability of their conduct, but in the literary quality of their inventor's work.

Still, in comparison to other dislocations for readers, the sensational sexual license of modernist fiction, though gleefully exploited in the gutter press, was only a minor disturbance. A novelist like D. H. Lawrence, to whom the life force was embodied in the promise and the act of sex—by no means necessarily heterosexual—found it natural (that is to say, healthy) to place Eros into the center of his work. But his notorious *Lady Chatterley's Lover* (1928) was a venture extreme even for him that underwent years-long vicissitudes before it could be legally published. Nor were negative reviews confined to the guardians of conservative morals: other modernists, like Virginia Woolf, were sternly critical of Lawrence's coarseness and ideological rigidity.

In short, modernist fiction undermined accepted criteria for literary verdicts—coherence, chronology, closure, let alone reticence—and turned inward, shockingly. Modernist mirrors reflected mainly the author. Consider a classic modernist instance: André Gide's *The Counter-feiters* (*Les Faux-Monnayeurs*) of 1926, his most ingenious construction. Its principal character, Edouard, is thinking about writing a novel, titled *The Counterfeiters* (of course!), that draws heavily on Edouard's diary from which Gide, its inventor, quotes at length. The novel called *The Counterfeiters* is, then, if it is about anything, about a novel called *The Counterfeiters*. It vividly epitomizes the modernist protest against conventional fiction writing. Humble realities were left behind, panting.

DEFYING MR. BENNETT

1.

IN THIS ELECTRIC ATMOSPHERE, it was only to be expected that modernist literary critics would make superficiality in commonplace novels their most vulnerable target. This critique survived the turmoil of the First World War, suggesting that it still had its uses. In one of her most spirited talks, "Mr. Bennett and Mrs. Brown," delivered in 1924 to a receptive audience at Cambridge, Virginia Woolf summed up her case against the literary establishment. Her theme was character in fiction, partisan perhaps, a little overstated, but no less powerful for that. Looking back more than two decades, Woolf famously declared that "on or about December 1910, human character changed." Unfortunately, she added, the best known British novelists, H. G. Wells, John Galsworthy, and Arnold Bennett—"the Edwardians," she called them—had failed to recognize, let alone join, that dramatic transition. Elsewhere she called the trio materialists, and materialism, which Symons had already denounced, was too narrow, too perfunctory, a take on character to generate lasting literature.

Wickedly, Woolf takes evidence on character from Arnold Bennett—wickedly because, though she shares Bennett's position on this single point, she will make him her principal victim as an author who has allowed his practice to compromise his principles. "'The foundation of good fiction is character-creating and nothing else,'" she quotes him as saying. "'Style counts; plot counts; originality of outlook counts. But none of these counts anything like so much as the convincingness of the characters. If the characters are real the novel will have a chance, if they are not, oblivion will be its portion.'" She can only agree: "I believe that all novels . . . deal with character, and that it is to express character—not to preach doctrines, sing songs, or celebrate the glories of the British Empire." This raises the question just how Bennett misapplies his principles in his work.

In response, Woolf recalls an elderly woman she had encountered on a recent train trip, and invents a name for her, Mrs. Brown, and part of a life history. How, Woolf asks, would the Edwardians have depicted Mrs. Brown? Wells would have painted a Utopian future for her; Galsworthy would have shown her a victim of industrial capitalism. And Bennett, Woolf's true prey, would have remained fixated on externals. She instances his description of Hilda Lessways in his eponymous novel, which includes what Hilda sees out of her window, what kind of house she occupies, what sort of neighborhood it stands in, all in detail. Then Bennett tells his readers that she hears her mother's voice, and Woolf pounces: "But we cannot hear her mother's voice, or Hilda's voice; we can only hear Mr. Bennett's voice telling us facts about rents and freeholds and copyholds and fines." There sits Mrs. Brown, "and not one of the Edwardian writers has so much as looked at her." Plainly, their conventions, their writer's tools, are "the wrong ones for us to use."

We can perceive the grounds of Woolf's objection all the better when we realize that the novel she was writing around this time was *Mrs. Dalloway*, in every conceivable respect the opposite of Bennett's *Hilda Lessways*. Defenders of the conventional novel, Woolf adds, use an alibi for their approach to character; she has the docile British novel-reading public say: "Old women have houses. They have fathers. They have incomes. They have servants. They have hot-water bottles." And do these facts of their lives not add up to recognizable old women, alive within the rich texture that Bennett and his fellows provide? Woolf coolly rejects this rationalization as self-serving propaganda by best-selling authors. "If you hold that novels are in the first place about people, and only in the second about the houses they live in, that is the wrong way to set about it." The prosecution rests.

2.

FRIEDRICH NIETZSCHE, we recall, had hoped in the 1880s that psychology would become the master discipline, the queen of the sciences. And the modernist novelists, as though listening to Nietzsche, tried to give him what he wanted by making fiction into deep-searching psychological explorations. If it is at all possible to assign a specific date to the birth of that venture, the most plausible year is 1887, which saw the publication of Edouard Dujardin's short novel, *Les Lauriers sont coupés*. Dujardin, better known as an editor than as a novelist, was active in French writers' campaigns against prosaic literary and philosophical schools like Realism and positivism. Following the traditions established by the Romantics writing more than seventy-five years earlier, he wanted to participate in re-enchanting the world that, he believed, the Enlightenment had reduced to dry and boring materialism. In 1885, he was among the founders of *La Revue Wagnérienne*, and, in the following year, of *La Revue Indépendante*, both mouthpieces of the Symbolists, a small but influential band of avant-garde writers for whom Zola's Realism was not avant-garde enough.

In Dujardin's novel, a signal contribution to modernism, almost nothing happens, which is to say that whatever happens does so behind a curtain. The book consists of ordinary conversations between an infatuated young man, the narrator; his pedestrian, rather cynical friend with whom he rehearses his amorous fantasies; and a lovely young actress who may or may not consent to have an affair with him. The prospective lovers talk and take a walk together; she gives him a rendezvous a few days hence, and he decides not to show up. That is all.

But Dujardin had a subtext: the protagonist's musings, his reflections, his responses to stimuli external and internal; in short, his conversations with himself. Dujardin called this technique the *monologue intérieur*, a private, silent speech. It is a relatively orderly form of the free associations let loose in pure stream of consciousness, in which the links are often resemblances of sounds and sudden memories. Both impose the burden of narrating subjective experiences on the character itself, much the way an actor may disclose his unspoken thoughts in an aside to the audience.

The interior monologue was a major step toward electing psychology as queen of the sciences. Dujardin, largely lost to the history of literature, later reported that his experiment sold just a few hundred copies, and was soon virtually forgotten. But among its few readers was James Joyce, and he did not forget it. Later, gratefully, he signed a copy of *Ulysses* to Dujardin, calling himself "an impenitent thief." We shall soon see what he made of his unapologetic appropriation.

3.

DUJARDIN, AN INVOLUNTARY PIONEER, venturing into a new kind of fiction, underscores the point that the modernist novel is an exercise in subjectivity. But this alone does not differentiate it from its Victorian forebears; there was nothing new about novelists' psychological investigations as such. Almost from its birth, certainly by the middle of the eighteenth century, modern fiction had claimed mental life as its domain. In the introductory chapter to *Tom Jones* (1749), Henry Fielding said so plainly: "The provision, then, which we have here made is no other than HUMAN NATURE." In important ways, he adds, what writers collect under that "general name" really boasts a prodigious variety. Hence it is virtually impossible "to exhaust so extensive a subject." Whether dressed in epistolary guise—a favorite among readers of novels down to the age of the French Revolution—or equipped with intrusive, all-knowing authorial comment on the feelings and the motives of fictional personages, the novel lived under the well-understood obligation to be a credible guide to human conduct. Serious fiction required plausible heroes and heroines who transcend stereotypes, acting out predictable roles. For novelists claiming to write literature, fictional characters had to be probable human beings with probable motives in probable environments facing probable conflicts.

The originality of the modernist novel, then, lay not so much in its discovery of the mental province as in re-mapping its territory; its experimental techniques were designed to dig deeper—far deeper—

than tradition-bound novelists had ever done. The novel in modernist hands became increasingly a novel of consciousness, and the devices that so offended much of the reading public were strategies to serve that purpose. Indeed, at times beyond consciousness: in *Lafcadio's Adventures* (1914), André Gide has the protagonist, Lafcadio, commit an "unmotivated" crime—that is, an act that is certainly caused by the actor, but whose stimulus is so securely buried in the criminal's unconscious as to defy rational explanation. Freud's techniques of investigation do not seem particularly remote or strange before such psychological enigmas.

By no means all the novelists listening for the still, sad music of humanity resorted to unconventional procedures. They enlisted long-established techniques for radical ends. The prolific novelist and thoroughly avant-garde editor Ford Madox Ford called these prudent innovators "Impressionists," writers more interested in their subjective responses to the reality of their creations than to numerical or statistical facts.* Cautious or bold, modern novelists sought to capture minds at work, dreaming, ruminating, hesitating, wishing, in conflict. A few of them, like Thomas Mann, the master of irony, educated themselves in psychoanalytic literature. But even novelists who were not reading Freud—one thinks of Marcel Proust—were asking Freudian questions. They were relentless and sensitive mind readers, attesting in their varying approaches to the range of the modern.

IN LONG RETROSPECT, it may seem that the modernist revolution in fiction progressed through a series of preordained steps to the summit of literary radicalism. But that is to visualize far too neat a succession of events. If we think of Dujardin, we know that a few novelists had already undertaken expeditions to the core several years before Joyce began. They were no less passionate about truth than the Realists of the nineteenth century, but they added another dimension to their defini-

---

* Ford himself displayed his literary virtuosity in *The Good Soldier* (1915), with a brilliantly imagined unreliable narrator, a splendid instance of what increasingly mattered in modernist fiction.

tion of reality. Among these pioneers, giants in the history of modernist fiction, two stand out: the Norwegian Knut Hamsun and the Austrian Arthur Schnitzler.

Hamsun was an eccentric among eccentrics, a grimly isolated figure in the history of the novel, the most subversive of modernists. A self-started, largely self-educated outsider, he remained an outsider for all of his large readership, despite the Nobel Prize he received in 1920. His first mature novel, *Hunger*, remains astonishing to this day. He had written some fiction before, with little public resonance. Born in provincial Norway in 1859, physically strong and mentally resilient, he worked on the family farm until at twenty he escaped to Oslo to pursue his destiny: literature. He lived at virtual starvation level, and then tried his luck in the United States, which he visited twice between 1883 and 1888, mainly laboring at a variety of menial jobs—farm worker, streetcar conductor, barber—and writing. His main accomplishment: an impudent short book aping other condescending travelers' reports, denouncing America as a country without manners, literature, and culture.

Then, in 1890, back in Oslo, he had his breakthrough. *Hunger* is an autobiography magically transformed into art. The narrator, literally penniless for days on end, often goes hungry, again and again loses his shabby rented room for failing to pay up, occasionally secures a few kroner for an article only to resume his subhuman existence once he has spent the windfall. For all the crudeness of his existence, he records the faintest motions of his mind, and the novel concludes with the nameless narrator signing on to a ship about to leave Norway. Until Joyce's later work, Hamsun's stream-of-consciousness technique was unsurpassed.

Hamsun's triumphant expressive performance was not a sudden inspiration or a casual enterprise: he would repeat it in later novels, and had thoughtfully prepared for it. In 1890, the year of *Hunger*, he published a pioneering essay in which he outlined the importance of capturing the most intimate moments of mental work: "They last a second, a minute, they come and go like a moving winking light; but they have impressed their mark, deposited some kind of sensation before they vanished." These are "secret stirrings that go unnoticed in the remote part of the mind, the incalculable chaos of impressions, the delicate life of the imagination seen under the magnifying glass; the random progress of these thoughts and feelings; untrodden, tractless journeyings by brain and heart, strange workings of the nerves, the whisper of the blood, the entreaty of the bone, all the unconscious life of the mind." Holding a magnifying mirror to the self, paying heed to the most evanescent impressions, recognizing the interplay of mind and body, accepting the apparent irrational trajectory of thoughts, all this and Hamsun's adjectives—"delicate," "random," "tractless," "unconscious"—make for a terse program for the modernist novel. It is literary psychoanalysis without the couch.

A decade later, in 1901, Arthur Schnitzler, then Austria's most modern playwright and novelist, employed internal monologues with striking finesse in a brilliant novella, *Leutnant Gustl*. Schnitzler offers not a word of commentary; Gustl's thoughts alone carry the story. It is as though Flaubert's ideal fiction, in which the author has become perfectly invisible, had been translated into German. Schnitzler's lieutenant, an aristocrat serving in the Austro-Hungarian army, conceited, empty-headed, self-absorbed, rather stupid, finds himself brooding about a duel with a corpulent, elderly civilian, to be fought early the next morning. The two men have had a trivial quarrel, provoked by Gustl, in a crowded cloakroom after a concert. Gustl spends the rest of the night wandering about Vienna, mortally afraid of the fate that likely awaits him. He briefly ponders shooting himself. He considers composing farewell notes to his parents and his sister, even though letter writing is not his strong suit. He recalls, with self-pitying regret, the faithful Adele whom he exploited and abandoned for all her tears because she had begun to bore him. ("In all my days I haven't seen a female cry that much. . . . In fact that was the sweetest thing I've ever experienced.") He wonders how his friends and his current mistress, Steffi, will mourn him after his sudden demise—if at all. Then his opponent suffers a fatal stroke, and the intensity of Gustl's relief is almost obscene.

The originality of *Leutnant Gustl* is overshadowed by the passion of Schnitzler's satire. A political liberal, he had no use for snobbery

(which he took to be the governing vice of his age), the duel (an aristocratic practice that he heatedly opposed), or misogyny (on which his
own record was admittedly somewhat less than spotless). *Leutnant
Gustl* is, in some 12,000 words, a stinging indictment of the Austro-
Hungarian monarchy. It attests that modernists did not hold the doctrine of art for art's sake consistently. Still, even in semi-political texts
like this, the sovereignty of the artist remained inviolate. As we shall
see more than once, some of the most successful avant-garde novels
and plays, even compositions and designs, had a political sting. A
Picasso on the left was a contemporary of Céline's on the right. But

Arthur Schnitzler, Austria's best known playwright, novelist,
and poet. A masterly psychologist.

that did not make them any less modernist, any less hostile to the products of the Academy, than more neutral works of art.

FOUR MODERN MASTERS

1.

HENRY JAMES, JAMES JOYCE, VIRGINIA WOOLF, MARCEL PROUST—a splendid quartet of novelists unsurpassed in their fiction. The list is open to selective enlargement: Thomas Mann, Joseph Conrad, D. H. Lawrence, William Faulkner? or an Indian or Korean Nobel laureate little known in the Western world? I have picked my four for this essay, rounded out with a fifth, Franz Kafka, largely because they are inescapable and because, for all their fundamental accord on the need to discard traditional techniques, they treated their departures from conventionality and their methods of penetrating to the inner recesses of their fictional creations in strikingly individual ways.

AT FIRST GLANCE, the place of Henry James among modernists remains somewhat problematic. His dozen or more novels and scores of short stories obey the classic rules: their plots move forward at a relentless pace, their denouements occur where convention has put them, at the end—there are fictions by James in which he dissolves the carefully tied knot of suspense in the last paragraph, even the last word. Their dialogue is, if at times high-flown, naturalistic; their author appears as an all-knowing presence; his language, though refined, should not drive the educated reader to a dictionary. Despite all these earmarks of literary orthodoxy, though, there is something about James's work, especially his late novels, that is amazingly new and unexpected. His explorations of consciousness shy at no complexity. Between his characters' weighty conversations and his authorial interventions (usually delicately nuanced reports on motives, feelings, responses), James weaves an intricate network of gradual clarifications that reaches into the secret heart of his puppets. It is significant that by 1916, the year of James's death at seventy-three, he was a well known writer across the

English-speaking Atlantic, but never a popular favorite. It took a generation of well-read and eloquent enthusiasts to place him in the top echelon of novelists, a most modern of modernists for all his ostensibly conformist procedures.

What gave James this stature was, as I have suggested, his surgeon's precision for the subtlest distinctions traceable in human thought and conduct. He pursued in his considerable output several favorite themes: the innocent American confronting urbane, often corrupt Europe; the artist at work struggling with himself and his public; the melodramatic invasion of evil—James's ghost stories are chilling. The three late novels he published at a rapid pace between 1902 and 1904, *The Wings of the Dove*, *The Ambassadors*, and *The Golden Bowl*, composed at breakneck speed, all of them substantial in size and authoritative in presentation, showed his antennae quivering with a refinement beyond which it seems impossible to go. These novels were, as salespeople in bookstores or railroad bookstalls would admit, not very easy to read, and so it took years before the reading public had been browbeaten into buying and even enjoying them. Yet outside the university and beyond its influence on literary journalism, this trio of masterpieces has never secured a sizable following. One can regret this but see why his avant-garde fiction was and remained caviar for the cultured elite.

2.

HENRY JAMES AND JAMES JOYCE are as different as two novelists could possibly be, hence it is of interest that T. S. Eliot, not given to praising modern writers unless they were French, was devoted to both. This ability to stretch his capacity for admiration across so wide a field of literature proves, if proof be needed, that the modernist impulse was a powerful uniting force. James was everything one might expect Eliot to be enthusiastic about: an American who had chosen to exile himself abroad—he settled in England, as Eliot himself would do, in 1876 at the age of thirty-three. And James was the most consistent, most concentrated writer professing literature, bravely, honestly at odds with the vulgarity rife among contemporary critics and reviewers and with the so-called educated public. His essays were trenchant, often melancholy attempts to rescue the literary vocation from democracy much as Eliot would labor to secure his calling in poetry.

Eliot's partiality for Joyce was less self-evident but most unequivocal and most importunate. He went about singing the praises of *Ulysses* (1922) among his friends and in print. "I hold this book to be the most important expression which the present age has found," he wrote in 1923; "it is a book to which we are all indebted, and from which none of us can escape." Ernest Hemingway, the master of the lapidary style, made the same point, only less genteelly. "Joyce," he wrote, "has a most goddam wonderful book." Here were heartfelt salutes from two modernist masters; and it is much to the point that Eliot should consider the novel appropriate to "the present age." He was responding, with a generosity rare for him, to a writer who was, as Baudelaire would have noted, in tune with his time.

JOYCE SPENT MUCH of his life abroad in self-chosen exile. At the end of *Ulysses* he listed the places of its composition: "Trieste–Zurich–Paris." But in a sense he never left home. Born in Dublin in 1882 and educated there, he fled at twenty from an Ireland he found awash in superstition and chauvinism, and lived on the Continent for most of his life. But a slender volume of brilliant short stories published in 1914, as its title, *Dubliners*, plainly underscores, has as its locale the city of his birth. So does *A Portrait of the Artist as a Young Man* (1916), a major rehearsal for his masterpiece, *Ulysses*, possibly the best known of all modernist fictions, in which two imagined characters traverse most of Dublin. And Dublin, finally, is the scene of *Finnegans Wake* (1939)—if "scene" is the right word for that dreamlike tapestry of puns and tireless linguistic experiments—a book that, technically speaking, is Joyce's most extreme modernist fiction, but one that pushes his alienation from ordinary language so far as to have deprived the work of virtually all readership.

Joyce bore all the stigmata of modernism at its most subversive: intellectual versatility, wealth of literary allusion, a playful mastery of foreign languages, an acrobatic imagination, and a willingness to trans-gress rules that had governed writing for centuries. He piled heresy upon heresy. *Ulysses* had been a slow birth. Several sections of the sub-stantial text had appeared in an avant-garde journal from 1918 on, and quickly aroused lively responses. Even before the novel was published in its entirety, more than fulfilling its promise, critics whom the frag-ments made exceedingly uneasy had been unable to deny its power. Writing in 1921, Richard Aldington, a prominent English Imagist poet and editor, cautioned against the destructive effects it was bound to have on Joyce's camp followers.

Aldington was a card-carrying modernist; in 1914 and 1915, he had overcome severe reservations to help serialize Joyce's previous novel in *The Egoist*. "True, *Portrait of an Artist* was sordid, but it had fine pas-sages; the contest between the 'idealism' of Dedalus [the hero, modeled on young Joyce himself] and the outer world of crass stupidity and ugliness was very moving." The book, Aldington confessed, had roused great expectations in him; "one felt that here was a man of extreme sensitiveness and talent." But *Ulysses* had disappointed his hopes. The new book, Aldington wrote, "is more bitter, more sordid, more ferociously satirical than anything Mr. Joyce has yet written." He thought it "a tremendous libel on humanity," clever no doubt and witty, but basically far too depressing. "There is laughter in *Portrait of an Artist*, but it is a harsh, sneering kind," far indeed from the healthy humor of Rabelais. The same was true of its successor. To be sure, *Ulysses* deserved wide attention. "From the point of view of art," Ald-ington granted, "there is some justification for Mr. Joyce; he has suc-ceeded in writing a most remarkable book," Yet, he persisted, "from the point of view of human life I am sure he is wrong."

Efficiently surveying Joyce's menu of stylistic devices, Aldington found them dazzling and seductive, however bad an example the novel would set. "Mr. Joyce has pushed the intimate detailed analysis of char-acter further than any writer I know." In short, the novel is "an aston-ishing psychological document." Indeed, "in nearly every case he achieves his 'effect.' He has done daring but quite wonderful things with words. He can be sober, ironic, disgusting, platitudinous, sarcas-

tic, just as he wishes." By introducing a moral dimension into his verdict on a literary work, Aldington was quite unintentionally raising a
persistent issue that at least some modernists, like Oscar Wilde, had
already tried to exorcise from literary criticism. But so pure a modernist commentator as Virginia Woolf agreed with Aldington in part.

3.

VIRGINIA WOOLF WRESTLED with Joyce's revolution for years. To her
mind, he was one of the few writers—Samuel Butler and Bernard
Shaw were two others—who had noticed, and even anticipated, what
she would consider to be, in her famous phrase, the spectacular
upheaval in human character of December 1910. But Joyce was complicated for her. In her notes on him, she had shown appreciation for his
attempt to get thinking into literature. This, of course, epitomized her
own enterprise. But in "Mr. Bennett and Mrs. Brown," she suggests
that *Ulysses* "seems to me the conscious and calculated indecency of a
desperate man who feels that in order to breathe he must break the windows. At moments, when the window is broken, he is magnificent. But
what a waste of energy!" It is an illuminating, if censorious, perspective
on Joyce; she thought *Ulysses* ill-bred and boring in part. This provides
yet another instance of how modernists could fail to see eye-to-eye on
essentials.

The passages that troubled Aldington—and Woolf—were only one
reason why *Ulysses* was kept out of the reading public's hands for
years. To begin with, one could not expect a wide distribution from its
publisher, Sylvia Beach, who brought it out under her imprint, Shakespeare & Company, named after her bookstore in Paris. Its first printing was all of 1,000 copies, and the bulk of the second and third
printings were confiscated by the British and American postal authorities for supposed obscenity. The officially sanctioned edition of *Ulysses*
did not appear until early 1934, with Random House in New York,
which had hoped for, and got, a historic decision by U.S. District Judge
John M. Woolsey—who had taken the trouble to read the novel
through—that it was literature, not pornography. A minor press as first

publisher, tortuous legal struggles, and a triumphant, intelligent judicial vindication. What could be more gratifying to a modernist?

BORROWING THE SAME BACKDROP for *Ulysses* from *Portrait of the Artist*—even, with Stephen Dedalus, the same character—Joyce has Dedalus and his fellow protagonist, Leopold Bloom, wander all over Dublin, visiting a tavern, a newspaper office, a lying-in hospital, a public library, a cemetery, a bookstore, a brothel. Joyce's insistence on writing about what he knows best, his strong sense of place for all his estrangement from Ireland, gives the novel a firm grounding in social realities.

But the novel's range of literary versatility is even more impressive. Yeats spoke in a guarded accolade of Joyce's "cruel playful mind like a great soft tiger cat." A single example of his verbal virtuosity may do: the characteristic episode at the lying-in hospital. Bloom comes to visit Mrs. Purefoy, who is about to give birth. In sheer exuberance, Joyce echoes the stages of her fetus's development with a comic history of the English language, mimicking Anglo-Saxon, Elizabethan, Miltonian, Bunyanesque, Victorian English in turn, to end up, as he told his friend, the painter Frank Budgen, with "a frightful jumble of Pidgin English, Nigger English, Cockney, Irish, Bowery slang and broken doggerel." Aldington was not alone in exclaiming that Joyce could do anything with words—anything. No wonder John Middleton Murry, an influential English literary critic and editor, called him "a half-demented man of genius." It seems as though his most admiring readers—always excepting T. S. Eliot—had to qualify their praise of the man who had written what might well be the novel of the century.

Even for literary revolutionaries, he was too revolutionary. Yet Joyce used his gifts not to display his ingenuity and scattered learning, but to make his portraits more tangible, more rounded, more lifelike than any novelist had been able to draw before him. Once he had found the right prose for a passage, he said, there remained the task of arranging it properly, to order the words perfectly. This explains some of the ornate passages in *Ulysses* that are more musical, more "poetic" than most prose. But it is the stream of consciousness flowing through the minds of his characters that the reader is most likely to retain. It turns up in one episode after another, and comes into its own in the concluding episode in the monologue of Molly Bloom, Leopold's wife, probably the most celebrated soliloquy in modern literature.

It takes up twenty-five printed pages without a single punctuation mark to slow down her racing associations; the emphatic period at the close comes like a small explosion. Joyce has reached the concluding episode in his epic, the thoughts of a modern Penelope, after he has arranged the encounter of the two protagonists toward which the novel has been aiming all along. It is late evening. Bloom has run into a drunken, helpless Stephen Dedalus in Dublin's Nighttown, the city's principal whorehouse district, and, with paternal solicitude, has brought him home. The trajectory of these men who had almost met several times during the day has reached its destined denouement, as the two, so different and yet so compatible, enact the age-old drama of familial love as father and son. And Molly Bloom awakens, to exemplify another kind of love, sexual love, which modernism found easier to explore.

Molly Bloom's soliloquy, vigorous and vulgar, travels across her mental map; her main subject, to which she returns over and over in almost clinical detail, is her erotic memories, past and present, real and fantasized, of the men she has had. She has no room for euphemisms, for she is, in Joyce's symbolic imagery, the voice of earth, with not a touch of the celestial; "yes I think he made them a bit firmer sucking them like that so long he made me thirsty titties he calls them I had to laugh yes this one anyhow stiff the nipple gets for the least thing." What she longs for most is what Leopold Bloom cannot fully give her: sexual gratification.

She may be a tough-minded bundle of energy, but neither vicious nor ungrateful. After revisiting several adulterous episodes, she turns her thoughts to Leopold at last and recalls the time in Gibraltar when he asked her to marry him. She closes with the word Joyce explicitly chose; it was, he informed Budgen, the most positive word in the language: "Yes." She repeats the word almost obsessively:

O and the sea the sea crimson sometimes like fire and the glorious sunsets and the figtrees in the Alameda gardens yes and all the queer little streets and pink and blue and yellow houses and the rosegardens and the jessamine and geraniums and cactuses and Gibraltar as a girl where I was a Flower of the mountain yes when I put the rose in my hair like the Andalusian girls used or shall I wear a red yes and how he kissed me under the Moorish wall and I thought well as well him as another and then I asked him with my eyes to ask again yes and then he asked me would I yes to say yes my mountain flower and first I put my arms around him yes and drew him down to me so he could feel my breasts all perfume yes and his heart was going like mad and yes I said yes I will Yes.

No wonder the modernist partisans of *Ulysses* enormously admired this declaration of love to life; no wonder the disapproving, blind to the bouquet of affections that are its principal exhibits, thought it a book desperately in need of censorship. But this, as we have seen so often, was the impact of modernism: it was shocking to the shockable.

JOYCE'S *ULYSSES* is at once the freest and the most disciplined of novels. In company with his exuberant libertinism, its productive tension between autonomy and control made it a novel that only a modernist, at once sovereign over and indebted to the past, could have written. Joyce was far from indifferent to the literary tradition: Dante, Shakespeare, especially of course Homer, pervade this novel. But he used the giants of the past for his purposes. With his imposing linguistic facility and fertile imagination, he seemed to himself in danger of losing power over his creation. Hence the device of writing a modern *Odyssey*, a serious burlesque of a classic that would keep his construction from disintegrating, with its strict form providing a sturdy framework. His use of the ancient tale, T. S. Eliot wrote perceptively, if rather too sourly, "is simply a way of controlling, of ordering, of giving shape and a significance to the immense panorama of futility and anarchy which is contemporary history." Joyce would not have endorsed Eliot's rejection of his own time, but he would have acknowledged that enlisting the Ulysses myth was a way of staying in charge of his overabundant supplies.

Joyce had other means of organizing this swarming mass, this Dublin of the mind. He placed words, images, motifs into strategic spots and, at the right moment, returned to them, giving with unobtrusive cross-references a continuity and coherence, a persistence of style and habits, that made the psychology of his inventions richly lifelike. Then, too, as he pointed out to Budgen, "my book is the epic of the human body," with each organ, like each episode of the book, in its place. Plainly, Joyce's ideal reader must, above all, be supremely attentive.

To such a reader, *Ulysses* quickly emerges as a dazzling parody: Bloom, a petty bourgeois, likable and down-to-earth, reexperiences the adventures of a noble hero during a single day in mundane, early twentieth-century Dublin—the date is June 16, 1904—and on a level far less exalted than that of Odysseus' legendary Greece. The counterpoint of this curious parallelism, between high and low, mythical and mundane, invites two possible interpretations. At first glance it appears only too obvious that any comparison between the Ulysses of Homer and the Ulysses of Joyce works as a devastating critique of the modern juxtaposed with the ancient. Yet the contrary reading is, though not quite so obtrusive, the one that Joyce must have intended. He gives Bloom a certain dignity and fundamental decency, an ability to confront life under inauspicious circumstances. Bloom is, in his fleshly way, one of Baudelaire's heroes of modern life.

He may be only a humble advertising canvasser with a wife who takes lovers, but he possesses a modicum of learning—certainly Molly Bloom appreciates it—and courage and curiosity all his own. And these qualities make him a worthy moral and emotional companion for Stephen Dedalus, for the young man, like his newfound substitute father, is a liberal who has risen above his parochial, constricted world, Catholic Dublin. Stephen is impatient with the cheap jibes against Jews that are the common coin in his circle and it is no accident that the paternal Bloom should be a Jew. But to Joyce, Ulysses is more than that: he is the complete human being in literature, more so, he said, than Faust making a bargain with the devil, more so than Dante traversing hell; he is son, father, lover, friend, warrior, companion at arms, a man of wisdom, and a good man into the bargain. Joyce, in search of disinterested subjectivity, parades before his readers one of the transcendent inventions of modernist literature. His Bloom, as he once casually noted, is Everyman—stripped, we may add, of all social surfaces, all the necessary hypocrisies that culture imposes.

4.

JAMES JOYCE AND VIRGINIA WOOLF obviously stood at the opposite extremes of the modernist literary sensibility: he sensual and she cool, he prolific with words and she parsimonious, his world large, crowded, and lavish, hers highly concentrated. Both Joyce's *Ulysses* and Woolf's *Mrs. Dalloway* cover a single day, but the first hits the target, as it were, with bursts of scattered machine-gun fire, the second with single shots from a sharpshooter. When in April 1918 Virginia Woolf and her husband, Leonard, had the opportunity of publishing early chapters of Joyce's novel in progress at their tiny Hogarth Press, she turned them down not just from practical reasons; she did not like what she read. "I don't believe that his method, which is highly developed," she wrote to her friend Lytton Strachey, "means much more than cutting out the explanations and putting in the thoughts between dashes." It was a typically perceptive remark that encapsulated her differences from Joyce in a single phrase: he put in the thoughts for which she substituted dashes.

Actually, Virginia Woolf was not so proper, or so frigid, as the Bloomsbury myth presumed her to be. She talks candidly, even fiercely, about love and hate—of couples' hatred for one another, of children struggling with their parents—as though she has peeled away layers of courteous circumlocutions to reach hidden ranges of primitive mental urges. One need not be an orthodox Freudian reader to discover oedipal conflicts in her novels; they are everywhere. James Ramsay, one of the Ramsays' eight children in *To the Lighthouse*, silently resents his father's assertion of authority: "Had there been an axe handy, a poker, or any weapon that would have gashed a hole in his father's breast and killed him, there and then," Woolf records his boyish rage, "James would have seized it."

Sexual love, too, was within her range. Granted, the erotic sphere was not her special passion in life or in fiction—not long after she got married, she told a friend that the charms of orgasm had been exaggerated. But at the very least Eros was a necessary analytic ingredient as

Virginia Woolf. "With their simple tools and primitive materials, it might be said, Fielding did well and Jane Austen even better, but compare their opportunities to ours!" Woolf wrote, and she beautifully took those opportunities in her own fiction.

Vanessa Bell (Virginia Woolf's sister and a highly regarded painter), jacket for Virginia Woolf's great *To the Lighthouse* (Hogarth Press, 1927).

she anatomized her characters; as a novelist, she followed Shakespeare's Polonius, offering her readers indirections to find directions out. On the concluding page of *Between the Acts*, published in 1941, the last novel she completed before she drowned herself the same year, she has a married couple that has presided over a daylong historical pageant in their village tensely confront one another: "Left alone together for the first time that day, they were silent. Alone, enmity was bared; also love. Before they slept, they must fight; after they had fought, they would embrace. From that embrace, another life might be born. But first they must fight, as the dog fox fights with the vixen, in the heart of darkness, in the field of night." She did not always employ the dashes.

VIRGINIA WOOLF HAS become such a celebrity, through biographies, picture essays, monographs, conferences, a veritable library of reminiscences about the Bloomsbury group, even movies, that her life requires little elucidation. She was born Virginia Stephen in 1882, the daughter of Sir Leslie Stephen, a formidable intellectual historian, eminent editor, mountain climber, and needy neurotic. Mr. Ramsay, in *To the Lighthouse*, is a recognizable portrait of him with all his striking flair and no less striking flaws, just as the true protagonist of the novel, his wife, the beautiful and powerful Mrs. Ramsay, stands for her mother. These parents obsessed their sensitive daughter in unhealthy ways, she thought, until middle age, when she managed to write herself more or less free. Labile, responsive to the finest touch like a harp, visited by extreme mood swings, she was often ill and at times mad. Unfortunately, the sexual games to which her older half brothers had subjected her, a gold mine for biographers (often hasty, half informed), have made hunting for the smallest clues to her secret nature almost irresistible. The seductive play left deposits, no doubt, but much remains sheer conjecture, mysterious and a little opaque. Virginia Woolf would have been a splendid character in one of her own novels.

She read voraciously always; and she wrote and wrote—letters, diaries, sketches, reviews, essays, feminist polemics, all luminously intelligent; and after a while, novels. Her mature fiction was the ultimate beneficiary, the essential point of her ruminations about the private theatre she carried about with her, and her reflections on being a woman in a man's world. She read and wrote like a professional anxious to learn her trade, anxious to make a contribution that would be recognizably unique. She found the first of her novels—*The Voyage Out*, published in

1915—torment to write and torment to let go, yet for all that travail it is still conventional in tone and technique. Not until she was middle-aged did she confidently see her way clear. "There's no doubt in my mind," she confided to her diary on July 26, 1922, with a splendid air of self-discovery, "that I have found out how to begin (at 40) to say something in my own voice." To be authentically herself, like no one else, no matter how admirable a model might be—this was the modernist incarnate speaking. Three quarters of a century before, Flaubert had praised Baudelaire's poetry for being unlike anyone else's. It was his highest compliment, and it was Woolf's highest aspiration, which made her most susceptible to breakdowns after she had completed a novel, awaiting the capricious, unpredictable public judgment.

Evolving her unmistakable tone, she listened to her literary language, testing it, diligently revising, thinking up new experiments. One of her later novels, *The Years* (1937), which follows six friends through their lifetime, published to wide approval after she had acquired a substantial reputation, remains a contentious text among Woolf's devoted followers. Some thought it the best book she had ever written, while others (this writer included) find it stilted and rather forced. But, interestingly enough, the final product was as astonishing to her as it would be for many readers. She had planned to write a novel about a single protagonist, herself, and with the writing began to spread herself among her characters. The lure of the new could strike unprepared modernists as strongly as the unprepared public.

The language that was accessible to her as a tactic of comprehension and communication proved to be enormously flexible. Like a seasoned animal tamer, Woolf cracked her whip on her prose and made the most feral brute cringe at her orders. She moved with ease from broken phrases to elegant formulations. She overrode rules and conventions when it suited her—"ghostlily" is a typical neologism. She used, with rich metaphorical expressiveness, likenesses borrowed from the nature she knew. Birds, flowers, gardens, water—especially waves, with their undulant fluidity—all familiar pictures in the mind of an educated Englishwoman who often visited, and at times owned, a country cottage, served her purposes. But she could also take dramatic leaps, invoking war, tyranny, blight, all suddenly lighting up, like unexpected bolts of lightning, strains within and among her characters. The issue was always the same for the modernist writer: "And now I ask, 'Who am I?'" It is the writer Bernard's query, repeating a question she asked herself more than once in the privacy of her diaries. He professes not to know the answer. But at her best, Virginia Woolf came as close to giving literary expression to, and resolution of, this conundrum as novelist ever did.

5.

IN 1922, THE BANNER YEAR of her finding herself as a true writer, Virginia Woolf discovered Marcel Proust with an excitement quite uncommon for her. It was also the year of Proust's death; only five sections of his masterpiece had been published at the time—the remaining three would come out during the next five years—but his claim to the highest rank among modernists was already beyond dispute. "Proust so titillates my own desire for expression that I can hardly set out the sentence," Woolf told her friend, the art critic Roger Fry. "Oh, if I could write like that! I cry. And at the moment such is the astonishing vibration and saturation and intensification that he procures—theres something sexual in it—that I feel I write like that, and seize my pen and then I don't write like that." No other contemporary writer came near producing that delicious erotic sensation in her—sex in life, we know, was less thrilling to her than sex in literature—but face-to-face with the French master, her self-confidence did tremble a little.

MUCH LIKE WOOLF, the mature Proust lived to write. Born in 1871 in Paris into an upper-middle-class family, his father a distinguished physician and his only too beloved mother from a prosperous Jewish clan, it took him some years to discover his supreme reason for living. But even as a young dilettante, soaking up the gratifications of a society that he would later dissect so pointedly, he was half-consciously preparing himself for his life's mission. The evolution of the novel's

Marcel Proust at the house of Reynaldo Hahn, composer and
one of Proust's early lovers (1905).

narrator and that of the novel's author are far from identical, yet their
consummations are strikingly similar.

Proust unquestionably was a genius, but one of his most impressive
traits was diligence. In his late twenties and early thirties, gathering up
the social capital he would expend a decade later in *A la recherche du
temps perdu*, he read intensely; developed a passing but passionate
engagement with John Ruskin's subjectivist aesthetic, which treated the
arts (not excluding architecture) as the mirror of society, particularly its

morals; and turned out sketches, stories, a long unfinished novel, none of them published in his lifetime. His experiments in love, discreet homosexual affairs—less discreet after his mother's death in 1906— flowered as literary raw materials. Together, these preoccupations matured into the modernist style that *A la recherche* would ultimately embody. The title states the work's dominant theme: life is the search for a past we have lost. We recapture it when we remember, and we remember not because we want to, but because some glowing, concrete experience compels us: Proust's narrator has his epiphanies as he feels irregular paving stones beneath his feet, starched napkins at his lips, and, most memorable of all, the taste of a madeleine dipped in tea.

His novel abounds in set pieces when memory will not be denied. But it also follows a master plan. The narrator goes through life mingling with high society, tasting the dubious pleasures of love, cultivating acquaintance with artists, traveling to thrilling places like Venice, improving his mind and tastes, and is always about to launch a literary career—though we hear little about this as the years go by. The closing volume, *Le Temps retrouvé*, rounds off a long life's history marked with humor, brilliant excursions into the making and unmaking of minds, voyeuristic observations of sexual couplings and startling discoveries about the prevalence of homosexuality in his circles, a good deal of futility and frustration. After spending some years in a sanitarium, the narrator returns to Paris to attend an elegant party of gray-haired men and women, his old friends and associates, now as elderly as he has become.

But Marcel has found his vocation: he will draw the portrait of his world by portraying himself, painting the portrait of the artist as an old man, voyaging through Time. By no means everyone is fated to become an artist, that rare being, who grows into himself from some internal compulsion, no matter how late. The narrator is among the chosen: he will write a great novel—and the novel the reader has just read is the novel the narrator will write. He has learned his life's lesson: the price the searcher for lost truth must pay is steep, even extortionate, but it is worth paying. Art alone can bridge the gaps between the intermittences of the heart. "The true life, life at last discovered and illuminated, the only life really lived, is that of the artist." Art alone can over-come the ravages of indifferent, pitiless Time. There are moments like these in modernist fiction when the underground affinities between it and the Romantics' glorifications of art rise to the surface.

It is worth recalling here that in *To the Lighthouse*, too, Virginia Woolf grants a gratifying consummation, the act of completing a long-delayed task. And, significantly, the task to be completed is a work of art. The opening part of the novel is set in the Ramsays' summer home in the Hebrides, followed by "Time Passes," the short, almost casual bridge to the third part, set ten years later and, like the first, in the Ramsays' summer home. The guests include all those who have survived the passing of time and the Great War. Most conspicuously absent is Mrs. Ramsay, who, we have been casually informed, has died suddenly. There is a family friend, Lily Briscoe, who, having failed to complete a painting on which she had labored a decade earlier, again sets up her easel out of doors and bravely tries to solve the problem. And Lily Briscoe finds the very brushstroke that had eluded her a decade before: "With a sudden intensity, as if she saw it clear for a second, she drew a line there, in the centre. It was done; it was finished. Yes, she thought, laying down her brush in extreme fatigue, I have had my vision." On a different scale but with a similar force, Proust and Woolf could write like partners.

They were partners, too, in a more ambitious scene, also involving Lily Briscoe. There is a short, memorable passage titled "The Intermittences of the Heart" in *A la recherche* that occurs in *Sodome et Gomorrhe*, the volume published just before Proust's death. It was a phrase that he had sometimes thought to use as the general title for his masterpiece. He well might have, because the expression tersely epitomizes one of Proust's most disheartening, and most irresistible, conclusions about the vicissitudes of existence: the human heart fails when its endurance and judgment are most needed. Life is many things, to be sure, but most conspicuously it adds up to a vast array of mistakes, of mis-matches, of sentiments out of phase with realities, of experiences not reflected in feelings. We get experiences wrong; everyone gets experiences wrong. Proust at the opening of "Intermittences" (a little

tediously) introduces a talkative foreign-born hotel manager who mal-
treats the French language in every sentence. He is a typical small
example of larger human failings.

But Proust wastes little time on such trifles. Rather, he gives illustrations of what he insists is only too common: we love too early and
too late, and too often the wrong persons; what we learn about those
we come to know intimately almost never matches our first, or even
our second, impressions. Love turns into hate or into indifference or
reverses its course, but not for logical reasons: the heart, as I have said,
fails. It has, in short, its intermittences. Life, therefore, is a perpetual
act of revising, of correcting, what we think we know; it is a school for
disenchantment. There are only a few, a very few and very precious
exceptions to this rule, like a mother's or grandmother's pure love for
her offspring.

This is the important case that Proust studies in "Intermittences of
the Heart." A little more than a year before, the narrator's loving and
beloved grandmother has died, but that loss, though he had experienced it affectionately enough, has not really hit home. Now, he is at
Balbec, the resort he knows so well, in search of good-looking young
women to meet, when memory strikes him like a blow: "On the first
night [at the hotel], as I was suffering from cardiac fatigue, I bent
down slowly and cautiously to take off my boots, trying to master my
pain. But scarcely had I touched the topmost button than my chest
swelled, filled with an unknown, a divine presence, I was shaken with
sobs, tears streamed from my eyes." It was the memory of his grandmother, "tender, preoccupied," who had done him the same service
years ago, now recaptured in a spontaneous recollection infinitely
more powerful than his casual, selfish, frivolous thoughts of her
during the months since her death. At the moment that the need for
her had been reawakened, "I knew that I might wait hour after hour,
that she would never again be by my side. I had only just discovered
this because I had only just, on feeling her for the first time alive,
real, making my heart swell to breaking-point, on finding her at last,
learned that I had lost her for ever."

Virginia Woolf made the intermittences of the heart as well, in her

own way. For her, too, they were trophies that the indefatigable archeologist of the mind unearths only after digging in hidden, often
uninviting spaces. In her novels, men and women love and hate, often
the same person across time or even at the same time. There are, too,
rare times (of exquisite interest to Woolf) when women love women.
The best marriage is flawed; the course of love, as Shakespeare had
already said three centuries earlier, never runs smooth. Ambivalence,
in short, is everyone's companion. To the world, Clarissa Dalloway
seems satisfactorily married; yet as she goes about preparing for a party
in the novel that bears her name, she ponders her friend Peter Walsh,
who had wanted to marry her and who would have been, she often
muses, more interesting than her solid, stolid husband.

Such couples, who recapture fragments of the past with delight and
dread, populate virtually all of Woolf's fiction to her last. I have
already quoted from the closing page of *Between the Acts*. "Before they
slept, they must fight; after they had fought, they would embrace."
Traditional novels, too, could not dispense with triangles, but it was the
peculiar strength of modernist fiction to recognize their instability, and
the coexistence of incompatible feelings that bedevil them. Around the
time that Virginia Woolf reached her peak as a novelist, Freud was
warning that the Oedipus complex is almost never a straightforward
experience.

And Woolf's *To the Lighthouse* has a page that reads like a reminiscence of Proust's narrator weeping over his dead grandmother. In the
third part, Lily Briscoe, sitting out of doors, as we have just seen, worries over her unfinished picture. And Mrs. Ramsay hovers about her.
"Oh Mrs. Ramsay! she called out silently, to that essence which sat by
the boat, that abstract one made of her, that woman in grey, as if to
abuse her for having gone, and then having gone, come back again. It
had seemed so safe, thinking of her." But suddenly it was no longer safe.
Lily Briscoe was bitterly angry, "(to be called back, just as she thought
she would never feel sorrow for Mrs. Ramsay again. Had she missed her
among the coffee cups at breakfast? not in the least)." She called Mrs.
Ramsay's name. "The pain increased." What did it all mean? "'Mrs.
Ramsay!' she said aloud, 'Mrs. Ramsay!' The tears ran down her face."

This is, to my mind, the truest, most radiant reconstruction of memory's power in the modernist manner, surely among the most moving pages of radical twentieth-century fiction. It stands like a collegial greeting, a friendly wave, from one giant of modernism to another.

KAFKA

FRANZ KAFKA BELONGS on any list of major novelists, no matter how select. But I am setting him apart from the others, for his place among modernist writers, though secure, is unique; he did not enlist in the modernist cause, or in any cause but that of literature, the only thing that provided him with pure pleasure. "Nothing else," he confessed in his notebook, "will ever give me any satisfaction." He was, one might say, an accidental modernist, simply writing as he felt compelled to write and in the process upsetting conventional, time-honored ways with fiction without explanation, let alone apology.

The history of his novels' survival is well known. Kafka did not live to experience his fame. He died in 1924 of tuberculosis, just shy of forty-one, known in his native Prague for a few odd but highly regarded tales, and a volume of four stories, *The Hunger Artist*, published in the year of his death. He left behind hundreds of pages of notes, drafts, and aphorisms, and three largely completed novels, with instructions to his closest friend, Max Brod, to burn them all. Fortunately for posterity, Brod after anguished reflection decided to disobey these directions, giving the world peerless fictions and profound perplexities.

The dazzled reviewers of Kafka's *The Trial* (1925) and *The Castle* (1926), both piously edited by Brod, loaded their appreciations with superlatives—"the most uncanny and strongest book of the last few years," "the only true story teller," "a secret master and king of the German language." Admittedly, these two novels—the third, perhaps best known among various titles as *Amerika*, is a lesser, though still interesting, effort—are masterpieces in their own fascinating way. But the nature of his secret mastery and literary royalty has remained a matter of abiding controversy: Kafka has been, and continues to be, more thoroughly analyzed than any other modern writer of fiction, and after decades of debate, he remains the most incurably controversial novelist of the twentieth century.

The very genre of his posthumous novels has remained open to question. Satires? But what did Kafka satirize—the state's authority, the business bureaucracy, the judicial system? He was doubtless a brilliant ironist, whose stance gave him an observer's distance from his suffering characters, their dilemmas and their disasters. But his satiric aims are far more comprehensive than any set of institutions; they embrace all humanity. Was he, then, perhaps a supreme nihilist at heart, whose conundrums do not permit any resolution? Whatever the answer, his texts are effective enough, a product of cool reporting punctuated by a dry humor to which his listeners cheerfully testified: they laughed heartily when he read drafts to them. Or was he a victim of ethnic self-hatred, in flight from his overpowering "racial" background by not mentioning the word "Jew" in print. His friendly interest in the young Zionist movement and the traveling Yiddish acting troupe visiting Prague suggests otherwise. Inescapably, postmodern readers have weighed in to argue, thus conveniently (and preposterously) evading the contents of his work, that his writing is really about writing.

Far more pious and far more popular, interpreters have tried to make a case that Kafka's novels are theological parables about the human condition, a quest for God. The "hero" of *The Trial*, the unfortunate Joseph K., is accused of an unspecified crime, never explained, struggling through a parade of frustrations and ending with his being executed "like a dog." The appalling fates that Joseph K. and other of Kafka's protagonists undergo might speak, however obliquely, of the impassable gulf between divine justice and paltry human understanding. Such a religious perspective dominated Brod's reading of his friend's work; he indignantly repudiated all attempts at understanding these fictions as worldly texts. Like a Jewish Pascal, for whom the abyss between God and man was beyond bridging, Brod's Kafka stands aghast at human guilt and impotence. Closely linked to his theological readings, there have been related interpretations, even more melodramatic, that have insisted on seeing him as a prophet of Nazism and the Holocaust.

In comparison, the secular minority of Kafka's readers have nothing quite so dramatic, but interpretations far more sensible, to offer.
In fact, while the worlds that Kafka constructed in his stories and
novels were deeply unsettling in their harshness and their cruelty,
they have no supernatural dimension. What is more, Kafka's fictions
lack the ecstatic excitement that is customary with evocations of the
divine. His style is always unruffled and precise, in a tone that everyone who has written on Kafka has praised as pitch-perfect. Some of
his most celebrated stories are matter-of-fact in the midst of the most
horrifying detail—in "Metamorphosis" the leading character wakes
up one morning as a large bug, while the protagonist of "The Penal
Colony" is a machine that inscribes a criminal's offenses on his body
with sharp needles and eventually kills him. Kafka does not seem to
have been made anxious by the terrifying situations and doomed
characters he invents; he writes, as I have said, with the detachment
of a seasoned reporter.

Kafka's work, then, is awash in disconcerting images. He was not
squeamish. But, strangely, an essential ingredient in modernism, the
burrowing after deeper emotional realities, seems to be largely absent,
in fact unequivocally excluded, from his writings. His leading characters are little more than marionettes in the hands of irresistible forces.
They may protest, they may seek to reverse the irreversible, but they
have little if any inner life. Indeed, whenever Kafka had an opportunity
to comment on the science of mind, he showed his disdain. "There is
no observation of the inner world, as there is of the external world," he
writes in one of his notebooks. It is an argument he rehearses often. He
notes that he knows more about the room in which he lives than about
the mind that inhabits him. "The inner world can only be lived, not
described," he adds. And in one terse aphorism he puts it bluntly:
"Psychology is impatience." This comment sounds innocent enough
until the reader discovers that Kafka is making a grave charge, since for
him impatience is the greatest, perhaps the only sin. Again, "Work as
pleasure," he writes, "inaccessible to psychologists." Twice in the
course of these jottings, he makes this curt (impatient?) observation:
"For the last time, psychology!"

YET THIS IS NOT ALL that we can say about Kafka's take on the inner
life. At least once, at a critical moment, Kafka displayed a secure grasp
on psychology: in the famous letter he wrote to his father. It shows that
he could subtly exploit the motives of others and his own when he
needed to. Kafka wrote his 10,000-word indictment—it would take several psychoanalytic sessions to get it all recited—in November 1919,
when he was thirty-six, no longer in his youth. He never mailed it, but
paradoxically, just because it contains such choice biographical detail,
students of Kafka have often steered clear of it for fear of being thought
naïve, of taking a single revealing piece of evidence to explain away
one of the greatest writers of his century. That is a mistake: the letter is
the most informative autobiographical statement he ever ventured, and
an unsurpassable clue to his work. Like Edgar Allan Poe's purloined
letter, Kafka's missive to his father offers invaluable information precisely because it appears to be so obvious. His penetrating judgments
are impossible to reconcile with his exclamation, "For the last time,
psychology!"

The ostensible motive for the letter—ostensible, for the deeper reason is revenge—was to answer a question his father had recently asked
him: Why was he, Franz, afraid of him? Franz responded by doing
what he did best, enumerating concrete and dazzling instances. Hermann Kafka embodied the domestic tyrant at the dinner table. "From
your easy chair," his son summed it up, "you govern the world." He
bullies his children, with Franz, the eldest surviving son, his favorite
victim; he disparages the boy's appearance, his studies, his character;
he denounces Franz's friends in the most boorish language even before
he has met them; he harshly insists on silence around the table; he
warns that he will beat them all with his belt. He never praises them.

Kafka recognized that his terrified responses to his father, which
had become habitual with him, had originated in the feverish anxiety
of a child facing an unbearable, self-satisfied, cynical adult who enjoys
issuing arbitrary commands. He knew rationally that Hermann Kafka
never carried out his threat to whip his children and was, when all is

said, something of a paper tiger. Hence Kafka does not fail to reproach himself for his lasting anxiety. But he was certain that his father had brought him up to be as distrustful of himself as of others. And it is true that Hermann Kafka may not have been solely responsible for making his son neurotic, irresolute, and self-hating, but he bore an overwhelming share in causing the human catastrophe that became Franz Kafka. One can see why some students of Kafka likened the fraught father-son relationship to an oedipal struggle. But it is a curiously truncated, failed triangle, for Kafka rarely mentions his mother, the great peacemaker who was invariably loyal to her husband in all these dinner table confrontations.

To read this account of an education to neurosis, especially since Kafka sets it forth in the most reasonable tone, is to recognize the sagacity of a casual comment by Thomas Mann that Kafka wrote the same story all his life, his autobiography. What he spread out in writing to his father was the pervasive pattern of that life he would apply repeatedly in his fictions: the frightened, vulnerable child unable to cope with capricious authority, projecting his apprehensions onto a gigantic screen, turning his father into a menacing cluster of often invisible and usually vicious powers. There is among Kafka's aphorisms one brief entry that lights up his essential experience, reexperienced in ever new guises: "*Ich habe niemals die Regel erfahren*"—I have never been told the rule. The rule he craved was one he never learned in his household: what is permitted or forbidden, acceptable or unacceptable. Could this barking monster at the head of the table really love him? Kafka was, we know, the indecisive, tormented young man engaged to be married to two equally young women (to one of them twice), wholly unsuited to marriage, a man who felt comfortable only, as I have said, with literature. Thus he magnified and disguised his father's pathetic power by making up vast, elemental authorities, an unshakable establishment that accuses Joseph K. of an unknown, probably imaginary crime, an establishment that hides behind fog and low-level employees to frustrate the access of K. (the protagonist in *The Castle*); an establishment that can convert humans into vermin, and all the rest of Kafka's chamber of horrors.

Beloved as his writing was, though, it was not strong enough to save him from himself. It could not free him from the anguish his father had implanted in him the way that writing had largely liberated Virginia Woolf from the looming shadows of her parents. He was compelled to retell the same story just once more, and he had an extraordinary facility for covering his self-revealing tracks. The repetition compulsion had him in its grip. This, given his staggering talents, produced works that have placed Kafka in the foremost rank of modern writers. In August 1914, when a war he hated had just broken out, he declared his love with particular vehemence: "My talent for portraying my dreamlike inner life has relegated everything else to the incidental." There were moments when that unloved nuisance, psychology, made an appearance in his consciousness, to help portray his dreamlike inner life.

From this perspective, we might imagine Kafka in dialogue with Freud. There is no indication that Freud read Kafka, but good evidence that Kafka read Freud, largely on Brod's urging. Freud's verdict on the human animal was severe; in his judgment, conflict was built into every child's developmental history even at its best. But Freud, the principled pessimist, believed that psychoanalysts might alleviate some fixations and enlarge the range of rationality. "Where id was," he famously wrote with some confidence, "there ego shall be." For his part, Kafka would have taken this tough-minded realism as just another instance of all too human self-deception. Uncomfortably close to nihilist despair, he saw life itself as the villain. The conflict between Kafka's unflinching bleakness and the attitude of other modernist writers could not be any greater. I recall the last word in *Ulysses*, the most positive in the language, that Joyce gave to Molly Bloom—"Yes." Kafka's last word in all its forms was "No."

THE POET OF POETS

1.

IN 1948, T. S. ELIOT WAS AWARDED the Nobel Prize for Literature. It was a signal honor, and a welcome breakthrough to modernism by the selection committee. In half a century—the first literature prize had

T. S. Eliot at his desk at the publishing house Faber & Faber.

been awarded in 1901—the judges had shown themselves reliably old-fashioned in their tastes. Virtually all the poets they had chosen before Eliot, with the impressive exception of Yeats in 1923, are now largely forgotten. And none of the novelists I have singled out for close attention in these pages was among the Nobel laureates.* Yet the 1948 choice for literature dared to ratify Eliot's international reputation, first established twenty-six years earlier, with his difficult, consistently unconventional set of five poems assembled under one title, *The Waste Land*.

Eliot was no longer completely unknown in 1922. His two previous volumes of poetry, *Prufrock and Other Observations* (1917) and *Poems* (1920), generally brief, overwhelmingly moody, and bravely experimental, had found resonance among the poetry-reading public. And

---

* Kafka's work was almost wholly unpublished at the time of his death in 1924. But the other novelists who loom large in this book should have been highly eligible candidates: after all, James lived to 1916, Proust to 1922, both Joyce and Woolf to 1941.

some of their disenchanted, oddly threatening lines gained a certain independent circulation:

> *I grow old . . . I grow old . . .*
> *I shall wear the bottoms of my trousers rolled.*

> *Shall I part my hair behind? Do I dare to eat a peach?*
> *I shall wear white flannel trousers, and walk upon the beach.*
> *I have heard the mermaids singing, each to each.*

> *I do not think that they will sing to me.*

Early and late, Eliot was not to be caught in the snares of optimism. The mermaids would not sing to him. But it was *The Waste Land*, no more sanguine than its precursors, that made Eliot an international literary figure.

2.

IF THE HORRORS OF THE WORLD WAR, with its unending lists of casualties, were not in themselves enough to call for the despair with which *The Waste Land* is abundantly endowed, Eliot brought from his youth something contrarian in his stance toward the solid bourgeois culture in which he was raised. It came to strike him as insensitive and complacent, certainly hostile to true poetry and thus deserving the harshest satire—with these verdicts, Eliot quite unwittingly joined the ranks of the modernist protest. Born in St. Louis in 1888 to a family of prosperous and pious Boston Unitarians, some of whom had migrated to Missouri for commercial reasons, he early came to see himself—to borrow one of his favorite descriptions—as a "resident alien." From his school days he wanted to be a poet, but who was to prove a usable model? "The kind of poetry that I needed," he recalled years later, "to teach me the use of my own voice, did not exist in English at all; it was only to be found in French." The poetry available to American seekers, he noted, was unrevealing, thoroughly unrewarding: "1909 and 1910 was stagnant to a degree difficult for any young poet to imagine." The years he chose to single out in this censorious look back were significant to him—Eliot had just graduated from Harvard, where he had been a restless, hardworking undergraduate, almost desperately in search of poetic guidance.

Yet by 1909, he had begun to take the first step to self-emancipation; late in the previous year he had chanced on Arthur Symons's stimulating polemic, *The Symbolist Movement in Literature*, published ten years before, and absorbed lessons he never forgot. Symons's tract was made up of appreciative pages on the French modernist poets—Verlaine, Rimbaud, Mallarmé. These *littérateurs* wrote verse on subjects one could not find in the publications of their American or English counterparts: trials with prose poetry, attempts to map a ideal world, themes intimate in untested ways, obscene love verses, ideas realized in feelings; in short, original ways of exploring the poet's inner world, of mastering the subjectivity that, as I have insisted, was an indispensable ingredient of modernism. That they were also shocking in their novelty goes almost without saying. Best of all, Symons introduced Eliot to the less well known Symbolist Jules Laforgue, whose emotional daring and acerbic wit struck Eliot as a possible version of himself—one he could aspire to become.

Laforgue had died of tuberculosis in 1887, at just twenty-seven, but left behind an impressive if slender body of work. The women in Laforgue's poetry are like Manet's Olympia, not some generalized goddess or legendary heroine but an individual Parisienne, with her square jaw, bold body, and unapologetic look. We may sincerely love a woman from the past like Diane the huntress, wrote Laforgue, yet be "really passionate about some working girl, about some young lady from a salon," who "alone makes us sob and moves us to the bottom of our entrails." He was after capturing real experience, using techniques old and new to encompass it, with clever neologisms, brilliantly manipulated free verse, impious speeches imputed to Jesus and the Virgin Mary, declarations of love to ladies of the night, an ironic take on life and a barely suppressed longing for death. "I don't go to church," he asserted in a late poem. "I am the Lord High Chancellor of Analysis."

It was a splendid posture for translating into lasting poetry the aggressive pessimism of two German philosophers, Arthur Schopenhauer and Eduard von Hartmann, whose disciple Laforgue became.

Laforgue was aware that his ideas might appear to be contradictory. "True, life is coarse, but, by God! when it's a matter of poetry," he wrote to one of his sisters in 1883, "let us say everything, everything (that is, above all, about the filthiness of life which must put a humorous melancholy into our verses), but let us say things in a subtle way." It was to Laforgue's humorous melancholy, unknown to poetry in the English language, its felicitous coexistence of slang and philosophy, candor and elegance, that Eliot responded enthusiastically. Here is a Laforgue quatrain in one of his fine late poems, "Solo de Lune," mourning a love affair that had gone awry:

> *We loved one another like two lunatics,*
> *We parted without talking about it,*
> *A depression kept me exiled,*
> *And this depression came to me from everything. Oh, well.*

Penetrating and informal, this was a model for Eliot to follow.

He made no secret of his debt. It appears visibly in the opening stanza of "Conversation Galante"—note the French title—from Eliot's first book of poems, in the volume named for his invention, J. Alfred Prufrock:

> *I observe: "Our sentimental friend the moon!*
> *Or possibly (fantastic, I confess)*
> *It may be Prester John's balloon*
> *Or an old battered lantern hung aloft*
> *To light poor travellers to their distress."*
>   *She then, "How you digress!"*

The tribute to Laforgue could not be more direct; plainly, his discontent with nature and the human world, even though saying things "in a subtle way," stood as Eliot's model. Finding his own voice, Eliot would spread his satire more widely than Laforgue and later, surer of himself as a writer, abandon it. Among his first targets: the genteel Bostonian tradition—his own; his maiden aunt Helen; his cousins Nancy and Harriet, faithful readers of that bourgeois beacon, the *Boston Evening Transcript*, from whom he sardonically distanced himself. Another target, which in later years, after the twelve-year reign of the Nazis over Central Europe, admirers of Eliot found hard to explain, or explain away, was Jews, or certain Jews:

> *On the Rialto once,*
> *The rats are underneath the piles,*
> *The jew is underneath the lot,*
> *Money in furs.*

The lower case in "jew" was not a typographical error.* Eliot, young and old, saw much in the world to despise, and not jews—or rather, Jews—alone.

ELIOT'S *WASTE LAND* brought his recently acquired techniques, joined to his growing if still tentative sense of estrangement from the vulgarity of his times, to an astonishing proficiency. It is true that Eliot showed the early drafts of his poem to Pound and that this intimate friend and indispensable impresario, poet, exile, translator, and Fascist radically edited the manuscript of *The Waste Land*, mercilessly cutting it down and persuading Eliot to take his advice most of the time. But on his own, Eliot had an uncanny ear, a gift for the *mot juste* that would stay in the reader's mind. *The Waste Land* is a veritable anthology of his linguistic bravado. It plays with rhymed or free verse, lines long and short, the diction of a working-class woman or of an educated gentleman, passages in French or German or Italian or demotic English, to say nothing of quotations and paraphrases from select sources, including one from the father of the modernists, Eliot's cherished Baudelaire:

---

* For Eliot's "political" anti-modern modernism, see below, pp. 397–401.

"You! hypocrite. lecteur!—" Eliot puts him to use, "mon semblable,— mon frère!"

Yet even those who valued the rhetoric of *The Waste Land* found it hard to discover the unity presumably underlying its five distinct sections. He planted haunting lines in it, chilling, brooding, and memorable: "I will show you fear in a handful of dust" and "These fragments I have shored against my ruins," to say nothing of that startling opening phrase, "April is the cruellest month." The poem was sprinkled with esoteric allusions and speakers of uncertain identity, with Oriental words (the poem's last word, "Shantih," twice repeated, is, Eliot tells the reader in his notes, a blessing from an Upanishad, in Sanskrit), and with lines, as I have noted, in German and French. Some of the sudden, apparently meaningless insertions in *The Waste Land*, like "HURRY UP PLEASE ITS TIME," only exacerbated readers' perplexity.* For many, the poem was, in short, a modernist nightmare.

A number of reviewers took refuge in the shrugging disclaimer that they could not understand it. But a few took their very bafflement as their real reason for praise. The novelist and poet Conrad Aiken, who had long been Eliot's friend though he retained his independent judgment, maintained that "the poem succeeds—as it brilliantly does—by virtue of its incoherence, not of its plan; by virtue of its ambiguities, not its explanations." It was an ingenious interpretation and a highly suggestive analysis.

A handful of critics, then, did fit the pieces of *The Waste Land* into a larger whole. Burton Rascoe, a widely read American book reviewer, saw the poem as a magnificent—and, in fact, a coherent—indictment of contemporary culture; "it gives voice to the universal despair or resignation arising from the spiritual and economic consequences of the war, the cross purposes of modern civilization, the cul-de-sac into which both science and philosophy seem to have got themselves and the breakdown of all great directive purposes which give joy and zest to

---

* English readers would not find the words "Hurry up, please, it's time," particularly puzzling, since they could recognize them as the warning pub keepers often used to alert their patrons of closing time. To Americans, though, they conveyed a certain urgency.

the business of living. It is an erudite despair." Perhaps the most economical and persuasive reading came from Northrop Frye: the poem
"is a vision of Europe, mainly of London, at the end of the First
World War, and is the climax of Eliot's 'infernal' vision." Frye's
choice of "infernal" is much to the point, for Eliot is portraying his
civilization in hell and coolly wanted his audience to take his infernal
vision almost literally. Even sympathetic readers noticed that he had
put much about damnation into the poem, little if any salvation. As a
modernist by disposition as much as by experience—and this subjective element must be added to round out Frye's reading—Eliot's disdain for the modern world was pronounced even before the Great
War. Whatever readers got out of *The Waste Land*, Eliot's literary
radicalism was beyond dispute. He had quickly made himself into the
modernists' poets' poet.

3.

ELIOT WAS AN INFLUENTIAL POET and, at the same time, an influential
analyst of poetry, with an agenda to explicate as much as to carry it out.
Few modernists were as willing to adopt the role of commentator on
their craft. One of his most frequently quoted programmatic statements came early, in "Tradition and the Individual Talent" of 1920,
where he pleaded for the historical mind-set as essential to the poet's
equipment. "The historical sense involves a perception not only of the
pastness of the past, but of its presence." He visualized the working
poet imagining all his predecessors from Homer to, well, himself, as
making up a pantheon of contemporaries. It would be to this illustrious
assembly that the new poet, as it were, recites his verse, not only
acknowledging his debts but also, if he is strong enough, changing the
relation in which members of the pantheon stand toward one another
and the newcomer.

In other words, for Eliot the past did not merely shape the present,
but the present could reshape the past. There was, he noted elsewhere,
no discredit attached to living off one's ancestors: "Immature poets
imitate," he wrote famously, "mature poets steal; bad poets deface what

they take, and good poets make it into something better, or at least something different." Far more intensely than other modernists, Eliot felt at home with his literary past, and freely filched from ancestors he appreciated—notably the French Symbolists and the English Metaphysical Poets—for his own work.

At the same time, he developed a thesis of the true poet's impersonality. A consistent anti-romantic, he had no use for confessional literature. "Poetry," he wrote, "is not a turning loose of emotion, but an escape from emotion, it is not the expression of personality, but an escape from personality." What he found essential in the modern poet, and thought very few poets really understood, was the "expression of 'significant' emotion, which has its life in the poem and not in the history of the poet." In Eliot's imagination, the poet floats above his world, seeing it all and using it all, and lending his voice without sharing the feelings he describes and evokes. But, as his most penetrating critics have observed, this technique of sublime indifference is psychologically implausible and, all through Eliot's work, demonstrably untenable. It was a defensive maneuver that permits the poet to voice the most outrageous iconoclastic view, and to introduce distasteful metaphors—"A rat crept softly through the vegetation / Dragging its slimy belly on the bank"—without expressly involving himself in them.

It may not matter too much whether Eliot enjoyed such repellent language or not. But for the student of modernism, this is more than a mere technical issue. If Eliot is right to link all poets, and right to describe their involvement with their poetry as a detached affair, he would have been a powerful exception to my definition of the modernist as triumphant in subjectivity and partly—only partly—defined by his social environment. But with all his felicities, Eliot was wrong. The emotions of engagement and of discontent are at the heart of all modernists, even though for many of them it added up to no more than disgruntlement with their own specialty. In any event, once he officially became a High Anglican in 1927, Eliot's references to both these notions disappeared from his writings. But what happened afterwards will occupy us later.

4.

TOGETHER, THESE WRITERS, novelists, and poets made a revolution in literature. "Revolution" is a hackneyed word, but what they accomplished, working separately and spreading their influence together, was nothing less. Ordinary prose and poetry went on as though these masters had never written a word, but to alert readers, to say nothing of the literary avant-gardes, they had changed their world forever. These modernists were self-aware, at times even self-conscious, about the impact they thought their professions desperately needed. Notably Virginia Woolf and T. S. Eliot spread word of the call for their writings in a cascade of essays, lectures, introductions, and reviews. Henry James, too, especially in the expansive, deeply thoughtful Prefaces he wrote for the New York edition of his novels (1907–19), commented sagely on his works, one by one. The young Proust had been an eager student of modern French and English literature and written about them, but in his later years he gave himself no time for mere commentary. Increasingly in ill health, he was racing against death, struggling and largely succeeding in completing what he knew was an unsurpassed masterpiece. James Joyce, too, preferred writing fiction to writing about writing, and in 1939, two years before his death, published *Finnegans Wake*, passing in its sheer obscurity other modernists, certainly his own *Ulysses*.

Like *Ulysses*, Joyce's last novel covers a single day and night; like *Ulysses*, its location is Dublin; and, like *Ulysses*, it ends with a woman's soliloquy. But *Finnegans Wake* is not, Joyce consistently maintained, comparable or complementary to *Ulysses*, which had been a book about the day. This was a book about the night. The whole in truth has the atmosphere of a dream, with large truths and small ones facing the reader in magical formulations. Hence the actions of the characters are more incidental than their musings and their author's pun-ridden narrative. A tavern-keeper, Humphrey Chimpden Earwicker, his wife Anna Livia Plurabelle, and their three children carry the tale, but they pale before Joyce's indefatigable play with language: inventive neologisms, continual wordplay, allusions to other fiction. For years, writing *Finnegans Wake* had obsessed Joyce; it had become for him, he said, more real than reality. His aggressive, unique style, which compels the reader to undergo the chore of deciphering Joyce's meaning, was punctuated by comprehensible passages of brilliant humor and exquisite prose. It was as though Joyce, having broken nearly every rule of novel writing in *Ulysses*, was determined in his last book to build up a monument beyond which the most venturesome modernist could not possibly go.

Yet even without *Finnegans Wake*, modernist writers had done their best to dismantle the conventions by which readers had lived for centuries. I have briefly cataloged their defiance: the retreat from plot, the subversion of treating material conditions, above all the fierce commitment to the inner life. These novelists and poets were Realists; only their redefined reality now mainly consisted in thoughts and feelings, domains of life that earlier writers had neglected or felt unable to capture and express. Hence the broken sentences of modernist prose and poetry, their glancing asides, their cavalier treatment of suspense (which only Henry James sustained in the traditional manner), their reversal of what really mattered for the progress of the story, their resort to esoteric foreign phrases—Eliot's *Waste Land* is full of them—that made modernist fiction and poetry so hard to read. So hard and so rewarding. For what modernist imaginative writing asked of its public was the kind of close attention that more genial authors, seeking only to entertain, did not exact.

Modernist writing, then, became a strenuous venture not just for its makers but also for its audiences. Not all creators and publics stayed all the way on what I have called the express train to the future; some got off as the offenses to traditional tastes seemed to become excessive. That, in view of some modernists' extremism, is hardly astonishing. After all, no one pushed the envelope of the customary harder than they—except for modernist composers.

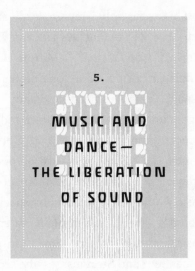

5.

MUSIC AND DANCE — THE LIBERATION OF SOUND

OVERTURES

AMONG ALL THE DOMAINS OF MODERNISM, MUSIC WAS the most esoteric. Arnold Schoenberg, the undisputed leader of the twentieth-century upheaval in music—for he aimed at nothing less—never secured a sizable audience and remains, more than half a century after his death, a specialized taste. Unlike avant-garde painting, or the novel, or architecture, which all entered the mainstream of taste after a time of trials, much avant-garde music is still avant-garde music. There has been, no doubt, as rich a variety of modernist approaches on offer by painters and novelists as in music, but the others managed to secure a certain following among a wider public; in contrast, composers resigned themselves to their fate as emotionally available only to a narrow elite. The highbrow musical scene—centering on progressive conservatories, their graduates, and their loyal friends—appears like a pot-pourri of styles, with impassioned advocates for new departures battling one another almost as energetically as they skirmished with determined defenders of tradition.

This apparently irreparable alienation survived through the decades with little weakening. As late as 1958 in a much-quoted essay, "Who Cares If You Listen?," Milton Babbitt, a sophisticated modernist, summed it all up. A serious modern composer, he wrote in civilized despair, "is, in essence, a 'vanity' composer. The general public is largely unaware of and uninterested in his music. The majority of performers shun it and resent it. Consequently, the music is little performed, and then primarily at poorly attended concerts before an audience consisting in the main of fellow professionals. At best, the music would be for, of, and by specialists." Overemphatic as it sounds, Babbitt's lament was a plain statement of fact about the high-level musical culture of his time. Only the two dominant modernists, Schoenberg and Stravinsky—the second far more than the first—could count on a rather more general reception. Babbitt's pungent assertion that the rest were all "'vanity' composers" was no doubt excessive. Dmitry Shostakovich, Francis Poulenc, Benjamin Britten, Sergei Prokofiev, to mention only the first modernist musicians who come to mind, have all been performed in many countries, even if in major concert halls across the civilized world the innovators have at best gained token concessions.

RESISTANCE TO INNOVATIVE form had not always been as powerful. Nineteenth-century musical life, long before Schoenberg, was awash in controversy among opinionated audiences and argumentative music critics, a modern profession to which a plethora of new daily newspapers gave unprecedented prominence. And the most celebrated composer of the age, Richard Wagner, aggressive and self-confident, whose ideologists claimed that his was the music of the future, was destined to inflame fierce responses wherever he went. But especially in his later years, he tasted stunning successes.

Born in Leipzig in 1813, Wagner had already seen his early operas on stage by 1848, when his participation in the failed German revolutions (on the "wrong" side) forced him into Swiss exile. This political radicalism did not last; Wagner's chief patrons would be, apart from rich bourgeois, Ludwig II of Bavaria, his infatuated sponsor royalty itself. His exile, though, gave him ample opportunities to elaborate his theoretical views on music and to draft his most celebrated composition: his version of the *Nibelungen* epic, a medieval German tale that ended up in Wagner's hands as four evening-filling music dramas.

Two features of Wagner's work will always be associated with him: a compositional contrivance and a theatrical ideal. He kept his complex action in order with *Leitmotifs*, a device he had not invented but used more lavishly than any other composer, an identifying label that gave musical notice just which character, and which mood, was on stage. (Debussy, not appeased, called it "a vague and high-flown charlatanism.") And he promoted the ambitious notion of the total work of art—*Gesamtkunstwerk*—in which all aspects of a performance, the music, the libretto, the costumes, the direction, the dances (if any), were unified as the expression of a single sovereign artist's imagination, in which music served the text. Wagner's tetralogy—*The Ring of the Nibelungen*—featured not just his music but his libretti.

Wagner's *Ring* poetry was awkward and artificial, largely a pastiche of pseudo-medievalism, but his gift for melody and harmony was utterly seductive. Above all, *Tristan und Isolde* (first performed in Munich in 1865) won him a much wider circle of excited and excitable partisans. In Paris, Baudelaire, that greatest of early modernists, was among them. Upon discovering the musician of the future in 1860, he wrote Wagner that hearing him had been the greatest musical experience of his life. In the German cultural orbit, especially after the annual Bayreuth Festival was launched in 1876, financed by Ludwig II, a spirited party of Brahmsians made often telling, at times labored, fun of the quasi-religious "orgies" attended by swooning Wagnerians. The devotees of Brahms denigrated Wagnerians as sickly, idolatrous, perhaps sexually dubious worshippers.

The Wagnerians shot back, calling Brahms a loud, boring reactionary who was in all important respects the antithesis of their demigod. It must have been Wagnerians who invented the catchy apocryphal tale of workmen in concert halls, sometimes set in London, sometimes in Vienna, putting up a laconic sign on doors: "*In case of*

Brahms, exit here." From the perspective of modernism, these battles were, though stimulating and durable, largely irrelevant, since Wagner, whatever one might think of his compositions, was bitterly hostile to the modern, to modernity, let alone to modernists. His choice of medieval legends was not an accident; it suited his claims for the innate superiority of German culture. His famous friendship with Friedrich Nietzsche suffered public shipwreck when the latter found the Christian tendencies of Wagner's last composition, *Parsifal* (1882), quite intolerable. Nietzsche objected not just to Wagner's newly emphasized religiosity but to his German chauvinism. Indeed, for Wagner, the most conspicuous modern phenomenon was assimilated Jews, to him an uncreative, mendacious, and money-grubbing race. To call Jews the most modern of moderns was clearly not a compliment either to the present-day world or to Jews.

MODERNISTS: PACESETTERS

1.

IF, FOR ALL HIS LASTING FAME and influence, Wagner, who ultimately did not challenge traditional tonality, does not belong among the founders of modernism, two of his younger contemporaries, Claude Debussy (1862–1918) and Gustav Mahler (1860–1911), were late nineteenth- and early twentieth-century pacesetters for its artistic self-liberation. The two had much in common: an iron-willed determination to follow their own internal commandments; a need to transcend, perhaps abolish, rules they had imbibed in their academic training, an overriding aspiration to achieve what the French-American modernist composer Edgard Varèse would later memorably call "the liberation of sound." They wanted harmonies that would, as Debussy once laconically put it, "drown tonality." Both knew that they were musical revolutionaries, though they were advocating, and carrying through, very different revolutions. And what they did not have in common—the music they wrote—was more important and more interesting than their shared aims.

All his life, Debussy wrestled with the dominant impact of Wagner, at once learning from and reacting against him. Born in 1862, he entered the Conservatoire at the age of eleven and suffered through, though also grudgingly benefited from, its severely scholastic school-ing. But already as a boy, when he irritated his piano teacher by devis-ing sacrilegious little preludes, he had been headstrong about taking orders only from himself. This would come to mean stretching the array of traditional harmony and experimenting with tonality beyond accepted bounds, all in the service of sonority. Everyone knows his *Prélude à l'après-midi d'un faune* (1894), which early documented his daring. He became a great emancipator of sound for its own sake and recognized, as a true modernist, that he was largely walking a lonely path. Many a composer, he wrote after 1900, "is engaged in listening modestly to the voice of tradition which prevents him, it seems to me, from hearing the voice that speaks within him." It was not a false mod-esty of which Debussy, the great subjectivist, would ever be guilty.

His defiant sense of himself as his only true source of inventiveness survived into maturity to serve him as a steadying anchor. Still, as a young composer, he had managed to win the coveted Prix de Rome in 1884, though not on the first try. In the following year, settled but not happily settled in Rome, he characteristically protested that the Acad-emy, though it had chosen him to spend three years composing in pre-sumably inspiring company, would not approve of his compositions. "Naturally, it considers that the path it prescribes is the only right one. But, it can't be helped! I am too fond of my freedom, and of my own ideas." All the feelings, and to some extent the idiom, of modernism— "I am too fond of my freedom"—are concentrated in this assertion.

Clearly, most of the music appreciated in academic circles was of no interest to him. Fleeing to distant centuries, to the masses of Orlando di Lasso and Palestrina, filled with the wonder of discovery, Debussy dis-paraged the pious effusions of "Gounod and Co." as expressions of "hysterical mysticism," which to his mind was nothing better than "a sinister farce." He was willing to forgive Gounod—after all, he was French and had escaped the influence of Wagner. Still, what he wanted was above all the truth, truth in the feelings experienced by the com-poser and truth in the compositions conveyed to his listeners. Sounding much like the psychological pointillist Knut Hamsun in his novel *Hunger*, Debussy noted, while still in Rome, how "difficult it is to render the thousand and one sensations of a character, while keeping the form as clear as possible," to capture "the lyrical emotions of the soul, and the whims of dreams." These hurdles, he believed, might be overcome only after the constrictions of academic prescriptions and proscriptions had been permanently retired.

The Academy, Debussy realized early, would never countenance such descents into the self. It followed a single, outmoded pedagogical line and narrow-mindedly confined its applause to granting the Prix de Rome, which Debussy, we know, accepted without gratitude. No wonder that one of the official reports about him from Rome to the Paris Academy bluntly expressed disappointment in this promising but disconcerting young prizewinner; he seemed addicted to writing music that is "bizarre, incomprehensible, and impossible to execute." Regrettably, this fellow Debussy was eager to astonish his listeners, steadily in search of unearned originality.

Throughout his life, Debussy returned to this favorite topic. "What a number of things one must first discover and then reject," he wrote in a late letter, "before one can express emotion naked and unadorned." Given the frowning academic atmosphere of his day and of its loyal supporters, his fortunes as the most contentious of composers were almost predictable. For his first masterpiece he chose to orchestrate *L'Après-midi d'un faune*, a poem by Stéphane Mallarmé, that avant-garde master of texture, suggestion, and indirection. He worked for more than two years in the mid-1890s on turning Maurice Maeterlinck's undramatic drama *Pelléas et Mélisande* into an unoperatic opera, filled with subtle atmosphere and internal monologues, but void of arias. Even though this unique opera did not uniformly please the public, it made him famous.

It also baffled, at least at first, most even among open-minded reviewers, though a few well-informed critics understood the groundbreaking nature of Debussy's work. The music critic Gaston Carraud, writing in 1902, argued that "in order to satisfy the noblest and most courageous of artistic ideals, M. Debussy . . . has created a music of his own." The influential piano and orchestral music Debussy wrote during the decade and a half that remained to him widened his appeal. And among them his large-scale pieces have kept him on the schedule of symphony orchestras.

The best known, most characteristic of these quasi-symphonies is the tone poem *La Mer* (1905). It is not program music; Debussy did not so much intend to write a portrait of the sea as to convey the feelings, perhaps the associations, aroused by the agitated spectacle. What made his music unforgettable was a happy, almost unique, blending of logic and expressiveness. It is not surprising that reviewers liked to call him a painter, and, disregarding all his objections, compare him to the Impressionists. This much was accurate about their all too easy comparison: Debussy's work was a delicate search, perfectly fitting into the world that modernist painters and poets were pursuing in their own way—the inner life and its felicitous portrayal.

FOR DEBUSSY AS A French composer, life was a campaign against two adversaries, not one: the Academy and Richard Wagner. The first came to him naturally and aroused no conflicts in him. As for the second, it is not that Debussy was a chauvinist, feeling obliged to hate a German composer simply because he was a German. Like many (though not all) modernists, he was cosmopolitan in disposition, at home in an often quarrelsome international family. The Société Nationale de Musique, founded in 1871 in the shadow of the humiliating defeat France had suffered in the war against Prussia, was not to Debussy's taste. He would allow himself to make malicious witticisms against Wagner, "the ghost of old Klingsor"—the wicked magician in *Parsifal*—a remark which his acquaintances spread around; but he also appreciated the composer's power, especially in *Parsifal*. His position was more nuanced than those French writers who insisted on calling Germans *boches*, or on the other side those who sustained the Wagner boom in Paris.

Debussy scorned such simplicities. After his second visit to Bayreuth, in 1889, which, it seems, he thought might clarify his feelings about Wagner (dead these six years but still a living succubus for him), he made a statement that illuminates his aims as a composer as lucidly as it let him come to terms with old Klingsor: "My conception of dramatic art is different. According to mine, music begins where speech fails. Music is intended to convey the inexpressible. I should like her to appear as if emerging from the shadowy regions to which she would from time to time retire. I should have her always discreet." Here was a vital, unbridgeable difference between these two masters: Wagner's music was never discreet.

2.

TANGENTIAL AS THE STUDY of Wagner may be for tracing the early twentieth-century evolution of modernism in music, a very different composer, Gustav Mahler, is highly instructive, for he illuminates with his astonishing symphonies, his illustrious career as a conductor, and the snail's pace of his gathering fame the meandering evolution of music down to the modernist rebellion. Born in 1860, the son of a Jewish distiller in Bohemia, Mahler started his musical career early: at the age of ten, he performed in his first concert as a pianist, and his future as a virtuoso seemed assured. But his ambitions were more exalted than that. In 1875, he began a five-year stint at the Vienna Conservatory, experimented with composing, and then, in 1880, he launched his career as a conductor. Discovering his gift for musical autocracy early, he briefly filled conducting assignments in several provincial capitals where in addition to sharpening his skills, he told a friend, he was "suffering for my masters." But each post was a promotion, until by 1883, still a young man, he was successively appointed to preside over the orchestras in Kassel and Prague, Leipzig and Budapest, Hamburg and, at last, from 1897 on, the Court Opera in Vienna. He had arrived.

Meanwhile, he wrote songs and symphonies. One trait that differentiated Mahler from Debussy was his extraordinary dual career.* There was, to be sure, nothing unusual about a composer on the podium,

---

* As a brilliant pianist, he could have chosen the vocation of a virtuoso performer. Instead, he opted for the double role of conductor and composer.

especially when conducting the premieres of his own compositions. But with Mahler these two professions weighed equally and beautifully fed one another, although his popularity waxed and waned. Many singers and instrumentalists admired him and found his demanding attention highly stimulating. And important composers, Brahms and Tchaikovsky among them, testified that he belonged among the very few first-rate conductors they had had the good fortune to hear. But even they would have admitted that Mahler was not an easy man to work for. Superbly prepared, he was fierce in insisting that his singers and players reach for their highest level, driving them toward as sovereign a performance as their capacities would allow.

Enrico Caruso, caricature of Gustav Mahler (1908).

The list of his reforms at the Vienna Opera, which he ran for ten years, was impressive and gratefully acknowledged by his audiences. He had invincible preferences for Wagner, and Debussy, as well as Mozart and Beethoven; in his early years as a conductor, if one of his local opera companies could manage only Rossini or Verdi, whom he did not particularly value, he felt relieved that the musicians in his charge would have no chance to brutalize his favorites. Showing himself a superb tactician when he could find the time, he subjected his natural impatience to iron self-discipline, and moved patiently to transform the time-honored habits of designers, performers, and audiences alike.

Thus Mahler offered his beloved Wagner as written, restoring the cuts that previous conductors had accepted without protest. He significantly reduced the prominence of the claque, those venal spectators who could be hired to cheer—or to boo—selected singers. He rescued stage sets from their Baroque overloaded massiveness. He made latecomers wait until intermission—this in Vienna! And he created cooperative dramatic ensembles that audiences greatly appreciated and had rarely experienced. No detail was too small for his baleful observant eye. And he felt himself at home in a mood of cultural renewal in the city: painters like Egon Schiele and Gustav Klimt, architects like Adolf Loos and Otto Wagner, the playwright and novelist Arthur Schnitzler, the savage, reform-obsessed cultural critic Karl Kraus, and the founder of psychoanalysis, Sigmund Freud, were only some of the modern spirits to which Mahler's devotion to high quality in the opera also belonged.

MAHLER'S ENFORCING of the highest standards, which guaranteed the supremacy of Vienna as the world's opera capital, had less to do with modernist experiments than with piety toward the masters, a respect for authenticity to which modernists for the most part sincerely subscribed. On the other hand, the nine symphonies he produced between the late 1880s and 1910 during his precious, longed-for summer vacations were radically novel creations, and not only to his mind. Mahler held on to traditional key signatures, but skirted the depths of dissonance and the limits of harmony. The size of his orchestra and the very length of his symphonic works marked him as an ally of the new. In explaining what he was doing in his symphonies, and more, what his symphonies were doing to him, he liked to mark the progress each made over its predecessor. His Third Symphony struck him as immeasurably superior to the Second, a mere child in retrospect.

To say that these expansive monsters meant much to him is to trivialize Mahler's feelings for his music. In 1909, not long before his death, he led his First Symphony in New York and wrote to his friend, the conductor Bruno Walter, that every time he conducted his work, "a burning painful feeling crystallizes itself in me. What kind of world is it that throws up such sounds and figures as a counter-picture? Something like the funeral march and the storm that breaks out seems to me a burning accusation against the Creator." The stakes were high, far beyond what a less metaphysics-spouting composer like Debussy would contemplate.

Nor did Mahler keep such sublime sentiments to himself. "Now imagine a work so *great*," he wrote in the summer of 1896 to the soprano Anna von Mildenburg, one of his loves, "in which actually the *whole world* mirrors itself." He did not like calling his orchestral works symphonies, for, as he commented on his Third, "in nothing do they cling to the traditional forms. To me 'symphony' means building up a world with all the methods of the available techniques. Its ever new and changing content determines its form by itself. In this sense I must first steadily learn again to create my expressive means anew." He came to detest the tone poems so popular in his day; his own programs told no specific tales, and were strictly private fantasies, aides in letting him build up a new world of sounds.* In 1906, commenting on the Eighth Symphony—his "most important work," he thought—he told his friend, the Dutch conductor Willem Mengelberg, "It is the greatest

---

* Interestingly enough, Richard Strauss, some of whose long-drawn-out musical meditations were close to literal translations of events—consider the hanging of Till Eulenspiegel in the tone poem of that name—denied what was palpably true, for him. "A poetic program is nothing but a pretext for the purely musical expression and development of my emotions, and not a simple *musical description* of concrete, everyday facts." The reader is entitled to regard artists' autobiographical declarations, including those of modernists, with a skeptical eye.

thing I have ever done. . . . Imagine that the universe had begun to sound and to ring. These are not human voices any more, but planets and suns circling."

He meant such apotheoses almost literally. In order to realize his grandiose programs, Mahler felt driven to employ the largest possible number of uncommon instruments such as the guitar, the mandolin, the post horn, and to seek his music in regions hitherto unexplored. He did not attempt to reach beyond the assistance that these newcomers could give the vivid and massive color portrait that made up each of his symphonies. At the same time, his implicit democratization of permissible notes and combinations made it almost inevitable that listeners would now and then hear what would strike them as trivial chords, trivial harmonies, trivial melodies. A composer who devoted a sizable movement in his First Symphony to variations on the canon "*Frère Jacques, Frère Jacques,*" even if unconventionally presented in a minor key, could hardly expect anything less. Shifting keys from major to minor, as he chose to do more than once, depending on the powerful resonance of percussion, Mahler enjoyed the vast volume open to drums and tympanum to make audible what he called, in his Third Symphony, "A Midsummer Noon's Dream."

THOUGH PROUD OF his technical competence, honing it as he did in his exalted and burdensome conductor's calling, Mahler saw himself like other creative musicians the servant of higher powers. However egomaniacal his rhetoric might sometimes seem, he did not confuse himself with God any more than other modernists did. "One is, so to speak," he wrote to a friend, "only an instrument on which the universe is playing." Describing how he felt virtually forced to compose his Eighth Symphony, he gave credit to the "spiritus creator" that "shook and whipped me for eight weeks until the greatest part was finished." He found the steps to a loftier rung on the ladder of accomplishment a frightening experience, as though he were pregnant with his compositions. "That is far, far larger than life size," he wrote about the Third Symphony, "and everything human shrinks like a realm of pigmies. I am gripped by true horror when I see what this is leading to, what path is reserved for music, and that I have been given the awful vocation of bearing this gigantic work."

Like Debussy, Mahler was principally concerned to establish the sovereignty of the sounds he invented and constructed, to let them blossom in his own and his listeners' minds. "My need to speak out musically, symphonically," he wrote to the music critic Max Marschalk in 1896, "begins only where the *dark* sentiments rule, at the door leading into the other world." Unconscious speaking to unconscious; one creator's subjectivity awakening others' subjectivities: this made his music suspect to traditionalists and at times overwhelming to more sympathetic audiences. In short—and this sort of talk could only amuse readers in the less overwrought Anglo-American cultures—he was convinced that he had been chosen "to be a destiny."

Though Mahler frequently resorted to conservative musical reminiscences, that destiny stamped him an avant-garde composer. The very volume and length of his symphonies—several of them take well over an hour—were potent pieces of evidence for their novelty. Yet not everything about them was innovation. Four of the nine completed symphonies incorporated singers, but one might (and most did) regard this feature as a nostalgic tribute to Beethoven. No doubt Beethoven's Ninth Symphony with its choral last movement had much to answer for.

Yet (to borrow his own excited language), whatever burst out of him like a mountain stream with all sluices suddenly opened while he was composing was music unknown to earlier symphony composers. It was as though the more or less conventional surfaces of his large-scale compositions covered, but barely concealed, untried harmonies, rhythms, and key relationships. His adventurous tonalities violated the traditional rules that composers had hitherto employed, and to pursue their course was to enter regions that could only dismay the habit-minded critic and stir the listener, whether pleasurably or painfully. He found it possible to incorporate popular music into his symphonies and demand the most sizable menu of sounds, all elements in the world he was building from materials that, he believed, had always lain within him.

Far more strenuously than Debussy, then, Mahler had to build up his reputation among leading composers against strong resistance. Yet in hindsight he belongs to the small clan of truly subversive composers, an exposed position assigned to him, interestingly enough, by Arnold Schoenberg, the most uncompromising of all modernists. At first hostile, as one might expect, Schoenberg had a lightning conversion in December 1904, after hearing the dress rehearsal of Mahler's Third Symphony in Vienna. He wrote Mahler a gushing letter, in as exalted a tone as Mahler used about his own compositions. The letter is worth quoting because it strikingly illustrates the poetic, indeed metaphysical, language common to German (or Germanic) musicians talking of their work and, just by the way, the confusing alliances among composers at the turn of the century. "In order to get hold in some measure of the unheard-of impression that your music made on me," Schoenberg told Mahler, "I may not speak to you musician to musician, but as man to man. For: I have seen your soul, naked, stark naked. It lay before me like a wild, mysterious landscape with its horrifying shallows and abysses, and by their side cheerful, charming sunny meadows, idyllic places to rest." Once launched in this confessional style, Schoenberg went on undismayed: "I felt the battles about illusions, I sensed the pains of the disillusioned one, I saw good and evil forces wrestling with one another. . . ." After such an accolade, what doubts remain about Mahler's place among the titans of music?

MODERNISTS: ARNOLD SCHOENBERG

1.

USUALLY, HISTORIANS OF music have treated Debussy and Mahler as "transitional" figures, as though they functioned as a kind of bridge between the virtually impassable gulf dividing classical composers and modernists. One can see why: had these composers not stretched accustomed harmonies to their very boundaries and at times even gone beyond them? But admirers of Debussy's *La Mer* or Mahler's Eighth Symphony could justly object to the general notion that their composers' work was a mere passageway from one extreme to another. The two greatest representatives of modernism, Schoenberg and Stravinsky,

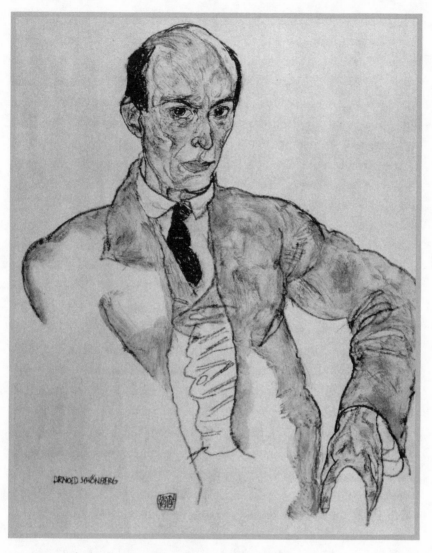

Egon Schiele, drawing of Arnold Schoenberg (1917).

made their revolutions from a variety of sources, from pitting long-forgotten traditions against the standard classics, from discontent with time-honored rules, and from the radical pressure not merely to defy these rules but also to construct wholly new foundations for music.

Born in Vienna in 1874 into a relatively poor Jewish family—they could nonetheless manage to have their visibly talented son take lessons in the violin—Arnold Schoenberg began composing as a boy and educating himself in music with the support of generous and appreciative friends. His parents, he would recall drily, were no more hostile to music than the average Austrian family. A true autodidact, often prompted by severe doubts, Schoenberg was persistently sure of one thing: that his composing manifested itself as an overriding internal compulsion. "My imagination," he wrote in 1912, "that is myself, for I am myself only a creature of this imagination."

Eleven years later, replying to an impresario in Berlin who had appealed to his "energy" to write something for him, Schoenberg replied that though this plea might be worth listening to, "unfortunately my energy is a very insubordinate being which is the foundation of its very existence. She is so unwilling to grant favors, and she does not even permit me to order her around. She is there or not, she does what she pleases." As he had told Vasili Kandinsky on January 24, 1911, in his first letter to the painter, he shared his new acquaintance's goal: pure subjectivity. It is "what you call the 'illogical,' and I call 'the elimination of the conscious will in art.'" The music he wrote, however deeply rooted in musical history it turned out to be, must all come from within.

For Schoenberg, this dependence on the subjective was not confined to musical theory; his private voyage through the confessions was tense and circuitous, and impinged on the texts he wanted to set. Raised as a Roman Catholic, he converted to Protestantism in 1898, a distinctly independent and sincere option for the citizen of a country beholden to Rome. But a display of anti-Semitism in postwar Austria, and, in 1923, his belief that his friend Kandinsky had been overheard making anti-Semitic remarks, propelled his thinking in a more familiar direction: he came home. In an irate letter to Kandinsky, he protested against the latter's reported bigotry, and professed himself a Jew. He now ceased worrying about the "organized fetters" that had once troubled him: he was and would firmly remain a Jew.*

---

* The story has never been cleared up. For the record, it was Alma Mahler, a rather unreliable gossip, who seems to have been Schoenberg's informant. Kandinsky always professed himself to have been shocked at Schoenberg's charge, and vehemently denied it.

Schoenberg did not fight his battles alone. And one of his enthusi-asts, Vasili Kandinsky, shows that the artistic frontier crossings so familiar in the arts were by no means unknown among modernists. It is an interesting story. On January 2, 1911, the Rosé Quartet traveled to Munich from Vienna with assorted performers to give a concert of recent compositions by Schoenberg. They included the sensational Second String Quartet, which came with an intriguing prehistory: its premiere in Vienna in December 1908 had caused a riot, and Schoen-berg was already fairly well known in advanced circles as the composer who had "abandoned tonality."

Among the expectant avant-garde audience was Kandinsky. Highly cultivated, sensitively responsive to music, a respectable cellist, he found Schoenberg's unfamiliar, partly atonal compositions a revela-tion. One aesthetic product of his sudden infatuation was a canvas he started the next day, *Impression III (Concert)*, which owes at least some-thing to nature: a large black splotch must stand for the grand piano on the stage; a cluster of primitively drawn shapes represents the audience. Kandinsky wrote to Schoenberg and the two men established a friend-ship, largely by correspondence. Both were at one in being determined to listen as much as they could to a single inspiration: themselves.

Not long after this fateful concert, the two friends became involved in an unexpected, historically important collaboration. Kandinsky, an inveterate joiner and organizer of cultural lobbies, had actively pro-moted the radical anti-naturalism he was developing, but found little response even among the "progressive" artists with which Munich was then abundantly supplied. But he found one convert, the painter Franz Marc, something of a nature mystic—he would become famous for his startling, beautifully painted *Tower of Blue Horses*—and late in 1911, the two decided to publish a collective volume of essays, photographs, scores, and illustrations, *The Blue Rider Almanac*, that would conve-niently gather together the truly new painting and its sympathizers in other fields. Kandinsky contributed some of his recent paintings and several polemical essays that firmly supported his case for a spiritual revolution in the arts. Marc was there with articles on modern art and, among the paintings, one featuring horses of various colors. And

Schoenberg, on whose participation Kandinsky fiercely insisted, was prominent with two paintings, scores of his compositions, and some provocative modernist prose. Books, we have heard often, have their fates; much of it is a matter of timing. The *Blue Rider Almanac*, which has become among cultural historians a monument to Expressionist German art in the years just before the war, enjoyed by no means so warm a reception on its first appearance in 1912.

SCHOENBERG ALSO FOUND support closer to his own professional circles. His two favorite pupils, Anton Webern and Alban Berg, both gifted composers, became his friends and dependable publicists. And concert managers, conductors, publishers, at least some of them, thought Schoenberg's music eminently worth performing. We hear of Schoenberg concerts in Leipzig, London, Amsterdam, Prague, Copenhagen. Yet Schoenberg trusted few among the middlemen of culture; he deluged them with precisely numbered instructions as to the quantity of required rehearsals, the quality of the singers, the need to have him conduct the first performance, to say nothing of voicing irritation with the inadequate respectfulness his correspondents had displayed. He took it all very seriously. "Recently," he wrote in 1914, "I have come to feel every inadequate presentation of a work of art more and more as a major crime, as immoral." A consciousness of his own vast importance is implicit in this pronouncement. One can see why Schoenberg disliked the business part of his existence: "nothing brings people closer than business. But I love distances."

All his life, then, Schoenberg erected some of the barriers of which he so bitterly (and often justly) complained. He never changed his tune, even on celebratory occasions. Collectively thanking the horde of friends and admirers who in 1949 had warmly congratulated him on his seventy-fifth birthday, he headed his reply pathetically with the declaration: "To be recognized only after one's death—!" He asked rhetorically why he had persevered "despite the resistance of the whole world." In his answer, he returned once again to his familiar thought of an irresistible inner pressure forcing him into a creative passivity that crushed any prudential considerations. The two more years he had to live did nothing to change this appraisal, at once gloomy and arrogant. Like other inspired prophets, he too "had had to say things, apparently unpopular, that had to be said." No doubt; but the embattled life of this principal modernist composer shows that the alienation between the producer and the consumers of high culture was at times a two-way street.

2.

SCHOENBERG'S ADVANCE to modernism came in 1907 and 1908, as he started to sketch out his Second String Quartet and several piano pieces. He had previously composed some appealing late Romantic works like *Verklärte Nacht*, but, driven by nameless forces he had barely started to comprehend, he began to investigate yet unharvested territory. In early 1910, in the program notes for an evening devoted to his compositions, he summed up what he had to expect—and had already experienced—for his uncompromising deviations, beginning with songs after poems by Stefan George, a cult poet for the German cultural elite. In those *Lieder*, "I succeeded for the first time to get close to the ideal of expression and form that has been occupying me for years. Before, I had lacked the energy and self-assurance to realize it. But now that I have finally taken this path, I am aware that I have broken through all the barriers of a past aesthetic."

Breaking through barriers—what could be a more eloquent, if hackneyed, metaphor to convey his bid for independence? It was a phrase that, among other aggressive statements, he used in the texts from Stefan George that he set for his Second Quartet. He was only too aware, he wrote, that he could already sense "the resistance I shall have to overcome"; he felt "the heat of the rebelliousness that will rouse even the calmest temper." Even those who "have believed in me thus far, will not want to see the necessity of this development." But (and this, as we have noted, he would repeat all his life) he could not help himself. He was obeying "an internal compulsion stronger than any training."

In 1909, in a letter to the composer and piano virtuoso Ferruccio Busoni, who had shown some interest in his innovations, Schoenberg detailed what this compulsion meant to him, highlighting the importance of each item by treating the list as though it were verse: "I strive for complete liberation from all forms / from all symbols of cohesion and / of logic. / Thus / away with 'motivic working out.' / Away with harmony as / cement or bricks of a building / Harmony is expression / and nothing else. / Then / Away with Pathos! / Away with protracted ten-ton scores from erected or constructed / towers, rocks, and other massive claptrap. / My music must be *brief.*" Hence his early confession of faith, which he would fully realize and even exceed, as he came to compose works of substantial length.

Schoenberg's radical program called for what he named the "emancipation of the dissonance"; one should see dissonance not as the adversary of consonance but as its extension. This was the program he meant to illustrate with his Second String Quartet, a work almost breathtakingly unconventional. What it did to its hearers was largely to deprive them of the expected signature of a stable key underlying the music. It had intervals of beauty recognizable to ordinary listeners in some passages, but to most ears, even well-schooled ones, much of the quartet was chaos. To make this impression all the more forceful, Schoenberg added a soprano for the last two movements—an innovation that underscored the sisterhood of music and poetry. And to make his subversive intentions all the more provocative, he opened the program with this quartet to intensify the listeners' shock. Eyewitnesses report, not without chagrin, that he succeeded beyond measure.

3.

IN THE YEARS THAT FOLLOWED, Schoenberg composed fairly little; between 1916 and 1923, he was largely busy pondering his mission and battling the infidels. Some of his early work, most notably *Pierrot Lunaire* (1912), even secured a certain following, though it rarely appeared in the standard repertoire of symphony orchestras. And this very *Pierrot* documents why: it dramatizes an avant-garde self-portrait of the artist as despised outsider. A selection of three sequences of seven poems each by the French lyric poet Albert Giraud, it takes as its dejected hero that old standby, the clown, here representing the modernist inescapably at odds with self-satisfied bourgeois society.

During these middle years, religion, never wholly absent from Schoenberg's preoccupations, came to take an increasingly conspicuous place in his consciousness. In 1922, again writing to Kandinsky—with whom, through the vicissitudes of war and revolutions, he had lost touch—he told him that for years, religion had been his "sole support," though admittedly "without all organized fetters." The parallels between Schoenberg's mental evolution and that of Stravinsky are beginning to become apparent.

He had given an early hint anticipating his preoccupation with God in a remarkable letter of 1912 to the German poet Richard Dehmel, known for his outspokenness in erotic matters, whose work Schoenberg highly esteemed. The composer confessed that he had "for a long time wanted to write an oratorio that should include how humanity today, which has gone through materialism, socialism, anarchism, which had been atheist, still retains a small remnant of the old faith (in the form of superstition). How this modern man quarrels with God (see also 'Jakob Wrestles' by Strindberg) and finally reaches the point of finding God and becoming religious. To learn how to pray!"

This projected oratorio, a vast scheme, was *Die Jakobsleiter* (*Jacob's Ladder*), for which he completed the first two of three parts by 1917, and intermittently resumed without ever bringing it to a close. After Dehmel had politely refused to undertake the text, Schoenberg wrote it himself, and it bears the mark of his workmanlike manner. The main voice in the oratorio is the archangel Gabriel, surrounded by and directing seekers, men aware of their sins, acknowledging their failure to pray. At the end, a gigantic chorus would join all forces on stage to sing the praises of prayer. Higher than the pilgrims whom Gabriel guides, there stands "the Chosen—*der Auserwählte*," closer to God than the others, a mortal who bears Schoenberg's features. The composer was never self-effacing about his place among other men (let alone women, that credulous sex), even though resentfully aware that the public failed to appreciate him. Had he not exclaimed as early as 1910 that his name "today already belongs to music history"? He was then just thirty-six years old.

Schoenberg spent much time learning how to pray, in and through music. It is perhaps appropriate that of all his major works, the powerful biblical opera *Moses und Aron*, composed between 1930 and 1932 but never completed—just like *Jacob's Ladder*, it lacks a third act—is the work most frequently, though still not regularly, performed. But humility in prayer did not preclude arrogance against the "masses." Schoenberg's rejection of the society around him—among all the anti-modern modernists he was one of the most bellicose—appeared most openly after the war.

His tone grew ever harsher: his only name for skeptics, adversaries, or opponents was "enemies." And his cultural politics, always patrician, only grew more exclusive. He numbered himself among "the better people," who, he said, made enemies more quickly than friends. In the fall of 1924, having been invited to conduct his *Serenade* at a musicfest organized and financially supported by the Austrian prince Egon Fürstenberg at Donaueschingen, he took the occasion to tell his friend Adolf Loos that the festival had "recently confirmed" his "dislike of democracy and the like." There was nothing new about such denunciations; Debussy had already inveighed against "the mediocrity of the herd mind."

IF SCHOENBERG HAD a fanatic's faith in the course he had shown the musical world, he was also obsessed perhaps as intensely, if less publicly, by the aspiration to make himself into a critic of contemporary society. It was, he thought, vulgar in tone, mercantile in ideals, and hopelessly indifferent to higher things. Its watchword was philistinism. As we have seen, Schoenberg was anything but a populist. "Inwardness," he wrote to the young conductor Hermann Scherchen in 1914, "the chaste, higher forms of feelings, seems to be denied to most humans." A cultural aristocrat, he was troubling himself only with fellow aristocrats; the mob, the *Pöbel*, was beyond the pale, and even some of the cultivated upper crust struck him as being less than loyal to his ideals.

Schoenberg's own social background was scarcely distinguished: his father had migrated to Vienna from Pressburg, married in his new home, and spent his life on the margins of the working class and the petty bourgeoisie. But being allowed to take violin lessons was a supreme moment in Schoenberg's life; almost the day he took up the instrument (we have his word for that), he began to compose, although, he adds, for some seven years he imitated whatever model came to hand. His atonality, the most original of musical styles, was a product of his thirties.

4.

REVOLUTIONARY AS IT WAS, atonality was not destined to be Schoenberg's final resting place as a composer and theoretician. During the war, he began to reflect on the need for a framework that might stabilize his emancipation of dissonance. He had achieved freedom and now he sought discipline—a governing organization that would in no way inhibit the musical elbow room he had gained from 1908 on. Thus he developed, in the greatest secrecy and with quiet experiments, what his disciple Anton Webern—who, with Alban Berg, immediately took to it—called the "twelve-tone law." It seems that Schoenberg first spoke of this in 1921 on a walk with his pupil and follower Josef Rufer, and told him in a moment of exultation: "I have made a discovery that will secure the preeminence of German music for the next hundred years."

However energetically Schoenberg tried to keep the outside world from his study door, the war and its consequences necessarily impinged on him. Rather like Debussy some thirty years earlier, he was not particularly nationalistic, but the loss of the war, the brutal peace treaties imposed on Germany and Austria by the Allies, and the continuing disdain from the West, notably the French, was more than he could tolerate. So much for his French and Russian rivals! He, the Austrian Jew, would write outstanding German music.

His technical discovery, which came to be called "serialism," looks rigid but is actually quite flexible. It takes each of the twelve notes of the chromatic scale, ordering them at the beginning of a piece, and using fragments of the scale, usually three notes, as the nucleus of a melody. Since these nuclei can be inverted, played upside down and backwards, they give the composer wide leeway within the desired frame—disciplined autonomy. It was, he warned, a difficult system to learn, but the order it imposed seemed to him amply worth the trouble.

In a long, didactic article of 1941 on this recent dispensation, Schoenberg said once again that he had not willed his manner of writing music; it had been imposed on him: "The method of composing with twelve tones grew out of a necessity." And in an interesting aside, he generalized his own iron-fisted self-assurance into a rule for all composers: "Whether one calls oneself conservative or revolutionary, whether one composes in a conventional or progressive manner, whether one tries to imitate old styles or is destined to explore new ideas—whether one is a good composer or not—one must be convinced of the infallibility of one's own fantasy and one must believe in one's own inspiration." All composers are puppets in the hands of that mysterious puppeteer, whether we call it God or Muse or the Unconscious.

5.

THIS CONQUEST OF ORDER that Schoenberg secured not long after the Great War coincided, and I believe interacted, with his increasingly vocal commitment to German musical history. He never regretted, and never rejected, his first innovations. But he came to place considerable weight on the debts he owed the past. Far from valuing the dubious distinction of being a kind of scarecrow in music made, as he put it, to frighten the peasants, he claimed to be keeping up good old tradition. "Good old tradition"—we shall see what the middle-aged Stravinsky would do with that. Meanwhile, it should be plain why Schoenberg should have told Rufer, on first revealing his twelve-tone method, that he wanted the world to see him as a link in that great and admirable German chain. He had at last found a place to stand.

Sometime in the early 1930s, in a draft for an article, Schoenberg

drew up an enlightening list of his "teachers." At the top, he named
Bach and Mozart; in the second tier, Beethoven, Brahms, and Wagner;
and then, for good measure, Schubert, Mahler, Richard Strauss, and the
highly regarded Max Reger. No Berlioz, no Debussy, no Ravel—the
absence of the French modernists powerfully attests to Schoenberg's
remaining musical patriotism. His originality, he added with a touch of
humility, rested on having immediately imitated the good things he had
seen. He was trying to integrate his revolutionary system into the honored German musical culture.

His most striking attempt in that vein came in 1937, when he set
Brahms's G-minor Piano Quartet for orchestra. It was one of his
favorite pieces by a composer he admired, a work too little known, he
thought, and abundant in thematic beauties that orchestrating it would
reveal. Four years earlier, just before emigrating from Hitler's Germany, he had written (and would eventually publish) a remarkable lecture on "Brahms the Progressive." Far from being the heavy-handed,
crusty conservative that listeners with forward-looking tastes had
every right to dismiss—Schoenberg maintained—Brahms had, especially in his late work, boldly experimented with thematic, harmonic,
and rhythmic devices of an inventiveness that did not look back to
Beethoven but ahead to, well, Schoenberg.

Yet history would not let him rest. In January 1933, Adolf Hitler
was appointed chancellor of Germany, and Schoenberg, who had been
living and teaching in Berlin, rapidly drew the consequences. He officially rejoined the Jewish confession, and left Nazi Germany precipitously in May. His first, brief stop was Paris, and then, in October, he
came to the United States, which was to be his home until his death in
1951. He was but one of a small army of distinguished refugees from
Nazi Germany and Nazi Austria who both saved their lives and transformed a country that had long—though quite inaccurately—been
called a land without culture.

Yet his loyalty to the great German tradition, wholly compatible
with his modernism, did not make Schoenberg's career easier. His
responses—to slights real and imagined, performances insufficiently
rehearsed, impresarios daring to revise or cut any of his scores—had

always been extreme and brought out the martinet who insisted point by point on conditions of performance that must not be touched under any circumstances. Now, growing old—apart from enjoying his single indulgence, tennis—his ill temper grew more marked. Of course, none of this reduces in the slightest the historic importance of the upheaval he made in music. It is perhaps too much to ask that the maker of a far-reaching revolution also have a sense of humor. To be a modernist was always harder than to go through life safely conventional. Whatever the causes, there is precious little laughter in Schoenberg's music.

MODERNISTS: IGOR STRAVINSKY

1.

THE CONTRAST BETWEEN Schoenberg's dominant earnestness and Stravinsky's frequent exhilaration could scarcely be more marked, yet both have an indefeasible claim to a place in the pantheon of modernist music. Born near St. Petersburg in 1882, Stravinsky could not have been better prepared for his calling if he had designed it himself. His father, Fyodor Stravinsky, was the leading bass baritone on the Russian opera stage and, into the bargain, a passionate bibliophile, who surrounded himself with scores and musical literature. In a volume of reminiscences, Stravinsky gave his parents scant credit for his spectacular career, but at least they provided him with piano lessons and encouraged him to persevere: they recognized his palpable talent at the keyboard, which included an enviable gift for sight-reading. All his life, he would compose at the piano.

There was nothing precocious about his growth into a composer, but he benefited from a stroke of luck, the kind of luck that has a way of blessing the well prepared. At the University of St. Petersburg, studying law, he made friends with Vladimir Rimsky-Korsakov, the composer's youngest son, and this connection, expanding from son to father and then to the whole clan, required only a few short steps. Before long, the celebrated Nikolay Rimsky-Korsakov made himself Stravinsky's informal musical adviser. The young student he counseled must have shown his brilliance early.

One of the most powerful figures in contemporary Russian music, Rimsky-Korsakov was a perplexing guide, for he seemed to be pointing in two directions. Famous for his operas and the orchestral *Sheherazade Suite* (1888), he took more pride in his technical accomplishment than in his popular compositions. Though a professor at the Conservatory, he was impatient with what he deplored as the unimaginative academicism, the merely formal lip service to rules, foisted on pupils in their training; yet at the same time he insisted on the need for fledgling composers to master the formal techniques of his métier, chiefly composition and harmony. Much like Picasso, who believed that the painters of his time did not study drawing enough, Rimsky-Korsakov championed the thoroughgoing teaching of music's fundamentals. This was precisely the advice the young Stravinsky needed and gladly took; through all his career, even the obstinate minority who disliked his compositions as empty of ideas acknowledged that he had superbly orchestrated them.

THE FIRST AFTER Rimsky-Korsakov to recognize Stravinsky's burgeoning genius was the great Russian impresario Sergei Diaghilev, ever in search of new talent for his traveling company, the Ballets Russes. Flamboyant, vain, deeply knowledgeable about the arts, confident in his grasp of each dramatic or musical detail—today one would call him a micromanager—he was an executive at once exciting and difficult. He was stubborn, jealous of any of his protégés' independent activities, addicted to imperious telegrams and hampered by infatuations that at times vitiated his judgment. But Stravinsky, not at all interested in or disturbed by Diaghilev's homosexual involvements, liked the man and got on with him: "that great personality," he called him in his autobiography. And for two decades, his musical production was closely linked to "the director." Only ten years older than Stravinsky, Diaghilev had a habit of command that suited the younger man to perfection.

In 1909, Diaghilev, bypassing more seasoned composers, commissioned Stravinsky to write a "Russian" ballet for him, offering him a text that he and his crew had soldered together from an old folk tale. It would become *L'Oiseau de feu*. Stravinsky complied, though he was still inexperienced in composing ballets, or in working to order. In those days, he would recall later, the ballet, long the province of aristocratic patrons and elderly lechers, was beginning to benefit from a revival in Russia, and he went to work, composing with unusual rapidity. On June 25, 1910, in Paris, headquarters of balletomanes, a select and knowledgeable audience witnessed the premiere of *The Firebird*. Not yet twenty-eight, for all the reminiscences a trained ear might trace to earlier composers, Stravinsky had provided the pleasures of heresy, and neither listeners nor critics were shocked by it. Overnight Stravinsky belonged to the world. He was no longer anyone's pupil, not even Rimsky-Korsakov's.

A year later, Stravinsky's second ballet for Diaghilev's company, *Pétruchka*, also premiered in Paris. The dancer Vaslav Nijinsky, his impresario's young lover, inarticulate, impulsive, but, once engaged, amazing on the stage, danced the title role and contributed to the ballet's breathtaking reception. But the triumph was really Stravinsky's. The music, more slender, more controlled than that of *The Firebird*, well-informed listeners including Debussy agreed, was remarkable for its radiance, its youthfulness, its sheer originality. Its success, Stravinsky wrote to a friend back in St. Petersburg, setting aside all reserve, "was colossal and increasing." Among the many reviewers enthusiastic over this new star, the French composer Alfred Bruneau, writing in the Paris daily *Le Matin*, perceptively identified the contribution that Stravinsky was beginning to make to musical modernism: "The sounds of the piano, mixed with those of the orchestra, give it a quite new character. Its orchestration, amusing, subtle, flavorsome, has an extraordinary sonic richness. Its form possesses complete freedom." It was precisely this freedom that Stravinsky had been aiming at from the first.

But his third ballet for Diaghilev, *Le Sacre du printemps*, which premiered in 1913 like its predecessors in Paris, provided a strikingly different experience. Anyone who knows just one thing about Stravinsky knows that the opening performance of *The Rite of Spring* provoked noisy demonstrations in the audience, booing, whistling, cat-calling, quarreling with neighbors. At last an avant-garde work received by the philistines as it should have been!

But this conventional perception is too facile. The audience was largely the same as its predecessors: the social elite, a few dozen of the composer's admirers ready to counter any audible manifestation with equally audible applause, and an unknown number of balletomanes who had already demonstrated their affection for Stravinsky's inventions. The reasons remain unclear. But we have evidence that Diaghilev had little objection to making his favorite Paris audience witness some scandalous music, dancing, and choreography. The original idea for the *Sacre* had been Stravinsky's, a stunning visual fantasy that had come to him while he was composing *L'Oiseau de feu*: a primitive rite in which a chosen virgin dances herself to death. The vision was enacted much as he had glimpsed it. But the music was indeed outrageous: thumping, static, and for many listeners, nerve-wracking. It had practically no conventional melodies; instead, the audience was treated to fortissimo, abrupt, frequently repeated chords like so many rhythmic explosions. This was anti-romanticism at its most ruthless. Interestingly enough, later presentations of the *Sacre*, whether in repeat performances or in a concert version, were consistently and warmly applauded. So rapid and uncontested a shift from pariah to classic was given to few modernists. But, then, Stravinsky was the exception that made the self-pity of those representing the rule, like Schoenberg—"to be recognized only after one's death"—all the easier to comprehend.

2.

THE MODERNIST CREDENTIALS of *Le Sacre du printemps* are unmistakably authentic, with its disquieting score and its birth in the composer's startling daydream. What of its predecessors? Ballet scores, however powerfully they bear the imprint of a single imagination, are a collective effort, and Stravinsky, though he was deeply involved in the shaping of all these productions, freely acknowledged that he also had others—conductors, choreographers, dancers, designers—to thank for his triumphs. Speaking in his autobiography of the applause that greeted *The Firebird* in Paris, he quickly adds, "I am, of course, far from attributing this success solely to the score."

Still, Stravinsky's precious individuality remains manifest, and dominant, in these early masterpieces. From his first years in music and throughout his lengthy composer's life—he died in 1971 at the age of eighty-nine, writing interesting music to the last—he insisted on being his own man. One day, debating with Maurice Ravel, himself a faultless modernist, the rules governing the alternation between major and minor keys, Stravinsky said he saw no reason to respect any set of laws: "*If I want to, I can.*" Had he boasted a coat of arms, he might have chosen this laconic sentence as his device.

There were other ballets to come, each of them sufficiently different from their predecessors, and all of them only cementing his international reputation. They confirm Stravinsky's often-repeated horror of repeating himself. The most contentious of them was *Pulcinella* (1920), an adaptation of pieces then attributed to Pergolesi, many of them hitherto unpublished. That concoction gave reviewers the chance to raise the vexed question of sacrilege against eighteenth-century music, but the ballet, delightful and imaginative, is very much Stravinsky's. Persuaded that he had once again made a revolution in composition, if a minor one, he described it as "a new kind of music, a simple music, with an orchestral conception different from my other works." He was vexed that he felt compelled to defend his originality, but it would not be the last time.

MEANWHILE, THOUGH, the vagaries of history had forced on Stravinsky's compositions an unexpected private importance. The 1917 Revolution in Russia, with the deposition of the czarist dynasty, the establishment of the Soviet Union, and its subsequent isolation by the hostile major powers, had stopped the dependable transfer of funds from his possessions on which he had regularly relied; he now had to live on his compositions alone to feed his numerous extended family and, from the early 1920s on, a permanent mistress. Vera Sudeykina was good-looking, much married, from a "good" family but a part-time bohemian, generous, charming, intelligent, and interested in the composer for all the irregularity of her situation. (She regularized it in 1940, marrying him a year after the death of his first wife.)

Fortunately, though, he proved himself a shrewd, exigent, and productive businessman; fortunately, too, he could now call on philanthropists who collected composers, mainly cultivated American magnates and still affluent European aristocrats. For Stravinsky, as for a sizable number of other avant-garde artists, the traditional age of patronage, presumably extinct in the bourgeois period, had survived all too well. Some millionaires raised horses, a significant few others sponsored painters or composers, suggesting a certain stability across centuries that historians in their search for clear-cut historical periods have often slighted.

From 1920, the Stravinskys made Paris their headquarters. They had already lived in the West for several years before the war, mainly in Switzerland, but now voluntary residence was transformed into enforced exile. Nor was this the only dramatic change in Stravinsky's life. He began to strip down his orchestration, to think small, to discard his exuberant "Russian" phase for what came to called his "neoclassical" period. This made him part of a widespread avant-garde retreat from emphatic statements or lush coloring that poets and painters, too, underwent; it was christened by the German collective name of *neue Sachlichkeit*, or new objectivity. This shift in Stravinsky did not entail a return to old-fashioned tonality. His works remained unconventional, his experimental modernism reimagined but largely untouched. Yet, as he confessed, his delight in discovering Pergolesi (or whoever he was) had opened the inexhaustible treasure-house of musical history, and Stravinsky made himself into an energetic tourist among eighteenth- and even seventeenth-century composers in piano works, orchestral pieces, operas, symphonies, and new ballets. He was disciplining his autonomy by widening his focus.

One of these works, the *Symphony of Psalms* of 1930, involved Stravinsky in yet more controversy, largely because his own accounts of his religious commitments are muddled and self-contradictory. Exasperation with artists called as witnesses to their motivations may not be an emotion that a professional historian should feel free to indulge, yet it is perfectly understandable: not that they refuse to testify, but that they testify too volubly and inconsistently. This much we know: for Stravinsky, as for Schoenberg, the 1920s propelled religion toward the center of his life.

THE YOUNG RUSSIAN STRAVINSKY, though showing little piety, had never repudiated his Greek Orthodox religion. But in exile, however French he became, he found the emotional prop of his church far more satisfying than he had in the pre-Revolutionary years. He was under strong pressure from French Catholic intellectuals like the philosopher Jacques Maritain to adopt the Roman version of Christianity, and it tempted him. But in the end he turned back to what he knew best. From 1927 on, he began to attend Orthodox services and to surround himself with decorative sacred objects. They helped to restore his bonds to the Russia he had grown up in and would probably never see again. This psychological turn of a modernist toward a lost emotional home should surprise only those who equate modernism with atheism. Religious belief and unbelief among modernists ranged across the widest possible spectrum, and was independent of their distance from conventionality in the arts.

It does not follow, then, that Stravinsky abandoned originality while he searched, as he put it, for order. He had grown uneasy about what had once been his supreme response to his passion for composition, his individualism. As he told a journalist not long after he had started putting icons on his piano: "Individualism in art, philosophy, and religion implies a state of revolt against God," and he had come to oppose this revolt. Individualism was, like atheism, he had come to believe, "contrary to the principle of personality and subordination before God." But such high-flying generalizations, though eminently quotable, did not affect his fundamental conviction that music is incapable of expressing feelings, including religious ones. Thinking of Wagner's Bayreuth, he vehemently objected to the notion of art as a creed. His newly intensified piety, then, was only one ingredient in that intellectual brew that fed his ever-varying neoclassical middle years. Hence the religious meanings of Stravinsky's *Symphony of Psalms*, if any, must remain indeterminate. He wrote it for the fiftieth anniversary celebration of the Boston

Symphony Orchestra in 1930, and was as astonished as his patrons that he had decided to set passages from the Old Testament for the occasion. He had won his sovereignty, and now he was shoring it up with control.

This would all too soon include the need to find another haven. The Second World War, which started in September 1939 with the Germans invading Poland, made France, where the Stravinskys had felt very much at home, an inhospitable place to wait out the hoped-for defeat of the Nazi war machine. In that month, the Stravinskys, all too aware of the imminent dangers in France, had decided to settle in Los Angeles, and for all its provincialism the city remained the center of their lives until his death in 1971 at the age of eighty-nine. Once the war was over, they regularly traveled to Europe to refresh their minds and their purse; Stravinsky conducted his music, both new and old, delivering lectures and harvesting honors. After Schoenberg's death in 1951, he remained the only titan of modernist music.

LESSER TITANS

2.

ATONALITY AND, EVEN MORE, serialism were the hallmarks of Schoenberg's modernism, and composers like Berg and Webern showed how much diversity such innovations made possible. But there were also other roads to modernism, independent of Schoenberg's inventions, and two composers, the Frenchman Edgard Varèse and the American John Cage, both fired up with truly eccentric ideas, competed with their Austrian contemporaries to create genuinely new music. They were lesser titans, but they had their audiences and their followers. However dry Schoenberg's technical treatises might appear—and they were!— the musical modernists were a colorful lot.

Varèse spent his career in a largely frustrating effort to find new instruments that would generate new tonalities. Schooled as an engineer and mathematician, he was the scientist as musician. The alliance of science—or, perhaps better, technology—with the arts was never to be closer among modernist composers than it was with Varèse. Like other European experimenters, he found in the United States, some-

Edgard Varèse, French-American modernist composer, in his New York apartment, April 14, 1959.

what to his surprise, the land of his future; in 1915 at thirty-two, no longer an apprentice, he came to visit and stayed. He married an American and took out American citizenship. Much like Duchamp, he experienced the enticements of heresy in New York and flourished in what he celebrated as the country most likely to release music from its stifling conventions.

In 1915, the year of his arrival in the United States, Varèse had laid out his program to an interviewer: "Our musical alphabet must be enriched. We also need new instruments very badly," and it seemed to him imperative for musicians to consult "machinery specialists." What he wanted was "new mediums of expression in my work. I refuse to submit myself only to sounds that have already been heard. What I am looking for are new technical mediums which can lend themselves to every expression of thought and can keep up with thought." It is an illuminating statement: in the company of other modernists, Varèse wished for mechanical aids for the sake of inward experience—lending themselves, as he put it, to every expression of thought, turning the most subjective impulse, above all feelings, into the objective correlative of a musical score.

The most familiar fruit of Varèse's transplantation was a piece for orchestra, *Amériques*, a brilliant accolade to his new homeland, completed in 1921 and premiered five years later. It was followed by a rash of orchestral pieces across the 1920s; nearly all of them heavily emphasized percussive instruments—possibly the best known, *Ionisation* (1931), used percussion alone—and turned the drum section into a more important feature than noisy accompanyist. Finally, after the end of the Second World War, newly invented electronic devices seemed to Varèse and his devotees like a belated response to his decades-old agenda.

In Varèse's time, and with his help, musicians' attitudes toward tones—even noise—were in ferment. His famous slogan advocating "the liberation of sound" stimulated reformers' minds. John Cage spoke for a consensus of avant-garde musicians when he paid tribute to his colleague's impact on his profession and the power of his thought: Varèse, he noted, "has often insisted upon imagination as a *sine qua non*, and the presence of his imagination is strong as handwriting in much of his works." For a modernist, committed to the primacy of the inner life in the creative musician, this was grand praise on Cage's part.

2.

JOHN CAGE WAS an authentic American radical. Composer, poet, lecturer, homemade philosopher, who died in 1992 at eighty, he was certainly the most eloquent—at least the most garrulous—among American modernists. He was by far the best known among the country's subversive composers, whose chief contributions to modernism postdate the Second World War. His very extremism in rhetoric and action discloses the length that some rebels against conventional music were ready to go. It is of some interest that Schoenberg, with whom

Cage studied for a short time, denied him the title of composer altogether and called him, in ambiguous appreciation, an inventor of genius.

The most extravagant of Cage's modernist creations is his intriguingly titled *4'33"*, the most stirring piece among the many products of his playfulness. Dating from 1952, it was always, not surprisingly, Cage's favorite. And it may well be the most extreme manifestation of modernist rebelliousness among all of its many domains. In this offering, a pianist "played" the piece sitting on a stage in front of a concert grand (though any other instrument would be perfectly acceptable). He held a stopwatch in complete silence, timing three movements that add up to four minutes and thirty-three seconds; and then, the number over, he got up and left. The well-prepared audience—Cage's listeners had, after all, to expect the unexpected—spent much time after the concert debating this novel "composition."

Fertile and imaginative, Cage had many surprises. But among his compositional principles, "indeterminacy" was the one most widely appreciated and imitated. The rule meant quite simply that a composer would set certain preconditions of performance in a piece he had written, such as its length, without specifying the necessary instrument or the musical content. Those were to be decided by the performer. As in *4'33"*, all "details" were open.

Not surprisingly, Cage made a fetish of unconventionality and of disregarding conventions, and, just by the way, of advertising his creativity. Success, for him, was a warning rather than a gratification; a call to conquer new frontiers. "If my work is accepted," he said, "I must move on to the point where it is not." He made this avant-garde duty a central feature of his mission in life. "I am devoted to the principle of originality," he said. "Obviously, the things it is necessary to do are not the things that have been done, but the ones that have not been done." He shared this frontier perspective, ever awake, ever restless, with other American composers intent on providing novelty at all costs, but he said so more often and more forcefully. Thus, taking note of traffic noise, Cage confessed, "I find it more beautiful than listening to music." In short, he came to receive all sounds as equally privileged, perhaps even more privileged, than those made by an ordinary musical instrument. A member of the audience dropping his program, another whispering to her neighbor, a third coughing, a fourth alert to rain pattering on the roof of the concert hall or an airplane flying close overhead, could become an integral part of a composition.

Cage's act of welcoming non-musical intrusions to musicmaking was typical of those progressive composers in the 1950s who increasingly refused to identify the instruments required to perform their novel works, or had soloists "prepare" a piano—its usual tone altered by strings tied together or encumbered with little wooden blocks. All this was intended to reduce, perhaps eliminate, the time-honored emotional impact of compositions, and to let each passage, each note, contribute to the listeners' pleasure. Anything but the conventional sound.

Cage was an anarchist, both in music and in politics. He intensely enjoyed explaining himself in talks, interviews, and recorded conversations. His creative imagination ranged adventurously, and he was not just compulsively cheerful but programmatically unafraid to take risks—or afraid not to. His agenda in a long life of composing was unpredictable, and he gave his audiences a copious menu of enjoyments and puzzles. Hazarding far beyond the most advanced nineteenth-century composers, he probably infuriated more listeners than he intrigued.

3.

IN SUM, THEN, Schoenberg's early twentieth-century assault on conventional tonality, though exceptional, was far from unique. It had reliable ancestors as well as understanding contemporaries. At least two early twentieth-century Utopians, Ferruccio Busoni, Italian born and German resident, and Alexander Scriabin, Russian virtuoso and composer, experimented with entirely new tonalities. Busoni, piano virtuoso and theoretician as well as composer, with his sweeping projected revisions of harmony, hoped, he said, to escape from "the tyranny of the major and minor system." And Scriabin, increasingly engaged in mysticism in his later years, pursued his system of baffling chords to promote universal happiness. An early manifestation of the importance of a Busoni or a Scriabin came in November 1918, when Schoenberg in Vienna founded the Society for Private Musical Performances, designed to counter the commercialism that governed concert managements. He would put on its programs the composers who were, in his judgment, making noteworthy contributions to the renewal of music, Mahler, Busoni, and other pioneers. Stravinsky, too, belonged to this small family of revolutions, and he remained on Schoenberg's catalog of admirable modernists to the end.

4.

IN THE LAST TWO DECADES of his long life—1951 to 1971—Stravinsky made two moves, together more far-reaching, more spectacular, than exchanging French for American residence: one to the twelve-tone method, the other back to ballet. As for the first, after Schoenberg's death in 1951 he turned his back on the neoclassicism that had sustained him through almost three decades, to adopt the twelve-tone method. In short, Stravinsky, the pronounced opponent of the Second Vienna School, ended up as Schoenberg and Webern's, especially Webern's, belated disciple, and did so creditably.

The public responses were twofold: indifference on the part of "ordinary" music lovers, who had no grasp on technicalities and were content simply to like or dislike Stravinsky's latest venture, and vehement displeasure on the part of those *au courant* with modernist music. They blamed Stravinsky for having waited with his conversion until the end of Schoenberg's life. Some said that Stravinsky was getting bored—or worse, getting boring—at a time when the twelve-tone scheme was all the rage in advanced circles. Others said that Stravinsky was trying to outdo the Austrians—"the first modern architecnologist of our time," an appreciative Stravinsky called Schoenberg—and to demonstrate that, though about to turn seventy, he could handle an unimpeachably modern idiom that other, lesser composers had struggled with for decades.

In the absence of credible testimony from the defector himself, this astonishing switch looks like a claim to competence in all possible unconventional styles, an uncanny flexibility that made Stravinsky the Picasso of modernist music. Like Picasso raiding one style after another and producing great art in them all, Stravinsky had tried his hand across the board of composition and was making impressive, characteristic music again and again.

As for the second "innovation," also dating from the 1950s, Stravinsky revisited the genre that had first made him famous many decades earlier: the ballet. The chief agent for this fertile return was the Georgian dancer and choreographer George Balanchine, who had lived in the United States since 1933, and after eking out a living choreographing musical comedies, ballet interludes in operas, and television specials launched the New York City Ballet in 1948, which became under his direction the most prestigious ballet company in the world. It would be a musical resource for Stravinsky through two decades. The composer of *The Firebird* was back.

THE BALANCHINE ERA

1.

THE EARLIEST ENCOUNTER of Stravinsky and Balanchine went back to 1925, under the aegis of Diaghilev. Their friendship started with Balanchine choreographing a revised version of Stravinsky's *Le Chant du rossignol*, first performed as a ballet five years earlier with choreography by Léonide Massine, then one of Diaghilev's personal and professional favorites. It solidified with an informal alliance, in large part a strategy designed to bear living under the "magician's" autocratic regime without surrendering any artistic integrity. It matured into two decades of the closest cooperation from the early 1950s on. Justly enough, observers of the collaboration have been awed by the harmonious, enormously productive blending of two very different artists to create one alluring ballet after another, significantly extending the traditional canon. Except for the virtual identity of Picasso and Braque in the Cubist period, which did not last nearly so long, no partnership between modernists can compete with Stravinsky and Balanchine's intimacy. It did not end with Diaghilev, but it all started with him.

I have already sketched Diaghilev's outsized presence, opinionated, imaginative, dictatorial, impressively informed about the arts, at times lighthearted about money. Not all his schemes for new soloists or composers, new scenery or new steps, were well advised or ever wholly divorced from the dancer he fancied at the moment. It was typical of him to cut passages from the Stravinsky-Balanchine ballet *Apollon Musagète* (1928) without bothering to consult the authors. Still, the historian assessing the share of dance in modernism must assign Diaghilev a conspicuous place. None of the ballets he nursed into the repertory could ever be performed in Russia, whether imperial or, after 1917, Communist—they were too modern for both regimes. In czarist days the conventions of nineteenth-century ballet still ruled, and after the Revolution, the Soviet state's increasing interference in artistic autonomy made the Ballets Russes' solid engagement with modernist choreography simply ineligible. This alone testifies to Diaghilev's consistent dedication to the joys of heresy. His headquarters were fashionable Monte Carlo and, of course more decisively for his reputation and influence, Paris.

As we recall, Diaghilev had demonstrated his adept instincts in 1909, the year he founded the Ballets Russes, in commissioning the still little known Stravinsky to compose the music for *The Firebird*. After its spectacular triumph, he repeatedly invited Stravinsky to write other, equally original ballets for him. And Balanchine, a meticulously trained dancer and technically sophisticated musician, was another Diaghilev discovery. Still quite youthful, Balanchine had shown himself a genius, nothing less, and that did not escape his first major patron.

Twenty years Stravinsky's junior and invariably respectful though never servile to his older friend, the Georgian Balanchivadze—it was of course Diaghilev who rebaptized him "Balanchine" and tried to mold his cultivation by dragging him to art museums across Europe—had joined the Ballets Russes in 1924, and was thrown into the role of choreographer with little fanfare. This, too, was, Diaghilev's notable adroitness, to disregard Balanchine's youth and inexperience—adroitness and a measure of desperation. The Ballets Russes had lost much of its élan: the splendid principal dancers of the early years had retired, and the

Parisian balletomanes' lust for innovation could hardly be satisfied by the talents available to him—except for Balanchine.

In the five years that remained to Diaghilev—he died in the summer of 1929, of diabetes, which he had taken self-indulgent, perhaps self-destructive, care to ignore in his sweets-laden diet—Balanchine choreographed ten more ballets for the Ballets Russes, but only *Apollon Musagète* to Stravinsky's music. It proved a historic moment. Balanchine would strip the piece even beyond its original spareness, purging what he considered redundant grace notes like colorful decor and costumes, and dropping the opening scene as excessively dramatic. This was modernist ballet reduced to its very bones.

Apollon is a silent conversation among four dancers—the boyish, rapidly maturing Apollo and three of the muses identified with music, Calliope, Polyhymnia, and Terpsichore, of whom Apollo chooses as his partner the last, who presides over dance. Their *pas de deux* became one of the memorable experiences in modern ballet. Not surprisingly, *Apollon* has sturdily survived the passage of time and the caprices of fashion, utterly distant in its simplicity and serenity from the crowded, gleaming spectacle that was traditional ballet, outrageous versions of which had been Stravinsky's specialty before the Great War. Written at a time when he was in the midst of his so-called neoclassical period, Stravinsky borrowed the alexandrine, a classical verse meter, from the giants of French literary neoclassicism, notably Racine and Boileau, to anchor his rhythm.

For this ballet at least, though, the true subversive in the partnership of choreographer and composer was Balanchine. In an uncommon attack of modesty, Stravinsky attributed the triumph of *Apollon* to Serge Lifar's dancing and Balanchine's choreography. Reminiscing half a century later in a rare burst of eloquence—it is a much-quoted statement—Balanchine singled out *Apollon* as a "turning point in my artistic life." Stravinsky's "score," he said, "was a revelation." It "seemed to tell me that I could dare not to use everything, that I could eliminate." This willed economy of means was the choreographer's way of finding an appropriate complement to Stravinsky's neoclassical compositions. "I began to see how I could clarify, by limiting, by reducing what seemed to be multiple possibilities to the one which is inevitable." For

George Balanchine and Igor Stravinsky. An indelible team for
modernist dance and composition.

the New York City Ballet he invented postures and gestures that (as he
knew perfectly well) grossly violated the rules that had long governed
his profession, and that were dimly foreshadowed in *Apollon Musagète*.

The works that Stravinsky composed during these years were strikingly unlike the conventional spectacle that so many balletgoers
adored; the ballets that Balanchine, his collaborator, barely in his twenties, made of them show that the label "classical modernism" need not

be an oxymoron. The famous slogan, "Less is More," that Ludwig Mies van der Rohe coined for architects, aptly applies to Balanchine's ballets. *Apollon Musagète* was one of Diaghilev's last triumphs, and he waxed ecstatic over it—not solely because his lover, Lifar, had so luminously filled the role of Apollo. Diaghilev was a consistent modernist, who with all his foibles was alert to a major revolutionary work.

2.

BALANCHINE'S DEBT to the incomparable impresario who first employed him and granted him abundant authority was limited to being pushed swiftly, indeed precipitously, onto the launching pad for his career. This was not a trivial matter; yet Diaghilev's death would do even more for scattering the modernist ballet across the world than he had ever been able to do during his lifetime. Two members of his old troupe, Serge Lifar and Ninette de Valois, who had shone as soloists, became choreographers and managers of their own companies, the first in Paris, the second in London. Others in his circle, choreographers like Fokine and Massine, also took their talents abroad. But among Diaghilev's brood, Balanchine soon showed himself beyond compare.

A momentous reason for Balanchine's rising to the pinnacle in his highly competitive domain and staying there for decades was his unrivaled musicianship. It was hard work being a modernist choreographer. He studied scores with exceptional sensitivity and, as it were, *saw* the music on stage. Far from merely illustrating it with his dancers' moves, he, in his words, made it visible rather than dominating or copying it. Balanchine did not aspire to make either the music or the dancing an accompaniment to the other. He wanted to allow audiences to hear the composer attentively while at the same time inducing them to follow his interpretations of what they were hearing. No wonder that he became—and remained—Stravinsky's most exciting choreographer.

SUDDENLY DEPRIVED OF reliable prospects with Diaghilev's death, Balanchine took fleeting employment in Paris and Copenhagen, and briefly ran a ballet company of his own. When in 1933 the young American Lincoln Kirstein, a serious balletomane and from a rich family, invited Balanchine to help him found an American company that would join Kirstein's taste backed with money to Balanchine's evident preeminence as a ballet master, Balanchine, at loose ends, accepted immediately. Ever the professional, he began by instituting a school to supply the future needs of an American company, the School of American Ballet. It proved a wise investment; outstanding performers like Tanaquil Le Clerc (later one of Balanchine's four wives) emerged as principal ballerinas in the 1950s with an international reputation.

But the American public was not to be rushed. It was not until April 1948, after disheartening frustrations and detours, that the New York City Ballet presented its first full evening performance at City Center. By then, Balanchine had lived in the United States for fifteen years without ever setting aside Kirstein's vision of establishing modern ballet in America. And it was not for another decade, until 1957, with his setting of *Agon* to Stravinsky's music, that Balanchine could be sure of a stable and enthusiastic public, which he kept to his death in 1983.

The history of *Agon* is yet another exemplar of patronage surviving into a bourgeois age. Kirstein, the intense, importunate, financially liberal benefactor, confronted self-propelled creative spirits who, instead of obediently falling into line with a wealthy man's suggestions, preferred to wait for the right moment, the right image, before feeling inspired to start a new ballet. After the long-lived *Apollon*, recently followed up with a Stravinsky-Balanchine creation, *Orpheus* (1948), Kirstein insistently begged for a concluding "third Act," perhaps featuring Apollo the builder of cities. But Balanchine and Stravinsky delayed and delayed until, discovering an ancient Greece of their own choosing, they came up with *Agon* (1957), a classical contest of wills, a largely abstract, virtually plotless ballet that called out for Balanchine's usual energy, speed, and clarity. Eight women and four men dressed in their practice outfits worked under glaring side lights.

Most notable among the contests that exemplify *Agon* was the famous *pas de deux*, performed by a brilliant white ballerina (Diana Adams) and an equally brilliant black male dancer (Arthur Mitchell), the first of his race to achieve the stellar rank of principal in the New York City Ballet. Balanchine was not being a civil rights activist before his time, but he was intent, characteristically, on dramatizing the sharpest possible contrasts, among others a very black hand on a very white arm. The moment, Melissa Hayden, a principal dancer in the company, recalled, was "really awesome." The modernism of Stravinsky's score was loosely based on seventeenth-century French dances reworked into the twelve-tone scale, which, we know, Stravinsky had recently made his own. As often in modernism, past and future were at peace with one another.

All this was astonishing enough. But the massive success of *Agon* was more astonishing by far, and with this the story departs from the customary fate of avant-garde offerings. Dancers, reviewers, and audiences showed themselves overpowered by what they had seen and wanted to see again. Stravinsky had been so skeptical about the public's probable reception of this highly concentrated, difficult piece that he did not even travel to the New York premiere. In replacement, friends sent him reviews and personal testimonials to prove his pessimism unfounded.

One of these messages stands out. "Just a note to tell you of our pleasure and excitement in performing *Agon*," Diana Adams wrote to Stravinsky. "I wish it were on each program. . . . The audience response is tremendous, they seem to love it, and several more performances have been added. I do hope you have seen the notices, they were marvelous. Congratulations, and thank you for our beautiful, beautiful score." There are not many such tributes in the history of modernism, and Adams's "our" is telling. As Balanchine and Stravinsky belonged to the New York City Ballet, the company belonged to them.

Overwhelming as his achievement proved, Balanchine of course did not corner the market on modernist ballet. He invented some numbers that were anything but radical: humorous, patriotic, even unashamedly traditional. His *Nutcracker*, to Tchaikovsky, was an evening-long celebration of the kind of ballet one could have seen well before Diaghilev, though what particularly endeared his company to new audiences was Balanchine's unprecedented, uncondescending use of children on stage, a novelty that would provide the New York City Ballet with steady, highly profitable standard fare during the Christmas season. And other modernists among choreographers like Frederick Ashton in London, Antony Tudor in New York, and John Cranko in Stuttgart proved themselves interesting competitors to Balanchine, with Tudor acting the psychoanalyst among choreographers. No one could have leveled the charge of superficiality against him; his characters' internal conflicts were a theme to which he repeatedly returned. But it was a criticism to which Balanchine was exposed.

THE HISTORIAN OF modernism dare not overlook this skeptical analysis. Of the two qualities I have singled out as defining modernism, Balanchine's success with the first, committing calculated offenses against conventionality, is beyond cavil. Balanchine's finest designs were rich to bursting with innovations, thrilling and shocking alike. But his investigation of the second, the exploration of subjective experience, was more problematic. His critics insisted that Balanchine's choreography valued technical virtuosity at the expense of his performers' hidden dimensions—that it was, in a word, heartless. No question, Balanchine's major ballets, especially the plotless ones—seeking to be only themselves, ballets—aimed at a rigor that allowed him to use his dancers' bodies as supremely flexible instruments in the making of forms, straining them to the utmost. He was not the first to liberate the dancer's body; that achievement belonged to avant-garde women virtuosos of an earlier generation like Loie Fuller and Isadora Duncan, and in Germany, Mary Wigman. But in its long heritage, ballet had never been so physically demanding as it became in Balanchine's hands.

Balanchine trained, and certainly noticed, ballerinas—and made that significant discovery in ballet, strong masculine dancers—who helped his inventions look easy, or at least appear manageable without imposing excessive physical stresses on the performers. Far from a sadist, he adjusted his choreography to the strengths of individual performers, and decorated his configurations with touches of humor, with a charming mischievousness. But the magnificent bodies who served to translate his balletic imagination into reality struck some viewers as unrevealing about the depths of their feelings, or for that matter Balanchine's own emotional subjectivity. He was as subjective as any abstract artist in listening to his impulses and his supremely personal reactions to the compositions he choreographed. Yet (at least for the doubters) the results appeared to be all too clever, too much like exercises in pattern-making. They seemed rather like one of Freud's case histories, which, though subtle investigations of minds in conflict, including their unconscious appetites and anxieties, were objective revelations of subjective states. The pleasures that a Balanchine ballet might give, his detractors charged, were the pleasures of geometry, rather like the gratification an art lover might obtain from one of Mondrian's famous grids: a detached, almost scientific appreciation of balances and contrasts of color rather than, say, the pleasures one might derive from one of Picasso's emotion-laden portraits of a mistress.

Yet the usual responses to Mondrian's art stand at the other extreme from Balanchine's motives as a ballet master. I spoke earlier of Mondrian's psychological predicaments, his intensifying fear of nature, which amounted to a fear of sexual intimacy. The most anxiety-producing of all natural phenomena for Mondrian was woman. The artist's carefully judged straight lines, his restrained, repetitive, unpatterned colored rectangles, his fierce rejection even of diagonals, document the power of his repressions. It is only because they were in some strange way so beautiful that most viewers of his paintings failed to see the panic behind his designs, the evasions beneath his apparently cool, uncommunicative canvases.

Balanchine's creations, in contrast, show that fear of woman was not an issue for him. He was not a distant, callous manipulator of submissive ballerinas. In fact, to judge from the warm response of his dancers and a fervent public to his work, "callous" is not the word that any of them would have applied to him. It is impossible to sum up Balanchine's massive output with a single theme. But one subject proved central to his designs: the worship of man for woman. It took many forms in his choreography. To cite only one of the ballets, a favorite that he enjoyed watching more than any other, the late *Stravinsky Violin Concerto* (1972):

Arthur Mitchell and Suzanne Farrell, two principal dancers in
George Balanchine's New York City Ballet.

"That sex rears its head in Balanchine's most cerebral Stravinsky ballets
is a given," wrote Anna Kisselgoff, the ballet critic of the *New York
Times*, in January 1999. He "created two of his most subtle studies of
male-female relations." Clearly, for Balanchine the wall between his
analytical and passionate inner lives was thoroughly porous.

We know that his life centered on women: he was married four
times, each time to a ballerina. If his "alabaster princess," Suzanne Farrell, his muse during his last two decades, had been willing, he would
have been married a fifth time. A fluent, appealing dancer, an innocent
seducer for whom he wrote dazzling, flattering roles, she seemed to
him the choicest combination of sheer femininity and artistic competence. Nor was his infatuation eccentric; his adoration was shared by
her sizable crowd of admirers. Being in love with Suzanne Farrell was
far from Balanchine's unique privilege. The infatuation did not interfere with his choreography: he made major ballets out of it. The portrait of Balanchine as the man without feelings, or unable to express
them, is a caricature.

3.

ALL THAT SAID, Balanchine was certainly more comfortable with a rationalist, though often aesthetically most pleasing, style of choreography than with dances aiming at confessional self-exposure. This is why the contrast with the creations of Martha Graham, America's undisputed high priestess of modern dance, is so striking. In dance, modernism drew on two distinct sources, both radical departures from tradition, with little overlap: modern ballet and modern dance. For Graham, the capture and dramatization of her deepest passions as the choreographer's and the dancer's sole true source of energy lay at the heart of her formidable productivity. Balanchine for his part reveled in what I have called the form-making pleasures by sublimating his feelings into deeply satisfying—at times even moving—contests among male and female protagonists. His erotic excitement, however overlaid by his spectacular technique, was stirring beneath the surface, without cheap explosions or pathos, yet adding up for performers and spectators alike to a profound sense of gratification. Martha Graham roused similar responses, but in her own, more directly sensual way.

She was an impressive, if highly individual beauty, with her penetrating eyes, good cheekbones, and a slender, supple body, though more well rounded than Balanchine's almost emaciated dancers. Born in California in 1894 to a professional family—her father was a physician with a specialist's interest in mental ailments—Graham was in her late teens when she discovered her life's vocation watching a performance by the American dancer Ruth St. Denis. After some delays, at twenty-one she enrolled in Denishawn, then perhaps the single serious dance company and school in the country, run by St. Denis and her husband Ted Shawn. She quickly learned what they had to teach and, alienated by the sentimental, quasi-religious atmosphere at the company—an ill-assorted amalgam of exotic influences and the doctrines of Christian Science—made herself independent. In 1926, after teaching dance for some time at the School of Music in Rochester, New York, and steadily evolving her unique personal style, she went public with her first work. She was then thirty-two years old, an age when other ballerinas might begin to think of retiring.

But Graham, her mission once fixed in her mind, never wavered. She choreographed dozens of solo dances with vastly ambitious themes —on Western Americana, on religion, on life and death, on women— staging each with a minimum of scenery and costume but with mounting mastery. Accessible to suggestions as long as they seemed portentous and profound to her, she enlarged her canvas; in 1929, she designed her first ballet for a bevy of dancers, and surrounded herself with a company of adoring disciples. But even here she was, and insisted on remaining, the sole ruler of her enterprise; she enjoyed her monopoly of power, steadily working to translate her most intense emotions into visual equivalents. Unwilling to turn over "her" roles to surrogates, she invariably made her part the principal one. Hers was an independently developed American counterpart to Mary Wigman's *Ausdruckstanz*, the Expressionist dance, which avant-garde performers developed during the Weimar Republic.

It was a risky mission to the heathens; for years Martha Graham danced in half-empty theatres. Having virtually no model to pattern herself after with the exception of a handful of steadfast allies, she worked largely on her own. But even without support, her cause, long unappreciated, would have sustained her. In fact, in her determination and her indifference to wealth and fashion, Graham, who spent much of her long life in principled poverty—she died in 1991 at the age of ninety-six—amply displayed the classic marks of the modernist. Having made some early concessions to vaudeville appearances, she stubbornly refused to participate in the commercial theatre, and for some years virtually starved. Then, after the Second World War, came public acceptance; her performances began to sell out and she was elevated into a national institution. But long before that, she had believed that she had something important to say to her culture; and, in good modernist fashion, she consistently stressed her contemporaneity. "No artist is ahead of his time," she said. "He *is* his time." The remark closes a circle in the history of modernism: Baudelaire, with whom this study was launched, had made the same observation more than a century before. In tune with other modernists recent or remote, whether composers or dancers, Martha Graham wanted most to live in her time.

6.

ARCHITECTURE AND DESIGN— MACHINERY, A NEW FACTOR IN HUMAN AFFAIRS

"THERE'S NOTHING MORE IMPORTANT THAN ARCHITECTURE"

1.

THE FIRST CLASSICS IN MODERNIST ARCHITECTURE appeared just a few years before the outbreak of the First World War. The trailblazers who designed them did not necessarily agree on much except for their antagonism to the academic establishment, the Ecole des Beaux-Arts, whose privileges they resented and taste they despised. The semi-official salons that certified time-honored principles—an awed affection for the Gothic style accompanied by an obedient reliance on trusted neoclassical facades, an invincible appetite for mechanical ornament—provided for modernists countless invitations to go their own independent way. A bank, traditionalists content with Beaux-Arts instructions would say, should look like a bank, which is to say, like a recognizable copy of an antique Roman structure—at least as imagined. In sharp contrast, a bank, innovative designers were beginning to say by mid-nineteenth century, should reject the habitual identifying marks and experiment with new shapes, untried materials, pleasing informal colors.

In their urgency to make things new, modernists enjoyed the most varied sources of inspiration, and no other short stretch in the history of their craft has ever been quite so rich in groundbreaking departures from what most clients still wanted: undemanding designs labeled by admirers and detractors alike as "historicist" and "eclectic." The majority of clients—always a majority even in the heyday of modernism—insisted on visualizing buildings reminiscent of the cherished past no matter how insipid or incorrect. They often drew on an incongruous assortment of backward-looking models—imitations of styles no longer worth imitating or blends of styles impossible to make coherent, let alone elegant.

Some of the early modernist structures, defiantly at odds with reigning tastes, make for an impressive list of innovations: Frank Lloyd Wright's Darwin Martin House in Buffalo, embodying years of experiments with an open plan gesturing to the outdoors (1904); Auguste Perret's apartment house in Paris manifestly constructed with that recent invention, reinforced concrete (1905); Walter Gropius's Fagus

Walter Gropius and Adolf Meyer, Deutscher Werkbund Exposition, Administration Building (1914). Radical modernism in architecture.

shoe tree factory, bathed in sunlight and ostentatiously lacking corner posts (1910); Adolf Loos's assertive, wholly unornamented Steiner House in Vienna, derided (to borrow a contemporary remark attributed to Emperor Franz Josef) as a scandalous house without eyebrows (also in 1910).

It is all too easy to underestimate the anxiety, soon transformed into rage, that these provocations aroused among conventional architects and most of their potential customers. The radicals were assaulting laboriously acquired principles, championing materials little known and little esteemed, showing no respect for prized habits going back to ancient Greece and Rome. Nor were the contests for the minds and pocketbooks of clients always a straightforward combat between two clearly defined adversaries. In France, where such disputes were fought out with particular passion, a third party, led by Eugène-Emmanuel Viollet-le-Duc, complicated the scene, and often the outcome, of these battles. Viollet-le-Duc, the celebrated lecturer on architecture (his forceful, dominant text, *Entretiens sur l'architecture*, was one of Frank Lloyd Wright's favorite books) and the most controversial restorer of churches and châteaux after midcentury, matched the protomodernists in his hostility to the Academy. Its rigid prescriptions, regular internal competitions, and highly publicized honors, like the Prix de Rome, all seemed to him rewards for commonplace nostalgia, thus unfortunately keeping them alive. For Viollet-le-Duc, the Gothic style was the ideal, but this did not mean that he was advocating slavish imitations of French cathedrals. Sounding much like a true modernist, he demanded contemporary solutions for contemporary problems, a modern architecture quite literally built on the foundations of Gothic.

THIS RHETORICAL MODERNITY was, of course, not drastic enough for modernists, who, with all their admiration for the classics, rejected such compromises with the past. Consider the pure commitment to the thrilling new as voiced by the young Italian architect Antonio Sant'Elia who, in 1914, affiliated himself with the Futurists, those feverishly progressive Italian propagandists, painters, and poets. One gets a sense of their appeal when one reads that in 1913, Sant'Elia's countryman Antonio Gramsci, still a student but well on his way to making himself a widely quoted Communist intellectual, had complained about "the present appalling poverty of artistic production." This scornful appraisal of their opposition, the respectable makers and guardians of taste, was widespread among modernists practically everywhere. In Britain, we recall, T. S. Eliot was grumbling about contemporary poetry in language that Sant'Elia would have endorsed for the architecture of his time.

For Sant'Elia, architecture, for all its built-in utilitarian qualities, was distinctly an art, and he declared recent technological inventions suitable for aesthetic judgments. Glass, concrete, and iron, he said, are "rich in the inherent beauty of their lines and modeling." Other Futurists echoed this promotion of humble materials. Umberto Boccioni, a Calabrian transplanted to northern Italy, almost as much a polemicist as a painter and sculptor, emphatically advocated an approach to the art of building essentially alien to current tastes. "In architectural creation," he warned, "the past weighs down on the mind of the client and of the architect." Hence, creativity must break away from tradition: "it has to start again from the beginning."

Like other Futurists, Boccioni, who died young in an accident in 1916, had rather indiscriminately gathered impulses from innovative movements in the arts but, as students of his movement have seen with some regret, never synthesized them into a new style. "Futurist painting, even Boccioni at his best," the art historian George Heard Hamilton has summed up its dilemma, "remains an unstable combination of Neo-Impressionist brushwork, harsh Expressionist colour, and Cubist drawing." It was the curt, provocative slogans embodying incessant motion—resounding activity, exciting rhythms—that were to be enough inspiration for the new painters. In short, for the Futurists at least, the past—Viollet-le-Duc to the contrary—was never a sound guide to the future, nor was the present.

Futurism embodied an ambitious, self-imposed assignment, one that Sant'Elia seemed most likely among Italian modernist architects to carry through. But his history is capped by pathos: he did not live to see his plans for a new city realized. The very war he had advocated so ferociously made him one of its casualties; as a good Futurist, Sant'Elia was as bellicose, as intent as his fellows on dragging Italy into the war that the country had first witnessed as a neutral bystander. Once Italy joined the Allies in 1915, he volunteered for service, and in October of the following year, he was killed at the front. A century earlier, Goethe had wisely warned his readers to beware of what they had wanted in their youth since they might get it in their adult years. Hence Sant'Elia's legacy is limited to brilliant ink drawings, some of them heightened with lively watercolor—apartment houses reaching into the sky, robust power stations and railroad terminals, avenues segregating various modes of transportation from each other. The ideal that nourished these sketches was epitomized by his Futurists' favorite one-word maxim that celebrates a world in constant, energetic action: dynamism.

THE NEED TO RETHINK architecture with a modernist's contempt for current tastes pervaded the Futurists' programmatic writings. The earliest of the group's manifestos, by the poet and editor F. T. Marinetti, founder of the movement and inventor of its name, is worth quoting at some length for its skill in tying aesthetic judgments to contemporary social conditions: "Such modern phenomena as cosmopolitan nomadism, the democratic spirit, and the decline of religions," he wrote in 1911, "have reduced to uselessness the great, decorative, imperishable buildings that once expressed kingly authority, theocracy and mysticism." The right to strike, equality before the law, the modern habits of hygiene and domestic comfort all required "large, popular, well-ventilated apartment blocks, absolutely comfortable trains, tunnels, iron bridges, large and fast ocean liners, hillside villas shrewdly sited toward the cool sweep of horizons, immense meeting halls and perfect bathrooms for the rapid daily care of the body." And he left his readers with what he called an "explosive" gift, the observation that "Nothing is more beautiful than the steel frame of a house in construction." It "symbolizes our burning passion for the coming-into-being of things."

In his comprehensive catalog, Marinetti recapitulated Futurist principles with private dwellings and public monuments alike: the need to expand the signification of beauty to the aesthetic aspects of what conventional judges had grievously overlooked; the overriding power of modern phenomena like rapid movement, growing secularism, and present-day physical culture; the superiority of imaginative becoming to static being—all this to be made manifest in buildings. In the light of this analysis, Sant'Elia's joining the Futurists seems virtually preordained. The drawings—some three hundred have survived—document his program to design a new city—*Città Nuova*—that would take account of the emerging features that Marinetti was celebrating. We moderns, Sant'Elia noted, echoing the master, "no longer see ourselves to be men of the cathedrals, the palaces, the podiums."

Born in Como in 1888, Sant'Elia moved to Milan for his architectural training and opened an office there. It was in Milan in 1912 that he helped to found an organization intent on propagating "New Tendencies"—*Nuove Tendenze*—and two years later, he led in organizing the group's first exhibition and wrote some of its programmatic prose. For many of its intellectuals, Italy seemed somehow left far behind the cultures of neighboring states, and discontent was rife from the Marxist left to reactionary monarchism. In that atmosphere, the temptation to explore—perhaps to adopt—alien doctrines was irresistible. True, the *Nuove Tendenze* was not so doctrinaire and not so political as Futurism, but it threw a bridge to the Futurists, who naturally secured the attention of the press.

2.

THE PREHISTORY OF FAR-REACHING "new tendencies" in building goes back more than one hundred and fifty years. Engineers—not architects—had led the way. Unencumbered by academic constraints and intent on solving practical problems, they devised impressive bridges plunging across hitherto uncrossable spaces, and bold exhibition halls or railroad terminals that were unself-conscious aesthetic masterpieces. The most extraordinary among nineteenth-century inventive architects was an amateur, Sir Joseph Paxton, a builder of conservatory gardens, who, assisted by competent engineers, designed the Crystal Palace to house the Great Exhibition in London of 1851. Built of iron and glass, and depending on machine-made parts alone, it was the most modern construction of the epoch. Incidentally, the astonishing fact that a good Victorian proposed this unparalleled design and that a committee of good Victorians authorized it may serve to refute the familiar charge that Victorians lacked taste and a sense of adventure.

By the 1850s, in fact, what was to become the dominant outlook of modernist architecture and design had been largely anticipated in two weighty words—"honesty" and "simplicity"—that avant-garde architects and critics used as artillery against their tradition-bound colleagues. Both traits were being widely proclaimed as ideals though they were still rarely, or timidly, applied. Honesty called for using available resources candidly rather than concealing them from view if they were "undignified." Painting one material to look like another was still a widespread practice, but more and more dissenting voices maintained that since wood and steel have a beauty of their own, architects should frankly display them. As for simplicity, many designers paying it lip service regularly violated that ideal with the alibi (not always groundless) that they were helpless before their patrons, who were insisting on showy detailing. To make the rhetoric of modernist architects salable required educating not only architects but their clients no less.

During the second half of the nineteenth century, some of that work, of course, was already being done. The English architect Charles Francis Annesley Voysey, who in 1882 opened his practice to design private houses and their accouterments, like charming printed linens, wallpapers, teapots, and furniture, was perhaps the most hopeful among transitional figures looking to a future of unencumbered design. In 1893, some years before the outspoken Viennese architect Adolf Loos had launched the notorious slogan "Ornament is Crime," Voysey had said in an interview, "The danger to-day lies in over-decoration; we lack simplicity and have forgotten repose." And, like a wholehearted modernist, he firmly declared himself determined to "live and work in the present." In the delightful country houses he designed, he realized the unconventional ideals of honesty and simplicity. The radical taste of a Gropius, even a Mies van der Rohe, was not too far distant.

MATCHING OTHERS OF their breed, and some of their immediate ancestors, a growing number of architects strove to be in tune with their time. The most consistent and forceful among artists who hailed the supremacy of the moment was the great American modernist Frank Lloyd Wright. Born in Richland Center, Wisconsin, in 1867 into an educated household—his father a lawyer and politician, who became a restless itinerant Baptist preacher, his mother from a well-to-do family, who had taken up the respectable profession of teaching—he traced his love of music and of learning to his parents. But his urge to be up-to-date seemed his own. "Every day life is the important thing," he wrote characteristically to one of his daughters in 1921, "not tomorrow or yesterday, but today. You won't reach anything better than the 'right now' if you take it as you ought." He spoke for others. The disputes common among Victorian builders and their clients about which historical style, Greek or Venetian or Renaissance, was superior to its rivals—that is to say, more "honest"—struck Wright, along with other modernists, as a reactionary escape from living in the present, a betrayal of their craft.

Such disputes, attempts to assign a proper place to novelty in architecture, were a pervasive subtext in the profession. Most significantly, this raised the question of the machine's proper place in construction. As the nineteenth century increasingly became an age of machinery, architects were compelled to take a stand. More and more, mechanical devices were replacing unaided human power, and not in factories alone. The typewriter, the transatlantic cable, the fast train, the elevator, the automobile, the vacuum cleaner, and, in building, materials like concrete and steel that made window walls possible, changed life in the factory, the office, and the home forever. What had once been the product of laborious (and expensive) manual fabrication was more and more being fashioned in large quantities, and far more cheaply. The question remained whether this revolution was a curse or a blessing. There were plausible arguments on both sides.

Thus the proponents of machine-made resources preached against obstinate resistance. The great worlds' fairs—in London, in Chicago, in Paris—which, starting at mid-nineteenth century, proudly exhibited new products available to anyone who could afford them, found a mixed reception among men and women of taste. They spawned objections, most eloquently after midcentury on the part of the English radical William Morris, who advocated integrity and consistency in the use of materials and sought to reestablish a vital link to medieval taste when workmanship, he believed, had given pleasure to maker and user alike.

To exemplify his conviction, Morris, who was at once poet, painter, designer, and shopkeeper to select customers, designed superb table linens and wallpapers, sturdy, appealing, patterned closely after nature. His age produced movements like the Arts and Crafts in England, or the Austrian *Wiener Werkstätte*, devoted to fine quality—and with that, necessarily, to high prices—and a determined critique of tasteless eclecticism. This conflict between quality and quantity became a stumbling block (especially for an ideologue who in his later years converted to socialism) that Morris could never overcome. Nor could others. Hence twentieth-century modernist architects and designers did their work amidst strident clamor over the machine.

One more point which, though patent, deserves to be underscored: more than all the other arts, architecture was a public enterprise that left perceptible, enduring traces. It required substantial investments and could not evade the lure (and threat) of partisan politics—the state's sponsorship or indifference, the exercise of public domain, officials meddling in aesthetic decisions by granting or withholding building permits, the power of the rich engaged in shaping policies. No wonder unconventional architects would come to think of themselves as historic figures. The American architect Philip Johnson, for decades a determined advocate of the modernist International Style, put it summarily in the early 1960s: "Monuments last much longer than words. Civilizations are remembered by buildings. There's nothing more important than architecture." Given the sublime self-importance habitual to many major architects, this statement is easy to translate: No one is more important than the architect.

"A HOUSE IS A MACHINE FOR LIVING IN"

A BUILDING, AS PHILIP JOHNSON might say, is likely to prove a more effective advocate for innovation than words, but one could not prove this from the verbal floods that modernist architects produced to stake their claims. Other artists, too, liked to explain themselves to the public, but they were tongue-tied amateurs compared to architect-partisans in their rivalries. Ideologically motivated architects expected to bring readers to their point of view with imperative proclamations and vigorous one-sentence paragraphs that excluded all nuances.

1.

IN 1901, THE RELATIVELY YOUNG, ever more thriving American architect Frank Lloyd Wright—he was then thirty-four—published an article titled "The Art and Craft of the Machine." It was perhaps the most influential amidst the avalanche of literature he would generate in a lifetime of spreading his vision in print. In this piece, lucidly though not tersely, Wright expounded the ideals he would try to realize in the houses he was being commissioned to design. He had no doubt about the beneficial significance of the machine—he never showed any doubt about anything in his numerous interviews and innumerable articles. "In the Machine," he wrote, "lies the only future of art and craft." It was the proper tool of, and for, the age; a potent instance of the present-mindedness we have come to expect from his tribe.

To praise the machine in 1901, Wright noted with his customary energy, was controversial because his colleagues had consistently misread the promise of recently invented mechanisms as they continued to design buildings that were pale and clumsy imitations of a largely irrelevant past. "Badgered into all manner of structural gymnastics," he noted, architects felt compelled to disguise structural steel with marble décor that added nothing to making a house a work of art. And so they turned their designs into swindles. When it came to disparaging fellow architects, Wright never minced words.

His call for honesty was a call for simplicity, another of his favorite terms. What we can learn from the machine is "that certain simple forms and handling are suitable to bring out the beauty of wood and certain forms are not." There were in fact several kinds of machine-made products that Wright loathed, such as mass-produced wood carvings, with their "elaborate and fussy joinery of posts, spindles, jig-sawed beams and braces." They were sentimental and overwrought. The implication was inescapable: to use the machine productively, to dominate it, required intelligence and manly decisiveness. Thus the article turned into a self-portrait.

Wright's essay stopped well short of the extreme position that the celebrated architect and painter Le Corbusier, born in Switzerland and settled in France, would adopt two decades later: "A house is a machine for living in." Actually, Sant'Elia would say it almost word for word just before the Great War: "The modern house is like a huge machine." But for his part, Wright steadfastly relied on another watchword to supplement (and complicate) his message of honesty and simplicity. Drawing on biology, the science of life, he used "organic" as an imprecise, highly elastic term of praise. To Wright, it meant the coherence of all elements in a complete design, including its furniture and its intimate relationship to nature—lawns and trees no less than chairs, tables, and doorknobs.* Hence, for Wright, design was an all-encompassing enterprise: to conceive a house called for working from the inside out, a procedure that his brethren in architecture, sold on making a good superficial impression, had all too flagrantly failed to adopt.

Wright's domestic architecture, just at the time he was becoming the designer of choice among affluent clients in Illinois and Wisconsin, echoed his strong views on family life. The roots of his convictions about domesticity (though they defy easy interpretation) must have run

---

* Ada Louise Huxtable points out: "It was Emerson's and Ruskin's ideas that were the philosophical source of Wright's 'organic architecture,' which had been dismissed by many as meaningless mysticism, or at best left open to any kind of interpretation. Like Emerson and the transcendentalists, Wright believed in the natural world as a source of physical and spiritual fulfillment."

deep. He often returned to his family history, not in order to find what to imitate but what to avoid, to design family dwellings in which all could live easily together. Reacting to his father, William Wright, who, forever in search of a better position, dragged his wife and children from one town to another, Frank Lloyd Wright grew up in perpetual insecurity. With no hope of obtaining the reassurance a boy needs from his father, his anxieties were exacerbated in 1885 when his parents divorced.

Wright's youth, then, was not a time to remember with pleasure, and, in retrospect, was most likely distorted by wishful fantasies. After a brief stint at the University of Wisconsin, he started his architectural career as a draftsman in the office of J. L. Silsbee, a prominent Chicago architect and a family friend, and then, fortunately, transferred to the firm of Adler & Sullivan, among a handful of progressive offices in the country, known well beyond Chicago for its skyscraper designs. Louis Sullivan, Wright's *"liebermeister"*—dear master—one of a handful of architects he ever took the trouble to praise, was for him the ideal employer, a man to argue with and to absorb from. Wright was fortunate in his teachers, in the way someone eager to learn will tend to choose guides able to teach. In 1893, he opened his own practice, and in the next few years developed the open floor plan and horizontal look that made him a household name among designers in the Midwest. That he lived in an upper-middle-class neighborhood and showed upper-middle-class tastes in his choice of wife and friends and entertainments only helped to make him socially as well as professionally highly acceptable among future clients.

WRIGHT'S OPEN PLAN converted a domestic dwelling, all but the bedrooms, from a set of enclosed containers into a freely flowing interior. He eliminated walls to make a single space that included what would have been separate dining and living rooms in a conventional house of the time. This radical innovation did not necessarily dictate a unique interaction of parents with children, since in a disciplinarian family, parental edicts as to what a child could or could not do became, as it were, the constitution regulating their conduct. But more probably,

Wright's floor plans encouraged casual exchanges—an intimacy that later generations would call "togetherness." He would repeatedly assert that they constituted freedom. He had thought them through, he liked to say, "from inside out."

These floor plans were not Wright's only innovation. He made much of built-in furniture—designed of course by himself—a bulky fireplace "*integral*" to the public space, a liberal ration of continuous strip or casement windows which, unlike conventional double-hung windows, were not, in Wright's words, "holes punched in walls." And the exterior, naturally deriving from "what had happened '*inside*,'" became his signature: a low-pitched roof underscoring the horizontal shape of the design and its closeness to the soil with wide overhanging eaves, built to shelter his houses from the often extreme elements and to diffuse light in the upper story. All told this added up—here was another favorite word—to "plasticity," an "indispensable element to the successful use of the machine." Setting aside Wright's inflamed rhetoric, the best of the houses he built after 1900 were immensely appealing, full of surprises.

Now, a century later, it is hard to visualize just how radical Wright's formulas really were. The houses practically every architect designed at the time, Wright noted in his *Autobiography*, simply "*lied* about every-thing." Considering his own designs, there were, he claimed, "no plans in existence like these at the time." All "boxes," he wrote, "were inside a complicated outside boxing." He "could see little sense in this inhibi-tion." And so "I declared the whole lower floor as one room, cutting off the kitchen as a laboratory, putting the servants' sleeping and living quarters next to the kitchen but semi-detached, on the ground floor. Then I screened various portions of the big room for certain domestic purposes like dining, reading, receiving callers." The "Prairie" houses (as he called them, even though not all of them were situated in the Mid-western plains) that he designed in the first decade of the twentieth cen-tury were very popular: his firm completed an average of ten houses a year, an impressive number for a relatively young company.

Wright's casual allusion to servants' quarters shows that he built houses mainly for the affluent. His early clients were for the most part

Frank Lloyd Wright, Robie House (1908–10). Wright was becoming famous
for his "Prairie" houses during this time, but this splendid realization was
actually built in Chicago.

businessmen and professionals, men with a modicum of education and
far from conservative Republicans, preferring Theodore Roosevelt to
Woodrow Wilson, by and large proud of their sophisticated sense for
the practical. There were even some among Wright's clients who
favored woman suffrage, and their taste was in general shared, and
encouraged, by their wives, a number of them college-educated, who
were active, if rarely in politics at least in socially conscious philan-
thropy. Departing from the usual anti-bourgeois sentiments of other
modernists, Wright appreciated the men of commerce for their sagacity
and adaptability and their wives for their open-mindedness. The
machine was not a threat to them. In short, dissenting from most fellow
modernists, he sought, and enjoyed, necessary support from figures in
the establishment who considered themselves enlightened patrons.
Wright's allegation, made repeatedly across the years, that he was
viciously derided, unjustly criticized, and sedulously neglected is quite

simply not true. It speaks of Wright's unconquerable desire to be the despised and ignored outsider that many avant-garde artists thought belonged to their status as revolutionaries.

2.

GIVEN HIS SOCIAL respectability and professional prestige, Frank Lloyd Wright could have prolonged his prosperous, comfortable existence for decades to come. His clients were impatient for his Prairie houses; he was widely being invited to lecture; he was publishing his designs, well illustrated, in journals of general circulation like the *Ladies' Home Journal*; in 1907, the Chicago Art Institute gave him a one-man exhibition, unprecedented for an architect working in the region. The following year, he completed one of his finest designs, the Robie House, placed right in Chicago. And then he seemed ready to throw it all away and ruin his career in an act of extreme willfulness. In September 1909, he left his wife and their six children and ran off to Europe with Mamah Borthwick Cheney, the wife of a close friend and neighbor. They lived in Germany and Italy for a year, then returned, though not contrite. Mamah Cheney secured a divorce, and Frank Lloyd Wright lived at his old address for a while before professing his permanent attachment to his lover—settling her, and as much as possible himself, in Taliesin, a retreat near Spring Green, Wisconsin, that he had been designing and constructing for some months.

Wright's ever-rising eminence made this escapade more than a local scandal. The architectural press continued to review his work impartially, that is in the main favorably, and a few prospective patrons were ready to overlook his indiscretions to employ his services. In Europe, indeed, his reputation and authority were assured by the publication in Germany, in 1910 and 1911, of two portfolios of designs for houses already completed. The United States was a different story. In the three years from 1912 through 1914, he completed only six buildings—quite a drop from his earlier annual average of ten. And then, paradoxically, an appalling tragedy that befell Wright partly restored him to the good graces of his community. In August 1914, while he happened to be in

Chicago, an immigrant from Barbados who served at Taliesin as a cook suffered a murderous psychotic episode during which he killed seven people, including Mamah Cheney and her two children. Mourning her in a printed eulogy, Wright continued to maintain her essential nobility. But more, he insisted, theirs had been a higher love to which only a few might legitimately aspire. Once the quintessential bourgeois, Wright now claimed the identity of a wounded bohemian. Some of his former social companions thought this might be a good time to forgive him.

A RELATIVELY BLANK interlude followed, lasting almost two decades. If clients turned their backs on Wright, though, it was not his notoriety so much as the startling recovery of tradition-ridden fashions for Tudor mansions and neoclassical banks. His only important commission was the Imperial Hotel in Tokyo (1913–22), which obliged him in late 1916 to start spending years in Japan. Wright had long taken an informed collector's interest in Japanese art. The fee for the commission was lucrative and his often lengthy absences from the United States most welcome to him. The Imperial Hotel showed its resiliency when it withstood the devastating earthquake of 1923; one of his Japanese backers sent him a famous telegram: "hotel stands undamaged as monument to your genius," a homage to which he took no exception.

But it was not until the 1930s, in his late sixties and early seventies, that Wright found his second wind as an architect. He designed numerous memorable commissions in his last years—he died in 1959 at the age of almost ninety-two—including a series of "Usonian" houses, which effectively and rather modestly accommodated middle-income clients. And two commissions guaranteed his immortality among modernists: the Kaufmann House at Bear Run, Pennsylvania—"Fallingwater" (1936); and the Solomon R. Guggenheim Museum in New York (1945–59), his most enduring monuments.

No one writing about Frank Lloyd Wright has failed to lavish praise on Fallingwater in the most glowing terms; it stands as one of the finest domestic dwellings, perhaps *the* finest domestic dwelling, of the twentieth century. It owes nothing to the past, something to the International Style he so vociferously loathed, and shows some traces to Wright's earlier work, as in its emphatic horizontal spaces and grand, easily flowing living room. Perhaps the most impressive feature is the way the house fits into its environment, a thoughtfully considered element in the design. Fallingwater, as Neil Levine, a specialist in Wright's architecture, has put it, "is ultimately about the cumulative effect of stone, water, trees, leaves, mist, clouds, and sky." A middle-sized three-bedroom holiday residence, it is built over a waterfall rushing below, with powerful cantilevered balconies that give the house a feeling of lightness and expansiveness but, at the same time, underscore its intimacy. The highly concentrated drama of Fallingwater is awe-inspiring.

As its public counterpart, the Guggenheim Museum is supremely confident, Wright's most commented upon legacy. Wright's own statement, once he had the commission in his pocket, was characteristic: it would be the first decent museum ever built. Dominating its surroundings on Fifth Avenue like a huge obese oyster, it has left its mark on art lovers of the most varied tastes. Naturally it had critics from the outset. It seemed eccentric and self-advertising to some; it forced viewers (several argued) to walk down a sloping ramp, made them look at paintings that, being flat, would clash with its curved walls, and compelled them to stand too close to the exhibits. As for the exterior appearance, detractors could not make peace with its opulent, swirling roundness, a unique departure from the solid rectangles firmly planted around up and down on Fifth Avenue. But decades after serving scores of visiting exhibitions, to say nothing of its permanent collection, the Guggenheim has, for all its troubles, proved its viability. This may be a compliment to the adaptability of museumgoers or, more likely, Wright's modernist, uncompromising genius. He was, as Ada Louise Huxtable has put it in her insightful biography, "a fascinating anachronism—a talented visionary and an unreconstructed romantic who produced designs, planning, and structural concepts that the twenty-first century is still absorbing." He was a supreme modernist happily at odds, as he saw it, with all other modernists.

3.

LUDWIG MIES VAN DER ROHE, much like Frank Lloyd Wright, attested to the pivotal place of the machine in his vocation. But unlike Wright, Mies preferred concise communications to the garrulous pronouncements that were Wright's forte. His famous three-word maxim, "Less is More," that plea for terseness, illustrates—tersely—the very point he wanted to make in his designs. It meant for him not just that the art of architecture consists in good part of eliminating superfluous decoration and fussy detail, but also that he valued the aid of mechanical, literally labor-saving devices in construction; he found them both aesthetically and economically desirable. Applying the principle of "Less is More" in his work gave his projects and executed buildings a stripped-down look that made each unmistakably a Mies van der Rohe.

Virtually all commentators on Mies, admirers and denigrators alike, have invoked the spirit of Plato to characterize his distinctive conspicuous minimalism. Mies never saw a right angle he did not like. "His own chaste taste gave these hollow glass shells a crystalline purity of form," Lewis Mumford, the eminent American historian and critic of architecture, wrote in 1964, in stern disapproval, "but they existed alone in the Platonic world of his imagination and had no relation to size, climate, insulation, function, or internal activity." And it is true that Miesian designs, whether intended for an office building, a school, or a private residence, seemed largely undistinguishable from one another. Plainly, Mies van der Rohe had turned his back on Louis Sullivan's much-quoted, generally accepted appeal for avant-garde individualism, "Form follows function." The marked family resemblance of Mies's designs displayed his program of realizing the Platonic ideal of eternal, unvarying principles, of universally applicable truths.

BORN IN 1886, MIES CAME by this quasi-scholastic disposition in his youth, in the Catholic school he attended until he was thirteen. But his education in architecture was thoroughly practical: helping out in his father's brick yard taught him the function of materials; late teenage years as an apprentice designer in Aachen, his hometown, gave him valuable experience as a draftsman. His stint in Berlin with the firm of Peter Behrens, a ubiquitous progressive architect, starting in 1908, when he was all of twenty-two, encouraged him to acquire a taste for the great Karl Friedrich Schinkel's century-old neoclassical public buildings spread across the center of Berlin—palaces, museums, churches—which, though they superficially looked very different from what Mies would become famous for, inspired him in his search for transparency and logic, that is, for architectural order.

In the historic fourteen years between 1900 and the outbreak of the First World War—a time that, we know, was flooded with important new music, new painting, new fiction, new theatre, the very years that Mies van der Rohe and Walter Gropius (whom we shall soon meet) entered the profession—architects, too, were in search of a new paradigm. Not all architects, of course; most of them, unhesitatingly acceding to their clients' faultlessly unoriginal tastes, designed for the thousandth time the traditional shapes that they, and their customers, felt most comfortable with—neo-Gothic, neoclassical, neo–Queen Anne. Yet among a few free spirits there was uneasiness about triumphant bad taste, and the sources of this discontent were often surprising: the commercial world, and the international market. Kitschy designs, whether of curtains or chinaware, might fail in the face of superior competition; and competing good design, whether in furniture or houses, might be visible, and available, from abroad.

Both of these causes for a modernist architectural upheaval were at work in prewar German high culture. The restless atmosphere among some of the country's leading designers did its part to promote untested ideas at the expense of long-honored traditions. In 1903, when Gropius was starting his studies at the Technische Hochschule in Berlin—he was twenty—the architect Hermann Muthesius returned to Germany after seven years in London attached to the German Embassy with the mission of reporting on English housing for possible German emulation. He was impatient to publicize the accomplishments of the domestic architecture to which his long residence had made him a passionate convert, and his slogan, almost like that of a politician running for office, became "reasonable *Sachlichkeit*," rational sobriety.

Then, in 1907, four years after his return, Muthesius was among the founders of the *Deutsche Werkbund*, an association of designers, artisans, educators, and manufacturers seeking to foster the "collaboration of art, industry, and artisanship," an agenda that, Muthesius shrewdly predicted, would be nothing less than a "struggle against existing conditions." The encounter of beauty, utility, and skill, the Werkbund hoped, would generate not points of tension but a complex though harmonious whole. It was in this organization that German designers worked to clarify the proper role of the machine, armed with (foreign, more pragmatic observers thought, confused by) metaphysical formulations. If not the country as a whole, then a highly select group of philosophically minded businessmen and designers would adopt modernism. This was the climate in which the young Mies van der Rohe could prosper.

THE FIRST PROJECTS that Mies sketched shortly after the First World War, two glass-walled skyscrapers, were never realized. But his boldness in choosing glass as the principal material, which even venturesome architects had so far largely confined to windows, gave Mies almost as much publicity as if they had been built. He carefully chose different materials for projects that followed: brick for one and concrete for two others, searching for the style that would let him formulate and express those perpetual qualities he thought underlay all architecture. By the end of the decade he had arrived, with two projects actually realized. In 1929, the Deutsche Werkbund commissioned Mies to take charge of the German Pavilion at an International Exhibition in Barcelona, and in 1930 he designed a private house for the Tugendhat family in Brno, Czechoslovakia. Both were much photographed and much talked about. And both showed the ultimate Miesian ideal of "Less is More."

The Barcelona pavilion was a fully apprehended realization of Miesian taste. Built as a temporary structure to be dismantled after the exhibition closed, it exhibited orderliness and sincerity, with pure expanses of glass and slim, stylish steel columns that held up the flat roof without sustaining external walls. Except for the furniture designed by Mies, it was empty: "the building itself was the object on view." The only art aside from Mies's lush, colorful, in fact sensual furnishings, dramatic and solitary, was Georg Kolbe's life-size statue of a nude, standing outside against a handsome green marble wall in a small pool. It must have occurred to more than one viewer walking through Mies's accolade to angularity that this naked young woman was the only curved object anywhere.

In comparison, the Tugendhat House, a two-story design, is marginally less chaste: the dining space is embraced by a semicircular wall of macassar ebony; the staircase joining the first to the second floor is inscribed within another semicircle; and the bedrooms upstairs are convenient and conventional. But the rest of the building is pure Mies: powerful horizontal lines, almost recalling Wright's ideal horizontality, anchor it into its hilly terrain. The street entrance is on the second

Ludwig Mies van der Rohe, Tugendhat House, Brno (1930).

floor, and the living area below literally looks down on the garden side of the house through vast, retractable window walls. Suitably, the furnishings are all of Mies's design; some taken from Barcelona, others designed specifically for the Tugendhat House, they fit stylishly into an overall impression of elegance and, in Huxtable's words, "austere luxury." With "the walls virtually gone," she writes, "the house held up only by the jewel-like chromed steel columns inside," the "shelter turned inside out" was "liberating in so many ways." Overall, the house was a passport to professional fame, a triumph of modernist architecture.

For Mies, the Tugendhat House was indeed a triumph, but one that exposed him to the charge of architectural authoritarianism. For the historian of modernism, the conflicts of testimony over the patron's role in this completed design are of particular interest because they are a rare specimen of candid self-exposure. Mies's account, not free of malice, is highly specific, detailing an unpredictable amalgam of tension and cooperation between an avant-garde pioneer and his affluent client. "Mr. Tugendhat came to me," Mies reported. "He was a very careful man. He did not believe in one doctor only—he had three." For a reader interested in the spectacle of a designer with unconventional tastes encountering a patron with conventional desires, this is a promising start.

As Mies reconstructs his decisive conferences with Tugendhat, it becomes painfully clear that to accept a commission from him must have been a willful misunderstanding on the architect's part. Tugendhat, it seems, had once seen one of Mies's

Mies van der Rohe, Tugendhat House, interior, Brno.

early houses, thought it well built, and wanted to commission a house like it, no doubt quite as well built. Mies, in short, cynically undertook to design the Tugendhats' house fully aware that the family was scarcely prepared to share his enthusiasm for the modernist style, especially in its uncompromising Miesian version. "I remember it was Christmas Eve when he saw the design. He nearly died." But Mrs. Tugendhat talked him round—all this, remember, reported by Mies—with her interest in modern art; he remembered that she apparently owned some van Goghs.

A few days later, Mr. Tugendhat came to Mies and told him to proceed with the building: "He said he did not like the open space; it would be too disturbing. People would be there when he was in the library

with his great thoughts. He was a businessman, I think. Later on he said to me, 'now I give in on everything, but not about the furniture.' I said, 'This is too bad.'" Undeterred by this expected news, Mies instructed the foreman of the construction crew to accept a shipment from his—Mies's—storage, and then, shortly before lunch, "say you are at his house with the furniture. He will be furious, but you must expect that." Indeed, as Mies had foreseen, Mr. Tugendhat wanted the furniture removed before he had even seen it, but after lunch he changed his mind. Mies's conclusion about the whole affair: "I think we should treat our clients as children." However lofty Frank Lloyd Wright might show himself in the course of decades, this would not have been his attitude.

Mies van der Rohe's contempt for Tugendhat and the whole class of Tugendhats is blatant enough; those "great thoughts" and all the rest of Mies's sneers bespeak his conviction that "bourgeois" and "philistine" are synonyms. True, Mies might have been trying to impress his listeners, whether the foreman or his client. But even if he had only been showing off, his arrogant comments are a plausible form for a modernist's exchange with a well-situated consumer to take. Modernists were by definition enemies of the cultural establishment; they needed an opponent, and if none was available, they could invent him. In realistic retrospect, they became only too aware that their deadliest adversaries were the totalitarian regimes so triumphant in the 1920s and 1930s, not the conservative consumers of high culture. The Tugendhat House after all was built, and built in the shape that Mies had designed for it.* Yet, leaving Hitler's Germany as late as 1937, he spent the second half of his career in flourishing exile in the United States, an unrepentant Miesian. Menaced everywhere by hard times, by Depression, dictatorships, and war, modernist design would show itself impres-

---

* By a piece of good luck, in the late 1960s I met a philosopher at the Free University in Berlin named Tugendhat, a son of the couple who had commissioned the celebrated Mies house. He energetically disputed the architect's disdainful characterization of his parents, noting that his mother in particular had excellent taste in art and was something of a collector. I have no independent confirmation of his statement, but in view of his parents' willingness to engage a famously uncompromising modernist, this account seems highly probable.

sively resilient, with sensible American clients hungry for a modernism that rescued what Nazified Europe was doing its utmost to destroy.

4.

THE MASTER BUILDER who welcomed the machine most emphatically was the imaginative, theory-obsessed Swiss architect Charles-Edouard Jeanneret, known as Le Corbusier, who designed his principal buildings, published his major writings, and devised his ambitious city plans after the First World War, in France, where he settled in 1917 at the age of thirty. Thirteen years later, he took French citizenship. Compared to other modernists, his body of work was relatively scanty, but his emphatic pleas for the widest possible employment of advanced technology in building made him an influential figure in contemporary architecture. It is in his best known, most widely translated book, *Vers une architecture* of 1923, a collection of previously published articles, that one finds his famous brisk formulation: "A house is a machine for living in." Le Corbusier insisted that "in building and construction, mass-production has already been begun; in face of new economic needs, mass-production units have been created both in mass and detail." He saw that a "style belonging to our own period has come about; and there has been a Revolution."

Had there been? The chapters surrounding these declarations of Le Corbusier's and the opinionated texts he poured out during the years leave little doubt that, self-assured and much-quoted as they are, they represented his wishes far more than a proven fact of contemporary society. What he meant to say is that in the modern world, innovators in all fields of activity had seized on the latest developments that technology had to offer—all but architects. "The various classes of workers in society today," he judged, "*no longer have dwellings adapted to their needs; neither the artisan nor the intellectual.*" Now architects were coming forward to overcome this deplorable lack.

More often than not, though, he would undercut his own optimism. He could maintain—and this is not the only occasion when Le Corbusier contradicted himself, putting his case into question—that

"Machinery, a new factor in human affairs, has aroused a new spirit," and then, again, "A great epoch has begun. There exists a new spirit." At the same time, in "Des Yeux qui ne voient pas," an intriguing chapter of *Vers une architecture*, he scattered pointed reminders to willfully blind fellow architects showing photographs of grain elevators, steamships, airplanes, and automobiles, all in praise of inventions that would have been unthinkable without modern materials for modern purposes—yet from which architects had refused to take instruction. Like Frank Lloyd Wright, then, the sense of being chosen—or condemned—to battle with superior forces in a civilization indifferent, even unsympathetic, to the new was a familiar modernist, if self-pitying, stance that he never abandoned. As a dreamer tirelessly proclaiming his servitude to the world of practice, he inescapably exposed himself to disappointments, mainly with schemes (fortunately) aborted.

Le Corbusier's claim to have been formed a willing slave to experience has a certain reasonableness. A largely self-made designer, he spent several apprentice years traveling to draw immortal models, including the classic temples of ancient Greece and Rome and the holy places of the fading Ottoman Empire, sketching, sketching. During this migrant phase, he worked for a time with protomodernists like Peter Behrens in Berlin and Josef Hoffmann in Vienna, to say nothing of the groundbreaking Auguste Perret in Paris. He was a serious painter, particularly in his early years, one among a small coterie of artists, the "Purists," working toward a contemporary aesthetic of lucidity and simplicity. They demonstrated their current relevance, as modernists well might, with smooth, pleasing, subdued still lifes of domestic products like pitchers and cups, and—a tip of the cap to Cubism—guitars. Le Corbusier's buildings were an integral part of his enterprise as a painter.

Ever given to resounding formulations, he perfected a catalog of essentials for housing, whether for a villa or a working-class settlement: ribbon windows, free facades, terrace roof, free ground plan, and free supports (*pilotis*). Some of these fundamentals were at home in the modernist vocabulary that architects had been elaborating since before the Great War: Gropius, Wright, and Mies van der Rohe had explored the free ground plan, the ribbon window, and the free facade. The *pilo-*

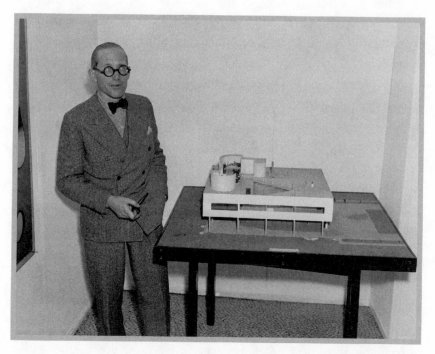

Le Corbusier (Charles-Edouard Jeanneret), Villa Savoye, at Poissy (1928–29), model. "A house is a machine for living."

tis that raised the house above the ground and the terrace roof were more characteristic of Le Corbusier, his special contributions to modernist design.

Hence Le Corbusier carried through his commissions in an unmistakable style: he preferred a cube or a rectangle to the emphatic wings and overhanging eaves that were Frank Lloyd Wright's special signature; with a flat roof providing space, often in a crowded urban environment, for sheltered gardening and sunbathing; and for the most part resting on trim posts or massive supports—boxes, they were called, on stilts. Probably the most successful, certainly the most photographed exemplar of this style is the Villa Savoye at Poissy, not far from Paris (1928–29). That famous house, Le Corbusier later said, is "a box in the air, pierced all around, uninterruptedly," raised on slender, regularly spaced pillars to dominate what was still then a rural landscape. That villa was, for him, the best possible representative of "*liberties taken*," a tribute to modernity, "liberties taken because they *have been won*, torn from the quickening sources of modern material. Poetry and lyricism brought forth by technics." In Le Corbusier's fertile schemes, radically incompatible grounds of action—aesthetics and technology—were, it seemed, happily joined, at least for him.

LE CORBUSIER'S AFFECTION for technology pervaded his prose no less than his designs. Hence seductive slogans appear and reappear in his writings: the modern private house as the architect's precious conquest or the spiritual foundation of materialism were triumphant battle cries for which a routine-ridden world, Le Corbusier dejectedly believed, gave him all too few opportunities. But he never rested content with erecting manors for the prosperous, those uncertain gates to fame. Throughout his career, he indefatigably drew, and occasionally built, housing for the poor and the lower middle classes, projects that he had in common with most other modernists. He drew up comprehensive plans for city after city on three continents, one after the other rejected for a wide gamut of reasons: emotional conservatism, conflicting interests, and rational resistance to schemes that would have displaced thousands of city dwellers. But from his first venture into urban planning in 1922 until his death in 1965, Le Corbusier kept returning to his earliest, vast city schemes. In all of them he tried to trump the English garden city and related proposals for being too diffuse, too timorous.

What the modern city needed, in his view, was to say farewell to the private house in favor of larger units, and to develop fully the segregation of functions—walking, driving, flying, domestic living. One result of these cogitations was the apartment block, *L'Unité d'Habitation*, which would bring together under one roof some 1,600 inhabitants— 350 families—and make room for playgrounds, primary schools, and shopping facilities. The other was Chandigarh, the new capital of Punjab, to be provided with government buildings largely designed by Le Corbusier. Prime Minister Jawaharlal Nehru courageously gave him the authority to preside as founding deity over major organized designs that European politicians refused to grant him.

Le Corbusier, Assembly Hall, at Chandigarh, India (1956). One of the very
few ambitious schemes he realized.

The *Unité d'Habitation*, several versions of which were built across
France in the 1950s, was a small miracle of ingenuity, a single regular
collective dwelling of eight double stories raised above the ground on
sturdy concrete piers. The apartments were of varying sizes, each with
a two-story living room. Among these habitations, the one in Marseilles (1946–52) became the most visited, most discussed, and most
contentious. Typically, Wright took the trouble to malign his competi-
tor: "that Corbusier thing in Marseilles," he said. "Massacre on the
waterfront." But Le Corbusier judged the *Unité* a success, a step
toward his often-drawn Utopia: mass housing dominated by cruciform
skyscrapers, a project he proposed several times, including his designs
for a rebuilt Paris, but never saw realized.

But Chandigarh, dating mainly from the early 1950s, grew into the most massive construction project of Le Corbusier's life. The Secretariat with its fleet of offices, the far smaller Palace of Justice, the Assembly Hall, along with a few other buildings, all read like a proud justification of his latest manner. Three and four stories high—an incurable shortage of financial resources prevented the architect and his colleagues from building more ambitiously—the august horizontality of these buildings suits their silent, severe background, the chain of Himalaya peaks. The buildings, poems in concrete, are recognizably Le Corbusier's, but not much was left from the house as machine. On the contrary, late Le Corbusier, amply equipped with fetching slogans, now spoke passionately about the human scale.

5.

THE CHANDRIGARH commission conveniently illustrates the importance of access to power for making major building projects a reality. A preeminent American architect, Louis Kahn, entrusted with designing the capital of Pakistan, Dacca, is another splendid instance of such access. As Le Corbusier's self-serving activities during the Vichy years show, he was no innocent on this front. After France's defeat by the Germans in June 1940, the country was largely run by the occupying forces. It became a time of cowardice, treachery, and demeaning compromises with the victor, ending only with liberation in 1944–45. For Le Corbusier, this shattering catastrophe was an opportunity. A long-standing admirer of Marshal Pétain, he saw the Vichy regime as a potential patron, intelligent enough to recognize the talents of a great builder like himself, authoritarian enough to have its orders enforced. To Le Corbusier, who claimed to be unpolitical, Vichy enjoyed all the advantages of the French spirit with none of its defects; the squabbles of corrupt politicians that had made France so notorious (and Le Corbusier so impatient) seemed at an end.

Vichy, then, promised what we know Le Corbusier regarded as a public architect's most gratifying and most dependable ally: order. Early in 1941 he was appointed to a provisional committee devoted to reconstructing war-damaged France; during those heady days he maneuvered to enlist the authorities in his far-reaching plans for Algiers, a city he undertook to turn into a centralized, powerful capital of France's colonial territories. Writing to General Maxime Weygand, then the country's Governor General of North Africa, he did not conceal his authoritarian hopes: "In the present administrative state, only the highest authorities of the country can permit the necessary innovations, create the useful precedents, authorize the ignoring of old regulations, permit the Plan to enter into life." What he was asking for, he said plainly, was "an order from above" and a "gesture of authority" that would cancel present plans and introduce a new one: Le Corbusier's.

Biographers of Le Corbusier have generally shied away from these political adventures, such as they were. One can see why. During the first two years of the Vichy regime, he behaved like one of its most committed supporters. He excoriated the vices of an uncontrolled, immoral press, singled out the French peasantry for its native vigor and clean principles and the purity of the French race, and praised the civilizing works of colonial administrators. Le Corbusier found these "sound"—which is to say, reactionary—notions, with their primitive nationalism and racial chauvinism, attractive for ideological and expedient reasons alike. They articulated, doubtless overstated, his grand simplicities about the contemporary world, and they were opportune convictions to trumpet in the hope of gaining Pétain's ear. But the Vichy regime, already mired in insoluble internal conflicts among conservatives, ideologues, and technocrats, showed little interest in his grand plans. If there are no Le Corbusier buildings between 1941 and 1945, France's Fascist interlude, that was not for his want of trying. He was lucky: the energetic, vengeful campaign after the war to purge Vichyites from public life spared Le Corbusier as perhaps too insignificant a collaborator. But his forays into influence-seeking, no matter how shabby the masters he was flattering, are a comment on the almost unlimited varieties of avant-garde politics. The promise of access to power was so potent an aphrodisiac that only a few, even modernists, failed to be susceptible to it.

"GOOD PROPORTIONS AND
PRACTICAL SIMPLICITY"

1.

IN 1932, NEW YORK'S recently founded Museum of Modern Art—it was just three years old—mounted an exhibition that boldly departed from its usual fare, contemporary paintings, showing the work of some forty leading architects from fifteen countries. The persuasive and controversial director of the museum, Alfred H. Barr, Jr., one of the true heroes of modernism, signally alert to European currents of art and energetically resolved to rouse his countrymen's interest in them, stood as a benevolent godfather. It was Barr who baptized the radical new architecture as "the International Style." Curated by the architectural historian Henry-Russell Hitchcock and the architect Philip Johnson, the show was a revelation. Frank Lloyd Wright, though then shackled by a lengthy creative block, had shown his countrymen one uniquely individual face of modernism. But the aesthetic possibilities of the straight line and the rectangle, the absence of ornament, the prominence of "inelegant" materials featured in the buildings being exhibited, were not yet very well known in the United States, and this exhibition tried to remedy that omission.

To capture this moment, which did for modernist architecture in the United States almost as much as the great Armory Show had done for modernist painting there two decades earlier, the two curators wrote an animated, amply illustrated little book that spread the name of this innovation to a larger public: *The International Style: Architecture Since 1922.* It was a style with few fathers and innumerable offspring, some of them stylish and many of them dull, as it increasingly came to dominate the design of office buildings in major American cities and elsewhere during the decades ahead.

Conservatives were not alone in complaining about this aesthetic nudity; there were detractors of modernist architecture even within the modernist camp. Sibyl, widow of the Hungarian designer László Moholy-Nagy, who sympathetically followed her husband's work at the

Bauhaus and later in Chicago, pointedly accused Mies van der Rohe of self-parodies in his later years. Other supporters of modernism became uncomfortable with the repetitive facades of mirrored skyscrapers and thought them soulless monsters, uninteresting in themselves and indifferent to their most important clients, the people who worked in them.* Yet the style also had important boosters, for all its unimaginative copyists: in 1959, Philip Johnson designed for himself a famous Miesian glass house in Connecticut, a pure rectangle in which only the bathroom walls reach to the ceiling. It was a fervent, indeed eloquent homage to the International Style. Later, Johnson designed an underground addition to house his art collection, and a conventional guesthouse, both implicit critical comments on the built-in limitations of glass walls.

2.

THE MOST IMPRESSIVE among the originators of the International Style was, beyond a doubt, Walter Gropius. His felicitous amalgam of imagination, craftsmanship, practicality, and, not to forget, didactic and ideological impulses, make him a superlative representative of German modernism. The young Gropius did not disdain the lessons that practical experience could impart. From 1907 to 1910, he worked in the office of Peter Behrens in Berlin, already praised here for his adaptability. When Gropius joined Behrens's atelier, his chief, unlike most German architects then working, had freed himself from traditional décor or that ornate novelty, Art Nouveau, to adopt a leaner, clearer vocabulary. In that year, 1907, Behrens was appointed artistic counselor to the Allgemeine Elektrizitäts-Gesellschaft (A.E.G.), Germany's largest supplier of electrical equipment. Here was an enlightened entrepreneur employing the services of an enlightened craftsman, a promising, unpolitical alliance that Gropius never forgot. Behrens designed massive factories, attractive and useful lamps, glass bottles, electric fans,

---

* "The last six years," Lewis Mumford wrote in 1954, "have brought forth a boom development in modern office buildings in Manhattan. With the exception of Lever House, these buildings have increased the congestion of New York's midtown business areas without adding much to the glory of its architecture."

typography for catalogs, whatever came his way at the A.E.G. It was an ideal atmosphere for Gropius to acquire firsthand knowledge about the intimate interplay of design and architecture.

After opening his own office in Berlin in 1910, Gropius spent much time dwelling on the public implications of architectural practice. It struck Gropius very early that the leading figures in his profession (always, of course, exempting Behrens) were snobbish in their social attitude and reactionary in their aesthetic judgment. These "arbiters of good taste," he recalled, largely confined their attention to "the small circle of the affluent," signally failing to respect the needs of modern industry and modern housing. "Even before World War I," he wrote years later, "I and some other architects grew alarmed to see that, more and more, the members of our profession were putting themselves into a straitjacket." This uneasiness would prove a most helpful preparation for the formation of the modernist protest.

In 1910, Gropius sent a memorandum to Emil Rathenau, chief of the A.E.G., that allows the historian to put his later recollections into their contemporary context. He allied himself with the proponents of the machine and of prefabricated, standard components in building. But he also spoke severely about speculative builders who care only for their profits. Current fashions in design, he noted harshly, are a deadly combination of "overloading and false romanticism" that had taken the "place of good proportions and practical simplicity." Denouncing the "inner disintegration"—*Zerrissenheit*—of German life that obstructed the formation of an up-to-date style—Gropius, too, as a good modernist, wanted to live and work in his time—he joined the social critics who for a century and more had been dismayed at the "fragmentation" of German culture. It was a problematic conclusion. To see the country as a lamentable age of experts blind to everything beyond their narrow enclave came close to nostalgia for a past that had never existed for the sake of a future that seemed exceedingly implausible.

Gropius, in short, gave the critique of his country's bad taste a German twist. He both defended the impact of the machine and mass production and at the same time flavored that argument with hard words against the "crass materialism" that tarnishes modern "mass civilization." The hunger for wholeness that beset so many thoughtful Germans beset him as well. It was not until the creation of the Bauhaus, a modernist institution at its purest, that he found a way of synthesizing these incompatible convictions.

3.

"THIS IS MORE THAN JUST a lost war," wrote Gropius in the fall of 1918, on leave from the Italian front and witnessing at home the revolution that would obliterate the German Empire. "A world has come to an end. We must seek a radical solution to our problems." Since 1914, when he was only thirty-one, he had been considered for the post of director for the School of Arts and Crafts at Weimar, in the gift of the odd, unpredictable Grand Duke of Saxe-Weimar. The tortuous negotiations over the authority of the school's director grew ever more enmeshed in politics with the disappearance of the dukedom during the revolution. The multiple traumas of vast losses in the war, the creation of a much-diminished Germany as a republic, the humiliating clauses of the Versailles Treaty holding the country responsible for the catastrophic hostilities just concluded, were potent ingredients in Germans' pervasive despair and wild hopes. The Bauhaus would be perhaps the greatest victory on the part of a country in the throes of abject defeat.

Gropius's creation was steadily short of funds; its students were almost invariably poor, though not in spirit; the right-wing Thuringian politicians from whom it had to secure subsidies had little use for the untraditional school that stressed collective decision making, seemed to reject all long-established styles, chose for itself an unprecedented modern title, "*Bauhaus*," and dared to hire an Expressionist like Lyonel Feininger—surely a Bolshevik!—to teach graphics and book design. When the founding manifesto of the Bauhaus appeared in late April 1919, it showed itself all the more provocative by having a Feininger woodcut, a stylized secular Expressionist cathedral, grace its title page. If the Bauhaus survived at all—which it did until the Nazi regime made it, as it were, commit suicide in 1933—that was due mainly to Gropius's negotiating skills, the infectious high morale of teachers and students, and, after 1925, the move to Dessau with the courageous support of that city's democratic mayor, Fritz Hesse, in the face of persistent, indefatigable opposition from Nazis and their political bedfellows.

IN TUNE WITH NEARLY all avant-garde institutions, the Bauhaus introduced itself to the public with a towering manifesto, towering in its aspirations but democratic in its tone. The voice was that of Gropius and his, too, was the conviction that to eradicate class distinctions at the Bauhaus was the most urgent prerequisite for its success. Artists of all descriptions must recognize their essential equality and their supreme duty to work together in old-fashioned concord. "*Architects, sculptors, painters, we must all turn back to the crafts.*" At the same time, all engaged in the building arts must acknowledge their equally essential kinship with industry, a cooperation free of snobbery. "Let us create *a new guild of craftsmen* without the class-separating presumption that would raise an arrogant barrier between craftsmen and artists."

Gropius, of course, was an architect, and the emphatic opening sentence of his manifesto bluntly described the "final aim" of all the diverse creative activities at the Bauhaus as "*der Bau!*"—the building. He wanted to restore "the architectonic spirit" that, like other reformers, he believed had been largely lost amidst Victorian eclecticism and the undeserved popularity of historicist architecture. But the aim was easier to proclaim than to realize. In a republic barely surviving, unsettled about its possible future in the concert of nations, laden with political extremists and rage at the extortionate Allies, the Bauhaus, too, was searching for a satisfying direction.

Some of its early irresolution was homegrown. If there were strong alliances among the staff of the Bauhaus, there were almost equally strong tensions. The required introductory half-year course, first run by Johannes Itten, a zealous, self-styled reformer of education with an eccentric mystical streak, was the very antithesis of the tough-minded Realism that Gropius had reached after years of flirting with

Expressionist self-expression. It was not until 1923, when Itten left and was replaced by László Moholy-Nagy, a firm believer, with Gropius, in "Art and Technology—a New Unity," that the anti-Utopians had an open field. "We want a clear, organic architecture," Gropius said in the same year, "whose inner logic will be radiant and naked, unencumbered by lying facades and trickeries; we want an architecture adapted to our world of machines, radios, and fast motorcars, an architecture whose function is clear." This is the ambiance in which Marcel Breuer was to design world-famous chairs and Herbert Bayer equally famous typefaces.

IN 1928, AFTER RUNNING the Bauhaus for ten years of an active directorship, worn more by politics than by architecture, Gropius decided to return to private practice. His successor, Hannes Meyer, attempted to remake the Bauhaus in a Marxist image. Yet powerful politicians in Thüringen demonized the school's tastes and projects— during the Weimar Republic every gesture, including the design of undecorated teacups, somehow became political. For die-hard fantasts dreaming of a Germany restored to great power status and revenged on its enemies, the Bauhaus was a symbol of decadence; in 1925, they managed to force it out of Weimar to the friendlier atmosphere of Dessau, not for its failures but for its successes. And, however embittered the battles over design remained, the paintings of Paul Klee and Vasili Kandinsky, the graphics of Lyonel Feininger and Gerhard Marcks, the furniture designed by Marcel Breuer and Ludwig Mies van der Rohe, were notable instances of modern art and utility that secured international responses.

Walter Gropius for his part devised one of his most successful structures during the Dessau years of the Bauhaus: the new school building, a grouping of four interdependent rectangles unapologetically modern, bearing his signature throughout, all thoughtfully differentiated. The fleet of small balconies interrupting the flat surfaces on the housing for pupils were a playful departure from the sober collectivity, as were the glass walls that surrounded the workshops and flooded them with dazzling sunlight. Not a stone in that school was old-fashioned, not a square foot was pure decoration.

The housing estates that Gropius designed after his resignation were equally pleasing, as long as one was willing to be pleased by plain surfaces; agreeable in shape, moderate in costs, immeasurably superior to the kind of dwelling common for the working classes. Here social sympathies and aesthetic preferences joined hands. As late as 1934, the year after the Bauhaus masters had decided to accept the inevitable and voted to close themselves down, Gropius still tried in letters to the authorities to save the new architecture by proving it inherently German—a futile, not very dignified gesture. It soon became plain that his front service during the First World War, and the indisputable "purity" of his "German blood," would bring him neither private nor public commissions. In the fall of 1934, he left for England. Mies van der Rohe, who had served as director of the clearly dying Bauhaus from 1930 to 1933, left Hitler's Third Reich for America in 1937. They took the International Style with them.

Walter Gropius, Siemensstadt Housing Development, Berlin (1930).
Social housing at its least shabby.

Frank Lloyd Wright, "Fallingwater," Edgar Kaufmann House (1936).
Perhaps the most celebrated modernist residence ever built.

"HITLER IS MY BEST FRIEND"

ALMOST FROM ITS BEGINNINGS, modernism was a cosmopolitan
affair. Few titles on modern architecture are more appropriate than the
book that Henry-Russell Hitchcock and Philip Johnson published in
1932 to accompany the important exhibition at the Museum of Modern
Art, *The International Style*. It may serve as a far more comprehensive
slogan than just in the history of architecture. No appraisal of Baudelaire's mind-set would be complete without including his translations
of Edgar Allan Poe's dark tales. In his advocacy of art for art's sake,
Oscar Wilde was more dependent on French literary critics than on his

English countrymen. T. S. Eliot's shocking *Waste Land* owed more to Jules Laforgue's French verse than to any English-speaking poet. The rapidly rising popularity of French Impressionists significantly remade the market in painting across Europe and the United States. Two of the greatest composers of the twentieth century, Schoenberg and Stravinsky, we will recall, ended up in Los Angeles, almost neighbors. And, more arresting even than any of these, the careers of modernist architects—most notably Gropius and Mies van der Rohe—reached their fulfillment in American exile, which did not feel like exile long.

As we know, from the early 1920s to the mid-1940s, the headquarters of modernism mov ed from Paris, London, and Berlin to New York and Chicago. American collectors had long been noted for their impassioned greed for European masterpieces and for their open purses. Now, with the political ascendancy of totalitarianism of the right and the left in Europe, artists and intellectuals of all stripes, kept from working or in danger of their lives, sought haven in the United States. Walter Cook, director of the Institute for Fine Arts in New York, used to say, undiplomatically but accurately enough, "Hitler is my best friend. He shakes the tree and I collect the apples." The list is long and distinguished, and it propelled American culture into the twentieth century.

Of course, not all eminent European immigrants were modernists. Nor were immigrant modernists necessarily fleeing from the Nazi or the Communist regimes. Marcel Duchamp and Edgard Varèse were only two French rebels who came to the United States before Hitler and stayed. Conventional academics, film directors, psychologists, musicians, sociologists, art historians, and others came by the hundreds and permanently enriched their new homeland. All of them, Jews and gentiles alike—for, common reports to the contrary, there were sizable numbers of non-Jewish, purely political refugees among them—had been unwelcome outsiders to their official culture. America gave these arrivals astonishing opportunities that so many Europeans could never have predicted. Surprisingly, the United States, a society (they generally believed) without traditions or high culture and enslaved to the dollar, showed itself rescuing—and appreciating—talented and unconventional artists.

Among the most spectacular results of America's benevolence to architectural radicals, not wholly disinterested—there was after all much to learn, much to profit, from them—was that by 1939, the year the Second World War erupted, the Bauhaus could have celebrated a well-populated reunion in the United States. László Moholy-Nagy, Gropius's close ally in championing the machine and the union of art and technology, moved to Chicago to start (unsuccessfully) a new Bauhaus and (more successfully) the Chicago Institute of Design, where he experimented with an impressive range of students— painters, sculptors, and photographers. Josef Albers, who since 1923 had taught the required introductory course at the Bauhaus with Moholy-Nagy, found his first home in the United States appropriately enough in the avant-garde Black Mountain College in North Carolina and later moved on to Yale as a widely recognized expert in color theory. Mies van der Rohe, who reached the United States in 1938, was invited to join the Illinois Institute of Technology, then moving to new quarters, and to design the new campus in faultless Miesian style— sober, lucid, severely geometric. The conspicuous apartment houses he built, also in Chicago, underscored his aesthetic of Less is More, and did their share in behalf of the recognition of an aesthetic reduced to its essentials: material and structure.

The most consequential of the *Bauhäusler* in the land of unlimited, modernist possibilities was Walter Gropius himself. During a three-year stopover in England, he left his mark with a brilliantly designed Impington Village College in Cambridgeshire with a local partner, Maxwell Fry. In 1937, he accepted an invitation from Harvard University to take a professorship of architecture; and a year later, he was appointed chairman of Harvard's Department of Architecture, a conspicuous post he held for fifteen years. Some time before his retirement—much though he enjoyed teaching, he did not want to stop designing—he formed a firm that, stressing his favorite mode of procedures, he characteristically named The Architects' Collaborative (TAC). With TAC he built schools, private houses, office buildings, embassies. And he would proudly show visitors the round office table where the partners at TAC sat in their discussions to offer their "stimulating and challenging" critiques. Gropius's commitment to the principle of cooperation did not compromise his romantic dedication to the image of the solitary creator. "The creative spark," he insisted, "originates always with the individual." Thus he gave a home to two modernist ideals, individualism and collegiality, often at odds.

ARCHITECTURAL CRITICS have given Gropius's later buildings mixed reviews, complaining of a certain tendency toward the monumental or the repetitious. The International Style, which he often represented at its best, was not without its problematic temptations. But certainly the house he built for himself and his family in 1937 at Lincoln, Massachu-

Walter Gropius in front of his house at Lincoln, Massachusetts (1937). Note the "unmodernist" circular staircase at right.

setts, shows important undogmatic detail.* An emphatically rectangular two-story building, amply supplied with large windows looking out on the gently rolling New England countryside, it is filled with Bauhaus furniture, including Breuer's best known chairs. It has a flat roof, a "vocabulary of typical New England materials and forms: wood painted white, brick chimney, screened porch, field stone foundation and retaining walls"—I am quoting from a publication of the Society for the Preservation of New England Antiquities—with "all of the fixtures and building supplies factory-made." Yet, "despite the use of American materials and vernacular forms, the appearance of the house is decidedly European."

The Gropius house, then, was largely a predictable product, predictable for the kind of home that a former director of the Bauhaus would want to live in. Yet it has one obtrusive, "inorganic" feature: a circular staircase connecting the first and second floors, plastered as it were onto the exterior of the building. It is only a small personal touch, but, precisely because it is so intimate, it testifies to the individualistic quality that so decisively distinguished modernist architecture from the Beaux-Arts historicist products whose pitiless critic it had been for decades. The explanation for that odd staircase is that Gropius's teenage daughter, who had a room upstairs, did not want her high school friends to have to traipse through the living room when they came to visit. Modernism with a human face.

"BEAUTY WAITING FOR US"

2.

TO SHIFT FROM MODERNIST architecture to modernist design is to take only a short step; in fact, for a significant number of gifted craftsmen with pencil in hand (or nowadays, computer at their service) it may not be a step at all. The architects I have discussed played with design; the designers I shall discuss played at architecture. Not rarely, the drafts-

---

* Marcel Breuer, Gropius's colleague from the Bauhaus who would also enjoy a distinguished career in the United States, collaborated in the design.

man was equally prominent in both subjects. Hence the pages that follow can be relatively brief. The parallels are not exact, but close
enough to have many a single statement unravel more than one problem. Thus we have a few Gropius chairs and desks, but they never
matched the lasting sales of Mies's and Le Corbusier's furniture pieces.
If Gropius's concentration of attention on building—and lecturing—
was exceptional, at least part of the explanation was that, as he once
famously said, he had spent 90 percent of his time as director of the
Bauhaus defending his creation against disbelieving conservatives and
hostile right-wingers. He certainly had less time for design than his fellow architects.

Most other modernists defied boundaries. They even devised a
rationale for their escape from dividing the labor of construction. As
usual, Frank Lloyd Wright put the matter forcefully: "The most truly
satisfactory apartments are those in which most or all of the furniture is
built in as part of the original scheme. The whole must always be considered as an integral unit." He could have added that freestanding furniture was particularly acceptable to modernist designers like him when
it recalled, or directly quoted, the architect's stylistic signature. Unity of
conception was essential to that most attractive result, unity of performance. "Everything in a room must be like an instrument in an orchestra," the Austrian playwright and journalist Hermann Bahr, open to all
the innovative streams that surrounded him, wrote poetically; "the
architect is the conductor, the whole should produce a symphony." Thus
Richard Wagner's ideal of the *Gesamtkunstwerk*, the comprehensive
work of art springing as a whole and with all its particulars from a single
inspired imagination, entered the domestic choices of the prosperous
Victorian and post-Victorian bourgeoisie, especially in Central Europe.

Architects and designers were so closely allied also because their
principal grievance was the same. Both lamented what they damned as
the shoddy taste of their potential customers: the sentimental passion for
cheap souvenirs—not always so cheap—brought home from vacations
abroad, the grandiose facades of private houses dimly evoking past masterpieces, the lame efforts at humor with tacky, "adorable" constructions
made of papier-mâché. The indiscriminate vengefulness of the reform-

ers was no doubt simplistic; some nineteenth-century designers, without the blessings of theory, had already manufactured domestic products plain enough to look in retrospect alien to those widely copied, widely criticized treasures from the Victoria and Albert Museum. They would have been at home in the Bauhaus workshops, some seventy years "ahead of their time."* In 1852, the American sculptor and prescient traveler Horatio Greenough had laid it down that "the redundant must be pared down, the superfluous dropped, the necessary itself reduced to the simplest expression, and then we shall find, whatever the organization may be, that beauty was waiting for us." These Victorians did not have the word "functionalism," but they practiced it.

By the end of the nineteenth century, in country after country, designers in search of honesty and simplicity had founded organizations aiming to wean the public from kitsch. The English Arts and Crafts Movement inveighed against the aesthetic poverty of potters, cabinetmakers, and silver smiths. It gathered up a small corps of national, and often nationalist, dissenters, producing from cosmopolitan London furnishings popular in Berlin and Vienna. Just as inventive was the Glasgow architect and designer Charles Rennie Mackintosh, celebrated for his Art Nouveau designs, who found a more sympathetic response on the Continent than in his home environment.

From the advanced vantage point of modernist design, the institutions intent on purifying taste seemed like halfhearted efforts to break loose from conventional dictates without following up their discontent with truly creative resourcefulness. In large part, for all their goodwill, these critics of conventionality suffered from ambivalence about that vexed question we have encountered before: what to do about the machine. The legacy of William Morris's medievalism was hard to shake off, and it was not until the later stages of their efforts that some subversives moved to accept twentieth-century industrial culture. The

* Readers might like to consult an astonishing, amply illustrated but relatively little known book, Herwin Schaefer, *Nineteenth-Century Modern: The Functional Tradition in Victorian Design* (1970). It would enable them to win bets by showing one of the illustrations and asking, "When do you think this easy chair—or teapot—was made?" The almost inevitable reply would be, "The Bauhaus, ca. 1922." And that would be off by about seventy years.

activist English architect and designer Charles Robert Ashbee, closely identified with Arts and Crafts, founder of the Guild of Handicraft (1888), and a friend of Frank Lloyd Wright's, did not acknowledge until 1911 that "modern civilization rests on machinery." It followed, for him, that "no system for the endowment, or the encouragement, of the teaching of art can be sound that does not recognize this." The road to Gropius and Moholy-Nagy, the complete modernists, was slowly being constructed mile by mile.

2.

RESISTANCE TO MODERNIST design came from all directions of the compass. It demonstrates the psychological effectiveness of consistent conservatism, an emotional defense of things as they are simply because they are; it was powerful enough to prevail even when it conflicted with naked self-interest. We have already seen Muthesius's prediction that in Germany the adoption of modern techniques and tastes would produce a "struggle against existing conditions." In fact, his lectures and his controversial book on the English house generated what his denigrators called "the Muthesius case." Anxious, angry artisans and manufacturers of useful and decorative objects rudely denounced him as "an enemy to German art" and some demanded that he be prohibited from continuing to mislead students of design with his subversive talk. Still, until the Nazis took over the country in 1933 with a thoroughness that overlooked no ingredient in German culture, the message of Muthesius and his associates found a certain hearing. With its stimulating periodical, *Die Form*, launched in 1925, the Werkbund spread word of new materials and new techniques, and at least some producers went along with its teachings. Among these moderns, the sheer existence of the Bauhaus stood as a sign of hope.

Yet mass production remained the principal barrier everywhere. It grated on tradition-minded makers of furniture, conservative craftsmen, unadventurous storeowners, and on cultural critics, as a vulgar betrayal of sacred standards. The German word *Typisierung*—"standardization" or "rationalization"—became a psychologically charged fighting label.

The very language of the debaters, often across frontiers, ornamented their verbal battles with philosophical profundities: the German Werkbund defined its task as the *Veredelung* and the *Durchgeistigung*, the "ennoblement" and the "thoroughgoing spiritualization," of products of common use. Other reform-minded countries—Britain, France, the United States—felt uncomfortable with such talk as pretentious and really meaningless, but their own stabs at letting objects speak for themselves were, if less oratorical, quite as sweeping.

Inescapably, the all too widespread disdain of Europeans for American civilization made its appearance in these controversies. In 1931, the German manufacturer Roger Ginsburger published a talk in *Die Form*, relating a story that briskly dramatizes the common, fierce opposition to what was identified as the American contribution to modern vulgarity. Ginsburger was speaking with a French manufacturer of door fittings and suggested to him that instead of continuing to produce and store three hundred types of door handles, some of which might find only a single customer a year, he concentrate on a single reliable and pleasing type in various sizes. This would save storage, advertising, and personnel, and permit him to sell his product more inexpensively than ever. To which his acquaintance rather pathetically replied, "I can see that you, too, are among the people who want to Americanize France." To Americanize: it was in those years a weighty and highly familiar charge.

SINCE ARCHITECTURE and design, far more, say, than poetry or painting, impinged on ordinary life and the bulk of people's aesthetic choices, organizations devoted to civilizing the general taste could not evade the commercial side of consumer interest. It was obviously one thing to draw unconventional designs, quite another to find customers for them. And two groups, the Wiener Werkstätte and the Bauhaus, the first a pale echo, the second an attempt at the realization of modernism, took divergent roads that designers could take to the sober reality of sales.

The spiritual father of the Wiener Werkstätte, or Vienna Workshop, was the prolific Austrian architect and designer Josef Hoffmann, as prominent in his field as Gustav Klimt was among Austrian painters. One of the founders of the Vienna Secession in 1897, he organized the Werkstätte six years later. His companions in the venture were the designer Koloman Moser, who in the first years worked closely with him, and Fritz Wärndorfer, a rich textile manufacturer imbued with modern tastes, far more interested in spending money than in making it. He was precisely the financier—well traveled, impassioned, obstinate, munificent—that the Werkstätte needed.

At first, Wärndorfer and Moser complemented Hoffmann to perfection. Born in 1870, Hoffmann had been trained in Vienna's Academy of Art, then a provincial backwater. "The atmosphere," he recalled years later, "was entirely uninteresting and inartistic"; in its halls, the great instigators of a new art and design—Charles Rennie Mackintosh, John Ruskin, William Morris, and Aubrey Beardsley, in the company of stimulating French and Belgian modern artists—simply went unmentioned. The complaints that less stale designers had been launching against official academies for many decades were also the complaints of the Viennese. Felicitous adjustments to current technological innovations seemed to be going on in other countries, but not at home. "We were seized with an endless longing," Hoffmann remembered, "to want and to attempt something other than what we saw every day."

What Hoffmann and his fellow rebels witnessed every day was the monumental, derivative Ringstrasse, recently completed, with its massive, dated, unadventurous public buildings in the center of Vienna. It was, to anyone even remotely interested in modernist attitudes, an inelegant accumulation of boring design that proved a perfect instance of what horrors to get away from. And they saw, too, the oversized historical machines by the fashionable painter Hans Makart, an immensely popular representative of Salon art. "It was a very unfavorable time for us young people," wrote Koloman Moser. "Everyone was completely enthralled by the Makart craze, with its playful ephemera and its dusty bouquets." In response, the periodical *Ver Sacrum*, the organ of the Vienna Secession, called for war on "the inactive slovenliness, the rigid Byzantinism, and all that tastelessness."

There was, then, in those days much to design against, and Hoffmann led the opposition in virtually every conceivable field. Among his houses—and he built important ones for fellow artists—the most widely discussed, really inimitable design remained the Stoclet family mansion in Brussels, built before the First World War. It was a spacious manor built, obviously enough, for a multimillionaire Belgian industrialist, magnificently decorated, including a stunning wall-length mosaic by Gustav Klimt in the dining room. Built across some six years, between 1905 and 1911, its plans underwent constant revisions by architect and client, which only added to the cost, already astronomic.* One did not have to be a tycoon to become a customer at the Werkstätte's sales outlets or the exhibitions to which it sent tempting samples, but it helped.

Obsessed with making shapes, it was with objects that Hoffmann gave his sharp pencil the freest rein. His fury for design was ubiquitous. He did furniture: sofas, beds, bookcases, tables, dressers, lamps, adjustable easy chairs, rocking chairs, mirrors, candelabra; he did domestic objects: wallpaper, clocks, samovars, vases, pitchers, glasses, cups and saucers, inkwells, rugs, trays, book jackets, even handbags; he did decorative items: jewelry, medals, monograms, combs, toys, necklaces. His gift for appreciation was catholic, his resourcefulness astonishing, even a little frightening. Hoffmann was supremely playful, and to appease his passion, he could find little use for the average consumer. His readers have not missed the prominence of his claim to realism in his self-presentations, but reality was far from the Werkstätte's ideal. Its cadre of well more than a hundred employees kept only the upper bourgeoisie in mind, an aristocracy of consumers. It is not that Hoffmann and the others disdained the machine; they acknowledged its mounting centrality

---

* Jane Kallir notes: "What the three-story, forty-odd-room house ended up costing will remain forever a secret, though it is known that the materials for Klimt's dining-room frieze alone came to 100,000 kronen. . . . Throughout the house only the best, most costly materials were used: real gold and jewels adorned the figures in Klimt's frieze, rare colored marble was carefully matched and affixed both to the exterior and to many of the interior rooms, the ultimate in craftsmanship, from marquetry to mosaic work, was applied to the decorative detailing. Not only did the Wiener *Werkstätte* supervise every detail, including a special silver service, but it also employed an army of outside artists and artisans on the project."

in the life of design, and there were times when they actually condescended to using some mass-produced items. But that modernist side of
their work remained marginal.

What is more, his sketchbooks give witness that Hoffmann would
never leave his designs alone; if there was one thing he loathed, it was
repeating himself. In 1903, he became interested in silverware, and his
first drawings showed unornamented, purely geometric shapes. Yet
their form did not follow their function, as truly modernist designs
would have done. The knives and forks were too long and slender to be
held comfortably, the spoons too shallow to be efficient. And soon,
Hoffmann started to embellish his cutlery, adding leaves, fruit, abstract
decorative edges. It was these later "improvements" that so irritated
Loos in his campaign against ornament in architecture and design. But
Hoffmann was never a consistent functionalist; his work was the triumph of imagination over utility.

3.

FROM ITS FOUNDING IN 1903 to its collapse in 1932 at the nadir of the
Depression, the Wiener Werkstätte was a losing enterprise that visibly
bore the seeds of its destruction. The Bauhaus survived the death of the
Werkstätte by one year. But the parallels between these two contemporaries are too inexact to serve as useful comparisons: the German institution was a state-subsidized school, a place for experiments and
innovative styles of life; its Austrian counterpart was a large private
shop with sales the principal interest. The objects the Werkstätte
showed were often elegant, usually well manufactured, and for the
most part handmade. Its language—mainly Hoffmann's—featured
some indisputably modernist declarations: "As long as our cities, our
houses, our rooms, our furniture, our belongings, our clothes and our
jewelry, as long as our language and sentiments fail to reflect the spirit
of our times in a plain, simple, and beautiful way, we shall be by a long
way behind our ancestors." But, however eager the Werkstätte's
spokesmen seemed to sound like good modernists—"reflect the spirit
of our times," "plain, simple"—their practice was markedly more con-

formist than this. The quality of their work was always more important to them than their sales figures.

The work program of the Wiener Werkstätte, published in 1905, was more revealing about its founders' true loyalties than they might have suspected. "The unlimited harm that appalling mass production on the one hand and thoughtless imitation of old styles on the other has caused among the arts and crafts has overrun the whole world like a gigantic flood. . . . In place of the hand the machine has taken over for the most part, in place of the artisan the businessman has taken over." Granted, "it would be insanity to try to counteract these streams." And yet—there would always be an "and yet" in such apologies—that is why the authors of the program had founded the Werkstätte, "to provide a spot of tranquility amidst the cheerful noise of the craftsmen." Their foundation, they said, should be particularly welcome to anyone who confesses his allegiance to Ruskin and Morris. "We cannot, and will not, compete with cheap prices." Indeed, "the surrogates in stylish imitations can only gratify the parvenu." This snobbish contempt could hardly have been more bellicose: the hand, threatened by "progress" and insufficiently appreciated, is vastly superior to the machine; price should not matter; above all, modish copies will satisfy only the newly rich. No wonder that during its decades of showing interesting designs to the world, the Wiener Werkstätte ruined two millionaires who passionately supported it until their resources ran out.

4.

THE MEN AND WOMEN of the Bauhaus, teachers and students alike, then, lived in a different world. Hoffmann's aesthetic was, for all its delight in unhackneyed results, often quite eclectic, depending more on his creative interests of the moment than on abstract principles of design. The Werkstätte prized ingenuity, sometimes at the expense of good sense; but in any event, what mattered most was that the villas and apartments of its clients, their decor and their furnishings, to say nothing of the fashionable ladies of the house wearing its clothes, exuded a sense of well-protected prosperity, no matter how dire the economic situation might be out of doors. Hence the respective significance of ornament and of machine-made production remained an unsettled conundrum for Viennese designers. It needed patrons who did not have to look at price tags, and when it could find no more, it discovered that industrial clients were unable to meet its bills, and all it could do was to close up shop.

For their part, the *Bauhäusler* wore the badge of poverty with pride and ingenuity. The teachers, especially in the introductory course, would regale students with terse maxims about the fundamentals that had brought them together: Tradition is the enemy. Mass-manufactured objects can be as good-looking as an artisan's unique product. Art and craftsmanship, now so fatally separated, belong together to stimulate one another. There were ideological tensions at the Bauhaus that Gropius, who preferred diplomacy to authoritarian edicts, would not resolve or simply declare out of bounds. Commitments to practicality continued to battle with Expressionist notions that had been stirring in the Bauhaus from the beginning. Feininger's famous woodcut of a cathedral in its founding manifesto was a gesture, but not an empty one. Yet the students were never swamped in Utopian rhetoric; they progressed toward expertise in the workshops they entered after passing through the preliminary course. They painted, constructed furniture, invented lighting fixtures, wove carpets, designed typefaces and teapots, all of them indifferent or antagonistic to the familiar legacies of their trade. They tried to understand not only what they were doing but why they were doing it. In their reminiscences, those who recorded their Bauhaus experience liked to recall the modest feasts they would organize with a glass or two of cheap wine when one of them had succeeded in completing a fine-looking and efficient desk or a distinctive, unconventional carpet.

They had good reasons to celebrate. The bulk of their income, first in Weimar and then in Dessau, came from state and local subventions, never quite adequate to provide sufficient study materials or subsidies to students who could not afford the fees. Hence the royalties students received for designs adopted by manufacturers helped them, and with that the Bauhaus, to meet their financial obligations.* For left-wing students, this fraternal pact between creative design and large-scale industry was less than welcome, but in principle, the Bauhaus, though devoted to a radical renewal of German society, never specified the political implications of the workable products the students contributed. I have noted it before: counterintuitive though this conclusion may be, the modernist imagination was compatible with all political systems that would tolerate it.

Through it all, Gropius insisted that there was no such thing as a Bauhaus style. One can see how important this disclaimer was to him: he was intent on underscoring the students' creative freedom. There was no authoritarian party line that would have compelled all the products of the Bauhaus to follow a single recognizable manner. Certainly the buildings he himself designed and those of Mies van der Rohe could never be mistaken for one another. There were some limits to imaginative enterprise that a modernist architect or designer would be unwilling to transgress: to overload a building with decor, to conceal or disguise materials in use, to ignore the function of the object to be designed.

Yet actually—as the brilliant romantic extravagances of Frank Lloyd Wright testify—even these fundamental rules could be bent to the will of an architect original and obstinate enough to insist that his own way was the only possible one. Still, setting aside a few striking exceptions, the working company at the Bauhaus and its followers at home and abroad—there were many—remained faithful to the principles announced from the early days of modernism by pioneers like Baudelaire and Daumier. They wanted to be in tune with their times, which meant in practice that they hoped to reshape their times in accord with their modernist commitments. What they aimed to make and spread through catalogs and exhibitions was objects at once hand-

* In 1923 (to mention only two of many instances) the Bauhaus pupil Otto Lindig designed a porcelain coffeepot, sturdy, bulky, all white, that the Staatliche Manufaktur in Berlin chose to produce for the general buying public. Two years later, the prolific Marcel Breuer devised a chair using tubular steel and leather strips, the first of generations of mass-manufactured modernist chairs that are still being turned out today and are still elegant.

some and affordable, not playthings for the rich but solid, and solidly modern, elements in ordinary domestic life.

Through it all, the place of the machine was never quite settled, not even among the modernists. As late as 1925, the Dutch architect and planner J. J. P. Oud, an influential, faultless member of the clan, registered his doubts. "I bend the knee before the miracle of technology, yet I do not believe that one can compare a steamship with the Parthenon." Indeed, "I long for a home that satisfies all the requirements of my love of comfort, yet a house is more to me than a machine—to live in." Modernists marched under many banners, with ideals that were at times incompatible with one another.

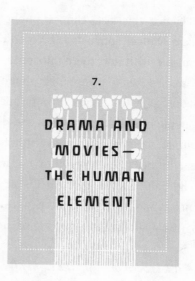

DRAMA AND MOVIES— THE HUMAN ELEMENT

F, AFTER MID-NINETEENTH CENTURY, A SINGLE CULTURAL institution urgently needed an infusion of fresh thinking, it was the stage. Not that theatregoers were loudly discontented everywhere. The three distinct publics we have discovered dividing the tastes for art inevitably appeared in the tastes for theatrical entertainment. We have met them before: lower-class and petty bourgeois audiences had their melodramas, operettas, and variety shows; the better educated could resort to well-made society comedies—though many of them, too, found the amusements offered to a working-class public entertaining enough. Only a narrow elite of cultivated consumers of high culture, spirits that fed avant-garde discontent everywhere, found reason to grumble. In most Western societies, they might at times count on some private stage to import a new, unconventional drama or on the royal or imperial houses in state-run theatres that featured the country's classics. But demand for modernism, inchoate as it was, easily outran supply.

Hence this last, choosy public encountered little but frustrations. The advanced journals it favored deplored the narrow choice of plays available to it and the conformist shows staged by servile bureaucrats more disposed to please their opinionated ruler than impassioned theatre lovers eager for drama of high quality. Imperial Germany is a striking example of such expectations and disappointments, especially after Wilhelm II, who meddled in everything, acceded to the throne. In 1888, the year he became emperor of Germany and king of Prussia, the playwright and theatre director Oskar Blumenthal dared to defy dominant opinion and to publicize his progressive aesthetic aims with a poetic prologue celebrating the opening of the Lessing Theater in Berlin:

It has been built for the right of the present,
For the high beckoning of the living.
We do not want to add new garlands
To old garlands on sacred sarcophagi,
And only cultivate the fame of the great departed—
We give ourselves to the spirit of these days.

It was an impeccable modernist agenda, with its emphatic present-mindedness, its claim to relevance, but destined to be realized only rarely.

Yet, when a modernist pioneer like Henrik Ibsen offered a new theatre, he managed to shock even audiences who claimed to be beyond being shocked. One main reason for Ibsen's spectacular, immensely controversial impact on the theatre of the late nineteenth century and beyond was his rare ability to imagine his way into the conflicts that were bedeviling contemporary society with no quick solutions in sight. Hostile to melodramatic tricks and indifferent to innovations, he raised commonplace people to the level of tragedy. Contradicting his supporters, he insisted that his so-called social dramas were at heart portraits of inner struggles. The very name of his most famous dramatic character, Nora, the protagonist of *A Doll's House* (1879), determined to go her own way in defiance of the conventional roles then assigned to respectable wives and mothers, became emblematic for the condition of modern woman. But Ibsen was not, as he repeatedly made clear to his admirers, a professional feminist. It was the human drama that fascinated him. No wonder that he taught generations of playwrights to be dissatisfied with surfaces. No wonder that he should have been one of Freud's favorite writers.*

The unremitting, even frantic search for a hit—in a private, unsubsidized theatre the sale of tickets was, of course, critical to its very survival—demanded compromises. And so did public authorities fixated on decency or fearful of seditious political opinion. Hence, between profit-obsessed impresarios on the one hand and reactionary government appointees on the other, cultivated consumers of the drama increasingly felt ready to welcome subversive flights from the usual fare. But most of the public and many of the critics refused to accept, let alone applaud, each shocking new production. It was usually only after exhausting battles with the censor, if then, that innovative plays, perhaps destined to claim a place in the permanent repertoire, might find an acceptable site.† Modernists had a great deal of educational work to do in the theatre—and, later, in the movies.

"MERDRE!"

1.

FOR THE HISTORIAN, the playbills after the mid-nineteenth century and, generations later, the programs of movie theatres are treacherous witnesses. The Alsatian poet Yvan Goll, successively Expressionist, Dadaist, and Surrealist, writing for avant-garde readers in the early twentieth century, called the stage "nothing but a magnifying glass." But it was a distorting glass, less a faithful reflection of social realities than of an author's preoccupations, or the shrewd merchandising of

---

* On March 1, 1909, addressing his Psychoanalytic Society in Vienna, Freud weighed Ibsen favorably against Gerhart Hauptmann, then Germany's most famous playwright. Hauptmann "always describes only himself and never the problem." In contrast, Ibsen, "with his consistency, unity, simplification of problems, with his art of concentration and concealment, is a great imaginative writer."

† Thus, a powerful instance, Victor Hugo's drama *Hernani*, which generated an impassioned debate over romanticism, was first performed at the official Comédie Française in 1830.

dramas or movies that an acceptable number of respectable bourgeois with a taste, and the money, for tickets presumably found appetizing. To deduce directly from a modernist play the culture from which it sprang was to slight the personal and professional elements in artistic creation, often highly individualistic, sometimes a little mad.

This characterization fits the most outrageous among the insurgent dramatists of the age, the French poet and alcoholic Alfred Jarry, working hard all his short life to cultivate his eccentricity. On December 11, 1896, when he was twenty-three, he presided over one of those historic premieres that mark some electrifying modernist occasions: the first—and next to the last—performance of his notorious play *Ubu roi*. It had started out as a puppet show for schoolfriends, lampooning a hated teacher, and ended up as a significant scandal from its opening word, uttered by the "hero," Ubu: "*Merdre!*"—"shitr." Eyewitnesses report—and we have several accounts from articulate modernists who were present, including W. B. Yeats—that it took a quarter of an hour before the wrought-up audience, some cheering, others hissing, calmed down enough to let the performance continue.

A glance at the French theatre of Jarry's time will underscore his offensiveness, his utter impudence. The well-made play, skating across the surfaces of a rapidly industrializing society, governed stages almost everywhere without a rival. Stock market speculation and the romantic adventures of the nouveaux riches supplied dramatists with plots. A few playwrights, like Georges Feydeau and Eugène Labiche, wove their exposure of hypocritical respectability and marital infidelity into farce. Most dramatists, like Alexandre Dumas *fils* and Emile Augier, treated the same problems with greater seriousness but hardly with greater psychological insight. Trivial and obvious moralizing was the rule, finding no room for mixed motives and unconscious drives. Pure heroes confronted vicious villains. *Ubu roi* did nothing to cure this superficiality, but its naked effrontery defied the popular drama in its time, too droll to be ignored.

Jarry's Ubu is an ogre, foul-mouthed, mean, uninhibited, sadistic, showing no trace of a restraining superego. He murders the king of Poland, usurping his throne, and engages in campaigns of terror at home and abroad, landing at last, defeated by superior military forces, in France. He appears a schoolboy's delight, violating every rule of polite manners and decent conduct. In the decade that remained to Jarry—he died prematurely in 1907 of tuberculosis hastened by dissipation, chiefly his beloved absinthe—he virtually transformed himself into his now celebrated persona, speaking, dressing, behaving as much like King Ubu as possible. Gathering supporters among such prominent and well-informed students of the theatre as Apollinaire, Jarry soon became the principal figure in entertaining anecdotes. One summer day, practicing target shooting in the garden behind his rented house, he heard a neighboring lady worrying out loud that his shots might hit her children. "If that should ever happen, madame," he eased her mind, "we should ourselves be happy to get some new ones with you." It is a remark that we can imagine Marcel Duchamp making.

Jarry's *Ubu roi* was too wispy and outlandish to serve as the foundation of an avant-garde drama—even with the rest of his oeuvre, his Ubu-esque sequels and invention of the ludicrous discipline "pataphysics," which he characterized as the science of imaginary solutions. Yet his ties to other modernist artists suggest that his uncompromising antagonism to established culture, including radical dissent, was not simply eccentric: Bonnard, Vuillard, Toulouse-Lautrec had helped Jarry with the scenery. And his performance—all his short life was a performance—became a beacon to playwrights and other literary modernists in later decades. André Breton, the undisputed chief of the Surrealists, discovered Jarry early, studied the work, including the unpublished texts, with care, and prized him as a foremost ancestor in the high company of Rimbaud. With all his sheer implausibility, Ubu, who is almost literally inhuman, had something to say about stupidity and beastliness: his character and conduct, just because they are so appalling, bluntly display pervasive aspects of human nature that earlier playwrights had only hinted at.

One may read Jarry's *Ubu* as acting out humanity at its worst, displaying traits that exist in some measure in everyone, magnified beyond prettifying bourgeois self-censorship and social performance. In his novel *Le Surmâle*, the protagonist, a champion cyclist with superhuman endurance, establishes a world's record by enjoying eighty-two orgasms in one day with the assiduous cooperation of a youthful American partner who keeps pace with him. Jarry may have been indifferent to psychology, but his work made it easier for later playwrights to investigate the unspeakable depths of their characters' private lives. It is not too much to say that he changed the theatre forever, literally as soon as the curtain went up. With *"Merdre!"* he had carved a breach in an age-old dividing wall separating utter candor from decent self-control: modernist playwrights would flood through to tell all.

2.

IF DECEMBER 11, 1896, the premiere of *Ubu roi*, was an unforgettable date in the calendar of the modernist stage, its successor, February 5, 1916, was equally memorable. It was the day when Dada, the anti-war movement, was founded in Zurich. The German poet, playwright, novelist, and pacifist Hugo Ball had procured the locale, provocatively named Cabaret Voltaire, just three days before. "Voltaire," suggesting that a writer born in the late seventeenth century could still arouse nostalgic fantasies about longed-for justice, freedom, and, above all good sense, discloses the depths of the organizers' despair. Sworn enemies of dominant irrationality, they were no more enamored of rationalism. In the light of appalling news from the eastern and western fronts, the Dadaists were equal opportunity nihilists.

The evidence supporting their posture was painfully obvious. After all, the war that had been raging for a year and a half was impartially, blindly, accumulating casualties on both fronts and showing no sign of flagging. Nor did there seem to be a serious opposition to the slaughter. With civilization in such desperate straits, it was only too comprehensible that the leading Dadaists should take their name from an accidental reference, found in a dictionary, to what in French baby talk means a hobby horse. That, in the light of conflicting claims to authorship, this should be the true history of "Dada" remains uncertain—a fact that in itself offers support for the notion that the world was lost to all rationality. To appeal to reason seemed to Dadaists as irrational as to support the insanity of generals and statesmen.

Neutral Switzerland, nearly surrounded by the interminable mass butchery on the western front, seems a curious setting for an anti-war, anti-art manifestation. But precisely the comfortable detachment of Zurich made the Cabaret Voltaire safe for dissidents from abroad—pacifists, conscientious objectors, avant-garde artists and writers scornful of their fellows' patriotic effusions. On that February evening, a tightly knit group of performers, none of them professional actors, first entertained a youthful audience with a deliberately chaotic program. Other evenings, no less extraordinary, followed. There were recitals of nonsense poems, a reading of *Ubu roi*, little plays, songs, dances in extravagant gear, a particularly startling simultaneous reading in which three Dadaists read three different poems at the same time—a feast of absurdity unleashed.

Short of burning down the Cabaret Voltaire as a demonstration, the founding Dadaists took their critique of contemporary culture and of its art to the outermost point.* No question it was theatre, but of a unique kind. When they took their ideas abroad, particularly to Berlin, Munich, and of course Paris, they found disciples who longed for a glimmer of sense in a world gone mad. But if there has ever been a doctrine that collaborated in its own destruction, it was Dadaism. This holds true even though the Dadaists solemnly swore that their thinking did not add up to a doctrine: "the true dadas," the Romanian playwright Tristan Tzara, the most quotable among them, laid it down, "are against Dada." Its most visible legacy was Surrealism, the doctrine of a tight clique dominated by André Breton complete with internal struggles, expulsions, and manifestos upon manifestos. It added up to a ripe mixture of automatic writing and efforts to portray the unconscious that made a certain noise, mainly in Paris, in the 1920s. Freud, an acknowledged inspiration to the

---

* The founders of Dada included Hugo Ball and his wife Emmy Hemmings, who sang *Lieder* in several languages; the energetic Romanian dramatist Tristan Tzara, a gifted writer of manifestos who exported Dada to France; Richard Huelsenbeck, a novelist and physician, who performed the same service for Germany; the Alsatian Jean (or Hans) Arp, who became an important modernist painter; and Marcel Janco, the second painter in the group and, after Tzara, the second Romanian.

This 1887 image (from Coquelin Cadet, *Le Rire*)
anticipated Duchamp's "improved" Mona Lisa by
thirty years.

Surrealists, was not impressed, and the occasional exchange of letters
between Freud and Breton led to nothing.

Historians have enlisted Marcel Duchamp among the Dadaists, an
association he denied, though he acknowledged that his essential view
of art was virtually identical with theirs. We recall that taking
Duchamp's "readymades" seriously—the mustachioed *Mona Lisa* or
the signed *pissoire*—would have destroyed any distinction between art
and non-art, and so would the Dadaists' campaign of making literal
nonsense the privileged aesthetic discourse. It was this rebellion against

rationality that made the Dadaists reverse the usual modernist aspiration to live in their own time. Their ideal was flight, and the suggestion
that they might engage in political activity struck them as a fundamental misreading of their non-doctrinaire doctrine. For Tzara and his fellows, the most unconventional contemporary cultural behavior only
emerged as effluvia from the swamp of stupidity.

Dada has well been called "organized insanity." The world, the
Dadaists were saying, has gone so incurably mad that the most reasonable agendas of reform are childish claptrap—their own apparently
childish claptrap was the only comment on the times that seemed to
them at all appropriate. All modernist schemes, the new painting, the
new poetry, the new architecture, and the rest, were at their most
respect-worthy doomed to fail. From Dada's perspective, modernism
in art and literature was at its core no better than the most hidebound
traditionalism. Not even Dada itself, the Dadaists insisted, could save
civilization. In their hostility to order, system, or doctrine, they refused
to make a program of their performances. In their often cheerful, imaginative declarations that the world is a truly hopeless place, their
extravagant exhibitions were modernist in their assault on good bourgeois ethics and aesthetics. In their programmatic way of refusing to
develop a program, they mounted a literary negativity that outstripped
any cultural criticism thought possible before; the Dadaists added up to
a particularly virulent case of anti-modernist modernism. That is what
Tristan Tzara must have meant when he said, "the true dadas are
against Dada." .

AN AUTOBIOGRAPHER AND OTHERS

1.

SEDUCTIVE, BRACINGLY persuasive as they were, Jarry and his incon-
stant heirs, the Dadaists, had no monopoly on modernist laments about
the current theatre. Far more instructive and far more influential, the
dramatist who exemplifies the revolution in the theatre most, well, dramatically was the Swedish novelist and playwright August Strindberg,
who provided radical impulses to the theatre more than once in a single

lifetime. Only a few choice spirits were fated to enlarge the capital of modernism significantly; Strindberg did so twice. It is like winning two Nobel Prizes—possible but exceedingly rare.

A restless and driven spirit, Strindberg was vastly productive from 1869, when he wrote his first play at twenty, to 1912, the year of his death. He poured out novels, stories, autobiographies, scientific papers (including some, not quite so scientific, on alchemy and amateurish chemistry), to say nothing of dozens of plays. For all the sheer personal interest of Strindberg's forceful tirades against liberated women, preoccupation with occult sciences, and his paintings, what matters most to the student of modernism is that, despite the improbability of such a vacillating, totally inconsistent figure in a great cultural revolution, his plays nourished the modernist theatre for decades. "Strindberg," said Eugene O'Neill, himself a disciple, in 1924, "was the precursor of all modernity in our present theater"; he was "the most modern of moderns."

For almost twenty years, he grew into being the most modern of moderns with slow deliberation, with apprentice work interesting only to specialists. He started his career as a drastic innovator in behalf of an unprecedented realism when two of his tragedies, *The Father* (1887) and, in the next year, *Miss Julie*, made him famous and introduced tough-mindedness as a plausible dramatic style. And in the late 1890s, not content with this breakthrough, and tormented after years of extreme anxieties resembling a religious conversion, Strindberg initiated an even more commanding innovation. In a series of plays—the three-part *To Damascus* (1898–1901), brilliantly kept alive in *A Dream Play* (1902) and *The Ghost Sonata* (1907), the most frequently performed among his later plays—without deserting his keenly observed psychological naturalism, he put the apparent illogic of dreams and unconscious preoccupations at center stage. Most of his characters lost their individual names; they were simply "The Daughter" or "The Old Man," a signal that Strindberg had transferred the primacy of his quest for intimate private revelations to the inward movements of symbolic personages whose travail claimed universal validity. In these dramas, he abandoned any hint of the old-fashioned plot, or rather, reworked it to focus on the spiritual (which is to say, the psychological) trajectory of modern pilgrims.

The episode that bisected his life was what he called the "Inferno crisis," a time of confusion and misery in the mid-1890s that Strindberg characteristically published in detail, a little fancifully elevating it to a massive breakdown. He seems to have endured several psychotic episodes—his friends unhesitatingly called them attacks of persecution mania—and a final religious reassessment. After declaring himself an atheist in his youth, he had returned to faith, but to a highly personal Christianity based on the doctrines of the eighteenth-century Swedish visionary Emanuel Swedenborg, which provided Strindberg with a sense of a divinely guaranteed physical order and moral purpose. Mysterious powers, he came to believe, govern all of life and lead sinful humans toward salvation.

IN *THE FATHER* AND *MISS JULIE*, Strindberg showed himself highly inventive in his choice of subject and technique: such open, offensive, erotic dialogue had not been heard quite that suggestively on stage before; the rapidity of his action and the economy of the dialogue, too, were largely a novelty. There was not an unnecessary line in these two dramas, and Strindberg treated explicitly what polite society had not discussed, did not begin to understand: the tense coexistence of love and hate, the energies of lust and sadism, the luxurious pleasures of revenge, the ascendancy of passion over reason. Ambivalence had rarely enjoyed such recognition.

In a remarkable text, soon hailed as a classic, Strindberg put into the preface to *Miss Julie* a modernist's program unequaled in its psychological subtlety. From his subjective vantage point, he argued that human nature is not cast in bronze, but open to the most disparate pressures, some from social demands and others, less easy to trace, from inner urges. Nor can desire and anxiety escape the conflicts that contradictory impulses arouse in the individual. In a hysterical period—and Strindberg insisted his culture was helplessly mired—contemporaries necessarily display an unsorted patchwork of qualities old and new that prove vacillating and are given to self-contradictions.

"As modern characters," he wrote in his impressive analysis, in a fine document of modernist protest, "living in an age of transition more urgently hysterical at any rate than the one that preceded it, I have depicted the figures in my play as more split and vacillating, a mixture of the old and the new." This meant that "my souls (characters) are conglomerates of past and present stages of culture, bits out of books and newspapers, scraps of humanity, torn shreds of once fine clothing now turned to rags, exactly as the human soul is patched together." He had written, he said, a "modern psychological drama," alert to "the subtlest movements of the soul." His bold venture had involved breaking with the "bourgeois concept of the immobility of the soul," a break that, since the bourgeoisie had so long dominated the stage, called for a new, thoroughly anti-bourgeois theatre. And it would not only be shocking to conventional sensibilities, but would break through to the core of the characters' minds. Here was modernist rhetoric in all its purity.

Thus Strindberg laid out the agenda for a theatre that would searchingly analyze modern personages for modern audiences, and *Miss Julie* itself boldly exemplified the intricate vision of human motives he wanted to see exhibited on the stage, making do with only three characters. Beyond being the theoretician of the modernist theatre, then, Strindberg was one of its most inventive practitioners. Inevitably he failed to live up consistently to his stringent, self-imposed demands. Yet in his best work, as in *Miss Julie*, which he called his "Naturalistic Tragedy," he did: a well-presented performance today is as likely to chill an audience as it must have more than a century ago. In fact, *Miss Julie*, in which a young valet first seduces his employer's daughter and then brutally talks her into committing suicide, was not his first essay in literary psychological investigation. The year before, after trying his hand with lesser works, he had completed *The Father*, in which a merciless, castrating wife reduces her husband to impotence and madness.

BUT STRINDBERG'S PROBING subjectivity, a realism beyond realism, which attacked new targets with new instruments, was not his contribution to the modernist theatre. In the plays of the late 1890s, he moved to symbolic personages whose travail is the lot of all humanity. And here, he abandons any hint of the old-fashioned plot. Strindberg's subjective principle is his tribute to human complexity. "The characters," he wrote in an Author's Note to *A Dream Play*, "are split, double and multiply; they evaporate, crystallize, scatter and converge. But a single consciousness holds sway over them all—that of the dreamer. For him there are no secrets, no incongruities, no scruples, no law. He neither condemns nor acquits, but only relates, and since on the whole, there is more pain than pleasure in the dream, a tone of melancholy, and of compassion for all living things, runs through these uncertain tales." Only a few years afterward, appreciative German Expressionist playwrights would lean heavily on Strindberg's late theatre, notably *To Damascus*, to dramatize the agony of modern man—which necessarily included in his dramas that most destructive, most powerful of beings: modern woman.

Though the spectrum of his plays and novels was wide, it was this subject, the emancipation of women, to which Strindberg obsessively returned. He was against it. Characteristically, visiting Germany in 1884, he was delighted to note that the country refused to permit women to register as students at universities. And he coarsely urged legislators not to fall into the trap of "granting civic rights to semi-apes, inferior creatures, sick children, sick and insane thirteen times a year at the time of menstruation, completely out of their minds during pregnancy, and irresponsible during the rest of their life, unconscious criminals, criminal, instinctively malicious animals who do not even know that that is what they are." Such inflamed rhetoric was typical when he turned to his favorite subject.

Strindberg's anti-feminist eruptions, all too perceptibly derived from his wives' appalling defects (as he came to see them), refer his readers back to one among his most memorable invented characters, Laura, in *The Father*. She is strong and vicious, plainly far better armored to survive the battle of the sexes than her husband, the Captain. Perhaps her most effective tactic in that war, fought almost literally to the death, is to raise doubts in her husband's mind whether he really is his daughter's father. Nothing less than his virility—and, with that, his sanity—is at stake. In a notorious article, "Woman's Inferiority to Man," published in Paris in 1895, Strindberg reiterated his habitual litany; in the midst of a far-ranging, often rude international debate over woman's true place, it secured him wide public attention. His three marriages, all to emancipated women who refused to sacrifice their careers to their husband, at once demanding and passive, ended as they must in bitter divorce. Strindberg, troubled, much like the Captain in *The Father*, by questions about his manliness, would end up accusing his wife of the moment of infidelity and an insatiable hunger for power. How could he have deceived himself by tying himself to a whore! Remember: it is one of the features of modernism to have a great artist make indelible contributions to the avant-garde while at the same time serving the forces of reaction.

2.

STRINDBERG DENIED that his work was autobiographical, though at times he acknowledged its debts to the private turmoil that seemed to accompany his every moment. Indeed, when he directly patterned novels or, less directly, plays, on his life, he was about as reliable as Frank Lloyd Wright, which is to say not at all. His publications were solidly rooted in his tempestuous experiences: his unresolved ambivalent feelings about his parents—it seems a pity that Freud, talking about the Oedipus complex, never used this prime instance as an example—his early failure to make a mark, other than scandal, in his native Sweden; his prolonged, repeated exiles in Berlin or Paris; his unhappy three marriages; the impact of music on his thinking; his feverish and credulous reading of psychology and mysticism; his talent for painting. A modernist in conduct as in beliefs, it seems as though Strindberg lived his life as a continuous experiment, recording appalling failures as faithfully as intoxicating triumphs. He was utterly changeable in his politics, his religion, his domesticity. Traveling to meet his second wife's parents, an encounter he did not anticipate he would enjoy, he wrote, "as always from the author's point of view, even if it does not work out, I'll always get another chapter for my novel!" If Strindberg wrote in order to live, he lived, too, in order to write.*

3.

STRINDBERG, WE HAVE to conclude, was an almost unconscious modernist. He professed to, indeed boasted of, being the most destructive of radicals all his life. In 1898, when he was almost fifty, he still pronounced himself determined to "paralyze the present order, to disrupt it." His wide-ranging experiments in literature, his persistent discontent early and late, his candor about his own life and that of his society, made him a natural candidate for the cultural rebellion that encompassed Impressionist, and later Cubist painters; composers who abandoned the tonal basis of their work; architects who defied all the historicist dogmas of their schools.

But the age also boasted superbly talented playwrights not necessarily committed to modernist departures. Rather, they were alert to social questions and to the modern post-Christian mentality that was, in the face of religious revivals, gaining converts. Anton Chekhov, for one, among the enduring short story writers and dramatists of the age, did not modify the traditional theatre, though the magical hold that his plays continue to exert on their audiences makes them somehow appear new and even, in their unsensational way, shocking and hard to classify—his late plays have been called, in a helpless attempt to capture their essence, exemplars of surreal naturalism. He had come to the theatre with the perspective of a medical man and as an accomplished writer of witty sketches. He combined a physician's commitment to grasp the causes of things with an alert sense of social realities. And he brought this background to the four consummate dramas he wrote in less than a decade between 1896 and 1904, the year of his death: *The Seagull, Uncle Vanya, Three Sisters*, and *The Cherry Orchard*.

---

* In an important essay, written from a psychoanalytic perspective, Robert Brustein, a learned specialist on the modern theatre, has explicitly denied that there was any distance between life and drama in Strindberg. His literary work, Brustein persuasively argues, "is one long autobiography," and then documents their intimate mutual involvement.

These masterpieces are reports of quiet frustration, of lives wasted and longings unfulfilled, of fates endured in resignation or cut short with a pistol shot—though not in his last and perhaps finest play, *The Cherry Orchard* (1904), which, he proudly noted, did not need a melodramatic suicide. However melancholy a life history he would invent for his creatures, Chekhov preserved a humorous distance from them. He strenuously objected to the way the renowned director Konstantin Stanislavsky at the Moscow Art Theatre distorted his sad comedies into virtual tragedies. In short, he was the poet of sentiment without yielding to sentimentality: a master of atmosphere without stage heroes or villains, ambitiously aiming all the while, as he did not hesitate to assert, at nothing less than truth and honesty. These are also conservative virtues, and if one insists on including Chekhov among modernists, his most dazzling contribution to the theatrical experience turns out to have been a refusal to surrender to brilliance. He was, if one may say so, the most old-fashioned among modernists.

THE LONG-LIVED George Bernard Shaw, who died in 1950 at the age of ninety-four, was another anti-romantic immortal with at best a casual attachment to modernist techniques. Though his favored subject, the failings of capitalist society, was utterly modern, he was imaginative but, for all his heresies, largely unconcerned with technical innovation. He poured out highly verbal (his critics called them wordy) plays and embroidered their theses with argumentative texts often longer than, and quite as eloquent as, the play they helped to explain. In the select company of Ibsen's British admirers—his pamphlet *The Quintessence of Ibsenism* (1891) vividly made the case—he wrote some impressive domestic plays, notably the early *Candida* (1894–95). Yet he also plainly enjoyed reimagining historic moments, inventing heroes and heroines without tumbling into hero worship—*St. Joan* (1923) remains the most famous. Others, like *Man and Superman* (1903), with a stunning dream sequence, or *Back to Methuselah* (1921), tackled ponderous scientific and philosophical issues. He exercised his talents, he said all his life, to give voice to political or cultural grievances: the fanaticism of doctors, the corruption of landlords, the strength of weakness, or, in the truly heartbreaking *Heartbreak House* (1919), the self-destruction of Western civilization. "My conscience," he wrote in a much-quoted self-appraisal, "is the genuine pulpit article; it annoys me to see people comfortable when they ought to be uncomfortable; and I insist on making them think in order to bring them to conviction of sin."

Shaw's ambitious intellectual exercises were openly tendentious, immensely serious and clever together, the work of a smart, self-assured pamphleteer, whose approaches to character (if not his conclusions) were conventional. He never saw an institution he did not find in desperate need of reform or an audience that was not parched for extensive instruction. He was a Socialist and an anti-Darwinian evolutionist, and endowed his work with earnest pleas. Yet among what he deprecated as his "shameless potboilers," there are plays like *Major Barbara* (1905) or *Pygmalion* (1912–13) that do not deserve so derisive a description; they survive by sheer wit and the author's good humor. Like Chekhov, then, Shaw worked at the margins of modernism. Along with Bertolt Brecht and, on a far lower level, the hired tools of Stalinism, he was a playwright most scornful of art for art's sake.

THE NEW MAN

1.

NO MODERNIST IS an island entire of itself. All of them, it hardly needs saying, lived within and responded to the world into which fortune had thrown them, if only, like the true radicals, to disparage its dominant features and offer alternatives to ruling aesthetic habits. Among their number, the most conspicuous representatives in theatre, as in architecture and design, were the German Expressionists, propagandists for a better world who gave the cultural atmosphere of the early Weimar Republic an appearance of unity. In the unsettling, almost literally world-shaking years stretching from around 1910 through the mid-1920s, their audiences associated these dramatists with like-minded poets, composers, architects, and painters. Ernst Barlach, a major sculptor known for his expressive touch, wrote several well-received plays on fraught subjects like the eternal struggle between generations. The Austrian Oskar Kokoschka, a painter who transmitted his dark vision of life in penetrating, uncompromising portraits, earned the uncertain distinction of inaugurating the Expressionist theatre with *Mörder, Hoffnung der Frauen* (1907), a short play that became notorious for its uninhibited treatment of sexuality. Practically all of these Expressionists were intensely serious. They rarely touched comedies; the importance of being earnest trumped all else.

If the German Expressionist theatre may claim a single founder, it was the chansonnier and dramatist Frank Wedekind. In 1891, he had written a notorious drama about the sorrows of puberty, *Frühlings Erwachen* (*Spring Awakening*), that the censors did not let him perform until fourteen years later. Then, in 1898, writing a disrespectful poem on Emperor Wilhelm II in a new satirical weekly, *Simplicissimus*, earned Wedekind a brief stay in one of His Majesty's fortresses. What the Wedekinds of his time would have welcomed most would have been a faithfully applied First Amendment protecting free speech.

For all their idiosyncrasies, then, the Expressionist playwrights offered a single emphatic message and a single emphatic technique. They, like their fellow insurgents, were proclaiming an overwhelming need for, and prophesied the coming of, a New Man in a culture that seemed naked without ideals and only thinly supplied with realistic expectations. And they were persuaded that they must speak, as other modernists built or rhymed or covered canvases, at the top of their voice, as it were, to trample upon the long-honored rules governing moderation about the inner discord that seemed to be the lot of every modern human. Some cultural clashes were doubtless stimulated by social conflicts, but in all of their plays they saw themselves as the voices of a culture in crisis. Indeed, that heavily laden German word for crisis, *Krise*, came easily to everyone's lips—not unjustly, in the devastating aftermath of 1918. The perpetuation of domestic political violence, the demands of foreign governments for reparations, the split on the left fostered by the Communist Party on Soviet instructions, made the future of the young Weimar Republic uncertain. It was only appropriate, then, that local skeptics should come to call the Expressionists' theatrical outpourings, with sarcastic disparagement, *Schrei-drama*—the scream-drama.

THE GERMAN EXPRESSIONIST theatre is of historical interest far beyond its merits as literature. For the devotee of high culture, including the open-minded shopper among literary options, its brutality, affectation, and primitive, largely unsublimated quality stand mainly as a striking artifact for the archeologist of the modern theatre. Never particularly urbane in tone or technique, these avant-garde playwrights usually reduced dramatic confrontations to an exhibition of clashing raw urges. But the favorable reception their productions enjoyed for some brief years, often staged by daring, highly original directors like Max Reinhardt, testifies that educated playgoers were in the grip of war or the calamitous peace that followed it.

Freud seems not to have commented on the Expressionist dramatists of his time, but if he had, he could have used their work as persuasive evidence for the existence, indeed the virulence, of the Oedipus complex. Since the earliest phases of modernism in the mid-nineteenth century, the profit-minded, philistine bourgeois had been the avant-garde's favorite enemy; among German Expressionists, the same enemy was not forgotten—one thinks of George Grosz's unsparing caricatures of the war profiteer, obese, *nouveau riche*, self-satisfied, sucking on a cigar, sneering at war-crippled veterans and exploiting young women exposed to his advances. But the Expressionists also concentrated their ire on a particular element in the bourgeoisie, the middle-class Father. He showed himself a versatile metaphor, standing for all despotic authority, for Emperor Wilhelm II, or, on a more intimate scale, the playwright's own father. The Father must be resisted, defeated, destroyed, for the sake of a more egalitarian, more decent world to come.

Among Expressionist playwrights, the attractiveness of the Father as villain was uncontested. The theme of Barlach's first play, *Der Tote Tag* (1912), was, as I have noted, the father-son relationship, as is true of several of the plays he wrote soon after. The playwright Walter Hasenclever's best known piece, *Der Sohn* (1913), dwells on the same oedipal theme still more explicitly. The Father, a typical middle-class domestic despot, keeps his twenty-year-old son a virtual prisoner at home, intending to make him enter a characteristic bourgeois life, dull, commonplace, safe. But the son gets away and in a melodramatic scene expounds to an audience of young men—the frothing long speech was a frequently used device in these plays—about the sins of the Fathers. Every son, he argues, should murder his own father. Still unnaturally innocent, he enjoys a night with a prostitute, an essential element in his education for life. After the police pick him up and take him home, he draws a handgun and the father dies of a stroke—an easy victory for the party of sons.

Probably the most extreme instance in this genre, Arnolt Bronnen's *Vatermord* (1920), made the oedipal triangle boorishly explicit. This play, interestingly enough, was directed by a young dramatist who had recently come to Berlin from Munich: Bertolt Brecht, apparently unfazed by Bronnen's elemental indecency. The elderly father in *Vatermord* is a sadistic domestic bully—Hasenclever would have recognized him; the mother lacks all respect for the incest taboo; the son, Walter, responds to her erotic overtures. As she faces her boy, naked, eager to consummate his seduction, the father interrupts the cozy scene. In the melee that follows, the son stabs his father to death, and the mother, covered in blood and sexually excited, pleads with her son to violate her. But he scornfully rejects her:

> Frau Fessel: *Come to me oh oh ohh come to me.*
> Walter: *I am fed up with you / I am fed up with everything /*
>   *Go bury your husband you are old / But I am young /*
>   *I don't know you / I am free /*
>   *Nobody before me nobody beside me nobody above me /*
>   *the father dead /*
>   *Heaven I am jumping up to you I fly /*
>   *Everything presses trembles groans laments is forced /*
>   *upward swells surges explodes flies / is*
>   *compelled higher / compelled higher / I /*
>   *I am in bloom*

Strong, independent, above all fatherless, Walter is the New Man. It should surprise no one that Bronnen, impressed by the Nazis' appeal to the irrational sources of "racial purity" they called blood and soil, eventually joined their cause.

THIS IS NOT TO SAY that these playwrights lacked all talent, however undisciplined their taste. But few of them ever learned to control their ecstatic oratory or ration their unbridled idealism. The most prolific and most gifted of them, Georg Kaiser, came closer than the rest of his company to writing plays as popular as they were agitated. He was indefatigable in his dramatic imagination. In his life as a writer—born in 1878, he died in 1945—he managed to complete fifty-nine plays, seven one-acters, two novels, and a quantity of poems and essays. The gamut of his plots, virtually inexhaustible, ranges from a satire on *Tristan und Isolde* (1913) to *Von Morgens bis Mitternachts* (1916), an intimate study of a bank clerk's fatal adventures with stolen cash. His best known play, *Die Bürger von Calais* (1914), staging Rodin's great life-size sculpture, takes a much-retold incident from Froissart's chronicle of the Hundred Years' War between England and France. Seven New Men in late medieval times perform acts of selflessness and duty, willing to sacrifice themselves for their fellow citizens. In 1918, Kaiser made his favorite impulse for pouring out plays perfectly plain: "What is the poet's vision?" he asked rhetorically, and had the answer ready. "There is only one: the renewal of humankind."

In his highly colored way, Kaiser was a complete modernist. He could have said with Kafka that literature is man's only worthwhile vocation, though he took that conviction to lengths that went beyond even Kafka's imagination. The most charitable progressive society would not have been prepared to allow Kaiser's vagaries to go unpunished. He wrote all the time, and sullenly resented any distractions, such as stopping to make a living, that might interfere with his priceless time at the desk. He insisted on stylish surroundings and total silence for his work; these, he said, put him above "hated reality." Self-sacrifice, so critical to his portrait of the New Man, was not his habit; he preferred to sacrifice others, like his wife, whose fortune was swallowed by the environment he fancied essential. One technique for keeping him undisturbed was to rent an elegant villa and, when his family's lack of money became acute, to pawn or sell the owner's furniture.

He performed this modernist pilfering twice. Finally tried for theft in early 1921, he defended himself with superb haughtiness. "Insane I am not," he told the court, "hence I must be right somehow. I cannot find my way into these obvious banalities. I don't get them. One does not put a Heinrich von Kleist or a Büchner before a court, that is unfair. One doesn't do such things." He went further still: "The sentence, 'Everything is equal before the law,'" he told the court, "is nonsensical. I am not just anybody. . . . We have so few independent productive people, that none of us should dare to renounce their achievement." The court was not impressed, and gave Kaiser six months in jail. The two months he still had to serve, having already spent four months in custody, he eased writing a play.

2.

EARNESTNESS DEFINED GERMANY'S Expressionist playwrights. But one of them, Carl Sternheim, endowed with merciless wit, was an exception. After venturing several experimental plays, he launched a series of comedies held together by dealing with "*Aus dem bürgerlichen Heldenleben*"—the heroic life of the bourgeoisie. His tone was virtually unique, in part borrowed from the style of the Expressionist troupe; to Sternheim's mind, it showed what he called "*Privatkurage*"—personal courage—a trait that Sternheim fully shared. Another Wedekind legacy was a sharply compressed, artificial style that he perfected.

The life of the bourgeoisie was heroic, to Sternheim, in its awareness of just how sharply its inner and external realities differed, and its willingness to act on that knowledge. The contemporary world, he wrote, was drowning in plush—a favorite metaphor for insincerity and duplicity. "A small official in a plushy world knows it is enough to evade embarrassments to *seem* to be plush amidst plush. He understands this like the rest of the world. What is new is that he knows, just for himself, an outrageous secret: if you conduct yourself toward the outside world civically and psychologically enough, you may be internally a brutal, hard, egotistic beast, then you may graze life for your own advantage and use." Sternheim withheld from his audience whether he approved of this knowledge.

The opening salvo in his cycle about bourgeois heroism was *Die Hose* (*The Panties*), in which Luise Maske, wife of the minor civil servant Theobald Maske, drops her underpants on a public occasion in the king's presence. She is lasciviously observed by Scarron, a poet, and Mandelstam, a hairdresser, who both promptly rent rooms in the Maskes' house to be close to the charming Luise. Sternheim produces his complex views with an extraordinary technique, the celebrated *Telegrammstyl*, which omits definite articles and forces German sentences into unprecedented, distinctly unique shapes. This makes his characters, including his petty bourgeois, seem forceful and energetic— that is, alien to the almost unanimous contempt for the bourgeoisie among modernists.

The Maskes have been married just a year, but this does not keep Luise Maske from finding her new boarder, Scarron, romantic and distinctly attractive, and Scarron from responding to her passionately. Yet Scarron is flighty. After a prostitute he just met the night before has shown herself superior to all other people he has ever known, he decides he must give up his room at the Maskes and be with her—without asking to have the year's rent paid in advance restored to him. Thus the tender intruder yields the field of battle to the prosaic Theobald Maske in the virtually invisible duel over the desirable Luise that Sternheim has been subtly developing.

But Sternheim paid an extravagant price for his linguistic originality. By the mid-1920s, the Expressionist drama seemed too strident to retain theatregoers' interest. The morale of Germans was buoyed by a growing acceptance of the Weimar Republic among other nations, an end to humiliating occupations of German territory, and a stunning resurgence of German culture. The "Golden Twenties" made consumers of culture increasingly impatient with histrionics, with intimations of doom, and with promises of total human regeneration. Sternheim's diction now came to seem too synthetic, too demanding a special dialect. The old rule for modernist departures surviving held for Sternheim's telegram style, too: if it was not absorbed into the mainstream after a time of testing, it would be reduced to a gesture of mere historical interest.

THE ONLY ALL-MODERN ART

1.

ALL MODERNIST ARTISTS felt their past looming over them, were busy denying it, demonizing it, cannibalizing it for subversive purposes, or elevating its most appealing exemplars into classics—all but one, the moviemakers. Moving pictures were born modern and, with the absence of any history, particularly receptive to inventors' ingenuity. After mid-nineteenth century, the prospects of setting photographs in motion drew the ingenious and the enterprising like a magnet. When on March 22, 1895, the Lumière brothers, Auguste and Louis, demonstrated to a select Parisian audience their movie *La Sortie des usines Lumière*, they were giants standing on the shoulders of giants.

The Lumières provided a second choice occasion at the end of that year, on December 28, when they showed an assortment of short films—all there was at the time—at the Grand Café on the Boulevard des Capucines in Paris. It was a spectacular occasion, with a varied menu that hinted at the virtually unlimited possibilities of the *Cinématographe*, the Lumières' machine. Viewers, who paid one franc apiece for the privilege, wondered at this stunning new entertainment that could accommodate humor, sentiment, anxiety, and tantalizing hints at erotic excitement. In some sense, the movies have never shown anything else; the rest is detail.*

---

* There are obvious objections to including the movies in the modernist spectrum: they were, and increasingly became, part of popular culture—collective enterprises largely depending on box office receipts or studio executives' advance judgments of what might or might not be a promising moneymaker. At the same time, and this is my justification, movies almost from the beginning were often enough battles between creative spirits—scriptwriters, directors, cinematographers, even actors—and their economic overlords, who could produce works of art or near misses.

OF COURSE, THE DOMINANT spur for experiments with cameras and light-sensitive substances essential to the modern miracle of motion pictures had been the recent invention and rapidly growing improvement of photography. From around 1839, Louis-Jacques-Mandé Daguerre and others had been able to produce precise, often quite beautiful images, and inventors all the way from impassioned tinkerers to the methodical genius of Thomas Alva Edison had competed to take that one more step—a giant step—beyond static pictures. By 1850, Maxime du Camp, traveling with his friend Gustave Flaubert, produced memorable photographic views of glorious ancient sights in Egypt and the Near East. In the next decade, Mathew B. Brady and his assistant photographers pitilessly documented the horrors of the American Civil War. And late in the 1860s, Julia Margaret Cameron captured prominent Englishmen of her acquaintanceship—her complaisant friends included Thomas Carlyle, Charles Darwin, and Alfred Lord Tennyson—with a prayerful concentration and a passion for inwardness that made her a modernist at heart. "My whole soul," she wrote in some autobiographical comments, "has endeavoured to do its duty towards [these great men] in recording faithfully the greatness of the inner as well as the features of the outer man." The modest notion that photography was by its nature confined to surfaces was soon overcome. And the movies, it turned out, could go further or, rather, dig deeper—even without the support of psychoanalysis which, some moviemakers hoped, would provide a key to the recesses of human nature in action.

The promising collaboration of movies and psychoanalysis had long been the subject of hopeful speculation. Not surprisingly, the chronological coincidence that the two were closely of the same age seemed to give grounds for optimism: 1895, the time of the Lumières' breakthrough, was the year before Freud gave his fresh, troubling discoveries the collective name of *"Psychoanalyse."* Except for the Surrealists, no party of modernists has been as eager as the makers of movies to benefit from, and provide benefits for, Freud's science. For many years, perhaps even more intensively in recent times, partisans of the future have maintained that each has much to teach the other in the unconventional—that is, modernist—study of human nature and its secrets.

In their materials, the two disciplines certainly have much in common, especially after the movie industry learned to use some of its unique devices to explore the minds of men and women in conflict with the world and themselves. Yet the union of movies and psychoanalysis was never more than a well-meant though not very productive shotgun wedding. Their relationship has been largely one-sided. Over the years, on rare occasions, psychoanalysts have interpreted movies to uncover hidden urges or anxieties of which their directors or scriptwriters might be as unaware as the actors speaking their assigned lines. But the contrary direction, with a movie successfully representing the central abstractions of psychoanalysis, has shown itself far more problematic.

In 1925, in a revealing episode, Freud himself expressed vehement reservations about an authentic psychoanalytic movie, even though Karl Abraham and Hanns Sachs, the analysts he trusted most among his adherents, strongly spoke in support of the project. However epochmaking, however essential to the history of modernism, Freud was a part-time revolutionary, subversive in nothing but his professional theories and techniques. He was nearing seventy, but still preserved an old-fashioned distrust for new toys like the telephone or the airplane. He would, he insisted, "personally have nothing to do with this film." Here was a founder of the twentieth-century mind who, as a reluctant modernist, kept moving pictures on the list of unnecessary innovations.

2.   ,

FOR ALL THE UNTOLD NUMBERS of movies made since their beginnings, they have never quite ceased to thrill, or at least astonish, viewers with their successive technical innovations—close-ups, montage, animation, split screen, sound, color, deep focus, special effects. At least for some years after their spectacular Parisian debut, they were largely the pastime of the masses, unreceptive to modernist experimentation. The so-called "better classes" ventured into the early movie theatres reluctantly, and did so with their characteristic condescension. The bourgeois passion for film, an essential prerequisite for the realization of the modernist impulse, took time to develop.*

This disdain for the moviegoing masses began to fade as a few enterprising moviemakers tried their hand at highbrow fare beyond just showing moving trains or slapstick pratfalls: an adaptation of a costume drama about Queen Elizabeth's loves or candid revelations about present-day slums. It was an ideal setting for an intrepid experimenter like the French magician Georges Méliès, who by 1900 had concocted scores of short narrative films, longer and far more imaginative than those the Lumières produced. And legendary performers like Charlie Chaplin and Mary Pickford, around whom viewers' extravagant private fantasies could form, rose as public idols far above the reputation of mere entertainers.

The domestication of movies in the culture of modern entertainment happened very quickly. In 1909, the *New York Times* for the first time reviewed a movie, an adaptation of Browning's *Pippa Passes*—one of the countless films that the American pioneer among pioneers, D. W. Griffith, shot for his first employer, Biograph, then at the top of the trade. Seven years later, the Harvard psychologist Hugo Münsterberg did not disdain publishing a scholarly monograph, *The Photoplay: A Psychological Study*. But such sober investigations remained relatively rare until at least 1928, when the advent of sound threatened a cataclysm in the film industry—a far-reaching, fascinating novelty that in fact would confine its feared devastations to actors who could not manage the transition to speaking on camera. Indeed, the flood of literature on film, much of it decidedly theoretical and at times exceedingly

---

* The snobbish reluctance of bourgeois to be seen in a moviehouse must have encouraged the use of more refined collective names in English, something more "elegant" than "moving pictures." The terms "cinema" or "film" seemed more refined, somehow—university faculties devoted to the study of what they did not want to call, well, "moving pictures," made other choices. I have used the terms interchangeably, making no attempt to impose value judgments, and for the most part have been satisfied with "movies."

pretentious, started to expand almost out of control only after the Second World War in the 1950s. It was then that the possible relationship of the movies to modernism could first be seriously broached.

The so-called *auteur* theory, first articulated in 1954 by the French director François Truffaut (though implicit long before) and promoted into a lively international issue among *cinéastes* by the American critic Andrew Sarris, was the most discussed intellectual product of these postwar years. Its central contention, the vehemently debated claim for the unique role of the "author" or director in the making of films, was both a simplified commonsensical recognition of his authority and a return to the romantic—and modernist—ideal of the lonely creative spirit set free. As detractors of the *auteur* theory hastened to point out, a movie, any movie, is a cooperative enterprise. Directors, actors, scriptwriters, cameramen, composers, designers of costumes or scenery, and in lesser roles hairdressers and makeup personnel, to say nothing of glib publicists working to convert their studio's wishful thinking into profitable realities, are indispensable members of every production team. At the same time, advocates of the theory, mainly advanced by French *cinéastes*, insisted that an aesthetically acceptable movie must show the hand of its principal maker, and that, however famous a star might be, that maker must be the director.

But craftsmanlike practice long predated such theoretical musings. In the more than three decades before critics started adulating the *auteur*, each country developed massive local organizations to meet an insatiable demand for affordable entertainment and, on rare occasions, for grim if aesthetically satisfying ventures that looked the horrifying recent war in the face.* Studios, then, everywhere turned out substantial quantities of silent films designed to let audiences escape, or at exceptional moments recall, a four-year-long conflagration whose murderous length and unexpected casualties nobody had anticipated. The early 1920s in Germany, the inaugural years of the persistently endangered Weimar Republic, saw the emergence of UFA, first a pub-

---

* This worship of the director was a spectacular departure for an industry in which at first his name had remained anonymous.

lic and then a private distribution company that found room for Expressionist, heatedly debated masterpieces like *The Cabinet of Dr. Caligari* (1919). For their part, French moviemakers retained their independence and opportunities for playfulness. But the principal developments in the organization of vertical near-monopolies supplying films and shaping demand came, of course, from Hollywood, ending up after repeated reorganizations with five major and several minor studios, each fostering and guarding its stars under contract.

It was the very complexity of making a movie that furnished, ironically enough, one reason why the *auteur* theory was so appealing: it eased the work of a critic by singling out one member of a collectivity for public acclaim or censure. In fact, the spread of that theory was a symptom that the movies had reached a certain maturity and had grown into proper fodder for debates among intellectuals. As the years went by, movies were exposed to the most divergent interpretations and rivaling ideologies. Leading film theorists welcomed Marxism, trendy, widely dominant in the 1930s and after, on loan from modern political thought; it delighted to "expose" the inner emptiness of the movies underneath all their complacent glitter. The Marxists saw film as a potent feature of the capitalist culture industry, a distinctive element in the superstructure with enormous political implications, in the right hands possibly a force for good as much as it was now a tool of reaction. Had not Sergei Eisenstein, that internationally acclaimed Russian film director and theorist, happily quoted Lenin in the late 1920s: "The cinema is the most important of all the arts"?

3.

COMPARED TO THE EASE with which left-wing writers adapted revolutionary principles to the deep reading of films, other theories such as poststructuralism, waves of feminism, and later postmodernism brought more esoteric critics largely speaking to other critics in their brave, not always successful efforts to elucidate the implicit cultural testimony of movies. By then, the question whether the motion picture is an art had been repeatedly and emphatically answered in the affirma-

D. W. Griffith, *The Birth of a Nation* (1915). The Ku Klux Klan rides to save endangered white womanhood. (This was Griffith's reading of Southern history.)

tive; it was, the proud assertion went, the peculiarly modern art of the twentieth century. D. W. Griffith, for years the world's best known filmmaker, had confidently used the term "art" as early as the First World War. And in 1919, Louis Delluc, a pioneering French film critic, editor, and director, clearly saw film's great claims and great future as an offspring of the machine age: "We are assisting at the birth of an extraordinary art which has already found its feet and is destined for future glories. The only modern art, the offspring of the machine and the human ideal." He spoke for other movie critics, a new journalistic specialty spawned to help shape the moviegoing public's taste, who were unanimous that a movie is not a dramatized play, or a novel adapted, or a collection of photographs set in motion. It is what it is, a movie, and must be judged on its distinctive terms, with its own vocabulary and its own aesthetic. And where there was modern art, there was modernist art lurking in the wings.

But the question What is a modernist movie? permitted no easy answer. Even if (against all probability) one could reach a consensus among critics and intelligent, alert viewers about the exceptional quality of a single production, this would say little about its historical import. One of the most influential movies ever made, Griffith's epic, *The Birth of a Nation* (1915), sternly enforced on its viewers the old debate over style vs. substance. Its racist reading of the Civil War and Reconstruction, with its bestial blacks and its noble members of the Ku Klux Klan, with its innocent, cultivated Southern states raped by invading carpetbaggers from Yankeeland, made this movie a hopelessly flawed masterpiece, as conspicuous for its flaws as for its mastery. It was only after viewers radically separated technique from content that they could credibly maintain its claim to a prominent place in modernist history.

Griffith, born in La Grange, Kentucky, in 1875, never grew away from his fierce sentimental attachment to the Southern version of the Civil War—his father had served as an officer in the Confederate Army—and made his most important movie a homage to his idealized, now shocking fellow Rebels. The ride of more than two score Klansmen in full regalia coming to the rescue of beleaguered innocent Southern womanhood is one of the movie's most stirring and disturbing episodes. That *Birth of a Nation* was poisoned by its bigotry is yet another useful reminder that "modernism" is not an automatic word of praise. Nor is a severe verdict on Griffith's most celebrated production an anachronistic response from a politically correct posterity. Many of its contemporaries gave verdicts just as scathing. Yet for all that, the film attracted unprecedented masses of viewers in many countries— one well-informed estimate of its worldwide audience suggests 150 million—and for years moviemakers everywhere, including the Soviet

Union, even those who found Griffith's message atrocious, acknowledged their debt to it.* His technical virtuosity carried all before it.

Griffith's artistic vision, then, though perfectly respectable at the time, was so oppressive—*The Birth of a Nation* was essentially about his impassioned reading of American history—that it frustrated any opportunity to develop even a trace of perceptive character portraits. Griffith strove for fidelity when it suited him—a set piece like the assassination of Lincoln might pass muster with professional historians. At the same time, when his obsessions were awakened, as in his need to lampoon the black-dominated South Carolina legislature after Emancipation as an obscene charade, he allowed his political agenda to take control. If Griffith had not agreed to cut certain passages on the urgent protests of the infant NAACP, his racist movie would have been even more incendiary than it was. The eminently quotable American economist and sociologist Thorstein Veblen spoke for necessary critical discriminations when he judged Griffith's most celebrated film coolly in the year of its release. "Never before have I seen such concise misinformation."

That said, *The Birth of a Nation* was far more ambitious, far more intricate, and far more expensive a spectacle than any other movie, including the literally hundreds of one-reelers that Griffith had shot before. The cost came to $110,000, some three times its original estimate, though its worldwide appeal made millions for the studio. In making the film, he had only a few settled devices to draw on—the industry, after all, was only twenty years old—many among them his own inventions or bold elaborations of his competitors' tinkering. For the most part he had to rely on his self-confidence, and gave it full play. He confronted practical complications and resolved them as they came up. In a word, Griffith was an American pragmatist: he cared about what worked and was willing to try the most daring experiments on the set, especially with the camera.

To his innumerable disciples, then, Griffith demonstrated the uses of cunningly orchestrated scenes of masses in action, imaginative

* The impact of *The Birth of a Nation* was not confined to moviemakers alone. Historians have documented that Griffith's racist interpretation of the Civil War and his sentimental glorification of the Ku Klux Klan did much to stimulate Klan activities across a number of states.

camera angles, incisive editing that kept the story moving, the most carefully constructed (and almost ruinously expensive) sets. Hence sober historians of the movies have justly given Griffith credit as an unsurpassed inventor, who introduced the split screen and the flashback, and ventured unprecedented play with the camera. *The Birth of a Nation* would stand for his admirers—a veritable Who's Who of moviemakers—as a brightly illuminated promise, reel after reel demonstrating far-reaching innovations. If the substance of Griffith's most stunning movie was, in a word, reactionary, his technical flexibility and sheer originality made him an unusual modernist, a brilliant technician who forever changed the making of movies into an unmatched artistic entertainment.

Griffith's later movies kept his reputation as an innovator alive. The memorable *Intolerance* (1916) had the most personal of origins. Smarting under the sharp criticisms of *Birth of a Nation* for its bigotry, he projected his injured conviction that he had been the victim rather than the perpetrator of racial prejudice. A complex sequence of four interrelated instances of intolerance in history—the Persian conquest of Babylon, the crucifixion of Jesus, the St. Bartholomew's Day butchery of French Huguenots in 1572, and a contemporary American instance, the killing of nineteen workers by Pinkerton guards during a strike—*Intolerance* must have been a moviemaker's most costly self-justification in the history of the industry. Vast elaborate sets, stunning multitudes of actors and extras, unprecedented shots of crowds in action, further enhanced his reputation as a technical genius. Unfortunately, the moviegoing public found it all too complicated, too determinedly solemn, in a word, disappointing. The losses plunged Griffith into life-long debt. Yet the impact of his work in his time went beyond mere appreciation. What was Griffith to the Soviet moviemakers, Sergei Eisenstein asked rhetorically in 1944, and answered: "A revelation."

EVEN INNOVATION is not enough to give a movie a place in the modernist catalog. There is, after all, *The Jazz Singer* (1927), the first "talkie," a tearjerker with Al Jolson in blackface belting out "Sit upon

Al Jolson in *The Jazz Singer* (1927), advertisement. Though otherwise undistinguished, it was the first serious effort at sound in the movies.

my knee, Sonny Boy." The few sentences that Jolson spoke in that film far outstripped in effectiveness his maudlin ballads; they proved a stunning surprise for its audiences, hitherto forced to rely on clumsy, intrusive printed intertitles. No wonder that Warner Bros. chose to advertise this novelty as their "supreme triumph." But although *The Jazz Singer* sufficiently fulfilled the first criterion for modernism, the lure of heresy, it did nothing for its essential second quality, the attentive search of the inner domain. It was novel but it was shallow. Membership in the modernist clan demanded more than this.

4.

OFTEN THE DIRECTORS DID NOT, or could not, follow the lead of the inventors. More than any other art, moviemaking was also a highly visible, heavily capitalized, anxious, and quarrelsome business. Movie attendance started out vast and grew vaster, quickly. By 1910, audiences in the United States had risen to 26 million a week. Granted, all the arts have always had more than a touch of commerce attached to them: painters had dealers, novelists had publishers, composers had impresarios, poets had angels to finance little magazines. However civilized film producers might on occasion be, cruel realities compelled them, as middlemen of culture continuously confronted with hard decisions in a callous competitive world, at least to study the balance sheet and strive to have profits exceed losses. The most feared phrase in the film industry was "running over budget."

Given the sizable number of specialized technicians working to bring a movie to completion, the paraphernalia needed to produce and distribute a movie are enormous compared to the undemanding economic machinery designed to keep the other arts available to the marketplace. And the power that tightfisted bankers or their pawns, apprehensive production chiefs, exercised over movie studios—questioning cost overruns, objecting to perceived moral laxity, vetoing expensive shots, assigning casting and "improving" endings—regularly damaged the final product, often reducing a strong script to banality. Just as in a convoy the slowest ship sets the pace for all, the never-ending struggle to produce a movie that would offend no one and at the same time bore the fewest viewers resulted in a compromise among compromises. The space available in the movie industry for bold modernist experiments was, in short, sharply limited. Still, what with the inescapable collectiv-

Fred Astaire and Ginger Rogers in *Top Hat* (1935). A characteristic
hit (one of several) for these two talented and charming performers
who provided unexcelled escape during the Depression.

ity of a production team and the often oppressive management by mon-
etary powers, what is surprising is not how few movies proved worth
seeing, but how many.

AT THE SUMMIT of modernist moviemaking, at least three innovators
rank with Griffith: Sergei Eisenstein, Charlie Chaplin, and Orson
Welles. No doubt, every historian of the movies, partisan of the *auteur*
theory or not, has a register of favorite directors—Ernst Lubitsch,

Jean Renoir, John Ford, Alfred Hitchcock, Luis Buñuel, Federico Fellini, Michelangelo Antonioni, Jean-Luc Godard, Akira Kurosawa, Ingmar Bergman.* But the three I have proposed as Griffith's most distinguished heirs were virtually unique in the epochal consequences of their experiments.

Eisenstein, Griffith's acknowledged successor as the leading creative spirit of moviemaking, was in a stronger position than his predecessor in background, character, and literary tastes, but the two shared decisive qualities: a restless originality and a commitment to an ideology. Born in 1898 to a prosperous and urbane middle-class Russian family—his father was an architect—Eisenstein came to artistic maturity in the heady, unusually open, early days of the Soviet regime, absorbing with the appetite of a human sponge avant-garde ideas in drama, painting, and psychology. And not only modernist ideas: he could knowledgeably quote Dickens as well as Tolstoy, Baudelaire as well as Goethe, Dante or Joyce as well as Marx. When he turned to the movies in 1923, he exploited all his intellectual acquisitions, especially the social implications of mental science. He never neglected to pay the closest attention, at once aesthetic and manipulative, to audience responses. Calculating the reactions of viewers played a large part in his cinematic decisions.

Among the half dozen movies he directed, virtually all in the 1920s, *Battleship Potemkin* (1925) was, and remains, Eisenstein's most notable venture. Celebrating the twentieth anniversary of the Russian Revolu-

---

* Probably more influential, though, was the rapidly maturing Italian movie industry, liberated from stifling Fascist "suggestions." The leading theorist of its new realism was the Marxist scriptwriter Cesare Zavattini, who pleaded as early as 1942, adopting a familiar modernist maxim, that directors "should unconditionally accept contemporary reality. *Today, today, today.*" Moviemakers, he maintained, should do without plots and actors, since both do violence to the day-to-day experiences that are common to all moviegoers. With often wounding openness, this neorealism became the mantra among a small team of remarkable directors, by no means all of them Marxists, historic figures in their craft, starting with Roberto Rossellini (*Roma, Città aperta,* 1945) and Vittorio De Sica (*Ladri di Biciclette,* 1948), followed soon after by Federico Fellini (*La Strada,* 1954) and Michelangelo Antonioni (*L'Avventura,* 1960). All were noted for their exquisite camerawork, superior acting, and the unsentimental treatment of delicate, often pathetic themes. These were years when independent-minded Italian directors came into their own, providing powerful ammunition to the supporters of the *auteur* theory.

Soviet poster of a capitalist pig squirming. The Russian script means "Third International."

tion of 1905, a failure that Bolshevik propagandists treated as a rehearsal for their successes in 1917, it recounts the triumphant mutiny of sailors on the *Potemkin* in Odessa Harbor, playing out only a few hundred yards away from the grisly massacre of civilians by government troops. Intelligently thought through frame by frame, and carefully rehearsed, it took little time to produce and stands as a homage to Eisenstein's imagination and genius. As a committed ideologue, he would eventually portray his directorial strategies as straightforward outgrowths of Marxist theory—or, as they had learned to say in the

Soviet ambiance, of Marxism-Leninism. Montage, the technique he perfected (he found an interesting example in Flaubert's *Madame Bovary*), using sharply contrasting shots that, as it were, comment on one another and thus intensify the impression they leave on viewers, became in his commentaries "dialectical montage." It was as though he wanted it known that Marx and Lenin had virtually written his scripts for him.

The unforgettable scene in *Potemkin*, the Odessa steps sequence, depicts czarist soldiers indiscriminately slaughtering ordinary citizens.* Visiting Odessa with his troupe to shoot several scenes, Eisenstein had become fixated on a broad flight of marble steps descending to the harbor. It is on this outdoor stage setting that a mother pushing her baby carriage and elderly women pleading with the troops for their lives are pitilessly mowed down. Eisenstein, a student of such matters, was fully aware of the resentment such barbarity was bound to arouse in his audiences and made the most of its dramatic opportunities. Nothing in *Potemkin* was more calculated to stoke indignation than this senseless massacre, superior even to the closely photographed rotten, maggot-infested meat that the *Potemkin*'s officers think good enough for the sailors' lunch. He alternated rapidly between panoramic shots showing victims being gunned down or trampled and the rhythmic sight of advancing military boots, and close-ups of ravaged, wounded faces. It was indeed a memorable passage, intended, like all of *Potemkin*, to make a political point, evil naval officers pronouncing the sailors' food to be perfectly palatable, evil czarist troops like so many killing machines butchering innocent Russians. We have seen it before: some of the most exciting innovations that modernists produced stemmed from sources of questionable merit.

The cinematic device Eisenstein developed in its most effective form

---

* As David A. Cook has pointed out, "*Potemkin* took ten weeks to shoot and two weeks to edit, and contrary to the prevailing mythology, its montage was not constructed according to some carefully rearranged and systematic plan. Eisenstein himself lent credence to this notion through his intricate structured analyses of the film in his later theoretical writings, but the truth is that, like *The Birth of a Nation* and *Citizen Kane*, *Potemkin* was less a matter of careful planning than an intense release of creative energy."

in *Potemkin*, the one always associated with his name, was montage. It secures his claim to being a true modernist in the art of the movies. With perceptive cutting, Eisenstein wrote in one of the many texts he devoted to it, "montage becomes the mightiest means for a really important creative remolding of nature." Handled by a master like himself, the contrivance could develop a certain subtlety, but in essence it was simplicity itself: the confrontation of incompatible events to make their close proximity enhance their impact. Every story has an element of montage in it; it is from making it appear seamless and natural, as Eisenstein did, that it derives its dramatic charge.

EISENSTEIN WAS MORE a casualty of the Soviet system than its beneficiary. His imaginative Marxism, far less a political straitjacket for him than it was for more unoriginal minds, fell afoul of bureaucrats uneasy with his idiosyncratic technical inventions, the ripe product of his individuality. He was as much of a modernist as the Soviet authorities would let him be, and their patience was far from predictable. He was lucky; the number of victims to Stalinism among intellectuals and artists was horrifying, especially among those who, like Eisenstein, were of Jewish background. Officials forced him to make changes small and large in his work; they accused him of "formalism," a favorite term of abuse that party hacks close to Stalin liked to apply indiscriminately to the music, drama, poetry, fiction—and movies—they considered too distant from the officially approved "Social Realism." They found him guilty of "bourgeois deviations."

Several of Eisenstein's projects were rejected by the authorities; his greatest work, *Battleship Potemkin*, continued to be available largely because of its immense popularity abroad. And the last movies he made, *Alexander Nevsky* (1938) and *Ivan the Terrible* (Parts One and Two, 1945 and 1946), were, in large part, triumphs of aesthetics over ideology. *Nevsky* recalled a historic thirteenth-century military clash with Russian troops victorious over Teutonic (which is to say, Nazi) invaders; Eisenstein made that movie at a time when a Nazi assault on the Soviet Union seemed imminent. Fea-

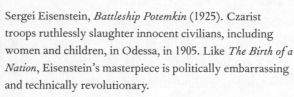

Sergei Eisenstein, *Battleship Potemkin* (1925). Czarist troops ruthlessly slaughter innocent civilians, including women and children, in Odessa, in 1905. Like *The Birth of a Nation*, Eisenstein's masterpiece is politically embarrassing and technically revolutionary.

turing a gigantic battle panorama and a superb score by Sergei
Prokofiev, with its slow-moving, grandiose set pieces, *Nevsky* seemed a
new genre, more opera than movie. Prokofiev, with his gift for neoclassical mimicry, melodic invention, and dramatic adaptability, a musician
whom biographers liked to call a "moderate modernist," was an ideal
partner for Eisenstein. And the late Eisenstein, even without Prokofiev,
left the same impression of a genius at work with *Ivan the Terrible* (Part
Three remained unfinished). In his last productions—Eisenstein died
prematurely in 1948 at fifty—the propagandist element receded and
pure art remained, a mild revenge by a director whose reading of Marxism differed in dangerous ways from that of the men in power.

5.

EISENSTEIN'S CONTEMPORARY, Charlie Chaplin—Chaplin is always
"Charlie," never "Charles"—took moviemaking in a radically different direction: inwards. In Chaplin's oeuvre, both essential elements of
modernism—the lure of heresy and the cultivation of subjectivity—
found their place. Obviously, his predecessors had occasionally provided insights into motivation, and love stories had never wholly
ignored feelings. But by and large directors had relied chiefly on plot,
one incident piled on another, to keep the audience interested, letting
the viewer imagine the feelings involved. With events chasing events,
whatever insightfulness was open to moviemakers, even if they were
interested, was mainly restricted to the close-up, a shot that gives an
actor's face unique control of the screen and can be an efficient device
for the presentation of emotions. It had first appeared around 1900 in
Griffith's movies, and served the director's sensibilities more than those
of the actor, usually a mere instrument in the director's hands. This
allocation of responsibility made no difference to Chaplin, who after all
directed and acted in his own creations.

Granted, Chaplin's emotional range was in general relatively narrow. What lurked behind his slapstick was pathos, and sentimentality
was an ever present danger of which Chaplin was keenly aware, even if
he did not always escape it. Most of the time, though, his mobile,

expressive face stopped short of cheap emotionality and was masterly in registering ambivalence, the coexistence of contradictory feelings that makes up so much of mental life. Chaplin, not very articulate about his skills as a performer, seems never to have claimed this talent. Nor did the corps of contemporary film critics, practically all of them in love with him, the unmatched clown. But the emotional potential he offered scriptwriters and directors (not, of course, excluding himself) was expansive, especially after the arrival of the talkies, although Chaplin himself resisted sound as long as possible.

6.

CHARLIE CHAPLIN WAS among the first movie stars to be treated as a star; the contracts that American studios bidding for his services offered him proved extravagantly lucrative. Already known as a promising comedian, he had first visited the United States as a young man with an English troupe of performers in 1910 and returned to stay. He would be transformed by, and transform, the fledgling movie industry. By 1916, he could command a salary of $670,000 a year in a newly signed contract with the Mutual Film Corporation, one among a handful of companies battling for supremacy in Hollywood. "Next to the war in Europe," boasted Mutual's publicist, "Chaplin is the most expensive item in contemporary history. Every hour that goes by brings Chaplin $77.55 and if he should need a nickel for a car fare it only takes two seconds to earn it." It was not his last raise; by 1917, he was earning over $1 million a year.

This was a dizzying reversal of fortune. Born in London in 1889 into a clan of unsuccessful music hall artists, Chaplin had been on the stage since childhood, visibly talented but invariably impecunious, though on his way to developing a reputation as a flexible actor with a limber body for physical humor and extraordinary features to mime the most varied moods. These qualities proved to be ideally suited to the demands of the one-reel movie short and to its heirs, and he found room for bringing his characters' responses to life even in his hastiest skits.

It was his choice to present himself as a single characteristic figure,

Charles ("Charlie," to everyone) Chaplin in *The Gold Rush* (1925), one of
the full-length classics in his middle years, reduced to eating his boot.

the little tramp, in which Chaplin, though ready to take any role at
short notice, quickly made himself famous, portraying and evoking the
intricately interwoven feelings of contentment and suffering. Charlie
constructed a personage effortlessly recognized among moviegoers
everywhere. He was the hobo reeking of penury in his unmistakable
posture and uniform—the shuffling walk, the wretched mustache, the
tight bowler hat, the two-sizes-too-small suit, the floppy shoes, the
antique walking stick. Such a character, complicated (one might say) in
his simplicity, was a splendid preparation for Chaplin's rapidly developing modernist style of moviemaking, in which he drastically
departed from the accepted rules of acting and directing alike. His
increasingly conspicuous emphasis on a mock-innocent critique of contemporary capitalist society further enriched his self-portrayal—and

brought him some determined detractors. He was not a model to other moviemakers; he was unique.

It did not take Chaplin long to graduate from acting the scripts of others to writing, and soon after that to directing, his own work with himself the inescapable principal. In the early shorts, and even more so later in the full-length features, he proved a meticulous craftsman, wearing out his actors and himself in ordering repeated retakes. In *The Circus* (1928), he has a scene with two lions in a cage, and Chaplin was in that cage with them every time. The confrontation was not only dangerous but expensive ($150 a day, including trainer); still, the total number of takes was over two hundred. This fanatical obsessiveness, to which his troupe of supporting actors had to adjust, was all the more exhausting for everyone because Chaplin seems to have held a Platonic image of each scene in his head, and would not stop until he had matched this ideal. He was partly aware that he was largely responsible for the occasional explosions on the set; writing later about one his masterpieces, *City Lights* (1931), he commented that he had worked himself "into a neurotic state of wanting perfection."

Whatever the psychological roots, Chaplin's longing for perfection explains his vehement discontent with what he judged to be imperfect takes. The great closing scene in *City Lights*, a triumph of delicately displayed mixed emotions—it was his lifetime favorite—is a splendid instance of his way with ambivalence. It was a moment he rethought, rewrote, and rehearsed for months, a moment for which he had no models and only his disciplined imagination to guide him. The movie tells the story of the tramp, as shabby as ever, and a blind flower seller, young, beautiful, and poor. After he discovers that she might regain her sight if a famous Austrian specialist were to operate on her, he schemes to find the money to send her to Vienna; in a number of variations, he becomes a street cleaner, even a corrupt boxer, with hilariously horrific consequences for him.

The key to the funds that will send his beloved flower girl to the eye surgeon is a millionaire whom Chaplin rescues from suicide attempts and who, when drunk, regards the tramp as his best friend but who, when sober, fails to recognize him. The results are tragicomic: Charlie

Charlie Chaplin,
City Lights (1931).
The tramp meets
the blind flower
seller.

gets the money he needs but is wrongly accused of having robbed his rich pal and is sent to jail. When he comes out of prison, more threadbare than ever, he drifts across town and happens on a charming flower store run by his protégée, now sighted, ever hopeful that her unknown benefactor, no doubt handsome and rich, will some day identify himself to her. The denouement is in the wings.

Noticing Charlie shrinking hesitantly by the door, the onetime flower girl forces some money into his hand and recognizes him from the days when touch had been her instrument for recognition. When the movie closes in heartbreaking close-ups, she asks him, as if to deny the obvious fact that her illusions about her rescuing angel have been discredited: "You?" He nods, and asks in turn, half expectant and all embarrassed, an unnecessary question: "You can see now?" He, of course, knows she does. And—it is now the end—she confirms what is so apparent, leaving viewers to devise their own fantasies about what if anything may come of the love between the tramp and the beauty. This recognition scene may skirt the boundaries of kitsch, but virtually no viewer has ever ventured to call it that. For the vast numbers who have seen *City Lights*, including the film critics, it remains Chaplin's finest moment.

WITHIN A DECADE, from the mid-1920s to the mid-1930s, Chaplin made three features, all comic masterpieces, *The Gold Rush* (1925), *City Lights* (1931), and *Modern Times* (1936). He wrote, produced, and directed them, took the hero's part, and composed the music. Charlie as hapless prospector in savage Alaska, cooking his boots and shoelaces; Charlie as factory worker caught in machinery from which he cannot escape, are scenes that remain in the memory. His next movie, though, *The Great Dictator* (1940), a venture into contemporary international politics, was a daring, abrupt departure from the character and the comedy that had made Chaplin world-famous. Taking advantage of a minor resemblance to Hitler—his mustache and that of the *Führer* looked vaguely alike—he constructed a fable in which the lives of a poor Jew (Charlie was neither the one nor the other) and of the Great Dictator, both of course played by Chaplin, intersect, with plentiful opportunities for playing off one against the other. The humor is grimmer than ever. Toward the end, the vagaries of the plot give the Jew a chance to deliver a heartfelt oration deploring present-day selfishness and cynicism ("Greed has poisoned men's souls—has barricaded the world with hate" and "We think too much and feel too little") and calling for a brighter future ("The way of life can be free and beautiful"). The speech was a collection of well-meaning chestnuts that displeased the angry left and the angry right alike, the one denouncing it as a naïve, politically meaningless plea for goodness, the other regarding it as a characteristic product of Communist pseudo-egalitarianism.

For Chaplin, the Hitler movie was a generally unexpected but in truth almost predictable step. Later, after learning about the concentration camps in Nazi Germany, he regretted having made *The Great Dictator*, which, with its brilliant incidents of slapstick, trivialized a monster. But his pronounced left-wing leanings, his very invention of the little tramp and his critique of the machine age in *Modern Times*, speak to his self-image as a spokesman for ordinary folk. He described himself as an "anarchist," and that term reflects his discomfort with all sorts of organized political institutions. That included the Soviet Union, a great favorite of radicals down to the Second World War. In 1938, Dan James, a wealthy Californian left-winger who came to know Chaplin well in those days, noted that "Whatever his exact politics, Charlie had a position of revolt against wealth and stuffiness. . . . He was certainly a libertarian. He saw Stalin as a dangerous dictator very early, and Bob [Meltzer] and I had difficulty getting him to leave Stalin out of the last speech in *The Great Dictator*. He was horrified by the Soviet-German Non-Aggression Pact" of August 1939. "He believed in human freedom and human dignity." Yet none of this kept certain critics of his views, including congressmen, from demanding that Chaplin, who had never taken out American citizenship, be deported.

An account of Chaplin's career as a genius in the movie industry, then, cannot evade his life away from the camera. A new breed, the publicity officials of movie companies, had come into existence to promote stars as public property, providing actors with euphonious names, spreading (if necessary, inventing) gossip about the stars' erotic adventures, all in the service of selling tickets. Chaplin was a natural target, or victim. His irrepressible attraction to nubile teen-age actresses brought him two sensational divorce suits, and even a trial—though he was acquitted—for having violated the Mann Act (1910), which prohibits the transportation of women across state lines for lubricious purposes. But the acquittal never acquitted him in the minds of his detractors, any more than it blackened his name among his admirers. His private life, coupled with his outspoken political opinions, made him a symbol to be celebrated or denounced.

All this left its mark on Chaplin. He made more movies after *The Great Dictator*, but found the country he had informally adopted increasingly unwelcoming to him. Then, in late October 1942, when Chaplin was fifty-three, he met Oona O'Neill, the seventeen-year-old daughter of Eugene O'Neill, and almost a year later they were married. Still making full-length features, *Monsieur Verdoux* (1947) and *Limelight* (1952), Chaplin finally drew the consequences of his endangered status and left the United States to settle down in Vevey, Switzerland, where he died in 1977. The father of eight children with Oona, laden with honors from the movie world and a knighthood in Britain, the anarchist lion retired as a contented bourgeois lamb. It was an astonishing ending to an astonishing life, not the kind of ending typical of modernists.

7.

THE TROUBLED CAREER of the avant-garde moviemaker Orson Welles far more closely resembles the chestnut of the unhappy modernist brought low by a culture unworthy of him. Certainly to modernist observers, the course of Welles's life, especially in its later years, serves to confirm that long-cherished legend about the unconventional genius doomed to defeat by mediocrity. Only posterity, then, more grateful and perceptive than his contemporaries, has done full justice to Welles's legacy.

The standing of Welles's first and finest film, *Citizen Kane* (1941), is secure. Those popular competitions that rank the world's "best" movies, periodically launched by magazine editors in search of circulation, invariably show it near or more often at the top.* And for this

---

* Plainly, such polls, reporting individual tastes, are too arbitrary, too subjective, to mean a great deal, though the consistent high ranking of Orson Welles's *Citizen Kane* seems utterly deserved. My own list of favorites holds no surprises: *La Femme du Boulanger* (1938), a half-pathetic and half-comic rural drama of infidelity and reconciliation, with the incomparable character actor Raimu; Howard Hawks's *His Girl Friday* (1949), a cool look at modern journalists, a brilliant remake of Lewis Milestone's *The Front Page* of 1931, with the suave Cary Grant and Rosalind Russell, the fastest-talking actress in Hollywood; Carol Reed's *The Third Man* (1949), about heartless black marketeers in postwar Vienna, from a script by Graham Greene, dominated from the moment of his first appearance by Orson Welles; and *Casablanca* (1942), with Humphrey Bogart, Ingrid Bergman, and Claude Rains. And, of course, *Citizen Kane*.

study it is of particular interest that *Citizen Kane* lavishly fulfills the two criteria that modernism requires: as a technical marvel and, at the same time, as a psychological detective story.

Orson Welles in *Citizen Kane* (1941), running for office. Universally hailed as the greatest movie ever made, with Welles, an authentic genius, producing, directing, acting, and participating in the script.

BORN IN 1915, WELLES was, like Eisenstein, embedded in a well-to-do family. He was something of a child prodigy, demonstrating his almost frightening precocity when other children his age were still quarreling in the sandbox. At four he discovered his life's vocation, working every role—author, director, acting each part—in a puppet theatre that an observant family intimate had given him. When he succumbed in 1939 to an invitation from RKO, a Hollywood studio in grave financial straits looking for a rewarding hit, he was already a widely known actor and director who had presided over unconventional productions of Shakespeare and experimental versions of Eugène Labiche and Marc Michel's old French comedy, *The Italian Straw Hat*.

Welles's legendary voice, which could intimidate or charm, speak with royal dignity or childish petulance, had been heard across the United States in his radio performances with his and John Houseman's Mercury Theatre. On one memorable evening, October 30, 1938, in a weekly dramatization of a piece of modern fiction, he had sent the nation (or a significant part of it) into collective hysteria with a naturalistic adaptation of H. G. Wells's *War of the Worlds*, a story of Martians invading the state of New Jersey. Despite an alert that he was broadcasting a piece of fiction, what with craftily phrased weather reports, police bulletins, and other official-sounding announcements, Welles persuaded untold thousands of listeners that the Martians were indeed landing in force. The panic was nationwide. In astounding numbers, anxious radio listeners called the police or newspapers or radio stations for advice and reassurance and fled their homes to their church or some public building. The result: Orson Welles found himself written up in *The New Yorker* and landed on the cover of *Time* magazine.

This, then, was the youthful genius, all of twenty-four, destined to rescue RKO. It took Welles more than a year to settle on the topic for his first movie: the biography of a vastly rich American newspaper publisher, Charles Foster Kane, who starts out as a young idealist but has permitted power to corrupt him and make him into a grasping, bullying, increasingly isolated reactionary. His blind need for ever more power invades his private life: he tries to force his second wife, a singer without talent or intellect, to pursue a serious career. Even with the organized support of his newspapers, she fails as she must, and at last, untouched by his earnest pleas and his fearful rage, she leaves him. All his power has not spared him the indignity of impotence. It is hardly necessary to add that the actor impersonating Charles Foster Kane was Orson Welles.

Citizen Kane begins with an ending: Kane, alone with great wealth and innumerable collectibles he has amassed, is dying; his last word is a baffling, whispered, barely decipherable name: "Rosebud." After an informative send-up of a familiar newsreel staple that gives the bare facts of the magnate's life, five of Kane's old intimates are interviewed in long flashbacks to explain, if possible, that odd farewell. As mountains of the junk he had indiscriminately gathered up to keep him company are thrown into the flames, one of the casualties of this drastic cleanup is a sled, named "Rosebud," which he had loved as a boy. The viewer sees it briefly, to leave the theatre with one puzzle solved, but with the emotional import of the youthful Kane's sled still open to speculation. Why a thing rather than a person as a final memory? Is it a commentary on Kane's inner emptiness, or perhaps the emptiness of a culture in which power counts more than morality? Welles brilliantly turned the career of an outsized American into a psychological mystery, with some of its solution emerging into view during the flashbacks.

WELLES WAS THE FIRST to acknowledge that not all of his fascinating departures from habitual moviemaking were of his design. He knew, for example, that a few venturesome directors had already placed a ceiling on their sets, as he would do. And some of his coworkers on *Citizen Kane* were men of exceptional talent. He worked closely with his cinematographer Gregg Toland, a professional open to, even eager for, experimentation. Welles and Toland tried out new camera angles, never before attempted lighting, and (Toland's specialty) deep focus shots that gave a figure in the background as clear a definition as another at the center of the action. When Welles credited his troupe in the concluding reel of the completed *Citizen Kane*, he placed Toland's name on the same page as his own—an unprecedented accolade. His appreciation of the chief script writer, Herman J. Mankiewicz, was less wholehearted. Mankiewicz wanted his name listed as the sole author of the script. But Welles, though perfectly ready to give Mankiewicz top billing, as he did, had the law and the facts on his side: he had done much of the writing and the editing. In any event, his imaginative absorption of others' discoveries and his own inventiveness, which the technically untutored audience would feel only as the film's intense grip on them, made *Citizen Kane* an unparalleled experience.

The reviewers responded with unusual, unanimous enthusiasm. Bosley Crowther in the *New York Times* flatly said that *Citizen Kane* "comes close to being the most sensational film ever made in Hollywood." William Boehnel in the *New York World-Telegram* agreed: "here is a film so full of drama, pathos, humor, drive, variety, and courage and originality in its treatment that it is staggering and belongs at once among the great screen achievements." And some reviewers insisted, rightly enough, on its cinematic inventiveness. "Technically," wrote Archer Winsten in the *New York Post*, "the result marks a new epoch." This was also the view of John Mosher in *The New Yorker*: "Something new has come to the movie world at last." For these insiders, the lure of heresy that *Citizen Kane* provided was nothing less than overwhelming. It resembled the sense of sudden discovery for painters in 1907, a discovery that changed the world of art forever, when the Salon d'Automne revealed Cézanne in his first posthumous exhibition.

The animated response of moviegoers presumed to know best could not make *Citizen Kane* a financial gold mine. It came in at under $850,000, hardly a staggering sum. But the story of the life and death of Charles Foster Kane had aroused the rage of the elderly newspaper magnate William Randolph Hearst, who took the film (not wholly without justice, for all of Welles's heated denials) to be an easily recognized portrait of him. Feeling slandered, Hearst, impassioned and unforgiving, mobilized his formidable resources to punish the young man who had dared to vilify him. He kept Welles's name, even other movies produced by RKO, out of the Hearst papers, and with his threats intimidated chains of movie theatres to forego showing the offending masterpiece. And, it must be admitted, the general public, without which no movie can make a profit, developed only a limited passion for it. What else could one expect of the vulgar democratic masses? a modernist might have asked. It was not until after the war that less ornate movie palaces, the new art houses in major cities that catered to choice, often foreign movies, would give *Citizen Kane* a permanent core of admirers, and the sincerest flattery by imitators. It was Welles's first movie, and the last over which he would have adequate financial backing and artistic control.*

He made many others, including an immediate successor, *The Magnificent Ambersons* (1942). A wistful look back at the decline of a provincial family in face of mechanization and modernization drawn from a Booth Tarkington novel—a lesser American counterpart to Thomas Mann's *Buddenbrooks*—the movie was drastically, ruthlessly cut down in Welles's absence by about a third, and further spoiled by added scenes designed to "clarify" the action. It remained a technical achievement, employing all the devices first tried out in *Citizen Kane*, but it failed at the box office, as did his version of Eric Ambler's highly successful espionage novel, *Journey into Fear*, released in 1943. As far as RKO executives could tell, their saviour had turned into a losing proposition.

THE REST OF WELLES'S LIFE, though it provided rewarding recompense from admiring moviemakers, critics, and students in university film departments, was shadowed by a desperate search for money and creative freedom. He was not starved for respectful recognition in flattering articles, medals, honorary degrees, even a knighthood in Britain. But such tributes, however gratifying, did not give him adequate resources to pay for ambitious projects that would bear his unique signature.

* To be precise, there is just one exception to this disheartening record: Welles's version of Kafka's *The Trial* of 1962.

Through the years, whether in Europe or during interludes in the United States, Welles's situation never improved drastically: he was looking to finance appealing visions that would run unencumbered, he hoped, all of them recognizably an Orson Wellses product. He worked as an entertainer at Las Vegas or New York television studios to amass the funds he needed. Late in his life television watchers could see him pathetically doing commercials for a California vintner, obese, miscast, wasting his golden voice as a spokesman for some undistinguished label. Welles died—at seventy in 1985—as he had lived, working on a new movie, a version, *his* version, of *King Lear*, with Welles (of course!) playing the dispossessed king.

There is something tragic about this life history, the stuff of a bleak modernist legend. Welles's country—or, more precisely, the movie industry and its financiers—failed to nourish one of its most brilliant geniuses. As those who worked with him could testify, he appears like a giant brought low by midgets who more than made up for their diminutive intellectual and artistic stature with money and its correlate, power. It was all part of an all too familiar story, a modernist's failure at the hands of the philistine. American culture may not have deserved him, but serious moviegoers with a taste for modernism will always have *Citizen Kane* as a lasting pleasure—and a bitter reproach.

8.

THE INSPIRED WORK OF postwar moviemakers, seconded by expert cinematographers and seasoned actors, gave earnest avant-garde periodicals like *Cahiers du Cinéma*, founded in Paris in 1951, much theorizing to do. The critics writing for the *Cahiers*, nearly all of them young and unfazed by the burden of tradition—François Truffaut, Jean-Luc Godard, Claude Chabrol, Eric Rohmer, to mention only the most celebrated—soon moved from writing to directing and established a style, the *nouvelle vague*, the new wave, that made a virtue of economic necessity. As impecunious producers, they brilliantly matched their technique to their severely limited financial resources. They preferred locations to studios, thus cutting the cost of their backgrounds, and in

editing their productions they freely used the jump cut, which permitted them to eliminate botched takes, even if that would disrupt their
continuity. This was a fundamental departure from Eisenstein's montage in favor of the *mise-en-scène*, "best defined as the creation of mood
and ambience," thus rendering a movie "not merely an intellectual or
rational experience, but an emotional and psychological one as well."
The French moviemakers of the 1950s made their self-conscious work
unconventional and psychologically searching, as modernist as movies
could become.

What is more, moviemakers had to confront the stern quality control of highly literate critics like Pauline Kael who, starting in 1967 for
The New Yorker, developed a large and loyal following for her acerbic
critiques and her enthusiastic discoveries. But the most dramatic source
of excitement and anxiety for the movie industry, exploding in the
1980s and drowning out other concerns, was the increasing application
of computer-generated imagery. It was as though the makers of movies
were belatedly appreciating the Futurists' infatuation with the machine.

Perhaps the weightiest reason supporting this radical disruption was
the promise of saving money. Computer programs could make the
weather more suitable to filming by adding rain or snow to a sunshiny
landscape, "reporting" fierce fights among prehistoric animals, constructing vast naval battles in a "pond" the size of a bathtub or, best of
all, digitally converting a small number of appropriately dressed extras
into an army or a mob, thus greatly reducing the daily expenses for having to hire hundreds who rarely did more than stand around. With the
aid of advanced computers, moviemakers could order up extraordinary
beings, often winged, who could make the most fantastic fable appear to
be within the range of possible events, or insert real actors into largely
artificial scenery. Year after year, digital ingenuity improved the effectiveness of these new devices. Hence annually, when the Motion Picture
Academy distributes its Oscars, it has had to make room for Best Special
Effects. One wonders what Orson Welles would have done with all
these inventions, since he did so much without them.

It is a hard question to answer. The future aesthetic significance of
the evolving digital share in productions, particularly its impact on the

psychological perceptiveness of movies, is almost impossible to predict. It is as though a music critic were to appraise an opera solely on the basis of its costumes and libretto. There is no guarantee that the contributions of technology to making a movie, so influential and apparently so promising, will necessarily improve it; in fact, they may reduce its claim to distinction. Technology the servant may become the master; it may starve that indispensable quality in modernism, the humane element. Thus it is highly possible that the mechanization of the movies is simply another symptom of the decay, perhaps the death, of the modernist enterprise.

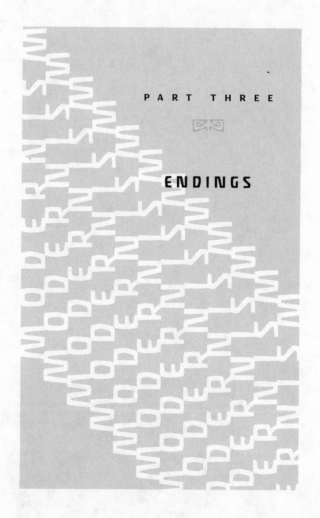

PART THREE

ENDINGS

New York crowds waiting in line for tickets to T. S. Eliot's
The Cocktail Party (1949). The difficult modernist poet as a
(relatively) popular playwright.

8.

ECCENTRICS AND BARBARIANS

THE PRECEDING FIVE CHAPTERS HAVE EXPLORED MAJOR and very diverse cultural domains in which modernism enjoyed a significant presence. It should have been apparent in these investigations that the careers of modernist arts and literature were far from smooth. The indifference and hostility of conservative tastes and the ideological objections of powerful institutions often limited, or delayed, a positive response to aesthetic innovators. Two sources of obstacles to modernist successes deserve more attention than I have given them this far; they were very unlike one another, yet could also curiously interact. They acted toward modernism, to borrow the title of this chapter, as eccentrics and as barbarians.

The first of these were sources of tension within the modernist camp. Themselves faultless modernists in their work, the eccentrics were indisputably aesthetic radicals rebelling against the traditional academic ideals that safeguarded the canon—the beloved and oppressive past—against unconventional newcomers who would introduce impermissible harmonic scales in music, illegitimate verse forms in poetry, or unacceptable intimacies in their fiction. The eccentrics, then—I am calling them the anti-modern modernists—were at one with their fellow dissenters in assailing the established, almost sacred truths in their professions. But they also rejected most if not all of their contemporary culture, including features that their fellow modernists found perfectly unobjectionable. In short, the eccentrics sought to practice and perfect their modernist departures, even though they expected to establish their way in the arts in a new, presumably better, society.

In sharp contrast, the barbarians—the German Nazis and the leaders of the Soviet Union—worked to destroy modernism as they enlisted the submissive arts in their ideological campaigns. The pages that follow, then, first consider modernists who were at the least ambivalent about, or more likely downright antagonistic to, their times and who embraced a past that was a design of their imagination more than the harvest of historical research. I shall then turn to the totalitarian regimes in Hitler's Germany, Stalin's Russia, and (to a lesser extent) Mussolini's Italy, as they dramatically first narrowed the conditions under which modernists in their countries had to work and then shut them down altogether.

In these perilous conditions, the internal struggles of the eccentrics were less conclusive, and more interesting. They eloquently testify to the wide reach of modernism. Incoherent though their patterns of thinking and feeling may look, there were modernists on the pattern of Degas, the most individualistic among the French Impressionists. In the mid-1890s, during the Dreyfus Affair, when the Jewish Captain Alfred Dreyfus was convicted—falsely—of betraying French military secrets to the Germans, Degas began to quarrel with his closest Jewish friends and allied himself with right-wing anti-Dreyfusard fanatics. He grew more heated about what he called the need to protect the honor of the French army at all costs than he was about the truth, or untruth, of the charges against Captain Dreyfus. Modernists, in a word, could find themselves anywhere on the map of ideas, no matter how unintelligible their views. They themselves might be unsure just where on the spectrum of opinion they really stood. Drastically as they dissented from the totalitarians, in reality their deadly enemies, the anti-modern modernists enlarged and further complicated the definition of the great movement that is the object of this study.

ANTI-MODERN MODERNISTS: AFTER STRANGE GODS

l.

THERE WAS NO MORE FITTING a poster boy for anti-modern modernists than T. S. Eliot. His friends and readers found him baffling: "he seemed too radical to conservatives," as his biographer Peter Ackroyd has summed it up, "and too conservative to radicals." Holding fast to conflicting opinions, he raised contemporary poetry to hitherto little explored diction, versification, and subject matter, and adopted his first masters among anti-bourgeois French literary rebels. But at the same time, Eliot the radical clung to traditional beliefs in his religion and his politics, the two inseparably intertwined.

In short, Eliot's sweeping subversion of contemporaneous poets' practice, an uncompromising, generally acknowledged modernism, was no obstacle to his discovering in High Anglicanism the inner peace, the fulfillment of his longing for certainty that had long eluded him. In 1927, five years after publishing *The Waste Land*, he was received into the Church of England, punctiliously undergoing the formal, long-established ceremonies. He took instruction; he was baptized and confirmed in accord with all the rules. Increasingly, he dressed, spoke, and tried to sound like an Englishman. A true loner, born in Missouri in 1888 and a discontented heir of Boston's Unitarian heritage, he had reached port at last.

Religion, which had never been far from his mind, now began to occupy ever more space in his poetry, and with his dismissal of modern individualism, it demonstrated to him the vital role of like-minded people of faith. "What have you if you have not life together?" he asked rhetorically in 1934 in the pageant *The Rock*, and answered his own question:

There is no life that is not in community,
And no community not lived in praise of GOD.

He was finally settled as a believer, and a year after his conversion he famously epitomized his "general point of view": it was that of a "classicist in literature, royalist in politics, and anglo-catholic in religion." However others might feel, there is no evidence that he saw any tension between adopting the highest of High Church Anglican doctrine and continuing to write his seditious verses.

Though concise and eminently quotable, Eliot's declaration of faith did him no favors; it categorized his perspectives in all too plain and set a way, as though he would never need intellectual breathing space and flexibility again. Actually, he remained a one-man crusader, an adventurer, if only in poetry, within the canonical limits he had set for himself. He began to write plays, starting with the verse drama *Murder in the Cathedral* (1935). Its ostensible theme is the assassination in 1170 of Archbishop Thomas Becket by royal agents in Canterbury Cathedral, but it is at heart a dialogue on worldly temptation and devout resistance. Though a surprising success in its staging, Eliot, unwilling to repeat himself, went back to poetry; his later plays had contemporary themes, yet were all tied to what a wise character in one of them, *The Family Reunion*, refers to as "sin and expiation."

Eliot's most ambitious project, though, became *Four Quartets* (1935–43), a cycle of four poems, reflections on time, order, and sinful man's precarious place before God. He begins the first, "Burnt Norton," with some high-flown, even intimidating reflections:

> *Time present and time past*
> *Are both perhaps present in time future*
> *And time future contained in time past.*
> *If all time is eternally present*
> *All time is unredeemable.*

But redemption may yet come. Eliot thus concludes the last quartet, "Little Gidding":

> *We shall not cease from exploration*

* * *

And all shall be well and
All manner of thing shall be well
When the tongues of flame are in-folded
Into the crowned knot of fire
And the fire and the rose are one.

Whether from fatigue or through maturity, Eliot (it is a rare gesture for him) ends with the possibility of eternal harmony, of salvation.

2.

AS ELIOT GREW INCREASINGLY famous, invitations to lectureships or introductions to other writers' books began to inundate him. They provided him with welcome space to comment on controversial issues beyond the technical questions confronting poets. In 1933, in *After Strange Gods*, the Page-Barbour Lectures at the University of Virginia, he gave his distaste for the contemporary world free rein, and supplied critics of his more and more reactionary politics with a wealth of damaging quotations—damaging to him. The cultural inferences he drew from his anti-modern modernism would never again be so patent. He flattered his listeners as doubtless enjoying "at least some recollections of a 'tradition,' such as the influx of foreign populations has almost effaced in some parts of the North, and such as never established itself in the West." Having contemptuously set aside the ur-American ideal of making a nation through generations of immigrants, Eliot candidly lamented the crowding-in of aliens from apparently inassimilable cultures. "You are farther away from New York; you have been less industrialized and less invaded by foreign races."

Eliot's use of "invaded" measured his disapproval of what the flood of recent newcomers had done to his former country. Massive immigration—and who were more numerous and conspicuous than East European Jews?—was, for Eliot, a cultural catastrophe. Certainly New York, as Eliot's close friend Ezra Pound harshly put it, was *"ganz verjudet"*—wholly judaized. The most desirable makeup of inhabitants in any society struck Eliot as so obvious as to make explanation virtually redundant. "The population should be homogeneous; where two or more cultures exist in the same place they are likely either to be fiercely self-conscious or both to become adulterated. What is still more important is unity of religious background, and reasons of race and religion combine to make any large number of free-thinking Jews undesirable." One unintended merit of *After Strange Gods* was that it refused to flee to euphemisms and circumlocutions.

The lectures showed Eliot's ethnology to be, in a word, primitive. Granted, the loose, irresponsible use of "race" was still common, and in deploying it Eliot was in good (which is to say, bad) company. But it exacted costs: in counting Jews among the races, Eliot was implying that Jewish qualities—all of them undesirable—are indelible. That is the key to his explicit objection to "free-thinking" Jews: they were cunningly trying to conceal their racial endowment, and, given that endowment, necessarily concealing it badly. Further, that one could count on their being skeptical about Christianity did not endear them to Eliot. This reading of Eliot's thinking on social coherence finds confirmation with his reliance on the term "homogeneous" to sketch his social ideal. Eliot nostalgically turned back literally centuries—some four centuries, to be precise—to a time when shared identity of cultural and, more important, religious beliefs were regarded as essential preconditions for order in a commonwealth. Yet Eliot spoke confidently, as he usually did. It was a fundamental truth for him that the United States was "worm-eaten by liberalism," a swear word for him.

It is a comment on Eliot's alertness to his readers that he never authorized *After Strange Gods* to be reprinted. The lectures were suffused with genteel bigotry, and probably would have proved embarrassing for him. But ample as the opportunities were, he never repudiated these passages either. His picture of the world he wanted and whose absence he desperately regretted, a world uniform in culture and creed, as thoroughly anti-modern as it was possible for a modernist to be, was always at the heart of his ideology. Eliot's literary modernism was of decisive importance to him and to readers of poetry everywhere. It radically transformed the way poets read and wrote poetry. But that unimpeachable modernism coexisted peacefully (at least for him) with a most intense anti-modernism. No doubt, the adequate definition of a modernist, already complicated enough, will have to accommodate the awkward quality of apparent self-contradiction—a tribute to the sheer complexity of human nature. The point of interest remains that Eliot never considered his positions self-contradictory at all.

ANTI-MODERN MODERNISTS: A LOCAL GENIUS

1.

THE FIRST TIME IN HIS life that someone called Charles Ives a "musical genius" was in 1888, when he was thirteen. The occasion was a concert conducted by the genius's father, George Ives, who happily presided over the premiere of one of his son's first relatively adult compositions, his *Holiday Quickstep*. The author of this accolade to his brilliance was a reporter in Ives's hometown weekly, the *Danbury News*, bowled over by a youthful local talent.

It was almost the last time, too, that this extravagant epithet was applied to Ives while he lived. When he died in 1954 at seventy-nine, the most lonely of loners among modernist composers, he was known only to a tiny self-selected band of enthusiasts, and tributes to his astonishing musical gifts mainly came half in jest from friends who had attended Yale with him. Ives was too diffident to make such grandiose claims, but he knew himself to be a serious musical innovator who was at the same time proud of the insurance brokerage house in which he made himself a millionaire and who in his spare time composed music nobody wanted to hear.

In the course of a hardworking, illness-haunted life, Ives was exceedingly prolific. During his most productive years, spanning from the last decade of the nineteenth century to the early 1920s, he wrote four symphonies, none of which saw a complete performance until 1951. Among them, the Fourth, probably Ives's most conspicuous claim to immortality, enjoyed a few partial exposures confined to one or two of its movements; it was not until 1965 that Leopold Stokowsky boldly placed the whole symphony—all of it—on one of his programs with the Philadelphia Orchestra and, to redouble his good deed, recorded it. Thus, more than a decade after Ives's death, the concertgoing public was introduced to a "new" masterpiece that had been kept waiting in the wings for almost half a century. It uses choruses; quotations from his own and others' works, reminiscences from hymns like "Watchman, Tell Us of the Night" and "Nearer, My God, to Thee"; conflicting pitches; and a ready openness to a non-denominational religious experience—all typical of Ives's unorthodox manner.

Similarly, Ives's "sets" for large orchestra—following Beethoven's Sixth (*Pastoral*) Symphony and Richard Strauss's *Till Eulenspiegel* aiming intermittently to imitate nature literally—long remained rarities. Other among Ives's pieces of music fared little better. In 1922, he brought out a comprehensive *114 Songs*, later cannibalized for shorter

Charles Ives in his last years. The modernist and anti-modernist composer.

collections published separately, yet they made few appearances at recitals. The finest of his piano pieces, the *Concord* Sonata, had been largely completed by 1913 but had no full public coverage until 1939, and what exposure it had received little applause and less attention. Ives, in these later years, spent much time and money having his music printed and sent around to those who just might be interested. It is not that Ives's music was a cultivated taste—it was too little performed to permit music lovers to cultivate it in the first place.

IN THE COURSE OF this study, we have encountered a sizable number of eccentrics, determined outcasts who, driven by divine discontent, obeyed their urge to write, or paint, or design, or compose works that Ibsen's "compact majority" scorned as amateurish handiwork, as a symptom of incompetence and perversity, or outright madness. In this honor roll of outsiders, Ives must occupy a leading place. He became the supreme hermit in his calling not through ignorance, opportunism, or neurosis, but through his culture. Danbury, Connecticut, formed him in two incompatible ways. His complicated gathering of attitudes makes Ives appear quite ambivalent. On the one hand, his native soil trained him as a stubborn citizen of small-town, conservative America, and on the other hand, as the kind of self-determined artist who simply felt compelled to go his own, which is to say modernist, way. His hometown environment, which boasted some 10,000 inhabitants when he was born, would never quite let him go.

Ives's principal, unforgettable inspiration was his father, George Ives, a widely admired soloist on the cornet and organist at a local church. The founder and leader of several bands that offered occasional concerts, he gloriously performed at the public holidays that the town patriotically celebrated and raucously enjoyed; the annual Danbury Fair each autumn was a memorable high point for him and thousands of delighted visitors. He liked unresolved dissonances, uncertain or conflicting keys, the injection of hymns or folk songs or patriotic ditties in serious music, virtually unplayable quarter tones—all irregular devices that students in conventional conservatories were taught to dis-

dain as the kind of sheer blunders their teachers would do their utmost
to eradicate.

Yet, a perceptive son and an adventurous experimenter even as a boy,
Charles Ives adopted his father's venturesome "mistakes" and gave
them a home in his compositions, including the most ambitious. He idealized his father-instructor, and called him, in addition to his wife, his
only teacher (an excessive tribute since Charles Ives, as a subscriber to,
and patron of, magazines on recent music, had other influences ready to
hand). But, thoroughly at home in his culture, as I have said, he must
have had it brought home to him that his father's choice of working as a
professional musician was an unpromising way to make a living.
Indeed, George Ives in his last years—he died prematurely in 1894 at
forty-five when Charles Ives was a freshman at Yale—took a job in his
family's bank. But the issue that most troubled the Iveses, father and
son, was not money so much as reputation. It was the common property
of philistine Americans, thoroughly shared by the worthies of Danbury,
that to be a musician by trade was not a proper career. Lacking gravity
and virility, it was the sort of living a real man would not adopt, especially when he had opportunities in the business world.

Charles Ives was penetrated by this atmosphere from boyhood. He
started his musical education with his father at the age of five and
could not overlook the astonishment and quiet disapproval of neighbors, even of family members, at George Ives's way of life. At the
same time, he thoroughly appreciated the loving, generous, fostering
manner that was the father's style with his evidently supremely gifted
son. "What my father did for me was not only in his teaching, on the
technical side, etc.," Charles Ives later wrote, "but in his influence, his
personality, character and open-mindedness, and his remarkable
understanding of the ways of a boy's heart and mind." This open-
mindedness allowed the father to be extraordinarily patient with his
son's playful musical ventures, some of them suggested by his own
tireless inventiveness. George Ives would at times ask listeners to sing
a song in one key and then accompany them in another. As long as you
know what you are doing, he told his son, you are free to break whatever traditional rules and restrictions—which he also taught his son

conscientiously—that try to hold you back from originality. In this benign climate, Charles Ives grew up with contempt for European, mainly German, technical edicts.

It looks, then, at first glance as though Charles Ives faced a stark choice upon graduating from Yale in 1898: to pursue full time the music he loved above anything else or a more "manly" career, the sort of which Danbury would approve. The truth is quite different and more serpentine. To a reader attuned to the high prestige that a career in the arts now carries with it, that moment must seem like a stark choice. Actually, it appears that Ives knew from the outset what he must do: he went into training in a New York life insurance company. A few years later, he established his own firm and prospered mightily.* For two decades, the choice seemed unexceptionable; he worked happily and productively in his life insurance company and, whenever he had some free time, he wrote much of his most interesting music.

2.

IN THE EARLY 1930S, when he was in his late fifties, Ives gathered up some informal reminiscences, mainly anecdotal, and included a passage explicitly justifying his career. He does not refer to the moment when he made the decision, probably because there was no such moment. In the contest between joining a commercial culture and opting for a romantic isolation, the victory of the culture was wholly unsurprising. "As a boy [I was] partially ashamed of it," he writes about his surpassing love of music, "an entirely wrong attitude," he added, "but it was strong—most boys in American country towns, I think, felt the same." Far from being an absentee from an American boy's ordinary life, Charles Ives was a fine athlete in school, a good baseball player and captain of his football team. Yet plainly this was not enough. "When other boys, Monday A.M. on vacation, were out driving grocery carts, or doing chores, or playing ball, I felt all wrong to stay in and play

---

* In his biography of Ives, Frank R. Rossiter writes, soundly enough, "it is doubtful there was any conscious decision [to go into business] at all."

piano. And there may be something in it. Hasn't music always been too much an emasculated art? Mozart etc. helped." Mozart, at least much of Mozart, was not emasculated.

With these memories, Ives reached for the heart of the matter as he understood it. There were, he observed, ample reasons for choosing life insurance. One met a variety of interesting people in business, which "widens rather than cramps up [one's] sensibilities." Besides, to disregard the claims of one's family and let its members go hungry by concentrating on one's ideals was, to Ives, unacceptable. "How can he let the children starve on his dissonances," he asked rhetorically, and duly cited his father's views. George Ives had "felt that a man could keep his music-interest stronger, clearer, bigger, and freer, if he didn't try to make a living out of it," especially if he had "a nice wife and some nice children."

These seemed like strong motives, but the first, his shame as a boy at failing to participate adequately in masculine pursuits, was the one that held special weight for Ives. Manliness was an obsession with him. His biographers have naturally found his heated rhetoric about the effeminacy of most music and musicians worthy of comment. It is so extreme, and depends so exclusively on a single metaphor: the composer as a feminized creature. Through the years, Ives gathered a fairly monotonous vocabulary of abuse to which he resorted freely—calling male music critics he disliked "Miss" or "Aunt"; mocking the professional specificity of a life insurance executive by estimating that "88⅔%" of modern music was "an emasculated art"; or describing conservative commentators on his volume of *114 Songs* as "musical pussies." He acknowledged that as a young composer he had actually enjoyed some effeminate compositions: "When I think of some music that I liked to hear and play 35 or 40 years ago—if I hear some of it now, I feel like saying, 'Rollo, how did you fall for that sop, those "ta tas" and greasy ringlets?'"

"Rollo" was a nickname Ives employed to epitomize the feminized musician, the good son who believes what dull, unadventurous authorities tell him. "In this I would include the *Preislied* [in Wagner's *Meistersinger*], *The Rosary* [by Ethelbert Nevin], a certain amount of Mozart,

Mendelssohn, a small amount of early Beethoven, with the easy-made Haydn, a large amount of Massenet, Sibelius, Tchaikovsky, etc. (to say nothing of Gounod), most Italian operas (not exactly most of the operas, but most of each opera). Some of Chopin (pretty soft, but you don't mind it in him so much, because one just naturally thinks of him with a skirt on, but one which he made himself)." Even that boastful profile in courage, Richard Wagner, whom Ives had esteemed in his early years, came to represent the party of effeminacy. He had "more or less of a good brain for technical progress," but had "put it to such weak uses—exulting, like a nice lady's purple silk dress, in fake nobility and heroism, but afraid to jump in a mill pond and be a hero. He liked instead to dress up in purple and sing about heroism—(a woman posing as a man)."

To Ives's mind, these "molly-coddling" musical "saps" or "lily-pads" are the lethal enemies of music. In 1934, in London, he attended a Sibelius program and "those groove-made chewed-cuds" made him fear that real music—*his* music—had no future. Sibelius's *Valse Triste* "(as brown-sugar-coddle as it is) is bigger than what [we] heard last night—for the first it is a nice lollipop, and it doesn't try to be something else—but those symphonies, overtures, etc. are worse because they give out the strut of a little music making believe it's big. Every phrase, line, and chord, and beat went over and over the way you'd exactly expect them to go"; they were "trite, tiresome awnings of platitudes, all a nice mixture of Grieg, Wagner, and Tchaikovsky (et al. ladies)." Worst of all was seeing "those young people standing downstairs, seriously eating that yellow sap flowing from a stomach that had never had an idea." They would go home, copy down "those slimy grooves" thinking they were "creating something," while actually they were "helping music decline—dying—dying—dead."

Charles Ives's unmodulated, unwarranted rage at most music—88⅔% of it!—hints broadly at a personal involvement more heated than mere abstract concern over its long-range prospects. However varied his targets, his criticism of fellow composers had only a single dimension: they all lacked manliness. We have entered the domain of speculation here, but it seems undeniable that Ives, all his protests to the contrary, had private reasons for buying into the ideology of the small-town provincial America in which he grew up. True, his own compositions, apart from the touches of youthful sentimentality he humbly acknowledged, were (he thought) free of the homosexual taint that others were flaunting, "emasculating America for money—that's the root of the snake. . . . A Nation Molly coddled by commercialized papp—America losing her manhood."* His own unresolved dissonances, phrases quoted from patriotic and religious tunes, and simultaneous employment of different keys, were all efforts on his part to keep music manly, which, he was only too sure, desperately needed it—as most probably did he.†

CHARLES IVES'S ANTI-MODERN modernism, then, was unique and embattled, an intermittent nightmare. Unlike T. S. Eliot and (as we shall see) Knut Hamsun, he was no reactionary in his politics, but grew into an engaged egalitarian and left-leaning liberal. He had, we know, as little use for Haydn as he did for Sibelius, and for the same reason. But his inner world was more conflicted than he allowed to reach consciousness. His preference for business over art was, as I have said, natural, perfectly inescapable for him. But his experience as a life insurance executive, which confirmed what he had learned as a child, kept him within shooting distance of his heritage, the ideals—I have called them philistine—of Danbury, Connecticut. It was his homage to that world that made him disdain most of the music written in his own time and that written in preceding generations. And his disdain of that musical world made him persist in his subversive techniques.

---

* It is entirely plausible that Ives's excessive, single-minded worries about the manliness of American musicians were prompted by more private concern about his own virility. In her substantial biography, Jan Swafford speculates that the diabetes from which Ives suffered may have produced impotence, which might certainly have exacerbated his preoccupations.

† There was a time when poetic justice caught up with Ives's impassioned distaste for homosexuality. In 1936, Ives's most effective amateur press agent, the composer Henry Cowell, was tried and convicted of sodomy. The friend who thought that Ives should know of this catastrophe and who knew of his attitudes asked Harmony Ives to inform her husband when she judged him ready. In fact, he took it very badly; in the four years that Cowell spent imprisoned in San Quentin, Ives never got in touch with his devoted friend. Only when Cowell was released and got married did Ives forgive him.

There is yet more to be said. As a modernist—it was a label that, like all labels, he disliked—Ives composed by setting aside the historic rules. As an anti-modern modernist, he detested the music that his contemporaries adored, and that he thought he might just trump with his departures from tradition that were his life in music. And his guides to these departures were significantly translated from inspiring American words that made his compositions both radically new and soothingly old. After all, the great *Concord* Sonata and the Fourth Symphony took as their programmatic guides a select number of New England Transcendentalists—Emerson and Thoreau, and, to a somewhat lesser extent, Hawthorne and the Alcotts. They would, he hoped, liberate him—and his listeners—from the traditional dependence that nearly all contemporary American composers still displayed. Idealizing Emerson as he idealized his father, Ives lived in the past as much as he did in the present, both remade to order.

ANTI-MODERN MODERNISTS:
A NORDIC PSYCHOLOGIST

ON APRIL 30, 1945, Adolf Hitler committed suicide in his bunker in Berlin, an irrevocable exit that would release worldwide rejoicing. But a week later, on May 7, the Oslo daily *Aftenposten* printed a short, mournful obituary for him. "I am not worthy to speak his name out loud," the author wrote. "Nor do his life and his deeds warrant any kind of sentimental discussion. He was a warrior, a warrior for mankind, and a prophet of the gospel of justice for all nations. His was a reforming nature of the highest order, and his fate was to arise in a time of unparalleled barbarism which finally felled him." It was about the last possible time for such a heartfelt tribute; one day later, German troops everywhere, including the occupying forces in Norway, surrendered to the Allies. Even if the necrologist's name had been concealed, any halfway educated Norwegian could have guessed it: the parade of personal diffidence ("I am not worthy"), the stern rejection of sentimentality, the awe before the manly "warrior for mankind," to say nothing of the appalling perversion of recent history, unmistakably pointed to Norway's most illustrious novelist and leading modernist: Knut Hamsun.

Hamsun's astonishing homage to a lost leader is even more drastic a rejection of modern civilization than Eliot's contempt for contemporary poetry or Ives's condemnation of composers as hopelessly effeminate. Beyond being a virtually unique outburst, it provides Hamsun with a passport to the eccentric country of anti-modern modernists. For, like Eliot and Ives, Hamsun was a revolutionary subverter of his specialty, fiction, but, like them, too, he turned his back on the social and political ideals that seemed only natural to fellow modernists. While an undisputed leader in the avant-garde of novelists, his political loyalties put him in an isolated minority among writers.

The text shocked many readers, but it wholly surprised few of them. For years, Hamsun had trumpeted his virulent contempt for "the masses," most of them, he believed, seduced by Bolshevism; made disparaging comments on parliamentary rule; and persistently held a dictatorship superior to democracy. This was not a senile attack of intransigent enthusiasm. As early as 1894, when he was thirty-five, with his first major novel, *Hunger*, just four years behind him, Hamsun had spoken highly of, and virtually identified himself with, the "independent and aristocratic loner," who has "no confidence in democracy, the choice of the masses, rule by the masses. He is repelled by the mob, and despises its essence." This political perspective was much on his mind and remained so. A year later, in his drama *At the Gates of the Kingdom*, he had a character eloquently reiterate this article of faith, voicing his devotion to "the born leader, the natural despot, the great commander, the one who is not chosen but who elects himself to mastery over the hordes on the earth. I believe and hope for one thing, and that is the coming again of the Great Terrorist, the Life Force, the Caesar." For Hamsun, the remote past ("the Caesar . . . coming again") was far more satisfying to contemplate than the chaotic liberal present.

Hamsun was of course not the only writer to be tempted by fascism. A few intellectuals and artists in France or Britain and elsewhere, weary of what they detested as bourgeois mediocrity and corruption,

Knut Hamsun at fifty—Gulliver in Lilliput.

found much to applaud in what they hailed as the energy, the manliness, the destruction of quarreling factions that Fascists, whether Italian or German, seemed to be offering as a strong and attractive alternative. But Hamsun was special: the only Nobel Prize laureate to adore Hitler; the subtlest of psychologists, who signally failed to read his infatuation with the Nazi and Italian regimes with whatever rationality remained to him.

In the political turmoil that overtook Europe after the First World War, the time, it seemed, had been ripe for the Caesar, much to Hamsun's delight. He had "great admiration and respect for Mussolini," he told his publisher in 1932. "What a man in the midst of these confused times!" As for Mussolini's junior partner in Germany—so the pair was seen at the outset in 1933, if not for long—Hamsun confessed during the Second World War, "above all, it is Hitler who has spoken to my heart." Back home, the aggressive, authoritarian politician Vidkun Quisling, the founder of the Norwegian Nazi Party whose name would become a synonym for traitor, was Hamsun's man: "If I had *ten* votes," he proclaimed before the elections of 1936, "he would get them."

THE SORE, WIDESPREAD distress over Hamsun, Hitler's fond obituarist, was easy to understand. Living in a remote and small country totaling roughly 3 million souls around 1900, Norway's citizens treasured any fellow citizen who gained international attention. This anxiety for recognition, if anything, only mounted after 1905, when Norway liberated itself from subjection to the Danish monarchy and became a wholly independent state. Henrik Ibsen, though he spent years of his life abroad, was the most celebrated among its national icons. But Ibsen died in 1906, and other great Norwegians, like the playwright, novelist, and poet Bjørnstjerne Bjørnson, died soon after. By that time, at forty-seven, Hamsun had already gathered considerable literary prominence, though he was not yet a best-selling novelist. He was, odd and unpredictable though his conduct, well placed to assume the position of Norway's leading celebrity; the Nobel Prize for Literature he was awarded in 1920 only underscored his stature. That is why, when Norwegians discovered or recalled Hamsun's pro-Nazi wartime utterances culminating in his farewell to Hitler, they preferred to think that the poor old man was no longer responsible for his words. It was a convenient if desperate alibi, all too easily discredited. In fact, he knew what he meant when he talked politics to his death in 1952.

The historian facing the extraordinary phenomenon of a modernist as Nazi is tempted to read his life in reverse, to search his earlier history for preparatory steps that point toward their repugnant consummation. But that is to disregard the paths Hamsun might have taken but did not take, to slight the astonishing range, the apparent incoherence, of his mental functioning. And that fails to acknowledge psychological complexity, a failure that Hamsun, the uncanny student of the human mind, would have found naïve. In short, to support fascism was not an inescapable consequence of his life's record.

Yet in retrospect it was likely enough. Hamsun allowed himself, for all his acumen, to generalize wildly about national character. One of his most solidly built mental constructs was the German-English duel he set up for himself from his youth on, with Germany the hero encircled and betrayed and England the cold, callous villain. Thus the Nazis, their charismatic leader in particular, for Hamsun the incarnation of the courageous, tough-minded German spirit, had a special attraction for him. Granted, the Germans had been the first to appreciate—and to buy—his novels, the first to study him as an important writer. But, more significantly, he came to look upon Germans as his racial kin, fellow members of a Nordic brotherhood—a racist perception that acquired ever-increasing prestige in his thinking after the Nazis' accession to power.

Nor did he regard the blessings that Germany bestowed as exclusively designed for his personal benefit: German educational institutions and German culture in general were, he believed, far in advance of those elsewhere. Far in advance: especially when contrasted with Britain, a country he hated with pathological intensity, a hatred particularly striking (no commentator on Hamsun has been able to evade it) because it was based on no more, at least consciously, than a short English train journey in his youth, and a few historical anecdotes presumably documenting the harshness and egotism of British imperialism. It was as though he needed to concentrate most of his rage and disgust—and he harbored inexhaustible stores of both—on one highly visible target. Given his obstinate trust in his intuitions, it was impossible for any impression he cherished—and he cherished all his impressions—to be modified, let alone jettisoned. Hence his idealization of Germany made Hamsun a natural candidate for conversion to the Nazis, who claimed to be restoring their country's masculinity, firmly returning women to their natural roles of housekeeper and childbearer, dedicated to eradicating the humiliations their nation had suffered at the hands of the Allies—mainly Britain—after the First World War, and stressing the purity of race. In key respects, the Nazis' program was Hamsun's program.*

HAMSUN'S AFFINITY WITH Nazi totalitarianism ran deeper even than this. It originated, I believe, as a response to some elemental habits of mind, untouched (as I have said) by his sophisticated psychology. For, even though he was unequaled in capturing the fleeting impressions and changes of mood that ran through him and made great modernist literature of them; even though at times he recognized his imperious need to be a minority of one, such insights did not carry through to his political choices.† He was born Knut Pedersen, a peasant, and for all his exposure to city life, always remained a peasant. Whenever he got an opportunity, he would practice the skills he had acquired as a boy, transforming the estates he acquired into farms that could serve as exemplars to the neighborhood. In later years, he invariably replied to questions about his profession tersely, "Farmer and writer." And he was a wanderer, representing his restlessness, his relentless search for solitude, by inventing outsiders for his novels who owed their existence to his characteristic unease. "Once upon a time I was like my comrades," he said. "They have kept pace with the times, I have not. Now I am like no one. Unfortunately. Thank God."

He thought he knew the city and what it did to its denizens. In a wandering life, spending long stretches in Norway's capital, he repeat-

---

* The late 1930s and early 1940s were the years, too, when Hamsun lent himself to anti-Semitic propaganda. In 1942, in a vicious article that appeared only in Germany, he wrote that Franklin D. Roosevelt was "a Jew in the pay of Jews, the dominant figure in America's war for God and for Jewish power."

† "It feels rather strange," Hamsun wrote in an early letter to the great Danish critic Georg Brandes on December 24, 1898, "to be a writer who is so at odds with all and everything."

edly turned to urban themes; his first significant fiction, *Hunger* (1890), was set in Christiania (later renamed Oslo), and so were others among his twenty-three novels. Yet for Hamsun urban life, beset by shallowness, cynicism, and materialism, and given over to a lust for progress (which he saw as a conspicuous symptom of hateful liberal power), was the fertile breeding ground for corruption and decadence. His lyrical evocation of the lonely countryside, his enthusiasm for isolation sought and lustily enjoyed, all brilliantly captured in the lyrical style that first brought him notice, was in dramatic contrast to the vice that was the city. Formal religion meant nothing to him, but nature brought out a poetic pantheism, and spoke to his most profound desire—to retreat to a rural purity, imitating his father. Intent as he was on rejecting modern Norway wholesale, he romanticized his early childhood as a "lost paradise, where the children lived in close harmony with the animals on the farm and the nature around them." This sophisticated primitivism made Hamsun a reliable ally to anti-modernists. Yet, at the same time, his modernism, worked out in his psychological reading of his literary characters, remained unimpaired.

This complex passion was more than a strategy for his fiction. When Hamsun was courting Marie Andersen, an actress some twenty-two years his junior who would become his second wife, he begged her, urged her, more important: ordered her, to give up the stage and reclaim the rural origins that were the source of all that was good about Norwegians. In tune with this demand, he created one of his most striking fictional figures, the mysterious Isak in *The Growth of the Soil* (1917), his most famous novel, who is a real, and magnificent, peasant. "A tiller of the ground, body and soul; a worker on the land without respite. A ghost risen out of the past to point the future, a man from the earliest days of cultivation, a settler in the wilds, nine hundred years old, and, withal, a man of the day." In this portrait, he trumped his fellow modernists in claiming his wanderers to be ancients and moderns at once, ghosts from long ago yet sound models for modern times.

None of this, I insist, makes Hamsun's anti-modern modernism or, for that matter, his obsession with Nazi Germany, a foregone conclusion. Others in his time had idealized the purity of peasant life and damned the dishonesty of city existence without drawing the political consequences that Hamsun thought perfectly natural. Nor does his exposure to psychiatry help to solve the riddle that is Hamsun. A short psychoanalysis he underwent in 1926 and 1927 with Norway's first analyst, Johannes Irgens Strømme, broke a particularly resistant writing block, but left no usable record and seems to have led to no noticeable adjustments in his mental economy. After the defeat of the Nazis, two Norwegian psychiatrists examined him in intensive question-and-answer sessions, eked out with Hamsun's own writings unpublished and published, including his fiction. In their report, these experts were gratified by the "absolute honesty" of their eighty-six-year-old patient, and took note of his difficult childhood (the "lost paradise"). Their conclusion: Hamsun had suffered from an inferiority complex brought on by the guilt feelings aroused by the strength of his instincts. He was not insane, but two relatively mild strokes suffered during the war had weakened his judgment and "permanently impaired" his "mental faculties."

For restored post-1945 Norwegian officials, this verdict was only too welcome; it spared them having to try their most famous compatriot in a criminal court, and perhaps to have him shot for treason, as they had Quisling shot in October 1945. But the psychiatrists' analysis was hardly persuasive, what with the feeble Adlerian diagnosis of an inferiority complex and Hamsun's visible self-control and intelligible answers to questions in the civil trial he had to undergo, answers that proved his mental faculties had not been "permanently impaired." He had no excuse for his politics. At the same time, though, it does not follow that his admiration for Hitler in any way compromises the peerless penetration of his early fiction. Other modernists could strenuously object to classifying Hamsun as one of them; no one so infatuated with mass murderers qualified for such an association. But there is no doubt that *Hunger*, with its profound psychological, almost psychoanalytic, exploration of usually neglected mental states, remains among the first classics of modernist fiction, proof that one could be anti-modern and a modernist at the same time.

BARBARIANS: HITLER'S GERMANY

1.

IF A SPRINKLING AMONG MODERNISTS, like Hamsun, welcomed the totalitarian regimes of the right and a far more sizable contingent of fellow travelers applauded the ascent of the left, the largest number of writers and artists became their prey, and among them modernists were prominent. Hitler's Germany, Stalin's Soviet Union, and (with less drastic consequences) Mussolini's Italy amassed victims among artists and intellectuals. An intelligent observer of his time, the aged Sigmund Freud, looking about him in early 1938, grouped these three dictatorships together:

> We find to our astonishment that progress has allied itself with barbarism. In the Soviet Union they have set about improving the living conditions of some hundred millions of people who were held firmly in subjection. They have been rash enough to withdraw the "opium" of religion from them and have been wise enough to give them a reasonable amount of sexual liberty; but at the same time they have submitted them to the most cruel coercion and robbed them of any possibility of freedom of thought. With similar violence, the Italian people are being trained to orderliness and a sense of duty. We feel it as a relief from an oppressive apprehension when we see in the case of the German people that relapse into almost prehistoric barbarism can occur as well without being attached to any progressive ideas.

Yet even in the collective ruthlessness against enemies real or imagined which these three dictators shared, they differed in purposes and targets, and demand to be treated separately as unique acts of regression.

Of the three, Nazi Germany was the most consistent in its suppression of any independent source of power, even of taste, linked to its cult of the charismatic leader. For German modernist artists and writers, who had supplied significant contributions to the theatre, the novel, poetry, painting, and architecture, Hitler's accession to office sounded their death knell. After he was invited to become Germany's chancellor on January 30, 1933, his trusted squads asserted their new power with demonic speed and frightening effectiveness. Across the country, the physical assaults on political opponents, including Socialist deputies to the Reichstag presumed immune from such treatment, multiplied in numbers and viciousness, and the country stood by, largely unmoved or even rejoicing. "The rapidity of the transformation that swept over Germany was astounding for contemporaries and is scarcely less astonishing in retrospect," Hitler's judicious biographer Ian Kershaw has summed up the prevailing German mood and the victors' momentum. "It was brought about by a combination of pseudo-legal measures, terror, manipulation—and willing collaboration. Within a month, civil liberties—as protected under the Weimar constitution—had been extinguished. Within two months, with most active political opponents either imprisoned or fleeing the country, the Reichstag surrendered its powers, giving Hitler control of the legislature. Within four months the once powerful trade unions were dissolved. In little over six months, all opposition parties had been suppressed or gone into voluntary liquidation." As early as March 1933, the new holders of power candidly announced the opening of a concentration camp, the first, at Dachau near Munich. The quest for total control over culture high and low, over business directors and bowling clubs, editors and soccer teams, advanced against tepid resistance and to widespread approval. Abruptly and without appeal, Germany's *Moderne* found itself and its daring innovations consistently and contemptuously denounced as "*undeutsch*"—un-German.

THE NATIONAL SOCIALIST regime's first blow against modernism was a by-product of anti-Semitism. With the Reichstag reduced to impotence, and backed by enabling legislation aiming to "purify" German society, the Nazis hastened to convert some of their long-professed anti-Jewish fantasies into reality. Jews were purged wholesale: Jewish civil servants, Jewish orchestra conductors and theatre impresarios, Jewish professors—not a large group but more numerous during the Weimar Republic than they had been in the German Empire—Jewish journalists, Jewish performing artists, Jewish painters and writers quickly found themselves unemployed and unemployable.

Of course, by no means all the German Jews expelled from their livelihood and often their homeland were modernists. Nor were a disproportionate number of them engaged in modernist causes. The orgy of dismissals was carefully targeted; it was enough to be a Jew to become an undesirable intruder among authentically Germanic talents. For, despite their undeserved reputation for *Kulturbolschewismus*, the bulk of Germany's Jews were far from favoring "cultural Bolshevism." Like most German gentiles, they were content with established tastes. When in 1937 the Nazis staged their carefully organized traveling exhibition pillorying what they called "Degenerate Art," the managers found only six Jews among the one hundred twelve artists scornfully selected for their so-called depravity. Yet culturally conventional Jews, too, were caught in the net of the government's racist program. An eminent conductor of the classics like Bruno Walter, whose specialties were Mozart operas and Mahler symphonies, escaped to Austria in the spring of 1933 under threat of violence if he dared to continue conducting on German soil. Leading scholars like the neo-Kantian philosopher Ernst Cassirer and the art historian Erwin Panofsky, neither of them remotely concerned with modernist art or literature but both of them Jews, were deprived of their professorships and had to find new platforms abroad, eventually, as so many of them did, in the United States.

Yet some of the involuntary exiles were full-fledged members of the modernist clan. Probably the most spectacular exemplar of a Jew dismissed simply because he was a Jew was the inventive, immensely versatile director of the Deutsches Theater in Berlin, Max Reinhardt. This civilized showman presented plays that modern audiences would find gripping no matter how old-fashioned their provenance. He revived German and French and Greek classics, offered a *Hamlet* in modern-day costume and a spectacular *Midsummer Night's Dream* on a revolving stage. His reward: being forced into American exile where he would continue his stunning, imaginative designs, though on a much-reduced scale.

Nor were all emigrants Jews. Bertolt Brecht, Weimar Germany's most interesting playwright, who outgrew an early Expressionist phase to adopt Marxist didacticism, left Nazi Germany on February 28, 1933, the day after someone had set fire to the Reichstag in Berlin* and at the same time that Brecht's recent plays were arousing the most vehement rejection in the provinces. In this literally incendiary atmosphere, Brecht conjectured that his arrest—sure to be followed by maltreatment—seemed a reasonable probability, and he fled abroad.

THE SCATTERSHOT AGGRESSION that the Nazis mounted against German avant-gardes soon concentrated on more precisely chosen targets. May 10, 1933, saw the notorious burning of the books, an obscene gesture that underscored the wide support that the Nazis, for all their viciousness, then enjoyed. The holocaust of condemned books, which included not only Jewish authors but such "Aryans" as the brothers Heinrich and Thomas Mann, was a riot of *ressentiments*, of vulgar Teutonism politicized. It was an emotional outburst against the memory of events and ideas like the "shame" of the November Revolution of 1918 that had put an end to the Hohenzollern Empire, and a presumably final farewell to liberalism, "worm-eaten" (to use Eliot's word) and all too widely shared. The rhetoric of the day was like an exultant funeral oration against modernism. Few remembered then—though thousands would recall it later—that a century before, the great German poet Heinrich Heine had said that in a country where they burn books, they will burn people.

The Action against the Un-German Spirit, at which as many as some twenty thousand books were burned in Berlin and smaller numbers in other German cities, had been attentively prepared in April by

---

* The question just who had set fire to the Reichstag has long been debated, though recent scholarship has thrown grave doubts on the charge (widely credited at the time) that the Nazis themselves were responsible as part of their plan to destroy Germany's constitutional rights. It now seems almost definite that the Dutch ex-Communist Marius van der Lubbe was, as he himself confessed, the sole arsonist. Whoever did it, the Nazis exploited the event with uncanny speed.

the German Students' Organization, intent on trumping the Nazis' own Student Federation with a set of twelve ferocious theses placarded all over the country, including the universities. Thesis Number Seven read: "When the Jew writes in German, he lies. He should be compelled to indicate from now on in books he wishes to publish in German: 'Translated from the Hebrew.'" The open mendacity of such oratory was unsurpassed and unsurpassable, but the book burning that followed from it found wholehearted backing among academics and students, to say nothing of firemen detailed to see that the fires did not grow out of control. It was not just crusty reactionaries still unreconciled to the Weimar Republic who celebrated the unceremonious disposal of "un-German" texts; an unconventional lyrical poet like Gottfried Benn and an influential philosopher like Martin Heidegger loudly endorsed the regime and helped to immobilize a crucial source for dissent. Manliness, patriotism, racial purity, identification with the people, the *Volk*, the contemptuous dismissal of cosmopolitanism, rationalism, and other enlightened ideals were the only intellectual styles the regime supported, and allowed. A new heroic day was dawning and a solid core of educated Germans wanted to be part of it.

2.

WERE SUCH ACTS SYMPTOMS of anti-modern modernism? Did the Nazi regime principally look toward the future or the past? More than half a century has gone by since the dismal end of Hitler's Thousand Year Reich, and there are still no answers to these questions. Nor can there easily be, since both Nazi ideology and Nazi actions pointed in divergent directions. On the one hand, the Nazis took technology to be a humble but valued servant; they celebrated modern inventions like the automobile and the airplane and used them ostentatiously as agents of military preparedness. They resourcefully began to rearm their country from 1933 on, and energetically reoriented German industry to serve the needs of a war in the not too distant future.

What also exhibits the Nazis' infatuation with the modern was their shrewd exploitation of that still young institution, the radio, for their propaganda. Nazi painters found a grateful subject in portraying a rustic German family gathered around their simple radio intently listening, with the caption, *"Der Führer spricht"*—The Leader is speaking. Abetting this practical modernity were Utopian Nazi ideologues who envisioned a new world dominated by a New Man, an Aryan world without Jews. And they worked toward that fundamental revolution with a great thoroughness—*Gründlichkeit*, the quality that believers in national character liked to ascribe to Germans—that left not the smallest space untouched, as they transformed Jews who had significantly contributed to the treasure of German culture into parasites. By the mid-1930s, *Gymnasium* pupils in Berlin and elsewhere were assigned a songbook that ascribed the words to the favorite tune, *Die Lorelei*, too popular to be dropped, to "unknown," when in fact Heine, a baptized Jew, had written the immortal text a century before.

Yet on the other hand, this New Man—and Woman—sported a curiously old-fashioned air. The imagined self-portrait prescribed heroic self-sacrifice for the German female with *Küche, Kirche, Kinder*—kitchen, church, children. Among the few political jokes that managed to circulate in that humorless society under the watchful eye of the Gestapo and of citizens eager to denounce neighbors lagging in their loyalty to the *Führer* was the "definition" of the Nazis' dream, the New Man: as blond as Hitler, as athletic as Goebbels, as lean as Göring. More seriously, if few Germans could meet the stern demands of the radical agenda for self-renewal, they could always fall back on the aura surrounding Hitler to remind them that they were being led by a *Führer* who bore the burden of laboring for others, suffering for others, *seeing* for others—a secular Jesus Christ.

There was something timeless about the cult of Hitler, a profession of abjectness that has intermittently appeared across the ages. The Germanic ideal that leading Nazis acknowledged—the New Man—was cobbled together from folk memories, literary inventions, and self-aggrandizing historical legends recent and remote.* The realities of his-

---

* Henry A. Turner, a distinguished historian of modern Germany, has noted that "the National Socialists sought their model in the past, looked, however, back not to the history but to a mythical and eclectically manufactured past. What they proposed was a flight from the modern world."

Vanessa Bell, jacket of Virginia Woolf's
To The Lighthouse (Hogarth Press, 1927).

Salvador Dali, *The Great Masturbator* (1929).

Piet Mondrian, *Composition with Red, Yellow and Blue* (1937–42).

Andy Warhol,
Brillo Box
(1964).

René Magritte, *La Trahison
des images (Ceci n'est pas une
pipe)* (1928–29).

Anthony Caro, *Early One Morning* (1962).

Jasper Johns, *Three Flags* (1958).

Andy Warhol, *Marilyn*,
silkscreen (1962).

Roy Lichtenstein,
Woman with
Flowered Hat
(1963).

Jasper Johns,
False Start (1959).

Roy Lichtenstein, *Crak!* (1963–64).

Frank Gehry, Guggenheim Museum, Bilbao (1997), exterior.

tory had no chance of competing with such Teutonic fantasies. For all the self-contradictory elements in Nazi thought, then, all in all, the past loomed larger in the official ideology than the future, a nostalgia at least partly disguised by modern embroidery.

3.

THIS FANCIFUL NEEDLEWORK did nothing to save German modernism. During their first year of power, the Nazis created a comprehensive Reich Chamber of Culture, which gathered in its subdivisions imaginative writers, the press, the theatre, the radio, music, and the arts under the aegis of the Propaganda Ministry, which is to say Joseph Goebbels, who was carrying out Hitler's explicit program. "We want to give back to our *Volk*," the *Führer* had said as early as February 1933, "a truly German culture, a German art, a German architecture, a German music, which will restore our soul." Hitler, enamored of slim, realistic, blond nudes and a worshipper at the shrine of Richard Wagner, was not likely to have much patience with German Expressionist paintings, graphics, and poetry, even though these adventurous arts were largely the accomplishment of recent gentile masters. And so, German modernists emigrated or fell silent.

The categorical proof that the Nazis had no use for cultural modernism came in July 1937 with a sensational exhibition, first shown in Munich and after that in thirteen other German cities, featuring *Entartete Kunst*—Degenerate Art. On its crowded walls or in its catalog one could see modernist art cleverly paired with paintings by permanent inmates of insane asylums, accentuating the childishness, sickness, even madness of paintings and graphics that had presumably been imposed on a passive, excessively patient German art. But the statistics—some 2 million viewers in Munich alone, another 1 million elsewhere—attest less to the persuasiveness of the Nazis' case than the public's fascination with the modern art that was being confiscated wholesale from German museums. If they were not incinerated in Berlin's chief fire station, the works ended up in a few privileged private collections or auctioned off abroad, profitably.

This organized demonizing of modernism was not without its built-in paradoxes. Just as some prominent Nazis pursuing the officially required investigation into their family ancestry discovered to their horror that, far from being pure Aryans, they had a Jewish grandparent, so some of the most ardent Nazis among German artists discovered, to *their* horror, that their modernist leanings made them outcasts from the pure Aryan art world now taking shape. Probably the most dramatic instance of such tragicomic failures was the Expressionist art of Emil Nolde. Among the paintings exhibited as exemplars of degenerate art, there were twenty-six Noldes, with the striking colors, distorted forms, and primitive outlines of his uninhibited canvases, exotic woodcuts, and superb watercolors. He had traveled and chosen to live most of his artistic life in half-seclusion in a remote North German village. His subjects varied from flower pieces and alien landscapes to intensely felt Christian scenes, all committed, as he put it, to "a profound spirituality, religion and tenderness."

For years Nolde had acted as an old-fashioned, self-isolated avant-garde artist. And yet he had early been a member of the Nazi Party in his district of Schleswig-Holstein and enthusiastically accepted the Nazis' worldview. Hence he found being publicly stigmatized extremely painful. The number of his paintings, drawings, and prints confiscated from museums by 1937 and for the most part destroyed has been recorded at 1,052, the largest for any single "degenerate" German artist. In 1941, he was officially forbidden to paint—an order he disobeyed in the silence of his out-of-the-way home—at a time when other Expressionists, like Karl Schmidt-Rottluff, were also censored out of artistic existence. Another modernist artist, the painter and sculptor Otto Freundlich, died in the Nazi extermination camp of Maidenak in March 1943, not because of his style but because of his "race."

FOR SOME YEARS, historians of Nazi culture have argued that while Germany's rulers between 1933 and 1945 politicized art, they at the same time aestheticized politics. It was the time when appearance competed with the attention given to substance. The massive spectacle of thousands of uniformed civilians, orderly in serried ranks all earnestly at attention, stiffly holding up standards dominated by a swastika; the shrewdly manipulated interplay of dazzling lighting and the breathtaking moment when the *Führer* manifested himself from the shadowy background to start one of his two-hour-long orations; the monumental neoclassicism that characterized the designs (and normally the buildings) of Nazi public architecture; the carefully nurtured mystique of the *Volk*; the notoriously seductive propaganda films of the 1934 Nuremberg Party Convention, and that of the Olympic Games in Berlin in 1936, both brilliantly filmed by Leni Riefenstahl—all were items in the rulers' agenda to enlist general enthusiasm for the thrilling and self-deceptive feeling of participating in a grand national adventure.

Whatever ingredients of modernist techniques the Hitler regime found useful to appropriate, then—and Riefenstahl's movies are a splendid instance of this—liberalism, that fundamental principle of

Leni Riefenstahl at work. Though she never fully acknowledged it, Riefenstahl was Hitler's favorite filmmaker.

modernism, the freeing of impulse and inventiveness from the commands of whatever authority might stand against it, was lost amidst the noise of the Nazis' retrograde revolution.

BARBARIANS: STALIN'S SOVIET UNION

1.

ALTHOUGH IN PRINCIPLE Soviet Communism stood at the other end of the world being manufactured in Nazi Germany, observers who were not imprisoned in Stalinist ideology increasingly discovered astonishing and disheartening affinities between the two. For all the continuing influence of pro-Soviet intellectuals in the West, more and more thought of the Nazi-Soviet Non-Aggression Pact of August 1939 as a perfectly natural development. In fact, the critical term "totalitarianism," which tersely asserted that the two regimes were brothers under the skin, uncannily alike for all their mutually hostile rhetoric, began to come into use among political scientists and journalists in the late 1920s. Certainly both regimes used their destructive powers to force avant-garde artists into a government-issued line and to silence whatever aesthetic opposition might remain. Their effect on the modernists within their borders was identical: compelled obedience and cooperation or silence, or, perhaps, death.

LIKE MODERNIST PAINTING and music and fiction elsewhere, the Russian versions of these cultural radicals go back to the nineteenth century. Backward and highly eclectic in whatever it could manage to borrow from the West, Russia's first avant-garde of note had emerged in the 1860s with an anti-establishment school of painters rebelling against the self-isolating ideology of the dominant St. Petersburg Academy. At one with other Russian reformers then and later, these protomodernists tried to address the foremost problem confronting every humane observer of their country: what to do for the majority of the people, the poverty-stricken, devout, often illiterate peasantry. When Dostoevsky wrote, "The question of the people and our view of them . . . is our most important question, a question on which our whole future rests," he spoke for most intellectuals and cultivated Russians. But the program of these modest radicals was not far-reaching; they called themselves, humbly, "the Wanderers," to stress their aspiration to send art exhibitions across the country spreading culture to the neglected masses. Their heirs would not stop there.

Only a few of these polite outsiders did memorable work—I am mainly thinking of Ilja Repin, an accomplished Realist known for his penetrating psychological perception. But their social discontent survived. By 1921, with the Bolsheviks securely in control of Russia's vast territory ending four years of civil strife, foreign intervention, and a brief war against Poland, artists enthusiastically supporting the new Soviet regime also saw themselves obligated to the people and the need to alleviate their aesthetic illiteracy. If in the West, the art for art's sake principle had been a triumphant claim to autonomy by unconventional artists, Russia's revolutionaries stood that value judgment on its head by denouncing the doctrine as a resource of reaction. With the making of a New Man, and with that a new art, in the offing, they believed that there was abundant room for modernists to work with the support of the young regime.

They had already done so well before the Revolution. The imaginative, versatile sculptor Vladimir Tatlin performed highly original experiments with a wide gamut of materials, providing heretical thrills for Russian viewers. And, even more decisive for the history of Russian modernists, Kazimir Malevich, the most important artist among them, was indebted to the Italian Futurists as well as to French models like Cézanne for his classical compositions and to the young Matisse for his color-drunken exuberance. From about 1910, Malevich began to simplify his figures; he reduced bodies to heavy circular shapes (highly inelegant in rendering arms and legs) and lavished color on his abstract canvases in lively contrasts. By 1913 he had reached what he called "Suprematism," straightforwardly rendering squares, circles, cruciform shapes, and rectangles, gradually complicating his canvases by playing these essential ingredients off one another. His famous *Black Square*, and the even more famous *Suprematist Painting: White on*

White, put painters as well as art lovers before a predicament similar to the one that Marcel Duchamp was posing with his readymades: Were these forms, in their very simplicity, the ultimate modern confection, or did they, as the left-wing painter and designer Alexander Rodchenko and other Constructivists insisted, announce the end of art?

Such burning issues, fiercely debated as the Russian Revolution engrossed the attention of intellectuals no less than that of politicians, easily translated into questions about the prospects of modernism. Was modernism perhaps the latest act in a long-running drama that had been playing for over two millennia and would retain its integrity and independence? Or was it a desperate bourgeois scheme to salvage a future it did not deserve? If these years of upheaval seemed a tempting time to engage in fundamental quarrels, at the same time, they were too agitated to have artists concentrate on such metaphysical conundrums. And so avant-garde artists went into the years of revolution no less baffled than others, facing unpredictable consequences.

2.

THE RECEPTION OF THE SOVIET UNION among modernists is a long, complicated, sad, often discreditable tale. It amounted to a love affair and, a little later, to its pathetic dissolution—being sorted out only now after the demise of the Soviet Union. This much has been clear for decades: the passionate early worldwide infatuation with the Soviets among progressive artists and writers was comprehensible if not wholly creditable. The czarist regime had inspired little esteem, and the triumphant revolution that overthrew it looked to many like a breathtaking alternative. After all, were not modernists anti-bourgeois, and was not the Soviet leadership just as hostile? It struck many as a shared conviction that appeared irrefutable and important.

But around 1920, as soon as the Bolsheviks' military successes became incontestable, a first question was in order. It was Russian bourgeois—at least the handful wealthy enough to travel to the West and to build lavish mansions for displaying their purchases—who were the first serious collectors of modernist paintings in Russia. Muscovite merchants had been avidly acquiring the new Western paintings for decades. Savva Mamontov, an immensely rich railroad magnate, and his cultivated wife, Elisabeth, had from the 1870s become the founders of a hospitable artists' center, as well as buying some of the revolution-ary paintings—mainly Impressionists and Post-Impressionists—for their pleasure.

This booty and that of fellow collectors gave Russian artists access to the latest news about the arts, mainly from Paris. Even more instructive to Russian painters yearning to experience the shock of avant-garde art at firsthand was the splendid, highly concentrated collection of Sergei Shchukin, a Moscow businessman who went beyond merely collecting Impressionists. In 1906, he bought his first Matisse and began to special-ize in that artist, elevating his own position from customer to patron—as long as the artist he patronized was Matisse. Picasso came later. In 1911, when Matisse visited Shchukin at home in Russia, he was elated to discover that his host owned twenty-five of his canvases (the last count, thirty-seven, would show him to be even more obsessive), and was just as elated to carry out two large-scale commissions for murals of *Dance* and of *Music*. It never occurred to devotees of the Soviet "experiment," as they liked to call it, that it had been the Russian upper middle class that had brought its country the latest, most radical art. True, the Sovi-ets once in power had enough intelligence to prize avant-garde paint-ings, if mainly to seduce foreign visitors: the collections of Shchukin and of his chief local rival, Ivan Morosov, an equally rich factory owner, were confiscated for a state museum. Here another question arose, even more troubling than the first: Would the Soviet Empire, with its ambi-tious aspiration not simply to transform the nation's economy but human nature itself, be able to generate an atmosphere welcoming, or at least not set in principle against, new art? The answer to that question had to be, after only a few years, a depressed negative.

With the passage of time, modernists at home and abroad had good reasons to discard their wishful fantasies about the Soviet Union as the culture to be looked forward to and possibly imitated. Some foreign observers were not captivated at all by the aesthetic promise of the new world giant. One early visitor, Bertrand Russell, who was in Russia in

1919, predicted that the turmoil he witnessed would end badly, in a Napoleonic dictatorship. Others got over their infatuation after one crisis in Soviet life or another. Later, between 1936 and 1938, with two years of sensational show trials of old Bolsheviks reaching defendants as highly placed as Bukharin and Radek, who offered in court elaborate and unbelievable confessions of high treason—all the accused were convicted—a commission of inquiry led by the American philosopher John Dewey soberly concluded in 1938 that the trials were a cruel farce.

By that time the *Partisan Review*, the bible of most New York intellectuals, turned away from Stalin to Trotsky, now in exile, while one of its most reputable contributors, the literary critic Edmund Wilson, having overcome his earlier sympathies for the Revolution and the Communist system, rejected the spectacle in a Moscow courtroom as a totally incredible melodrama unworthy of a civilized country. A little later, in August 1939, the Soviet pact with the Nazis further thinned the ranks of fellow travelers, but far from completely. When in 1950, the disenchanted left-wing English journalist R. H. S. Crossman edited a widely noted book of confessions with the stark title *The God That Failed*, it could count on a warm reception from former fellow travelers. The distinguished roster of contributors featured revealing essays from onetime true believers like the black American novelist Richard Wright, the self-exiled Italian novelist and political critic Ignazio Silone, and the cosmopolitan Arthur Koestler, to say nothing of such reformed fellow travelers as André Gide.

But even then, the nests of Soviet followers remained articulate and influential. One American academic, Frederick Schuman, a political scientist, published a substantial postwar study of the Soviet Union that dismissed reports of labor camps quite simply: since the estimated numbers of prisoners held in those hells on earth varied markedly from critic to critic, the most reasonable conclusion must be that they were, one and all, mere inventions by anti-Communist zealots. Though there were some modernists in this shrinking heap, most had come to understand that cultural life in the Soviet Union was nothing better than humiliating, often dangerous slavery. Since 1932, Russia's culture czars had decreed that the only acceptable style in any art—

including fiction, poetry, painting, opera, architecture, certainly movies—was Socialist Realism, an ideal steeped in monotonous vulgarity. A lame joke made the rounds internationally: What is the ideal plot for a Soviet love story? Answer: Boy meets tractor, boy loses tractor, boy gets tractor. To the modernist victims of Soviet repression, driven to inactivity, betrayal of their talent, or suicide, there was nothing amusing about it.

IT WAS NOT THUS at the beginning. Russian modernists who welcomed the Revolution were welcomed by it. Even avant-gardes badly split in internecine quarrels—Tatlin found Malevich's "un-Socialist" abstractions literally intolerable—tried to claim the Revolution as their own. "Cubism and Futurism," wrote Malevich in 1920, "were the revolutionary forms in art foreshadowing the revolution in the political and economic life of 1917." Lenin's Commissioner of Enlightenment, Anatol Lunacharsky, in charge of cultural life in the new regime, was a playwright with a strong interest in aesthetics; he had long lived in Western Europe, and proved a civilized and, among Bolsheviks, an unusually tolerant official. Besides, in the first years, Lenin had problems more pressing on his mind than the mobilization of poets and painters, including a devastating drought in 1921. That totalitarian control of the arts did not come sooner than it did was at least in part a matter of the weather.

The fate of modernists in such a regime was all too unsurprising. Vasili Kandinsky, who had returned to Russia from Germany in 1914, now consistently abstract in his paintings, worked for a time in the Commissariat for Public Instruction, where he drew up plans for the reform of art schools, and had some say in the government's purchase of paintings to be distributed among various provincial museums. But he soon found that his pronounced commitment to the autonomy of art was not destined to prevail. He left the Soviet Union for Weimar Germany in 1922 to teach at Gropius's Bauhaus. Malevich, too, enjoyed a limited measure of authority and stayed on: he taught in the new Gallery of Artistic Culture until 1928, but his masters compelled him to regress to representational art, which he had spent most of his life fiercely rejecting.

The situation of composers was no better; the combat they had to engage in with their superiors in the bureaucracy, battles they would invariably lose, were degrading experiences. The enforcers of Socialist Realism in music let Prokofiev know that the Soviet people deserved better than the "decadent" or "formalist," which is to say "bourgeois" compositions—three favorite Soviet terms of abuse—that he had brought home with him in 1936 after almost two decades in New York and Paris. That return, it is important to note, was wholly voluntary. But, once back, duly chastened, he took to composing music that, as he put it, was "serious-light," necessary "for the mass audience that the modern Soviet composer must strive to reach," music "primarily melodious, and the melody should be clear and simple."

Dimitry Shostakovich was harder to deal with; the lighthearted humor of Prokofiev that marks much of his music seemed a less formidable antagonist to the regime than Shostakovich's earnestness. Growing into a difficult experimental composer after his early conventional work, in short a modernist, Shostakovich was brutally slapped down by the official keepers of the new dispensation. In January 1936, *Pravda*, the official organ of the Communist Party, ran a wholly unexpected political assault on him. Its target: Shostakovich's opera, *Lady Macbeth of the Mtsensk District*, first performed in 1932, which had been an immense critical and popular success in Moscow (ninety-seven performances), Leningrad, and in the provinces, as well as abroad. This shocking critique, "Chaos Instead of Music," did more than just force one composer into the Socialist Realist line; it was a warning to all other composers within the party's ken, as it furiously assailed *Lady Macbeth* for its "petty-bourgeois innovations" and its "deliberately dissonant, confused stream of sound." What followed is hard to measure. Some of Shostakovich's later symphonies (but not all) show attempts to be comprehensible; his chamber music, especially his quartets, seems more untrammeled. But *Pravda*'s blunt assertion of power remained uncomfortably unforgettable.

As one searches for the place of modernism in Soviet literature or movies or music or painting, it becomes inescapable that the term "totalitarian," mentioned before, seems wholly justified. However distinct the origins of the Nazi and the Soviet courses of action toward anti-establishment high culture, they became almost identical. This was the regime, with Stalin's paranoia at its destructive height, that had five leading Yiddish writers, once in high favor, executed on the same day, August 12, 1952. This was the regime that compelled Boris Pasternak to refuse the Nobel Prize he had been awarded in 1958 for his unconventional novel, *Dr. Zhivago*. Only an extreme effort at denial could keep the old romance in the West with Stalinism alive. The sheer brutality of the regime, exacerbated by the vulgarity of its cultural dictates—exemplified in the sudden assault of the Communist Party on Shostakovich's *Lady Macbeth* in 1936—made modernist enterprise virtually impossible; the glorious early achievements of Soviet culture like Malevich's abstract canvases and Tatlin's Utopian designs proved all too ephemeral. Their sad history serves to underscore a point made at the outset: among the indispensable preconditions of modernism, political freedom must rank high.

BARBARIANS: MUSSOLINI'S ITALY

1.

ITALIAN FASCISM CONFRONTED the fine arts and literature in its own way. Granted, its ideology, its way to office, and the two decades of its rule came to bear arresting resemblances to those of the later Nazi regime and linked it to Hitler's Germany as another exemplar of totalitarian rule, of mass politics with elitist trimmings. Like the Nazis, Italian Fascists came into power legally; they promoted their *Duce*, Benito Mussolini, from a loquacious, boastful, and clever politician into a superhuman embodiment of omniscience and omnicompetence; they freely resorted to naked physical assaults on politically inconvenient opponents; they labored to erase all traces of modern feminism and trade unionism; they put the making of a new, higher type of humanity on their program; they made increasingly exigent demands on ordinary citizens, invading their privacy whether it involved sports or music les-

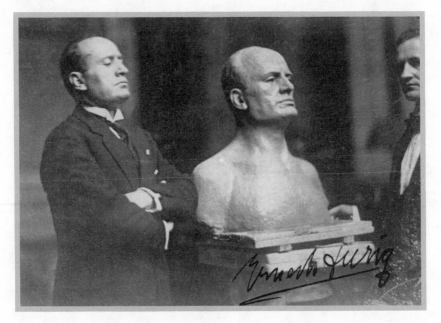

Mussolini and bust. The dictator's jaw—firm, aggressive, never open to compromise—was justly famous.

sons, theatrical performances or art exhibitions. And like them, they added a partisan hymn, *Giovinezza*, to be played and sung with the national anthem, characteristically trumpeting Youth as the guiding principle of the ruling party.

The prehistory of Italian art had well prepared the country's painters and architects for Fascist rule. A few years before the First World War, the Futurists, that tightly knit group of Italian painters, poets, and designers, had startled the public at home and abroad with their noisy manifestos and their stunning canvases devoted to the celebration of such modern phenomena as speed and dynamism. The Futurists' public declamations, in large part written by their leader and self-appointed spokesman, Marinetti, and noted for their fierce antitraditional and uninhibited tone, broadcast their case for bellicosity, together with calls for manliness. They were a blatant symptom of discontent with a foreign policy of compromise, and the anxiety about what many termed a nationwide failure of male self-confidence. This ideology made them ideal forerunners for the Fascists' ambitious, if vague, agenda. Thus several elements of modernism entered Fascist culture with no need for translation.

The excitement that Futurism generated was partly due to the parlous condition of the constitutional Italian monarchy. The fervor with which in 1914 and after the Futurists and their admirers pushed the country toward joining the Allies in their war against the reactionary German and Austrian empires lived off their expectation that an Italy at war would generate overdue changes at home. All too many Italian intellectuals disdained the politics of their country as boring, corrupt, and split to the verge of civil war. Rightist interventionists, not persuaded by the Futurists' *antipassatista* rage, anticipated a restoration of law and order; their temporary leftist allies hoped for the revolution that, they believed, would surely follow Italian international activism.

The partisans for war got their wish in May 1915 as Italy joined the Allied camp. But the fighting and its aftermath left most Italians profoundly disillusioned. They widely regarded their country's share in the booty distributed in 1919 after victory as paltry, downright insulting. Like Germans, who were of course among the losers, Italians seemed ready for dramatic departures. The years that followed were times of domestic instability, with politicized workers occupying factories, and right-wing squads, thuggish and vicious, attacking Communists in the streets and usurping control of whole towns. The Fascists' "March on Rome" of October 1922, which propagandists quickly raised to mythic status, brought them into power. In truth, Mussolini comfortably took the train, and the eminent Italian historian Gaetano Salvemini contemptuously called the dramatic takeover a "comic opera"; but it remained an uncontested Fascist victory.

THE NEW REGIME, as I said, had its own ways of dealing with the issues of high culture. At first exceptional, as the years went by, it increasingly resembled Hitler's Germany; in October 1936, the Fascists concluded an alliance with Nazi Germany—the "Axis"—and two years later, in an egregious act of flattery and an expression of its weakness in the face of its northern ally, the Fascist regime promulgated anti-Semitic racial laws. And yet: for all these resounding echoes, Italian fascism did not imitate the Nazis' systematic and effective subjugation of the avant-garde, though its pressure on the country's creative spirits increased. Among totalitarian countries, Italy was, then, unique when it came to the arts. The long-lived metaphysical painter Giorgio de Chirico, who survived the tragicomedy of fascism, noted frankly in his autobiography: "For the sake of truth it must be said that the Fascists never forbade people to paint as they wished. The majority of the Fascist hierarchy was in fact modernists enamored of Paris." Adopting tactics that Nazis could never understand—they would not have permitted gestures of independence from anyone—Mussolini largely left painters alone.

He declared otherwise, though rather uncertainly. In 1926, opening an exhibition of twentieth-century Italian painting, the Duce had called for "a new art, an art of our times, a Fascist art." But only two years after, he coolly undermined the extremists' grandiose notion that being a good Fascist was a guarantee of artistic accomplishment: "The party card does not give talent to those who do not already possess it." For students of modernism, these were curiously ambivalent statements. To proclaim the need for an art of one's own time was to echo the calls of nineteenth-century modernists like Baudelaire or Manet, but to define it as Fascist art was to subject it to a political agenda, a demand incompatible with modernist claims to autonomy. Even more problematic, to separate artistic talents and political loyalties was to champion the politically neutral thesis of art for art's sake. It was behind such screens of inconsistencies that Italian painters preserved a measure of independence.

The experience of Arturo Toscanini during the Fascists' twenty-one-year rule vividly underscores the differences between them and the Nazis.* Well before the "March on Rome," before it had become clear whether Mussolini's political program would be right- or left-wing, Toscanini, at the time an enthusiastic nationalist, had lent his name to

---

* Toscanini was, of course, not a modernist, but his stubborn insistence on his autonomy as an artist is a perfect parallel to the modernists' implicit (and at times explicit) demand for freedom from political censorship. This story significantly differentiates the Italian and the German versions of totalitarianism.

the just-born Fascist Party. But its reliance on street gang violence as a suitable tactic alienated him. "If I were capable of killing a man," he said, "I would kill Mussolini." Taking considerable chances, he never changed, never cooperated. As the conductor at Milan's La Scala he repeatedly refused to play *Giovinezza*; disregarding the government's orders with contempt, he openly called himself an anti-Fascist. Thugs beat him up, which did not make him modify his stance; instead, he made international news with his "stubbornness."

Toscanini showed himself consistent against other totalitarians as well. In 1933, after Hitler's accession to power in Germany, he refused to preside over the annual Wagner festival at Bayreuth, where he had been the first foreign-born conductor to be so honored, a gesture he repeated in February 1938 at Salzburg, after Austria's chancellor, Kurt von Schuschnigg, had felt compelled, only a month before the *Anschluss*, to yield to German threats. Toscanini lived to tell the tale, mainly in a dazzling career of conducting major American orchestras constructed around him. Mussolini, near the violent end of his life, paid Toscanini a supreme tribute by acknowledging that, for all his bad behavior, he was the greatest of conductors. Can one imagine Hitler letting Wilhelm Furtwängler live after such provocations?

2.

THE RULERS OF THE NEW ROME were not imprisoned by doctrine, or passionate about whichever doctrine of the moment they favored. They acted pragmatically (to hear them talk) by responding to each threatening situation as they must. And murder was among their weapons: in 1924, the government-inspired assassination of Giacomo Matteotti, a Socialist deputy, caused a tremendous scandal; only the notorious, almost proverbial disunity of the anti-Fascist opposition saved Mussolini's regime from a devastating public response. Amid increasingly cold-blooded measures, the government resorted to *confino*, condemning some fifteen thousand to internal banishment in which they incarcerated inconvenient citizens with house arrest in remote southern regions, eliminating them from political action without physically murdering them. Carlo Levi, one victim of the *confino*, a painter and writer who gave up his medical career for the sake of his literary calling, was probably its most memorable casualty. After the Fascist nightmare was over, he published a beautiful book, *Christ Stopped at Eboli* (1945), about his forced exile in the godforsaken southern district of Lucania (Christ made a stop at Eboli but did not trouble to visit the place to which Levi had been banished). It is a humane, unsentimental, deeply moving essay on one of fascism's sorriest aspects that most Italians never had a chance to see. Others evaded *confino* by fleeing the country. The political theorist and novelist Ignazio Silone wrote his anti-Fascist books in Switzerland; the historian Gaetano Salvemini ended up teaching at Harvard. Much like the stream of refugees from Nazi Germany who signally enriched American and British culture, Italy, too, had its share of enforced cultural transfer, if in smaller numbers. Modernists could only benefit from such migration.

In the two decades of Fascist rule, unwelcome political writings were, expectedly, the most consistent targets of repression, although, in contrast with the speed and mercilessness of the Nazis toward democratic or "decadent" writers and journalists whether Jews or gentiles, Italian administrators in charge of the new political order often took their time. Yet by 1925, tough laws meant the destruction of a free press; during the late 1920s, relatively liberal periodicals, often the highly personal voice of their editor's literary taste and political views, were for the most part compelled to cease publication. And by the early 1930s, Italian composers with modernist leanings found it hard to escape political controls.

In this increasingly anxiety-producing atmosphere, the Fascist regime—at least until it passed the anti-Semitic laws in 1938—exploited the arts without prescribing their contents. Some cousins to modernism like Marinetti largely supported Mussolini's New Rome as long as the Duce stressed its novelty. In useful contrast, the government enlisted great art, mainly the classics of the Italian Renaissance, to serve Fascist foreign policy with grand exhibitions sent to Western capitals, a fine instance of shrewd cultural imperialism that was indifferent toward modernism. As Italy grew more imperial and, with its military assault on Abyssinia in 1935, more frankly aggressive on the international stage, its demands on artists, modernists and others, to conform to political commands grew more urgent. But it never decreed the wholly servile art that had come to be automatic in Nazi Germany and the Soviet Union. The principal effect of fascism on the arts, then, was negative, less significant for what it produced than for what it kept from being produced. Yet in the quarter century between the outbreak of the First and that of the Second World War, other, culturally less crippled countries had almost comparably thin records of lasting accomplishments in the arts. This was what W. H. Auden baptized the Age of Anxiety, a time of resentment, rearmament, irreparable and unappeasable social tensions, the easy turn to violence in international fascism and communism, and worldwide Depression.

I HAVE EMPHASIZED throughout that there is no automatic link between political views and artistic talents—even Mussolini, we have seen, knew that. But the yawning absence of Nazi Germany from the creative venture we call modernism; the almost as complete dereliction of the Soviet Union, with only a handful of gifted (and lucky) artists like Pasternak and Prokofiev surviving; the repeated, futile calls for an "Italian modernism," only confirm what was posited before: cultural institutions, including politics, must, in cooperating, generate social conditions that make the emergence or survival of modernism possible in the first place. The eccentric explorations of the anti-modern modernists, which stand at the opposite end of totalitarian control of culture high and low, have this in common with their counterpart: they prove, each in his own way, how much room modernism needs to breathe.

9.

LIFE AFTER DEATH?

After the end of the second world war, modernist artists demonstrated with their fiction, their painting, and their architecture that they had managed to survive the ordeals of totalitarianism, persecution, and war. They were battered but full of energy.* Yet their subversive principles, especially beginning in 1945, still faced mortal threats, some old, some new. For one, the irrepressible democratization of high culture left casualties among discriminating modernists—the topic will occupy us in the pages that follow. This final chapter, Life After Death?, proposes the doubts about the long-range survival of modernism, and, of course, it unmistakably hints that somewhere, somehow, it had already died.

Indeed, whatever giants remained, trying to continue at home in the competitive derby of originality, confronted in this postwar era the skeptical allegation that they had no

---

* Stalin, to be sure, lived on until 1953, and after his death, the Soviet regime kept up its repressive cultural policies for years.

future to look forward to. In any event, the old guard, cherished for its exhilarating, often imperishable contributions to the treasure-house of art and literature, was aging or gone. Matisse died in 1954; Picasso would live on to 1979, but his latest enthusiasm, modernistic versions of classics like Delacroix's *Women of Algiers*, Velázquez's *Las Meninas*, or Manet's *Déjeuner sur l'herbe*, though they found their admirers, proved too fragile a structure on which to build notable new departures. Again, T. S. Eliot, whose poetry had fundamentally changed the literary climate of more than one generation, was gone by 1965, and so was Wallace Stevens ten years before him, and they had produced no creditable heirs. The international school of architects was under fire largely for being so long-lived, with no seriously competing theory to follow it. True, there were a handful of promising dramatists—Ionesco, Beckett, Pinter—whose plays hinted that their theatre might produce a long-lived modernist repertory; but their enterprise was a striking exception rather than a life raft for modernism. There was much talent and little genius. The last ballets that Stravinsky composed for his younger friend Balanchine had quite a sad air of farewell about them. And for many, including men and women of goodwill, the burden of the recent past, the crimes decreed by their states and performed by their loyal fellow citizens, was almost more than they could bear.

CLEARING THE SLATE

1.

FOR ARTISTS, the year 1945 imposed far harder tasks than their fathers had been forced to perform after the year 1918. Each of these two dates, of course, marks the ending of a great war, and, after both, Germany was stigmatized as an aggressor and punished by the victors. But the world that emerged after the peace treaties of 1918 and 1919 generated few striking innovations in high culture. Much to the contrary, the ending of the Second World War, which left the map of European countries—except for that of Germany—largely intact, confronted those who presumably cared about high culture with gross moral failures and irrepressible horrors to explain, expiate, or evade. In 1949, the

German philosopher and cultural critic Theodor Adorno, a principal of the *Marxisant* Frankfurt School, famously said that "after Auschwitz," it would be "barbaric" to write poetry. And though Adorno's despairing conclusion won few converts, he had raised a fundamental question about the relevance of beauty and humanity to a civilization whose favorite ideological weapon, of all states wielded by the "land of poets and thinkers," had been mass murder.

2.

IN 1945, THEN, GERMAN writers and artists certainly had the heaviest burden to bear. Not undeservedly: too many, most unforgivably among the educated, had welcomed the Nazi regime and willingly joined forces with it or at least accommodated themselves seamlessly. The swarm of professors, members of academies, managing directors of museums or publishing houses, theatres or orchestras, and others who, in 1933, participated without protest or with gusto genuine or feigned in the purge of Jews and political undesirables from the universities, the arts, publishing, journalism, and the rest, was shockingly large. Consistent German modernists—an avant-garde painter like Max Beckmann or a modern architect like Walter Gropius (who, it must be said, after a futile attempt to ingratiate himself with the regime, found that there was no place for him in the New Germany)—were in a sense fortunate: Hitler gave them no opportunities to flourish.

Equally fortunate were, in a perverse sense, many among the country's half million Jews, who had had good reason to believe themselves to be fully German and were now (to put it mildly) grossly cheated of their patrimony. Their increasing stigmatization made them, too, begin to think of leaving their ungrateful fatherland. And there were those whose life was literally in danger; an outspoken anti-Nazi playwright like Carl Zuckmayer, whose dramas were taboo from 1933 on, fled, as others would do, to the United States. But these refugees did not outweigh the influential Germans who had managed to work with the gangsters in charge, stars in the firmament of their culture who could have found gainful and honorable employment abroad, a soprano like

Elisabeth Schwarzkopf, a prestigious poet like Gottfried Benn, or (by now a trite, inescapable instance) a philosopher like Martin Heidegger.

Their treason to civilization produced an outpouring of understandable hectoring from émigrés. Thomas Mann, who had been abroad when the Nazis took power and after the war settled in Switzerland (offering with this gesture a harsh critique of his native country and of his recent host, the United States), published in October 1945 a devastating declaration in a South German newspaper, the *Augsburger Anzeiger*: "It might be superstitious, but in my eyes books that could be printed from 1933 to 1945 in Germany are less than worthless, and they are not good to handle. An odor of blood and shame sticks to them. They should all be pulped." That may sound undiscriminating, sweeping aside the handful of heroes and heroines who would not desert their aesthetic principles or abandon their Jewish friends. But Mann hit the heart of the predicament that German writers faced in 1945: their language had been thoroughly contaminated by Nazi concepts and terminology and needed to be cleansed to make it usable once again. Mann's statement was a solemn warning just how hard it would be to restore Germany, a country that had long been productively involved in the making and progress of modernism, to its pre-Nazi stature.

How hard and how desperately necessary: from the beginning of Germany's liberation, the young writers who, as it were, defying Adorno, still wrote fiction and poetry were fully aware that they were handling toxic instruments. The older generations of German writers had little to teach their successors; not even an anti-Nazi like Erich Kaestner, a prolific author of novels and world-famous children's books, found much of an echo. The alibi of having gone into what apologetic writers came to call "inner emigration" during Hitler's Reich struck many of the new writers, even when it was demonstrably sincere, as too freely used. To stay in the country but cooperate with the ruling mob as little as humanly possible was all very well, but not enough. In any event, after the surrender, post-Nazi German authors soon had other authors to draw on: writers, both German and foreign, whom the Nazis had banned and burned.

Hence German novelists and poets, compelled by recent history, were drawn to modernism without necessarily aiming at it. Two years after their country's unconditional surrender to the Allies, growing out of informal get-togethers of writers who met to discuss literary issues and to read some of their work in progress, a small cadre formed that they modestly called *Gruppe 47*. It held annual meetings and awarded a prize, all in the service of a new, purer *Literatur*, and it managed to survive for twenty years. Marcel Reich-Ranicki, an East European Jew with an abiding love for German literature and for two decades the country's most powerful book critic, "the Czar" who regularly attended Group 47 affairs, noted in his autobiography that it "had neither statutes nor directors, it was not an association, not an assembly, not a club and not a society. There was no list of members." In a country often lampooned about its rage for order, this anti-organization must have seemed a most un-German invention but, considering the venomous quagmire the Nazis had left behind, precisely what was needed. And in 1959, it gained instant international recognition through the reflected light of a remarkable novel, *Die Blechtrommel*, by Günter Grass, a Group 47 regular.

Grass's *The Tin Drum* must be the most sensational debut of a novelist since Flaubert's *Madame Bovary*. The author was young—thirty-two—and relatively little known. Born in Danzig of German-Polish parents, he had studied art, spent some years in Paris, and poured out Surrealist poems and rather bizarre plays. They were testimony that one privileged key to the restoration of writing worthy of being called civilized would be to contribute to subversive aesthetic ideologies, which is to say modernism in action. But nothing had prepared the world of readers, and perhaps Grass himself, for *The Tin Drum*. A very substantial volume, it is an eclectic mixture of pitiless reportage and episodes of what came to be called "magic realism." With its candid erotica, it was heedless of the once dominant "dignity of literature," but at the same time it boasted a vast, brilliantly managed vocabulary that raised the book to the most sophisticated literary level.

The narrator and "hero" of *The Tin Drum*, Oskar Matzerath, is nearing thirty. A dwarf and a hunchback, he had chosen not to grow in stature beyond three years. With cool, cruel eyes, he observes the Nazi regime around him, but his true, indeed his only, interest is his own survival. With virtually no superego to check his impulses, he is responsible for several deaths but always succeeds in escaping blame. All this feverish activity in Grass's terrible world of (for the most part) ordinary men and women demands iron self-control, and he had mastered it. With "his natural exuberance and a language that was incredibly rich," the critic Peter Demetz has justly observed, Grass "made a mockery of the worn-out slogans about the death of the novel or the fatal sterility of the German idiom."

Grass did more: he made a mockery, too, of the widely credited assertion that second efforts in literature never live up to the first. His next two novels completed what he called the Danzig Trilogy: *Cat and Mouse*, a shorter text, in 1961; and, two years after, *Dog Years*, as voluble and as imaginative, as sensual and as magic-ridden—and almost as successful—as *The Tin Drum*. But the first in the trilogy remains Grass's historic masterpiece, in part because it came first, in part because no one, not even Grass himself, could outdo its energy and its felicitous amalgam of dramatic coherence and episodic drive. It was a seventeenth-century *Schelmenroman*—a picaresque novel—in modernist dress.

IT WOULD BE WORSE than naïve to claim that a single novel, or a single novelist, could even begin to wipe out the barbarities of a regime that had had an ample dozen years to encompass the ruination of German culture. The 1950s and much of the 1960s were years of the great denial in defeated Germany. That embarrassing question by a German son or daughter, "What did you do in the war, Father?," achieved proverbial status, particularly because it rarely received an honest answer. Besides, the division of Germany in the 1950s into the Stalinist East and the capitalist West, not to be canceled by reunification until 1990, raised the most awkward questions; more and more writers escaped the Socialist paradise in the East, an obedient satellite with Socialist Realism as its watchword, to throw themselves on the uncertain mercies of a high-capitalist, free-enterprising (its critics said, Americanized) state.

This was the clouded, heavy atmosphere into which *The Tin Drum* exploded. Grass was, of course, not alone, notably accompanied, even slightly anticipated, by several other novelists like Wolfgang Koeppen, less well known in the Atlantic culture than he should be. Koeppen published three works of fiction in the 1950s, laden with irony, his target the postwar prosperity of Germany. His rapidly recovering country disgusted him as superficial, materialistic, and only too anxious to repress horrific memories of the Nazi Reich. In each novel he employed modernist stylistic devices. Thus, in *Pigeons in the Grass* (1951), he compressed into a single day the dealings of a diverse complement of characters in search of hedonistic pleasures. In *The Hothouse* (1953), he captured unadmirable German politicians in conferences and meetings, as the protagonist is driven to suicide unable to accept the power of former Nazis in Bonn, ruthlessly exposing their characters with generous portions of interior monologues. And in *Death in Rome* (1954), relying on the same technique, he angrily exposed in detail the irreparable generational conflicts between Nazi fathers and anti-Nazi sons. Oedipus was alive and unwell in post-Nazi Germany. Koeppen's frank disenchantment with postwar Germany and his rage were just as unusual as Grass's political activity in behalf of the mildly Socialist Social Democratic Party. As a rule, German avant-garde writers of fiction had not dipped into the swamp of practical politics. Grass broke that, as he did so many other German conventions.

FOR THEIR PART, a handful of German avant-garde painters were less reluctant than their writing brethren to face the shameful legacy their country had left them to deal with. Directly, or more often indirectly, they recalled the Nazi years with a kind of appalled urgency. Some, the most prominent among them, with chips on their shoulder, were migrants from East to West Berlin. The first was Georg Baselitz, who moved in 1957 at the age of nineteen, followed four years later by Gerhard Richter, then thirty-one. These, and other modernists like them, had to deal with two opponents: the Socialist Realism they had happily left behind and the uncomfortable, heavily derivative abstractions that West German painters were producing in bulk. In defiance, Baselitz and his followers insisted on figurative paintings, but lacking proportions and all refinements of touch, as though their makers were not particularly talented amateurs. Baselitz's *Grosse Nacht im Eimer* (*Great Night Down the Drain*) (1962–63) has a grossly distorted standing nude grasping an enormous penis, his face and figure smeared with flecks of paint. Despite all of Baselitz's disclaimers ("I had never intended to be provocative. My aim was to distance myself from . . . abstract painting"), it looks as though, by defying the canons of good taste and rules of skillful painting, the artist has told everyone—West and East, the whole bourgeoisie, to say nothing of German fathers—how little he thinks of them.

3.

THE FRENCH WERE, OF COURSE, among the victors in the war, but they too had memories to trouble their conscience, if not quite so acutely as the Germans. It was easy enough to override the protests of French literary men and execute the Fascist novelist and critic Robert Brasillach as a traitor. It was even easier to gratify the impulse for self-righteous vengefulness by humiliating young Frenchwomen, shaving their heads and mocking them for *collaboration horizontale* in taking lovers among the occupying troops, whether from sexual loneliness or for money or simply a pair of rare silk stockings. There were boisterous, well-attended spectacles of *épurations* across the country. Although France was finally to grant women the vote at this very time (August 1944), the popular pleasure in their humiliation through these circuses smacks of barely concealed reprisals against women—as though the rectification of an old female grievance, which prominently figured (with rare exceptions like Strindberg and Hamsun) on the modernist agenda, aroused the resistance of Frenchmen caught in a new dispensation.

But the adept small merchants who prospered during the German occupation and the slavish Vichy government, and then conveniently discovered their patriotic sentiments as Allied troops moved toward Paris, were harder to pin down because they were more ordinary. The comic novelist Jean Dutourd, in an immensely successful if minor tale, *Au Bon*

Beurre (1952), sarcastically exposed the opportunism rampant among the French petty bourgeoisie in a time of troubles. These were the turncoats who knew the right moment to start shouting: "Vive de Gaulle!" For four years beginning in June 1940, General de Gaulle had been an indefatigable spokesman for anti-Vichy forces, making the Free French case from London. Then, from August 1944 with the liberation of Paris to his death in 1970, with one notable interruption, the tall, austere, cultured, and almost royal de Gaulle was a magical figure for his country.

Many among the new recruits adoring de Gaulle, like many among them making excessive, often largely imaginary boasts about heroic exploits in the Resistance (resembling the professions of Germans to have detected among their ancestors a Jewish grandparent), showed symptoms of half-conscious feelings of guilt for their callousness, servility, or xenophobia—or of their desperate search for an alibi. But, fortunately for its recovery, French culture made literature of it all. If (to paraphrase Voltaire) Jean-Paul Sartre had not existed, it would have been necessary to invent him.

Among commentators on Sartre—and there were many—one personal issue provoked debates from the outset: was he a philosopher dabbling in literature or a *littérateur* toying with philosophy? For Sartre, this was a pseudo-problem: he saw both as aspects of a single, energetic, well-pondered intellectual posture. When he was philosophizing, he leavened his treatises with stylish passages; when he was writing a play or a novel, he dramatized their plots, such as they were, with his Existentialist principles. Whether fiction or philosophy, these attitudes were indisputably modern. Strenuous and unconventional, Existentialism was thrilling in its originality and subjective in its orientation; its appeal to the century-old writings of the Danish theologian Søren Kierkegaard suggested not the wealth of its ancestry but its paucity. Yet for some years, as Existentialists proposed heterodox answers to perennial questions, its gravity and calls for courage enjoyed international circulation. And modernists could put both facets of Sartre's work, fiction and philosophy, to use. If they needed a philosophy—which they really did not—his Existentialism, first adumbrated in the late 1930s, would have been a strong contender.

It was much remarked that Sartre should have placed the human animal at the forefront of his thought. Existentialism, he maintained in an endlessly quoted lecture of 1946, is a "humanism," a vague term open to divergent interpretations: most readers took it to mean that the author was forcefully asserting human concerns to be fundamental, far more so than the abstract categories of metaphysicians. True, in *Huis clos* (*No Exit*), a play first performed in 1944, Sartre makes a character say in one of those quotable phrases in which his work abounds, "*L'Enfer, c'est les autres*"—Hell is the others. But this terse bon mot is not representative of Sartre's thought; he was not a misanthrope, except against bourgeois.

In his judgment, the individual is condemned to be free—free, in that he makes himself the author of his own being; condemned, in that this freedom entails the weightiest responsibilities. And these duties are particularly onerous because there is no God to guide and restrain human deeds. While several theologians developed a Christian Existentialism to compete with Sartre's, the indispensable core of his belief—or better, unbelief—was atheism. Humans are thrown into the world to make their way on their own. Their godless life, bereft of an authoritative moral order imposed by a deity, exhibits the absurdity and essential meaninglessness of existence. It resembles the human situation after the Oedipus complex has been resolved with the death of the father which, granting new freedoms, imposes new obligations. Existentialism, in short, was the most demanding of philosophies.

For France in 1940, defeated in war and occupied by enemy troops, Existentialist duties were naturally translated into political demands, and Sartre proved a suitable model for his fellow freethinkers: he served in the French army, was captured, escaped in 1941, joined the Resistance, and kept on philosophizing. A brilliant debater, he expounded his thought in treatises, essays, novels, and plays. It was the Second World War, he said later, that had awakened his mind to politics, giving his ethical views a practical orientation—just as the First World War had recruited the architect Walter Gropius to the realistic good cause of left-wing politics.

But in the 1950s, Sartre's political commitments pushed him into indefensible positions. His views were complicated by the conflict over the French colony of Algeria striving for independence. That eight-year-long clash, fought with unexampled ferocity on both sides and ending in 1962 with Algeria's triumph, placed Sartre into fierce opposition to his government's policies, which permitted something he strongly condemned—the use of torture.

Compared to the emotions that this "French-French" war aroused in Sartre, his feelings about the Soviet Union were simplicity itself. As an opinionated avant-garde commentator, he had situated himself almost inevitably on the left, and that required him—as it did every French intellectual and millions of ordinary voters—to have views on Soviet domestic and foreign policies. In the wake of the egregious failures of other political parties, the French Communist list of candidates was a respectable choice for many French voters to take, and Sartre joined them. For half a dozen years he allowed his detestation of the middling class to override his more judicious observations of French and Soviet realities. He had convinced himself that the United States, then in the grip of Senator Joseph McCarthy's "anti-Communist" crusade, was launching a new fascism, while the Soviet Union, with all its blatant defects (which he once had liberally condemned), was supporting the good cause of world peace. This infatuation collapsed in October 1956, when USSR troops crushed a popular revolt in Hungary, an invasion that Sartre flatly denounced as "Soviet aggression." But his apologetic shifts of front about "the great Bolshevik experiment" did not lessen the influence of his philosophical ideas over contemporary culture.

4.

FORTUNATELY FOR HIM, Sartre's erratic political itinerary, far from wholly creditable, mattered less to the public than his novels and plays, which directly and indirectly presided over two powerful literary post-war ventures: the Theatre of the Absurd and the *Nouveau Roman*. In the 1950s, playwrights experimented with a world made for futility, for miscommunication and endless disappointment. The actors in the Theatre of the Absurd did not discuss ideas, they exemplified them. In one absurdist drama, Eugène Ionesco's *Rhinocéros* (first staged in 1960), an innocent citizen watches with revulsion as his fellows, including his pretty secretary, turn into rhinoceroses in a contagious rage for conformity. In another, Samuel Beckett's *Waiting for Godot*, two characters talk past one another under a barren tree while they are waiting, it seems, for God. In short, what the dramatists of the absurd shared was a defiance of every time-honored convention the theatre had unreservedly employed for centuries.

The most celebrated avant-garde dramatist of the absurd, the acknowledged teacher of the others, was the Irish writer Samuel Beckett, a major novelist as well as playwright, who did much of his work in French. In his best known, most widely performed play, *En attendant Godot* (written in 1948), he experimented with spare, often inconsistent anguish, with genial wit and amusing verbal twists. Beckett's principal message, then, learned less from Sartre than from Schopenhauer and his own experience, was that life is a catastrophe from birth, that isolation is a necessary element in the human condition, and that salvation, even though promised, will never come. Nor will self-knowledge. Whatever one undertakes, Beckett noted in one of his much-quoted sayings, one must fail, and one's only recourse is to fail again, if better the next time.

This was difficult doctrine. When the *New York Times* critic Brooks Atkinson reviewed the premiere of *Waiting for Godot* in New York in 1956, he begged off—"Don't expect this column to explain" the play, he wrote—but concluded that this "mystery wrapped in an enigma," with its "strange power," did transmit "some melancholy truths about the hopeless destiny of the human race." This, Beckett's enthusiastic commentators have insisted, is not a complete reading of his work, but it approached most of what his readers and listeners took away from seeing or reading him.

Among those whose refused to explain *Waiting for Godot* was Beckett himself. When his friend, his American director Alan Schneider, asked him for the meaning of this undramatic drama, Beckett replied: "If I knew, I would have said so in the play." This was not teasing or tormenting his interrogator. It was a simple truth for him that not only are the answers unknowable, but the most fundamental questions, about birth and even more about death, are not susceptible to neat clarification. What was clear was Beckett's depressed revision of Descartes's celebrated proof for human existence: I suffer, hence I am.

THE UNNAMABLE, THE LAST in a trilogy of Beckett novels (1951–53), famously ends with an admission of anguished ignorance paired with the duty to persist: "I don't know, I'll never know, in the silence you don't know, you must go on, I can't go on, I'll go on." Curt and ambivalent, this is the most radical possible rejection of ordinary consistency, extreme, uncompromising modernist philosophizing. The predecessors of *The Unnamable*, the novels *Molloy* and *Malone Dies*, had smoothed its way. All three are terse first-person fictions, for the most part long monologues leaping fitfully from topic to topic, arbitrarily shifting chronology, spending gloomy time (just as arbitrarily) over unimportant inconveniences. In the first sentence of *Molloy*, Beckett's eponymous hero shows him, anxiously seeking his mother, to be already in his mother's room. Malone desperately attempts to discover his true self, but recognizes that it will always be hidden. And *The Unnamable* is the culmination of such inquiries, a resolution as absurd to pursue as it is to stop pursuing it.

Among many heartfelt accolades to Beckett, the most quotable one came from Harold Pinter. The leading English practitioner of absurdist theatre, Pinter had gone to school to Beckett. "The farther he goes," he wrote of his preceptor, "the more good it does me. I don't want philosophies, tracts, dogmas, ways out, truths, answers, nothing from the bargain basement. He is the most courageous, remorseless writer going, and the more he grinds my nose in the shit the more I am grateful to him." And yet, for all the portentousness of his praise, Pinter insists: "His work is beautiful." That in 1969 the determined outsider Beckett should have been awarded the Nobel Prize for Literature, the supreme honor for an insider, shows that the selection committee shared Pinter's enthusiasm: "His work is beautiful." It seems only appropriate that in 2005, Beckett's best known pupil, Pinter, politically

Samuel Beckett, the Irish-French avant-garde playwright and novelist whose work remains, decades later, highly controversial.

even more fanatical an adversary of middle-class establishment thinking, joined him by being awarded the Nobel Prize for Literature.

Other dramatists of the absurd, all deeply in Beckett's debt, were less austere in their dramas. If Samuel Beckett could assemble his characters on a blasted heath, Harold Pinter found a well-appointed living room sufficiently threatening. Beckett had life itself as the enemy; his fellows could concentrate on political and social systems they found hateful. Pinter, a poet and actor before he turned prolific playwright, developed unmistakable stage talk—his dramatic situations secured the uncertain honor of being immortalized as "Pinteresque"—in which his characters convert seemingly innocuous conversations into confrontations rife with deep-lying and frightening hostility. His violence may be verbal, but it is no less violent for that.

5.

IN EUGÈNE IONESCO's eccentric, often hilarious dramas, the modernist Theatre of the Absurd returned to nineteenth-century preoccupations and completed the circle of avant-garde rage against the conventional order. Ionesco, more brilliantly than anyone, invariably had the "bourgeoisie" in his gun sights, as fiercely as any Flaubert or Baudelaire. Just as the forerunners of his tragic farces (as he called them) had identified every symptom of conventionality and philistinism as "bourgeois," Ionesco chose this mocking badge of identity for stage characters suffering from their anxious orderliness, their ritualistic self-denial, their paralyzing fear of originality. In 1960, already a seasoned playwright, he spoke of his "ten-year fight against the bourgeois spirit and political tyrannies."

By that time, he had already, in his first dramatic hit, *La Cantatrice chauve* (1950), identified what he called the "universal petty bourgeoisie," a cast of interchangeable people, "the very incarnation of the commonplace, of the slogan, of *conformism*, wherever and whenever it occurs." Drawing on the idiotic conversations in an instruction book of English phrases—Ionesco, trying to study English, claimed that it was this volume that had made him a dramatist of the absurd—he exhibited personages who had "forgotten all meaning of emotions" and had "forgotten how to be." Taking his stage characters from every rank in society, his indefatigable imagination invented the most astute variations. This is how he reports on that process:

I set to work. Conscientiously I copied whole sentences from my primer with the purpose of memorizing them. Rereading them attentively, I learned not English but some astonishing truths— that, for example, there are seven days in the week, something I already knew, that the floor is down, the ceiling up, things I already knew as well, perhaps, but that I had never seriously thought about or had forgotten, and that seemed to me, suddenly, as stupefying as they were indisputably true.

Ionesco had two points to make, the reign of the platitude and the terror of being/non-being, of death, and the two coincided in his plays. True language at its best conveys feelings, and at its worst (that is, in our times) finds the atrophy of feeling manifesting itself in common speech and trivializing or denying being. Hence variations were not merely possible but essential; and by the mid-1950s, Ionesco had mastered chilling and witty versions with an international following.

THE DRAMATISTS OF the absurd were not alone in their modernist experiments. They had abundant company, concentrated like them on Paris, among authors of fiction, the little club writing the *Nouveau Roman*—Nathalie Sarraute, Claude Simon, Robert Pinget, Alain Robbe-Grillet, Michel Butor. They were not Sartre's mindless disciples, even though they learned some of their techniques from his *L'Age de raison* and *Le Sursis* (both 1945), the opening two volumes of a planned tetralogy, *Les Chemins de la liberté*. But, more important, they felt liberated by his innovations to play boldly with literary devices. With little happening in their novels, they could closely examine the mental travail of their fictional characters.

The writers whose work in the 1950s literary journals quickly grouped under the single rubric of the New Novel were highly self-conscious about the craft they thought it necessary to revolutionize, and they approached it with an earnestness that appealed to, and was shared by, Sartre. They were intellectuals, not entertainers. Nor were they, in their aversion to coherent scenarios or traditional accounts of motivation, the grateful heirs of nineteenth-century Realists. Rather, without using the term, they were card-carrying modernists, each following a chosen track—a highly individualistic collectivity.

The writer of fiction, Sarraute argued in *L'Ere du soupçon* (1956), the first gathering of theoretical reflections by a new novelist, must aim

at constructing believable human beings whose rapid succession of intimate movements—a smile, a gesture, a shrug—even if the observer hits
the target foursquare, will always remain an impossible ideal for interpretation. Sarraute was exceptionally well read in foreign literature—
her programmatic statement could have been a late revision of Knut
Hamsun's agenda. But the *nouveaux romanciers* were not keen to be
labeled anyone's adherent, unless of course it was Dostoevsky; Sarraute criticized even Proust for a certain shallowess, though she
admired him, and she disparaged Virginia Woolf by happily quoting
her self-criticism as being psychologically naïve.

In effect, the new novelists were offering no more than a second
edition of prewar modernist critiques of fiction; they added up to a
wavelet of avant-garde writers who were echoing the very reservations
that their modernist forebears had launched against their traditionalist
fellows. One need think only of Strindberg denouncing the novelists of
the 1880s, or Virginia Woolf four decades later, more subtly yet still a
little unfairly, denigrating the novels of Arnold Bennett. To the mind of
the postwar new novelists, the most unconventional authors of the previous generation had failed to capture the movements of their characters' psyches. Such verdicts speak well for their independence of mind,
but not for their literary judgment.

BORN IN 1902, Nathalie Sarraute was the oldest among the *nouveaux
romanciers*. Her essential interest, throughout her long career as novelist, playwright, and essayist, was in what she called "tropisms." Those
physiological responses that make a plant turn toward a strong external
presence like light or heat suggested to Sarraute the reactions it is an
author's highest obligation to capture. Hence the trivial, the banal, the
commonplace rather than dramatic clashes provide access to the "myri-
ads of little movements" that make up mental life. In the unnumbered,
untitled short sections of *Les Fruits d'or* (1963), perhaps her most interesting, most maddening novel, she puts speakers through their paces
without preparation and without identification. Its protagonist (as
reviewers already complained upon its publication) turns out to be not

a person but a novel, and a mediocre novel at that, titled (of course!) *Les Fruits d'or*.

This imagined-book-as-hero gives Sarraute's irony ample room to play freely over her text. Fragments of conversation alternate with anonymous reflections, broken, incomplete, sometimes deliberately philistine. One voice finds the novel "amusing . . . I laughed." (The ellipses are Sarraute's throughout.) "There are scenes. . . . When he misses his train . . . or when this personage, you'll remember, is looking for his umbrella, but that is irresistible . . . the real Charlot" (which is to say, Charlie Chaplin). "A style . . . A force . . . Better than Charlot." The New Novel, she writes, "provokes a mysterious and salutary sort of emotional turmoil which will make it possible to apprehend at a single blow, as in a flash of lightning, the whole object with all its nuances, its possible complexities and even—if by chance there should be some—its abysses. Anyway, there is nothing to lose and, it seems, everything to gain." But this encouraging clap on the novelist's shoulder is at its most innocent quite problematic, as audiences wrestled with modernist texts that made few if any concessions to them. I have called Sartre's Existentialism a demanding philosophy; France's new novelists were no less demanding on readers.

THE OVERRIDING INTEREST of the new novelists, then, was that of the classic modernists: to write against the grain of contemporary fiction, to discard all hints of traditional principles like the logical sequence of events, which only forces an ordering, and therefore misleading, device on a disorderly world. Such concerns as suspense or character development were, to them, signposts pointing to obviousness and superficiality. The *nouveaux romanciers*, in short, imposed on their readers the stiff task of recognizing fictional characters without supplying them with the usual aides. In Claude Simon's *Histoire* (1967), a paragraph almost invariably breaks off in the middle of a sentence, and its successor is not at all related to its predecessor. It followed that these fictions could count on a more loyal, perhaps even a numerically larger, audience in courses offered by French departments in American colleges than they could on the free market in Parisian bookstores. It was in that academic atmosphere that the puzzles set by the new novelists were analyzed with a zest that most French readers must have found astonishing.

The most popular of these new novelists was Alain Robbe-Grillet, who secured much of his celebrity by enlisting aid from the outside: the movies. The best known of his cinematic excursions was *Last Year at Marienbad*, made in 1961 from one of his novels into a film by Alain Resnais, a modernist movie that won the grand prize at the Venice Film Festival with a script by the author of the novel. Robbe-Grillet underscored its nonconformity by keeping the "action" obscure, left largely to hints, with affected dialogue that has nothing in common with straightforward speech. It centers on a triangle, ironically the most conventional of plots. A year before the movie starts, an unknown and unnamed, probably unattached man (X) has fallen in love with a woman (A) he had met at Marienbad, and persuaded her to leave the man (M) she is with (her lover? her husband?). But she makes X wait for a year, and that year is now over. Practically all the talk we hear is delivered to A by X, who compulsively remembers all the places they had visited together in and around their elegant spa the year before. She ineffectually resists his seductive reweaving of their recent involvement, and it seems almost definite that in the end they will leave Marienbad together.

The prevailing climate of this movie reinforces the novelist's effort to suggest everything and explain nothing. Its characters are shown wearing different outfits within a single scene; the background, like the park surrounding the castle, is photographed with special effects, trees throwing no shadows while the persons near them do; the only drastic action is an unbelievable rape scene—perhaps a fantasy. Audiences leaving the theatre were likely to be mystified, and guessing at the subject matter to which they had just been exposed. The question just whom modernist novels, or movies, were intended for was one that had been difficult to answer for decades. The *nouveaux romanciers* only exacerbated it. But their very presence, indirectly buttressed by modernist painters like Jean Dubuffet, the most impassioned of antibourgeois artists, did its part in strengthening the conviction, certainly among the French, that France was once again a major player on the chessboard of high culture.

AN AGE OF INGENUITY

1.

THE POSTWAR THREATS to the survival of modernism ran deeper than a mere shortage of outstanding talents. It had to face, once again, the revival of a fundamental philosophical objection that went back to Duchamp and was confirmed by contemporaries without necessarily quoting, or even knowing about, their French inspiration.* What is art? Or, perhaps better, What is not art? One consequential implication of these questions were technological advances like the perfecting of color movies, television, jet airplanes, and other blessings of the machine age; these speeded the democratization of high culture and thus raised more intensely than ever basic issues about the possible place of modernism, that aristocratic way to the arts, in the post-1945 culture.

One momentous change in the population of modernists came as the Americans joined the battle. In the new postwar world, they began to take an active part in cosmopolitan modernism. Their most ambitious bid for autonomy came with Abstract Expressionist painting, enlisting followers across the Atlantic. The French even had two names for it, *tachisme* and *art informel.* Thus the world of art entered a new phase: its most prominent artist, Jackson Pollock, was soon almost as famous in Europe as he was at home in the United States.

Like other such collective sobriquets, Abstract Expressionism, too, covered over noticeable diversities. But with the powerful exception of Willem de Kooning, whose disturbing series *Women*, dramatically distorted, was recognizable as a misogynistic gesture, the pictures they produced were distinctively non-figurative. Although commentators on Pollock's work—and he kept them busy with his

---

* "Jasper Johns has been described as a follower of Duchamp," the art historian Barbara Rose has justly objected, "although nothing in his work implies that he was even aware of Duchamp until after 1960."

canvases—detected hints of representational elements like the human figure, the general public saw them as being as close to pure painting as they could imagine. In a Pollock, the viewer, unlike the spectator of an Impressionist painting, was likely to see more at a second look than at the first.

THE PLACE OF JACKSON POLLOCK in the modernist pantheon is secure. In fact, combining both of its defining elements—unconventionality and subjectivity—he belongs among the most representative of modernists. His huge "drip" paintings, done mainly between 1947 and 1950, shocked viewers, who found them eccentric, perplexing, in a word heretical, although there were those who thought them somehow magnificent. Pollock himself insisted that the roots of his art were profoundly personal. The true source of his inspiration, he said, was the unconscious. But, despite his record of undergoing some Jungian analysis and finding the Jungian rather than the Freudian atmosphere truly congenial, students of Pollock's art failed to reach a consensus on just how much of his painting stemmed from unconscious pressures, how much of it from a deliberate, conscious practice. Pollock was sure he had the answer. "My painting does not come from the easel," he said. "On the floor, I am more at ease. I feel nearer, more a part of the painting, since this way I can walk around it, work from the four sides and literally be *in* the painting." He added, significantly, "When I am *in* the painting I'm not aware of what I'm doing. It is only after a sort of 'get acquainted' period that I see what I have been doing."

Clement Greenberg, the most powerful modernist art critic of the time and a partisan of Abstract Expressionism, hailed Pollock as the finest of the painterly painters, ahead even of his most formidable European competitors—Greenberg often made comparative evaluations as though they were horse races. By 1943, when Pollock was thirty-one, he had his first one-man show at Peggy Guggenheim's avant-garde gallery, Art of This Century; but his real celebrity came four years later when he began showing his drip paintings, celebrated as much for their mode of production as for their results.

We have photographic records of Pollock building up these works layer by layer. The canvas, unstretched, lies on the floor of his studio, the painter stands over it and either pours, or, wielding a large brush, spreads the paint, constructing what may become a pattern in which drops from the brush and irregularities of the smearing contribute to the design. In a

characteristic instance, *Number 2*, a very large horizontal painting of 1949—it is over fifteen feet wide—dizzying colored lines from thin to thick interweave with black lines to make for a complicated pattern on a plain brown background. The sheer subjectivity of modernist art has never been expounded more aggressively than in this picture.

Pollock, then, made himself a privileged observer of his own work, as it gradually revealed to him what, he claimed, he had had in mind all along. His brooding canvases made heavy demands on the spectator. After all, nothing could be more remote from traditional techniques of putting paint on canvas than the artist dripping it as he walked around that canvas. Still, Pollock's productions found appreciative echoes among lovers of modern art, puzzled but impressed.

Other viewers, however, unaccustomed to his revolutionary procedures, his particular claim to immortality, found it hard to clarify their responses. But Greenberg set the tone of the market by seeing a pattern emerge from apparent chaos: "Pollock wrestles aesthetic order from the look of accident— but only from the look of it." This important fact, wrote Greenberg in 1969, may be hard to decipher at first. "The haphazardness of Pollock's execution, with its mazy trickling," meant that the artist's "dribbling, whipping, blotching, and staining of paint" appeared to be swallowing up and extinguishing every element of order. "But this is more a matter of connotation than of actual effect. The strength of the art itself lies in the tension (to use an indispensable jargon word) between the connotations of haphazardness and the felt and actual aesthetic order, to which every detail of execution contributes." Settling in New York in 1930, Pollock explored wide

Jackson Pollock, the celebrated Abstract Expressionist, at work on a drip painting in 1949.

possibilities of avant-garde painting, and famously joined it with his celebrated and controversial drip paintings. Whatever the success of these canvases with which Pollock reached the climax of his aesthetic experiments, the venture itself was an extreme form of modernist rebelliousness. His drip canvases were not a bid for artistic freedom but, in fact, its realization.

ABSTRACT EXPRESSIONISM could draw on a living modernist past, on its detestation for conventional Realism, on models largely taken from Surrealism, and in the end on its own naked encounter with the act of painting. Greenberg maintained that art tells us what we already feel, and neither he nor his favorite painters thought this act of communication a rational process. In this new dispensation, gifted painters—homegrown Americans and European refugees alike—fiercely appropriated the opportunities that an art with no obligations to mimetic accuracy gave them. The empty canvas was for them an invitation to free aesthetic play, controlled only by technique, subject only to the internal demands of their art, a thoroughly modernist game.

Inescapably, this artistic playfulness developed more than a single style. Barnett Newman produced outsized canvases painted in a single color disrupted only by a single, narrow, vertical line, going Mondrian one better. Harold Rosenberg, Greenberg's only serious rival for the papacy of contemporary art criticism in the United States, wrote in *The New Yorker* that Newman was "after bigger game than providing stimulus to the spectator's retina. His program was to induce emptiness to exclaim its secret," an ambitious if rather mysterious agenda he shared with such fellow Abstract Expressionists as the erudite and cultivated Robert Motherwell, whose stark abstractions were celebrations of Eros, and whose *Elegies to the Spanish Republic* series was a painterly tribute to a regime overthrown by Fascist forces. The objections of Abstract Expressionists, then, to "retinal art" were congruent with Marcel Duchamp's lifelong denigration of art that appeals to the eye alone.

Duchamp's influence was ubiquitous. He was the most quoted prophet—and agent—of art's pitiable future; his sweeping suggestion, half a century old by 1960, that anything—*anything*—could be denominated a work of art, including his own work, required no research and no erudition. That notorious snow shovel and a slightly mutilated postcard-size copy of Leonardo da Vinci's *Mona Lisa*, two of Duchamp's most famous inventions, were graphic illustrations of his bleak prediction about the fate of art.

2.

WHAT MADE THIS RADICAL proposition so potent after 1960 was that Pop Art gave it a spectacular resurgence. The emergence and triumphant career of Pop Art proved a decisive moment in the history of modernism, in which these new fashionable painters sought to reduce high and low art to a single category. It was, as we shall see, a shotgun wedding that produced little marital felicity. Pop was boldly scrambling accepted categories in the arts—unconventional with commonplace painting, originality with facsimile, socially engaged art with art for art's sake—thus largely reducing to futility the already strenuous effort to define the nature of art and to predict its fate.

The Pop artists were fortunate in their tutors, chiefly Hans Hofmann. A German-born, European-trained painter and respected teacher who settled in the United States in 1932 in his early fifties, he founded art schools in Provincetown and New York and taught by example as well as precept. His late style, which drew its dynamism from the interplay of rectangular patches of brilliant contrasting colors, expressed his conviction that the supreme springs of art are subjective. "Creative expression," he taught, is "the spiritual translation of inner concepts into form," and he alerted his students that "imitation of objective reality is therefore not creation but dilettantism, or else a purely intellectual performance, scientific and sterile." These axioms might stand as terse statements of twentieth-century modernist painting.

AND SO, THE YEARS around 1960, after Americans had been asserting themselves in the global derby of artistic ingenuity for a few years, propelled modernism into a time of crisis—to employ an overused term that is fully appropriate here. No branch of the arts demonstrates this more vividly than painting, which experienced a rush—better, an avalanche—of new schools rivaling with, and succeeding, one another with dizzying rapidity. "There are Assemblage, Pop, and Op," wrote Greenberg in 1969. He naturally had mixed feelings about his catalog. "There are Hard Edge, Color Field, and Shaped Canvas; there are Neo-Figurative, Funky, and Environmental; there are Minimal, Kinetic, and Luminous; there are Computer, Cybernetic, Systems, Participatory—and so on." Virtually all of them, I must add, claimed membership in the family of modernism.

Some of these claimants were authentic extremists. In 2005, in a lengthy survey of performance art, Barry Gewen, an editor of the *New York Times Book Review*, addressed the issue of what he called the "anything-goes problem." As he knew, this dilemma went back almost a century, to Duchamp, but in the hands of the particular bomb throwers he was listing, the issue took on new relevance. Gewen's review, "State of the Art," repays extensive quotation.

> In 1975, Chris Burden had himself crucified on the roof of a Volkswagen. He was creating a work of art. A decade later, Hermann Nitsch staged a three-day performance in which participants disemboweled bulls and sheep and stomped around in vats, mixing the blood and entrails with grapes. Another work of art. Rafael Ortiz cut off a chicken's head and beat the carcass against a guitar. Ana Mendieta, who had a retrospective at the Whitney last year [2004], also decapitated a chicken and let its blood spurt over her naked body. As one commentator has observed, "animals are not safe in the art world." Neither are the artists. They have sliced themselves with razor blades, inserted needles in their scalps, rolled naked over glass splinters, had themselves suspended by meathooks and undergone surgical "performance operations" during which spectators could carry on conversations with the artist-patient. In 1989, Bob Flanagan nailed his penis to a wooden board.

At one point in his painful and repellent catalog of sadistic and masochistic self-exhibitions, Gewen found himself constrained by his place of publication: "A Viennese artist, Günther Brus, performed a now famous—or at least notorious—work in which he urinated and defecated on a stage, then masturbated while singing the Austrian national anthem. (Other aspects of this piece cannot be described in a family newspaper.)" At last, the triumphant philistine will say, the good bourgeois has nailed the revolutionary—almost literally. But one example of the pseudo-modernist aesthetic ventures that Gewen mentions has long enjoyed a certain celebrity. "In 1960, the French artist Yves Klein made a series of 'anthropometries,' using women's nude bodies as paintbrushes," saved for posterity by a photograph showing a slender, beautiful naked model being dragged through mud serving as paint. Beauty, it seems, is irresistible. This is modernist freedom reduced to absurdity.

Typically, many of the postwar innovators issued manifestos. The Minimalists, mainly sculptors, makers of "three-dimensional" pieces, concentrated on what they considered the essence of art with no ideological admixtures, covering the floor in an art gallery with square tiles, or leaning a painted board against a wall. Meanwhile, the "Fluxus" group, named in 1961 by George Maciunas, a Lithuanian immigrant to the United States, started a cosmopolitan team that turned once again toward the amusing playfulness of the Dadaists and of Duchamp, asserting the indispensability of the artist, very broadly defined, including the inspired amateur. The painter, Maciunas said, "must demonstrate that anything can be art and that anybody can do it." Half a decade later, in 1967, Germano Celant, an Italian art critic, named this kind of art—anti-American, anti-technological, impatient with photography, and nostalgic for old-fashioned craftsmanship—*Arte povera*, and successfully exported it. The 1960s, in short, were an overloaded storehouse of experimentation, but none of the ingredients had sufficient aesthetic energy or appeals to beauty to last.

Characteristically, these frantic days were swamped by what came to be called "Happenings." This was a little misleading; for all their suggestive name, these spectacles did not simply happen. They were meticulously scripted, rehearsed, highly theatrical; Pop artists like Jim Dine were glad to act in them. Happenings presented nonsensical scenes at times accompanied by a chamber orchestra. In one early performance, Dine, soon known for attaching three-dimensional objects like neckties to his canvases, quickly sketched an automobile and just as quickly erased it, only to start again. The most likely site for such performances that sustained this genre was a self-consciously modern art gallery.

I shall not go into detail about still other schools, earth art, installations, and the rest. Despite their confident tone, despite their popularity among gallerygoers, it was impossible to say whether their various self-proclaimed liberations eased the viewers' responses or made them more frustrated: that depended largely on the taste of the installer. There were a few cultural critics who celebrated the diversity of art now available as a kind of Protestant pluralism, but others, more perceptive, thought it a major symptom of avant-garde culture in trouble, particularly for modernism. The skeptic, including this writer, must wonder whether Gewen's most disturbing samples of life in contemporary art did not smell suspiciously like symptoms of death waiting in the wings.

3.

THE MOST ALARMING OF these warning signs, though not immediately interpreted as such, was Pop Art. Its very cheerfulness obscured its destructive implications, obscured its significance not just to outsiders but to its practitioners from the earliest days on. Certainly neither of the pioneers, Jasper Johns and Robert Rauschenberg, gave an inkling of how much their work, and that of their closest allies, might mean to the general history of art. In the late 1950s, the two were intimates who shared a studio and presented one another with choice specimens of their work, and it was Johns in particular who was, and would remain, the subtlest craftsman among the Pop artists, with an elegance of touch that conquered even Clement Greenberg—partially. He painted maps, flags, targets, numbers flat on, all objects familiar to everyone, with fidelity, and raised once again insistent misgivings about the relationship of artifact to art.

Johns's accounts of his canvases only deepened their mysteries. In 1958, Lawrence Alloway, an English critic with a passion for American Pop Art, heard Johns "clarify" his already notorious canvas of three American flags, each centered on the larger one behind it: "Somebody said, 'It's not a flag, it's a painting.' Johns said, "But that's not what I meant. It's not a painting, it's a flag.'" Since this statement could so easily be reversed to claim the opposite—"It's not a flag, it's a painting"— its explanatory value added up to nothing. But Johns seemed not so much interested in making his pictures comprehensible as in opening new possibilities for responding to a banal object once it had been dignified by converting it into an artistic subject.

Some Pop artists were deliberately provocative, apparently eager to evoke a wry smile with their outlandish productions. Claes Oldenburg specialized in constructing pieces of sculpture open to the most varied interpretations or, most agreeably, to no interpretation at all. Virtually addicted to edibles usually bulked up to unnatural size, he made *Hamburger with Pickle and Tomato Attached* (1963), which required no imagination, indeed vetoed any imagination. *Soft Pay-Telephone* of the same year is a concoction made of kapok covered by vinyl and mounted on a wooden panel, the whole looking like a life-size imitation of, well, a soft pay-telephone. The later *Giant Chocolate* (1966) is simply, grossly, itself. At times, Oldenburg's constructions seemed to invite ironic commentary. The famous gargantuan stand-up red lipstick fastened in rigid verticality onto caterpillar tracks (1969) may constitute a critique of the contemporary military-erotic complex. Perhaps; perhaps not.

AROUSING AMUSED SHOCK, Pop artists came to claim their privileged place in the history of art. The best known of them developed distinctive personal styles that shared just one, but an all-important, quality with the others. The principal source of a Pop artwork was, as everyone knows, a subject borrowed from popular culture—an ordinary artifact of daily use like a comb; a familiar item like an American flag; a slightly doctored version of a panel from a comic book; a frontal, unsentimental nude; a bronzed can of beer. These improbable works

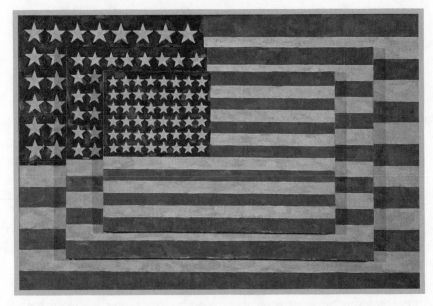

Jasper Johns, *Three Flags* (1958). One of the pioneering Pop artist's most celebrated canvases.

were all too easy to understand, a refreshing move away from the interpretative obscurities that their predecessor, Abstract Expressionism, had imposed on museumgoers. Yet, even for the most unashamed borrowers among Pop artists, the sheer investment of artistic labor their work required was far greater than a quick look would suggest. Hence they indignantly protested when critics dropped their canvases into the bin of popular art. It was, they insisted, high art.

But this indignation was not wholly convincing; it left too many issues unresolved. Were the messages of James Rosenquist's gigantic, apparently miscellaneous canvases a critique of American capitalism or a love letter to its technological supremacy?* Was the pseudosociological doctrine that all works of art are on the same level exemplary of the fashionable rejection of rank-obsessed qualitative discrimination or a deep insight into art in the modern world? Were the "low" subjects that

---

* We have evidence independent of his artwork that Rosenquist was a vehement critic of the military-industrial complex and the cheap, seductive vulgarity of most popular culture.

abounded in Pop paintings a denigration of kitsch or an attempt to assimilate it? For Greenberg, Pop Art (always excepting Jasper Johns) was merely "Novelty art," no doubt "diverting" but not "really fresh," an art that raised more difficulties than it settled. Its displays of sheer ingenuity were, Greenberg argued, essentially shallow, mere fun. The charge was that influential artists were throwing all painting into a single pot, not taking it seriously but presenting their work as simply amusing and wanting it to be enjoyable for everyone. But this bluntly exposed the radical way that Pop Art was subverting the modernist ideal by reconciling the irreconcilable, assimilating two essentially distinct areas of art, high art and low, which modernists had thought it crucial to keep apart.

THE FIRST RESPONSES of collectors to Pop Art were mixed, but before long these canvases developed into a highly visible staple among progressive galleries, daring and affluent collectors, and, soon after, museums devoted to modern painting. True, older critics were uneasy with this flood of astonishing novelties; their abandonment of time-honored canons was too abrupt, too scandalous to escape resistance. Yet it became undeniable that Pop Art was entertaining, at the least intriguing; its sense of humor, so rare among modernists, and its smiling affection for eccentricity, provided welcome relief to admirers of such difficult art as Pollock's and Newman's.

Among Pop artists competing for attention in a crowded and noisy market, Roy Lichtenstein was probably the strongest performer, outdoing everyone except Andy Warhol (to whom I shall turn in a moment). The viewer's flash of recognition generated by Lichtenstein's paintings, carefully redrawn from comic strips, was only the most famous product of his appropriations. His comical, dead-on "copy" of one of Picasso's distorted portraits of women, and a series of paintings of 1965 that had brushstrokes as their subject, invited divergent readings of his work. Students of that work have noted—it is impossible to overlook—that Lichtenstein was among the most enjoyable modernists to make the incompatible compatible. Of course, all Pop productions transgressed

Roy Lichtenstein, *Woman with Flowered Hat* (1963).
A wry tribute to Picasso.

the time-honored boundaries between serious and playful art. But what made Lichtenstein's version of Pop so alluring was that the "low" sources from which he drew his best known subjects were themselves exemplars of low art, not just numerals or hamburgers but "paintings" by little known, largely anonymous craftsmen working for the cartoon industry.

The act of compelling low art and high to work together—that is, to make high art from low—could not be more dramatic than in Lichtenstein; his most prominent borrowings read like comments on Freud's view of human nature, with forceful displays of sexuality and aggression. They single out weeping young beauties ruminating on what might have been, and American airmen blasting enemy planes out of the air. *Hopeless* (1963) has a pretty girl brooding, her eyes filled with tears; "That's the way—it SHOULD have BEGUN!" she is musing to herself, "but it's hopeless!" And in the same year, Lichtenstein did *Wham!* in which an American fighter pilot's silent soliloquy runs: "I pressed the fire control . . . and ahead of me rockets blazed through the sky," his target lethally enveloped in vivid red and yellow flames. The patent kitsch of the first and the hint at sadism of the second made this sort of painting characteristic of the Pop school.

4.

THE IRRESISTIBLE ENLARGEMENT of the catalog listing subjects appropriate for art, which the Pop painters and sculptors did so much to encourage, reached an outer edge with Andy Warhol's *Brillo Box*, exhibited in 1964 at the New York Stable Gallery. It resembled John Cage's "composition" *4'3"* in its decisiveness. That non-musical piece, we recall, consists wholly of a silence lasting precisely four minutes and thirty-three seconds. The American philosopher Arthur Danto, particularly attuned to developments in the arts, the more outrageous the better, saw *Brillo Box* as an extraordinary revelation, marking nothing less than the death of art. It seemed that Duchamp, who, we well know, had worked half a century earlier toward the same destructive aim, had apparently failed to reach his goal.

Andy Warhol's box that was not a box was neither a painting nor exactly a sculpture, but a three-dimensional container, an identical twin (which is to say, a not quite identical twin) of the box that wholesalers use to pack Brillo pads by the dozen for distribution to retailers. The questions that Warhol's *Brillo Box* raised were most troubling, if highly familiar: What is a work of art? How do you distinguish between one of them and the rest of creation?

This did not mean—the proponents of the thesis were quite firm on this point—that the making and selling of art would stop, and artists in their world would consist solely of painters without commissions and dealers without customers. Prosperous people wanted, and probably would continue to want, something decorative to hang on their walls. Some commonsense distinctions would no doubt occur to the commercially alert crowd that made a living off art. What is more, the directions that modern art and literature were taking after mid-twentieth century were overwhelmingly produced by artists richly endowed with ingenuity. Certainly, without imitating the fanatic's performance in which she smeared the blood of the chicken she had just killed over her naked body, the Pop artists did more than their share devising, and showing, works of art that, however greatly they pleased art buyers of their time, would have baffled or irritated the most imaginative pioneers of the previous generation. And so, at least to some observers, all the talk about the death of art was reversible: were not the very obituary writers opening the way to a new, living art?

It was Andy Warhol's mission to enliven this debate and make it familiar to the broad newspaper-reading public. In the course of a stunning career, he established himself as an authentic celebrity, keeping his glamorous reputation alive with inspired experiments that at times surprised even him. To be sure, not all the ingredients in his fame were works of art, unless one counts as art his far-flung, polymorphous social life, his photo ops with boxers and movie stars, financial moguls, even royalty in Washington, Paris, London, and Teheran. But even without his spectacular socializing, Walhol did enough to fill the gossip pages in the daily press.

WARHOL WAS BORN in Pittsburgh in 1928, the son of Czech immigrants, to a close-knit and disciplined family of the Byzantine Catholic persuasion. His family name was Warhola, and his decision in late adolescence to drop the final vowel was an early token of his lifelong passion for notoriety; to his mind the shorter "Warhol" was more euphonious, more suitable to public notice than the name he was born with. From boyhood on, he was a passionate and facile draftsman, filling with his sketches whatever pieces of paper he could wangle, leaving little doubt that art would be his life's vocation. Before he was twenty-five, he was doing highly paid commercial art, advertising fashionable shoes or illustrating stories in monthly magazines. This blessing—his income soon rose to high five figures—was also a curse: his work for *Glamour* and *Mademoiselle* struck fellow artists as a betrayal of their craft and it would take years before he could shed the hated aura of being a whore to capitalism.

This was not Warhol's only handicap. Timid, afraid (as some of his classmates put it) of everything, he had his schoolmates laugh at him—a classic Mama's boy. During repeated stretches of childhood ailments, he was often alone with his mother while his two brothers were in school, and those episodes only strengthened his affection; Mrs. Warhola, it seems, was the only woman he ever loved. In 1949, when Warhol, after graduating from the Department of Painting and Design at Carnegie Tech, moved from Pittsburgh to New York, he brought her to live with him. It was an exciting time for a young artist to be in New York, filled with adventurous notions about art; it was the time, too, that Jackson Pollock was concentrating on his most radical paintings. While there was much about his adult life that Warhol would keep private from his mother, he always took care to introduce his special friends to her.

He became famous largely through sheer hard work. One telling feature of making himself at home in the exclusive circles of the beautiful people whose doings filled the society pages was his facility in generating epigrams and surprising self-revelations that rapidly circulated. Indeed, unlike the proverbial sayings attributed to Yogi Berra, the great catcher of the New York Yankees, many of whose entertaining and laconic paradoxes were coined by others, Warhol's memorable remarks were his own. He freely acknowledged his passivity: "I want everybody to think alike," he told *Art News*. "I think somebody should be able to do all my paintings for me." Or, a telling abdication: "I feel the less something has to say the more perfect it is. Who wants the truth?" Life as a man was a great strain: "I'd like to be a machine, wouldn't you?" he asked a reporter from *Time*. "I've never been touched by a painting," he admitted to another interviewer. In 1975, aided by an intelligent assistant, he put a raft of his sayings and responses in order and published the fascinating farrago in *The Philosophy of Andy Warhol: (From A to B and Back Again)*, a storehouse of astute remarks and risqué anecdotes mixed in with banalities. This was the man who memorably said that in the future everyone would be famous for fifteen minutes, but who did his utmost to escape being condemned to that kind of insubstantial celebrity. Straining toward a bloated self-image, he longed to be famous all the time for all time.

Warhol's modernism survived his unforced, profitable commercial ties. In the early 1960s, though he rarely spoke about art, admitting only that he "hated" Abstract Expressionism, he joined the Pop revolution. His first breakthrough, suggested by a friend, came with renditions of Campbell's soup cans, silk-screened and sold individually or in groups. His painting of Marilyn Monroe, made just days after her suicide, came next and established him as a leader among the Pop clan. After all, Warhol's precisely copied Campbell's soup cans and Monroe's unforgettable features aggressively defied all established canons of painting, and were a trump card in the Pop assault on the conventions.

Though gratifyingly lucrative, Warhol's career as a painter was only intermittent. By the mid-sixties, he had become attached to the movie business, and even announced that he was through with art. For the most part, he directed the movies himself and superintended details; mainly improvised, they usually elaborated a dirty joke or sexual situation and sometimes provided a severe test of his audience's patience. *Sleep* (1963), an uncompromising six-hour assault on the very idea of drama, showed one of Warhol's friends sleeping, nothing more. But *Blow Job* (1964), the most appreciated among his underground productions, was a high point in what I am calling the age of ingenuity. For thirty-three intense minutes, the camera stares unblinkingly at an actor's face, and the viewer sees nothing but his mounting excitement and his relaxed denouement.

Warhol movies were, in short, crude in every meaning of the word. In retrospect they seem to fit the 1960s: a time of international uncertainty, student rebellions against war, noises of a sexual revolution, after eight years of the stolid days marking the Eisenhower presidency. But by the early 1970s, Warhol returned to his first craft. As he had

Andy Warhol, *Blow Job* (1964). This is all the viewer sees.

become something of an international figure, he discovered that he could make far more money as a painter than as a movie director, and making money was a crucial element in every one of Warhol's plans. Invariably based on a photograph, a Warhol portrait cost $25,000 at the beginning, with a discount for extra copies, fees that had roughly doubled by the time of his death in 1987.

IN LAUNCHING HIS CAREER as a director and as a virtual wholesaler of graphics, Warhol relied on a cadre of hangers-on, some picked for their erotic appeal, some for their needed efficiency, the whole assembly known as the Factory; it included several heterosexual males and a few women required to serve as "superstars" for his movies. Though notoriously silent and detached, the qualities he allowed to rise to the surface—or could not help expressing—were by no means inaccessible. His love of money and of fame, and his detachment from men he professed to love, were obvious enough. So was, as his choice of subjects revealed, his imagination of disaster (to borrow Henry James's phrase), his loving concentration on car crashes, electric chairs, and poor Marilyn Monroe.

If he shared Duchamp's thinking about the impossibility of separating art from non-art, Warhol's grip on that anti-modernist stance was far more uncertain and far more mercenary than Duchamp's amused, largely disinterested stance. With Warhol, a whine of disappointment would in the end often take back his boldest pronouncements. "Everything is art," he said to a *Newsweek* interviewer in the mid-1960s. "You go to a museum and they say this is art and the little squares are hanging on the wall. But everything is art, and nothing is art. Because I think everything is beautiful—if it's right." What is particularly noteworthy in this declaration is Warhol's yawning indifference to art, including his own.

5.

POP ART, by forcing what I have called a shotgun marriage between high art and low, energetically assailed what gave life to modernism: its subversive and quality-minded discriminations between the two domains, a separation that rescued innovative artists and writers from common bad taste. It seems now, decades later, as though the Pop artists' hardworking cheerfulness was (as already hinted) a symptom and agent of irredeemable retreat from the wholehearted anti-establishment convictions that had animated modernists all the way back to Baudelaire and Flaubert. Few of the 1960s innovators had illusions about producing a lasting addition to the pantheon of art that transcends the occasion and moment of its making. Even fewer had any conscious intention of helping to speed the end of a great tradition.

Though the Pop artists' contributions to the roster of ingenious novelties were imaginative, enjoyable, and almost inexhaustible—one thinks of Oldenburg's phallic lipstick and Lichtenstein's heartbroken cartoon damsels—they deliberately excluded a concern with inwardness, that indispensable ingredient of modernism. They dwelled on surfaces and almost ostentatiously kept away from psychology. Their art had all the impact of a witty cartoon in a weekly magazine, appealing and entertaining for quick consumption, but in the long run flat, stale—and profitable.

The yearning for heresy remained. It is interesting that the sophisticated French mock-primitivist painter Jean Dubuffet should declare, "I feel a need that every work of art should in the highest degree lift one out of context, provoking a surprise and a shock." The idea is only too familiar to readers of these pages, but the situation in which the startling nature of the artwork seemed necessary to modernism had changed. The Pop artists, too, could provide shocks, but their collective effort at turning cartoons or numerals into high art struck modernists as an unacceptable blurring of artistic categories and in effect an assault on their reforming mission. So much for an age of ingenuity!

SUCCESS

1.

THERE WAS YET ANOTHER ingredient in the arts from the 1960s that became particularly problematic for modernism: success. From its very beginnings in mid-nineteenth century, it had posed difficulties. For the traditional avant-garde, on principle hostile to the bourgeois buying public, to sell was more or less to sell out. To encounter articulate, affluent, even passionate lovers of modernist work among the buying classes was, of course, welcome; indeed, to outsiders who had no chance of being exhibited in mainstream salons to secure a following, it was essential. But success was in a way a betrayal of the true social role of an avant-garde, which was, after all, intent on striking at the complacent establishment, whether in art or literature. The eventual triumphs of Pop painting raised this old dilemma all over again.

In January 1964, the year of Warhol's *Brillo Box*, Dorothy Seiberling, the art editor of *Life*, wrote a short piece on Roy Lichtenstein for her popular weekly, provocatively titled "Is He the Worst Artist in the U.S.?" This title was all the more memorable since fifteen years before, the same critic, writing for the same magazine, had published an equally short piece, "Jackson Pollock: Is he the greatest living painter in the United States?" Seiberling did not answer her questions, only observing that the two artists were controversial, and gave her readers no guidance just what to think of their work. Why did Pollock's *Number Nine* stop precisely at the width of eighteen feet? "His studio," a caption told the reader, "is only 22 feet long." Its asking price, $1,800, *Life* noted, made it cost $100 a foot, a pair of observations strongly implying that the reader need not take such odd productions too seriously.

A look at critics discussing Pop Art in the pages of the *New York Times* reveals first uncertainty and then surrender. Reviewing the opening of the "New Realist" show (in a word, Pop) at the Sidney Janis Gallery in late October 1962, Brian O'Doherty seemed playfully helpless: "It's mad, mad, wonderfully mad. It's also (at different times) glad, bad and sad, and it may be a fad." He suggested that it might be "a rearguard action by the advance guard against mass culture—the mass culture that pushes the individual below the line into the lowest common denominator." Welcoming the exhibitors' assault on "a majority they indulgently despise," he remarked on their use of "wit, satire, irony, parody, all the divisions of humor." The ruling principle of the show was, of course, to demonstrate that current popular culture is "bad." In any event, "With this show 'pop' art is officially here." Returning to this radically innovative exhibition a few days later, full of praise and doubt, O'Doherty underscored the possibility of the Pop Art exemplars being for the most part "entirely ephemeral." It might well be a "definite trend, a possible movement." But "At the moment, most of it falls under the heading of clever—very clever—journalism."

This seems to have been the first consensus among professional judges: Pop was an amusing excursion, but surely it lacked staying power. In late December of that year, O'Doherty summed up the season: "Pop sold." Still, "most people predicted that it would be a flash in the pan." One is reminded of other increasingly accepted modernist artists like Cézanne, who, in the eyes of a presumably wise judge of radical art like Mary Cassatt, must be merely a passing fad. As for himself, O'Doherty was by no mean certain. He saw no major trends in the offing but, quickly covering his rear, he added, "apart perhaps from Pop."

In January 1964, John Canaday took up where O'Doherty had left off, finding that his skepticism overrode his infatuation with the new. Despite a gifted sculptor like George Segal, with his fascinating dead white plaster life-size sculptures constructed from living models, Pop Art was already giving "signs of beating itself to death." It "selects its motifs from the inexhaustible and malodorous limbo of debased things that make up our landscape—the worst comic strips, the trashiest commercials, the smut magazines, the badly designed utilitarian objects, such ubiquitous paraphernalia as TV sets and all such organic, indispensable and anonymous gear as radiators, steam pipes—anything." Canaday's catalog was grim and accurate enough, but there was in fact no sign that their creators were about to beat themselves to death.

To be sure, Canaday added, this Pop explosion was meant to be satire, but it was bad satire. Its producers "relish the inanities and perversities that they have adopted as a pictorial vocabulary; they seem to enjoy exposing what is hateful only as a compensation for something missed." In short, he concluded, "there is virtually no pop art of any importance in itself . . . the premise of the movement, if it proves to be one, lies in a premise that has been prostituted before it could prove itself."

Those are strong words, but Canaday took them back partly in late 1964. It is curious to read the contemporary critics of Pop; nearly all of them, repelled by its vulgarity but baffled by its popularity, made strong statements but felt compelled to subvert their own certainty. Pop Art, commented Canaday, was, strangely enough, finding paying collectors and giving every sign of staying around at least for some time. It was, he noted with a swipe at professional art historians, "bulldozing its way through the academy which was, as usual, following fashion by teaching Pop and thus legitimizing it." And thus it remained. In March 1966, the respected critic Hilton Kramer observed that Pop Art had proved an astonishing artistic and social success and had been taken up by "gossip columnists, fashion writers and even political commentators," who "were quick to seize on pop as a subject to be exploited." The reason was obvio us: "Serious art, which had in the past been regarded as difficult, mysterious and private, was found, with the proliferation of pop, to be amusing and easy, a matter of laughter rather than tears." And this, of course, was precisely the point: art that claimed to be serious was easy to understand and enjoy—a relief from the work of unriddling the likes of Jackson Pollock.

2.

AS POP ART RETAINED, and even increased, its popular acceptability, critics from the late 1960s on labored to explain its astonishing longevity. In September 1971, Robert Brustein, then dean of the Drama School at Yale, charged that the United States was suffering from "cultural schizophrenia," unable to decide between high art and low, and even unable to differentiate between them. While the democratic impulse of Pop is not central to Brustein's diagnosis, it quietly informs his argument. The favorite subject in his symptomatology was the classicist Erich Segal, a specialist in ancient Roman drama. He had become famous with *Love Story*, a best-selling novel—sentimental in the modern manner, about two Harvard students—and successful movie no less maudlin. Segal would, Brustein noted, "respond to an invitation to play the piano by pounding out the theme from *Love Story*—this was not just to invite ridicule, it was to court it. In Segal, the media interviewers had found the perfect patsy—a performer willing to play the fool on demand in return for continued exposure in front of the public." In a word, Pop attitudes were actively playing to degrade cultural values. Their effect on modernism, easy to see now half a century later, was still relatively obscure, though the failure of critics to stem the tide of Pop was becoming increasingly apparent.

The year after, also writing in the *New York Times*, Hilton Kramer, a strong partisan of modernism, recalled the tenth anniversary of the sensational exhibition of "New Realism" at the Janis Gallery in 1962. It had been a "howling success," Kramer glumly recalled, but immediately added, "it was also, as so many successes are nowadays, a very great disaster." He went back more than a century to find a comparison. "Not since the Pyrrhic victories of the Pre-Raphaelites in Victorian London had the taste and standards of the professional art world been so radically debased. For a sizable portion of the art public, the whole notion of artistic seriousness was altered—altered downward." It was indeed happening as Kramer saw it, but Pop seemed irresistible.

The financial rewards to modernists did not have too long to wait. In 1978, Ralph Tyler published a sobering survey of that touchy topic. In his fetchingly titled "The Artist as Millionaire," he observed that while detailed figures were still hard to come by, there were some remarkable numbers worthy of thoughtful reflection. Since defecting from the Soviet Union in 1961, the fees for the great modern ballet dancer Rudolf Nureyev had climbed to over $10,000 for a single performance, a millionaire's pay that Mikhail Baryshnikov would later match. Around the same time, Sir Georg Solti, who had been presiding over the Chicago Symphony Orchestra, could count on over $500,000 annually, mainly through guest appearances. Success was paying off in the cultural domain, and modernist artists and performers were not left behind.

Granted, unconventional artists did not necessarily find all the stunning sums flowing directly into their pockets. Most of the hitherto liter-

Roy Lichtenstein, *Crak!* (1963–64).

ally incredible prices were achieved at auctions, and dealers, too, took hefty commissions. De Koonings were going for around $180,000, almost matched by Rauschenbergs for about $150,000. In retrospect from, say, a quarter of a century later, these prices seemed downright modest. In the early 1970s, when Andy Warhol might realize $135,000 at auction, so grand a return seemed almost beyond his most avarious dreams. Only a decade later, he could sneer at so piddling a reward.

Normally, the leading earner among the Pop painters was, and remained, Jasper Johns. In 1970, a sizable Johns canvas already went for $240,000. His work soon did better, much better. When the wealthy Connecticut collectors Burton and Emily Tremaine disposed of a Johns canvas they had bought from the Leo Castelli Gallery for $900, they sold it to the Whitney Museum for a million dollars. By the 1990s, such prices were no longer impressive. In 1994, Lichtenstein's *I . . . I'm Sorry*, one of his blond cartoon beauties dropping a regretful tear, went for $2,477,500 at a Sotheby's auction in New York; a year later, Christie's slightly outdid its principal rival with Lichtenstein's *Kiss II*, a handsome young cartoon couple in a hot embrace, which was knocked down for $2,532,500. By this time, Warhols had stabilized at roughly $2 million, if not more. There had been a few, a very few, comparably wild prices in the late nineteenth century, particularly for Salon artists like Gérôme and Meissonier, but they were rare exceptions. Late in the twentieth century, they were becoming commonplace.

It has seemed destined to last. Riches amassed by Hollywood producers, makers of patent medicines, lucky speculators, real estate moguls, or owners of mundane companies like a fleet of taxis in New York were being redistributed among "progressive" dealers, adroit auctioneers—and artists. During the 1980s, while this tide of prosperity lasted, Japanese billionaires began to swamp the Western art market, indulging in sudden passions for van Gogh and other Post-Impressionists. In an unintended tribute to the sheer power of money in shaping capitalist high culture, competing collectors and curators, shrewdly nourished by middlemen, drove prices through the roof and have kept them there. The numbers are stunning. In 1988, the press reported—one can sense the bated breath—that Jasper Johns's *False*

Jasper Johns, *False Start* (1959). In 1988, this painting brought $17 million at auction, an instance of the vast inflation that exceptional canvases had begun to produce—unprecedented prices that have not yet begun to moderate.

Start of 1959 had first been sold for $2,500 and had just realized $17 million, a record for a living artist, more expensive than most Rembrandts, even authentic ones. Since then, even these prices have been put into the shade. In 2006, a painting by Picasso of 1905, not particularly renowned, managed to break the $100 million barrier. In the same year, Tobias Meyer, an auctioneer at Sotheby's, said that he could list quite a number of people "who don't care whether an art work costs ten or twenty million dollars more or less," and no one is likely to challenge Meyer's boast.

The extraordinary inflation of prices in art is another instance of how the old, firm distinction between respectable and subversive art, which, we know, has central consequences for the fate of modernism, has been fading away. There have been other times in the past when some very rich individuals or institutions were willing to pay all they had, even more, for the art they craved. But the condition of art since the 1960s has become an international fashion, and modernism has been caught up in it. For the appetites of late nineteenth and early twenty-first-century collectors are neutral in their behavior toward modernism. No one can predict whether the affluent art lover will buy one of Kandinsky's abstractions or Bouguereau's idealizations of mother and child. For the market it is all the same.

NONE OF THIS should be taken to suggest that the threefold hierarchy of tastes, first analyzed a century earlier, has been wholly dismantled. The cultured elite that alone nourishes modernism, the philistine bourgeoisie that professes to understand the movement, the benighted masses that have no use for it, still exist. But their boundaries have been breached. With steady advances in the modern technology of leisure and its apparatuses, the artistic choices of the masses reaching deep into the tastes of the middle classes have become more pronounced as they are increasingly subjected to advance testing and manipulation. More menacing still is the broadening of what the cultural critic Dwight Macdonald has baptized as "Midcult": the soft-centered misreading of classical music (Leopold Stokowski's Bach), the unthinking repetitions of modern architecture (the business skyscrapers on Park Avenue), all offspring of sophisticated calculation. The makers of these entertainments claim to have seriously contributed to modernist culture, but they have only scrambled and dis-

torted the frontiers of what used to be clear distinctions. The sizable
share of Pop Art in causing this grand confusion, this so-called high
art that uniformly used low art as its inspiration, is undeniable. The
"howling success" of Pop, as Hilton Kramer put it in 1972, was indeed
a "very great disaster" for modernism.

Differences in the quality of tastes can easily be documented by
anecdotal evidence, but there are also some quantitative measures. *To
the Lighthouse*, published by the Woolfs' Hogarth Press in May 1927,
had a first printing of 3,000 copies, which had to be supplemented by
another 1,000 in June. This was quite impressive for Virginia Woolf,
and she was duly impressed. In 1965, defending its status as a good
seller, Leonard Woolf noted that the novel had sold 253,000 copies in
the United States and Great Britain. But the thousands of copies sold
(even before American colleges began to use it as a text) almost vanish
before the many millions that cheap romances sold in the last quarter of
the twentieth century. In October 2005, the Romance Writers of America proudly advertised that in 2004, their total sales amounted to $1.2
billion; 54.9 percent of all paperbacks were romances, and indeed 39.3
percent of all fiction sold that year was romances.

SIGNS OF LIFE

1.

GRAND PERIOD TERMS like "Renaissance" or "Mannerism," no matter
how instructive they may be as markers, can never be securely brack-
eted between specific dates. A play or a composition, a painting or a
novel in the "wrong" time period, too early or too late, will always turn
up to damage such misplaced specificity. If we accept Pop Art as signal-
ing the death knell of modernism, we must then not be surprised to discover major works of art or literature beyond its presumed life cycle.
And there were, in the second half of the twentieth century, intriguing
hints of modernist life after death.

Such symptoms ranged all the way from triviality to grandeur. In
October 2001, I read a story in the *New York Times* that I clipped for
later use without knowing then what that use might be. Its hero was

Damien Hirst, painter and maker of installations, the most ingenious among the Young British Artists, a clan of conceptual painters who had gained notoriety by exhibiting animal carcasses, displayed in tanks filled with formaldehyde to *épater la bourgeoisie*. On October 19, 2001, Hirst's dealer, the Eyestorm Gallery in London, gave a party to celebrate the opening of a one-man Hirst show, for which he constructed a pile of organized chaos representing the detritus of a painter's studio. It consisted, Warren Hoge, the *New York Times* reporter covering the story, wrote, "of a collection of half-full coffee cups, ashtrays with cigarette butts, empty beer bottles, a paint-smeared palette, an easel, a ladder, paintbrushes, candy wrappers and newspaper pages about the floor," an assemblage sure to sell in six figures the next day.

But after the party was over and the guests were gone, a cleaner came upon Hirst's installation, and later admitted that he had "sighed because there was so much mess. It didn't look much like art to me. So I cleared it all in bin bags, and I dumped it." To his credit, Hirst found the episode "hysterically funny" and, using some snapshots and his memory, reconstructed his precious "sculpture." The lesson of this mishap is obvious: the "mess" that the cleaner discarded was, to its maker and his potential customers, a faultlessly modernist piece, an act of aggression against conventional three-dimensional objects. In short, the traditional hierarchy of tastes had survived into the twenty-first century, if not for the artist, then for the man who cleaned it up. Was there life after death for modernism? Were its obituaries of around 1960, as Mark Twain would have said, exaggerated? The emergence of a few major avant-garde figures after the decade suggests that perhaps they were.

By this time, the prospects for the preconditions indispensable to a flourishing modernism had become hard to read. The cleaner who threw Damien Hirst's installation into the garbage because it did not look like art to him beautifully represents the untutored majority, to whom modernist deviations were a matter of puzzlement or supreme apathy. He did not rise to the level of the philistine, which remained the preserve of culturally conservative middle-class audiences consisting of prosperous, opinionated burghers who didn't know anything about art but knew what they liked.

This has not, in itself, wholly ruined the possible survival of modernism. To keep modernist fiction or architecture or painting alive has always been the work of a minority, and at best a minority it must remain. The democratization of high culture, far from destroying this segregation, has marginally revised, and probably somewhat enlarged, the number of elite consumers on whom modernism so vitally depends. Serious curricula educating the young in classical music, museum outreach programs supplying youngsters with more self-confidence in their own childish artworks, school drama classes organizing performances of pupils doing major plays, all sow seeds that may ripen into settled good taste and philanthropic emotions as the child grows into a citizen with cash to spare.

All this uncertainty, all this essential imprecision, raises doubts about the hundred twenty years I am tentatively allocating to modernism. History is invariably less orderly than historians like to make it. Even if the early 1960s experienced the death of modernism, the emergence of writers like Gabriel García Márquez or, as we shall see, architects like Frank Gehry right into the twenty-first century may well invalidate the obituaries. It may be that among novelists now working, or now maturing, one may turn out to be another Marcel Proust, another Virginia Woolf. It may be that among composers now working, or now maturing, one may turn out to be another Igor Stravinsky, another Charles Ives. This is why I have given my concluding chapter the deliberately indecisive title "Life After Death?" A revival of modernism is neither impossible nor assured.

2.

ANECDOTES ARE OF COURSE never enough. They may point to larger realities; by the late 1960s, most playwrights of the absurd, for example, had a few followers, like Edward Albee, who continued their work. But there is more significant evidence of modernist literature after death: the fiction of García Márquez, a splendid representative of a lively Latin American literature. His novels and long stories urgently demand, and just as urgently resist, interpretation. They are filled to bursting with highly improbable twists and turns, and far from self-explanatory; the verdicts of a competent analyst seem needed on every page. At the same time, to scrutinize his work with caliper and microscope in hand threatens to slight his impressive narrative flow, overlook the riches of his fertile imagination, miss the humor in the amusing, often very funny terse speeches he gives his characters, in a word, to be blind to his exceptional gifts for creating another world teeming with memorable incidents and personages. Perhaps the most fruitful solution is to read his novels twice, once as a reader open to pleasure and once as a critic savoring the details.

BORN IN 1928 IN ARACATACA, a small town in northern Colombia near the Caribbean coast, Gabriel García Márquez spent his early years, it would seem, mainly preparing himself to grow into a writer. This absorbing passion put him at odds with his father, who wanted him to complete his legal studies—a defiance of paternal authority far from easy in his culture, yet consistent with modernist themes. But it was a risk the son was willing to take. His family, with its long-cherished, sometimes savage peasant beliefs joined to a credulous Roman Catholicism, gave the boy, who more than anything else wanted to write it all down, a superlative education in cultivating his imagination, an enviable writer's instrument. He craved to make a world suffused with the red blood of reality touched by the miraculous. It was in tracing his characters' convictions, their superstitions and traditional beliefs, that he made their inner lives, their needs and fears, central to his vision.

Literary historians have generally described the style García Márquez matured in years of eclectic experimentation with the oxymoron "magical realism," the mutually fostering coexistence of mundane day-to-day life with phenomena outside the possibilities of nature. Literary historians have looked as far back as Nikolai Gogol and Henry James, as widely apart as Rainer Maria Rilke and D. H. Lawrence, to find storytellers who deployed this stylistic device decades before the term was invented in the 1920s, and they have crowned García Márquez its most eminent practitioner. It neatly, economically encapsulates two incompatible perspectives, which encompass tough-minded narration in which ordinary characters lead ordinary lives in ordinary surroundings—these are not fairy tales—yet some of whom act in ways, or undergo experiences, irreconcilable with what readers know to be possible. In one novel, a stunningly incomparable beauty is one day rapt from the earth to heaven; in another, a dictator who has been in power for perhaps two hundred years can change the weather at will; among the curses that afflict García Márquez's hapless Colombians is a years-long plague of collective insomnia. Compared to these marvels, a married military man of García Márquez's invention who makes seventeen sons with seventeen mistresses, each of the boys named after him, is positively commonplace.

Rejecting the verdict of literary historians, García Márquez has spurned the label of "magical realist" and insisted that he is simply a realist. One can see why. His prose, he has said, reproduces the literally wonderful stories that his loving, simple, and credulous grandparents had lavished on him when he was a boy living with them in a house "full of ghosts." And it is true that some of the wildest tales his elders told him, filled with irrational dread, appear in his fiction virtually unrevised: the Buendía family, given to incestuous marriages between cousins, tensely awaits each legitimate birth in the fear that the infant will appear with a pig's tail, the mark of the objectionable, until one day a newborn really does bear the infamous mark. Yet these makers and victims of such fantastic events are humdrum persons, subject to all the universal laws of physics and chemistry that dominate the lives of their fellows—all laws perhaps but one.

There is more to García Márquez's special realism than this. And his particular contribution to modernist literature lies in his highly original vision of reality. As he sees his provincial Colombia, it lives, as it were, at the edge of fantasy. Things happen there that would not, and could not, happen anywhere else. Taking this perception as his guide, he was stone by stone constructing a new Caribbean that would unmistakably be his bailiwick. From the 1950s to the mid-1960s, he published a great deal of fiction, widely appreciated and winning prizes; in retrospect, they read like so many preparatory sketches. Then, in 1967, he completed *One Hundred Years of Solitude*, first published in Buenos Aires. He was thirty-nine.

In that tour de force, which made García Márquez world-famous, he unrolls the history of the town of Macondo, whose citizens permanently alternate between excitement and disillusionment "to such an extreme that no one knew for certain where the limits of reality lay. It was an intricate stew of truths and mirages," with the mirages as necessary to the storyteller as the truths. Hence the border between unvarnished fact and imaginative tale is impossible to specify, let alone keep intact. One amorous couple enjoy intercourse eight times a day, adding three times more during the siesta. A destructive rain falls ceaselessly for several years. The face of a young beauty is so dazzling that men who get a glimpse of it are changed forever. A frequent visitor to Macondo, the gypsy Malquíades, has several lives to live, and can read the future, in hair-raising detail, of the Buendías and their town's life and decay. This, the realist García Márquez holds, is how things are in the world he has made.

His technique, in short, is an amusing modernist variation on the kind of routine mundane description that was the common coin of less imaginative realists. García Márquez's early reading of Kafka left its mark: the strange, in real life impossible experiences of Kafka's characters—think "Metamorphosis"—told in a calm, businesslike prose reappear translated to the Caribbean, a hotter, less doom-ridden climate than Kafka's unidentified Central Europe but hospitable to the kind of cool voice that could produce *The Castle* and *The Trial*—and the imagined history of Macondo. Like Kafka, too, García Márquez wrote psychological novels without invoking psychology. Seen from a distance, the cosmopolitan range of modernist experimentation in fiction is nowhere more marked than in his work.

IT FOLLOWS THAT GARCÍA MÁRQUEZ'S stories and novels are far from self-explanatory—the main reason why his work calls out for interpretations—and that, not surprisingly, critics have dissected them with the most up-to-date literary instruments that academics can borrow. They have measured his phrases and counted his repeated favorite words, searched for political parallels and exclaimed over his opening sentences.* Since García Márquez has been forthcoming in interviews and memoirs—*Living to Tell the Tale*, the first of a planned three-volume autobiography, was published in the United States in 2003 when he was seventy-six—we are well informed about his professional parentage. The principal influence on him, cultivated in years of attending—or rather, not attending—law school at Bogotá, was, in addition to Kafka, William Faulkner. Hence two advanced modernists, with García Márquez giving Faulkner the credit for creating his obsession with a writer's career, presided over his life. Kafka and Faulkner, a remarkable choice of dissimilar literary fathers who had little in common except for dwelling at the top rank of modernist masters.

In *Living to Tell the Tale*, which covers his childhood and youth, García Márquez reports in some detail how much his irresistible fantasies cost him at home. Resolute in his decision, he dropped out of law school to take a job with a newspaper. The years that followed were a long apprenticeship, when he did journalism and practiced modernist techniques of fiction in his stories: unreliable narrators, unexplained shifts in perspective, the invasion of supernatural moments, the barely controlled flights of imagination.

IN SOME EARLY STORIES, García Márquez had already played with a fictitious Colombian settlement he named Macondo, and in *One Hundred Years of Solitude* he recites its history from founding to inglorious collapse. Macondo represents a rich though digestible mixture of Colombian life, including its dramatic growth and interminable civil wars, with one family, the Buendías, serving as a pseudo-historical spine through the generations. It is fiction, though serenely reported as a chain of facts by the all-knowing narrator in—I cannot but repeat—

* See, for an example, the seductive opening sentence in *One Hundred Years of Solitude*: "Many years later, as he faced the firing squad, Colonel Aureliano Buendía was to remember that distant afternoon when his father took him to discover ice."

the patented Kafkaesque style. The result was immense popularity, not just among the literary elite. Much like Charles Dickens a century before him, García Márquez delighted several distinct registers of taste at once; even readers who could not respond to his finer devices found enough in his fiction to welcome it with enthusiasm. In a chapter on the successes of the avant-garde, *One Hundred Years of Solitude* would occupy a prominent place.

Which leaves the question what this novel is actually about. Conjectures as to just what García Márquez had in mind with this all-embracing panorama have been raised and answered in the most various ways. It is a family chronicle, but also more than that. Just as Thomas Mann's classic *Buddenbrooks* bursts the limits of the family chronicle by presenting the decay of the commercial bourgeois Buddenbrooks clan as a shaping element in German social history (a genre that was a great favorite around the turn of the twentieth century), García Márquez has history happen to Macondo. The railroad comes, as does, even more weightily and destructively, a powerful Fruit Company that brings American "progress" to Macondo as it satisfies an irrepressible appetite for bananas in the United States and in the process has government troops kill an unknown number of strikers. There is harsh reality in his realism, we note; Yankee imperialism, the target of bitter reproach in contemporary Latin American literature, also makes its appearance. But magic remains central.

Yet the novel is also punctuated by a less conspicuous subtext that merits closer attention than it has received: the pathos of solitude. García Márquez's exuberant humor, which won him untold thousands of readers, has been gratefully noticed, but his melancholy side, which makes intermittent appearances in this text, deserves closer attention. The book has "solitary lovers." The many illegitimate sons of one of the novel's principals, Colonel Aureliano Buendía, share "a look of solitude." Rebeca, a character whose sad life receives ample space, finds that "solitude had made a selection in her memory"; she had undergone "many years of suffering and misery in order to attain the privileges of solitude." Indeed, solitude almost never manifests itself as a privilege in *One Hundred Years of Solitude*. Far more often, a personage suffers from his "solitary sadness," and the learned gypsy Melquíades returns from death because "he could not bear the solitude." One spear carrier, "a bony, jaundiced man," García Márquez notes, is "marked forever and from the beginning of the world with the pox of solitude." That the reader should encounter the haunted word, *soledad*, in the very title of this novel, is surely a sign that the author has assigned it a marked prominence. To reinforce this impression, García Márquez, who rarely left any particulars of his writings to sheer accident, returns to it in the closing sentence, with his assertion that "races condemned to one hundred years of solitude did not have a second opportunity on earth." The miracle that gave Melquíades the gift of several lives will not be reenacted for the citizens of Macondo.

It is far easier to recognize this theme than to understand it. García Márquez draws a fundamental, if not always lucid, distinction between love and sex. There is a good deal of the latter in his writings, and less of the former. Many of his men, and a few of his women, are erotic athletes, more distinguished for the quantity of their erotic encounters than their quality. Yet their activity in bed—and not in bed alone—is not always simply the blind gratification of their biological urges. Among frequent instances of lovemaking, perhaps the most conspicuous one comes near the end of the novel. A married couple in the Buendía clan rediscover each other as lovers and spend virtually all their waking moments in sexual wrestling of the most extravagant intensity and the most untraditional positions, some of them newly invented by the wife. But their almost crazed repeated performances are something better than sheer animal exercises: "both of them," their inventor insists, "remained floating in an empty universe where the only everyday and eternal reality was love."

The obverse side of this happy juncture of love and sex is its cheerless divorce. In *The Autumn of the Patriarch* (1975), another, though less celebrated masterpiece, García Márquez's protagonist is an aged dictator who, near death, when it is too late, after untold decades of sexual indulgence and untrustworthy comradeships, has "learned of his incapacity to love." This is not the author dropping into sentimentality, proclaiming "All you need is love." He knows better. His character's late discovery is an essential counterpart to the relationships he idealizes. Solitude is humans' dark companion in the absence of love.

AFTER THE SPECTACULAR popular and critical success of *One Hundred Years of Solitude*, García Márquez continued to write novels, exploring his family's and his country's history. One of them, *Love in the Time of Cholera* (1985), is a dazzling treatise on the vagaries of love, with a traditional triangle stretched very much out of shape. Two shy, immensely respectable teenagers, Florentino and Fermina, lovers mainly by mail and both still virgins, break up as she abruptly decides that the man she adores is somehow unworthy of her. She marries the most eligible local bachelor, a physician, and shares a long, relatively happy marriage. Meanwhile Florentino, at first hesitantly and then energetically, embraces the joys of sex—the author, who greatly likes precise figures, specifies the number of his affairs at 622—without ever ceasing to love Fermina. After her husband's death, with the pair now in their seventies, Florentino, ever faithful, resumes his suit. The story ends as it must: the two ancients finally, at long last, finish up in bed together—happily. Their liaison, like others in García Márquez's fiction, is free of guilt feelings for both partners, largely because it is prompted and facilitated by genuine affection. Love does not conquer all in his work, but without it, conquest is not worth having.

3.

GARCÍA MÁRQUEZ'S FICTION was shaped by life experiences—researching *Love in the Time of Cholera*, he learned with unfeigned delight that his septuagenarian parents were still practicing, and taking pleasure in, sexual intercourse, and he freely used their domestic coitus in the novel. But life as a Latin American writer also pushed him toward a grimmer sector of reality: the all too prevalent phenomenon of dictatorships in other Latin American countries and his own. For half a century and more, before García Márquez tackled it directly, several eminent novelists had tried their skills on the *caudillo*, as enamored of their subject matter as they detested its real-life protagonists. Hence it was sensible for him to leave the country of *The Autumn of the Patriarch* unnamed; it is, as the author put it, "a synthesis of all the Latin American dictators, but especially those from the Caribbean," with the traits of ancient Roman dictators, whom García Márquez had studied for the purpose, thrown into the mix.

The story begins (if so commonplace a word as "story" fits at all) with the death in the president's palace of a man who has served the dictator for many years as his perfect double. After the population breaks out in a paroxysm of impromptu festival, the real dictator takes his revenge on those who welcomed his disappearance and seeks out those who had mourned over his body to reward them appropriately. The autocrat in *The Autumn of the Patriarch*, known as "General," is all a Latin American dictator is supposed to have been, and often was: sadistic and desperate for affection, vengeful and ignorant, superstitious yet shrewd, narcissistic and (not wholly unjustly) paranoid. When in 1982 García Márquez delivered his oration in Stockholm upon accepting the Nobel Prize for Literature, he entertained his listeners with true horror stories about Caribbean dictators.

This self-imposed assignment—to stage the life and death of a tyrant—called forth all the stylistic devices that critics have called magical realism. García Márquez has divided his fairly short text into six unnumbered and untitled chapters, giving the impression of the tight, solid unity of a short story. The world that readers see emerging is enslaved to the dictator and all his caprices. His book fortifies this impression by casting each chapter into a single paragraph, and the closing one into a single sentence. The comma is king, pitilessly linking one phrase to, and dividing it from, another.

It is this pervasive linguistic irrationality that García Márquez, in brilliantly told anecdotes, documents with steadily shifting narrative voices that effortlessly move from one speaker to another, often within a single sentence. We hear an anonymous participant in the final phase of the General's life; the dictator addressing his mother; a local prostitute; and at times the mother herself. One and all, they dramatize the point that political theorists have long made about despotism: The General,

Gabriel García
Márquez (left)
receiving the Nobel
Prize for Literature
from the king of
Spain in Stockholm,
1982.

sick, arbitrary, unpredictable, like his fellows elsewhere, is the deadly
enemy of reason.

When it comes to the psychology of politics, *The Autumn of the
Patriarch* and what I have called the subtext of *One Hundred Years of
Solitude* meet and join. García Márquez has said that his dictator novel
was a "poem about the solitude of power." Readers have usually put
the emphasis of this pronouncement on power, but it speaks about solitude just as prominently. The General, we read, is a "solitary despot."
He felt menaced even in the "solitude of his bedroom." His clumsy,
unsuccessful attempts to rape the maids in his house lead to "solitary

tears," and after a massacre of his enemies, he goes to sleep "more alone than ever." He had exercised "the solitary vice of power," making it sound like masturbation. Being without love—I have quoted this passage before—the General has had a life not worth living. If this is magic realism, the magic lies mainly in the author's ability to conjure up a world, not omitting the inner world of a notoriously exceptional human being.

4.

ONE REASON for García Márquez's worldwide reputation, though by no means the only one, is that he had so few competitors at the summit of literature. Karl Marx once meanly said about John Stuart Mill that his eminence was due to the flatness of the surrounding landscape. If applied to García Márquez, this remark would be highly unfair. But it is true that nowadays there are virtually no novelists whose announcement of a new work of fiction would make lovers of high literature rush out to a bookstore and buy it. Günter Grass, perhaps, and V. S. Naipaul might be suitable candidates for the living pantheon, even though both have given the world some weak performances. But who else?

Not that there are no talented novelists in our time; the level of skillful, often astonishing fiction may be as high as it has been for decades. But the contrast with the years of high modernism is striking and disheartening: reports of a forthcoming volume by Proust or Joyce, by Faulkner or Virginia Woolf, promised a major cultural event. This is simply no longer true. Granted, the classic modernist novels I have discussed found resistance among shocked readers or prudish government officials, or might be so baffling that they defeated honest efforts to master their intricacies. Joyce pushed the dissection and reconstruction of prose to an extreme that nobody could surpass without landing in sheer incoherence.

Plainly, this strange novel could not serve as a model for later subversive writers, but it remains—and will remain—a solitary monument to a bold, learned, and unduplicable venture, serving as Joyce always did to affront dominant literary pieties. But one *Finnegans Wake* is about as many examples as modernism at its most venturesome can safely digest. It belongs among works that make modernist experiments the stuff of immortality, but it says nothing about the future of the movement. There are, we know, later avant-garde novelists, witness the work of Gabriel García Márquez, and there may be yet more.

The same possibilities hold true for other domains of modernism. Orson Welles, for all the universal admiration he won among directors with *Citizen Kane*, did find worthy successors like the Italian Realists and the French *nouvelle vague*. And the International Style of architecture has finally found an heir in Frank Gehry's imaginative designs. At the same time, music or painting still await their Stravinskys or their Picassos. That is all we now know.

CODA: AND GEHRY AT BILBAO

1.

I AM GOING TO END *MODERNISM* AS I STARTED IT, ON A PERSONAL note. I want to explore, briefly, my experience with one of Frank O. Gehry's most electrifying buildings, the Guggenheim Museum in Bilbao. This sort of individual treatment strikes me as appropriate for such a project as mine: while generalizations are indispensable (the Impressionists, the Expressionist playwrights, the partisans of the *auteur* theory), the real achievements, whether a poem or a symphony, always come back to a single talent at work. Even when I dealt with the fundamentals of modernist ideology (the lure of heresy and the crucial task of subjectivity), my ultimate resort has always been the lone productive artist feeling and thinking, adopting or rejecting a tradition, making it new. Hence this Coda, which links the author with his subject.

Bilbao: Its very location caught my attention. A drab industrial port in the Basque country of northwestern Spain, until recently of little interest to foreign visitors, has now secured, thanks to Gehry's modernist masterpiece, a select place on the map of the international tourist trade. People come by the thousands to wonder at the museum. So did I, and I can testify that the visit, to borrow the highest praise the *Guide*

Michelin has to offer, *Vaux le voyage*: it is worth a detour.

When, in 1991, Thomas Krens, director of the Guggenheim Museums, commissioned Frank Gehry to design one of its new branches in Bilbao, the architect was sixty-two years old and widely recognized as an original designer for a diverse menu of buildings. Two years before, he had been awarded the coveted Pritzker Prize,

Frank Gehry, Guggenheim Museum,
Bilbao, exterior (1997).
Photographs by Dr. Gabriele Katwan.

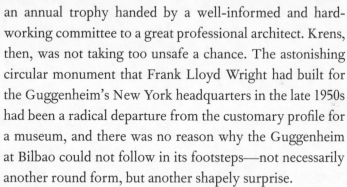

an annual trophy handed by a well-informed and hard-working committee to a great professional architect. Krens, then, was not taking too unsafe a chance. The astonishing circular monument that Frank Lloyd Wright had built for the Guggenheim's New York headquarters in the late 1950s had been a radical departure from the customary profile for a museum, and there was no reason why the Guggenheim at Bilbao could not follow in its footsteps—not necessarily another round form, but another shapely surprise.

Gehry was prepared to venture further into unconventionality than he had ever gone before. The computer, a fairly recent arrival in his office for which he had a rather skeptical affection, simplified the labors of an architect tired of the expected, ever-repeated straight angles; and he was firm on its essentially servile function. "The computer," Gehry said, "is a tool, not a partner, an instrument for catching the curve, not for inventing it." It permitted him to visualize, and audaciously experiment with, complex shapes that would define the proposed museum both inside and out.

I FIRST SAW GEHRY'S GUGGENHEIM at Bilbao in the summer of 2000, and, in a word, I was overwhelmed. Perhaps this is not the best term for my response; I was not awed into silence, but took pleasure from the first from the wealth and elegance of the forms that rose up around me. I had lived enough and seen enough to resist easy enthusiasms, but walking around this museum over and over, and then circling it quite as often, I concluded that "enthusiasm" was the only fitting name for my feelings. Here was modernist architecture at its most thrilling, though, I admit, distant from my old favorites by classic modernists like Gropius or Mies van der Rohe.

Since the 1980s, perhaps even a little before, Gehry had joined the clan of modernists, and had designed an array of structures particularly noted for their violence against time-honored modern straight lines—enlivening solid elevations with unlooked-for curves, dramatizing the bulk of an apartment house with a nipped-in waist, pitting masses against one another with irregular angles, calling for flat roofs with a certain pitch to them. By 1990, he had grown even more adventurous with the roofline, producing swooping variations that disciplined what might look at first glance like chaos. A secure sense of the architect in control coupled with a dazzling air of playfulness—of architecture as art—made his buildings provide a sense of naturalness, almost of inevitability. Few critics objected; his buildings were, in a word, likable.

A chronological look at Gehry's career shows a gratifying evolution. Born in Toronto in 1929 and moving with his family to Los Angeles in 1947, he progressively liberated himself from slavery to the unmitigated rectangle of the International Style without falling into the lighthearted games of uncommon colors and redundant balconies of postmodern designers. If his plans were startling, they were startling on architectural terms. "I used to be a symmetrical freak and a grid freak," he recalled in a confessional mood. "I used to follow grids and then I started to think and I realized that those were chains, that Frank Lloyd Wright was chained to the 30–60 grid, and there was no freedom in it for him." And freedom was precisely what he wanted for himself. He was, then, ready for Krens, and Krens, once the museum was in place, testified, "The thing about Bilbao is the surprise of it."

Surprise was the right response to my first viewing; the museum at Bilbao is a succession of architectural thrills. Greatly impressed with Frank Lloyd Wright's atrium in the New York Guggenheim, surrounded by an ever-rising rotund ribbon from which, walking along, the visitor may enjoy the pictures fairly close up, Krens had hoped for a similar effect in Spain. The New York Guggenheim had been a major conversation piece in the late 1950s and was still fascinating in the 1990s; it was, after all, almost outlandishly different from other museums. There was, for Krens, no reason why Bilbao might not follow suit. Gehry was perfectly willing to produce an impressive atrium, but not a copy of Wright's. The Fifth Avenue original, he told Krens, "was antithetical to the art."

Hence he designed a tall central hall rising over 150 feet from floor to ceiling that lets visitors look up to the complex roof, or to the stylish glassed-in elevators that take them to the second and third floors. Light pours in everywhere from strategically placed windows and the skylights on the roof, providing a welcome air of buoyancy. Off to the side I could see the largest, longest gallery. That room was, at the time of my stay, featuring the skillfully arranged if aesthetically awkward historical survey of the motorcycle, an exhibition on loan from the Guggenheim headquarters in New York. It looked as though most of the visitors in that hall were young Spaniards who had dragged their more or less reluctant girlfriends along to get a close look at the fascinating exhibits.

Whenever I shifted my spot, only moving some three or four feet, I discovered a different assortment of curves, of weight-bearing, slightly twisted pillars, of curved internal bridges, of enticing balconies, all of them enlivened by museumgoers wandering about the spaces. Gehry designed two sets of three straightforward rectangular galleries devoted to a permanent exhibition of modern paintings, taking their old-fashioned shape as right for the kind of established modernist art shown there. But eleven galleries designed for temporary exhibitions were adventurously distinct from one another. There are, as I have said, many surprises at Bilbao—most, perhaps all, of them agreeable.

The exterior provides still other surprises. The museum backs on the Nervion River, a landscape visible from many of the windows. Its front faces the town, a local museum, and the university. And from certain streets, the Bilbao Guggenheim rises up as a harmonious, if highly unorthodox, pile, with the hills behind it as a sober backdrop. The dense, jumbled diversity of shapes awakens the viewer's imagination: the museum looks from one perspective as though a massive airplane had hit a large building and been left in place; from another it seems to show a group of richly curved buildings rather carelessly shoved together by a giant's hand. The whole, especially at first glance, seems something of a puzzle, inviting art lovers to proceed and look, and look. What can this odd sculpture mean?

The word "sculpture" is deliberate. Gehry has used the tantalizing phrase "expressionist architecture" to depict his more recent work, and his designs amply support his description as an artist. He has acknowledged that "crossing the line between architecture and sculpture is something that's been difficult for me." Crossing the line—here, in this tearing down of boundaries, is another witness to Gehry's modernist cast of mind. Interestingly, he has never defined the respective domains of the two, but in his architectural work he has manifestly brought them together.

This does not mean that he has ever lost the architect's craftsman-like concentration on his commissions. Gehry has been well known in the profession for his intimate relationship with clients, doing research into each client's intentions, and fostering the exchange of ideas between builder and customer. Talking about Bilbao after completing the assignment in 1997, he said with feeling, "I love to go back to Bilbao. They're all part of my family now." How much this means becomes evident when we remember Mies van der Rohe's condescending, even contemptuous attitude toward the Tugendhats when he designed a house for them in the late 1920s. Gehry's contrasting manner proves that there is no reason why a modernist master must keep so much distance from his clients.

It has been typical of Gehry to turn to artists for company and cooperation and to art for ideas and incentives. Discussing a vacation house he designed for one of his favorite clients, the advertising executive Jay Chiat, he noted that "our inspiration was Duchamp's painting," the celebrated *Nude Descending a Staircase, No. 2*, shown in the New York Armory Show. This glance back to that vastly influential exhibition of 1913, which acquainted thousands with the latest European aesthetic rebels, illustrates the longevity of the first American experience with modernist art. And Gehry made friends with the Pop sculptors Claes Oldenburg and his wife, Coosje van Bruggen, involving them in several of his commissions. In a word, he prepared himself to be a sculptor without abandoning architecture. It was my sense of being in the hands of an artist who had not abandoned his dominant professional allegiance that made my stay at Bilbao unforgettable, and prepared me for the study you have before you.

2.

WHAT, IF ANYTHING, can Bilbao do for modernism and its possible revival in years to come? I cannot safely offer confident predictions. I am a historian, not a prophet, and must leave the future to the future. Still, enough evidence has been marshaled in the preceding pages to suggest that the array of modernist acts I have offered adds up to a historical period, complete with its times of prosperity and disruption, self-confidence and self-denigration. It dates roughly from the early 1840s to the early 1960s, from Baudelaire and Flaubert to Beckett and beyond to Pop Art and other dangerous blessings. During these decades, it survived two world wars and the murderous hostility of totalitarian regimes; again and again found new unconventional masters, whether in sculpture or the novel, to shock the shockable; and moved its headquarters from Paris to New York. To venture greater precision is to ignore the imprecision of the boundaries that attend every period.* We obviously cannot delight in innovative poems not yet written, or innovative museums not yet built; meanwhile, we celebrate García Márquez's long productivity and Frank Gehry's mastery of the computer, and have at least some reason to hope for more of the same.

From this wary perspective, I venture to suggest that for all the modernists' original verve, all their energetic recklessness expended to combat the conservative establishments in the arts—all of those tiresome works whether written, painted, designed, or composed—a fullfledged revival of their crusades is not very likely. Instead, we may expect a full recognition that modernism has become a secure part of our historical past, as interesting as any other cultural period that we have put behind us. It has become an age whose dimensions we recognize and whose accomplishments we value. Some of its most impressive products are now taught as our patrimony in schools and universities—Virginia Woolf's *To the Lighthouse*, James Joyce's *Ulysses*, Edvard Munch's *The Scream*, Paul Cézanne's studies of Mont Sainte-Victoire, Walter Gropius's Bauhaus in Dessau, Samuel Beckett's *Waiting for Godot*, T. S. Eliot's *Waste Land*, Orson Welles's *Citizen Kane*, and other classics that continue to provide pleasure as intense if not as thrilling as they gave their first audiences.

The principal reason for the tentativeness of this forecast is the democratization of culture that has pervaded Western civilization, beginning after the French Revolution. We have seen that modernism is not a democratic ideology. But this does not make it necessarily incompatible with democratic politics. Free speech, a free press, a wide suffrage, a tolerant culture do not automatically damage or discredit the supremacy of the elite essential to avant-garde literature and the arts, the sufficient numbers of individuals and committed groups to promote concerts of difficult composers, exhibitions of difficult

---

* Thus the art historian T. J. Clark has stated, with what seems to me unwarranted precision, that his book *Farewell to an Idea* "was written after the Fall of the Wall. That is, at a moment when there was general agreement, on the part of masses and elites in most of the world, that the project called socialism had come to an end—at roughly the same time, it seems, as the project called modernism."

painters, printing of difficult poets and novelists, clients for difficult architects, even consumers for difficult movies.*

The survival of distinct audiences for high culture, the most conspicuous element in democratization, has made the future of modernism only too precarious. For, with the rapidly advancing technology of entertainment listed earlier—recordings, radio, color illustrations, talking movies, television, computer innovations—the commercial manufacture of culture has become ever more influential an activity. It is not, as conservative cultural critics have maintained, that culture has been commodified: it has always had a commercial angle to it, even among the ancient Greeks and Romans. But the sophistication of the cultural trades, the ease and speed of communications that are of particular interest to the middle classes, have encouraged compromises that cannot help but favor the marginalization of future avant-gardes. We live in an age of musical comedies.

IT WAS CLEAR from the beginning that modernism could establish itself as a powerful cultural phenomenon only when economic, political, and cultural conditions were supportive. History shows that these conditions developed in this favorable direction from mid-nineteenth century on. Concretely, this means that modernism lived off adventures, and it was triumphant mainly because these conditions were congruent for perhaps a century or more—if repeatedly diverted by war, intermittent religious revivals, and the wrecks left by fascism and communism. Yet the old Duchampian claim that anything can be art, the dream that Pop Art turned into reality, has been more destructive of modernism than the more obvious challenges.

There may indeed be a revival of massive modernism some day. Considering the fiction of a García Márquez and the architecture of a Frank Gehry, we can imagine artists not yet known, perhaps even not yet born, who may provide a new birth of life after death. There have been some

* As Dwight Macdonald has written in his famous assault on bourgeois culture, as it were reminding himself of an important proviso: "From *Tom Jones* to the films of Chaplin, some very good things have been popular."

brilliant moments in the history of modernism that invite us to speculate about similar possible moments in the future: the virtually simultaneous publication of Flaubert's *Madame Bovary* and Baudelaire's *Les Fleurs du mal* in 1857; the sensational memorial exhibition of Cézanne at the Salon d'Automne in 1907, which made him famous almost overnight; the explosion of Dada at the Cabaret Voltaire in Zurich on February 5, 1916. Whether the fantasies about a repetition of such events will ever come true is beyond my competence to foresee. At the very least we can say that modernism has had a hundred and twenty years to throw its products—often exquisite and always new—onto the cultural market, providing confusion, astonishment, and delight. It has had a good long run.

NOTES

A CLIMATE FOR MODERNISM

4   *"as I would like to do in paint"*: Henri Matisse to Pierre Bonnard, in Elizabeth Cowling et al., *Matisse/Picasso* (MOMA, 2003), 292.

6   *"bourgeoisophobus"*: Gustave Flaubert to Louis Bouilhet, December 26, 1852, in *Correspondance*, ed. Jean Bruneau, 5 vols. (1973–), II, 217.

6   *"Antiborghese"*: Emily Braun, *Mario Sironi and Italian Modernism: Art and Politics Under Fascism* (2000), 50.

7   *"the magic inherent in the universe"*: Oldenburg in Dore Ashton, "Monuments for Nowhere and Anywhere," *L'Art vivant* (July 1970), repr. in *Idea Art*, ed. Gregory Battcock (1973), 12.

12   *"deplorably dull"*: For these comments quoted and summarized, see G. Bernard Shaw, *The Quintessence of Ibsenism* (1891; ed. 1912), 3–4.

12   *"for any young poet to imagine"*: T. S. Eliot, Introduction, *Literary Essays of Ezra Pound* (1954), xiii.

13   *"a Christmas present"*: See Werner Hofmann, *Turning Points in Twentieth-Century Art 1890–1917*, trans. Charles Kessler (1969), 18.

13   *"necropolises of art"*: Camille Pissarro to Lucien Pissarro, in Theodore Reff, "Copyists in the Louvre, 1850–1870," *Art Bulletin*, XLVI (December 1964), 553n.

13   *"Ecole des Beaux-Arts"*: Paul Gauguin to Emil Schuffenecker, October 8, 1888, in Paul Gauguin, *The Writings of a Savage*, ed. Daniel Guérin, trans. Eleanor Levieux (1996), 24.

13   *"utilitarian acts of cowardice"*: F. T. Marinetti, *Manifeste initiale du Futurisme*, *Le Figaro*, February 20, 1909, in Jean-Pierre de Villiers, ed., *Le premier manifeste du futurisme* (1986), 51.

14   The *"perspiring philistine"*: Robert Louis Stevenson, "Walking Tours," *Essays by Robert Louis Stevenson*, ed. William Lyon Phelps (1918), 32.

15 *Picasso should have "failed to advance"*: Piet Mondrian, "Toward the True Vision of Reality" (1941) in *Plastic Art and Pure Plastic Art and Other Essays*, ed. Robert Motherwell (1951), 10.

16 *"the void of modern art"*: Salvador Dali, *The Secret Life of Salvador Dalí*, in Francine Prose, "Gala Dalí," *The Lives of the Muses: Nine Women and the Artists They Inspired* (2002), 198.

16 *"the natural friends of the arts"*: Charles Baudelaire, "Salon de 1846," *Oeuvres complètes*, ed. Y.-G. Le Dantec, rev. Claude Pichois (1961), 874–75.

16 *"those who would pluck it"*: Guillaume Apollinaire, "La Jolie Rousse," *Calligrammes, poèmes de la paix et de la guerre (1913–1916)* (1966), 184.

19 *"no home in Europe but Paris"*: Friedrich Nietzsche, *Ecce Homo* (1908), *Werke*, ed. Karl Schlechta, 3 vols. in 5 (6th rev. ed. 1969), II, 1090.

20 *"enriched by commerce and trade"*: Memoir of Sir Charles Eastlake, in Charles Locke Eastlake, *Contributions to the Literature of the Fine Arts*, 2nd ser. (1870), 147.

24 *"by means of education"*: Alfred Lichtwark, "Publikum," *Erziehung des Auges: ausgewählte Schriften*, ed. Eckhard Schaar (1991), 25.

26 *"the most diverse educational paths"*: Ibid., 26.

27 *well, a new age*: Holbrook Jackson, *The Eighteen Nineties* (1913), 22.

PART ONE: FOUNDERS

CHAPTER 1: PROFESSIONAL OUTSIDERS

34 *"external to the artist and the artist himself"*: Charles Baudelaire, "Salon de 1859," *Oeuvres complètes*, ed. Y.-G. Le Dantec, rev. Claude Pichois (1961), 1099.

34 *"the feeling I attach to it"*: Ibid., 1076.

36 *these "new lips"*: Ibid., *Les Fleurs du mal* (1857), 140.

37 "mon semblable—mon frère!": Ibid., 6.

37 *"the heroism of* modern life": Charles Baudelaire, "The Painter of Modern Life," ibid., 1155.

38 *"the most widely read poet in France today"*: Edna St. Vincent Millay, Preface to *Baudelaire, Flowers of Evil*, trans. and ed. Millay and George Dillon (1936; ed. 1962), xxx.

38 *"which is the first of all qualities"*: Flaubert to Baudelaire, July 13 (1857), in Flaubert, *Correspondance*, ed. Jean Bruneau, 5 vols. (1973–), II, 744.

39 *"devils, fetuses, demons, cats, and vermin"*: Gustave Bourdin, *Le Figaro*, July 5, 1857, in Enid Starkie, *Baudelaire* (1957; ed. 1971), 364–65.

39 *"its niceties of language"*: Flaubert to Baudelaire, July 13 (1857), in Flaubert, *Correspondance*, II, 74.

40 *"the manner in which they are treated"*: Baudelaire, "M. Gustave Flaubert, Madame Bovary—La Tentation de Saint Antoine" (1857), *Oeuvres complètes,* 652.

40 *"in tune with 'The Nature of Things'"*: C. K. Stead, *The New Poetry: Yeats to Eliot* (1964; ed. 1967), 145.

42 *"to assert its* necessity": T. S. Eliot, "Baudelaire" (1930), Eliot in *Selected Prose,* ed. John Hayward (1953), 187.

48 *"supreme Scholar!"*: *I Promise to Be Good: The Letters of Arthur Rimbaud;* trans. and ed. Wyatt Mason (2003), 33.

49 *"The very heart of today"*: Wilde, quoted in Richard Ellmann, *Oscar Wilde* (1988), 169.

53 *"useful place in a home is the latrine"*: Théophile Gautier, *Mademoiselle de Maupin* (1835–36), ed. Geneviève van den Bogaert (1966), 45.

54 *"aspires toward the condition of music"*: Walter Pater, "The School of Giorgione," *Studies in the History of the Renaissance* (1873), 111.

54 *"by her mother to a young girl"*: A. C. Swinburne, *Notes on Poems and Ballads* (1866; with *Atalanta in Calydon,* ed. Morse Peckham, 1970), 338.

54 *"must follow him"*: "Spiritual Contents in Painting," *Die Grenzboten.*

57 the Master's *"precious relics"* had been preserved: Eduard Hanslick, *Aus meinem Leben,* 2 vols. (1894; 4th ed. 1911), 265–66.

58 *"Amen. Amen"*: From the last speech of Louis Dubedat, George Bernard Shaw, *The Doctor's Dilemma: A Tragedy* (1906), Act 4.

58 *"the future attitudes of the general populace"*: See Emily Braun, *Mario Sironi and Italian Modernism: Art and Politics Under Fascism* (2000), 92.

59 *"every trick learned from his masters"*: William Butler Yeats, *The Trembling of the Veil* (1922), in *Autobiography* (1965), 93.

60 *"One or the other has to go"*: Ellmann, *Oscar Wilde* (1987), 581.

61 *"Little Nell without laughing"*: Ada Leverson's recollection of Wilde's best known bon mot, endlessly recited in the literature—ibid., 469.

61 a *"long and lovely suicide"*: Wilde to H. C. Marillier (December 12, 1885), in *The Complete Letters of Oscar Wilde,* ed. Merlin Holland and Rupert Hart-Davis (1962; ed. 2000), 272.

61 *"believe in their probability"*: Wilde, "The Decay of Living," in *Intentions* (1891), quoted in *The Artist as Critic: Critical Writings of Oscar Wilde,* ed. Richard Ellmann (1969), 294.

62 *"is the object of living"*: Wilde, "Note" (New York Public Library, Berg Collection), in Ellmann, *Oscar Wilde,* 310.

62 *"some deliberate artistic composition"*: Yeats, *Trembling of the Veil,* 90.

66 *"the bovine rage of the Philistine"*: Ernest Newman, "Oscar Wilde: A Literary Appreciation," *Free Review,* June 1, 1895, in *Oscar Wilde: The Critical Heritage,* ed. Karl Beckson, (1970), 90.

67 *"Victorianism was ready to pounce"*: Ellmann, *Oscar Wilde*, 431.

67 *"our view of things"*: St. James's *Gazette*, editorial, May 27, 1895.

68 *"Books are well written or badly written"*: Wilde, *The Picture of Dorian Gray* (1891), vii.

68 *"decision half of his renown"*: Yeats, *Trembling of the Veil*, 192.

CHAPTER 2: IRRECONCILABLES AND IMPRESARIOS

70 *"absolutely no use for the masses"*: Claude Debussy, *Monsieur Croche the Dilettante Hater* (1927), trans. B. N. Langdon Davies (1928), 66.

71 *"a monstrosity—bazaar, music hall"*: Camille Pissarro to Lucien Pissarro (April 21, 1900), in Camille Pissarro, *Letters to His Son Lucien*, ed. John Rewald (1944; 3rd rev. ed. 1972), 340.

72 *"great moral depravity"*: Jean-Léon Gérôme in Kirk Varnedoe, *Gustave Caillebotte* (1987), 198, 201.

72 *with unhealthy and decadent art*: Hervey de Saisy in ibid., 209.

77 *"has been too much neglected"*: Eugène Boudin, in François Mathey, *The Impressionists* (1961), trans. Jean Steinberg (1961), 237.

79 *"in the history of modern art"*: Renato Poggioli, *The Theory of the Avant-Garde* (1962), 132.

80 *taught in academies and studios alike*: Stephen F. Eisenman, "The Intransigent Artist *or* How the Impressionists Got Their Name," in Charles S. Moffett with Ruth Berson et al., eds., *The New Painting: Impressionism 1874–1886* (1986), 53.

80 *"I don't give a damn"*: Phoebe Pool, *Impressionism* (1967), 52.

81 *"the expression of what I've experienced by myself"*: Monet to Frédéric Bazille, in Kermit Swiler Champa, *Studies in Early Impressionism* (1973), 23.

83 *the "vapid fineries"*: John Ruskin, *Modern Painters*, 5 vols. (ed. 1897), III, 59.

83 *"hope to advance to the first rank"*: Sir John Everett Millais, Bart., in *The Life and Letters of Sir John Everett Millais* by his son John Guille Millais, 2 vols. (1899), I, 380.

84 *"consequently suggestive of high culture"*: Charles W. Furse (1892), in Robert Jensen, *Marketing Modernism in Fin-de-Siècle Europe* (1944), 140.

84 *"on Boulevard Haussmann"*: *Alfred Sisley*, ed. Mary Anne Stevens (1992), 272.

85 *making more than 200,000 francs*: See Paul Hayes Tucker, *Claude Monet: Life and Art* (1995), 103, 134, 158.

87 *"the Irreconcilables"*: See Viola Hopkins Winner, *Henry James and the Visual Arts* (1970), 50.

91 *"included in the most beautiful collections"*: Paul Durand-Ruel, letter in *L'Evènement*, November 5, 1885, in Anne Distel, *Impressionism: The First Collectors*, trans. Barbara Perroud-Benson (1990), 23.

92 "*appeals with convincing force*": "The Ethics of Art," *Musical Times and Singing Class Circular*, XXX, May 1, 1889, 265.

92 "*the failure of thought*": Henry James, "Criticism" (1891), *Selected Literary Criticism*, ed. Morris Shapira (1963), 167–68.

95 "*into a work of art*": Gustav Pauli, Introduction to Alfred Lichtwark, *Briefe an die Kommission für die Verwaltung der Kunsthalle*, 2 vols. (1924), I, 13.

95 "*and demand new achievements from them*": Alfred Lichtwark, "Museen als Bildungsstätte" (1903), *Erziehung des Auges*, 47.

96 "*aimed solely at the passing effect*": Lichtwark, *Briefe an die Kommission*, June 24, 1897 (from Brussels), I, 271.

97 "*we will not arrive at culture*": Ibid., June 26, 1892 (from Paris), I, 97.

97 "*its vanity and its narrow outlook*": Ibid., June 16, 1898 (from Paris), I, 322–23.

98 "*will remain the great survivors*": Ibid., 323.

99 "*distributed in Hamburg by the hundreds*": Ibid., April 24, 1897 (from Paris), I, 250–52.

PART TWO: CLASSICS

CHAPTER 3: PAINTING AND SCULPTURE

105 "*endowed with particular clearsightedness and sensibility*": Giorgio de Chirico, *Valori Plastici* (April–May 1919), in *Metaphysical Art*, ed. Carlo Carra et al. (1971), 91.

105 *famous or notorious*: In John C. G. Röhl, *Wilhelm II. Der Aufbau der Persönlichen Monarchie* (2001), 1025.

107 "*in politics that anarchy reigns*": Mary Cassatt to Louisine Havemeyer, September 6 and October 2, 1912, and March 1913, in Frances Weitzenhoffer, *The Havemeyers: Impressionism Comes to America* (1986), 207, 208, 210.

107 *denounced Matisse, as a swindler*: Arthur Schnitzler, *Tagebücher*, ed. Peter Michael Braunwarth et al., 10 vols. (1987–2000), *Tagebuch*, V, 17 (February 8, 1913); *Tagebuch*, III, 375 (December 21, 1908); *Tagebuch* IV, 321 (April 4, 1912).

109 "*shackled by the need of probability*": Gauguin, *Intimate Journals*, in Robert Goldwater, *Gauguin* (n.d.), 92.

110 "*I have tried to express*": Van Gogh, *Dear Theo: The Autobiography of Vincent van Gogh*, ed. Irving Stone with Jean Stone (1937; ed. 1995), 383–84.

111 "*than the photographer's*": Van Gogh to his sister Wilhelmina J. van Gogh, in *Complete Letters of Vincent van Gogh*, 3 vols. (1958; ed. 1978), III, 437.

112 "*ferocity of a productive egotism*": See Debora Silverman, *Van Gogh and Gauguin: The Search for Sacred Art* (2000), 5, and chap. 12.

112 "*being complete abstraction*": Gauguin to Emile Schuffenecker, in ibid., 262.

118 *"an exceptional painter"*: Ensor to Jules Du Jardin (October 6, 1899), *Lettres*, ed. Xavier Tricot (1999), 272.

119 *"angels which attended my cradle"*: J. P. Hodin, *Edvard Munch* (1972), 11.

120 *to develop . . . his inner turmoil to the full*: See Gerd Woll, "Angst findet man bei ihm überall," in *Munch, Liebe, Angst, Tod*, ed. Ulrich Weisner (1980), 315.

121 *"a kind of egotism"*: Munch to Eberhard Griesebach (1932), Richard Heller, "Edvard Munch, Die Liebe und die Kunst," ibid., 297.

122 *"naked individuality"*: Stanislaw Przybyszewski quoted in Wolfdietrich Rasch, "Edvard Munch und das literarische Berlin der neunziger Jahre," in *Edvard Munch: Probleme, Forschungen, Thesen*, ed. Henning Bock and Günter Busch (1973), 200.

125 *"is the classic of tomorrow"*: Elie Faure, Preface to exhibition catalog, in James D. Herbert, *Fauve Painting: The Making of Cultural Politics* (1992), 9.

126 *"which expresses the painter's experience"*: Louis de Marsalle [pseud. for E. L. Kirchner], "Über die Schweizer Arbeiten von E. L. Kirchner" (1921), in *E. L. Kirchners Davoser Tagebuch*, ed. Lothar Griesebach (1968), 196, 195.

129 *"also play a certain role in my art"*: See Gotthard Jedlicka, "Max Beckmann in seinen Selbstbildnissen," in *Blick auf Beckmann: Dokumente und Vorträge*, ed. Hans Martin Frhr. von Erffa and Erhard Göpel (1962), 112.

130 *"by universal law different from each other"*: Vasili Kandinsky, *Sturm Album* (1913), xv.

131 *"in its power to bestow happiness"*: Wilhelm Worringer, *Abstraction and Empathy* (1908), trans. Michael Bullock (3rd ed. 1910), 13.

131 *"stronger and more intense than ever"*: Hans K. Roethel, with Jean K. Benjamin, *Kandinsky* (1977; ed. 1979), 138.

132 *"let there also be a new romanticism"*: Kandinsky to Will Grohmann, November 21, 1925, in ibid., 116.

134 *"the seed of the future"*: Kandinsky, *On the Spiritual in Art* (1912), trans. Michael T. Sadler (1913), 2.

134 *"their mysteries rather than reveal them"*: Roethel, *Kandinsky*, 82.

136 *"the experience of objectlessness"*: Vladimir Malevich, *Die gegendstandlose Welt* (1927), passim.

138 *his back to the park's lush greenery*: Motherwell's verbal communication to the author, December 1968.

141 *"in accord with the spirit of modern times"*: Piet Mondrian, "Toward the True Vision of Reality" (1941), in *The New Art—The New Life: The Collected Writings of Piet Mondrian*, ed. and trans. Harry Holtzman and Martin S. James (1986), 338.

141 "a liberation from the oppression of the past": Piet Mondrian, "Plastic Art and Pure Plastic Art" (1936), in *Plastic Art and Pure Plastic Art and Other Essays*, ed. Robert Motherwell (1951), 42.

143 *"not the beginnings of art, but of disgust"*: Tristan Tzara in William S. Rubin, *Dada, Surrealism, and Their Heritage* (1968), 12.

143 *"a moral safety valve"*: Richard Huelsenbeck in ibid., 15.

143 *"useless and impossible to justify"*: Francis Picabia, in Hans Richter, *Dada: Art and Anti-Art* (1965), 76.

144 *"to establish the idiotic everywhere"*: Tzara, ibid., 67.

145 *except for seeing . . . as Dadaists revived*: Harold Rosenberg, "Pro-Art Dada: Jean Arp," *The De-Definition of Art: Action Art to Pop to Earthworks* (1972), 80.

145 *"that lamentable expedient which is painting"*: André Breton, *Surrealism and Painting* (1965), ed. and trans. Simon Watson Taylor (1972), 6.

146 *"the undirected play of thought"*: Breton, *Surrealist Manifesto* (1924), in William S. Rubin, *Dada, Surrealism, and Their Heritage* (1968), 64.

146 *"in provoking an emotional shock"*: James Thrall Soby, *René Magritte* (1965), 9.

148 the *"capital importance of his intervention"*: Breton, "René Magritte," *Surrealism and Painting*, 270.

149 he wished to *"assassinate painting"*: See Fundacio Joan Miró, *Guidebook*, ed. Rosa Maria Malet (1999), 55.

149 *"and an atrocious egoism"*: Orwell in Hilton Kramer, "Dalí" (1970), in *The Age of the Avant-garde: An Art Chronicle of 1956–1972* (1973), 251.

149 *"association of delicious phenomena"*: Breton, "Salvator Dalí: The Dalí Case," *Surrealism and Painting*, 133–34.

151 *in a feverish creative rush . . . between March and early May 1933*: See *Picasso for Vollard*, intro. Hans Bollinger, trans. Norbert Guterman (1957), xi.

152 *"under what circumstances"*: Brassaï [pseud. Gyula Halsz], *Picasso and Company* (1964), trans. Francis Price (1966), 100.

153 *"It makes me do what it wants"*: Pierre Daix, *Picasso* (1965), 250.

159 *"It would be crude"*: Richard Penrose, "Beauty and the Monster," in Daniel Kahnweiler et al., *Picasso 1881–1973* (1973), 181.

165 *"It helped liberate me completely from the past"*: Duchamp in Pierre Cabanne, *Dialogues with Pierre Cabanne* (1964), trans. Ron Padgett (1971), 31.

167 *"of my being with anyone else"*: Calvin Tomkins, *Duchamp: A Biography* (1996), 267.

167 *"the great 'saboteur'"*: Robert Motherwell, Introduction to *Dialogues with Pierre Cabanne*, 12.

169 *"Copy nature!"*: Matisse quoting Rodin, in Matisse, "Notes of a Painter, 1908," *Matisse on Art*, ed. Jack D. Flam (1973), 39.

169 *"a living and suggestive synthesis"*: Raymond Escholier, *Matisse from Life* (1956), trans. Geraldine and H. M. Colville (1960), 138.

170 *"both in number and in concept"*: David Smith, in a symposium on "The New Sculpture" (1952), quoted in *David Smith*, ed. Garrett McCoy (1973), 82.

170   *"Impressionism freed painting from chiaroscuro"*: Smith, "The Artist and Nature" (1955) in ibid., 119.

172   *"instead of emotional energies"*: Valentiner quoted in Andrew Causey, *Sculpture Since 1945* (1998), 27.

175   *"our greatest living sculptor"*: Smith, "The Artist and Nature," in *David Smith*, ed. McCoy, 118.

175   *"the real meaning of things"*: Sir Herbert Read, *Modern Sculpture: A Concise History* (1964), 187.

CHAPTER 4: PROSE AND POETRY

183   *"without that sympathy"*: Thomas Hardy, "The Science of Fiction," *New Review* (April 1891), 318.

184   *"and its authentic speech"*: Arthur Symons, Introduction, *The Symbolist Movement in Literature* (1899), 10.

185   *"Nothing happens"*: May Sinclair, "The Novels of Dorothy Richardson," a review of Dorothy Richardson's *Pilgrimage* (1915–38), *The Egoist* (April 1918), 58.

186   *"human character changed"*: Woolf, "Mr. Bennett and Mrs. Brown," 1924 lecture repr. in *The Captain's Death Bed and Other Essays* (1950), 91.

187   *"the glories of the British Empire"*: Ibid., 97.

187   *"the wrong ones for us to use"*: Ibid., 106.

187   *"the wrong way to set about it"*: Ibid., 106–07.

189   *"to exhaust so extensive a subject"*: Henry Fielding, *Tom Jones* (1749), Bk I, chap. 1.

192   *"all the unconscious life of the mind"*: From the title of Hamsun's essay, *From the Unconscious Life of the Mind* (1890).

192   *"the sweetest thing I've ever experienced"*: Arthur Schnitzler, "Leutnant Gustl" (1900), *Die erzählenden Schriften*, 2 vols. (1961), I, 357.

196   *"from which none of us can escape"*: Eliot, "Ulysses, Order and Myth," *The Dial* (November 1923), 480.

196   *"has a most goddam wonderful book"*: Ernest Hemingway to Sherwood Anderson, March 9, 1922, in Richard Ellmann, *James Joyce* (1959; rev. ed. 1982), 529.

196   appropriate to *"the present age"*: Eliot, "Ulysses, Order and Myth," 480.

197   *"I am sure he is wrong"*: Richard Aldington, "Mr. James Joyce's *Ulysses*," *Literary Studies and Reviews* (1924), 201.

198   *"But what a waste of energy!"*: Woolf, "Mr. Bennett and Mrs. Brown," *The Captain's Death Bed*, 109.

199   *"a great soft tiger cat"*: W. B. Yeats in Ellmann, *James Joyce*, 531.

199   *"Bowery slang and broken doggerel"*: James Joyce to Frank Budgen, March 20, 1920, in *Selected Letters*, ed. Richard Ellmann (1975), 250.

199 *"a half-demented man of genius"*: Middleton Murry in Ellmann, *James Joyce*, 531–32.

200 *"the nipple gets for the least thing"*: Molly Bloom's soliloquy in Joyce, *Ulysses* (1922), corrected text, ed. Hans Walter Gabler et al. (1986), 620.

201 *"and yes I said yes I will Yes"*: Ibid., 643–44.

202 *"which is contemporary history"*: Eliot, "Ulysses, Order and Myth," 483.

202 *"the epic of the human body"*: Joyce to Budgen, see Ellmann, *James Joyce*, 436.

203 *"putting in the thoughts between dashes"*: Woolf to Lytton Strachey, April 23, 1918, in *The Letters of Virginia Woolf*, 6 vols. (1975–80). Vol. II (*1912–1922*), ed. Nigel Nicolson and Joanne Trautman (1976), 234.

204 *"James would have seized it"*: Virginia Woolf, *To the Lighthouse* (1927; ed. 1937), 273–74.

206 *"in the field of night"*: Virginia Woolf, *Between the Acts* (1941), ed. Stella McNicol, intro. Gillian Beer (1992), 129.

207 *"to say something in my own voice"*: Woolf, July 26, 1922, *The Diary of Virginia Woolf*, ed. Anne Olivier Bell and Andrew MacNeillie, 5 vols. (1977–84), II, 186.

208 *"and then I don't write like that"*: Virginia Woolf to Roger Fry, May 6, 1922, in *Letters*, II, 525.

211 *"is that of the artist"*: Marcel Proust, *A la recherche du temps perdu* (1913–27; 3 vols. Pléîade ed. 1966), "Le Temps retrouvé," III, 895.

212 *"learned that I had lost her for ever"*: Ibid., "Sodome et Gomorrhe," II, 756.

213 *"The tears ran down her face"*: Woolf, *To the Lighthouse*, 268–69.

216 *"can only be lived, not described"*: Kafka, *Hochzeitsvorbereitungen auf dem Lande und andere Prosa aus dem Nachlass* (1953), 3rd Octavheft, 72.

216 *"Psychology is impatience"*: Ibid.

216 *"inaccessible to psychologists"*: Ibid., 8th Octavheft, 153.

217 *"you govern the world"*: Kafka, "Brief an den Vater," ibid., 169.

218 *all his life, his autobiography*: See Thomas Mann, "Homage," in Kafka, *The Castle*, trans. Edwin and Willa Muir (2nd ed. 1941), xi.

218 "Ich habe niemals die Regel erfahren": Kafka, "Fragmente." *Hochzeitsvorbereitungen*, 232.

219 *"has relegated everything else to the incidental"*: Kafka, August 6, 1914, *Tagebücher, 1910–23* (1951), 261.

221 *as a "resident alien"*: See Peter Ackroyd, *T. S. Eliot: A Life* (1984), 24.

221 *"only to be found in French"*: T. S. Eliot, "Yeats," *On Poetry and Poets* (1957), 252.

222 *"to the bottom of our entrails"*: Jules Laforgue, *Oeuvres complètes*, 8 vols., III: *Mélanges posthumes*, in *Selected Poems*, ed. Graham Dunstan Martin (1998), Introduction, xxiii.

222 *"the Lord High Chancellor of Analysis"*: Laforgue, "Sundays" [dernier vers], ibid., 229.

223 *"but let us say things in a subtle way"*: Laforgue to his sister, May 1883, in ibid., V, 21.

223 *"Oh, well"*: "Nous nous aimions comme deux foux / On s'est quitté sans en parler. / Un spleen me tenait exile / Et ce spleen venait de tout. Bon"—Laforgue, *Selected Poems*, 240.

223 *"She then, 'How you digress!'"*: T. S. Eliot, "Conversation Galante," *Prufrock and Other Observations* (1917), in *The Complete Poems and Plays of T. S. Eliot* (1952), 19.

224 *"Money in furs"*: Eliot, "Burbank with a Baedeker: Bleistein with a Cigar," *Poems* (1920), in ibid., 24.

225 *"its ambiguities, not its explanations"*: Ackroyd, *T. S. Eliot*, 127.

226 *"It is an erudite despair"*: Lawrence Rainey, *Revisiting the Waste Land* (2005), 110.

226 *"The climax of Eliot's 'infernal' vision"*: Northrop Frye, *T. S. Eliot* (1983; rev. ed. 1968), 72.

226 *"the pastness of the past, but of its presence"*: T. S. Eliot, "Tradition and the Individual Talent," *The Sacred Wood: Essays on Poetry and Criticism* (1920; 7th ed. 1950), 52.

227 *"or at least something different"*: Eliot, "Philip Massinger," ibid., 125.

227 *"and not in the history of the poet"*: Eliot, "Tradition and the Individual Talent," ibid., 59.

CHAPTER 5: MUSIC AND DANCE

232 *"music would be for, of, and by specialists"*: Milton Babbitt, "Who Cares If You Listen," Strunk's Source Readings in Music History, *The Twentieth Century*, ed. Robert P. Morgan (1950; rev. ed. 1998), 36.

233 *"a vague and high-flown charlatanism"*: Debussy, *Monsieur Croche the Dilettante Hater* (1927), trans. B. N. Langdon Davies (1928), 17.

234 *"the liberation of sound"*: Varèse in Robert P. Morgan, *Twentieth-Century Music* (1991), 312.

234 *"drown tonality"*: Edward Lockspeiser, *Debussy: His Life and Mind*, 2 vols. (1962; 2nd ed. 1966), I, 198.

235 *"the voice that speaks within him"*: Debussy, *Monsieur Croche*, 19.

235 *"and of my own ideas"*: Léon Vallas, *Claude Debussy: His Life and Works*, trans. Maire and Grave O'Brien (1933), 34.

235 *"a sinister farce"*: Ibid., 37.

236 *"the whims of dreams"*: Ibid., 35.

236 *"impossible to execute"*: Academy on Debussy, ibid., 41.

236 *"naked and unadorned"*: Ibid., 178.

236 *"M. Debussy"*: Ibid., 131.

237 *"the ghost of old Klingsor"*: Lockspeiser, *Debussy*, 91.

238 *"have her always discreet"*: Ibid., 84.

238   "*suffering for my masters*": Gustav Mahler to Friedrich Löhr (1882), in Jens Malte Fischer, *Gustav Mahler: Der fremde Vertraute* (2005), 149.

241   "*against the Creator*": Ibid., 200.

241   "*the* whole world *mirrors itself*": Mahler to Anna von Mildenburg, summer 1896, in ibid., 340.

241   "*to create my expressive means anew*": Ibid., 339.

241   "*concrete, everyday facts*": Strauss to Rolland, July 1905, in *Richard Strauss and Romain Rolland: Correspondence*, ed. Rollo Myers (1968), 29.

242   "*planets and suns circling*": Mahler to Willem Mengelberg, August 1906, in Fischer, *Gustav Mahler*, 635.

242   "*an instrument on which the universe is playing*": Mahler to Anna von Mildenburg, summer 1896, in ibid., 340.

242   "*until the greatest part was finished*": Mahler to his wife Alma, summer 1906, in ibid., 636–37.

243   "*of bearing this gigantic work*": Mahler to Natalie Bauer-Lechner, in ibid., 341.

243   "*leading into the other world*": Mahler to Max Marschalk (1896), in ibid., 637.

244   "*evil forces wrestling with one another*": Arnold Schoenberg to Mahler, December 1904, in ibid., 586.

246   "*only a creature of this imagination*": Schoenberg to Ferruccio Busoni, July 28, 1912, in *Arnold Schoenberg, Briefe*, selec. and ed. Erwin Stein (1956), 29.

246   "*she does what she pleases*": Schoenberg to Fritz Windisch, August 30, 1923, in ibid., 105.

246   "*the conscious will in art*'": Schoenberg to Vasili Kandinsky, January 24, 1911, in Fred Wasserman, "Schoenberg and Kandinsky in Concert," *Schoenberg, Kandinsky, and the Blue Rider*, ed. Esther da Costa-Meyer and Fred Wasserman (2002), 25.

246   "*organized fetters*": Schoenberg to Kandinsky, July 20, 1922, in *Briefe*, 70.

248   "*more and more as a major crime, as immoral*": Schoenberg to Hermann Scherchen, February 1, 1914, in *Briefe*, 45.

248   "*But I love distances*": Schoenberg to Josef Stransky, September 9, 1922, in ibid., 77.

249   "*that had to be said*": Schoenberg's response to congratulations on his seventy-fifth birthday, September 16, 1949, in ibid., 301.

249   "*through all the barriers of a past aesthetic*": Schoenberg, program note, early 1910, in Willi Reich, *Arnold Schoenberg, oder Der konservative Revolutionär* (1968; ed. 1974), 58.

249   "*stronger than any training*": See ibid.

250   "*My music must be* brief": Schoenberg to Busoni, August 1, 1909, in *Ferruccio Busoni, Selected Letters*, ed. Antony Beaumont (1987), 389.

251   "*sole support*": Schoenberg to Kandinsky, July 20, 1922, in *Briefe*, 70.

251   "*To learn how to pray!*": Schoenberg to Richard Dehmel, December 13, 1912, in ibid., 30.

252   "*today already belongs to music history*": Schoenberg to Emil Hertzka, March 7, 1910, in ibid., 18.

252   "*dislike of democracy and the like*": Schoenberg to Adolf Loos, August 5, 1924, in ibid., 126.

252   "*the mediocrity of the herd mind*": Debussy, *Monsieur Croche*, 32.

252   "*denied to most humans*": Schoenberg to Hermann Scherchen, February 1, 1914, in *Briefe*, 44.

253   "*for the next hundred years*": See Reich, *Arnold Schoenberg*, 139.

254   "*one must believe in one's own inspiration*": Schoenberg, "Composition with Twelve Tones," *Style and Idea: Selected Writings of Arnold Schoenberg*, ed. Leonard Stein (1950; 2nd ed. 1975), 218.

257   "*that great personality*": Igor Stravinsky, *An Autobiography* (1936), 28; though largely ghostwritten, this book remains a useful source for Stravinsky's views.

258   "*was colossal and increasing*": Stravinsky to Vladimir Rimsky-Korsakov, June 16/29, 1911, in Stephen Walsh, *Stravinsky. A Creative Spring: Russia and France, 1882–1934* (1999), 163.

258   "*Its form possesses complete freedom*": Alfred Bruneau in ibid.

259   "*solely to the score*": Stravinsky, *Autobiography*, 29.

260   "If I want to, I can": Walsh, *Stravinsky*, 198.

260   "*different from my other works*": Ibid., 312.

262   "*and subordination before God*": Ibid., 504.

265   "*can keep up with thought*": Varèse in Morgan, *Twentieth-Century Music*, 306–07.

265   "*handwriting in much of his works*": John Cage, "Edgard Varèse" (1958), in Cage, *Silence, Lectures and Writings* (1961), 85.

266   "*but the ones that have not been done*": David Revill, *The Roaring Silence: John Cage, a Life* (1992), 13.

266   "*more beautiful than listening to music*": Ibid., 123.

267   "*the tyranny of the major and minor system*": Busoni in Morgan, *Twentieth-Century Music*, 36.

268   "*the first modern architecnologist of our time*": Stravinsky on Schoenberg in Charles M. Joseph, *Stravinsky Inside Out* (2001), 248.

271   "*that I could eliminate*": See Charles M. Joseph, *Stravinsky and Balanchine: A Journey of Invention* (2002), 74.

275   "*really awesome*": Ibid., 257.

275   "*our beautiful, beautiful score*": Ibid., 256.

278   "*his most subtle studies of male-female relations*": Anna Kisselgoff, *New York Times*, January 7, 1999, in Joseph, *Stravinsky and Balanchine*, 337.

280   "*He is his time*": Agnes De Mille, *Martha: The Life and Work of Martha Graham: A Biography* (1956; ed. 1991), 126.

CHAPTER 6: ARCHITECTURE AND DESIGN

284 *"appalling poverty of artistic production"*: Gramsci in *Antonio Sant'Elia*, ed. Dore Ashton and Guido Ballo (1986), 13.

284 *"start again from the beginning"*: Boccioni in ibid., 28.

284 *"and Cubist drawing"*: George Heard Hamilton, *Painting and Sculpture in Europe, 1880–1940* (1964), 184.

285 *"burning passion for the coming-into-being of things"*: Marinetti (1911), in *Antonio Sant'Elia*, 17.

286 *"the cathedrals, the palaces, the podiums"*: Sant'Elia in ibid., 23.

287 *"live and work in the present"*: C. E. Annesley Voysey, *Studio*, I (1894), 234.

288 *"if you take it as you ought"*: Frank Lloyd Wright to Catherine and Kenneth Baxter, February 7, 1921, in Robert C. Twombly, *Frank Lloyd Wright: An Interpretive Biography* (1973), 236.

289 *"There's nothing more important than architecture"*: Johnson in Charles Jencks, *Modern Movements in Architecture* (1973), 50.

290 *"the only future of art and craft"*: Wright, "The Art and Craft of the Machine" (1901), in Twombly, *Frank Lloyd Wright*, 46.

290 *"all manner of structural gymnastics"*: Ibid.

291 *"jig-sawed beams and braces"*: Wright, *An Autobiography* (1932; 2nd ed. 1943), 150.

291 *"is like a huge machine"*: *Antonio Sant'Elia*, 27.

291 *"physical and spiritual fulfillment"*: Ada Louise Huxtable, *Frank Lloyd Wright: A Penguin Life* (2004), 27.

293 *"from inside out"*: Twombly, *Frank Lloyd Wright*, 66.

293 *"to the successful use of the machine"*: Wright, *Autobiography*, 142.

293 *"dining, reading, receiving callers"*: Ibid.

294 who favored woman suffrage: See Leonard K. Eaton, *Two Chicago Architects and Their Clients: Frank Lloyd Wright and Howard Van Doren Shaw* (1969), 38, and 81, 85.

295 *In the three years . . . he completed only six buildings*: See Twombly, *Frank Lloyd Wright*, 113.

297 *"leaves, mist, clouds, and sky"*: Huxtable, *Frank Lloyd Wright*, 209.

297 *"that the twenty-first century is still absorbing"*: Ibid., 244.

298 *"insulation, function, or internal activity"*: Mumford in Jencks, *Modern Movements*, 96.

300 a *"struggle against existing conditions"*: Hermann Muthesius, "Die Bedeutung des Kunstgewerbes" (1907), in Peter Gay, *Art and Act: On Causes in History: Manet, Gropius, Mondrian* (1976), 114.

302 was *"liberating in so many ways"*: Huxtable, letter to the author, March 12, 2001.

304 *"we should treat our clients as children"*: Mies van der Rohe in Gay, *Art and Act*, 142.

304 *built in the shape that Mies had designed for it*: Tugendhat (son of the owners of the house and a professor of philosophy at the Freie Universität Berlin) in conversation with the author, mid-1960s.

305 *"a machine for living in"*: Le Corbusier, *Towards a New Architecture* (1923), trans. Frederick Etchells (1927), 10.

305 *"there has been a Revolution"*: Ibid., 13.

305 "neither the artisan nor the intellectual": Ibid., 14.

306 *"There exists a new spirit"*: Ibid., 84, 12.

309 *"Massacre on the waterfront"*: Twombly, *Wright*, 276.

313 *"the glory of its architecture"*: Lewis Mumford, "Skin Treatment and New Wrinkles" (1954), in *From the Ground Up: Observations on Contemporary Architecture, Housing, Highway Building, and Civic Design* (1956), 96.

314 *"the small circle of the affluent"*: Walter Gropius, "Tradition und Kontinuität in der Architektur," *Apollo in der Demokratie* (1967), in Gay, *Art and Act*, 115.

314 *"putting themselves into a straitjacket"*: Ibid., 52.

314 modern *"mass civilization"*: Gropius, "Der stilbildende Wert industrieller Bauformen," *Der Verkehr, Jahrbuch des Deutschen Werkbundes* (1914), 29–32.

315 *"a radical solution to our problems"*: Gropius to James Marston Fitch, in conversation. See Peter Gay, *Weimar Culture* (1968), 9.

316 *"an arrogant barrier between craftsmen and artists"*: Gropius, Manifesto for opening of the Bauhaus, April 1919, in Hans Wingler, *Das Bauhaus 1919–1933: Weimar, Dessau, Berlin* (1962), 39.

316 *"the architectonic spirit"*: Ibid.

317 *"an architecture whose function is clear"*: Ibid.

320 *"and I collect the apples"*: Quoted in Erwin Panofsky, "Three Decades of Art History in the United States: Impressions of a Transplanted European," *College Art Journal*, 14 (Autumn 1954), 16.

322 Their *"stimulating and challenging"* critiques: Gropius interview with the author, July 1968.

322 *"originates always with the individual"*: Walter Gropius, *Four Great Makers of Modern Architecture: Gropius, Le Corbusier, Mies, Wright* (1961), 227.

323 *"the house is decidedly European"*: Nancy Curtis, *Gropius House*, in Reginald Isaacs, *Gropius: An Illustrated Biography of the Creator of the Bauhaus* (1983; ed. 1986), 232.

324 *"must always be considered as an integral unit"*: Quoted in Edward Lucie-Smith, *Furniture: A Concise History* (1979), 162.

324 *"the whole should produce a symphony"*: Bahr in Eduard F. Sekler, *Josef Hoffmann. The Architectural Work* (1985), 33.

326 *"that does not recognize this"*: Nikolaus Pevsner, *Pioneers of Modern Design: From William Morris to Walter Gropius* (1936; rev. ed. 1960), 26.

327　*"the people who want to Americaniʒe France"*: Roger Ginsburger, "Was ist Modern?" (1931), in *Die Form: Stimmen des Deutschen Werkbundes 1925–1934*, ed. Ulrich Conrads et al. (1969), 70.

328　*"other than what we saw every day"*: Hoffmann, lecture on February 22, 1911, in *Josef Hoffmann Designs*, ed. Peter Noever (1992), 231.

328　*"and all that tastelessness"*: *"dem thatenlosen Schlendrian, dem starren Byʒantinismus, and allem Ungeschmack"*—the not so vivid phrase in the text is as close a rendition as it is possible to give. Koloman Moser, "Mein Werdegang," *Vielhagen und Klasings Monatshefte*, X (1916), 255.

329　*"artists and artisans on the project"*: Jane Kallir, *Viennese Design and the Wiener Werkstätte* (1985), 54.

330　*"a long way behind our ancestors"*: Ibid., 29.

331　*"can only gratify the parvenu"*: Josef Hoffmann and Koloman Moser, *Arbeitsprogramm der Wiener Werkstätte von 1903–1932*, Ausstellung des Bundesministeriums für Unterricht (1967), 21–22.

331　*modish copies will satisfy only the newly rich*: See ibid.

334　*"a machine—to live in"*: J. J. P. Oud, "Ja und Nein: Bekenntnisse eines Architekten," *Europa Almanack 1925* (1925; ed. 1993), 18.

CHAPTER 7: DRAMA AND MOVIES

336　*"to the spirit of these days"*: Bärbel Reissmann, "Das Lessing-Theater," in Ruth Freydank et al., *Theater als Geschäft, Berlin und seine Privattheater um die Jahrhundertwende* (1985), 127.

337　*"nothing but a magnifying glass"*: Goll in Martin Esslin, *The Theatre of the Absurd* (1961), 268.

337　*"is a great imaginative writer"*: Freud, "Mit seiner Geschlossenheit, Einheit, Vereinfachung der Probleme, mit seiner Kunst der Konzentration, und des Verdeckens . . ." *Protokolle der Wiener Psychoanalytischen Vereinigung*, 4 vols., II, 1908–1910, ed. Herman Nunberg and Ernst Federn (1967; ed. 1977), 174.

339　*"happy to get some new ones with you"*: Jarry in Roger Shattuck, *The Banquet Years* (1958), 167.

339　*had helped Jarry with the scenery*: See Esslin, *Theatre of the Absurd*, 261.

341　*"the true dadas are against Dada"*: Tzara in Tomkins, *Duchamp*, 191.

343　*"organiʒed insanity"*: Ibid., 190.

344　*"the most modern of moderns"*: O'Neill in James McFarlane, "Intimate Theatre: Maeterlinck to Strindberg," in *Modernism: A Guide to European Literature, 1890–1930*, ed. Malcolm Bradbury and James McFarlane (1976; ed. 1991), 326.

346　*"immobility of the soul"*: Strindberg, Preface, *Miss Julie* (1888), *Miss Julie and Other Plays*, trans. and ed. Michael Robinson (1998), 59–60.

347　*"these uncertain tales"*: Author's note to *A Dream Play* (1901), ibid., 176.

347 *"that is what they are"*: Olof Lagercrantz, *August Strindberg*, trans. Anselm Hollo (1979), 160, 169.

349 *"I'll always get another chapter for my novel!"*: Ibid., 247.

349 *"to disrupt it"*: Ibid., 91.

349 *"is one long autobiography"*: Robert Brustein, "August Strindberg," *The Theatre of Revolt: An Approach to the Modern Drama* (1964), 88.

351 *"to bring them to conviction of sin"* George Bernard Shaw, "Epistle Dedicatory," *Man and Superman* (1903).

355 *"the renewal of humankind"*: Georg Kaiser, "Vision und Figur," *Das neue Deutschland*, vol. I, no. 10 (1918).

356 *"none of us should dare to renounce their achievement"*: B. J. Kenworthy, *Georg Kaiser* (1957), xix.

356 "Privatkurage": Carl Sternheim, "Privatcourage" (1924), in *Gesamtausgabe*, ed. Wilhelm Emrich, 10 vols. (1963–76), VI, 309.

360 *"the features of the outer man"*: Julia Margaret Cameron, "Annals of My Glass House" (a fragment of autobiography), in Mike Weaver, *Julia Margaret Cameron, 1815–1879* (1984), 157.

363 *"the most important of all the arts"*: David A. Cook, *A History of Narrative Film* (1981; 4th ed. 2004), 115.

364 *"the machine and the human ideal"*: Liam O'Leary, *The Silent Cinema* (1965), epigraph.

366 *"have I seen such concise misinformation"*: Thorstein Veblen in Cook, *History of Narrative Film*, 66.

366 *made millions for the studio*: See ibid., 64.

367 *"A revelation"*: Sergei Eisenstein, "Dickens, Griffith, and the Film Today," *Film Form* (1956), trans. Jay Leyda (1957), 201.

369 *had risen to 26 million a week*: Cook, *History of Narrative Film*, 32.

373 *"an intense release of creative energy"*: Ibid., 128.

374 *"creative remolding of nature"*: Eisenstein, *Film Form*, 5.

377 *"it only takes two seconds to earn it"*: Publicist for Mutual Film Company, in David Robinson, *Chaplin: His Life and Art* (1983), 157.

381 *"The way of life can be free and beautiful"*: Chaplin's famous concluding speech in *The Great Dictator*; in ibid., 504.

382 *"human freedom and human dignity"*: Dan James in ibid., 489.

PART THREE: ENDINGS

CHAPTER 8: ECCENTRICS AND BARBARIANS

397 *"and too conservative to radicals"*: Peter Ackroyd, *T. S. Eliot: A Life* (1984), 157.

398 *"and anglo-catholic in religion"*: Eliot, *For Lancelot Andrewes* (1928; ed. 1970), 7.

398 "*sin and expiation*": Agatha in *The Family Reunion* (1939), Part II, Scene II, in *The Complete Poems and Plays of T. S. Eliot* (1952), 275.

398 "*All time is unredeemable*": Eliot, "Burnt Norton," *Four Quartets*, ibid., 117.

399 "*And the fire and the rose are one*": "Little Gidding," *Four Quartets*, ibid., 145.

399 "ganz verjudet": Pound in Anthony Julius, *T. S. Eliot, Anti-Semitism, and Literary Form* (1995), 155.

400 "*free-thinking Jews undesirable*": Eliot, *After Strange Gods: A Primer of Modern Heresy* (1933), 15.

400 "*worm-eaten by liberalism*": Ibid., 13.

404 "*the ways of a boy's heart and mind*": Charles Ives, "Memories," *Memos*, ed. John Kirkpatrick (1972), 113–15.

405 "*it is doubtful*": Rossiter, *Charles Ives and His America* (1975), 84.

406 "*Mozart etc. helped*": Ives, *Memos*, 131.

406 "*and some nice children*": Ibid., 130–31.

406 "*musical pussies*": Ibid., 131.

406 "*those 'ta tas' and greasy ringlets?*": Ibid., 134.

407 "*(pretty soft . . . but one which he made himself)*": Ibid., 134–35.

407 "*(a woman posing as a man)*": Ibid., 134.

407 "*dying—dying—dead*": Ibid., 136.

408 *may have produced impotence*: Jan Swafford, *Charles Ives: A Life with Music* (1996), 406–07.

409 "*unparalleled barbarism which finally felled him*": Knut Hamsun, obituary for Hitler, May 7, 1945, *Aftenposten*, in Robert Ferguson, *Enigma: The Life of Knut Hamsun* (1987), 386.

410 "*and despises its essence*": Ibid., 347.

410 "*the Life Force, the Caesar*": Hamsun, *At the Gates of the Kingdom* (1895), in ibid., 391.

412 "*in the midst of these confused times!*": Hamsun to Harald Grieg, November 5, 1932, in ibid., 331.

412 "*Hitler who has spoken to my heart*": Ibid., 362.

412 "*he would get them*": Hamsun, open letter to *Fritt Folk*, October 17, 1936, in ibid., 333.

414 "*Unfortunately. Thank God*": Hamsun, quoted as epigraph to ibid.

414 "*for God and for Jewish power*": Ferguson, *Enigma*, 365.

414 "*at odds with all and everything*": Hamsun, *Selected Letters*. Vol. II, *1898–1952*, ed. Harald Naess and James McFarland (1998), 23.

415 "*and the nature around them*": Ferguson, *Enigma*, 9.

415 "*withal, a man of the day*": Hamsun, *The Growth of the Soil* (1917), trans. W. W. Worster (1971), 434.

416 his "*mental faculties*": See Ferguson, *Enigma*, 338–410.

417 "*attached to any progressive ideas*": Sigmund Freud, *Moses and Monotheism:*

Three Essays (1939), *The Standard Edition of the Complete Psychological Writings of Sigmund Freud*, ed. and trans. James Strachey et al., 24 vols. (1953–75), XXIII, 43. For my take on Freud, see *Freud: A Life for Our Time* (1988).

418   *"or gone into voluntary liquidation"*: Ian Kershaw, *Hitler, 1889–1936: Hubris* (1998), 435.

419   *selected for their so-called depravity*: See Hal Foster, Rosalind Krauss, Yves-Alain Bois, and H. S. Buchloh, *Art Since 1900: Modernism, antimodernism, postmodernism* (2004), 281.

421   *"'translated from the Hebrew'"*: Saul Friedländer, *Nazi Germany and the Jews*, 2 vols. Vol. I: *The Years of Persecution, 1933–1939* (1997), 59.

422   *By the mid-1930s . . . a century before*: Author's personal experience in the Goethe Reform Gymnasium in Berlin, 1935–36.

422   *"a flight from the modern world"*: Henry A. Turner, Jr., "Fascism and Modernization," in Turner, ed., *Reappraisals of Fascism* (1975), 120.

427   *"our whole future rests"*: Dostoevsky, *A Writer's Diary, 1873–1876*, trans. Kenneth Lanz (1997), 349.

431   *"economic life of 1917"*: Malevich in Daniel Bell, *The Cultural Contradictions of Capitalism* (1976; ed. 1996), 18.

432   *"clear and simple"*: Prokofiev in S. Shlifstein, *Sergei Prokofiev: Autobiography, Articles, Reminiscences* (2000), 100.

433   *"confused stream of sound"*: *Pravda* in Orlando Figes, *Natasha's Dance: A Cultural History of Russia* (2003), 479.

436   *"who do not already possess it"*: Emily Braun, "The Visual Arts: Modernism and Fascism," in *Liberal and Fascist Italy, 1900–1945*, ed. Adrian Lyttelton (2002), 203.

437   *"I would kill Mussolini"*: Harvey Sachs, *Toscanini* (1978), 154.

CHAPTER 9: LIFE AFTER DEATH?

444   *"They should all be pulped"*: Quoted in Peter Demetz, *Postwar German Literature: A Critical Introduction* (1970), 48. I have slightly amended this quotation by substituting the word "pulped" for "destroyed" (*eingestampt*).

445   *"There was no list of members"*: Marcel Reich-Ranicki, *Mein Leben* (1999), 404–05.

446   *"fatal sterility of the German idiom"*: Demetz, *Postwar German Literature*, 214.

448   *"from abstract painting"*: Beate Stärk, *Contemporary Painting in Germany* (1994), 7.

452   *"I would have said so in the play"*: Richard Coe, *Samuel Beckett* (1964), 2.

453   *"His work is beautiful"*: Pinter text from www.google.com (no source given).

455   *"the bourgeois spirit and political tyrannies"*: Richard N. Coe, *Eugène Ionesco* (1961), 12–14.

455   *"forgotten how to be"*: Ionesco, "La tragédie du langage: Comment un manuel pour apprendre l'anglais est devenu ma première pièce," *Spectacles*, 2 (1958), 5.

456   *"as they were indisputably true"*: Ibid., 3.

457   *disparaged Virginia Woolf . . . as being psychologically naïve*: Nathalie Sarraute, *L'Ere du soupçon: Essais sur le roman* (1956), 97–99.

457   *the novels of Arnold Bennett*: Note the title of Sarraute's first book, *Tropismes* (1939).

458   *"the real Charlot"*: Sarraute, *Les Fruits d'or* (1963), 126–27.

458   *"Better than Charlot"*: Sarraute, *L'Ere du soupçon*, 21–22.

460   *"until after 1960"*: Barbara Rose, *American Art Since 1900: A Critical History* (1967), 217.

461   *"I see what I have been doing"*: Jackson Pollock, "My Painting," *Possibilities* (sole issue, Winter 1947–48).

463   *"every detail of execution contributes"*: Clement Greenberg, "Jackson Pollock: Inspiration, Vision, Intuitive Decision," *The Collected Essays and Criticism: Modernism with a Vengeance, 1957–1969*, ed. John O'Brian (1993), 246.

464   *"to exclaim its secret"*: Harold Rosenberg, *The De-Definition of Art: Action Art to Pop to Earthworks* (1972), 91.

465   *"scientific and sterile"*: Hofmann in Rose, *American Art Since 1900*, 152–53.

466   *"Participatory—and so on"*: Greenberg, "Avant-Garde Attitudes, New Art in the Sixties" (1969), *Collected Essays and Criticism*, 294.

467   *"(other aspects . . . a family newspaper)"*: Barry Gewen, "State of the Art," *New York Times Book Review*, February 10, 2005.

467   *"and that anybody can do it"*: Maciunas in Hal Foster, Rosalind Krauss, Yve-Alain Bois, and Benjamin H. D. Buchloh, *art since 1900* (2004), 468.

469   *"'it's a flag'"*: Lawrence Alloway, *American Pop Art* (1974), 69.

471   *but not "really fresh"*: Greenberg, "Post-Painterly Abstraction" (1964), *Collected Essays and Criticism*, 197.

475   *"I've never been touched by a painting"*: Victor Bockris, *Warhol, the Biography* (1989; ed. 1993), 180, 179, 163, 145.

478   *"everything is beautiful—if it's right"*: Ibid., 210.

480   *"'pop' art is officially here"*: Brian O'Doherty, "Art: Avant-Garde Revolt," *New York Times*, October 31, 1962.

480   *"clever—very clever—journalism"*: Brian O'Doherty, "'Pop' Goes the New Art," *New York Times*, November 4, 1962.

481   *"prostituted before it could prove itself"*: John Canaday, "Hello, Goodbye," *New York Times*, January 12, 1964.

481   *"and thus legitimizing it"*: John Canaday, "Pop Art Sells On and On—Why?" *New York Times*, March 31, 1964.

482   *"laughter rather than tears"*: Hilton Kramer, "Look! All Over! It's Esthetic . . . It's Business . . . It's Supersuccess!" *New York Times*, March 29, 1966.

482   *"exposure in front of the public"*: Robert Brustein, "If an Artist Wants to Be

Serious and Respected and Rich, Famous and Popular, He Is Suffering from Cultural Schizophrenia," *New York Times*, September 26, 1971.

482　*"a very great disaster"*: Hilton Kramer, "And Now . . . Pop Art: Phase II," *New York Times*, January 16, 1972.

487　*fiction sold that year was romances*: See Julia Briggs, *Virginia Woolf: An Inner Life* (2005), 186. The advertisement on romances was in the *New York Times Book Review*, October 16, 2005.

488　*"hysterically funny"*: Warren Hoge, *New York Times*, October 20, 2001.

492　*"an intricate stew of truths and mirages"*: Gabriel García Márquez, *One Hundred Years of Solitude* (1967; trans. Gregory Rabassa, 1970), 230.

494　*García Márquez has history happen to Macondo*: See ibid., 416, 154–55, 224, 419, 50, 400, 422.

495　*"and eternal reality was love"*: Ibid., 412.

495　*"learned of his incapacity to love"*: Gabriel García Márquez, *The Autumn of the Patriarch*, trans. Gregory Rabassa (1975), 255.

497　*"especially those from the Caribbean"*: Raymond L. Williams, *Gabriel García Márquez* (1984), 111.

498　a *"poem about the solitude of power"*: Ibid., 121.

499　*"the solitary vice of power"*: García Márquez, *The Autumn of the Patriarch*, 4, 6, 47, 31.

CODA

504　*"not for inventing it"*: Quoted on back cover of *Gehry Talks*, ed. Mildred Friedman, with Michael Sorkin (2002); see also Sorkin, "Frozen Light," in ibid., 32.

505　*"there was no freedom in it for him"*: "Commentaries by Frank Gehry," in ibid., 140.

505　*"the surprise of it"*: Quoted in Friedman, "The Reluctant Master," in ibid., 22.

505　*"was antithetical to the art"*: Gehry, "Commentaries," in ibid., 140.

506　*"something that's been difficult for me"*: Ibid., 208.

507　*"our inspiration was Duchamp's painting"*: Ibid., 183.

508　*"project called modernism"*: T. J. Clark, *Farewell to an Idea: Episodes from a History of Modernism* (1999), 8.

509　*"some very good things have been popular"*: "Masscult and Midcult" (1960), in Dwight MacDonald, *Against the American Grain: Essays on the Effects of Mass Culture* (1962), 7.

BIBLIOGRAPHICAL
ESSAY

This bibliography is highly selective. I have focused on the texts that proved most helpful to me, usually offering brief comments; a comprehensive, let alone exhaustive account of what I read or consulted during the five years it took me to write *Modernism* would have swelled it beyond rational limits. Some entries—like those, say, on Impressionism—imposed detailed coverage, but with most of them I have been more economical.

A CLIMATE FOR MODERNISM

The number of scholars addressing modernism, its meaning and its history, is rapidly growing after many decades of neglect. Few have been daring (or deluded) enough to produce a study sweeping across all the areas they might have included in their purview. The most inclusive, hence to me most serviceable, volumes have been compilations of texts, chiefly *The Modern Tradition: Backgrounds of Modern Literature*, ed. Richard Ellmann and Charles Feidelson, Jr. (1965), and *Modernism: An Anthology of Sources and Documents*, ed. Vassiliki Kolocotroni, Jane Goldman, and Olga Taxidou (1998). Both are imaginative, with the latter putting more weight on recent practitioners (Brecht, Adorno). *The Cambridge Companion to Modernism*, ed. Michael Levenson (1999), gathers sophisticated essays on literature, art, theatre, even movies. In comparison, *Aspekte der Modernität*, ed. Hans Steffen (1965), is heavy and Teutonically "deep." Samuel Lublinski, *Die Bilanz der Moderne* (1904) and *Der Ausgang der Moderne: Ein Buch der Opposition* (1909), are the first efforts (after Nietzsche) at defining modernism.* The philosopher Robert B. Pippin has thoughtfully restudied

---

* In an important review essay, at once substantial and thoughtful, Robert Wohl, "Heart of Darkness: Modernism and Its Historians," *Journal of Modern History*, 74 (September 2002), 573–621, generously examines several recent titles, notably Christopher Butler, *Early Modernism: Litera-*

the German intellectual tradition—Nietzsche, Heidegger—to trace modernism largely to it, in *Modernism as a Philosophical Problem* (1991; 1999).

Certain general histories have served me well, notably J. W. Burrow's *The Crisis of Reason: European Thought: 1848–1914* (2000), which shrewdly travels across the intellectual transformation of Europe. Elie Halévy, *The Era of Tyrannies* (1938; trans. R. K. Webb, 1965), a compendium of pieces on socialism and on "the World Crisis, 1914–1918" by a great historian, remains rewarding, as does Hajo Holborn, *The Political Collapse of Europe* (1951), a reflective interpretation of the European order crumbling. H. Stuart Hughes, *Consciousness and Society: The Reorientation of European Social Thought 1890–1930* (1958), is an important but now somewhat neglected study. Other informative texts include Hartmut Kaelble, *Historical Research on Social Mobility* (1977; trans. Ingrid Noakes, 1981); Charles Kindleberger, *Economic Growth in France and Britain, 1851–1950* (1964); W. O. Henderson, *The Industrial Revolution in Europe: Germany, France, Russia, 1815–1914* (1961); George Lichtheim, *Europe in the Twentieth Century* (1972), a beautifully written survey; and David S. Landes, *The Wealth and Poverty of Nations: Why Some Are So Rich and Some So Poor* (1998), an impressive historical effort to answer the hard conundrum of the subtitle.

For the early onset of the "bourgeois reign," Emma Rothschild, *Economic Sentiments: Adam Smith, Condorcet, and the Enlightenment* (2001), brilliantly and learnedly sets the stage, as does Albert O. Hirschman's *The Passions and the Interests: Political Arguments for Capitalism Before Its Triumph* (1977). Both examine the historic conflicts between reason and passion and the disposition for self-subversion to outline the growth of modern capitalism.

Avant-gardes have enjoyed original research, which has usually stressed the unmitigated hostility of advanced artists toward bourgeois society—often oversimplifying it. See George Boas, *Vox Populi: Essays in the History of an Idea* (1969), which pursues the influence of "the people" through the centuries. Peter Bürger, *Theory of the Avant-Garde* (1974; trans. Michael Shaw, 1980), a widely quoted *Marxisant* work, distinguishes, like Theodor Adorno, modernism from the avant-garde—as I do not. See *"Theorie der Avantgarde." Antworten auf Peter Bürgers Bestimmung von Kunst und bürgerlicher Gesellschaft*, ed. W. Martin Lüdke (1976). John Carey, *The Intellectuals and the Masses: Pride and Prejudice Among the Literary Intelligentsia, 1880–1939* (1992), is salutary in harshly exposing snobbish prejudices against cultural democracy. Despite a memorable chapter on Wyndham Lewis's racist and pro-Fascist views, Carey oversells his weighty denunciations by, for instance, denigrating Virginia Woolf as an incurable elitist on the basis of selected passages, and by disregarding her left-wing politics. Theda Shapiro, *Painters and Politics: The European*

---

ture, *Music, and Painting in Europe, 1900–1916* (1994); William R. Everdell, *The First Moderns; Profiles in the Origins of Twentieth-Century Thought* (1997); Peter Nicolls, *Modernisms* (1995); and Bernard Smith, *Modernism's History: A Study in Twentieth-Century Thought and Ideas* (1998). Each offers his own definitions, varying from one another and from mine.

Avant-Garde and Society, 1900–1925 (1976), is a pioneering essay in the social history of art.

The matter of virility has been largely ignored by historians (including this author), though it is certainly indispensable for understanding leadership, and thus avant-gardes. But see David D. Gilmore, *Manhood in the Making: Cultural Concepts of Masculinity* (1990), a comparative anthropological study. Gerald N. Izenberg, *Modernism and Masculinity: Mann, Wedekind, Kandinsky Through World War I* (2000), is relevant to the period of modernism. Harvey Mansfield, Jr., *Manliness* (2006), defends familiar anti-feminist slogans in this polemic, and is useful mainly as a reminder of traditional views. Robert A. Nye, *Masculinity and Male Codes of Honor in Modern France* (1993), is an outstanding experimental venture. Renato Poggioli, *The Theory of the Avant-Garde* (1962; trans. Gerald Fitzgerald, 1968), is excellent and much quoted. José Ortega y Gasset, *The Revolt of the Masses* (1931; trans. 1932) is a classic statement supporting the idea of a cultural aristocracy. And Charles Russell's *Poets, Prophets, and Revolutionaries: The Literary Avant-Garde from Rimbaud Through Postmodernism* (1985) is a sensitive historical survey in search of dependable definitions.

Subjectivity, of crucial significance for the definition of modernism, has been relatively little studied. *Introspection in Biography: The Biographer's Quest for Self-Awareness*, ed. Samuel H. Baron and Carl Pletsch (1985), records a conference, with papers heavily (though not uncritically) indebted to psychoanalytic thinking. One key text from earlier times is Wilhelm Worringer, *Abstraction and Empathy* (1908; trans. Michael Bullock, 1910), an influential monograph on the share of the subjective in creative work. Sigmund Freud, a good bourgeois in his literary and artistic tastes, was a radical modernist on human nature and is, though not prominent, the crucial background to my portrait of modernism. I have used, in addition to the German texts, the *Standard Edition of the Complete Psychological Works*, ed. James Strachey et al., 24 vols. (1953–73). My own biography, *Freud: A Life for Our Time* (1988), sums up my attitude to the man's life and work; it has a detailed bibliographical essay. As for Friedrich Nietzsche, a philosopher for whom subjectivity was decisive and who makes a cameo appearance, *Werke*, ed. Karl Schlechta, 3 vols. in 5 (6th rev. ed. 1969), is the most usable.

PART ONE: FOUNDERS

CHAPTER 1: PROFESSIONAL OUTSIDERS

The hero of modernist life with whom I begin this study is Charles Baudelaire, though it would not have been irrational to have launched it with a Romantic poet or composer instead. His works are handily presented in *Oeuvres complètes*, ed. Y. G. Le Dantec, rev. Claude Pichois (1961), which packs his poetry and prose (all but the translations of Edgar Allan Poe) into a single, well-annotated volume. His letters have been gathered up in *Correspondance Générale*, ed. Jacques Crépet and Claude Pichois, 6 vols. (1947–53). Among the bulky literature that has piled up, one contribution, by Erich Auerbach, "The Aesthetic Dignity of the *Fleurs du mal*," stands out as a persuasive reading, easily accessible in *Baudelaire*, ed. Henri Peyre (1963), 149–69. Margaret Gilman, *Baudelaire the Critic* (1943), examines a prominent aspect of his literary work. Lois Boe Hyslop, *Baudelaire: Man of His Time* (1980), closely links the man to his society. Jean-Paul Sartre, *Baudelaire* (1947; trans. Martin Turnell, 1949), is suggestive—Sartre is rarely boring—but eccentric. Three other thoughtful French titles, Henri Peyre, *Connaissance de Baudelaire* (1951), Claude Pichois, *Baudelaire. Etudes et Témoignages* (1967), and Paul Valéry, *Situation de Baudelaire* (1926), repay close scrutiny. Among biographies in English, Enid Starkie, *Baudelaire* (1957; ed. 1971), retains its place. In French, Claude Pichois and Jean Ziegler, *Baudelaire. Biographie* (1987), remains unsurpassed. A shortened version in English by Pichois (trans. Graham Robb, 1988) retains much fascination but drops important details. And Roger L. Williams, *The Horror of Life* (1980), chooses Baudelaire as the first of five French writers—Jules de Goncourt, Gustave Flaubert, Guy de Maupassant, and Alphone Daudet are the others—ruined by syphilis. Among the translations of Baudelaire's *Les Fleurs du mal* into English, *The Flowers of Evil*, ed. and trans. George Dillon and Edna St. Vincent Millay (1936; ed. 1962), is probably the most intriguing.*

Richard Ellmann, *Oscar Wilde* (1988), is the life of choice, scholarly and elegant, though inclined to take Wilde's philosophizing more seriously than I think it deserves. *The Artist as Critic: Critical Writings of Oscar Wilde*, ed. Ellmann (1969), fully covers Wilde's lectures and his important and other publications on aesthetics. Ellmann has also edited *Oscar Wilde* (1969), a compilation of critical essays with comments from Yeats, Gide, Joyce, Shaw, and Alfred Douglas, Wilde's most notorious love. *The Letters of Oscar Wilde*, ed. Rupert Hart-Davis (1962), from the original manuscripts, supplemented with *More Letters of Oscar Wilde* (1985), add up to a treasure-house of informative and dazzling writing. Among the writings, *The Picture of Dorian Gray* (1891) has been edited often, perhaps best by Isobel Murray (1974). The *Autobiography* (1965) of William Butler Yeats, who came to know Wilde fairly well, has keen observations. Among Lord Alfred Douglas's self-serving autobiographical texts, none is reliable; *Oscar Wilde and Myself* (1914) sets his tone. H. Montgomery Hyde, *The Trials of Oscar Wilde* (ed. 1962), and its sequel, *Oscar Wilde: The Aftermath* (1963), are dependable accounts of Wilde's legal entanglements in 1895, his conviction, and his life in prison. Melissa Knox, *Oscar Wilde: A Long and Lovely Suicide* (1994), is a bold and knowledgeable experiment in psychoanalytic biography that deserves serious reading. Regenia Gagnier, *Idylls of the Market-*

---

* There is help for the reader of Baudelaire without French: Jonathan Mayne, trans. and ed., *The Mirror of Art: Critical Studies by Baudelaire* (1955; ed. 1956), features the poet's three *Salons* and several papers on art, including "The Life and Works of Eugène Delacroix." Jonathan Mayne, trans. and ed., *The Painter of Modern Life and Other Essays* (1965), adds an important discussion of "Constantin Guys, The Painter of Modern Life" as well as "On the Essence of Laughter."

place: Oscar Wilde and the Victorian Public (1986), explores the fascinating, inconsistent reception of Wilde the man and the writer. *Oscar Wilde: The Critical Heritage*, ed. Karl Beckson (1970), supplies necessary texts.

Other titles consider some of Wilde's "teachers." See esp. Holbrook Jackson, *The Eighteen Nineties* (1913). For Walter Pater, in essential ways Wilde's guide in aesthetics as a strong English partisan of art for art's sake, see above all his celebrated *Studies in the History of the Renaissance* (1873). Of A. C. Swinburne's many works, his *Notes on Poems and Ballads* (1866), printed with *Atalanta in Calcydon* (1865), ed. Morse Peckham (1970), is the main text to read. Incidentally, an instance of hero worship for great men (Goethe), Eduard Hanslick's autobiography, *Aus meinem Leben*, 2 vols. (1894; 4th ed., 1911), is particularly instructive since generally Hanslick was known for disdaining such adulation. Charles Locke Eastlake, in *Contributions to the Literature of the Fine Arts*, 2nd ser. (1870), offers contemporary evidence for a shift in the class loyalties of art collectors, at least in Britain.

THE FUNDAMENTAL IDEA of art for art's, or literature for literature's sake, to which Wilde was so ostentatiously committed, has not been studied a great deal. Albert Guérard, *Art for Art's Sake* (1936), is instructive. And see George Boas, "Il faut être de son temps," *Journal of Aesthetics and Art Criticism*, I (1941), 52–65, which analyzes the idealizing of contemporaneity to which I have given space in my text. Among nineteenth-century authors, the most conspicuous proponent was the novelist, poet, critic, and reviewer Théophile Gautier, who deserves more notice by historians of literature than he has so far received. Of the few serious studies, Joanna Richardson, *Théophile Gautier: His Life and Times* (1958), is the most interesting one. Gautier states his case in the famous long preface to his *Mademoiselle de Maupin* (1835; trans. Joanna Richardson, 1981), published when its author was all of twenty-three. Gautier launched this preface, more famous than the novel it introduces, with a sentence stunning in its self-confidence: "One of the most ridiculous things which we have the happiness to live in is undoubtedly the rehabilitation of virtue." For the rest, the claim that art needs and deserves full autonomy and can function only if there is no whiff of utility came to be widely taken for granted, especially among modernists.

CHAPTER 2: IRRECONCILABLES AND IMPRESARIOS

Pride of place belongs to the man who, more than anyone else, shaped Americans' taste in modern art: see Sybil Gordon Kantor, *Alfred H. Barr, Jr., and the Intellectual Origins of the Museum of Modern Art* (2003). As the initial director of MoMA, and later as its chief curator, as a privileged buyer and organizer, and a distinguished writer on art, Barr set a tone and struck out in a direction that only a trustee could find objectionable. He was a hero of modernism.

Barr's first exhibition included Cézanne, Seurat, van Gogh, and Gauguin, thus widening the common view of the Impressionists as the first recognizable avant-

garde. And the mid-nineteenth-century landscape artists were its most gifted predecessors. See the rich study by Jean Bouret, *The Barbizon School and 19th-Century
French Landscape Painting* (1972; trans. 1973). See also the illuminating catalog, *Jean-
François Millet*, Robert L. Herbert, ed., with Roselie Bacou and Michel Laclotte
(1975); and *Théodore Rousseau*, ed. Hélène Tussaint (1967), and Peter Galassi, *Corot
in Italy: Open-Air Painting and the Classical-Landscape Tradition* (1991), are both
attractive and dependable. Joseph C. Sloane, *French Painting Between the Past and the
Present: Artists, Critics, and Traditions from 1848 to 1870* (1951), sorts out the complex
history of painting in a transitional period. *Charles Gleyre, ou les illusions perdues*
(1974), is a catalog published a century after the death of an impressive if conventional draftsman. For interesting accounts of the "enemy," the academic art of the
Salons, see Patricia Mainardi, *Art and Politics of the Second Empire: The Universal
Expositions of 1855 and 1867* (1987) and *The End of the Salon: Art and the State in the
Early Third Republic* (1993), astute essays in cultural history.

John Rewald, *The History of Impressionism* (1946; 4th ed. 1973) has earned the reputation of being the "cornerstone" of studies in this subject. *The New Painting: Impressionism, 1874–1886*, ed. Charles S. Moffatt, Ruth Berson et al. (1996), conveniently
reproduces the eight original Impressionist exhibitions. See Robert L. Herbert,
Impressionism: Art, Leisure, and Parisian Society (1988), as a beautifully argued exploration of the Impressionists' modernist urban commitment. *Les Archives de l'Impressionisme. Lettres de Renoir, Monet, Pissarro, Sisley et Autres: Mémoires de Paul
Durand-Ruel, Documents*, 2 vols., ed. Lionello Venturi (1939), is an invaluable collection of relevant materials. Anne Distel, *Impressionism: The First Collectors* (1989;
trans. Barbara Perroud-Benson, 1990), impressively demonstrates that the earliest
enthusiasts for this modernist style were not proverbial American parvenus or Russian millionaires. Kermit Swiler Champa, *Studies in Early Impressionism* (1973), is typical of the massive recent scholarship. It fits well with Theodore Reff, "Copyists in
the Louvre, 1850–1870," *Art Bulletin*, XLVI (December 1964). Meyer Schapiro,
Impressionism: Reflections and Perceptions (1997), sums up the lifelong interest of an
influential master commentator. Robert L. John House, with Anne Dumas et al.,
Impressions of France: Monet, Renoir, Pissarro and Their Rivals (1995), is a thoroughly
documented comparative catalog. Among popular accounts, Phoebe Pool, *Impressionism* (1967), probably remains the most satisfying.

Of the biographical studies of Impressionists, the following—a concise selection—
stand out: Beth Archer Brombert, *Edouard Manet: Rebel in a Frock Coat* (1995), an
impressive life of the exemplary, powerful, and reluctant half-member of the clan.
T. J. Clark, *The Painting of Modern Life: Paris in the Art of Manet and His Followers*
(1985), is confrontational but, giving Manet's reviewers ample space, helps to outline
contemporary artistic culture. (In this connection, see also George Heard Hamilton,
Manet and His Critics [1954].) Paul Hayes Tucker ably rehearsed his impressive
Claude Monet: Life and Art (1995) with *Monet in the 90s: The Series Paintings* (1990).
Theodore Reff, *Degas: The Artist's Mind* (1976), is a persuasive essay by a profes-

sional specialist. Carol Armstrong, *Odd Man Out: Readings of the Work and Reputa-tion of Edgar Degas* (1991), is a brilliant analysis of this elusive modernist. See also Sue Welsh Reed and Barbara Stern Shapiro, *Edgar Degas: The Painter as Printmaker* (1984). As for Pissarro, in some measure every Impressionist's tutor, Richard R. Brettell, with Joachim Pissarro, *The Impressionist and the City: Pissarro's Serial Paint-ings* (1993), makes a significant contribution. Pissarro's fascinating communications to his painter-son, *Letters to His Son Lucien*, ed. John Rewald with the assistance of Lucien Pissarro (1943; trans. 1944), offer intriguing clues.

Maryann Stevens, *Alfred Sisley* (1992), helps rehabilitate a somewhat neglected mem-ber of the clan. Charles F. Stuckey, William P. Scott, with Suzanne D. Lindsay, *Berthe Morisot, Impressionist* (1987), and Anne Higonnet, *Berthe Morisot* (1990), are both dependable. Walter Pach, *Renoir* (1983), and Barbara Ehrlich White, *Renoir: His Life, Art, and Letters* (1984), are solid studies. Kirk Varnedoe, *Gustave Caillebotte* (1987), gives a vivid and rewarding account of an intelligent collector and talented painter, whose legacy of his splendid Impressionists to the French state made for a noisy contro-versy between modernists and anti-modernists in the 1890s. Marie Berhaut's *catalogue raisonné, Caillebotte, sa vie et son oeuvre* (1978), is full and authoritative.

For the intricate subject of aesthetic middlemen, I have relied on a collection of monographs, which, together, permit a close look at the modernist enterprise. I had completed this manuscript only to happen upon a pertinent statement by Mary Cas-satt: "In these days of commercial supremacy, artists need a 'middleman' who can explain the merits of a picture to a possible buyer, and who can point to the fact that there is no better investment." Some art dealers have been candid about their tastes and profits. Among the most revealing are Daniel-Henry Kahnweiler, with Francis Crémieux, *My Galleries and Painters* (1961; trans. Helen Weaver, 1971), and Ambroise Vollard, *Recollections of a Picture Dealer* (1937; trans. Violet M. MacDon-ald, 1946). *Ein Fest der Künste: Paul Cassirer, Der Kunsthändler als Verleger*, ed. Rahel E. Feilchenfeld and Thomas Raff (n.d.), is a substantial collective effort to do justice to a dealer, publisher, and passionate supporter of the modernists.

The great French literary historian and critic Charles-Augustin Sainte-Beuve wit-nessed the early decades of modernism, even though his uncounted learned essays show that his gift for appreciating the new (with the conspicuous exceptions of Flaubert and Baudelaire) was not highly developed. Selections from his famous *Causeries de Lundi* are easily available. The definitive, still incomplete, Pléiade edition has his masterly study of seventeenth-century Jansenism, *Port-Royal*, 5 vols. (1840–59), ed. Maxime Leroy in 3 vols. (1952–55), and 2 vols. containing the *Premiers lundis, Portraits littéraires*, and other works (1966–), also well edited by Leroy. Wolf Lepenies, *Sainte-Beuve. Auf der Schwelle ʒur Moderne* (1997), beautifully portrays France's most distinguished nineteenth-century critic as standing on the threshold of modernism. See also a recent biography by Nicole Casanova, *Sainte-Beuve* (1995).

The literature on collectors is sizable. For a summary look, see Gay, *Pleasure Wars* (1998), esp. chap. 4, "Hunters and Gatherers." *Splendid Legacy: The Havemeyer Col-*

lection, ed. Alice Cooney Frelinghuysen et al. (1993), is noteworthy for illuminating the way that rich American collectors endowed American museums with important modernist paintings. It should be read in tandem with Louisine Havemeyer, *Sixteen to Sixty: Memoirs of a Collector* (1930; ed. 1961). Her husband Harry Havemeyer, who collected Rembrandts, appears prominently in a 2-vol. catalog by Hubert von Sonnenburg, *Rembrandt/Not Rembrandt in the Metropolitan Museum of Arts; Aspects of Connoisseurship* (1995).

For two great Russian supporters of modernism, patrons and collectors of modernists alike, see the thrilling exhibition catalog *Monet bis Picasso. Die Sammler Morosow, Schtschukin. 120 Meisterwerke aus der Eremitage, St. Petersburg, und dem Puschkin Museum, Moscow,* ed. Georg-W. Költzsch (1994). Dianne Sachko Macleod, *Art and the Victorian Middle Class: Money and the Making of Cultural Identity* (1996), is enlightening on British bourgeois as art collectors. So is David Robertson, *Sir Charles Eastlake and the Victorian Art World* (1978), which moves beyond biography to cultural history, and Robin Hamlyn, *Robert Vernon's Gift: British Art for the Nation, 1847* (1993), which is short but meaty. John Rewald, "Chocquet et Cézanne" (1969), is reprinted in Rewald, *Studies in Impressionism,* trans. and ed. Irene Gordon and Frances Weitzenhoffer (1986), a pleasing survey of artistic questions that intrigued him.

For German collectors and their ties to museum directors, there is Wolfgang Hardtwig, "Drei Berliner Porträts: Wilhelm von Bode, Eduard Arnhold, Harry Graf Kessler. Museumsmann, Mäzen und Kunstvermittler—Drei herausragende Beispiele," *Mäzenatentum in Berlin. Bürgersinn und kulturelle Kompetenz unter sich verändernden Bedingungen,* ed. Günter and Waldtraut Braun (1993). For all its clumsy title, this is a significant contribution to the study of the German bourgeoisie and the arts. For the leading anti-modernist in Germany, Emperor Wilhelm II, see the reliable, extremely detailed report on his intrusions on the country's museums and museum directors in John C. G. Röhl, *Wilhelm II. Der Aufbau der Persönlichen Monarchie* (2001), the second in a projected 3-vol. life, a devastating, exhaustive study.

The literature around cultural middlemen is rapidly growing. A few titles must make do. The influential museum director and cultural educator of the German bourgeoisie, Alfred Lichtwark, covered in this chapter, has a sensible study by Carolyn Kay, *Art and the German Bourgeoisie: Alfred Lichtwark and Modern Painting in Hamburg, 1886–1914* (2002). Lawrence W. Levine, *Highbrow/Lowbrow: The Emergence of Cultural Hierarchy in America* (1998), penetrates the class differences in a "classless" society. Robert Jensen, *Marketing Modernism in Fin-de-Siècle Europe* (1994), focuses on art around 1900, and on the public impact of the radical German critic, historian, and polemicist Julius Meier-Graefe. As for dealers, Lionello Venturi, *Les Archives de l'Impressionisme* (see above, p. 536), is invaluable. So is Peter de Mendelssohn, *S. Fischer und sein Verlag* (1970), for an account of the most consistent German avant-garde publisher. For the great Austrian music critic Eduard Hanslick, there is Peter Wapnewski, ed., *Eduard Hanslick. Aus dem Tagebuch eines Rezensenten. Gesammelte*

Musikkritiken (1989), a shrewdly chosen anthology of reviews by Vienna's "czar" of music critics. See Daniel-Henry Kahnweiler with Francis Crémieux, *My Galleries and Painters* (see above, p. 537), and Ambroise Vollard, *Recollections of a Picture Dealer* (1936; new foreword by Una E. Johnson, trans. Violet M. McDonald, 1978). The German art dealer and publisher Paul Cassirer is worthily celebrated in *Ein Fest der Künste: Paul Cassirer, Der Kunsthändler als Verleger,* ed. Rahel E. Feilchenfeld and Thomas Raff (see above, p. 537). See also an interesting collection of autobiographical statements by dealers such as Leo Castelli, Sidney Janis, Betty Parsons, and others, who specialized in modernist painters: *The Art Dealers,* ed. Laura de Coppet and Alan Jones (1984). René Wellek, *A History of Modern Criticism, 1750–1950,* 8 vols. (1955–91), is an exhaustive and impressive scholarly account. Albert Dresdner, *Die Entstehung der Kunstkritik im Zusammenhang der Geschichte des europäischen Kunstlebens* (1915; ed. 1968), which focuses on eighteenth-century origins, is an old study well worth reviving.

PART TWO: CLASSICS

CHAPTER 3: PAINTING AND SCULPTURE

The most consistently stimulating review of twentieth-century art is almost certainly Robert Hughes's highly personal, usually convincing, and often dazzling *The Shock of the New* (1980; 2nd ed. 1991), a series of lectures for the BBC, skillfully translated into print. A second weighty conspectus is the collaborative, oversize artifact by Hal Foster, Rosalind Krauss, Yve-Alain Bois, and Benjamin H. D. Buchloh, *art since 1900: modernism, antimodernism, postmodernism* (2004), drenched in usable information and provocative opinions, almost frantically up to date, and enamored of extremes. Among the most rewarding general texts, George Heard Hamilton's *Painting and Sculpture in Europe, 1880–1945* (1993), is a masterly synthesis; see also Richard R. Brettell's concise and imaginative *Modern Art 1851–1929: Capitalism and Representation* (1999); Charles Edward Gauss, *The Aesthetic Theories of French Artists: From Realism to Surrealism* (1959; ed. 1966); and Werner Hofmann, *Turning Points in Twentieth-Century Art 1890–1917,* trans. Charles Kessler (1969). Walter Abell, *The Collective Dream in Art: A Psychologial Theory of Culture Based on Relations Between the Arts, Psychology, and the Social Sciences* (1957), utilizes Freudian explanations only to criticize them as essentially inadequate; yet the book is a promising start. James R. Mellow, *Charmed Circle: Gertrude Stein and Company* (1974), sets the Parisian atmosphere after 1900.

For coverage of the most significant painters between the Impressionists and the twentieth-century modernists, a leading place belongs to John Rewald, *Post-Impressionism from van Gogh to Gauguin* (1963; 3rd ed. 1978); it is, like all Rewald's work, solid. Robert L. Herbert, *Peasants and "Primitivism": French Prints from Millet to Gauguin* (1996), draws attention to a somewhat understudied corner of the visual art. Debora Silverman's lucidly argued *Van Gogh and Gauguin: The Search for Sacred*

Art (2000) also belongs here, as does Naomi E. Maurer, *The Pursuit of Spiritual Wisdom: Van Gogh and Gauguin* (1998). *The Letters of Vincent van Gogh to His Brother, 1872–1886*, 2 vols. (1927), and *Further Letters of Vincent van Gogh to His Brother, 1857–1890* (1929), brought together as *The Complete Letters* (1978), ed. Robert Harrison, trans. Johanna van Gogh-Bonger and C. de Dood, are a strong, indeed indispensable source. See also Bogomila Welsh-Ovcharov, *Vincent van Gogh and the Birth of Cloisonism* (1981).

The conventional art that I have called the modernists' "enemy" is smartly dissected by Albert Boime in *The Academy and French Painting in the Nineteenth Century* (1971). Two monographs by Patricia Mainardi, already mentioned, *Art and Politics of the Second Empire* and *The End of the Salon* (see above, p. 536), well cover the French scene in and after mid-nineteenth century. Jerrold Seigel, *Bohemian Paris: Culture, Politics, and the Boundaries of Bourgeois Life, 1830–1930* (1996), helpfully examines the French middle classes at their margins; though bohemianism is not central to my study of modernism, this work clarified with its sheer intelligence my understanding of bourgeois tastes. Gerald M. Ackerman, with Richard Ettinghausen, *Jean-Léon Gérôme, 1824–1904* (1972–73), approvingly and tersely treats a celebrated academic painter unforgiving, despite all his spectacular success, of avant-garde artists. For one branch of modernism, that of raucous entertainment, see Phillip Dennis Cate and Mary Shaw, *The Spirit of Montmartre: Cabarets, Humor, and the Avant-Garde, 1875–1905* (1996). Harrison C. White and Cynthia A. White, *Canvases and Careers: Institutional Change in the French Painting World* (1965), have amassed a valuable study in the sociology and economics of nineteenth-century French art. *The Second Empire: Art in France Under Napoleon III* (1978), is a rich, charming catalog filled with art and artifacts.

David Sweetman, *Paul Gauguin: A Life* (1995), is impressively documented. See also the sophisticated reading by Robert Goldwater, *Gauguin* (1983), and Richard Brettell et al., *The Art of Paul Gauguin* (1988). Wayne Andersen, *Gauguin's Paradise Lost* (1971), is, among biographies, the most daring and most interesting, seeing the painter through a psychoanalytic lense. *Correspondance de Paul Gauguin: Documents, Témoignages* (1984), is obviously instructive. In Gauguin's literary output, the *Intimate Journals*, on which he worked until shortly before his death, are probably the most revealing (1902–03; trans. Van Wyck Brooks, 1936). Meyer Schapiro, *Van Gogh* (1982), is a profound essay. Mark Roskill, *Van Gogh, Gauguin, and the Impressionist Circle* (1970), reconstructs van Gogh's artistic world. And see two highly informative catalogs by Ronald Pickvance, *Van Gogh in Arles* (1984) and *Van Gogh in Saint-Rémy and Auvers* (1986).

The all-important 3-vol. *Complete Letters of Vincent van Gogh*, cited above, especially to his brother Theo, have been expertly selected by Ronald de Leeuw, *The Letters of Vincent van Gogh* (1990; trans. Arnold Pomerans). Silverman's *Van Gogh and Gauguin*, just cited, is naturally applicable here, too. Robert Goldwater's *Gauguin* (1983) is a rewarding study, as is Goldwater, *Primitivism in Modern Painting* (1938;

enlarged ed. 1986). See also Gauguin's private journal, *Avant et après* (1902–03, trans. Van Wyck Brooks, 1923).

Paul Cézanne has benefited from the most careful scholarly attention. One early appreciation, still very much worth reading, came from England, more concretely, the Bloomsbury circle: Roger Fry, *Cézanne: A Study of His Development* (1927). Among the more recent biographies, John Rewald, *Paul Cézanne: A Biography* (1948), became a model for later biographers; Jack Lindsay, *Cézanne: His Life and Art* (1969; ed. 1972), and Richard Verdi, *Cézanne* (1992), all do the job they had assigned to themselves. Among monographs, I profited most from Fritz Novotny's careful study of the painter's perspective: *Cézanne und das Ende der Wissenschaftlichen Perspektive* (1938); and Robert J. Niess, *Zola, Cézanne, and Manet: A Study of "L'Oeuvre"* (1968), which examines with scholarly probity the intricate, tragicomic history of two fond school-mates—Emile Zola and Paul Cézanne—and their breakup. And, finally, there is a wonderful catalog for an exhibition at the Museum of Modern Art, New York, by Theodore Reff et al., *Cézanne, The Late Work* (1977).

The Belgian modernists, notably James Ensor, are captured in a substantial volume, *Les XX and the Belgian Avant-Garde: Prints, Drawings, and Books ca. 1890*, ed. Stephen H. Goddard (1992), a revealing exhibition catalog whose essays go beyond its narrow assignment; its bibliography seems exhaustive. For Ensor, the most amusing and terrifying painter before ca. 1900, when his inspiration ran out, see John David Farmer, *Ensor* (1976), a catalog that does not slight Ensor's fascinating graphic work, skeletons and all.

For the "Wild Beasts" of French art, we have James D. Herbert, *Fauve Painting: The Making of Cultural Politics* (1992). With all its relative brevity, Joseph-Emile Muller, *Fauvism* (1967; trans. Shirley E. Jones, 1967), is abundantly instructive, finding room for a dozen Fauves, giving particular prominence to Matisse. As for the latter, there is now a fine, exhaustive 2-vol. biography by Hilary Spurling, *The Unknown Matisse: A Life of Henri Matisse: The Early Years, 1869–1908* (1998), and *Matisse the Master: A Life of Henri Matisse: The Conquest of Color, 1909–1954* (2005). This abundant work, however, does not make Alfred H. Barr, Jr.'s, admirable presentation, *Matisse: His Art and His Public* (1951; ed. 1966), in any way obsolete. *Matisse on Art*, ed. Jack D. Flam (1973; ed. 1995), is a worthwhile anthology of comments.

The Norwegian painter and graphic artist Edvard Munch, a great subjective Realist who took most of his obsessive motifs from his inner life, has inspired some impressive scholarship. See *Munch: Liebe, Angst, Tod*, preface Ulrich Weisner, ed. Arne Eggum et al. (1980), which has some excellent contributors like Reinhold Heller, "Edvard Munch, Die Liebe und die Kunst," and Gerd Woll, "Angst findet man bei ihm überall." *Edvard Munch. Probleme—Forschungen—Thesen*, ed. Henning Bock and Günter Busch (1973), includes, among other interesting papers, Wolfdietrich Rasch, "Edvard Munch und das literarische Berlin der neunziger Jahre." See also Patricia G. Berman and Jane Van Nimmen, with two lengthy essays, *Munch and Women: Image and Myth* (1997), spotlighting one of Munch's favorite subjects in art and life. Reinhold Heller, *Munch: The Scream* (1973), examines Munch's most famous picture. There is also an exhibition catalog impressively introduced by Robert Rosenblum, *Edvard Munch: Symbols and Images* (1978), with important contributions by Arne Eggum and others. The most compact short treatment is J. P. Hodin, *Edvard Munch* (1972).

The German Expressionists were discovered abroad mainly after the Second World War. See esp. Paul Vogt, *Expressionism. German Painting 1905–1920* (1978; trans. Robert Erich Wolf, 1980), which casts its net very wide. So does Horst Uhr, *Masterpieces of German Expressionism at the Detroit Institute of Arts* (1982). Peter Selz was among the first to recognize its historical importance in *German Expressionist Painting* (1957). Selz's *Emil Nolde* (1963) was almost as pioneering. G. F. Hartlaub, *Die Graphik des Expressionismus in Deutschland* (1947), focuses on a central preoccupation of German painters, woodcuts, engravings, and the rest.

For individual Expressionists, see Wilhelm R. Valentiner, *E. L. Kirchner, German Expressionist* (1958), and *Ernst Ludwig Kirchner 1880–1938* (1979), a catalog for the Berlin Nationalgalerie. See also *Ernst Ludwig Kirchner: The Dresden and Berlin Years*, ed. Jill Lloyd and Magdalena M. Mueller (2003), a catalog which, breaking off at 1918, captures his work at its most creative. See also Louis de Marsalle [pseud. for E. L. Kirchner], "Über die Schweizer Arbeiten von E. L. Kirchner" (1921), in *E. L. Kirchners Davoser Tagebuch*, ed. Lothar Griesebach (1968). Some of the entries show modernism at its worst; writing on the influential and by now elderly Max Liebermann in 1925, Kirchner notes: "he has surely wanted much that is beautiful, but as a Jew he could not manage it." To Kirchner, the old anti-Semitic slur that Jews—*as Jews*—could not reach the summit of art, beauty, was simply true. *Ernst Ludwig Kirchners Selbstbildnisse*, ed. Roland Scotti (1997), proved essential for self-portraits; its bibliography is particularly valuable. Peter Selz, *Emil Nolde* (1963), is an essential American monograph. *Lovis Corinth 1858–1925*, ed. Felix Zdeneck et al. (1985), has an important essay on Corinth's self-portraits by Joachim Heusinger von Waldegg. Horst Keller, et al., *Lovis Corinth. Gemälde, Aquarelle, Zeichnungen und druckgraphische Zyklen* (1976), is one of several exhibition catalogs for one-man exhibitions of Corinth's work. Charlotte Berend-Corinth, *Mein Leben mit Lovis Corinth* (1947), gathers the intimate memories of Corinth's articulate widow and buxom model.

In my opinion, Max Beckmann was Germany's most interesting modernist painter, meant to last. *Blick auf Beckmann. Dokumente und Vorträge*, ed. Hans Martin Frhr. von Erffa and Erhard Göppel (1962), has some, to me, highly helpful essays, including Gotthard Jedlicka, "Max Beckmann in seinen Selbstbildnissen." *Max Beckmann*, ed. Sean Rainbird (2003), a splendid catalog for an international exhibition, is beautifully illustrated, with some excellent essays. *Max Beckmann: Self-Portrait in Words: Collected Writings and Statements, 1903–1950*, ed., trans., and annot. by Barbara Copeland Buenger, with Reinhold Heller and assistance from David Britt (1997), has much of value for the historian. Beckmann, *Leben in Berlin. Tagebuch 1908–09*, ed. Hans Kinkel (1966), is an interesting youthful diary. We must include Peter Selz et al., *Max Beckmann* (1964), and Wendy Weitman and James L. Fisher, *Max Beckmann Prints from the Museum of Modern Art* (1992). Horst Uhr, *Masterpieces of German Expressionism at the Detroit Institute of Art* (1982); and Paul Vogt, *Expressionism. German Painting 1905–1920* (1980), have a great deal of information on Kirchner, Beckmann, Nolde, and other Expressionists.

Will Grohmann, *Wassily Kandinsky: Life and Work*, trans. Norbert Guterman (1958), is very substantial, beautifully illustrated, and includes a *catalogue raisonné*. Hans K. Roethel, with Jean K. Benjamin, *Kandinsky* (1977; ed. 1979), does the essential work. Erika Hanfstaengl, *Wassily Kandinsky. Zeichnungen und Aquarelle* (1974), is a highly instructive catalog of Kandinsky's lesser known but no less significant drawings and watercolors. Sixten Ringbom, *The Sounding Cosmos: A Study on the Spiritualism of Kandinsky and the Genesis of Abstract Painting* (1970), throws new light on his mysticism. It should be read in conjunction with Kandinsky's best known text, *On the Spiritual in Art* (1912; trans. Michael T. Sadleir, 1913). See also Kandinsky fitting uneasily into Russian revolutionary art in Camilla Gray, *The Russian Experiment in Art, 1863–1922* (1962), a comprehensive summing up. For a fascinating account of Kandinsky's little known middle years, Clark V. Poling, *Kandinsky: Russian and Bauhaus Years* (1983), is excellent.

Gray's book also provides a dominant space for Kazimir Malevich, who, until the Soviet government forced him to return to figurative painting, was a leading abstractionist, famous for his revolutionary all-white canvas and his other "Suprematist" work. See an important exhibition catalog, *Kasimir Malevich, 1878–1935*, intro. Camilla Gray (1955), and Matthew Drutt et al., *Kazimir Malevich: Suprematism* (2003). His own "treatise," *The Non-Objective World* (1927; trans. Howard Dearstyne, 1957), is naturally of real interest; its definition of art is reminiscent of art for art's sake: "the expression of pure feeling, seeking no practical values, no ideas, no 'promised land'" (p. 78). Sophie Lissitzky-Küppers, *El Lissitzky, Life—Letters—Texts* (1967), is a beautifully illustrated volume celebrating her hushand's life as a major, internationally respected designer; but it loses much authority through her omission (only some gentle hints get through) of *anything* wrong in the Soviet Union.

For Piet Mondrian expressing and repeating himself, see *The New Art—The New Life: The Collected Writings of Piet Mondrian*, ed. and trans. Harry Holtzman and Martin S. James (1986). For another selection, see *Plastic Art and Pure Plastic Art and Other Essays*, ed. Robert Motherwell (1951). Michel Seuphor, *Piet Mondrian* (n.d.), is a bulky, detailed, handsomely produced biography. *Piet Mondrian: 1872–1944: Centennial Exhibition* (1971), a catalog published by the Guggenheim Museum, has a series of short essays. For a brief life, there is Frank Elgar, *Mondrian* (trans. Thomas Walton, 1968).

NOT SURPRISINGLY, Picasso must be the most widely discussed modernist. John Richardson, *A Life of Picasso*, 2 vols. (1991, 1996), has the story to 1917 so far; careful and extraordinarily well informed, it is well on its way to become the authoritative biography. Juan-Eduardo Cirlot, *Picasso: Birth of a Genius* (1972), has a rich *catalogue raisonné* down to 1917. Jean Clair et al., *Picasso érotique* (2001), is a stunning catalog of Picasso's artistic games with candid, imaginative sexual art. Wayne Andersen, *Picasso's Brothel: "Les Demoiselles d'Avignon"* (2002), is a reading of an oddly mysterious masterpiece; Anthony Blunt, *Picasso's "Guernica"* (1969), is another close reading. *The Posters of Picasso*, ed. Joseph K. Foster (1964), shows his versatility. Mary Mathews Gedo, *Picasso: Art as Autobiography* (1980), goes unapologetically in the Freudian direction, while *Picasso for Vollard*, intro. Hans Bollig, trans. Norbert Guterman (1956), collects Picasso's magnificent set of 100 graphics, complete. David Douglas Duncan, *The Private World of Pablo Picasso* (1959), a photographer's intimate record, belongs with Françoise Gilot and Carlton Lake, *Life with Picasso* (1964), an account by what must have been Picasso's most articulate and thoughtful lover. One of Mondrian's essays, "Toward the True Vision of Reality," in Motherwell, ed., *Plastic Art and Pure Plastic Art*, records his disappointment in Picasso's "failure" to push his painting to full abstraction. John Berger, *Success and Failure of Picasso* (1965), is a critique from the left.

Picasso's (and Braque's) great venture into Cubism has been intelligently analyzed more than once—see John Golding, *Cubism: A History and an Analysis, 1907–1914* (1959; 2nd ed. 1968); Robert Rosenblum, *Cubism and Twentieth-Century Art* (1962; rev. ed. 1966); and Douglas Cooper, *The Cubist Epoch* (1970). The three volumes are closely related in their conclusions. For one among Picasso's lesser rivals, see the exemplary self-advertiser, Salvador Dali, *The Secret Life of Salvador Dali* (1942). In contrast, another, far more appealing avant-garde Spaniard, Joan Miró, is attractively presented by *Fundació Joan Miró, Guidebook* (1999), ed. Rosa Maria Malet, a delightfully illustrated introduction.

Marcel Duchamp, the supreme anti-artist, has of course not lacked commentary. Calvin Tomkins, *Duchamp: A Biography* (1996), is now the standard life. Pierre Cabanne, *Dialogues with Marcel Duchamp* (1967; trans. Ron Padgett, 1971), is a valuable set of conversations held shortly before Duchamp's death. *Marcel Duchamp* (1973), ed. Anne d'Harnoncourt and Kynaston McShine, gathers up a satisfying collection of essays. Octavio Paz, *Marcel Duchamp: Appearance Stripped Bare* (1969; trans. Rachel Phillips and Donald Gardner, 1990), is brilliant. Jerrold Seigel, *The Private World of Marcel Duchamp: Desire, Liberation, and the Self in Modern Culture* (1995), better than its title, offers a very readable and thoughtful set of reflections. John Golding, *Marcel Duchamp. The Bride Stripped Bare by her Bachelors, Even* (1972), analyzes Duchamp's curious masterpiece (if that is what it is) in detail. Jeffrey Weiss, *The Popular Culture of Modern Art: Picasso, Duchamp, and Avant-Gardism* (1994), takes Duchamp (and Picasso) from the unusual perspective of popular art, and their links with it. *The Spirit of Montmartre: Cabarets, Humor, and the Avant-Garde, 1875–1905*, ed. Phillip Dennis Cate and Mary Shaw (1996), already cited (see p. 540) is a delightful supplement to Weiss's *Popular Culture*.

Modernist sculpture has been well studied. Sir Herbert Read, *Modern Sculpture: A Concise History* (1964), is a judicious introduction. It can be supplemented with

Andrew Causey's excellent survey, *Sculpture Since 1945* (1998), with a fine bibliographical essay. Rosalind E. Krauss, *Passages in Modern Sculpture* (1977), is a stimulating, highly original guide through the cacophony of recent work. Carola Giedion-Welcker, *Contemporary Sculpture: An Evolution in Volume and Space* (1937; rev. and enlarged ed. 1956), belongs in this company.

For individual sculptors, see above all Carola Giedion-Welcker's *Constantin Brancusi* (1959), which tackles the best known, most elegant, modernist sculptor; see also Sidney Geist, *Brancusi* (1968). Krauss's *Terminal Iron Works: The Sculpture of David Smith* (1971) is a knowledgeable monograph on America's most famous modernist. Will Grohmann, *Henry Moore* (1960), is a German appraisal; Herbert Read, *Henry Moore* (1965), should be added. James Johnson Sweeney, *Alexander Calder* (1951), is an attractive exhibition catalog. A. M. Hammacher, *Barbara Hepworth* (1968), analyzes the work of Britain's best known woman sculptor.

CHAPTER 4: PROSE AND POETRY

Erich Auerbach, *Mimesis: The Representation of Reality in Western Literature* (1946; trans. Willard R. Trask, 1968), is a classic that I first read in 1954; it has meant much to me throughout my career. Malcolm Bradbury and James McFarlane, eds., *Modernism: A Guide to European Literature* (1976; preface added 1991), have enlisted the right authorities, offering ample essays on their specialties, including German and Russian modernism, and chapters on modernist cities. From the vast literature on Vienna as a modernist city, I select only two: Kirk Varnedoe, *Vienna 1900: Art, Architecture and Design* (1986), and Allan Janik and Stephen Toulmin, *Wittgenstein's Vienna* (1973). For French fiction, see Margaret Gilman, The *Idea of Poetry in France* (1958). The second half of Martin Turnell's *The Novel in France* (1950) and all of Henri Peyre's *French Novelists of Today* (1955; 2nd rev. ed. 1967), far more detailed, are relevant to this study. Arthur Symons, *The Symbolist Movement in Literature* (1899), put the French Symbolists on the literary map not only of France.

The issue of literature for literature's sake, though not confined to France, was born there. Théophile Gautier, *Mademoiselle de Maupin* (1835), published when the author was twenty-three, is the model statement. Apart from this preface, literary historians have rather shunted this gifted and versatile man of letters aside—the far from skimpy *Cambridge Companion to the French Novel from 1800 to the Present*, ed. Timothy Unwin (1997), mentions Gautier just once in passing. See P. E. Tennant, *Theophile Gautier* (1975).

I have dealt in detail with Arthur Schnitzler, life and world, in *Schnitzler's Century: The Making of Middle-Class Culture, 1815–1914* (2002). The best biography of this fascinating playwright and novelist, whom Freud admired for his psychological penetration, is Giuseppe Farese, *Arthur Schnitzler. Ein Leben in Wien 1862–1931* (1997; trans. from the Italian by Karin Krieger, 1999), but there is more to be said. Hartmut Scheible, *Arthur Schnitzler* (1976), is a skimpy life that briefly has most of the essentials.

Arthur Schnitzler, *Briefe, 1875–1912*, ed. Therese Nickl and Heinrich Schnitzler (1982), and *Briefe, 1913–1931*, ed. Peter M. Braunwarth, Richard Miklin, Susanne Pertlik, and Heinrich Schnitzler (1984), are abundant, and elaborately annotated. Over the years Schnitzler carried on correspondences with single *Briefpartnern* published separately. So were his *Aphorismen und Betrachtungen. Buch der Sprüche und Bedenken* (1967). The bulk of his writings has been collected in *Die erzählenden Schriften*, 2 vols. (1961; 2nd ed. 1970), and *Die dramatischen Werke*, 2 vols. (1962; 2nd ed. 1972).

Schnitzler's *My Youth in Vienna* (1968; trans. Catherine Hutter, 1970), is a fairly candid autobiography that may supplement, and partially correct, Stefan Zweig, *Die Welt von Gestern. Erinnerungen eines Europäers* (1944), the fluently written reminiscences of a born teller of tales, a long-term best-seller, much quoted, but which, when it came to analyze the Viennese bourgeoisie, consistently overstated its sexual hypocrisy. John W. Boyer, *Political Radicalism in Late Imperial Vienna: Origins of the Christian Social Movement 1848–1897* (1981), is a sober study of modern (anti-Semitic) mass politics so ravenous in Vienna from the 1880s on. For an informative collection of essays in the cultural history of Vienna, see *Glücklich ist, wer vergisst . . . ? Das andere Wien um 1900*, ed. Hubert Ch. Ehalt, Gernot Heiss, and Hannes Stekl (1986), a set of frank examinations of sexuality, domestic violence, schooling of the poor, the emergence of psychoanalysis, and other easily overlooked features. Two important monographs put Schnitzler into his ethnic environment: Marsha Rosenblit, *The Jews of Vienna 1867–1914: Assimilation and Identity* (1983), and Steven Beller, *Vienna and the Jews 1867–1938: A Cultural History* (1989).

For the "anti-modernist" party, see esp. Margaret Drabble, *Arnold Bennett: A Biography* (1974); for its special pleading for Bennett, see John Carey, *The Intellectuals and the Masses* (cited above, p. 532).

James Joyce's *Ulysses* is best read in the corrected text, Hans Walter Gabler et al. (1986). Richard Ellmann, *James Joyce* (1959; rev. ed. 1982), is the standard life, impressively done. Ellmann has also edited Joyce's *Selected Letters* (1975). Between the first and second editions of the biography, he published several beautifully pondered essays and lectures on Joyce, all worth reading: *Ulysses on the Liffey* (1971), *The Consciousness of Joyce* (1977), and *James Joyce's Hundredth Birthday: Side and Front Views* (1982). T. S. Eliot, "*Ulysses*, Order and Myth," *The Dial* (November 1923), constitutes a tribute from Joyce's most celebrated admirer. Edna O'Brien, *James Joyce: A Penguin Life* (1999), is a lovely short biography by the eminent Irish novelist. Richard M. Kain, *Dublin in the Age of William Butler Yeats and James Joyce* (1962), is an inspired guide to the time that Joyce wrote *Portrait of the Artist as a Young Man* and was beginning to think about *Ulysses*. An indispensable vademecum, Stuart Gilbert, *James Joyce's "Ulysses": A Study* (1930), takes the reader through Joyce's text, episode by episode. Robert Humphrey, *Stream of Consciousness in the Modern Novel* (1954), is a modest, responsible inquiry into the modernist novel's well known technique.

New biographies of Proust (and special studies of his ocean of a novel) seem to be appearing every year. I have mainly used the older 2-vol. life by George D. Painter,

Proust, The Early Years (1959), and *Proust, The Later Years* (1965), useful particularly for treating *A la recherche du temps perdu* as "a creative autobiography," closely linking Proust's life to his art. André Maurois, *Proust: A Biography* (1950; trans. Gerard Hopkins, 1958), is, as one would expect from this author, smoothly narrated, and depends heavily on unpublished correspondence. Finally, William C. Carter, *Marcel Proust: A Life* (2000), was ideal for my purposes; bulky and authoritative, it synthesizes much previous research. Among the earliest commentaries, a deep reading that has not lost its luster is Samuel Beckett's *Proust* (1931), published not long after the final volume of *A la recherche* came out. In the same year, Edmund Wilson included a stunning chapter on *A la recherche* in his *Axel's Castle: A Study in the Imaginative Literature of 1870–1930*, that, as Roger Shattuck, a major expert on Proust, put it, was "an essay on the *Search* as a Symbolist novel—the perfect complement to Beckett's study."

Shattuck himself first addressed the novel in his brief, highly suggestive technical essay *Proust's Binoculars: A Study of Memory, Time and Recognition in "A la recherche du temps perdu"* (1962). His later *Proust* (1974) proved a subtly pondered guide how to understand the man and read his masterpiece. In 2000, Shattuck revised his earlier efforts in *Proust's Way: A Field Guide to "In Search of Lost Time,"* retaining and expanding some of his earlier insights. Randolph Splitter, *Proust's Recherche: A Psychoanalytic Interpretation* (1981), and J. E. Rivers, *Proust and the Art of Love: The Aesthetics of Sexuality in the Life, Times, and Art of Marcel Proust* (1980), both concentrate on Proust's homosexuality; the latter, Rivers, in fact busily justifies this sexual taste and worries over homophobic stereotypes. Neither fully convinces me, for the author's sexual orientation—a complex business in any event—rarely acts as the sole determinant of a writer's work. Céleste Albaret, *Monsieur Proust*, ed. Georges Belmont (1973; trans. Barbara Bray, 1976), a deeply moving book, collects the intimate (and it seems utterly reliable) memories of Proust's housekeeper, who was close to him during the last decade of his life.*

A WRITER AS ACTIVE and appealing as Virginia Woolf has amassed a very library of commentaries and editions. See *The Diary of Virginia Woolf*, ed. Anne Olivier Bell and Andrew McNeillie, 5 vols. (1977–84), and *The Letters of Virginia Woolf*, ed. Nigel Nicolson and Joanne Trautmann, 6 vols. (1975–80), both ample, usually delightful, and deeply revealing. Many of her essays were published in her lifetime; many more of them, edited by her husband, after her death. They include *The Common Reader, First Series* (1925), esp. as annotated by Andrew McNeillie (1984); *The Second Common Reader* (1932); the eventually very influential *A Room of One's Own* (a pair of lectures

---

* The reader of Proust must also seriously consider his other writings, often introductory to his life's work. They are all easily available in French—and in English. *The Complete Short Stories by Marcel Proust*, comp. and trans. Joachim Neugroschel (2001); and *Marcel Proust on Art and Literature, 1896–1919*, trans. Sylvia Townsend Warner (1964), which includes the important essay "Contre Sainte-Beuve," are both satisfactory.

given at two women's colleges in Cambridge in 1928, rev. and exp. 1929); *The Complete Shorter Fiction of Virginia Woolf*, ed. Susan Dick (1985; 2nd enlarged ed. 1989); and several collections of reviews and articles like *The Captain's Death Bed and Other Essays* (n.d.). Her celebrated related essays on women's education, in behalf of women entering the world of the professions, and against war, *Three Guineas* (1938), show her at her most mature. And this abundant fountain of learning, energy, and wit, never inactive for long, has been caricatured in the movies as a steadily depressed female!

Biographies abound. Quentin Bell, *Virginia Woolf: A Biography*, 2 vols. in 1 (1972), was the first serious effort, written by a nephew with long-range memories. Hermione Lee's *Virginia Woolf* (1996) has been widely, and wisely, praised; it is the most detailed life, and, prominently including rational comments on Woolf's mental breakdowns, the most sensible. Julia Briggs, *Virginia Woolf: An Inner Life* (2005), perceptively and instructively discusses sales figures on Woolf's fiction. Elizabeth Abel, *Virginia Woolf and the Fictions of Psychoanalysis* (1989), is a brave psychoanalytic reading of Woolf's most successful novels—*Mrs. Dalloway* and *To the Lighthouse*—but is in my opinion too subtle (compare with Hermione Lee!). Still, the book raises important questions about art and its psychic background in modernism. Sonya Rudikoff, *Ancestral Houses: Virginia Woolf and the Aristocracy* (1999), is an elegantly written reflection on Woolf's affection for what she called the "mandarin" aspects of life—raising that vexed issue of "aristocratic" modernism.

FRANZ KAFKA: Kritik und Rezeption, 1924–1938, ed. Jürgen Born, assisted by Elke Koch, Herbert Mühlfeit, and Mercedes Treckmann (1983), greatly eases the historian's awareness of the reception of Kafka's work. Especially considering that upon his death in 1924, Franz Kafka was almost wholly unknown, even in Prague, his current worldwide reputation as the very model of modernist writing is indeed astonishing, but explicable. It has grown rapidly; by 1977, Heinz Politzer, an authentic expert, could speak of an "academic Kafka-Industry" without fear of contradiction. What would he call it now? The German publishing house Fischer is in the midst of bringing out a fully annotated Kafka. *The Trial* (1925; trans. Willa and Edwin Muir, 1937; Malcolm Pasley, ed., 2 vols., 1990), was the first in that critical edition. A sign of poetic justice, *The Trial* was the first of Kafka's posthumous masterpieces to reach publication. *The Castle* (1926; trans. Edwin and Willa Muir, 1930) was the second great novel to see print. A casual observation in Thomas Mann's "Homage," which appeared in the English-language version of *Das Schloss*, left a decisive impact on my understanding of Kafka. The last of his novels, a lesser effort first titled *Amerika* and later *Der Verschollene* (1927; trans. 1946), has undergone wide-ranging changes in title and contents.

Kafka's *Hochzeitsvorbereitungen auf dem Lande und andere Prosa aus dem Nachlass* (1953), ed. Max Brod, is a sizable all-important miscellany, a principal witness to his achievement, filled with aphorisms, notes, and fragments. *Diaries, 1910–13*, ed. Max Brod (1951; trans. Joseph Kresh, 1949), and *Diaries 1914–23*, ed. Max Brod (1951; trans. Martin Greenberg and Hannah Arendt, 1949) get close to the writer. See also

Sämtliche Erzählungen, ed. Paul Raabe (1970), and *Description of a Struggle and Other Stories* (1953; trans. Willa and Edwin Muir, Malcolm Pasley, Tania and James Stern, 1979). *Beim Bau der Chinesischen Mauer. Prosa und Betrachtungen aus dem Nachlass*, ed. Max Brod and Hans Joachim Schoeps (1931), contains more unpublished Kafka prose. His letters, too, especially those to the women he loved, have their own large significance: *Briefe an Milena*, ed. Willy Haas (1952; trans. Tania and James Stern, 1953); *Briefe an Felice*, ed. Erich Heller and Jürgen Born (1967; trans. James Stern and Elizabeth Duckworth, 1973); and *Letters 1902–1924*, ed. Max Brod (1958). Gustav Janouch, *Conversations with Kafka: Notes and Reminiscences* (1968; trans. Goronwy Rees, enlarged ed. 1981), contains trustworthy notes on conversations between "Dr. Kafka" and the twenty-year-younger student Janouch during Kafka's last four years.

Kafka's intimate, Max Brod, who famously disregarded his promise to destroy his friend's unpublished writings, thus saving abiding modernist literature for the world, also became his friend's propagandist in the years after. See Max Brod / Franz Kafka, *Eine Freundschaft. Reiseaufzeichnungen*, ed. Malcolm Pasley, with Hannelore Rodlauer (1987), interesting diary entries written separately on joint trips from 1909 to 1912. Brod, *Der Prager Kreis* (1966), and his autobiography *Streitbares Leben* (1969), add considerable information about Kafka. Brod's three works explicitly taking his best friend as their subject are *Franz Kafka, Eine Biographie* (1954); *Franz Kafkas Glauben und Lehre* (1948); and *Verzweiflung und Erlösung im Werk Franz Kafkas* (1959), all energetically testifying to Brod's unshakable (but in my judgment unacceptable) view that his friend was a profound religious teacher.

Der junge Kafka, ed. Gerhard Kurz (1983), collects interesting essays on Kafka's literary beginnings. Hartmut Binder, *Der Schaffensprozess* (1983), bravely attempts through close reading to grasp Kafka's creative processes, not without success. Erich Heller's fine essay, *Franz Kafka*, ed. Frank Kermode (1974), relying mainly on Kafka's letters to Felice and the two major novels, comes to conclusions remarkably near to my own: "The vicinity of literature and autobiography could hardly be closer than it is with Kafka: indeed, it almost amounts to identity." See also, among many other commentators, Heinz Politzer, *Franz Kafka: Parable and Paradox* (first English version 1962), a major contribution to well-informed readings. Mark M. Anderson, *Kafka's Clothes: Ornament and Aestheticism in the Hapsburg Fin-de-Siècle* (1992), far from merely amusing (which it is), also has much to say about Kafka's style. E. T. Beck, *Kafka and the Yiddish Theatre: Its Impact on His Work* (1971), has significant comments on a still-puzzling topic. In his usual slashing manner, Frederick Crews, "Kafka Up Close," *New York Review of Books*, February 10, 2005, takes as his target several recent interpreters of Kafka, most savagely Stanley Korngold, whose Gnostic readings he finds, not undeservedly, unhelpful. Among recent biographies, Ernst Pawel, *The Nightmare of Reason: A Life of Franz Kafka* (1984), is most sophisticated psychoanalytically.

THE WORKS OF T. S. Eliot, the poet I have chosen to concentrate on in this book, are conveniently available in *The Complete Poems and Plays* (1952). Eliot's widow,

Valerie, was responsible for bringing out his most famous work, *The Waste Land: A Facsimile and Transcript of the Original Drafts Including the Annotations of Ezra Pound* (1971), which has become standard. The most meticulous review of this epoch-making poem is Lawrence Rainey, *Revisiting The Waste Land* (2005), which deals superbly with its making, publication, and reception. Among biographies, I found Peter Ackroyd, *T. S. Eliot: A Life* (1984), most satisfactory, at once well informed and cool. Just about all of Eliot's criticism, indispensable to any assessment including his political views, is in print. His two most substantial texts, *The Idea of a Christian Society* (1940) and *Notes Towards the Definition of Culture* (1949), have sometimes been published together under the joint title *Christianity and Culture*.

Among the other prose collections are *The Sacred Wood: Essays on Poetry and Criticism* (1920), his earliest summing up, often reprinted; *For Lancelot Andrewes: Essays on Style and Order* (1928); and *The Use of Poetry and the Use of Criticism: Studies in the Relation of Criticism to Poetry in England* (1933), all of them indispensable. *After Strange Gods: A Primer of Modern Heresy* (1934), the Page-Barbour Lectures at the University of Virginia, stands as a text with some uncomfortable comments on secular Jews that Eliot never had reprinted. John Hayward, *T. S. Eliot: Selected Prose* (1953), had a certain resonance with its very economy and omissions. There is a fine critical edition of *The Waste Land*, a facsimile and transcript, which includes Ezra Pound's annotations, ed. Valery Eliot (1971).

Some prestigious modern critics have done their share of expressing their views on the essential among modernist poets. I learned most from Northrop Frye, *T. S. Eliot* (1963), as learned as it is brief. F. O. Matthiessen (with additional chapter by C. L. Barber), *The Achievement of T. S. Eliot: An Essay on the Nature of Poetry* (1935; 3rd ed. rev. and enlarged 1959), is an important piece of lucid and largely appreciative criticism. *T. S. Eliot: The Man and His Work*, ed. Allen Tate (1966), is an enjoyable gathering of personal reminiscences and literary criticism. Even though there had long been, apart from scattered muttering, no single critique of Eliot's distaste for "free-thinking Jews," it began to stimulate considerable uneasiness among his readers after the war. A rational study by the eminent English critic Christopher Ricks, *T. S. Eliot and Prejudice* (1988), opened a debate beyond mere feelings. The most powerful and most angry participant was a lawyer with literary tastes, Anthony Julius, whose *T. S. Eliot, Anti-Semitism, and Literary Form* (1995) shook the vast community of Eliot's admirers with carefully documented and subtly reasoned conclusions. For an organized defense, see *T. S. Eliot and Our Turning World*, ed. Jewel Spears Brooker (2003).

CHAPTER 5: MUSIC AND DANCE

My principal source for the history of modernist music was Robert P. Morgan's *Twentieth-Century Music* (1991), a beautifully informed, scrupulous account with ample musical examples; on the whole focusing on the composers rather than on political events. It partly supplants Paul Henry Lang, *Music in Western Civilization*

(1941), who stylishly and exhaustively covers the whole ground from the ancients onward, and concludes with the Spenglerian question about the decline of the West. *Strunk's Source Readings in Music History, The Twentieth Century*, ed. Robert P. Morgan (1950; rev. ed. 1998), is a first-rate collection of articles and passages from monographs on which I have heavily relied. Rudolph Reti, *Tonality in Modern Music* (1958; ed. 1962), briefly analyzes the key issue (forgive the pun) in modernist music. Edward Lippman, *A History of Western Musical Aesthetics* (1992), is a welcome panorama with emphasis on modern thought. Full of ideas, it seems too committed to Adorno, who—and it matters to this chapter—in a comparative study of the two giants in twentieth-century modernism, Schoenberg and Stravinsky, *Philosophy of Modern Music* (1949; trans. A. G. Mitchell and W. V. Blomster, 1973), sees the first as progressive and the second as reactionary. To me this is a distorted, even brutally oversimplified categorization. Andreas Liess, a good European, kept his passion for German-French understanding through the Second World War, and published an attractive essay on the musical lives in his favorite two countries: *Deutsche und französische Musik in der Geistesgeschichte des neunzehnten Jahrhunderts* (1938; enlarged ed. 1950). In 1916 (pre–Weimar Republic, of course, but continuing to be useful), Paul Bekker, *Das deutsche Musikleben*, offered a sociological portrait of German musical life, including musical society, musicians, and critics. E. D. Mackerness offers a concise but very informative *Social History of English Music* (1964). See also Martin Cooper, *French Music from the Death of Berlioz to the Death of Fauré* (1969); and Michael P. Steinberg, *Listening to Reason: Culture, Subjectivity and Nineteenth-Century Music* (2005), a civilized stroll from Beethoven across Wagner to Mahler and the way to modernism.

Claude Debussy, *Monsieur Croche the Dilettante Hater* (1921; trans. B. N. Langdon Davies 1928), is a witty rumination on the music public, modern composers like Richard Wagner and Richard Strauss, conductors, and other vexing matters (available in *Three Classics in the Aesthetic of Music* (1962), along with Charles Ives, *Essays Before a Sonata*, and Ferruccio Busoni, *Sketch of a New Esthetic of Music*). For Ives, see below. See also Edward Lockspeiser, *Debussy: His Life and Mind*, 2 vols. (1962; 2nd ed. 1966); Léon Vallas, *Claude Debussy: His Life and Works* (1927; trans. Marie and Grace O'Brien, 1933); and Léon Vallas, *Les Théories de Claude Debussy, musicien français* (1928).

Of the numerous biographical studies, Henry-Louis de La Grange, *Gustav Mahler, chronique d'une vie*, 3 vols. (1979–84), is very detailed; in contrast, Wolfgang Schreiber, *Gustav Mahler in Selbstzeugnissen und Bilddokumenten* (1971), is very terse. Among Theodor Adorno's vast output on music, his *Mahler: A musical physiognomy* (1960; trans. Edmund Jephcott, 1972) is exceptionally lucid and worth reading. But we can now enjoy (it appeared soon enough to make a difference to this chapter) Jens Malte Fischer's *Gustav Mahler: Der fremde Vertraute* (2003)—elegantly written, amply documented, and knowledgeably argued. It also contains an elaborate bibliography; a translation into English would be most desirable. Walter Frisch, *German Modernism:*

Music and the Arts (2005), learnedly though agreeably analyzes the German musical scene from Wagner to Pfitzner.

For "lesser" modernists, see above all Edward J. Dent, *Ferruccio Busoni: A Biography* (1931), and Busoni's *Selected Letters*, ed. Antony Beaumont (1987). Edgard Varèse, that fascinating French modernist, has been well captured by Malcolm MacDonald, *Varèse: Astronomer in Sound* (2003). John Cage's own *Silence: Lectures and Writings* (1961) may be read along with David Revill, *The Roaring Silence: John Cage, a Life* (1992). For Charles Ives, there are first of all his own writings: *Essays Before a Sonata, The Majority, and Other Writings*, ed. Howard Boatwright (1962), and *Memos*, ed. John Kirkpatrick (1972), a collection of critical importance to understanding Ives's mind. Frank R. Rossiter, *Charles Ives and His America* (1975), performs his self-appointed task well. So does Jan Swofford's even more substantial biography, *Charles Ives: A Life with Music* (1996). The late Stuart Feder, a psychoanalyst and trained musician, and thus ideally prepared, published a psychoanalytic life at once intrepid and cautious—*Charles Ives: "My Father's Song": A Psychoanalytic Biography* (1992). Feder's central argument that Ives was possessed all his life with, and by, his musical father is not so very surprising; someone untrained in psychoanalysis but familiar with Ives could reach very similar conclusions. The difference lies in Feder's ability to recognize this dependence across his subject's life, and in persuasive technical conjectures. *Richard Strauss and His World*, ed. Bryan Gilliam (1992), offers a heady harvest of essays on Strauss's music, his life, and the reception of his work. See also *Richard Strauss and Romain Rolland: Correspondence*, ed. Rollo Myers (1968).

Style and Idea: Selected Writings of Arnold Schoenberg, ed. Leonard Stein (1950; trans. Dika Newlin, 1975), features influential and some astonishing essays such as "Brahms the Progressive." Arnold Schoenberg, *Briefe*, selec. and ed. Erwin Stein (1958), proved most revealing. Walter Frisch has analyzed Schoenberg's path to modernism in *The Early Works of Arnold Schoenberg, 1893–1908* (1993). Willi Reich, *Arnold Schoenberg: A Critical Biography* (1968; trans. Leo Black, 1971), is, as Charles Rosen has objected, not very critical, but its long quotations were worth the perusal. Reich has also written a biography of a famous pupil of Schoenberg's, *Alban Berg: Leben und Werk* (1963). Charles Rosen's own *Arnold Schoenberg* (1975) is a knowledgeable terse examination of the Schoenbergian revolution. Esther da Costa-Meyer and Fred Wasserman, *Schoenberg, Kandinsky, and the Blue Rider* (2002), gives a good account of Schoenberg's engagement in other modernist arts, as well as of Kandinsky. It belongs with *Arnold Schoenberg / Wassily Kandinsky: Letters, Pictures, and Documents*, ed. Jelena Hahl-Koch, trans. John C. Crawford (1984), the strange correspondence documenting a strange friendship; musicologists have brooded on this largely epistolary alliance as a major biographical event. See *Schönberg and Kandinsky: An Historic Encounter*, ed. Konrad Boehmer (1997), including an important, wide-ranging essay by Reinhold Brinkmann, "The Fool as Paradigm: Schönberg's *Pierrot lunaire* and the Modern Artist."

Stephen Walsh's two volumes, *Stravinsky: A Creative Spring, Russia and France, 1882–1934* (1999) and *Stravinsky: The Second Exile, France and America, 1934–1971*

(2006), are the most persistent to treat Stravinsky's life and works in the detail they deserve, and in my opinion largely succeed. (Walsh's account has not gone unchallenged. Robert Craft, an intimate of the Stravinsky household, has published several volumes on his life with Stravinsky that differ in many details.) Igor Stravinsky, *An Autobiography* (1936), came out while Stravinsky was still in Europe; but much of it, ghostwritten, requires considerable caution in reading. Charles M. Joseph, *Stravinsky Inside Out* (2001), and Paul Henry Lang, ed., *Stravinsky: A New Appraisal of His Work* (1962), positive as they are, also feature some skeptical appraisals. Charles M. Joseph, *Stravinsky and Balanchine: A Journey of Invention* (2002), is a meticulous account of a great collaboration.

FOR A GENERAL PERSPECTIVE on modern ballet and dance, there is now the monumental tome by Nancy Reynolds and Malcolm McCormick, *No Fixed Points: Dance in the Twentieth Century* (2003), objective, circumstantial, and clearly committed to modernism. See also Bernard Taper, *Balanchine: A Biography* (1984): though more recent and readable lives exist, this now "ancient" biography retains its charm with its close proximity to the choreographer and his genius. Joseph's *Stravinsky and Balanchine* (see above) fits precisely here. In a deeply felt and beautifully written review, Toni Bentley, a former dancer in Balanchine's company, mourned the abuse of Balanchine's name by his own former company, strongly (and rightly) preferring the life by Robert Gottlieb, an experienced balletomane, *George Balanchine: The Ballet Maker* (2005), to that by Terry Teachout, *All in the Dances: A Brief Life of George Balanchine* (2005). One collection, largely of interviews of those who well knew Diaghilev, Balanchine's first master, is amusing and valuable: John Drummond, *Speaking of Diaghilev* (1997). See also *André Levinson on Dance: Writings from Paris in the Twenties*, ed. Joan Acocella and Lynn Garafola (1991); *The Diary of Vaslav Nijinsky*, ed. Joan Acocella (unexpurgated ed. 1995; trans. Cyril Fitzlyon, 1999); and Agnes De Mille, *Martha: The Life and Work of Martha Graham, a Biography* (1991), a love letter, but from a lover who knows what she is talking about.

CHAPTER 6: ARCHITECTURE AND DESIGN

Modernist architecture is the most conspicuous and enduring witness to the revolt of the twentieth century against the historicism and eclecticism of the nineteenth. *The Beaux-Arts and Nineteenth-Century French Architecture*, ed. Robin Middleton (1982), is a collection of short but solid essays. Henry-Russell Hitchcock, a prolific historian of architecture, started with *Modern Architecture: Romanticism and Reintegration* (1929). He followed this up with a modest-looking but radical catalog for an exhibition at MoMA in New York, written with Philip Johnson, *The International Style: Architecture Since 1922* (1932), which became a guide to modernism, leaving its mark on possible clients and excited architects alike. Their masters are essentially mine. Nicolaus Pevsner, *Pioneers of Modern Design from William Morris to Walter Gropius* (1936; Penguin ed. 1960), which largely underwrites the Hitchcock/Johnson line, has been a widely accepted historical survey that sees a straight line from Victorian to modernist rebels. Walter Gropius was their hero, as he is mine. For a slashing (to my mind over-done) critique of this view, see Charles Jencks, *Modern Movements in Architecture* (1973), which proposes a "pluralistic development," and in general finds more fail-ures in the modernist canon than I can endorse. Vincent Scully, Jr., *Modern Architec-ture: The Architecture of Democracy* (1961, reprinted several times), is a concise essay supported by ample illustrations and a generous, far from uncritical survey of current masters. Note also Scully's bibliographical comments. For Louis Mumford's many critiques of modern architecture from a humanist's perspective, see *From the Ground Up: Observations on Contemporary Architecture, Housing, Highway Building, and Civic Design* (1956). *Die Form: Stimme des Deutschen Werkbundes, 1925–1934*, ed. Ulrich Conrads et al. (1969), has rescued intelligent comments from neglect.

Hans M. Wingler, *Das Bauhaus: 1919–1933. Weimar, Dessau, Berlin* (1962), is an enormous, well-organized, invaluable collection of documents. *Bauhaus 1919–1928*, ed. Herbert Bayer, Walter Gropius, and Ise Gropius (1959), is an abundantly illus-trated and far shorter account of all but the Bauhaus's last five years. Gillian Naylor, *The Bauhaus* (1968), is a short survey. Among books published by the Bauhaus, the most interesting one is on its theatrical performances: *Die Bühne im Bauhaus*, ed. Oskar Schlemmer, László Moholy-Nagy, and Farkas Molnar. Henry Van De Velde, *Geschichte meines Lebens* (ed. and trans. Hans Curjet, 1962), is a detailed autobiogra-phy of the widely traveled Belgian designer and architect who thought highly of Gropius.

The Bauhaus experience was far- and deep-reaching enough to produce some memorable reminiscences. See the informative if somewhat self-congratulatory *Con-cepts of the Bauhaus: The Busch-Reisinger Museum Collection*, with commemorative essays by insiders like T. Lux Feininger, Herbert Bayer, and Ise Gropius (1971). Sibyl Moholy-Nagy, *Moholy-Nagy, Experiment in Totality* (1950; 2nd ed. 1969), a candid, intimate, moving life written by the widow of Gropius's closest ally at the Bauhaus, tells much of German life after the Nazis' accession to power. *Bauhaus und Bauhäusler. Bekenntnisse und Erinnerungen*, ed. Eckhard Neumann (1971), is full of stimulating, if rather brief, reminiscences. Also see Lothar Schreyer, *Erinnerungen an Sturm und Bauhaus* (1966). And see Julius Posener, *From Schinkel to the Bauhaus* (1972), for terse, intelligent lectures.

For the first director of the school, see Reginald Isaacs, *Gropius: An Illustrated Biogra-phy of the Creator of the Bauhaus* (1990, abridged version of the original); a far more sub-stantial German translation, *Walter Gropius. Der Mensch und sein Werk*, 2 vols. (1983–84), gives a fuller account. Gropius lectured and published many of his talks. See, among other collections, *The New Architecture and the Bauhaus* (1935); *Architecture and Design in the Age of Science* (1952); *The Scope of Total Architecture* (1954); and *Apollo in der Demokratie* (1967). Joseph Hudnut, *Architecture and the Spirit of Man* (1949), is an eloquent defense of modern architecture from the man who was dean at the Harvard

School of Design in the 1930s. Gropius plays a prominent role in Anthony Alofsin, *The Struggle for Modernism: Architecture, Landscape Architecture and City Planning at Harvard* (2002), an engrossing story from the inside. And see the chapter on Gropius in Peter Gay, *Art and Act. On Causes in History: Manet, Gropius, Mondrian* (1976).

For some instructive essays on Ludwig Mies van der Rohe, see *Four Great Makers of Modern Architecture: Gropius, Le Corbusier, Mies van der Rohe, Wright*, the record of a 1961 symposium at the Columbia School of Architecture (1963). The indispensable papers in that necessary volume are Peter Blake, "A Conversation with Mies"; Howard Dearstyne, "Miesian Space Concept in Domestic Architecture"; and James Marston Fitch, "Mies van der Rohe and the Platonic Verities," this last rightly making much of Mies's "Platonism." Arthur Drexler, *Ludwig Mies van der Rohe* (1960), is adoring and very brief, if systematically illustrated; it makes one long for a sizable, independent biography.

Maurice Besset, *Who Was Le Corbusier?* (1968; trans. Robert Kemball, 1968), is an earnest, well-illustrated biographical effort to explain this elusive Swiss architect, painter, and tireless city planner, who, after taking instructive tours through major architects' offices in several countries, settled in Paris.* But neither Besset nor most of "Corbu's" other biographers have found it necessary to mention (or necessary to finesse) that during the war years Le Corbusier was an impassioned follower of Vichy. This holds true of the otherwise useful Stamo Papadaki, *Le Corbusier: Architect, Painter, Writer* (1948), of Besset's biographical study (just cited), and others. The most sustained exception is Robert Fishman, *Urban Utopias in the Twentieth Century: Ebenezer Howard, Frank Lloyd Wright, Le Corbusier* (1977), which has a carefully researched chapter titled "Vichy"—see his extensive original treatment, "From the Radiant City to Vichy: Le Corbusier's Plans and Policies, 1928–1942," in *An Open Hand: Essays on Le Corbusier* (1977), ed. Russell Walden, 244–83. The architect's politics were shifting from syndicalism to authoritarianism. "France," he said, "needs a Father. It doesn't matter who; it could be one man, two men, any number" (Fishman, 265). Norma Evenson, *Le Corbusier, the Machine and the Grand Design* (1968), tersely surveys Le Corbusier's many unrealized and one realized city plan (for Chandigarh, the new capital of Punjab). Le Corbusier's commitment to the machine ("A house is a machine to live in") may be his lasting legacy.

Hugh Morrison, *Louis Sullivan, Prophet of Modern Architecture* (1935), is a most useful biography of a pioneer whose teachings, unlike anyone else's, Frank Lloyd Wright gladly acknowledged. Wright has had, despite notable failures, some serious biographers, especially Robert C. Twombly, *Frank Lloyd Wright: An Interpretive Biography* (1973); Meryl Secrest, *Frank Lloyd Wright* (1992); Neil Levine, *The Architecture of Frank Lloyd Wright* (1996); and, definitely to be added, the life by the eminent architectural historian and critic Ada Louise Huxtable, *Frank Lloyd Wright: A Penguin Life* (2004), as witty and elegant as the rest of her work. Wright's *An Autobi-*

---

* As a young man he switched from Charles-Edouard Jeanneret to an old family name.

ography (final version, 1943) is grandiloquent and melodramatic, like most of his published writings, better evidence for his personal style than for the events in his life. Leonard K. Eaton, *Two Chicago Architects and Their Clients: Frank Lloyd Wright and Howard Van Doren Shaw* (1969), is an interesting study of Wright's customers.

AS FOR DESIGN, most of the major architects discussed in the previous paragraphs were also designers, and many of the texts devoted to them fit into this section. Certainly, the Bauhaus and its leading spirits belong here, too; their belief in the machine and, at the same time, high-quality modern design, stands in powerful contrast to its Austrian counterpart. Jane Kallir, *Viennese Design and the Wiener Werkstätte* (1986), is an important catalog analyzing the Bauhaus's Austrian contemporary and rival. *Josef Hoffmann Designs,* ed. Peter Noever (1987), contains a broad assortment of articles on Vienna's most famous and most versatile designer, with 481 illustrations. It may be supplemented with Eduard F. Sekler, *Josef Hoffmann: The Architectural Work* (1982; trans. John Maas, 1985). For Hoffmann's closest associate, see Werner Fenz, *Koloman Moser: Graphik, Kunstgewerbe, Malerei* (1984). See also [Josef Hoffmann and Koloman Moser], *Arbeitsprogramm der Wiener Werkstätte. Modernes Kunsthandwerk von 1903–1932* (1967). Easily the best catalog of Viennese modernism is Kirk Varnedoe, *Vienna 1900: Art, Architecture & Design* (1986).

Robert Macleod, *Charles Rennie Mackintosh* (1968), is a satisfying account of a Scottish designer with enormous influence on the Continent. Edward Lucie Smith, *Furniture: A Concise History* (1979), is a suggestive brief account. To conclude, Herwin Schaefer, *Nineteenth Century Modern: The Functional Tradition in Victorian Design* (1970), is far too little known: it proves conclusively that the over-designed, often kitschy pieces prominently displayed at the Victoria and Albert Museum in London did not have a monopoly in the Victorian decades.

CHAPTER 7: DRAMA AND MOVIES

The two great Scandinavian founders of the modernist theatre, Ibsen and Strindberg, have been satisfactorily presented in English. The knowledgeable critic and director Robert Brustein's *The Theatre of Revolt: An Approach to Modern Drama* (1964) offers impressive assessments of both, as well as Chekhov, Shaw, Brecht, Pirandello, O'Neill, and Genet (1964). Michael Meyer, *Ibsen: A Biography* (1971), is the standard life in English; to be supplemented with *Ibsen: The Critical Heritage*, ed. Michael Egan (1972), an illuminating collection of reviews and commentaries. George Bernard Shaw, *The Quintessence of Ibsenism* (1891), remains a vigorous contemporaneous defense of that controversial playwright. The exhaustive introduction to the 5-vol. German edition of Ibsen's *Sämtliche Werke* (1907), by Julius Elias and Paul Schlenther, over 180 pages long, is by its very existence a tribute to the playwright's international reputation. Brian W. Downs, *Modern Norwegian Literature 1860–1918* (1966), places Ibsen into the context of his literature.

Olof Lagercrantz, *August Strindberg* (1979; trans. Anselm Hollo, 1984), is the best biography of Strindberg in English. A catalog for an exhibition in London of his other passionate interests throws much light on the playwright's gifts and his persistent isolation: *August Strindberg: Painter, Photographer, Writer*, ed. Olie Granath (2005).

Ruth Freydank et al., *Theater als Geschäft: Berlin und seine Privattheater um die Jahrhundertwende* (1985), is a suggestive survey of drama in Germany's capital around 1900. *The Theory of the Modern Stage: An Introduction to Modern Theatre and Drama*, ed. Eric Bentley (1968), a soundly edited and shrewdly selected anthology of modernist theoreticians like Bertolt Brecht and Luigi Pirandello, also includes several nineteenth-century pioneers. Martin Esslin, *The Theatre of the Absurd* (1961), covers the ground for modernist playwrights. Note also the relevant chapters in Bradbury and McFarlane, *Modernism* (see above, p. 545).

Hans Richter, *Dada: Art and Anti-Art* (1965), is an indispensable account from an insider. The splendid Dada exhibition at MoMA in New York, with its lavish catalog (2006) that emphasizes the international aspects of this non-movement, came just in time before I completed this manuscript. For its successor (more or less), Surrealism, see Sarane Alexandrian, *Surrealist Art* (1969; trans. Gordon Clough, 1970), which gets excellent mileage from limited space. William S. Rubin assesses *Dadaism, Surrealism and Their Heritage* (1968) in an informative and wide-ranging catalog. André Breton, *Surrealism and Painting* (1965; trans. Simon Watson Taylor, 1965), combines necessary texts, including the original of 1928, *Artistic Genesis and Perspective of Surrealism* (1941), *Fragments* (1961), *Environs* (n.d.), and *Further Affluences and Approaches* (1963–65), the last filled with accolades to Surrealist artists. Mark Polizzotti, *Revolution of the Mind: The Life of André Breton* (1995), is an appreciative, full life. For an imaginative, internationally appreciated study of Surrealists, there is James Thrall Soby, *René Magritte*, exhibition catalog (1965), economical and informative, to be read with Louis Scutenaire, *René Magritte* (1948; 2nd ed. 1964), and Suzi Gablick, *Magritte* (1971). See also Soby, *Magritte*, like his earlier entries a catalog for an exhibition at MoMA in New York.

Though Breton does not mention Alfred Jarry often, he acknowledged "that great poet" as "the master of us all." Indeed, for the French avant-garde theatre, Jarry (*"Merdre!"*) may claim paternity to modernist drama. The relevant chapter in Roger Shattuck's elegant *The Banquet Years* (1958) retains its authority. Artaud's influence remains powerful. Naomi Green, *Antonin Artaud: Poet Without Words* (1970), intelligently sets the stage. Artaud's best known programmatic work is *The Theatre and Its Double* (1938; trans. Mary C. Richards, 1958), essays that develop the idea of the theatre as especially suitable to manifestations and to transmission of cruelty and inhumanity. We may supplement it with an *Artaud Anthology*, ed. Jack Hirshman (1965). In an important article, "Antonin Artaud," *Encounter*, vol. 39, no. 2 (1967), 44–50, Nicola Chiaromonte has demonstrated that Artaud's demand for a "pure" theatre of cruelty is really self-contradictory. Martin Esslin, *Antonin Artaud* (1976), continues his expert work of high-level criticism started with *Theatre of the Absurd*. One of

Artaud's friends, the mime, actor, and theatre director Jean-Louis Barrault, a consistent adversary of traditional dramaturgy, went public in *Réflexions sur le théâtre* (1949). Italy's most celebrated modernist playwright, the Nobel laureate Luigi Pirandello, the supreme skeptic about human identity, has five of his plays (including his two masterpieces, *Six Characters in Search of an Author* and *Henry IV*), collected in *Naked Masks* (1952), ed. Eric Bentley. James Knowlson, *Damned to Fame: The Life of Samuel Beckett* (1996), reads like the life's work of a specialist—affectionate, thorough, vast, but also meticulous.

For all the rapidity with which I have dealt with German Expressionist drama, scholars of German culture have, since the war, expended enormous energy on it (as well as on its poetry). H. F. Garten, *Modern German Drama* (1959), has a long chapter on the Expressionist playwrights. Claude David, *Von Richard Wagner zu Bertolt Brecht. Eine Geschichte der neueren deutschen Literatur* (1959; trans. Hermann Stiehl, 1965), is an excellent survey by a French scholar. Walter H. Sokel, *The Writer in Extremis: Expressionism in Twentieth-Century German Literature* (1959), is an authoritative study. *Expressionismus. Aufzeichnungen und Erinnerungen der Zeitgenossen*, ed. Paul Raabe (1965), offers a fascinating collection of reminiscences by contemporaries. *Der deutsche Expressionismus. Formen und Gestalten*, ed. Hans Steffen (1965), includes painters and poets along with playwrights. Volker Klotz, *Bürgerliches Lachtheater. Komödie, Posse, Schwank, Operette* (1980), is an earnest study of the sadly neglected topic of German humor in the theatre. Peter Uwe Hohendahl, *Das Bild der bürgerlichen Welt im expressionistischen Drama* (1967), is a rare attempt to apply the sociology of literature to the attitude of avant-garde Expressionist playwrights toward the bourgeoisie. Richard N. Coe, *Eugène Ionesco* (1961), is terse but rewarding.

For Carl Sternheim, see the brief, clever essay by Hellmuth Karasek, *Sternheim* (1965); F. Eisenlohr, *Carl Sternheim* (1926); and Carol Petersen, "Carl Sternheim," in *Expressionismus: Gestalten einer literarischen Bewegung*, ed. Hermann Friedmann and Otto Mann (1956). See also above all the introduction to Vol. I of his collected writings by Wilhelm Emrich, the editor of the complete works (1963). For Georg Kaiser, we have E. A. Fivian, *Georg Kaiser und seine Stellung im Expressionismus* (1946), and a reliable English monograph by B. J. Kenworthy, *Georg Kaiser* (1957).

The standard history of movies from their beginnings is David A. Cook, *A History of Narrative Film* (1961; 4th ed. 2004); very detailed and very reliable (I have used it with confidence), it boasts a vast Selective Bibliography. Liam O'Leary, *The Silent Cinema* (1965), is a quick trip with lots of adjectives, which stresses rather superficially the movies' psychological insights. *Endless Night: Cinema and Psychoanalysis, Parallel Histories* (1999), ed. Janet Bergstrom, is a tentative try to throw a bridge between two different specialties. Hugo Münsterberg, *The Photoplay: A Psychological Study* (1916), is the first serious psychological investigation of the new art by an eminent European scholar. The psychologist Rudolf Arnheim collected several essays, mainly from the 1930s, in *Film as Art* (1966). Klaus Kreimeier, *The UFA Story: A History of Germany's Greatest Film Company, 1918–1945* (1996), searchingly accounts for this near-monopoly—its movies, its actors, and its directors, not forgetting its "triumphant" role in Nazi moviemaking. See also *Film Theory and Criticism: Introductory Readings, etc.*, ed. Gerald Mast and Marshall Cohen (1974; 3rd ed. 1985).

Robert M. Henderson, *D. W. Griffith: His Life and Work* (1972), and Richard Schickel, *D. W. Griffith: An American Life* (1984), are major contributions by experienced movie historians. Yon Barna, *Eisenstein*, trans. Lisa Hunter (1973), and *The Battleship Potemkin: The Greatest Film Ever Made*, ed. Herbert Marshall (1978), give readers a sense of the appalling pressures under which Eisenstein, a cultivated and well-read Marxist, had to work. See also his *Autobiography*, trans. Herbert Marshall (1983). In sharp contrast, Jay Leyda and Zina Voynow, *Eisenstein at Work* (1982), is a quick run-through of Eisenstein's career as a moviemaker, with the usual pro-Soviet lacuna, setting aside the obstacles he faced most of his director's life. Béla Balázc, *Der Film: Werden und Wesen einer neuen Kunst* (1949; trans. Alexander Sacher-Masoch, from the Hungarian, 1961), devotes a chapter to montage, Eisenstein's favorite technique. David Robinson, *Chaplin: His Life and Art* (1983), is a responsible biography; Gerald D. McDonald, Michael Conway, and Mark Ricci, *The Films of Charlie Chaplin* (1965), has brief synopses of his output, adding a few words from contemporary reviewers, from his most primitive one-reeler to the end of his career. And see Parker Tyler, *Chaplin: Last of the Clowns* (1972).

Within a growing pile of publications on Welles, Frank Brady, *Citizen Welles: A Biography of Orson Welles* (1989), stands out as an informative life. See also Robert L. Carringer, *The Making of Citizen Kane* (1985), which details the creation of what most moviegoers would agree is the most remarkable movie ever made. The list of writers on Welles with high reputations is exceptionally long: André Bazin's *Orson Welles* (1950; trans. Jonathan Rosenbaum, 1978) and Peter Bogdanovich's *The Cinema of Orson Welles* (1961) try to move beyond *Citizen Kane* to his later productions, few of which are widely known but some of which are masterpieces. And see Pauline Kael, Herman Mankiewicz, and Orson Welles, *The Citizen Kane Book* (1971), an intriguing account. The most disturbing of these accolades—for, however cool they may try to be, they stand as tributes—is Clinton Heylin, *Despite the System; Orson Welles versus the Hollywood Studios* (2005). The author's research is exhaustive and his rage at the philistines who destroyed whatever Welles hoped to build is plain—and, I must add, largely justified.

PART THREE: ENDINGS

CHAPTER 8: ECCENTRICS AND BARBARIANS

For T. S. Eliot, see above, pp. 549–50.

Charles Ives, after decades of neglect, is not only being performed once in a while these days but also studied. The first collection of his mainly unknown writings began to be compiled toward the end of Ives's life; see *Essays Before a Sonata, The Majority, and Other Writings*, ed. Howard Boatwright (1962), followed by an even more intimate compendium, *Memos*, ed. John Kirkpatrick (1972), which contains most of his unpublished notes and memoirs—a priceless source. Frank R. Rossiter, *Charles Ives and His America* (1975), is a well-grounded biography that stresses Ives's utter isolation as a key to his conduct. The late Stuart Feder's life, *Charles Ives: "My Father's Song": A Psychoanalytic Biography* (1992), is the work of a doubly appropriate specialist.

KNUT HAMSUN, pioneering psychological novelist, incurable Nazi supporter, and Nobel Prize–winning stylist, has been brought to life by Robert Ferguson, *Enigma: The Life of Knut Hamsun* (1987), the candid, now standard biography in English. Hamsun's brilliant early novels, notably *Hunger* and *Pan*, are easily available. *Knut Hamsun: Selected Letters*, Vol. 2: *1898–1952*, ed. and trans. Harald Naess and James McFarlane (1998), has important passages. Leo Löwenthal has a fascinating long essay, "Knut Hamsun: Zur Vorgeschichte der autoritären Ideologie," *Zeitschrift für Sozialforschung*, vol. VI, no. 2 (1937), which, typically for the Frankfurt School, depends on Freud and Marx at the same time.

THE TOTALITARIAN COUNTRIES need less bibliographical attention; in writing these sections, I have worked through the major texts in political history, but I do want to list some recent or exceptional titles. Robert O. Paxton, *The Anatomy of Fascism* (2004), by the leading expert on Vichy France, rescues the term "Fascism" for Nazi Germany. For that country, see still my old favorite, Karl Dietrich Bracher, *The German Dictatorship: The Origins, Structure, and Effects of National Socialism* (1969; trans. Jean Steinberg, with a short intro. by Peter Gay, 1970), a classic historical survey that briefly goes back to the German Romantics, and with its very title helped to demolish the then fashionable German apologists who blamed Nazi barbarism on modernity or machine civilization—but not Germany. Saul Friedländer, *Nazi Germany and the Jews*, Vol. I: *The Years of Persecution, 1933–1939* (1997), brilliantly analyzes the Nazis' murderous obsession with the Jews. Vol. II, when it appears, can only get more appalling about the land of *"Dichter und Denker*—Writers and Thinkers." Ian Kershaw, *Hitler, 1889–1936: Hubris* (1998) and *Hitler, 1936–45: Nemesis* (2001), comprehensively and convincingly make the *Führer* the true protagonist of his obscene satyr play. In an important monograph, Henry Ashby Turner, Jr., *German Big Business and the Rise of Hitler* (1985), demonstrates that big business—the usual villain for most historians studying the triumph of the Nazis—had a comparatively modest part in it. George L. Mosse, *The Nationalization of the Masses: Political Symbolism and Mass Movements in Germany from the Napoleonic Wars Through the Third Reich* (1975), wrestles with historians' crucial issue of how the scholar must deal with "the people." *I Shall Bear Witness: The Diaries of Victor Klemperer*, and its sequel, *To the Bitter End* (1995; trans. and abr. Martin Chalmers, 1998–99), is one of the few truly great diaries in the German language, by a German Jew who survived. Peter Demetz, *Postwar German Literature: A Critical Introduction* (1970), offers a neat survey of after-1945 German writers: eight poets, six playwrights, and eight novelists. In 1986, he revisited the subject with *After the Fires: Recent Writing in the Germanies, Austria and Switzerland,* a thoughtful survey that closes with an admiring chapter on Günter Grass.

For Soviet history and the place of the arts, see esp. W. Bruce Lincoln, *Between Heaven and Hell: The Story of a Thousand Years of Artistic Life in Russia* (1998), with more hell than heaven, and James Billington, *The Icon and the Axe: An Interpretive History of Russian Culture* (1966), both highly recommended by Orlando Figes, *Natasha's Dance: A Cultural History of Russia* (2002), and both deserving of his praise. Figes's own recent work is beautifully informed; the chapter "Russia Through the Soviet Lense" gives the sad, often appalling details of the lives of modernists in the Workers' Paradise. John E. Bowlt, *Laboratory of Dreams: The Russian Avant-Garde and Cultural Experiment* (1996) explores Utopian trends among revolutionaries. David Elliot, *New Worlds: Russian Art and Society, 1900–1937* (1986), focuses on the exciting early days of cultural fervor. Among the directions that searchers for a New Man found particularly seductive was psychoanalysis, an interest that Freud did not reciprocate. Anne Applebaum, *Gulag: A History* (2003), is a powerful indictment of the Soviet system as a pitiless police state. See also Martin Miller, *Freud and the Bolsheviks: Psychoanalysis in Imperial Russia and the Soviet Union* (1998). An essay by Laura Engelstein, "Zwischen Alt und Neu: Russlands moderne Frauen," summons up the difficult yet exciting atmosphere of revolutionary Russia for six modern women artists, in *Amazonen der Avantgarde,* ed. John E. Bowlt and Matthew Drutt (1995).

Mussolini's Italy is more complicated. *Liberal and Fascist Italy, 1900–1945,* ed. Adrian Lyttelton, is an outstanding volume in the *Short Oxford History of Italy* (2002). Emily Braun's chapter in that collective enterprise, "The Visual Arts: Modernism and Fascism," lucidly makes the case that the state largely (not wholly) let the arts go their own way. For a comparable perspective, see Ruth Ben-Ghia, *Fascist Modernities: Italy, 1922–1945* (2001). For the very viability of the term "Fascism," see the interesting collection, *Reappraisals of Fascism,* ed. Henry A. Turner, Jr. (1975), particularly the editor's own contribution, "Fascism and Modernization." The pre-Fascist strand in artistic propaganda has been widely canvassed: see the first Futurist manifesto, by F. T. Marinetti, *Manifeste intiale du Futurisme* (*Le Figaro,* Feb. 20, 1909), in Jean-Pierre de Villiers, ed., *Le premier manifeste du futurisme* (1986). Günther Berghaus, *Futurism and Politics* (1996), is one reading of that once widely applauded intellectual and aesthetic aggressiveness in Italy and abroad. See also Joshua C. Taylor, *Futurism* (1961), and *Futurism and the International Avant-Garde,* ed. Anne d'Harnoncourt, trans. John Shepley, with an essay by Germano Celant (1980). The piece by Celant fits into the "aristocratic" strand of modernism. "The effects of 'massification,'" he writes, "from which society suffers today, include generalized conformity, in accordance with which the area reserved for personal and private choices is greatly reduced," and more of the same about indoctrination, public passivity, and the "management of culture." Emily Braun, *Mario Sironi and Italian Modernism: Art and Politics Under Fascism* (2000), follows a painter who gladly stayed with the regime. See also Simonetta Falasca-Zamponi, *Fascist Spectacle: The Aesthetics of Power in Mussolini's Italy* (1997). Philip V. Cannistraro and Brian R. Sullivan's reading of Margherita Sarfatti, a respected critic and Mussolini's long-term (Jewish) mistress, *Il Duce's Other Woman* (1997), is a study in her power, more than just gossip. And see Richard Etlin, *Modernism in Italian Architecture 1890–1940* (1991), which illuminates another part of the modernist forest. For the work of the Futurist architect Antonio Sant'Elia, see Esther da Costa Meyer, *The Work of Antonio Sant'Elia: Retreat into the Future* (1995). *Metaphysical Art*, ed. Massimo Carrà, with Patrick Waldberg and Ewald Rathke (1968; trans. Caroline Tisdall, 1971), is an enlightening collection of texts by Italian painters after World War I, most notably that strange, mysterious Giorgio de Chirico (for whom see also Soby, *Giorgio de Chirico* [1941]).

CHAPTER 9: LIFE AFTER DEATH?

Barbara Rose, *American Art Since 1900: A Critical History* (1967), is a firmly argued survey that puts Pop into its context. So does Henry Geldzahler, *American Painting in the 20th Century* (1973). Kirk Varnedoe and Adam Gopnik, *High and Low: Modern Art and Popular Culture* (1990), is a controversial catalog that touches on the central theme of this chapter. In the literature on Abstract Expressionism, I was particularly interested in Michael Leja, *Reframing Abstract Expressionism: Subjectivity and Painting in the 1940s* (1993), filled with original ideas, esp. on Pollock's Jungianism. Among the most illuminating and economical treatments of the Pop painters is Lawrence Alloway, *American Pop Art* (1974), a rapid, affectionate study that carries authority. See also *Pop Art: A Critical History*, ed. Steven Henry Madoff (1997).

Victor Bockris, *Warhol: The Biography* (1989; 2nd enlarged ed. 2003), in its detail and objectivity actually sustains the claim of its subtitle. Wayne Koestenbaum, *Andy Warhol; A Penguin Life* (2001), is exceedingly clever, written from the inside by a sympathetic observer, but not uncritically so; Koestenbaum's detailed essay on "Sources" is too accommodating, but worth consulting. Stephen Koch, *The Life, World and Films of Andy Warhol* (1973; rev. ed. 1991), is scholarly, elegantly written, an important essay on Warhol's favorite sideline, the movies. Andreas Brown, *Andy Warhol: His Early Works, 1947–1959* (1971), shows the draftsman before Pop Art. Some of his writings, usually reduced to order by an intelligent assistant like Pat Hackett, give access to Warhol the man. I recommend Warhol's *a (a novel)* (1965), which, despite the praise it has received, is virtually incomprehensible; and see *The Philosophy of Andy Warhol: From A to B and Back Again* (1980), an extremely revealing compilation of sayings and reminiscences (probably more revealing than its author intended), as well as *The Andy Warhol Diaries* (1989). *Edie: An American Biography*, ed. Jean Stein with George Plimpton (1982), tells the life of Edie Sedgwick, one of Warhol's most memorable and pathetic "superstars" at the Factory. The aesthetician Arthur Danto, who has made a specialty of contemporary art as a reviewer for *The Nation*, has repeatedly singled out Warhol's showing of Brillo boxes in 1964 as the end point of art; most recently in a collection titled *Unnatural Wonders: Essays from the Gap Between Art and Life* (2005). The art critic Donald Kuspit has offered a rather similar diagnosis, *The End of Art* (2004).

For other selected Pop artists, see Lawrence Alloway, *Roy Lichtenstein* (1963), tribute to an entertaining Pop master by an English enthusiast; and Michael Lobel, *Image Duplicator: Roy Lichtenstein and the Emergence of Pop Art* (2002), a subtle, perhaps a bit too subtle reading of this artist. Mary Lee Corlett, *The Prints of Roy Lichtenstein: A Catalogue Raisonné, 1948–1993* (1994), makes a major contribution to our understanding of the artist. *Jasper Johns* is an exhibition catalog at the Jewish Museum (1964); and see Max Kozloff, *Jasper Johns* (1974), a terse, vigorous account, done after Johns's success was assured. See also Walter Hopps and Susan Davidson, *Robert Rauschenberg: Retrospective* (1997). For other press attention, consult my choice of articles from the art pages of the *New York Times* in the Notes.

RAYMOND L. WILLIAMS, *Gabriel García Márquez* (1984), is a succinct, well-informed life. See also George McMurray, *Gabriel García Márquez* (1977), and Mario Vargas Llosa's study of this fellow master, the "deicide": *Gabriel García Márquez: Historia de un deicidio* (1971). My own favorite biographical study is Gene H. Bell-Villada, *García Márquez: The Man and His Work* (1990), which expends valuable pages on the novelist's cultural and literary background and whose meticulous chapter on *The Autumn of the Patriarch* I found particularly useful. As of this writing, we now have the first volume of García Márquez's autobiography planned for 3 vols., *Living to Tell the Tale* (2002; trans. Edith Grossman, 2003), which is naturally extremely enlightening. *Magical Realism: Theory, History, Community*, ed. Lois Parkinson Zamora and Wendy B. Faris (1995), places the genius.

CODA

Frank Gehry has enjoyed a great deal of attention for the last three decades and more. I refer the reader chiefly to *Gehry Talks: Architecture and Process* (1999; 2nd rev. ed. 2002), with essays by Mildred Friedman and Michael Sorkin, and, most important, a candid, almost continuous commentary by the architect himself. It deserves to be matched with *Frank O. Gehry: The Complete Works*, ed. Hadley Arnold, with essays by Francesco dal Co and Kurt W. Forster (1998), a generously and beautifully illustrated volume that takes the reader from the mid-1950s well beyond the Guggenheim Museum at Bilbao. Valuable as these texts are, they are no substitute for going to Bilbao.

ACKNOWLEDGMENTS

This book is not my fault. Naturally I take full responsibility for it, but I want to record its origins fairly. In early fall 2001, my editor at Norton, Bob Weil, called me with an idea—his idea. I had a contract with his house—still have—to write a psychoanalytic-historical study of liberalism. I had the title, complete with a subtitle, *The Liberal Temper: Human Nature in Politics*, and had just begun to think about the project. I had laid out the ground for the enterprise with "Liberalism and Regression," an address to a semiannual conclave of American psychoanalysts, in which I spelled out my first thoughts about the intimate intercourse between politics and psychoanalysis. Bob Weil proposed that I hold off on this venture and instead undertake a study of modernism. I recall asking him, "Do you mean painting or literature?" His categorical reply was "everything." I objected that I did not know everything nor ever would, but this sensible disclaimer did not diminish the urgency of his suggestion. In due time I became intrigued, and the result is the book you are holding in your hands.

Obviously, a text with that wide a range necessarily depends heavily on the kindness of others (during my five years of reading for and writing *Modernism*, I consulted specialists who read and discussed with me portions of my text, much to its benefit). If I have overlooked any of them, I can only say in apology that they must have been lost in the crowd of my thoughtful and helpful experts.

I begin with Bob Weil, a close reader and an imaginative editor, whose immensely valuable suggestions helped to focus my labors. I trust he has not come to regret his original inspiration. Bob's assistant, Tom Mayer, to whom too I am grateful, consistently removed obstacles along the way. In addition, I owe particular thanks to Ann Adelman, my civilized copy editor, who missed nothing and made important and subtle comments throughout.

During my forty-six years of marriage to Ruth Gay, she read and beautifully improved every one of my writings—all except *Modernism*. Her deteriorating health, which ended with her death from leukemia on May 9, 2006, made this project not our usual cooperative, almost joint affair, but a far more isolated one.

Through all my all-too-prolonged venture, I had valued support, which greatly contributed to my ability to complete what seemed at times irrelevant to my life. My old friends (we mostly go back to the time when Harry Truman was president) Bill and Shirley Kahn, Al and Ruth Burstein, and Gladys Topkis have been there through the years when I needed them, partnerships in affection that have meant a good deal to me. While this book was nearing completion, my three stepdaughters, Sarah Glazer Khedouri, Sophie Glazer, and Elizabeth Glazer, were touching presences for their mother, and thus for me. Our—my—beloved friend from Berlin, Gaby Katwan, psychoanalyst and conversationalist, left her mark on *Modernism*. (And we enthusiastically discovered Frank Gehry's Guggenheim Museum in Bilbao together.) My long-lasting conversation with Bob Webb (our cordiality was not impaired by our coauthoring a textbook on modern European history), as with Dick and Peggy Kuhns, has happily survived more than half a ceutury of more than just agreeable talk. The same holds true of Jerry and Bella Berson, and my Yale colleagues Henry A. Turner and John Merriman. I am much indebted to Janet Malcolm, bold and brilliant stylist. I must also gratefully acknowledge the marvelous life-serving presence of Zenaida So (known affectionately a "Zany") as *Modernism* was in the making. Among what sometimes appears like a small army of physicians, I am particularly obliged to Dr. Elizabeth Jacobson for her interest and kindness.

Rosemary Ramsey has put me in her debt by replacing chaos with order among my books, and chasing elusive source notes. I am also obliged to former students, long since my friends: MeikeWeerer and Helmut Smith, Mark Micale and Robert Dietle. In addition, Jeremy Eichler, Carolyn Kay, and Robert Wohl have given me welcome assistance. Merek Royce Press served effectively as a knowledgeable physician (or is it psychiatrist?) to my obstreperous computers.

My European contingent has been no less rewarding. Two Cambridge history professors, Quentin Skinner and Stefan Collini, have been invaluable friends for many years, as have Maarten Brands and Frouke Wieringa, who have often welcomed me to Amsterdam, and may claim a real share in the making of this book. Gaby Katwan naturally belongs in this paragraph as well.

AS THE FOUNDING DIRECTOR of the Lewis and Dorothy Cullman Center for Scholars and Writers at the New York Public Library, I had the pleasure, starting in 1999, of having an abundance of consultants, fifteen different fellows each year, at my fingertips. I exploited them freely. I feel particularly in debt to Marian Kaplan and Douglas Morris, a pair of able historians who came to mean a great deal to me both intellectually and socially. Among other fellows to whom I owe grateful acknowledgment, I single out (not unfairly I hope) Stacy Schiff, Carol Armstrong, Harvey Sachs, Colm Toíbín, Andy Delbanco, and Christopher Fleck. Pamela Leo proved the ideal assistant director in my tiny domain; she was throughout my four-year tenure, and continues to be now, a true friend and associate. Among supporters in the

Library staff, I want to single out Anne Skillion, an intellectual in the guise of an editor, with whom I singularly enjoyed exploring things that mattered.

Some of the Center fellows did more than freely discuss my varied topics with me, and sagely improved chapters in this book: Ada Louise Huxtable on architecture, Herbert Leibowitz on T. S. Eliot, Claudia Pierpont on dance, Walter Frisch on music, Rachel Hadas on poetry, and Harvey Sachs on Toscanini. I could not have invented a better-informed and more consistently supportive team of authorities. I repeat that they are, of course, not to be held responsible for whatever eccentric views I may have smuggled into the text.

Among these readers, two had the stamina and patience to stay with my manuscript as steady and steadying presences: the art historian Emily ("Mimi") Braun and the American historian Doron Ben-Atar. Doron, as they would say in Washington, kept me on message, praising, criticizing, suggesting improvements. And Mimi served as a brilliant guide to modern and contemporary art not only tactfully (and liberally) making my prose more precise but also educating me by exploring art exhibitions with me. I have dedicated *Modernism* to these two in the deepest gratitude. Without them, I would no doubt have completed this study, but it would have been a far slower and far less enjoyable chore.

—Peter Gay

CREDITS

iv: © 2007 Artists Rights Society (ARS), New York / ADAGP, Paris / Succession Marcel Duchamp. © The Philadelphia Museum of Art / Art Resource NY.

7: © 2007 Artists Rights Society (ARS), New York / SIAE, Rome. Emily Braun, *Mario Sironi and Italian Modernism: Art and Politics under Fascism*. Cambridge: Cambridge University Press, 2000. Illustration from *Le Industrie Italiane Ilustrate*, March 1920.

14: Illustration from *Parodie*, December 1869 (engraving; b/w photo), © Bibliothèque Nationale, Paris, France / The Bridgeman Art Library.

17: © The New Yorker Collection 1958 Stan Hunt from cartoonbank.com. All rights reserved.

20: Oil on canvas, © Fogg Art Museum, Harvard University Art Museums, USA / Bequest from the Collection of Maurice Wertheim, Class 1906 / The Bridgeman Art Library.

25: Oil on canvas; portrait of Alfred Lichtwark (1852–1914).

32: © Hamburger Kunsthalle, Hamburg, Germany / The Bridgeman Art Library.

52: © Bridgeman-Giraudon / Art Resource, NY.

63: © Time & Life Pictures, courtesy of Getty Images.

65: Regenia Gagnier, *Idylls of the Marketplace: Oscar Wilde and the Victorian Public*. Palo Alto: Stanford University Press, 1986. Topham Picture Library.

72: Oil on canvas, © Musée Marmottan, Paris, France / Giraudon / The Bridgeman Art Library.

74: Oil on canvas, © Private Collection / The Bridgeman Art Library.

78: Oil on canvas, © Musée Marmottan, Paris, France / Giraudon / The Bridgeman Art Library.

82: Watercolor, with touches of gouache, over graphite, on off-white woven paper, 206 x 173mm, Gift of Mrs. Charles Netcher in memory of Charles Netcher II, 1933.1, the Art Institute of Chicago. Photography © Art Institute of Chicago.

85: Oil on canvas, © Metropolitan Museum of Art, New York, USA / The Bridgeman Art Library.

86: © Scala / Art Resource, NY.

90: Anne Distel, *Impressionism: The First Collectors*, trans. Barbara Perroud-Benson. New York: Harry Abrams, 1990. Bibliothèque Nationale, Paris.

102: © 2007 The Munch Museum / The Munch-Ellingsen Group / Artists Rights Society (ARS), New York. © Erich Lessing / Art Resource, NY.

132: Peter Gay, *Weimar Culture: The Outsider as Insider*. London: Secker & Warburg, 1968.

139: © Tate Gallery London / Art Resource, NY.

147: © 2007 C. Herscovivi, Brussels / Artists Rights Society (ARS), New York. © Banque d'Images, ADAGP / Art Resource, NY.

150: Oil on canvas © Museo Nacional Centro de Arte Reina Sofía, Madrid, Spain / Index / The Bridgeman Art Library. © 2007 Salvador Dali, Gala-Salvador Dali Foundation / Artists Rights Society (ARS), New York.

154: © Albright Knox Art Gallery, Buffalo, New York, USA / Giraudon / The Bridgeman Art Library. © 2007 Estate of Pablo Picasso / Artists Rights Society (ARS), New York.

156: Oil on canvas, © Pushkin Museum, Moscow, Russia / Giraudon / The Bridgeman Art Library. © 2007 Estate of Pablo Picasso / Artists Rights Society (ARS), New York.

158: © 2007 Estate of Pablo Picasso / Artists Rights Society (ARS), New York. Bibliothèque Nationale de France, Paris, Départment des estampes et de la photographie, collection particulière. Barcelone, Museu Picasso, MPB. Reprinted from *Picasso Erotique*, the catalog to the museum show, Réunion des Musées Nationaux.

163: *The Evening Sun*, New York, March 20, 1913.

165: Color lithograph, © Private Collection / Photo © Boltin Picture Library / The Bridgeman Art Library. © 2007 Artists Rights Society (ARS), New York / ADAGP, Paris / Succession Marcel Duchamp.

166: ©1963 Julian Wasser. All rights reserved.

169: Hirshhorn Museum and Sculpture Garden, Smithsonian Institution, Washington, DC.

171: Digital Image © Museum of Modern Art / Licensed by SCALA / Art Resource, NY.

176: © Philadelphia Museum of Art / Corbis.

178: Tate Gallery, London, Great Britain.

193: © Imagno, Hulton Archive, courtesy of Getty Images.

204: © Hulton-Deutsch Collection / Corbis.

205: © Estate of Vanessa Bell, courtesy of Henrietta Garnett.

209: © Snark / Art Resource, NY.

220: Peter Ackroyd, *T. S. Eliot: A Life*. New York: Simon & Schuster, 1984. By permission of Houghton Library, Harvard University.

239: Courtesy Lebrecht Music and Arts Photo Library.

245: © Erich Lessing / Art Resource, NY.

264: Robert P. Morgan, *Twentieth-Century Music*. New York: W. W. Norton & Company, 1991.

272: © Martha Swope.

278: © Martha Swope.

282: Peter Gay, *Art and Act: On Causes in History—Manet, Gropius, Mondrian*. New York: Harper & Row Publishers, 1976.

294: © 2007 Frank Lloyd Wright Foundation, Scottsdale, AZ / Artists Rights Society (ARS), New York. Photograph by Frank Scherschel, Time & Life Pictures, courtesy of Getty Images.

301: © Miroslav Ambroz / GreatBuildings.com.

302: © Miroslav Ambroz / GreatBuildings.com.

307: © 2007 Artists Rights Society (ARS), New York / ADAGP, Paris / FLC. © Bettman/Corbis.

309: © 2007 Artists Rights Society (ARS), New York / ADAGP, Paris / FLC. © Art Resource NY.

318: © 2007 Artists Rights Society (ARS), New York / VG Bild-Kunst, Bonn. Peter Gay, *Art and Act: On Causes in History—Manet, Gropius, Mondrian*. New York: Harper & Row Publishers, 1976. Photograph courtesy of the Museum of Modern Art, New York.

319: © 2007 Frank Lloyd Wright Foundation, Scottsdale, AZ / Artists Rights Society (ARS), New York. © Corbis.

322: Peter Gay, *Art and Act: On Causes in History—Manet, Gropius, Mondrian*. New York: Harper & Row Publishers, 1976. Courtesy of the Architects Collaborative.

342: Eugene Bataille (Sapeck), photo-relief illustration for Coquelin Cadet, *Le Rire*. Paris: Paul Ollendorff, 1887. Schimmel Fund. *The Spirit of Montmartre*, ed. Philip Dennis Cate and Mary Shaw, trans. Eileen Hennessy. New Brunswick, NJ: Jane Voorhees Zimmerli Art Museum, Rutgers University, 1995.

364: Courtesy of the Everett Collection.

368: © Snark / Art Resource, NY.

370: © John Kobal Foundation, Hulton Archive, courtesy of Getty Images.

372: Richard Pipes, *Russia under the Bolshevik Regime*. New York: Random House, 1994.

374: Courtesy of the Everett Collection.

378: © Bettmann / Corbis.

380: © Sunset Boulevard / Corbis.

384: Courtesy of MPTV Image Vault.

394: Peter Ackroyd, *T. S. Eliot: A Life*. New York: Simon & Schuster, 1984. John Topham Picture Library.

402: © Bettmann / Corbis.

411: Robert Ferguson, *Enigma: The Life of Knut Hamsun*. New York: Farrar, Straus & Giroux. 1987.

425: © Corbis.

434: © Bettmann / Corbis.

454: © Lipnitzki, from Collection Roger Viollet, courtesy of Getty Images.

462: © 2007 The Pollock-Krasner Foundation / Artist Rights Society (ARS), New York.

470: Oil on canvas © Whitney Museum of American Art, New York, USA / The Bridgeman Art Library.

472: © Estate of Roy Lichtenstein.

477: © 2007 The Andy Warhol Museum, Pittsburgh, PA, a museum of Carnegie Institute. All rights reserved.

483: © Estate of Roy Lichtenstein.

485: Oil on canvas, © Private Collection / Lauros / Giraudon / The Bridgeman Art Library.

498: Photograph by Bertil Ericson, AFP, courtesy of Getty Images.

502: Photographs by Gabriele Katwan.

Color inserts:

August Renoir, *The Swing*. © Réunion des Musées Nationaux.

Andy Warhol, *Brillo Box*. © 2007 Andy Warhol Foundation for the Visual Arts / Artists Rights Society (ARS), New York. Photograph courtesy of Corbis.

Andy Warhol, *Marilyn*. © 2007 Andy Warhol Foundation for the Visual Arts / Artists Rights Society (ARS), New York. Photograph courtesy of Corbis.

Guggenheim Museum, Bilbao. © Alantide Phototravel / Corbis.

INDEX

Page numbers in *italics* refer to illustrations.